WEBSTER'S NEW WORLD™

DICTIONARY
—— of the ——
VIETNAM WAR

Edited by Marc Leepson
with Helen Hannaford

Webster's New World™
An Imprint of Simon & Schuster Macmillan
New York

Macmillan General Reference
A Simon & Schuster Macmillan Company
1633 Broadway
New York, NY 10019-6785

A Webster's New World™ book

MACMILLAN is a registered trademark of Macmillan, Inc.

Library of Congress Cataloging-in-Publication Data

Webster's new world dictionary of the Vietnam War / edited by Marc Leepson with Helen Hannaford.
    p. cm.
  Includes bibliographical references.
  ISBN 0-02-862746-6 (pbk.)
  1. Vietnamese Conflict, 1961–1975—Dictionaries.   I. Leepson, Marc, 1945– .
II. Hannaford, Helen.
DS557.7.W38 1998
959.704'3'03–dc21

                            98-42916
                              CIP

Cover photograph courtesy of the U.S. Army

Manufactured in the United States of America

02 01 00 99 98 — 5 4 3 2 1

This book is based on licensed content from *Encyclopedia of the Vietnam War* published by Macmillan Reference USA, © 1996 by Stanley I. Kutler.

Contents

Maps

Preface

Very few aspects of the American war in Vietnam have been without controversy. But there is one thing that everyone who has studied the war agrees on: During the long American experience in Vietnam, very few American policy makers had more than a superficial knowledge of Vietnamese history, politics, culture or society.

Webster's New World Dictionary of the Vietnam War is intended to provide detailed facts on the who, what, where, when, and how of the main events and people involved in the war. It contains over 1,500 concise entries that cover the broadest spectrum of topics, including:

- The relevant histories of Vietnam and its neighbors, Cambodia, Laos, and Thailand

- The history of the French colonial experience in Vietnam

- The post–World War II political and military histories of the former Republic of Vietnam (South Vietnam) and the Democratic Republic of Vietnam (North Vietnam)

- The military and diplomatic history of the American war in Vietnam

- Profiles of the prominent Americans and Vietnamese from both North and South who served in the Vietnam War

- The U.S. political environment in which the war was waged and the domestic anti-war movement

- Descriptions of noteworthy cities, provinces and other geographical areas in North and South Vietnam

- The war's legacy in the United States, ranging from the history of the American Vietnam veterans movement to significant books, films, and plays relating to the war

The appendices include

- A detailed chronology, covering the geopolitical emergence of Vietnam and Southeast Asia from the early 7th century to 1995.

- The full text of the Paris Peace Accords and the Gulf of Tonkin Resolution.

- The orders of battle for the U.S., South Vietnamese, and North Vietnamese forces.

The very nature of this work suggests that it is by no means a definitive account. We have steadfastly avoided any supposition, commentary, or theorizing about the "why's" of the Vietnam War. We have focused instead on providing simply the facts from which readers can draw their own conclusions and make their own connections between cause and effect. For in-depth articles and essays which do discuss the "why's," please consult the *Encyclopedia of the Vietnam War,* edited by Stanley I. Kutler, the outstanding work published by Macmillan Publishing, USA from which this dictionary is derived.

We are confident, though, that every significant aspect of the war is covered in these pages. The entries have been extensively cross-referenced to lead readers to each aspect of an issue—from the people, equipment, and places to the dates, policies, and battles. We believe that the wealth of information contained in these pages will provide historians, students of the war, and general readers seeking information about the Vietnam War with a sound and comprehensive starting point for research.

Marc Leepson
Editor, *Webster's New World Dictionary of the Vietnam War*
Middleburg, Virginia
August 1998

Acknowledgements

This work was not done in a vacuum. Faunette Johnston, my multi-talented editor, has shaped every aspect of this book. We were immeasurably aided by the dictionary's associate editor, Helen Hannaford.

Thanks also goes to the publisher and staff at Macmillan Library Reference and to Stanley I. Kutler and his many contributors for making the source material from the *Encyclopedia of the Vietnam War* available.

I also would like to acknowledge the much-needed and much-appreciated support and assistance I have received from colleagues including Bob Butler, Jim Churchill, Pat Duncan, Bill Ehrhart, Gayle Germise, Bill Gibbons, Bill Hammond, Skip Isaacs, Michael Kelley, Steve Matthews, Debbie McLaughlin, Angus Paul, Mokie Porter, Michael Pretzer, Dennis Pyles, Shaun Shaughnessy, Sandy Stencel, Col. Harry Summers, Bill Thomas, Sharon Thorn, Sheila Whetzel, David Willson, and Bob Wilson.

A special thanks goes to my unwavering family support group: my wife, Janna Murphy Leepson, and our children, Devin and Cara.

List of Contributors

Dale Andradé
Daniel T. Bailey
Ellen Baker
William C. Berman
Thomas R. Cantwell
Timothy N. Castle
Graham A. Cosmas
Rotert Dallek
David A. Dawson
Jean Delmas
Vincent H. Demma
William J. Duiker
Kelly Evans-Pfeifer
Jennifer Frost
Glen Gendzel
Amy Golden
Ellen D. Goldlust
Jeffrey Greenhut
John F. Guilmartin, Jr.
K. E. Hamburger
William M. Hammond
Han Tie
George C. Herring
Arnold R. Isaacs
Victor Jew
Benedict Kiernan

Stanley I. Kutler
Adam Land
David W. Levy
Edward J. Marolda
Thomas J. McCormick
Alfred W. McCoy
Robert J. McMahon
Allan R. Millett
Thomas Myers
Ngo Vinh Long
James S. Olson
Leo P. Ribuffo
Randy W. Roberts
Andrew J. Rotter
William Paul Schuck
Robert D. Schulzinger
Jack Shulimson
Paul M. Taillon
Sandra C. Taylor
Carlyle A. Thayer
Thongchai Winichakul
Steven J. Tirone
William S. Turley
Brian VanDeMark
James W. Williams
Yoneyuki Sugita

Common Abbreviations and Acronyms Used in This Work

AAA	antiaircraft artillery
AB	Air Base
ABC	American Broadcasting Company
Adm.	admiral
AFB	Air Force Base
AID	Agency for International Development
ARVN	Army of the Republic of Vietnam
BBC	British Broadcasting Corporation
Brig.	brigadier
Capt.	captain
CBS	Columbia Broadcasting System
CIA	Central Intelligence Agency
CIDG	Civilian Irregular Defense Group
CINCPAC	Commander-in-Chief, Pacific
cm	centimeter(s)
Col.	colonel
Comdr.	commander (naval rank)
COMUSMACV	Commander, U.S. Military Assistance Command, Vietnam
CORDS	Civil Operations and Revolutionary Development Support
COSVN	Central Office for South Vietnam
CTZ	Corps Tactical Zone
D	Democrat
diss.	Dissertation
DMZ	Demilitarized Zone
DRV	Democratic Republic of Vietnam
ed.	editor (pl., eds.); edition
e.g.	*exempli gratia*, for example
et al.	*et alii*, and others
fl.	*floruit*, active during
Gen.	general
HE	high explosive
HEAT	high explosive antitank
HQ	headquarters
i.e.	*id est*, that is
JCS	Joint Chiefs of Staff
JGS	Joint General Staff
kg	kilogram(s)
km	kilometer
Lt.	lieutenant
MAAG-V	Military Assistance Advisory Group–Vietnam
MACV	Military Assistance Command, Vietnam
Maj.	major

mm	millimeter(s)
MR	Military Region
NBC	National Broadcasting Company
NCO	noncommissioned officer
n.d.	no date (of publication)
NLF	National Liberation Front
no.	number (pl., nos.)
n.p.	no place (of publication)
NVA	North Vietnamese Army
p., pp.	page
PAVN	People's Army of Vietnam
pl.	plural
PLAF	People's Liberation Armed Forces
PRC	People's Republic of China
PRG	Provisional Revolutionary Government
pt.	part (pl., pts.)
Pvt.	private
R	Republican
Rein.	Reinforced
Rep.	Representative
ret.	retired
rev.	revised
RF/PF	Regional Forces/Popular Forces
RVN	Republic of Vietnam
RVNAF	Republic of Vietnam Armed Forces
SAM	surface-to-air missile
SEATO	Southeast Asia Treaty Organization
sec.	section (pl., secs.)
Sen.	Senator
Sgt.	sergeant
U.K.	United Kingdom
U.S.	United States
USAF	United States Air Force
USARV	United States Army, Vietnam
USMC	United States Marine Corps
USN	United States Navy
USS	United States Ship
USSR	Union of Soviet Socialist Republics
VC	Viet Cong
VNAF	Republic of Vietnam Air Force
VNN	Republic of Vietnam Navy
vol.	volume (pl., vols.)
WWII	World War II

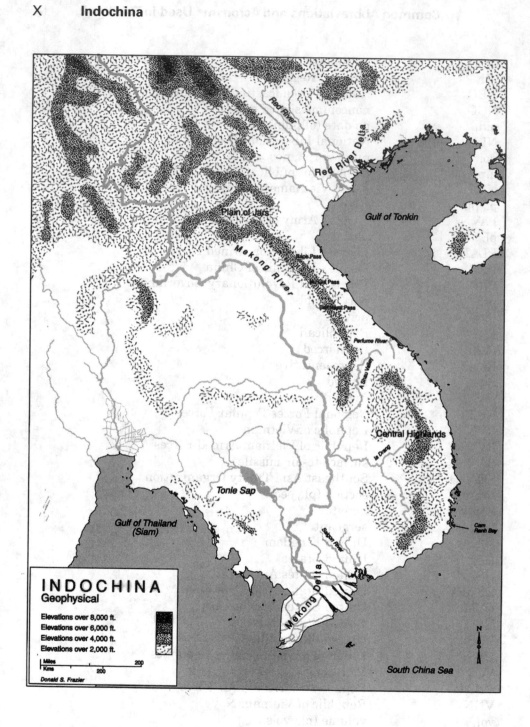

Red River

Red River Delta

Gulf of Tonkin

Plain of Jars

Mekong River

Bach Pass

Mu Gia Pass

Mu Gia Pass

Perfume River

A Shau Valley

Central Highlands

Ia Drang

Tonle Sap

Gulf of Thailand
(Siam)

Saigon River

Cam
Ranh Bay

Mekong Delta

South China Sea

INDOCHINA
Geophysical

Elevations over 8,000 ft.
Elevations over 6,000 ft.
Elevations over 4,000 ft.
Elevations over 2,000 ft.

Miles   200
Kms   200

Donald S. Frazier

N

A-1 Skyraider. Single-engine, propeller fighter-bomber used in many combat operations by the U.S. Navy, U.S. Air Force and South Vietnamese air force to provide close air support for American and South Vietnamese ground troops.

A-4 Skyhawk. Single-engine, single-seat jet attack bomber. The most extensively used combat aircraft flown in the Vietnam War by U.S. Navy and Marines.

See also: Linebacker and Linebacker II Operations.

A-6 Intruder. A close-air support, dual-engine jet bomber equipped to deliver rockets, bombs, guided missiles and small nuclear weapons. Designed especially to fly long distances at low altitudes in all weather conditions.

See also: Linebacker and Linebacker II Operations.

A-7 Corsair II. Carrier-based, single-engine, light-attack all-weather bomber first deployed in Vietnam by the U.S. Navy in December 1967.

See also: Linebacker and Linebacker II Operations.

A-26 Bomber. Propeller-driven, piston-engine World War II–era light bomber used by the U.S. Air Force in Vietnam in air commando unit operations in support of the South Vietnamese beginning in 1961. Replaced by the B-57 jet bomber in February 1965.

Abernathy, Ralph David, Rev. (1926–1990), civil rights activist, Baptist minister, head of the Southern Christian Leadership Conference, 1968–1977. A leader, along with Roy Wilkins and Martin Luther King, Jr., in the mainstream civil rights movement during the Vietnam era, Abernathy also was active in the American antiwar movement.

Abrams, Creighton W. Jr. (1914–1974), general, U.S. Army; commander, U.S. Military Assistance Command, Vietnam, 1968–1972; U.S. Army chief of staff, 1972–1974. Creighton W. Abrams, Jr., was commissioned into the cavalry as a member of the West Point class of 1936. Abrams, one of the most noted tank commanders of World War II, led Gen. George Patton's armored relief column to Bastogne during the Battle of the Bulge. Abrams was Army vice chief of staff during the U.S. buildup in Vietnam and Gen. William Westmoreland's deputy MACV commander early in 1967. His primary responsibilities were modernizing the Army of the Republic of Vietnam (ARVN) and, in cooperation with Robert W. Komer, managing pacification programs in South Vietnam. After the 1968 Tet Offensive,

Johnson assigned Abrams as COMUSMACV. Abrams's tasks were to oversee the Vietnamization of the war and, in 1969, to proceed with the withdrawal of U.S. forces at an accelerating pace.

With the 1972 signing of the Paris peace accords, President Nixon chose Abrams as U.S. Army chief of staff. His main task in that position was rebuilding a U.S. Army that was in disarray. The army and the armed forces as a whole underwent a precipitate reduction in size and experienced a sense of alienation from American society. Also during Abrams's tenure, the draft was ended; the military services became entirely volunteer forces, with attendant short-term disruption. Abrams died of lung cancer in 1974 while chief of staff.

See also: Accelerated Pacification Campaign; Army of the Republic of Vietnam; Cambodia; Central Office for South Vietnam; Joint Chiefs of Staff; Krulak, Victor; Menu, Operation; State, Department of; Vann, John Paul; Weyand, Frederick C.

Accelerated Pacification Campaign (APC). The Accelerated Pacification Campaign began on 1 November 1968 and ran for three months in an attempt to take advantage of the Viet Cong's heavy losses during the Tet Offensive. Planned by CIA analyst Robert Komer, the program was carried out by his successor, William Colby. APC was intended to improve security in contested hamlets in South Vietnam by coordinating military operations and pacification teams, and to deny Viet Cong guerrillas their traditional access to the countryside. By the end of the campaign, 1,100 formerly contested hamlets were considered secure, and communist control reportedly dropped from 17 percent to 12 percent.

See also: Colby, William; Komer, Robert W.

Accuracy in Media. A conservative media watchdog organization that in 1985 produced two programs, *Television's Vietnam: The Real Story* and *Television's Vietnam: The Impact of Media,* which strongly criticized what was described as the "liberal bias" of *Vietnam: A Television History,* the documentary series produced by the PBS station, WGBH.

Acheson, Dean (1893–1971), U.S. secretary of state, 1949–1953; one of the "wise men," unofficial advisers to President Johnson during the 1960s. Dean Acheson began his tenure as secretary of state supportive of Southeast Asian nationalism. By 1950, however, he saw Vietnamese nationalism as a front for Soviet or Chinese communism, and therefore supported former emperor Bao Dai, rather than Ho Chi Minh, the nationalist-communist Viet Minh leader. On 26 March 1968,

Acheson sharply repudiated his previous endorsement of the Johnson administration's escalation policy, declaring that the United States could not prevent a North Vietnamese victory and, consequently, should seek to end the war.

See also: European Defense Community; Lattre de Tassigny, Jean de; Nitze, Paul H.; State, Department of; Wise Men.

Adams, Eddie (1933–), Associated Press photographer who, on 1 February 1968, during the Tet Offensive, took what is perhaps the most famous photograph of the Vietnam War: a close view of Gen. Nguyen Ngoc Loan, chief of the South Vietnamese national police, holding a pistol to the head of a cringing prisoner moments before pulling the trigger outside the Au Quang Pagoda in Saigon. Adams won the Pulitzer Prize for photography in 1969, among other awards, for that much reprinted photograph.

Adams, Sam (1933–1988), Central Intelligence Agency (CIA) analyst, 1963–1973. Adams reviewed agent field reports about the strength of Viet Cong and People's Army of Vietnam (PAVN) forces and came to the controversial conclusion that the U.S. military intentionally underestimated the number of enemy troops to bolster claims of progress and to justify further escalation. Adams's charges became the basis for a controversial *60 Minutes* television segment that resulted in Gen. William Westmoreland's multimillion-dollar libel suit against the CBS network.

See also: Central Intelligence Agency.

Ad Hoc Task Force on Vietnam. Formed by President Johnson in February 1968 following the Tet Offensive, the task force, chaired by incoming Secretary of Defense Clark Clifford, was called together to evaluate Gen. William Westmoreland's request for 200,000 additional American troops and to recommend future American military action in Vietnam. On 7 March, the task force recommended increasing the troop total by 23,000, calling up reserve units, increasing the draft and extending the tour of duty in Vietnam. The members of the task force who argued against Westmoreland's request were Deputy Undersecretary of Defense Paul Nitze, Undersecretary of State Nicholas Katzenbach and Assistant Secretary of Defense for International Security Affairs Paul Warnke. Those favoring the larger escalation included Joint Chiefs of Staff Chairman Gen. Earle Wheeler, Special Assistant to the President Walt W. Rostow, and presidential adviser Gen. Maxwell Taylor.

See also: Clifford, Clark; Nitze, Paul H.; Rostow, Walt Whitman; Taylor, Maxwell D.; Westmoreland, William C.

ADSIDs. *See* Air-Delivered Seismic Intrusion Devices

Advanced Research Project Agency (ARPA). A Department of Defense unit responsible for testing new weapons and methods of fighting. ARPA teams operated in Vietnam throughout the war. In 1961, under the code name Project Agile, ARPA teams conceived of using herbicides as a counterinsurgency technique. Beginning in November, herbicides were used in conjunction with ground operations. Tests also were carried out to create "fire breaks" or open areas along South Vietnam's borders in August under ARPA.

See also: Agent Orange; Chemical Warfare.

Advisers, U.S. The first American military advisers sent to Vietnam arrived in Saigon in September 1950 as the U.S. Military Assistance Advisory Group Indochina (MAAG). The group became known as MAAG-Vietnam in 1954 following the formation of the Republic of Vietnam (RVN). These early U.S. military advisers worked with all the branches of the RVN military and accompanied RVN units in the field. In 1961, at the end of the Eisenhower administration, there were 900 American military advisers in Vietnam. The number grew to 16,300 by the end of 1963. MAAG operations became part of the U.S. Military Assistance Command Vietnam (MACV) in 1964. After the large American troop buildup

in 1965, American military advisers continued to work with South Vietnamese Army units. The advisory effort also included thousands of military personnel, Foreign Service officers, and others working through the U.S. Civil Operations and Revolutionary Development Support (CORDS) program and U.S. Special Forces who were sent to work among the Montagnard tribal groups of the Central Highlands.

See also: Army of the Republic of Vietnam; Civil Operations and Revolutionary Development Support; Johnson, Lyndon B.; Taylor, Maxwell D.; Taylor-Rostow Report.

Aeromedical Evacuation. In Vietnam, medical evacuations (known as medevacs) by helicopter, or "dustoffs," became the norm. Helicopter evacuation teams carried critically wounded soldiers directly to military hospitals, replacing the intermediate aid stations that had previously stabilized casualties. As a result, about 98 percent of those wounded on the battlefields of Vietnam survived after reaching a medical facility.

See also: Medical Support, U.S.

Aerospace Rescue and Recovery Service (ARRS). U.S. Air Force unit made up of specialists trained to rescue downed air crews. Working out of U.S. air bases in Thailand and South Vietnam, the first ARRS units went into South Vietnam in April 1962. They had officially claimed 3,883 personnel rescued when the unit departed Vietnam in 1973.

See also: Search and Rescue.

African-Americans. Although African-Americans largely supported the Vietnam War until the late 1960s, polls indicate that they turned overwhelmingly against the war more rapidly and in greater proportion than white Americans. Many prominent civil rights leaders initially refrained from challenging Lyndon Johnson's policies. In January 1966, however, Martin Luther King, Jr., spoke out against the war. More militant African-Americans, such as members of the Student Nonviolent Coordinating Committee (SNCC), railed against what they called the "white man's war."

African-American military personnel supported U.S. policy toward Vietnam in the initial years of the war. Since the desegregation of the armed forces during the Korean War, African-Americans had viewed the military as a haven for economic advancement, and attempts by the military to address racial bias, such as discrimination in off-base housing, had drawn praise from many prominent African-American career military personnel. African-Americans' enthusiasm reflected and reinforced the generally high morale of the armed forces early in the war.

By 1968, however, there was a new critical attitude among African-American soldiers. Influenced by the influx of African-American draftees and the expanding civil rights movement, black soldiers questioned the continuing patterns of racial inequality in the military. For instance, in 1969 African-Americans accounted for 13.3 percent of all the personnel in the U.S. Army and Marine Corps, but they made up only 3 percent of the officer corps of the Army and less than 1 percent of the Marine officer corps. Moreover, many African-Americans, who often lacked technical training, performed the lowest level menial duties in rear areas. The military justice system, as congressional and U.S. military studies confirm, dealt more harshly with African-American soldiers than with white soldiers. Although the precise racial makeup of U.S. casualties in Vietnam remains disputed, evidence indicates that there was a disproportionately high number of casualties among African-Americans, particularly for the initial years of the war. Pentagon statistics report that blacks suffered nearly 25 percent of U.S. fatalities in late 1965.

U.S. draft policies contributed to the disproportionate number of African-American soldiers in dangerous or less desirable duties. "Project 100,000," begun by the Johnson administration in 1966, lowered mental and physical requirements for inductees. Justified as a social welfare scheme, the project promised remedial and technical education for the "New Standards Men." In practice, the approximately 360,000 draftees (40 percent African-American) received limited training, and the result of the program was that many of the poorest Americans were sent to combat duty in Vietnam.

In 1967, a race riot erupted at the U.S. Army stockade at Long Binh. In 1969, the Marine base at Camp Lejeune, North Carolina, experienced virtual warfare between black and white Marines who had just returned from Vietnam. Racial incidents also occurred on the U.S. aircraft carrier *Kitty Hawk* en route to Vietnam in 1972 and on U.S. bases in Germany in the early 1970s. Racial friction in the U.S. armed forces subsided in the mid-1970s. The onset of the volunteer army, and new racial programs instituted by the U.S. military contributed to the decline. Since the Vietnam War, the armed forces have attracted increasing numbers of African-American men and women. In 1991, African-American soldiers accounted for nearly 25 percent of the U.S. military personnel.

See also: King, Marting Luther Jr.; Project 100,000.

Agency for International Development (AID). A part of the State Department, the Agency for International Development originated in 1961, taking over the functions of its predecessors, the International Cooperation Administration and the Development Loan Fund. AID became the principal U.S. agency responsible for designing and implementing nonmilitary U.S. development and assistance programs. Providing loans and grants (over $2 billion per year by 1965), AID programs emphasized long-range plans to build the economies of less developed countries and directed aid to the areas of health, agriculture, population planning, education, and energy. The agency also sent specialists abroad to support its projects and train foreign nationals. Between 1962 and 1975, South Vietnam received by far the largest portion of AID economic assistance. In 1967 alone the agency's budget allocated more than $550 million for Vietnam, the majority through the Commercial-Import Program (CIP). Between the early 1960s and 1972, AID tried to establish self-help projects, schools, health clinics, and farming cooperatives in Vietnam. The agency provided funds for the construction and renovation of 20 hospitals and the building of more than 170 district, 370 village, and 400 hamlet maternity dispensaries. More than 774 AID-contracted U.S. physicians served 60-day tours in AID-built hospitals. AID workers in 1966 set up village elections in "secure" areas.

Although Congress had separated military and economic assistance in its 1961 legislation, policymakers considered foreign assistance to Southeast Asia part of containment policy. Particularly in South Vietnam, they saw long-term economic development as insurance against revolution, and a significant part of AID assistance went to police forces and counterinsurgency programs. In 1955, the International Cooperation Administration, under the cover of a Michigan State University advisory group, had financed a team of Central Intelligence Agency (CIA) specialists to teach South Vietnamese police forces and intelligence services techniques that could be used against the Viet Cong guerrillas. In the mid-1960s, AID's Office of Public Safety coordinated an effort to enlarge and upgrade the South Vietnamese police force, emphasizing "law enforcement" with more local roots for the rural population. AID representatives, however, were most successful when working with villagers individually or with the Hoa Hao and the Catholics, the only two independent organizations in rural areas that were able to resist Viet Cong guerrilla infiltration.

See also: Central Intelligence Agency; Colby, William; Commercial-Import Program; Michigan State University Vietnam Advisory Group.

Agent Blue. A herbicide sprayed by U.S. forces in Vietnam primarily to eradicate rice crops suspected of being used by the enemy. Named for the blue identifying markings on its barrels.

See also: Agent Orange; Agent White; Chemical Warfare; Ranch Hand, Operation; United Nations.

Agent Orange. The herbicide sprayed most extensively in Vietnam in an effort to kill vegetation to deny cover to the enemy. Some 11 million gallons of Agent Orange, which contains dioxin, an extremely toxic byproduct, were sprayed by U.S. Air Force personnel from C-123 planes in the program known as Operation Ranch Hand from 1962 to 1970. Named for the color of a band that marked the drums, Agent Orange was considered nontoxic to humans and animals except in very large doses. However, since the early 1970s epidemiological evidence has strongly suggested a link between dioxin and many debilitating illnesses, rashes, tumors, and birth defects. Long-term effects include the destruction of coastal mangrove forests and claims of widespread health problems by Vietnamese authorities and U.S. veterans, who successfully sued the Veterans Administration for recognition of Agent Orange–related disabilities. A 1984 court settlement awarded $180 million to U.S. soldiers who suffered health ailments from exposure to Agent Orange. In 1997 the Department of Veterans Affairs began compensating the children of Vietnam veterans suffering from the birth defect spina bifida due to their parents' exposure to Agent Orange in Vietnam.

See also: Air Force, U.S.; Chemical Warfare; Cleland,

Joseph Maxwell; Ranch Hand, Operation; United Nations; Veterans, American; Veterans, Vietnamese; Zumwalt, Elmo R. Jr.

Agent White. The herbicide Agent White comprised about 14% of the total of the U.S. herbicides sprayed in the Vietnam War. Agent White was used to kill brush and weeds to try to deny cover to the Viet Cong and the North Vietnamese Army.

See also: Agent Blue; Agent Orange; Chemical Warfare; Ranch Hand, Operation; United Nations.

Agnew, Spiro T. (1918–1996), governor of Maryland, 1967–1969; U.S. vice president, 1969–1973. As Richard M. Nixon's vice president, Agnew harshly criticized antiwar protesters and the media. He repeatedly attacked the media for its "liberal eastern bias." Agnew's efforts contributed to Nixon's "silent majority" strategy to marshal support in the wake of antiwar protests. Agnew resigned in October 1973, following allegations of criminal conduct while governor and vice president. He was succeeded by Gerald R. Ford, Jr.

See also: Ford, Gerald R. Jr.; Nixon, Richard M.

Agricultural Reform Tribunals. The Democratic Republic of Vietnam (DRV) operated agricultural reform tribunals between 1954 and August 1956 as part of its Marxist campaign against landlords in rural North Vietnam. Few peasants owned more than a few acres, but because the tribunals had quotas of landlords to fill, thousands of alleged landlords were killed and thousands more were banished to labor camps, many of them victims of unsubstantiated accusations. The tribunals sparked a peasant revolt in November 1956 in Ho Chi Minh's native province, Nhge An, and he sent in a division of North Vietnamese Army troops to quell it.

Agroville Program. With the help of U.S. and British experts, in 1959 South Vietnam's President Ngo Dinh Diem began a wholesale resettlement program that forced the resident population into so-called Agrovilles— and later on, strategic hamlets— in an effort to weed out communists and control the population. Borrowed from a similar British concept used in Malaya, Agrovilles were communities built by the government as a means of protection from the insurgents. Peasants, however, resented being uprooted and then being forced to build the Agrovilles themselves. Peasant resistance and insurgent attacks led to the program's abandonment in 1961.

See also: Ngo Dinh Diem; Pacification; Strategic Hamlet Program.

AID. *See* Agency for International Development.

Aiken, George (1892–1984),
U.S. senator (R-Vt.), 1941–1975;
member, Senate Foreign
Relations Committee,
1954–1975. Aiken initially supported U.S. military intervention
in Vietnam. By 1966, however, he
opposed the war as a mistaken
policy and urged President
Johnson to declare the United
States the winner, withdraw the
troops, and end the war.

Air America. A creation of the
Central Intelligence Agency, Air
America became one of the CIA's
largest commercial proprietary
corporations. A conglomerate airline wholly owned by the CIA, it
supported covert and paramilitary activities in Laos, Vietnam,
and Cambodia, where it ferried
people and supplies when the
use of U.S. military aircraft was
undesirable. Air America flew
visiting VIPs, prisoners, U.S.
casualties, CIA operatives and
transported opium grown by
U.S.-backed Hmong tribesmen in
northeastern Laos. The sale of
opium was key to the Hmong's
financial survival, and Air
America proved vital to maintaining this drug-based lifeline.
Air America eventually proved to
be too visible, and revelations
about its illegal activities led to
cutbacks by the CIA.

See also: Agency for
International Development;
Central Intelligence Agency;
Colby, William; Golden Triangle;
Hmong; Pathet Lao.

Aircraft Carriers. In response
to the Gulf of Tonkin incidents in

August 1964, the U.S. Seventh
Fleet stationed aircraft carriers
off the coast of Vietnam in the
South China Sea. The aircraft
launched from the carriers flew
missions over North Vietnam,
South Vietnam, Laos and
Cambodia. At least two carriers
were in place until the war
ended in 1975. Altogether, 19
U.S. aircraft carriers saw service
in the South China Sea during
the Vietnam War.

See also: Kitty Hawk, USS; *New
Jersey,* USS; *Oriskany,* USS;
Yankee Station.

**Air-Delivered Seismic
Intrusion Devices (ADSIDs).**
Devices dropped from planes
and helicopters that buried
themselves in the ground and
had sensors that could detect the
movement of enemy troops.

See also: Barrier Concept;
McNamara Line.

Air Force, U.S. The U.S. Air
Force, established in 1947, was
the preeminent air force in the
Vietnam War. The U.S. Army controlled more aircraft (mainly
helicopters) and the U.S. Navy
and Marine Corps performed
many of the same missions, but
the U.S. Air Force dropped more
destructive ordnance than the
others combined and left its
mark on the conflict through a
strongly held belief in the strategic decisiveness of centrally
controlled air power. The Air
Force lost 2,257 aircraft, 1,737 of
them combat losses, including 33
helicopters and 2,584 personnel
killed in action (KIA). The Air

Force combat commitment to Vietnam began in late 1961 when President Kennedy sent air commando units equipped with propeller-driven, piston-engine A-26 bombers, T-28 ground attack-trainer aircraft, and C–123 transports modified to spray defoliants, notably Agent Orange, and insecticides. In 1964–1965, there was a massive Air Force buildup in Southeast Asia under President Johnson. Air Force operations were controlled by the Seventh Air Force (2nd Air Division before April 1966) in Saigon except for B52 Arc Light strikes, which began on 18 June 1965 and were controlled directly by SAC.

The Air Force's war was divided into five campaigns. The first, in South Vietnam, was waged in support of ground forces primarily by aircraft based there. These included tactical fighters, notably F-100s, F-4s, and propeller-driven piston-engine A-ls, and a large tactical airlift fleet, notably C-123s and C-7s obtained from the army. The second was the Rolling Thunder offensive against North Vietnam, which began on 2 March 1965 and was driven by Secretary of Defense Robert McNamara's theory of graduated escalation that featured tight control of targets, and even tactics, by President Johnson. Thailand-based F-105 and F-4 fighter bombers were Air Force mainstays of the war over North Vietnam. Fought in conjunction with carrier-based Navy air power, the campaign was waged in the face of unprecedented dense concentrations of antiaircraft artillery, Soviet-built SA-2 surface-to-air missiles (SAMs), and limited, but effective, use of MiG-17 and MiG-21 interceptor aircraft. The Air Force response to these defenses included standoff jamming aircraft, which used electronic counter-measures (ECM) to jam defensive radar while out of antiaircraft range, and specialized "Wild Weasel" anti-SAM strike fighters. Rolling Thunder was severely curtailed by President Johnson on 31 March 1968 and cancelled on 31 October as part of a U.S. peace initiative. President Nixon's Linebacker and Linebacker II campaigns, March to October and 18–29 December 1972, respectively, were extensions of Rolling Thunder. The third was an interdiction campaign against the Ho Chi Minh Trail, the network of communist supply lines in southern Laos and northeastern Cambodia, and conducted under the code names Steeltiger, Tiger Hound, and Commando Hunt. This campaign was waged primarily by Thailand-based Air Force units. The later stages featured the extensive use of small, air-dropped seismic and acoustic sensors to detect the movement of troops and vehicles along the trail, forming the so-called McNamara Line. The fourth campaign (December 1963 to February 1973) was in northern Laos in support of the Royal Laotian Army, guerrillas trained and supplied by the Central

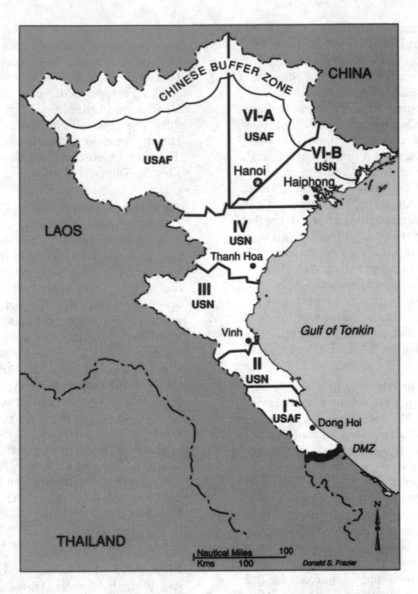

U.S. Air Force–U.S. Navy Route Packages. *Imposed in December 1965 by Adm. U.S. Grant Sharp, CINCPAC, the so-called route packages divided responsibility for bombing operations over North Vietnam between the U.S. Navy and the U.S. Air Force. As the map indicates, coastal targets were primarily reserved for carrier-based Navy aircraft; inland targets were usually allowed to longer-range Air Force aircraft mostly operating from bases in Thailand and South Vietnam. Operations were strictly forbidden within a buffer zone along the Chinese border. (Map adapted from Barrett Tillman and John B. Nichols,* On Yankee Station. *Naval Institute Press, 1987.)*

Intelligence Agency (CIA), and Thai ground forces. The fifth campaign was in support of the Lon Nol government of Cambodia and lasted from March 1969 until August 1973.

The airlift capacity of the Air Force also played a major role in the Vietnam War. After the initial buildup, most military personnel arrived in Vietnam and returned home aboard MAC transports and civilian jetliners operating under MAC contract. Turboprop C-130 transports were used throughout Southeast Asia and the Pacific. Air force airborne forward air controllers (FACs), who directed air strikes from propeller-driven light aircraft, were a major feature of the war in South Vietnam, along the Ho Chi Minh Trail, and in northern Laos. Technical and tactical air force contributions to the U.S. war effort included the extensive use of air refueling; the development of fixed-wing, side-firing gunships (notably the AC-47 and AC-130); and the creation of a specialized combat rescue organization based on long-range, air-refuelable HH-3E and HH-53C helicopters.

The casualty profile differed sharply from that of the Army and Marine Corps but resembled that of the Navy in that most KIAs were officer aviators. Casualties, defined as those killed in action or wounded seriously enough to require hospitalization, comprised only 1.2 percent of Air Force personnel who served in Southeast Asia, as opposed to 22.5 percent for the Marines and 9.5 percent for the Army. However, 65 percent of those killed in action were officers. The median rank of air force KIAs was captain (653 lost); more majors were killed in action (399) than first lieutenants (236) and nearly as many colonels (184) as lieutenant colonels (187).

See also: Ap Bia; Arc Light; Bien Hoa; Brown, George S.;

Commander-in-Chief, Pacific; Defense, Department of; Easter Offensive; Hoopes, Townsend; Linebacker I & II, Operations; Medical Support; Menu, Operation; Philippines; Plain of Jars; *Pueblo* Incident; Ranch Hand, Operation; Rolling Thunder, Operation; Search and Rescue; Tan Son Nhut.

Airmoble Assault Units. The U.S. Army developed new helicopter-borne air mobile assault units and tactics in the Vietnam War. The helicopter revolutionized every aspect of operations, from fire support to medical evacuation, establishing itself as a significant new weapon of war. The rapid insertion and extraction of U.S. Army units by helicopter and the use of air cavalry helicopter gunships for fire support became hallmarks of Army airmobile operations throughout South Vietnam. The 1st Cavalry Division (Airmobile) became the first air mobile division in the U.S. Army in July 1965.

See also: Helicopters.

Airmobile Divisions. The U.S. Army was by far the largest user of helicopters and fielded entire airmobile divisions with helicopter transport, reconnaissance, and fire support. Most notable of these was the 1st Cavalry Division (Airmobile).

See also: Helicopters; Ia Drang.

Air Power. The U.S. Air Force was the largest player in the air power arena. Air power played a crucial role in sustaining South Vietnam militarily, inflicted heavy losses on North Vietnamese and Viet Cong forces, and reduced the toll on U.S. and allied ground forces. However, air power did not win the war and detractors argue that it could not have done so. Advocates respond that air power was not given a chance, citing the success of the Linebacker campaigns in achieving President Nixon's objectives and arguing that President Johnson and Defense Secretary McNamara's micro-management of Rolling Thunder doomed it to failure.

See also: Arc Light, Operation; Air Force, U.S.; Linebacker and Linebacker II Operations; Radford, Arthur W.; Rolling Thunder, Operation.

Alessandri, Marcel (1893–1968), French Army major general. General Alessandri commanded the French Army in Tonkin during WWII. He was relieved of his command in 1950 following severe French losses against the Viet Minh in northern Vietnam.

See also: Franco–Viet Minh War.

Algerian Crisis. The 1958 uprising in France's North African colony of Algeria can be traced in some respects to the catastrophic French defeat in May 1954 at Dien Bien Phu in Vietnam. The loss at Dien Bien Phu led to France's withdrawal from its Indochinese colonies. The defeat in Indochina hardened French resolve to stand firm in its North African colony; the Viet Minh victory, correspondingly, inspired Algerian nationalists, who perceived the vulnerability of the colonialists.

See also: Ten-Pin Theory.

Ali, Muhammad (1942–), born Cassius Clay; American heavyweight boxing champion (1964–1967). Drafted in 1966, Ali, a Black Muslim, unsuccessfully applied for conscientious objector status on religious grounds. When he refused to report for duty, he was stripped of his boxing title. In June 1967 Ali was convicted of violating the Selective Service Act, fined $10,000, and sentenced to five years in prison. The Supreme Court reversed the conviction.

See also: African-Americans.

All for the Brotherly South Campaign. After the U.S. bombing campaign of North Vietnam began in 1964, the Democratic Republic of Vietnam mounted a political campaign called "All for the Brotherly South" *(Tat Ca Cho Mien Nam Ruot Thit)* to rally support for the war against the United States. This was partly because to all Vietnamese destruction of the land, houses and graveyards had deep cultural meaning. It was a political campaign, designed to bolster spirits in the north for the war against the south, not a military campaign.

It is the tradition of the Vietnamese people to fight those who destroy their ancestors' graveyards or bring foreigners in to destroy the fatherland. Because the Vietnamese considered the Red River Delta region the cradle of their civilization, and because the United States tried to bomb it heavily, many Vietnamese, whether from the North or South, were ready to sacrifice everything to rid their country of the foreign destroyers of their traditions.

See also: Red River Delta

All-Volunteer Force (AVF).
The name given to the U.S. military after President Nixon ended the draft in January 1973.

Alpha Company Incident. A widely publicized incident of combat refusal that occurred in August 1969 when, after five days of intense fighting at a remote fire base near Da Nang during which 10 men were killed and 20 wounded, Company A of the 3rd Battalion, 21st Infantry, 23rd Infantry "Americal" Division, refused an order to move back into the battle zone. This was the first recorded instance of combat refusal in the Vietnam War.

Alvarez, Everett Jr., Lt. (jg)
(1937–), U.S. Navy pilot whose A-4 fighter bomber was shot down in a retaliatory air raid against North Vietnam on August 5, 1964. Alvarez became the first U.S. prisoner of war

(and the longest held, for eight years) in North Vietnam.

See also: Pierce Arrow, Operation.

Amerasians. After the end of the Vietnam War, Amerasian children—the sons and daughters of U.S. servicemen and Vietnamese women—were a significant and visible group in Vietnam. Amerasian children, particularly those of African-American parentage, were ill-treated and discriminated against in Vietnam and most sought to emigrate to the United States. Amerasians also exist in other countries where Americans served, in Korea, Laos, and Thailand. The most commonly accepted estimate of the number of Amerasians in Southeast Asia is 30,000, but estimates range from 10,000 to 200,000. Of these, most (65–75 percent) were fathered by Euro-American soldiers, the rest by African-Americans.

In 1982, Congress passed legislation accepting Amerasians as U.S. citizens. However, because the United States and Vietnam had not established diplomatic relations, Amerasians in Vietnam were excluded from the bill. After much criticism, the U.S. government qualified for entrance to the United States any person born in Vietnam between 1 January 1962 and 1 January 1976 who was fathered by a U.S. citizen. Amerasian emigration from Vietnam proceeded slowly until the Amerasian Homecoming Act of 1987 set a timetable for bringing all Amerasians and their family members to the United States. By 1990, some 22,000 Amerasian refugees had settled in the United States.

American Friends of Vietnam.

Private U.S. anti-communist organization formed in 1955 to support South Vietnam. Professor Wesley Fishel of Michigan State University led the organization, which consisted largely of American mainstream liberals. Charter members included Sen. John F. Kennedy, the historian Arthur M. Schlesinger, Jr., and Norman Thomas, the perennial socialist presidential candidate. The group acted as an unofficial lobby for the government of Ngo Dinh Diem until support for Diem waned in the early 1960s. The organization became active again in 1965 after a wave of teach-ins on college campuses questioned President Lyndon Johnson's Vietnam policies. National Security Council aide Chester Cooper recommended using pro-administration Vietnam experts not officially tied to the White House to defend Johnson's policies. The administration turned to the Friends of Vietnam to organize this effort. In 1965 and 1966, the Friends organized a speaker's bureau of pro-administration Vietnam experts and arranged more than one hundred speeches, many on college campuses.

See also: Fishel, Wesley; O'Daniel, John W.

American Friends Service Committee.

Founded in 1917 by American Quakers (Friends) to relieve the sufferings of European civilians in World War I, the group was active in the American anti–Vietnam War movement beginning in 1963. The committee took part in many non-violent types of demonstrations to lobby for a political settlement to the war.

Amnesty.

Following the end of the draft in 1972 and the withdrawal of all U.S. troops from Vietnam the following year, approximately 281,300 civilians, including draft fugitives, nonregistrants, convicted draft offenders, and expatriates, along with an estimated 566,000 military personnel, were eligible for some form of amnesty. Civilians needed amnesty to have legal charges dismissed or to return from exile. Some specifically sought amnesty for moral reasons: they considered amnesty an acknowledgment by the government that those who had opposed the war were in fact morally correct, while a pardon would be an admission that they had been wrong but were being forgiven by the government. Veterans with less-than-honorable discharges needed amnesty to erase the negative stigma. Deserters required amnesty to free them from the threat of legal action by the U.S. military and, most likely, incarceration in a military prison for having been absent without leave (AWOL). The U.S. government took no official action on the issue for several years.

Conservatives and veterans' groups opposed amnesty, especially for draft resisters. President Gerald Ford began amnesty action with a clemency program of "earned reentry" based on case-by-case reviews and the option of alternative service, for civilians and military personnel. Few participated in the Ford program. The 1976 Democratic Party platform advocated amnesty for all who were "in legal or financial jeopardy because of their peaceful opposition to the Vietnam War." President Jimmy Carter's first action as president in 1977 was to issue an unconditional "blanket pardon." Former military personnel were offered a "Special Discharge Review Program" with case-by-case reviews and the possibility of discharge upgrades.

See also: Carter, Jimmy; Ford, Gerald R. Jr.

Amphibious Landing Operations.

A military assault from the open sea by a landing force across the shore. During the Vietnam War, U.S. amphibious capability was nearly the exclusive domain of the amphibious task groups of the Seventh Fleet. The groups usually consisted of a Marine Corps battalion landing team (a self-sustaining U.S. Marine infantry battalion reinforced with small support detachments) and a helicopter squadron. The most successful amphibious operation in the war was the first,

Operation Starlite, which took place in August 1965 when three Marine Corps battalions surprised a Viet Cong Regiment on the Van Tuong Peninsula near Chu Lai. From 18 to 24 August, the U.S. Marines killed more than 600 Viet Cong soldiers, but sustained heavy casualties themselves, including 51 dead and more than 200 wounded.

After Starlite, the Seventh Fleet Marine SLF, in coordination with the U.S. Military Assistance Command, Vietnam (USMACV), conducted more than seventy amphibious raids along the entire coast of South Vietnam. None were as successful as Starlite. Most resulted in largely unopposed landings. Still, the Marine SLF units helped keep North Vietnamese and Viet Cong coastal forces off balance and served as a means to reinforce allied units already engaged. Until late 1967, the SLF units also permitted MACV some leverage because they did not count against "in-country" troop strength figures. For the Marine Corps command in Vietnam, III Marine Amphibious Force (III MAF), the amphibious forces provided a means of refitting and replenishing units stationed ashore in I Corps through a system of battalion and helicopter rotations to and out of SLF units. For much of 1968, during the Tet Offensive, the battle for Khe Sanh, and the heavy fighting along the demilitarized zone (DMZ), marine SLF battalions spent extended periods ashore, acting as additional

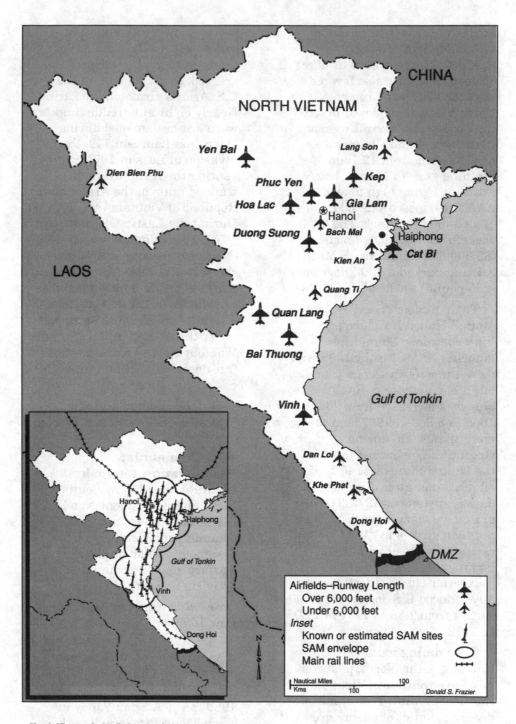

North Vietnam's Air Defenses. *SAM sites as of early 1969; key airfields as of 1972. (Map adapted from Barrett Tillman and John B. Nichols,* On Yankee Station. *Naval Institute Press, 1987.)*

artillery (AAA) batteries atop tall buildings in Hanoi. Restricted targets, such as dikes or hospitals, were also favored sites for AAA emplacements. North Vietnam deployed practically every antiaircraft weapon in the Soviet and Chinese arsenals, ranging from 12.7mm machine guns to 130mm heavy artillery. Flying high to avoid AAA fire exposed U.S. pilots to guided-missile attack. The SA-2 was effective to 26,000 meters (85,000 feet), could reach Mach 2.5, and packed a 130-kilogram (285-pound) warhead.

The notorious "SAM Triangle" around Hanoi, Haiphong, and Vinh contained 60 multiple-launcher SAM sites by 1966, and more than 150 sites one year later. The number of SAM launches increased from 200 in 1965 to 3,500 in 1967, and to more than 4,200 during Operation Linebacker, in which the United States lost 15 B-52s and 11 other aircraft in just 12 days in December 1972. The use of evasive maneuvers, SAM suppression strikes by "Wild Weasel" aircraft equipped with radar-homing missiles, and electronic countermeasures (ECMs) gradually reduced U.S. losses per 1,000 sorties from 2.38 in 1967 to 1.80 in 1972.

Even during halts in the bombing of the North, pilots on missions over South Vietnam or the Ho Chi Minh Trail ran a deadly gauntlet of enemy fire from small arms, machine guns, and mobile M38/39 37mm or ZSU 57mm AAA batteries. Slow moving, low flying helicopters proved especially vulnerable to ground fire as the war progressed, casting doubt on the U.S. Army's airmobility doctrine. Nearly eight hundred helicopters were lost or damaged during Operation Lam Son 719, the invasion of Laos in 1971, preventing the resupplying of trapped units of the Army of the Republic of Vietnam (ARVN). During the Easter Offensive in 1972, North Vietnamese Army (NVA) troops equipped with shoulder-fired SA-7 Strella portable SAMs inflicted significant losses on combat support aircraft. U.S. air superiority was never threatened in the Vietnam War, but North Vietnam attained "air deniability" that limited the use of that superiority.

See also: Rolling Thunder, Operation; SAMs; Smart Bombs.

Anti-Communist Denunciation Campaign.
Instituted in 1955 by South Vietnamese President Ngo Dinh Diem, the Anti-Communist Denunciation Campaign was designed to conduct ideological warfare against communist activists in South Vietnam.

See also: National Assembly Law 10/59.

Apache Snow, Operation.
An operation conducted by U.S. and South Vietnamese forces in May 1969 in the A Shau Valley in Thau Thien Province, less than two kilometers (one mile) from the Laotian border. The fight

against two NVA battalions for Ap Bia Mountain (also known as Hill 937 and Hamburger Hill) was one of the bloodiest battles of the Vietnam War. In 10 days of fighting, 70 Americans were killed, and the hill was taken, only to be abandoned several days later.

See also: Ap Bia; Hamburger Hill.

Ap Bac. South Vietnamese village in Mekong Delta, 65 kilometers (40 miles) southwest of Saigon. In early January 1963 Army of the Republic of Vietnam (ARVN) forces attacked Viet Cong guerrilla positions in the area. The guerrillas inflicted heavy casualties on the South Vietnamese, largely because of the poor performance of some ARVN officers. Although the Viet Cong forces eventually abandoned their positions, their success against the ARVN forces provided them with an important psychological boost.

See also: Army of the Republic of Vietnam; People's Liberation Armed Forces.

Ap Bia. Ap Bia mountain, in the A Shau Valley near the Laotian border with South Vietnam, was the site of one of the bloodiest battles of the Vietnam War. From 10 to 20 May 1969, as part of Operation Apache Snow, Army of the Republic of Vietnam (ARVN) units and elements of the U.S. Army's 101st Airborne Division fought to take the mountain from an entrenched Viet Cong

force. Both sides sustained high casualties in an engagement U.S. troops called "Hamburger Hill." Though they succeeded in occupying the hill, the ARVN and U.S. forces withdrew one week later.

See also: Apache Snow, Operation; A Shau Valley; Hamburger Hill.

APC. *See* Accelerated Pacification Campaign.

Apocalypse Now (1979). Francis Ford Coppola's epic film, a surreal reworking of Joseph Conrad's *Heart of Darkness* set in Vietnam and Cambodia.

Arc Light, Operation. Code name for high-altitude B-52 bombing raids in support of U.S. and Army of the Republic of Vietnam (ARVN) operations in South Vietnam and Laos. Dropped from B-52s flying above 30,000 feet, the bombs could not be seen or heard until they exploded, and caused enormous destruction in the impact areas. The first Arc Light strike targeting communist forces' rear areas occurred on 18 June 1965, marking the debut of U.S. Air Force Strategic Air Command (SAC) firepower in Vietnam; the last was on 18 August 1973. Prior to Arc Light, B-52s were used exclusively as part of the U.S. strategic nuclear force and as a pillar of the SIOP (Single Integrated Operational Plan), the U.S. war plan for a nuclear exchange with the Soviet Union.

Arc Light strikes were first mounted from Andersen Air Force Base in Guam, more than 3,200 kilometers (2,000 miles) from Vietnam. Beginning in July 1967, B-52s also operated from the U Tapao Royal Thai Naval Base near Bangkok, only some 800 kilometers (500 miles) from the target areas. Arc Light strikes were largely confined to South Vietnam, which absorbed more than 80 percent of the total. Targets immediately across the Laotian border were hit from December 1966 on, and there were occasional strikes against transportation and infiltration targets in southernmost North Vietnam.

The B-52s bombed by radar, at first using radar reflectors brought into the target area by helicopter and later under guidance from ground-based Skyspot radars. Most Arc Light strikes were against North Vietnamese Army (NVA) or Viet Cong base areas. Intelligence suggested, and postwar accounts confirmed, that the strikes were highly destructive, greatly feared, and had a serious impact on the morale of North Vietnamese and Viet Cong forces. Arc Light tactical support of ground troops began in mid-November 1965. These strikes were employed within 900 meters (3,000 feet) of friendly troops and were especially effective against NVA forces at Khe Sanh in 1968 and Pleiku and An Loc in 1972.

See also: B-52; Khe Sanh; Menu, Operation; Niagara, Operation.

Argenlieu, Georges Thierry D' (1889–1964), French high commissioner for Indochina, August 1946 to April 1947. Appointed by French President Charles de Gaulle, French Naval Vice Admiral d'Argenlieu zealously reestablished French authority in Indochina following World War II. He preempted the Fontainebleau Conference by unilaterally and without authority declaring the Republic of Cochinchina in southern Vietnam. The bombardment of Haiphong in November 1946, which he ordered, led to open warfare with the Viet Minh in December. Argenlieu was recalled to Paris in 1947 because of his extreme unpopularity among the Vietnamese, French socialists and communists.

See also: Bidault, Georges; Fontainebleau Conference; Le Van Kim.

Armstrong, Dwight (1952–) and **Karleton** (1948–). Residents of Madison, Wisc., Karl and Dwight Armstrong, along with two University of Wisconsin students, David Fine and Leo Burt, were arrested in connection with the bombing of the university's Army Mathematics Research Center on 24 August 1970, an incident in which researcher Bob Fassnacht was killed. In 1973 Karl Armstrong was tried, convicted, and sentenced to 23 years in prison. His sentence was later reduced to 10 years after Dwight Armstrong pleaded guilty to second-degree murder and received a 7-year sentence.

See also: Burt, Leo; Fassnacht, Robert; Fine, David; University of Wisconsin Bombing.

Army, U.S. The U.S. Army entered the Vietnam War gradually. President Kennedy in 1961 sent in Special Forces and military advisers, helicopter companies and other support units to assist the Army of the Republic of Vietnam (ARVN). By the end of 1963 the United States increased the number of Army advisers and support troops to nearly 16,000. In 1965, President Lyndon Johnson sent U.S. combat divisions to South Vietnam. By late 1968, the U.S. Army force in Vietnam, then at its peak strength, included seven infantry divisions, four independent infantry brigades, and an armored cavalry regiment, along with large combat and service support elements and a substantial advisory contingent—a total of more than 365,000 men and women. U.S. Army troops in Vietnam probably were the best supplied and equipped and received the most rapid and effective medical care of any fighting force in any U.S. war.

The Army broadly had two primary missions in Vietnam: the destruction of North Vietnamese and Viet Cong military units, and the development of an ARVN capable of bringing government control to the countryside, ultimately replacing U.S. forces in South Vietnam. While

U.S. troops defeated large NVA units when they were able to engage them, the NVA and Viet Cong regularly evaded combat and withdrew to base areas in Cambodia, Laos, and North Vietnam where the Americans, because of Johnson's decision to limit the war, were not allowed to pursue them. The U.S. Army advisory and assistance effort never overcame the ARVN's leadership, training and motivation deficiencies. By the war's end, U.S. Army casualties in Vietnam totaled more than 47,000 dead, more than 200,000 wounded, and nearly 2,000 captured or missing in action.

See also: Body Count; Casualties; Defense, Department of; Helicopters; Medical Support, U.S.; Military Assistance Advisory Group–Vietnam (MAAG-V); Military Assistance Command-Vietnam (MACV); Order of Battle, U.S. Military (Appendix B); Pacification; Project 100,000; Special Forces, U.S. Army.

Army-Navy Mobile Riverine Force. The U.S. Navy's Riverine Assault Force (Task Force 117), one of the main units of the U.S. Naval Forces, Vietnam, was the naval component of the joint Army-Navy Mobile Riverine Force, which was authorized in mid-1966 and deployed in Vietnam early in 1967. It eventually consisted of two brigades of the U.S. Army 9th Infantry Division, which operated with the U.S. Navy river assault squadrons of Task Force 117 in the upper Mekong Delta. MACV abolished the force in August 1969.

See also: Market Garden, Operation; Market Time, Operation.

Army of the Republic of Vietnam (ARVN). Created by the United States in 1955, the ARVN was the land forces component in the Republic of Vietnam Armed Forces (RVNAF), which included a navy and air force. The ARVN's mission was to neutralize North Vietnam's People's Army of Vietnam (PAVN) and its southern ally, the National Liberation Front (NLF), also known as the Viet Cong.

The first Vietnamese military force created by a Western nation to fight Vietnamese opponents dates from 1879. In that year, the French organized the *Régiment de Tirailleurs Annamites* (the Annamite Rifles) in Saigon; four years later, a companion unit, the *Régiment de Tirailleurs Tonkinois* (the Tonkin Rifles) was formed in Hanoi. Together they helped colonial army units enforce French policies in Vietnam. France believed its presence in Vietnam was "just," based on Western perceptions of empire, and it took steps to attain a variety of goals at local expense. For example, during World War I, some 48,000 Vietnamese laborers were conscripted and sent to the western front in Europe: 10,000 died and 15,000 were wounded, a casualty rate in excess of 50 percent. The Vietnamese were praised for their sacrifices in government reports, but there were few welfare or repatriation benefits for them. Veterans received little, if any, psychological support or material rewards for their services to France. In 1940 there were 60,000 Vietnamese troops, mostly conscripts, serving in the French colonial army in Vietnam; North African (40,000) and European (20,000) troops provided the remainder. France expected a degree of loyalty from the Vietnamese troops that did not materialize, however, because of the conclusion of World War II, continued Vietnamese antagonism toward colonial rule, and Vietnamese resentment over French collaboration with the Japanese occupation of Vietnam. By October 1946, 39,610 Vietnamese troops had deserted, more than 50 percent of the Vietnamese contribution to the colonial army's strength in Vietnam at that time.

Two years later, the French Indochina War against the Viet Minh had intensified and the colonial army had yet to find a military solution. Furthermore, defense priorities in Europe required a decrease in the number of French personnel serving in Vietnam, and growing antiwar sentiment among the French public had increased to the point at which government officials felt insecure about France's position in the war. Funding was unreliable; without U.S. assistance the

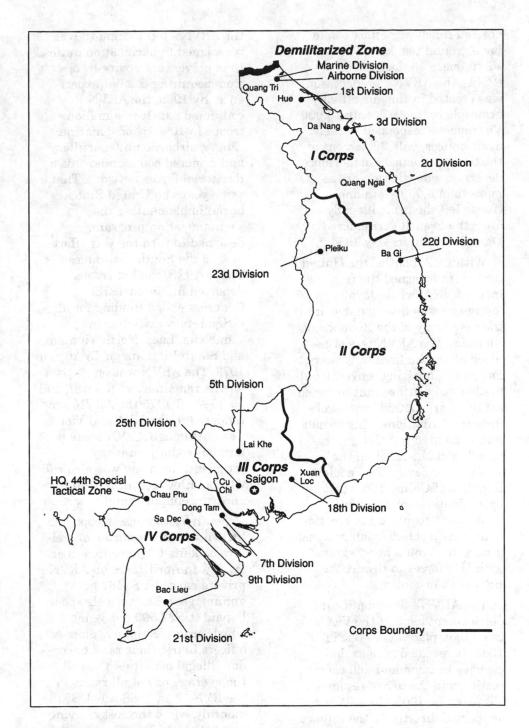

ARVN Divisions, December 1972. *The map shows ARVN divisional headquarters as located after the Easter Offensive. Note that the Airborne and Marine divisions, though headquartered in Saigon, were operating in and around Quang Tri City, which was retaken in the closing stages of the offensive. (Map adapted from William E. Le Gro,* Vietnam from Cease-Fire to Capitulation. *Center of Military History, 1981.)*

entire French war effort would have ground to a halt. The Vietnamese National Army (VNA), the ARVN's predecessor, was created in this unsettled atmosphere. In 1953 only 10,000 Vietnamese responded to their draft notices, only 20 percent of the desired quotas. Furthermore, desertion was widespread, as more than 4,000 Vietnamese troops left the army illegally after the French surrendered at Dien Bien Phu in May 1954.

Within 12 months, the United States transformed the fragmented VNA, whose loyalty to foreigners was questionable, into the new Army of the Republic of Vietnam. The ARVN was organized along the lines of Western forces, emphasizing conventional methods of warfare that included artillery, armor, and large-scale infantry formations. This format complemented the U.S. government's global outlook in the 1950s: specifically, the People's Republic of China (PRC) had been identified as a potential threat that required the creation of armies in select Asian nations, armies that could be integrated with U.S. forces to thwart the PRC's expansionism.

The ARVN's first significant engagement against the Viet Cong took place at Ap Bac in 1963. It revealed serious deficiencies in command and control, tactics, and the use of resources. However, by 1965, the ARVN, supported directly by the influx of U.S. combat forces, seemed to be a strong military force. However, in 1966, 50 percent of

the ARVN's total strength was reassigned to pacification duties, thus preventing novice troops from acquiring combat experience. By 1969, the ARVN contained nearly one million troops in 10 divisions; marine, ranger, airborne units; artillery and armored commands; plus a territorial forces network. That same year, the United States began implementing the Vietnamization program, designed to turn the war effort over to the South Vietnamese. The last U.S. combat troops departed in March 1973. Congress ended funding for all U.S. military activities in Cambodia, Laos, North Vietnam, and South Vietnam on 15 August 1973. The ARVN was on its own for the remainder of the war, and on 30 April 1975 the ARVN surrendered to the NVA and Viet Cong. Although ARVN units performed credibly on many occasions, the army was also rife with apathy, corruption, indifference, unreliability, and desertion.

South Vietnamese troops had little material, financial, or welfare benefits to guarantee their loyalty. In April 1968, an ARVN private earned US$467 per annum; generals were also poorly paid (US$2,500 per year), which prompted many senior officers to use their rank to conduct illegal activities. Overall, the average pay of all ranks in the RVNAF in 1968 was US$108 monthly, while the cost of living was between US$117 and US$120. Thus, Vietnamese soldiers, sailors, and airmen could not exist on their wages.

Desertion was a fundamental cause of the ARVN's demise and South Vietnam's downfall. Between 1965 and 1972 approximately 840,000 troops deserted, 120,000 per year. Desertions exceeded casualties by 6 to 1. The average deserter was aged 17–21, held the rank of private, and had served less than six months. The ARVN had the highest desertion rate (60 percent) of all ground units; the Regional Forces (23 percent) and Popular Forces (17 percent) accounted for the remainder. The ARVN's infantry divisions, those closest to the conflict, had the greatest number of deserters. The 25th and 5th divisions, located in III Corps Tactical Zone (CTZ) near Saigon, had the worst desertion rates: between 1965 and 1972, the 25th Division lost more than 8,400 troops, 1,200 men annually; the 5th Division ranked second. Within the ARVN's elite forces, the rangers had the greatest overall desertion rate (55 percent), followed by the airborne unit (30 percent) and the marines (15 percent). Of the entire RVNAF, 80 percent of all desertions occurred in the ARVN's combat units, 12 percent in the navy, and 8 percent in the air force.

In July 1973, Congress passed Public Law 93-50, which ended funding for U.S. military activities in Cambodia, Laos, North Vietnam, and South Vietnam. The greatest consequence of the law, which took effect on 15 August, was that the ARVN no longer had U.S. air support. Financially, South Vietnam asked for $1.45 billion for the calendar year 1975, but Congress provided only $700 million. In December 1974 and January 1975, PAVN forces attacked Phuoc Long province, northeast of Saigon, to determine how the United States would react to PAVN military actions. Outnumbered and outgunned, the ARVN fought with determination, but at great cost; the 18th Division and the 7th Ranger Group lost 4,500 troops killed or wounded by the PAVN's sustained artillery barrages. The congressional legislation had prohibited intervention by U.S. air power, and the ARVN was on its own for the remainder of the war.

See also: Abrams, Creighton; An Loc; Ap Bac; Ap Bia; Arc Light, Operation; B-52; Ban Me Thuot; Cambodian Incursion; Cao Van Vien; Civilian Irregular Defense Groups; Colby, William; Da Nang; Desertion; Dong Xoai; Duong Van Minh; Easter Offensive; Enclave Strategy; Fishhook; Helicopters; Ho Chi Minh Campaign; Hue; Ia Drang; Joint General Staff; Long Binh; Military Assistance Command, Vietnam; Military Assistance Advisory Group—Vietnam; Montagnards; Pacification; Pleiku; Provincial Reconnaissance Units; Quang Tri; Reeducation Camps; Regional/Popular Forces; Special Forces, ARVN; Tet Offensive; Tran Van Don; Trang Sup; Vann,

John Paul; Veterans, Vietnamese; Vietnamization; Westmoreland, William; Xuan Loc.

Arnett, Peter (1934–), Associated Press correspondent in Vietnam, 1962–1975. The longest-serving reporter in South Vietnam. Arnett, a native of New Zealand, often clashed with officials over his critical reporting of problems within the South Vietnamese government and the U.S. military. Arnett was regarded by many of his peers as the best Vietnam War correspondent.

ARPA. *See* Advanced Research Projects Agency.

ARVN. *See* Army of the Republic of Vietnam.

A Shau Valley. Located in Thua Thien province, near Laos; main entry point of the Ho Chi Minh Trail into South Vietnam. The A Shau Valley was a vital conduit into the northern military region of South Vietnam. North Vietnamese forces vigorously defended the valley against repeated U.S. and South Vietnamese attacks, none of which succeeded for more than a brief period. The noted battle at Ap Bia (also known as "Hamburger Hill"), took place in the valley from 10 to 20 May, 1969.

See also: Ap Bia; Hamburger Hill.

Associated Press. Oriented toward local markets, most newspapers in the United States relied upon news services such as the Associated Press (AP) for the news they carried of the war and refrained from assigning full-time reporters to South Vietnam on a consistent basis. The AP had eight reporters in the field at the height of the war in January 1968.

See also: Arnett, Peter.

Associated State of Vietnam (ASV). In March 1949, the French colonial authorities created the Associated State of Vietnam, with former emperor Bao Dai as chief of state. The ASV consisted of all the territory included in the Vietnamese Empire, which in the late nineteenth century had been divided by the French into three separate regions: Cochinchina, Tonkin, and Annam. Until the French defeat at Dien Bien Phu in 1954, the ASV collaborated with the French in seeking to prevent a communist victory. On 26 October 26, 1955, the ASV prime minister, Ngo Dinh Diem, formally established the Republic of Vietnam.

See also: Bao Dai; Ngo Dinh Diem; Vietnam, Republic of.

Atrocities. Often considered synonymous with war crimes, atrocities are defined by various international treaties and conventions. In the U.S. armed forces, these conventions are incorporated into the Uniform Code of Military Justice, and breaches of them by U.S. soldiers are supposed to be prosecuted through the military judicial system. These rules of warfare are quite extensive and complex. In general, atrocities are considered inhumane acts such as murder, torture, rape, robbery and other abuse against prisoners of war and noncombatants. Many abuses result from the chaos of the battlefield, the decentralized character of operations, and the widely varying discipline and training of the participating forces. Most instances of killing of captured or wounded soldiers and mutilation of the dead fall into this category, as do individual acts of murder, rape, and robbery by soldiers of both sides—crimes common among fighting men from time immemorial. Common, too, was the exaction of food and other supplies from peasants by soldiers of both Vietnamese factions, although the Viet Cong guerrillas regularized theirs as a form of taxation.

The Vietnam War witnessed many types of atrocities by both sides. U.S. forces used some weapons and tactics that came very close to or crossed the line of the permissible, notably the widespread employment of riot gases and herbicides, although a legal and moral defense can be made for the use of both. On the other hand, U.S. bombing of North Vietnam, while far from pinpoint in precision, avoided the sort of indiscriminate area attacks common in World War II. On the allied side, U.S. forces in the main treated prisoners in conformity with the Geneva and Hague conventions; but South Vietnamese troops, despite continual U.S. efforts to improve their conduct, often brutalized prisoners. South Vietnamese prison camps often fell short of international standards, as the well-publicized case of the Con Son "tiger cages" attested. North Vietnam, which considered captured U.S. airmen war criminals, subjected them to torture and abuse and compelled them to participate in anti-U.S. propaganda broadcasts. Viet Cong guerrillas in the south used terror, including systematic murder and kidnapping of civilians. The execution of some 2,800 persons in Hue during the 1968 Tet Offensive by North Vietnamese forces was an unusually large-scale atrocity. Peasants under Viet Cong control planted mines and booby traps that killed and maimed U.S. soldiers, provoking fear, hatred, and a desire to retaliate among the GIs. Those feelings, combined with poor unit leadership and training, contributed to the largest single U.S. atrocity of the war, the slaughter of several hundred civilians by soldiers of the American Division at My Lai in March 1968.

See also: Con Son; Geneva and Hague Conventions; My Lai; Tiger Cages.

Attleboro, Operation. A military engagement that took place in September 1966 near the Soui Da Special Forces Camp in Tay Ninh Province, in which elements of the U.S. 1st, 4th, and

25th Infantry Divisions inflicted heavy casualties on the 9th Viet Cong Division and the 101st NVA Regiment, forcing them to withdraw into Cambodia.

Attrition Strategy. Attrition strategy guided the U.S. war effort in Vietnam from start to finish. U.S. commanders, denied permission to invade North Vietnam, tried to break the will of communist forces by killing their soldiers and destroying their equipment until they gave up. The assumption was that losses would grow unacceptable and that North Vietnam would withdraw support for insurgency in South Vietnam.

Attrition strategy failed because the Viet Cong and North Vietnamese controlled the pace and intensity of battle. They began most military engagements and pulled back when battles turned against them. They sought sanctuary across borders that Americans could not cross and received supplies from foreign sources that Americans could not interdict. North Vietnam lost about three percent of its population to battle, a level nearly unprecedented in the history of warfare, but continued to fight on.

See also: Westmoreland, William.

August Revolution. Following Japan's surrender in August 1945, and just three days after calling for a general insurrection on 16 August, Ho Chi Minh and his Viet Minh seized power in Hanoi, initiating the August Revolution against the Japanese and the resurgent French. On 2 September Ho Chi Minh proclaimed Vietnamese independence and the establishment of the Democratic Republic of Vietnam (DRV).

See also: Ho Chi Minh; People's Army of Vietnam; Vo Nguyen Giap.

Au Lac State. Legendary Vietnamese kingdom in the northern mountains south of China, started by the mythical King An Duong Vuong. "Lac" is the oldest name for the Vietnamese people.

Auriol, Vincent (1884–1966), president of the Fourth French Republic, 1947–1954. On 8 March 1949, Auriol exchanged letters at the Elysee Palace in Paris with former emperor Bao Dai, which paved the way for Bao Dai to return to Vietnam as emperor and head of the Associated State of Vietnam within the French Union.

See also: Élysée Agreement.

Australia. Australia's military involvement in Vietnam began in 1962, when it sent a 30-man jungle warfare specialist group, the Australian Army Training Team Vietnam, to train South Vietnamese troops. In April 1965 Australia deployed its first combat troops. By September 1965, Australia had added artillery, air reconnaissance, and engineers.

In contrast to the United States, Australia rotated entire regiments, rather than individuals, into and out of Vietnam; but like the United States, it conscripted soldiers to fill its ranks. Australia coordinated its military forces with those of New Zealand. In 1966 Australia established a base camp in Phuoc Tuy province. It added air force and naval units in 1967; the number of Australian troops reached a peak of 7,672 in 1969. By 1971, all personnel had returned to Australia. The Australian Army Assistance Group was created in March 1972 to train South Vietnamese and Khmer Republic forces and remained until January 1973. A total of 386 Australians were killed in action and 2,193 wounded in Vietnam. Australia also provided some $10.7 million in civil services to South Vietnam from 1966–1970.

See also: Four-Party Joint Military Commission; Free World; International Reaction; Manila Conference.

AVF. *See* All-Volunteer Force.

AWOL. Absent without leave. In the United States military, desertion is defined as being absent without leave for more than 30 days.

See also: Desertion.

B-52. Large U.S. Air Force strategic bomber. In Vietnam B-52s dropped huge quantities of bombs from high altitude in support of U.S. and Army of the Republic of Vietnam (ARVN) ground operations in South Vietnam, along the Ho Chi Minh Trail, on Cambodia in Operation Menu raids, and in the Linebacker "Christmas bombing" of North Vietnam. Designed for the U.S. Strategic Air Command as a nuclear bomber by the Boeing Aircraft Company, the eight-engine B-52 was the first true intercontinental jet bomber and one of the most successful military aircraft ever built. The B-52's precursor was the B-47, a Boeing medium bomber of radical design, which entered service in the early 1950s. The B-47's thin, swept-back wings and jet engines suspended from underwing pylons inspired not only the B-52, but also the Boeing 707, the first successful commercial jet, and its basic military version, the C-135, the KC-135 tanker version of which played a major role in Vietnam. The B-52 design began as a turboprop in 1945–1946 and solidified in 1948 when the Pratt and Whitney J-57 engine, far more efficient earlier turbojets, promised to combine jet speed with long range. Far-sighted Air Force procurement officials stipulated that the bomber have a conventional as well as a nuclear ordnance capability. The B-52's immense 185-foot wingspan and capacious fuselage enabled it to fly above the range of Soviet antiaircraft artillery, and to drop enormous loads of 500-, 750-, and 1,000-pound high-explosive, general-purpose bombs from altitudes well above 30,000 feet, out of sight and hearing from the ground. On occasion, time-delay fuses were used for area denial and harassment, and armor-piercing 1,000-pound bombs were used to penetrate underground facilities. Bombs, typically dropped by three-aircraft cells in closely spaced strings, fell in long strips, leaving enormous swaths of destruction from blast and cratering. The Air Force purchased 742 B-52s in models A through H between 1953 and 1962. The first Arc Light strikes were carried out in Vietnam by B-52Fs modified to carry twenty-four 750-pound bombs externally on underwing racks. The B-52Fs were replaced beginning in December 1965 by B-52Ds with "Big Belly" bomb bays, modified to carry eighty-four 500-pound bombs or forty-two 750-pound bombs, a total bomb load of some 60,000 pounds, as opposed to 38,000 pounds for the model F. Many older B-52s were retired from service in the 1960s, and about half the B-52s used in the Linebacker campaigns were G models, optimized for the nuclear role with "wet" (i.e., fuel-filled) wings and less than half the conventional bomb load of the model Ds. Until Linebacker, B-52s were used only in low-threat areas and the crews fought a remote, almost antiseptic, war—which earned them the sobriquets "monkey killers" and "splinter makers" among tactical aircrews, the implication being that the B-52s, attacking well above the range of enemy guns, destroyed only jungle vegetation and animals. Despite initial heavy losses, B-52s proved highly effective in the 1972 "Christmas bombings," destroying railroad yards and industrial targets in North Vietnam with minimal damage outside the target areas.

See also: Arc Light, Operation; Commando Hunt, Operation; Haiphong; Harassment-and-Interdiction Fire; Ia Drang; Lam Son 719; Linebacker and Linebacker II Operations; Menu, Operation; Rolling Thunder, Operation; SAMs; Tunnels.

Babylift, Operation. Program begun by President Gerald R. Ford to evacuate South Vietnamese and Cambodian orphans to the United States before the communist takeovers of those countries in April and May 1975. Operation Babylift began on April 4, 1975, and ended May 9, 1975, bringing some 2,600 orphans to American sponsoring families.

Ba Cut (?–1956), nickname of Le Quang Vinh, the leader of the politically powerful and militarily strong Hoa Hao Buddhist sect in South Vietnam from April 1947 until his arrest by the South Vietnamese government in April 1956. Ba Cut was publicly guillotined at Can Tho in July 1956.

See also: Hoa Hao; Ngo Dinh Diem.

Ba Dinh Square. The site in Hanoi of Ho Chi Minh's mausoleum.

See also: Ho Chi Minh.

Baez, Joan (1941–), American folksinger who took an active part in the antiwar movement. From 1964–1974 Baez withheld 60 percent of her income taxes to protest the war. She took part in acts of civil disobedience and sang at protest rallies around the country, calling for an immediate end to the war. In 1979 Baez spoke out against human rights violations in Vietnam.

Balaban, John (1943–), writer, poet. Balaban, a conscientious objector who spent three years in Vietnam during the war with International Voluntary Services, is the author of, among other books, several volumes of Vietnam War–related poetry and the acclaimed memoir, *Remembering Heaven's Face* (1991).

Ball, George W. (1909–), U.S. Undersecretary of State, 1961–1966. In 1961 Ball predicted "the most tragic consequences" if the United States committed to a military role in Vietnam, and said that within five years 300,000 United States soldiers would be mired in a hopeless war. In the Johnson administration,

Ball continued to argue against U.S. military escalation in Vietnam. From 31 May 1964 to 21 April 1966 he submitted 18 memoranda and talking papers in which he refuted the arguments for expanding the war. In 1964, he said that an air war would not demoralize the North nor strengthen the South and that North Vietnam might send army regulars into South Vietnam, thus forcing the United States to match their troop commitment. Ball's views encountered stiff resistance from Dean Rusk, Robert McNamara, and McGeorge Bundy. He resigned in September 1966.

See also: Clifford, Clark; Forrestal, Michael; Hawks and Doves; Ngo Dinh Nhu; Wise Men.

"Ballad of the Green Berets, The." A song written and sung by former Special Forces Sgt. Barry Sadler, an homage to the U.S. Special Forces, that made its way to the top of the popular music charts in 1965.

Ban Me Thuot. South Vietnamese town in Darlac province in the Central Highlands. In a major battle fought 10–11 March 1975, Ban Me Thuot was captured by three North Vietnamese Army (NVA) divisions, prompting President Nguyen Van Thieu to withdraw all South Vietnamese forces from the Central Highlands. This withdrawal of the Army of the Republic of Vietnam (ARVN) forces and the flow of refugees

collapsed into what journalists dubbed the "Convoy of Tears," in which thousands died from starvation and NVA or ARVN shellfire.

See also: Central Highlands.

Bao Dai (1913–1997), emperor of Annam (1925; reigned 1932–1945); the last emperor of Vietnam (1949–1955). Born Prince Nguyen Vinh Thuy, Bao Dai was crowned emperor of French-controlled Annam in 1925. He collaborated with the Japanese during WWII, and when Ho Chi Minh proclaimed the Democratic Republic of Vietnam in 1945, he abdicated and retired to the French Riviera. In 1949 the French, desiring a Vietnamese figurehead for the newly proclaimed Republic of Vietnam, restored him as emperor. In 1950 the United States recognized his regime. He was uninterested in ruling the country and had no real power. Much of the U.S. monetary aid funneled to the South Vietnamese to defeat the Viet Minh was deposited by Bao Dai outside the country for use upon his eventual departure. Bao Dai installed Ngo Dinh Diem as prime minister in 1954, swearing him to defend Vietnam against the communists, and if necessary, against the French. Five months later, in 1955, Diem deposed Bao Dai in a referendum. The Emperor then went into permanent exile in France.

See also: Associated State of Vietnam; Binh Xuyen; Elections,

South Vietnam, 1955; Élysée Agreement; Fontainebleau Conference; France; Ngo Dinh Diem; Vietnam, Democratic Republic of; Vietnamese National Army.

Bao Ninh (1952–), literary pseudonym of a former North Vietnamese Army soldier whose brutal and disturbing first novel of the American war and its aftermath, *The Sorrow of War,* was a bestseller in Vietnam. It was published to critical acclaim in the United States in 1995.

See also: Veterans, Vietnamese.

Barrel Roll, Operation. The code name for covert American air operations over northern Laos from December 1964 to February 1973. The object of the massive bombing campaign was to destroy the Ho Chi Minh Trail and communist bases.

See also: Pathet Lao.

Barrett, Elizabeth, U.S. Navy commander, who served as ranking officer for the Naval Advisory Group in Saigon from 1972 to 1973.

See also: Women, U.S. Military.

Barrier Concept. Roger Fisher of Harvard Law School proposed building a 100-kilometer (60-mile) anti-infiltration barrier across the demilitarized zone (DMZ) and Laos to interdict the flow of personnel and supplies along the Ho Chi Minh Trail in 1966. After scientists at the Institute for Defense Analysis

added technological details, Lt. Gen. Alfred D. Starbird took charge of the plan. In an October 1966 memo, Secretary of Defense Robert McNamara called for "an interdiction zone covered by air-laid mine and bombing attacks pinpointed by air-laid acoustical sensors." Construction of the so-called McNamara Line began with Operation Dye Marker in April 1967, when U.S. Marines cleared 11.6 kilometers (8 miles) of land along the DMZ and sowed it with barbed wire, mines, and sensors. Problems soon developed: the government of Laos rejected a cross-border barrier; PAVN shelling slowed construction; and U.S. military commanders never embraced a static "jungle Maginot line," complaining it would tie down thousands of men who could better be used for search-and-destroy missions. By 1968, the diversion of U.S. manpower for defense of Khe Sanh halted construction of the barrier.

See also: Air-Delivered Seismic Intrusion Devices; McNamara Line.

Barry, Jan (1943–), journalist, veterans' advocate. Barry, who served with the U.S. Army's 18th Aviation Company in Vietnam in 1962–1963, co-founded Vietnam Veterans Against the War and is the author of several volumes of Vietnam War–related poetry.

Basic Training of Pavlo Hummel (1971). Produced on Broadway, it is the first of a trilogy, with *Sticks and Bones* (1972) and *Streamers* (1976), of award-winning plays by the playwright David Rabe, who served with the U.S. Army in Vietnam.

Baskir, Lawrence (1936–), co-author, with William Strauss, of *Chance and Circumstance: The Draft, the War and the Vietnam Generation* (1978), an authoritative study of the some 27 million men of the Vietnam generation and their experiences with the Selective Service System.

See also: Selective Service.

Bay Vien (?–1972), born Le Van Vien; leader of the Binh Xuyen, Saigon's powerful 1940s and 1950s criminal organization. Through payoffs to Emperor Bao Dai and with French approval, Bay Vien became a general in the South Vietnamese Army and head of the national police. After the Diem government defeated the Binh Xuyen in 1955, Bay Vien fled to Paris.

See also: Binh Xuyen.

Beckwith, Charlie A. (1929–), U.S. Army Special Forces colonel. Beckwith, who joined the Special Forces in 1958, served in Laos in 1960. In Vietnam he commanded long-range reconnaissance forces with the 5th Special Forces Group in 1965–1966, and a 101st Airborne Division battalion in 1967–1968. Beckwith later helped establish Delta Force, the elite Special Forces counter-terrorist unit.

See also: Special Forces, U.S. Army.

Béhaine, Pigneau de (1742–1799), French Bishop of Adran who recruited a private mercenary army of French troops that helped Nguyen Anh wrest control of Vietnam from the Tay Son family in 1792, after which Nguyen Anh became the Emperor Gia Long. Béhaine had hoped that his aid to Nguyen Anh would restore French influence in the area, but the emperor was suspicious of French activities and limited their influence in his kingdom.

See also: Gia Long.

Ben Suc. South Vietnamese village 50 kilometers (30 miles) from Saigon in Binh Duong province. During the Vietnam War Ben Suc, in the heart of the Iron Triangle tunnel complex, was controlled by Viet Cong guerrillas. As part of Operation Cedar Falls in January 1967, some 30,000 U.S. and South Vietnamese troops razed the village. All six thousand residents were forcibly relocated so the village could become a free-fire zone. The tunnels beneath the village were soon rebuilt. One year later, Ben Suc served as a base for Viet Cong guerrillas during the Tet Offensive.

See also: Cedar Falls, Operation; Iron Triangle; Tunnels.

Ben Tre. South Vietnamese city, capital of Kien Hoa province in the Mekong Delta. Ben Tre fell to Viet Cong guerrillas during the 1968 Tet Offensive. Half the city, with a population of 35,000, was destroyed by U.S. bombs and shells as U.S. forces retook it in February 1968, killing or wounding about two thousand civilians in the process. Ben Tre was described by a U.S. Army major as the village that "It became necessary to destroy . . . in order to save it."

See also: Ngo Dinh Diem; Nguyen Thi Dinh; Tet Offensive.

Berger, Samuel D. (1911–), U.S. deputy ambassador to South Vietnam, 1968–1972. Berger acted as liaison between the United States and the South Vietnamese government and military. He believed that South Vietnamese president Nguyen Van Thieu could serve as the head of a viable civilian, anticommunist government and urged the United States to support Thieu. Berger also supported the invasions of Cambodia and Laos.

Berrigan, Daniel (1921–), Jesuit Catholic priest who became active in the antiwar movement in 1964. In May 1968, Daniel, his brother Philip Berrigan, also a Catholic priest, and seven others broke into Selective Service offices in Catonsville, Maryland, and destroyed draft records to protest the war. The Berrigans and their associates became known as the "Catonsville Nine." All were convicted for conspiracy and destruction of government property. Daniel Berrigan served 18 months in prison for the crime.

See also: Berrigan Brothers; Berrigan, Philip.

Berrigan, Philip (1923–), a U.S. Army veteran of World War II, Philip Berrigan became an ordained Catholic priest in 1955. Like his brother Daniel, Philip Berrigan became active in the antiwar movement in 1964, and was convicted for his role in the May 1968 break-in at the Selective Service offices in Catonsville, Maryland. He served 32 months in prison before being paroled in December 1972.

See also: Berrigan, Daniel; Berrigan Brothers.

Berrigan Brothers. Daniel Berrigan (1921–), and Philip Berrigan (1923–), American Roman Catholic priests; active spokesmen for Clergy Concerned about Vietnam (later Clergy and Laity Concerned About Vietnam [CALCAV]), an interdenominational peace group. Daniel gained national prominence in 1965 when church superiors ordered him to travel to Latin America to halt his antiwar activities. This action provoked protests from Berrigan's supporters led by his brother Philip, and church superiors allowed Daniel to return to the United States in early 1966. By 1967, the Berrigan brothers urged peace advocates to engage in civil disobedience. In 1968, they and other members of the "Catonsville Nine" used homemade napalm to burn hundreds of records from a Maryland draft board. Tried and convicted,

Daniel and Philip Berrigan respectively served 16 and 32 months in federal prison in the early 1970s. Both brothers, critical of the proliferation of nuclear weaponry, continued their peace activism and civil disobedience during the 1970s and 1980s.

See also: Berrigan, Daniel; Berrigan, Philip.

Bertrand Russell Peace Foundation. The group headed by the Englishman Sir Bertrand Russell that conducted what it termed the "International War Crimes Tribunal" in May and November 1967 in Stockholm and Copenhagen investigating American conduct of the Vietnam War. The tribunal concluded that the United States violated many international treaties and the United Nations charter.

See also: International War Crimes Tribunal; Russell, Bertrand.

Bevel, James, Rev. (1936–), civil rights leader with the Southern Christian Leadership Conference. A close associate of Martin Luther King, Jr., Bevel called for an alliance between the civil rights movement and the antiwar movement. In January 1967, Rev. Bevel was named director of the Spring Mobilization to End the War in Vietnam, a coalition composed of academics, students, and Old and New Left organizations that organized large antiwar demonstrations in New York and San Francisco on 15 April 1967.

Bidault, Georges (1899–1983), premier of the French provisional government, July to December 1946; premier of French Fourth Republic, October 1949 to June 1950; minister of foreign affairs, 1947–1948, 1953–1954; minister of defense, 1951–1952; leader of the Christian-Democratic party that he helped found after WWII. As foreign minister Bidault was a stalwart proponent of the maintenance of the postwar French empire. He allowed High Commissioner Georges d'Argenlieu to pursue aggressive policies in Vietnam, including the November 1946 bombardment of Haiphong. Eight years later, when defeat at Dien Bien Phu appeared imminent, Bidault asked the Eisenhower administration to intervene. When Dien Bien Phu fell, Bidault reversed himself and sought a French withdrawal.

See also: Dien Bien Phu.

Bien Hoa. South Vietnamese city, capital of Bien Hoa province. Some 32 kilometers (20 miles) from Saigon, Bien Hoa became a large U.S. air base and the headquarters of III Corps. Viet Cong guerrillas attacked the South Vietnamese air base at Bien Hoa on 1 November 1964. A predawn mortar bombardment destroyed 6 and damaged 14 of the 20 B-57 bombers stationed there, killing 5 Americans and 2 South Vietnamese. By 1969, 220 U.S. Air Force and 75 South Vietnamese air force planes were based at Bien Hoa. The base was overrun during the North

Vietnamese Spring Offensive of April 1975.

See also: Australia; Ho Chi Minh Campaign; Korea, Republic of; Xuan Loc.

Bigart, Homer (1907–1991), veteran *New York Times* war correspondent who covered the Vietnam War in the 1940s, 1950s and early 1960s. A skeptic about the success of U.S. military involvement in Vietnam, Bigart had a strong influence on Neil Sheehan, David Halberstam and other younger correspondents.

Bigeard, Marcel (1916–), French Army general. Bigeard, a veteran of the French Resistance during WWII, served in Indochina from 1945–1954. He specialized in jungle warfare and, as a major, headed the 6th Colonial Parachute Battalion that parachuted into Dien Bien Phu on 20 November 1953. Bigeard was captured the next year by the Viet Minh and later released.

See also: Dien Bien Phu.

Big Minh. *See* Duong Van Minh

Big Red One. Order of Battle, U.S. Military (Appendix B); U.S. Army, 1st Infantry Division.

See also: Order of Battle, U.S. Military (Appendix B).

Binh Dinh. South Vietnamese province some 300 miles north of Saigon. In operations such as Irving, Pershing, and Thayer,

U.S. forces fought Viet Cong and NVA forces in the coastal plain of the province near the large city of Qui Nhon.

Binh Gia. Town in Quang Ngai province on Vietnam's coastal plain. On 29 May 1965 Viet Cong forces attacked Binh Gia, destroying two South Vietnamese battalions, which dropped their weapons and fled. The performance of the South Vietnamese troops led Gen. William Westmoreland to send a message on 7 June to Adm. Ulysses S. Grant Sharp, Commander-in-Chief, Pacific in which Westmoreland concluded that the South Vietnamese could not defeat the Viet Cong without massive U.S. assistance.

Binh Long. Province some 75 miles north of Saigon near the Cambodian border. The provincial capital, An Loc, was the site of a large NVA-ARVN Battle during the 1972 NVA Easter Offensive.

See also: An Loc; Loc Ninh.

Binh, Nguyen Thi. *See* Nguyen Thi Binh

Binh Xuyen. Saigon's preeminent criminal organization from the 1940s to 1955, named for a village south of the Saigon-Cholon area. Binh Xuyen originated from a fusion of bandit gangs, some of whose members were released from the penal colony of Poulo Condore (Con Son) by the Japanese during

WWII. Under the leadership of Bay Vien, the Binh Xuyen became a well-disciplined paramilitary organization serving whichever client paid the best—the Japanese, the French, or the Viet Minh. The Binh Xuyen joined alternately with the Hoa Hao and the Cao Dai religious sects challenging the French for power. In September 1945 the gang, which was involved in protection rackets, drugs, gambling, prostitution, and other vices for which Saigon was known, became politically active. Joining a Viet Minh–sponsored general strike, it infiltrated a Saigon suburb, killed 150 French and Eurasians, and mutilated many hostages. By the early 1950s, the gang rivaled the Viet Minh guerrillas as threats to Premier Ngo Dinh Diem's government. In spring 1955 some 40,000 Binh Xuyen troops, along with the sect armies, attacked Diem's army but were defeated and retreated to Cholon. Although U.S. adviser Edward Lansdale and others encouraged Diem to compromise, he insisted on eliminating the gang. Ngo Dinh Nhu's success in breaking up the gang convinced the Americans of Diem's viability against the communists, who acquired members from the defeated organization.

See also: Bay Vien; Cao Dai; Hoa Hao; Ngo Dinh Diem; Nguyen Chanh Thi.

Bird, Thomas A. (1947–), playwright, director. Bird, who served with the 1st Cavalry Division in Vietnam in 1965–1966, is the founder and artistic director of the Vietnam Veterans Ensemble Theatre Company (VETCO). He has produced or directed nearly two dozen VETCO productions, including *Tracers* (1980), widely considered the definitive theatrical production about American participation in the Vietnam War.

See also: Tracers.

Blackburn, Donald D. (1917–), U.S. Army general who planned Operation Kingpin, the unsuccessful November 1970 raid to free U.S. POWs at the Son Tay prison camp.

See also: Kingpin, Operation; Simons, Arthur D. "Bull"; Son Tay Raid.

Blacks. *See* African-Americans

Bloods: An Oral History of the Vietnam War by Black Veterans (1984). Wallace Terry's book that provided an in-depth examination of the African-American experience in the Vietnam War in the words of those who fought. A critical and popular success, *Bloods* is one of the few books that examines the role of African-Americans in the Vietnam War.

Blum, Léon (1872–1950), socialist Prime Minister who headed the French Popular Front coalition government in 1936–1937. Blum refrained from introducing sweeping political changes in France's Indochinese colonies following the suppressions of insurrections for fear of encouraging secession.

Boat People. *See* Refugees

Body Count. Unlike previous wars, the Vietnam conflict was a war of attrition rather than a war for territory along a specific front. Guerrilla fighting in the dense jungles involved ambushes, quick firefights, and retreats to bases. Troops did not hold ground, the traditional measure of military success. Since territorial measures were not applicable, the body count became the measure of military success for the United States. The body count was just that: casualty statistics to indicate the damage U.S. and Army of the Republic of Vietnam (ARVN) forces inflicted on the Viet Cong guerrillas (VC) and North Vietnamese Army (NVA) regulars. Body counts were regularly announced to the media to indicate how the conflict was progressing. Some argue that the use of body count desensitized U.S. troops and officers and contributed to tensions between Vietnamese civilians and the U.S. military. As the war continued, pressure from U.S. officials in Washington, who wanted to show the American public that the war was going well, led to routine inflation of body counts. The exact figure is indeterminable, but most agree that the counts were routinely and significantly exaggerated.

See also: Attrition Strategy; Five O'Clock Follies; R&R; Ticket Punching.

Boeing Aircraft Company. American aerospace company that built, among many other military aircraft, the eight-engine B-52, the first true intercontinental jet bomber that was widely used in the Vietnam War. Boeing also produced the Boeing 707, the first successful commercial jet, and its basic military version, the C-135, the KC-135 tanker version of which also played an important role in Vietnam.

Bolo, Operation. Code name for highly successful January 1967 U.S. Air Force operation in which U.S. F-4 fighters protected Rolling Thunder bombing attacks over North Vietnam.

See also: Rolling Thunder, Operation.

Bond, Julian (1940–), civil rights and antiwar activist. Bond co-chaired the September 1966 National Conference for New Politics, a large gathering of activist civil rights and peace groups. In that year the U.S. Supreme Court invalidated the Georgia state legislature's refusal to seat Bond, a newly elected representative, because of his antiwar statements.

Bonior, David E. (1945–), U.S. representative (D-Mich.), 1977– . Bonior, who served in the U.S.

Air Force from 1968–1972, founded the Vietnam Veterans in Congress caucus in 1979 and became a leading congressional advocate for Vietnam veterans' issues.

Booby Traps. Concealed explosives or other deadly devices activated by human contact. Viet Cong guerrillas extensively used booby traps such as hidden pits with stakes in them (known as punji stakes) or hand grenades or other explosives attached to trip wires. These weapons accounted for more than 10 percent of all Americans killed or wounded during the Vietnam War.

See also: Claymore Mines; Post-Traumatic Stress Disorder; Punji Stakes.

Boonie Hat. Nickname for full-brim cotton caps sometimes worn by U.S. soldiers in jungle operations, derived from the word "boondocks," first used by U.S. troops in the Philippines after the Spanish-American War.

Borneo. *See* Malaysia

Born on the Fourth of July (1976). A searing Vietnam War and postwar memoir written by former Marine Ron Kovic, who was severely wounded in the war. The book was the basis for the Hollywood film of the same name directed by Oliver Stone in 1986.

See also: Kovic, Ron.

Bouncing Betty. U.S. soldiers' nickname for versions of a land mine used by U.S. and Viet Cong forces that is buried in the ground and, when tripped, bounces some 3 feet in the air before exploding.

See also: Mine Warfare, Land.

Bowles, Chester (1901–1986), U.S. undersecretary of state, 1961; ambassador to India, 1963–1969. In 1961, Bowles opposed recommendations for increased military support for the regime of South Vietnamese President Ngo Dinh Diem, urging instead that Vietnam, like Laos, be made neutral. Bowles was dismissed and reassigned as roving ambassador. During the Johnson administration, Bowles headed a 1968 mission to Cambodia.

See also: Ngo Dinh Diem.

Boyne, Walter J. (1929–), author; retired U.S. Air Force colonel; director, National Air and Space Museum (1983). Boyne, the author of 28 books of fiction and nonfiction, served as a U.S. Air Force pilot from 1951–1974. He commanded the Air Force's 635th Services Squadron at U Tapao in Thailand in 1968–1969. Boyne's books include the best-selling novel *The Wild Blue* (1986), which he co-wrote with Steven Thompson.

Bradley, Omar N. (1893– 1981), general, U.S. Army; first

chairman, Joint Chiefs of Staff
(JCS), 1947–1953. During the
Indochina War, General Bradley,
a noted WWII general, helped
draft JCS contingency plans to
assist the French by bombing
and blockading China in 1952.
After retirement, Bradley visited
Vietnam in 1967 and declared
his full support for the war
effort. In 1968, he was one of the
few "wise men" of President
Johnson's special advisory group
to advise against withdrawal
from Vietnam.

See also: Joint Chiefs of Staff;
Wise Men.

Braestrup, Peter (1929–1997),
journalist, author. A former
Saigon bureau chief for the
Washington Post, Braestrup's two-
volume study, *Big Story* (1977), is
a detailed examination of the
American media's performance
during and after the 1968 Tet
Offensive. He concluded that the
"generalized effect of the news
media's contemporary output"
was "a distortion of reality—
through sins of omission and
commission—on a scale that
helped shape Tet's repercussions
in Washington and the [Johnson]
Administration's response."

See also: Tet Offensive.

Brezhnev, Leonid (1906–1982),
first secretary general of the
Soviet Communist Party,
1964–1982. Brezhnev replaced
Nikita Khrushchev in 1964 and
immediately changed the Soviet
Union's Vietnam policy. Under
Khrushchev, the Soviet Union
was not very active in promoting

communism in Southeast Asia;
China was North Vietnam's chief
source of aid. Brezhnev, however,
did not want the USSR to cede
Asia to Chinese influence, and
consequently involved the Soviet
Union more deeply in the
Vietnam War. The USSR significantly increased military aid to
North Vietnam, particularly
high-technology equipment such
as surface-to-air missiles (SAMs)
and sophisticated radar systems.
By the early 1970s Brezhnev
began to view détente with the
United States as more vital to
Soviet interests than a communist victory in Vietnam. Aid to
Vietnam was costly and the USSR
desired an end to the conflict.

Nixon and Kissinger tried to
make a U.S./USSR nuclear arms
reduction agreement contingent
on the Soviet Union pressuring
North Vietnam to negotiate.
Although Brezhnev rejected such
linkage, he did not cancel his
May 1972 Moscow summit with
Nixon despite the initiation of
the U.S. Linebacker bombing
campaign against North
Vietnam.

See also: Khrushchev, Nikita.

Brezhnev-Nixon Summit. *See*
Dobrynin, Anatoly

**Bright Shining Lie, A: John
Paul Vann and America in
Vietnam** (1988). Highly praised
biography of American Vietnam
War adviser John Paul Vann and
a history of the American war in
Vietnam by former *New York Times*
Vietnam War correspondent Neil
Sheehan. The book was awarded

the Pulitzer Prize for general non-fiction and the National Book Award for nonfiction.

Bright Light, Operation. Code name for U.S. Joint Personnel Recovery Center (JPRC) POW rescue operations in Laos, Cambodia, and North and South Vietnam during the Vietnam War. Bright Light operations freed some 500 South Vietnamese POWs and recovered 110 American bodies; no captured Americans were rescued from enemy prison camps.

Brink, Francis G. *See* Military Assistance Advisory Group–Vietnam

Britain. *See* Great Britain

Brothers in Arms (1986). William Broyles, Jr.'s, celebrated book in which the author, who had served in Vietnam as a Marine Corps lieutenant, reported on his 1984 trip back to Vietnam and reflected on his service in the war.

Brown, George S. (1918–1978), general, U.S. Air Force; commander, Seventh Air Force, 1968–1970; Air Force chief of staff, 1973–1974; chairman, Joint Chiefs of Staff, 1974–1978. From August 1968 to September 1970 George S. Brown, a highly decorated WWII veteran, commanded the Seventh Air Force in Vietnam. During the confirmation hearings in 1973 for his appointment as chairman of the Joint Chiefs of Staff (JCS),

Brown defended his concealment of the secret bombing of Cambodia under sharp questioning from Congress. As JCS chairman he criticized Congress for withholding aid when South Vietnam collapsed.

See also: Jones, David C.

Brown, H. Rap (1943–). A black power advocate during the 1960s and 1970s who criticized the nonviolent civil disobedience tactics of Martin Luther King, Jr., Brown and other militants condemned the Vietnam War as a conscious effort by white politicians to carry out genocide against African-Americans.

Brown, Sam (1943–), became a leader in the student antiwar movement in 1966 while at Harvard Theological Seminary. He organized student volunteers for Sen. Eugene McCarthy's 1968 presidential bid, and in 1969 helped found the Vietnam Moratorium Committee, a group of antiwar activists. Brown chaired the group, which sponsored the largest (to that time) antiwar demonstrations throughout the country on 15 October 1969, and in Washington, DC, on 15 November 1969.

See also: Moratorium Day; Vietnam Moratorium Committee.

Browne, Malcolm W. (1931–), foreign correspondent. Brown covered the Vietnam War for the Associated Press (1961–1965) and for ABC News (1965–1966). He won the Pulitzer Prize for international reporting in 1964.

Broyles, William Jr. (1944–), former Marine Corps lieutenant who served in Vietnam, Broyles returned in 1984 and wrote *Brothers in Arms* (1986), a celebrated book about that trip and his service in the war.

See also: Brothers in Arms.

Bruce, David K. E., (1898–1977), as U.S. Ambassador to France in 1949 Bruce convinced Secretary of State Dean Acheson not to implement a U.S. State Department proposal that would have backed more independence for Vietnam from the French. Bruce, who later served as Under Secretary of State, and U.S. Ambassador to West Germany, Great Britain, and China, served as an American negotiator to the Paris Peace talks.

See also: Habib, Philip; Nixon, Richard M.

Bryan C. D. B. (Courtlandt Dixon Barnes) (1936–), author of the powerful nonfiction book, *Friendly Fire* (1976), which told the story of the death of an American infantryman, Michael Mullin, by a U.S. Army artillery round. The book, based on Bryan's *New Yorker* magazine article, was made into a 1979 television movie of the same name.

See also: Friendly Fire.

Bucher, Lloyd (1928–), U.S. Navy commander. Bucher commanded the U.S. intelligence ship *Pueblo,* which was captured during the height of the Vietnam War by North Korea on 23 January 1968, and held for 11 months.

See also: Pueblo Incident.

Buddhists. Buddhism is the dominant religion in Vietnam. In contrast to Confucianism's concern for social order and hierarchy, Buddhism emphasizes a faith that transcends politics and society and promotes equality and community among individuals. Although strongly anticommunist, Buddhists had little political influence under South Vietnamese President Ngo Dinh Diem. The Catholic Diem largely appointed Catholics to fill important government positions. In addition to suppressing political opposition, Diem issued edicts that limited the religious freedom of Buddhists. On 8 May 1963, the government prohibited Buddhists from carrying flags on the birthday of the Buddha. Crowds gathered in Hue to protest, and government troops fired to disperse the dissidents, killing nine people. Diem's government blamed Viet Cong guerrillas for the deaths. The Buddhist leadership organized protests against the Diem regime. On 11 June, in Saigon, Quang Due, a Buddhist bonze (or monk), set himself on fire to protest the regime's policies. Vast demonstrations in the cities broke out, followed by the self-immolation of six more bonzes. On 21 August, Diem's brother,

Ngo Dinh Nhu, raided the Buddhist Xa Loi pagoda in Saigon; more than thirty bonzes were killed. Similar raids were carried out in other cities. These repressive actions against Buddhists encouraged the successful military coup against the Diem government in November 1963.

Over the next three years, Buddhists continued to protest the military governments and the U.S. presence in Vietnam, and to demand elections and the return of a civilian government. Buddhist leaders organized the United Buddhist Church of Vietnam in January 1964, which was widely supported. Sharp divisions existed among Buddhists, however; Thich Tri Quang, the militant leader of Buddhists in Hue and Da Nang, and Thich Tam Chau, a political moderate in Saigon, disagreed on goals and tactics for the Buddhist movement. Buddhist opposition challenged and undermined the governments of General Nguyen Khanh and of Tran Van Huong in 1964 and 1965. Protests against the military junta of Generals Nguyen Cao Ky and Nguyen Van Thieu failed, however. In March 1966, the United Buddhist Church demanded that the junta hold elections for a civilian government, and urban popular protests and divisions within the military followed. In response, General Thieu convened a National Political Congress and promised to hold elections, while General Ky, who refused to relinquish power, planned a military action. In May, with the tacit approval of the United States, Ky ordered troops to Da Nang, where hundreds of civilians were killed and wounded, and laid siege to Hue to crush all opposition.

In May 1966, Tri Quang, the Buddhist leader of Hue, was placed under house arrest, and Buddhists largely abandoned political activity. During the last years of the war, the Buddhists were an insignificant political force.

See also: Confucianism; Hue; Lodge, Henry Cabot Jr.; Ngo Dinh Diem; Nguyen Cao Ky.

Buffalo, Operation. Code name for a series of combat actions taken by elements of the Third U.S. Marine Division from 2 July to 14 July 1967, near the Demilitarized Zone.

Bui Diem (1923–), Republic of Vietnam's ambassador to the United States, 1966–1972. Bui Diem served as the liaison between the U.S. government and South Vietnam on many issues, including conditions for peace negotiations. In 1968, Bui Diem was the liaison between President Nguyen Van Thieu and Anna Chennault, who worked behind the scenes to support Richard Nixon's presidential candidacy in the belief that Nixon would take a harder line against the Democratic Republic of Vietnam than would Hubert Humphrey, the Democratic U.S. presidential candidate.

See also: Vietnam, Republic of.

Bui Phat. A refugee slum on the edge of Saigon. Bui Phat was an example of slums in many South Vietnamese cities created by peasants who migrated from the north to the south in the wake of the 1954 Geneva Accords. These shanty towns expanded as South Vietnamese also became refugees, a result of U.S. bombings, the establishment of free-fire zones, and the use of search-and-destroy tactics. The people in these slums, who represented 40–50 percent of the population of South Vietnam, became economically dependent on the U.S. presence in Vietnam and resisted efforts by Viet Cong guerrillas and Buddhists to organize protests against the U.S. presence.

Bui Tin (1928–), officer, People's Army of Vietnam (PAVN); journalist; government official. Bui Tin joined the Viet Minh in 1945 and fought at Dien Bien Phu. In 1963, he infiltrated South Vietnam to gather intelligence for the North Vietnamese. He later became a colonel in the PAVN. Bui wrote for the Communist Party newspaper, *Nhan Dan,* and the army newspaper, *Quan Doi Nhan Dan.* He accepted the South Vietnamese government's surrender as the ranking PAVN officer in Saigon in 1975. In 1990, while in Paris on official business, Bui Tin released a "citizen's petition" that was extremely critical of the regime of the Socialist Republic of Vietnam, which resulted in his expulsion from the Communist party.

Bumbry, Alonza B. (Al) (1947–), professional baseball player. Bumbry, a 1968 graduate of Virginia State University, was called to active duty through ROTC in June 1969. He served 11 months in Vietnam as a U.S. Army infantry platoon leader. A year after his 1971 Army discharge, Bumbry began his 13-year Major League Baseball career. He is one of only a handful of U.S. professional athletes who served in the Vietnam War.

Bundy, McGeorge (1919–1996), national security adviser, 1961–1966. Bundy was a key player in the formulation of U.S. Vietnam policy from the early advisory role through escalation. Under Kennedy, Bundy sought to insure a democratic South Vietnam without having the United States assume sole responsibility for the war. After Kennedy's assassination, Bundy became more prowar. By late 1964, he favored a bombing campaign against North Vietnam and an expanded United States combat role. After the initial troop commitment, Bundy supported subsequent buildups, arguing that unilateral de-escalation would devastate U.S. credibility. He also believed that a strong military presence would strengthen the U.S. and South Vietnam in peace negotiations. By 1966, Bundy began to question the escalation. These concerns led to his resignation. Later, as one of the "wise men," he supported de-escalation and eventual withdrawal in the watershed 1968 meeting.

See also: Ball, George W.; National Security Action Memorandum (NSAM) 288; National Security Council; Nuclear Weapons; Pentagon Papers; Rolling Thunder, Operation; SIGMA; Wise Men.

Bundy, William P. (1917–), Central Intelligence Agency (CIA), 1951–1961; assistant secretary of defense for international security affairs, 1961–1963; assistant secretary of state for Far Eastern affairs, 1964–1968. Along with his younger brother McGeorge, William Bundy had a significant hand in drafting U.S. policy in Vietnam. He advocated a U.S. military presence in Vietnam, but did not initially favor a ground combat role. Bundy instead pushed for air strikes against military and industrial targets in the North and the mining of Haiphong harbor. By 1964 Bundy believed that the administration needed congressional approval for further action in Vietnam. And so, he and aides drafted the Gulf of Tonkin Resolution, which provided Johnson with the authority to escalate the conflict as he saw fit. In 1964–1965, Bundy headed a working group to formulate U.S. policy recommendations. He opposed a large U.S. troop buildup, fearing that the war would become the responsibility of the United States, although he supported a limited combat troop commitment of 100,000 men. By 1967, Bandy walked the

line between the prowar and antiwar factions within the administration.

See also: Gulf of Tonkin Resolution; Appendix E.

Bunker, Ellsworth (1894–1984), U.S. ambassador to South Vietnam, 1967–1973. A former U.S. ambassador to Argentina, India, Italy, and Nepal, Bunker was sent to Saigon by President Johnson in 1967. Bunker ignored repression in South Vietnam, strongly supported the Saigon government, and revamped U.S.–South Vietnamese pacification and counterinsurgency efforts. He openly endorsed President Thieu in 1967 and 1971. Bunker supported President Nixon's policy of Vietnamization and the 1970 Cambodian invasion. He accompanied Henry Kissinger during the stormy sessions that persuaded President Thieu to accept the Paris peace accords in 1973. Bunker resigned after the ceasefire. "I'm an old-fashioned patriot," he once said. "I have always assumed that my country was fundamentally right in its dealings with others."

See also: Read, Benjamin.

Burdick, Eugene (1918–1965), co-author, with William J. Lederer, of the 1958 novel, *The Ugly American*, which was made into a 1963 movie of the same name. The book, set in a thinly veiled Vietnam, is a Cold War parable of what American political and diplomatic blindness could produce in Southeast Asia.

Edward G. Lansdale was the model for the character Edwin Hillendale.

See also: Lansdale, Edward G.; *Ugly American, The.*

Burt, Leo (1948–), with Karl and Dwight Armstrong and David Fine, was responsible for planting the bomb that on 24 August 1970 killed researcher Robert Fassnacht at the Army Mathematics Research Center on the University of Wisconsin Madison campus. The act was intended to protest Vietnam War–related research. Burt, a University of Wisconsin student, fled to Canada and remains at large.

See also: Armstrong, Dwight and Karlton; Fassnacht, Robert; Fine, David; University of Wisconsin Bombing.

Bush, George (1924–), U.S. representative (R-Tex.), 1966–1970; U.S. ambassador to the United Nations, 1971–1973; U.S. envoy to China, 1974; director of the Central Intelligence Agency (CIA), 1975–1976; vice president, 1981–1989; president, 1989–1993. George Herbert Walker Bush endorsed U.S. involvement in Vietnam as a member of Congress and supported the escalation policies of Presidents Johnson and Nixon. Bush did not denounce antiwar protesters, and had a reputation of balancing his support for the war with understanding for its opponents. As president, Bush claimed that the Persian Gulf War victory laid to rest what he called the "Vietnam Syndrome," the fear of military entanglement inspired by the experience of the Vietnam War.

See also: Embargo; Vietnam Syndrome.

Butler, Robert Olen (1943–), novelist and short story writer whose collection of stories of Vietnamese expatriates, *A Good Scent from a Strange Mountain* (1993), won the Pulitzer Prize for fiction. A former U.S. Army intelligence specialist in Vietnam, Butler deals significantly with the Vietnam War in his novels: *The Alleys of Eden* (1981), *On Distant Ground* (1985), *The Deuce* (1989), *They Whisper* (1994) and *The Deep Green Sea* (1998).

Buttinger, Joseph (1906–), German-born author and refugee relief worker. Buttinger, an officer of the private American Friends of Vietnam lobbying group, worked in South Vietnam with refugees from the north in 1954 and 1958. His books on Vietnamese history include *Vietnam: A Dragon Embattled* (1967).

See also: American Friends of Vietnam.

Byrne, Gerald (1944–), magazine publisher. Byrne served with the U.S. Marines as an air control officer at Marble Mountain and in Phu Bai in Vietnam in 1968–1969. He became publisher of *Variety* magazine in 1989.

C-130 Hercules. U.S. Air Force transport aircraft widely used in the Vietnam War from 1965–1975.

CALCAV. *See* Clergy and Laity Concerned About Vietnam

Calley, William L. Jr. (1943–), second lieutenant, U.S. Army, 23d Infantry Division (American), 1967–1969. Calley was the only U.S. soldier convicted of a crime in the 16 March 1968 incident in which U.S. troops killed hundreds of South Vietnamese— mostly women, children, and elderly—in the hamlet of My Lai, part of the northern coastal village of Song My. Calley directed his platoon's activities in the atrocity and was subsequently charged with killing 109 Vietnamese. In March 1971 a court-martial convicted Calley of the premeditated murder of at least 22 people and sentenced him to life in prison. The secretary of the army reduced the sentence to ten years, and Calley was paroled in November 1974.

See also: My Lai.

Ca Mau. The southernmost province in southern Vietnam. Ca Mau is a peninsula that sits on the southern edge of the U Minh Forest in the Mekong Delta. The Ca Mau peninsula is covered with dense jungle and features one of the world's largest mangrove swamps. The area was heavily defoliated by U.S. forces during the Vietnam War.

Cambodia. Southeast Asian nation adjacent to Vietnam that became a battleground during and after the American war in Vietnam. Cambodian King Norodom signed a treaty in 1863 that allowed France to make Cambodia a French protectorate. That relationship lasted until Japan occupied Indochina in 1940. The French continued to administer Cambodia, and in 1941 France made Prince Norodom Sihanouk, Norodom's grandson, king. Sihanouk proved an astute political operator, not the figurehead the French had sought.

After the Japanese defeat, Ho Chi Minh's fight for independence in Vietnam inspired many Cambodians to oppose French rule. Sihanouk launched an international campaign for Cambodian independence in 1952. After the 1954 defeat at Dien Bien Phu, France granted Cambodia independence. As king, Sihanouk was not permitted to participate in the country's first democratic elections. He abdicated in 1955, and easily won election to the presidency. His power rested on his ability to maintain Cambodia's neutrality.

Sihanouk tried to preserve peace in Cambodia as the conflict in South Vietnam escalated in the early 1960s. He believed that North Vietnam would win its war against the South, and broke relations with South Vietnam. After Diem's assassination in November 1963, he renounced U.S. aid.

In 1965, Sihanouk severed diplomatic relations with the U.S. and allowed North Vietnam to build base camps in eastern Cambodia to facilitate the deployment of equipment and soldiers along the Ho Chi Minh Trail. When the U.S. committed ground troops to South Vietnam in 1965, the intensified fighting forced more National Liberation Front guerrillas to seek refuge across the Cambodian border.

In early 1969, President Nixon approved covert bombing of NLF sanctuaries in Cambodia. The bombing campaign's failure to eradicate the North Vietnamese and NLF bases in Cambodia, led Gen. Creighton Abrams to call for a ground invasion of Cambodia. Knowing that Sihanouk would not approve such a plan, the U.S. government approached Lon Nol, a career officer who was Sihanouk's prime minister. Sihanouk was ousted in a March 1970 coup by Lon Nol and Sirik Matak. The U.S. immediately recognized their government.

Confident of Lon Nol's support, Nixon sent U.S. and Army of the Republic of Vietnam (ARVN) troops and B-52 bombers into eastern Cambodia in April 1970. The invasion ignited domestic protests in the U.S., and when the troops withdrew at the end of May they had failed to achieve their major objectives, particularly the capture of the Vietnamese communist command post for operations in South Vietnam.

After the invasion, the U.S. provided military support for Lon Nol's government from 1970 to 1973. In late 1974 a war-weary U.S. Congress slashed aid shipments. On 17 April 1975 Cambodian communist troops, the Khmer Rouge, marched into Phnom Penh. Khmer Rouge cadres killed all educated people. They tortured and slaughtered thousands of government officials, military officers, teachers, doctors, engineers, and anyone else thought unsuitable for "reeducation." By the end of 1978, about 1 million people (one seventh of the population) had been killed or had died of starvation or disease.

Disputes between the reunited Vietnam and the Khmer Rouge's Democratic Kampuchea led to a 1979 Vietnamese invasion and occupation of Kampuchea. The Khmer Rouge leadership fled to rural areas, where it joined two other groups (one led by Sihanouk) in armed opposition to the government. The Vietnamese-backed regime lasted until United Nations–supervised elections in 1993, which resulted in a coalition government representing three of the country's four major factions.

See also: B-52; Bowles, Chester; Brown, George S.; Cambodian Incursion; Central Office for South Vietnam; Daniel

Boone Operation; Ford, Gerald R.; Geneva Conference, 1954; Heng Samrin; Ho Chi Minh Trail; Jones, David C.; Khmer Rouge; Kissinger, Henry; Laird, Melvin R.; Lon Nol; Menu, Operation; Normalization; Phnom Penh; Pol Pot; Schlesinger, James R.; SEATO; Sihanouk, Norodom; Special Forces, ARVN; United Nations; Van Tien Dung.

Cambodian Incursion. The U.S. Army–led series of operations that began 1 May 1970 against North Vietnamese and National Liberation Front (NLF) bases inside Cambodia. The aim was to destroy enemy sanctuaries, a tactical strike advocated by top generals since 1967. In the main operation, some 12,000 U.S. Army and 8,000 ARVN troops attacked a 160-kilometer (100-mile) long border region northwest of Saigon. U.S. command expected a decisive battle, but the enemy retreated quickly to the west, offering limited resistance. Allied forces captured huge stocks of abandoned supplies, advancing 30 kilometers (19 miles) into the country before departing on 30 June. During the two-month operation, North Vietnamese and Viet Cong forces lost an estimated 11,000 men while U.S. and ARVN forces suffered 976 fatalities (338 American) and 4,500 wounded.

Sending ground forces into Cambodia provoked fierce reactions in the U.S. More than 100,000 protesters demonstrated in Washington on 9 May, joined for the first time by many politically moderate citizens. Several prominent National Security Council officials resigned. In May 1970, U.S. campuses experienced the most intensive period of protests in history, with demonstrations occurring on 1,350 college and university campuses. On 4 May, Ohio National Guard troops fired on a crowd of Kent State University demonstrators, killing four students and wounding nine. Ten days later, Mississippi police fired on unarmed black student protesters at Jackson State University, killing two and wounding twelve.

See also: Central Office for South Vietnam; Cooper, John Sherman; Daniel Boone, Operation; Defense, Department of; Enclave Strategy; Fulbright, J. William; Gulf of Tonkin Resolution; Hardhats; Kennedy, Edward M.; Kent State University; Lam Son 719; Nixon, Richard M.; Rogers, William P.; Rules of Engagement; Toan Thang, Operation; Appendix E.

Cam Lo. U.S. Marine base camp in Quang Tri Province near Dong Ha, 14 kilometers south of the DMZ and the site of many military engagements beginning in the summer of 1966.

Camp Carroll. Fire base established in 1966 and named for a U.S. Marine killed in battle nearby. Located in Quang Tri Province, halfway between the Laotian border and the coast, Camp Carroll was used, successively, by U.S. Marine, Army and

South Vietnamese Army units primarily as a site for 175mm artillery guns.

Cam Pha. North Vietnamese port that was mined, along with Haiphong, Hon Gai, and Thanh Hoa, by President Nixon in May 1972.

Cam Ranh Bay. A coastal city 200 miles northeast of Saigon in Khanh Hoa province. Cam Ranh Bay was the largest of six seaports the U.S. built in South Vietnam. Some 25,000 navy Seabees, army engineers, and civilians built the deepwater port, which opened at the end of 1965. It had prefabricated concrete piers, a 10,000-foot jet runway, warehouses, fuel storage tanks, cargo cranes, hospitals, and barracks. Cam Ranh Bay, the home of the U.S. Army's 22nd Replacement Battalion,, fell to the North Vietnamese Army in 1975 and became a Soviet naval base.

See also: Seabees.

Canada. Canada was officially neutral throughout the Vietnam War, neither openly criticizing U.S. policy nor providing war materiel. Canadian diplomats occasionally served as envoys between Washington, D.C., and Hanoi, and Canada was an original member of the International Control Commission, set up in 1954 as part of the Geneva Accords. Beginning in 1964, Canada sent $9.3 million in development assistance to South Vietnam, mostly medical supplies

and training. Tens of thousands of Canadians either enlisted or were drafted into the U.S. Army during the Vietnam War; an estimated 30,000 Canadians served with U.S. forces in Vietnam. Canadian diplomats occasionally served as envoys between Washington, D.C., and Hanoi, and Canada was an original member of the International Control Commission, set up in 1954 as part of the Geneva Accords. An estimated 30,000 Americans fled to Canada to evade the draft during the war.

See also: International Commission for Supervision and Control.

Can Lao. Created in 1954, *Can Lao Nhan Vi Cach Mang Dang* (Revolutionary Personalist Labor Party) was South Vietnamese president Ngo Dinh Diem's secret network of political supporters, organized and controlled by his brother, Ngo Dinh Nhu. Comprised mostly of highly placed Catholic refugees from the north, the Can Lao during the height of its power had more than 20,000 followers who did intelligence work for Diem and Nhu. They were rewarded with payoffs and political favors. The organization disintegrated after the brothers were assassinated in November 1963.

See also: Ngo Dinh Diem; Ngo Dinh Nhu.

Cao Bang. Province on the North Vietnam–China border. During a North Vietnamese offensive in October 1950,

French forces in Cao Bang tried to evacuate the area. Viet Minh knowledge of the French plans, combined with poor French strategy, resulted in the massacre of fleeing French troops by Gen. Vo Nguyen Giap's forces. The collapse of Cao Bang led the French to abandon Lang Son and other important posts in the region, leaving behind valuable military equipment and greatly weakening the French position in northernmost Vietnam.

See also: Lattre de Tassigny, Jean de.

Cao Dai. The *Cao-Dai Tien-Ong* ("His Excellency the Grandfather Immortal") is a South Vietnamese religious sect that originated in the Tay Ninh area in the 1920s and became a formal religion in 1926. Cao Dai followers believe that the main founders of all great religions are incarnations of the one supreme God (Cao Dai). Followers venerate as saints such figures as Sun Yat-sen, Vietnamese prophet Trang Trinh, Joan of Arc, Victor Hugo, Julius Caesar, Buddha, Jesus, and Confucius. In the early 1950s the Cao Daists favored the Progressive Forces Alliance, a party opposed to President Ngo Dinh Diem's authoritarian rule, and formed a private army. They joined another religious sect, the Hoa Hao, and the Binh Xuyen crime organization to oppose Diem militarily in 1955. Diem's forces crushed them. After its defeat, the Cao Dai split into a dozen or more factions, but continued as a

religion. The government of the Socialist Republic of Vietnam recognized the sect as a religion in 1986, and it continues to exist in Tay Ninh.

See also: Binh Xuyen; Hoa Hao.

Cao Van Vien (1921–), general, Army of the Republic of Vietnam (ARVN); chief, Joint General Staff, 1965–1975. Gen. Cao Van Vien retained the top military post in South Vietnam through many government upheavals. He belonged to the so-called Young Turks faction that took power in 1964, and he was a close ally of President Thieu. Gen. William Westmoreland met weekly with Vien, who resisted U.S. pressure to reform the ARVN or to replace corrupt officers. Vien proposed the withdrawal from the Central Highlands that led to communist victory in April 1975. After gaining asylum in the U. S., Vien worked at the U.S. Army Center for Military History. He became a U.S. citizen in 1982.

See also: Joint General Staff; Young Turks.

Capps, Walter H. (1934–1997), U.S. Representative (D-Calif.), January to October 1997. Before coming to Congress, Capps was a professor of religious studies at the University of California in Santa Barbara for three decades. In 1979 he created and taught a highly acclaimed and extremely popular course on the Vietnam War, which continued after his election to Congress. In the course, Capps made extensive use of guest speakers including Vietnam veterans and their families, Vietnamese expatriates, and antiwar activists.

Caputo, Philip (1943–), Journalist, novelist, and author of *A Rumor of War* (1977), a critically acclaimed, best-selling memoir that tells the story of his 1965–1966 tour of duty as a U.S. Marine Corps lieutenant in Vietnam. Caputo's other books include the Vietnam war–influenced novel *Indian Country* (1987) and "In the Forest of the Laughing Elephant," a novella set in Vietnam that is part of his 1997 book *Exiles*.

Caravelle Group. The name for the 18 former South Vietnamese government leaders and politicians who met at Saigon's Caravelle Hotel in April 1960 to demand reforms within Ngo Dinh Diem's government. These reforms included more democracy, civil rights guarantees, and recognition for political opponents. The group also called for economic reforms and an end to corruption. Most of its members were arrested following an unsuccessful November 1960 coup attempt.

Carmichael, Stokely (1941–), a founder of the militant civil rights group, the Student Nonviolent Coordinating Committee in the early 1960s, and the prime minister of the Black Panther Party in 1968–1968. Carmichael, along with other black power advocates such as H. Rap Brown, Bobby Seale, and Eldridge Cleaver took issue with the nonviolent civil disobedience tactics of Martin Luther King, Jr. Carmichael's rhetoric of protest and violence fractured the civil rights movement directly and the antiwar movement indirectly.

See also: Brown, H. Rap; Cleaver, Eldridge; Seale, Bobby; Student Nonviolent Coordinating Committee.

Carrying the Darkness (1985). A highly regarded anthology of poetry about the Vietnam War written by Vietnam veterans, antiwar movement veterans and others edited by W. D. Ehrhart, a poet and memoirist who served with the U.S. Marines in Vietnam.

See also: Ehrhart, W. D.

Carson, Rachel (1907–1964), biologist whose book, *Silent Spring* (1962), sensitized international opinion about the dangers of pesticides in the environment, including the herbicides such as Agent Orange used by the U.S. in Vietnam.

See also: Agent Orange.

Carter, Jimmy (1924–), governor of Georgia, 1970–1976; U.S. president, 1977–1981. As governor, James Earl Carter backed President Nixon's Vietnam policy and urged his fellow governors not to oppose the war and undermine public support. As a

Democratic presidential candidate in 1976, however, Carter denounced the Vietnam War as "immoral" and "racist." In 1977, President Carter issued a blanket pardon for draft resisters, an action he believed necessary to begin national reconciliation. Carter explored the possibility of normalization of relations with the Socialist Republic of Vietnam, but Vietnamese demands for war reparations, and Vietnam's 1979 invasion of Cambodia foreclosed such a policy change.

See also: Amnesty; Desertion; Komer, Robert W.; Vance, Cyrus R.; Vietnam Syndrome.

Carver, George A, Jr. (1930–1994), special assistant to the director of the Central Intelligence Agency (CIA) for Vietnamese Affairs, 1966–1973. Carver's negative reports on the war's progress influenced Secretary of Defense Robert McNamara to turn against escalation of the war in 1967 and 1968.

See also: Central Intelligence Agency; McNamara, Robert S.

Case-Church Amendment. Legislation sponsored in 1973 by Republican Sen. Clifford Case of New Jersey and Democratic Sen. Frank Church of Idaho to cut off all funding for the Vietnam War. The legislation was approved by Congress, and went into effect on 15 August 1973.

See also: Case, Clifford P.; Church, Frank.

Case, Clifford P. (1904–1982), U.S. senator (R-N.J.), 1954–1978; ranking Republican on the Senate Foreign Relations Committee. Case criticized the war from 1967 onward, arguing that the conflict represented an unwarranted extension of executive power, that the South Vietnamese government could not become viable as the U.S. military increasingly took over its responsibilities, and that the war could not be won without "the destruction of South Vietnam and much of American might itself." In 1973 he co-sponsored a piece of legislation with Democratic Sen. Frank Church of Idaho to cut off all funding for the Vietnam War. The legislation was approved by Congress, and went into effect on 15 August 1973.

See also: Case-Church Amendment.

Castries, Christian de (1902–1991), French army officer; commander of the French garrison at Dien Bien Phu, 1953–1954. De Castries had an impressive record as a tank commander during World War II. That experience proved worthless as Dien Bien Phu became a muddy siege with the French dug in into World War I–like trenches. De Castries, who received a battlefield promotion from colonel to brigadier general at Dien Bien Phu, stayed with his men and was taken prisoner when the garrison fell in May 1954.

See also: Dien Bien Phu.

Castro, Fidel. *See* Ten-Pin Theory

Casualties. Casualties in war are traditionally defined as military personnel killed, wounded, or missing in action (MIA). By that definition Vietnam War casualties from 1945–1975 totaled at least 1.75 million deaths for all participants and more than twice that many wounded.

During 1945–1954, France and its Indochinese client states lost 94,581 military personnel killed and 78,127 wounded.

The U.S. lost 58,159 killed, including 8 women, and 304,000 wounded from 1959–1975. Some 74,000 of the wounded survived as quadriplegics or multiple amputees. During 1968–1969, 300 or more U.S. servicemen were killed in a single week, and in April 1969 the total reached 33,641, surpassing the total number killed in the Korean War. About 18 percent of U.S. fatalities were from causes other than enemy action including disease, auto accidents, airplane crashes, friendly fire, homicide, suicide, and drug overdose.

The Republic of Vietnam Armed Forces suffered some 224,000 killed and more than 1 million wounded. The Royal Laotian Army and its guerrilla auxiliaries lost many thousands in the undeclared war in Laos, as did regular and irregular Thai forces fighting there.

During the U.S. phase of the war, an estimated 300,000 South Vietnamese civilians were killed by both sides and 65,000 North Vietnamese civilians were killed by U.S. bombs. Tens of thousands of North Vietnamese peasants were executed in the 1954–1956 land redistribution campaign; at least 2 million Cambodians were killed by the Khmer Rouge during 1975–1978; and tens of thousands of boat people died at sea fleeing Vietnam after 1975. Tens of thousands of Laotian civilians were killed by U.S. bombs and anti-guerrilla operations.

Catholic Church. *See* Catholics; Paul VI; Spellman, Francis Joseph.

Catholic Peace Fellowship. A militant, nonviolent Catholic group set up in the spring of 1965 to resist the Vietnam War. The fellowship's leaders included Philip and Daniel Berrigan and Thomas Merton. Members of the foundation helped Catholic conscientious objectors avoid the draft.

See also: Berrigan Brothers.

Catholics. During President Ngo Dinh Diem's 1954–1963 rule, Roman Catholicism dominated South Vietnamese politics and government. Diem cultivated Catholics' support with political patronage and business favors. As a result, Catholics, although a minority of the population, held the prominent political and military appointments under Diem. Catholics' privileged position alienated the majority Buddhist population.

After the Geneva Accords of 1954, some 700,000 Catholics, fearing religious persecution, left North Vietnam to live in South Vietnam.

Diem established ties with influential fellow Catholics in the U.S., including Senators Mike Mansfield, John F. Kennedy and Cardinal Francis Joseph Spellman. These and other U.S. Catholics helped form the "Vietnam Lobby," which advocated support for Diem's government and, later, U.S. military intervention in Vietnam.

After the military coup against Diem and his 1963 assassination 1963, Catholic influence in South Vietnam waned. With the fall of Saigon in 1975, many Catholics close to the government fled Vietnam.

See also: Agency for International Development; Buddhists; Can Lao; Mansfield, Mike; Ngo Dinh Diem; Nguyen Van Thieu; Paul VI; Reeducation Camps; Spellman, Francis Joseph.

Catonsville Nine. *See* Berrigan Brothers; Berrigan, Daniel; Berrigan, Philip

Catroux, Georges (1877–1969), French governor general of Indochina, August 1939 to July 1940. Catroux was recalled by the French Vichy government following Germany's invasion of France. He then joined the French Free forces.

See also: Vichy France.

Cedar Falls, Operation. A 17-day search-and-destroy operation by some 30,000 U.S. and South Vietnamese troops in January 1967 aimed at destroying the Viet Cong tunnels in the 60-square-mile Iron Triangle, 50 kilometers (30 miles) from Saigon in Binh Duong province. During the operation the VC-controlled village of Ben Suc was destroyed and its 6,000 inhabitants relocated. Although many tunnels were destroyed, Viet Cong troops returned to the area six months later.

See also: Ben Suc; Iron Triangle; Search-and-Destroy.

Cédile, Jean (1908–), Free French representative to the government of Cochin China, August 1945 to October 1946. Cédile parachuted into southern Vietnam and was captured by the Japanese. After his release he worked to re-establish French authority as quickly as possible.

See also: Franco–Viet Minh War.

Central Highlands. The isolated plateau at the southern end of the Truong Son Mountains in west-central South Vietnam is called *Cao Nguyen Trung Phan,* or Central Highlands. It covers 52,000 square kilometers (20,000 square miles) of tropical and bamboo forest interspersed with tea, tobacco, and coffee plantations. The principal towns are Dak To, Kontum, Pleiku, and Ban Me Thuot. The area's predominant ethnic groups are the

Rhade and the Jarai, semi-
nomadic natives who were called
Montagnards (highlanders) by
the French and *moi* (savages) or
ngoui throng (hillbillies) by the
Vietnamese. In 1962, the U.S.
Army Special Forces organized
the Montagnards into Civilian
Irregular Defense Groups. An
estimated 200,000 highland
tribesmen died during the
Vietnam War; most of the
600,000 survivors became
refugees.

Viet Cong attacks on Pleiku
triggered the first large-scale
U.S. bombing of North Vietnam
in February 1965. In October
1965, the U.S. Army 1st Cavalry
Division stopped a major North
Vietnamese Army (NVA) offen-
sive across the Central
Highlands. Fierce battles around
Kontum and heavy U.S. bombing
blunted the NVA's Easter
Offensive in 1972. North
Vietnam's final offensive began
at Ban Me Thuot in March 1975.
South Vietnamese Army defenses
crumbled rapidly after with-
drawing from the Central
Highlands.

See also: Ban Me Thuot; Easter
Offensive; Ho Chi Minh
Campaign; Ho Chi Minh Trail;
Kontum; Montagnards; Pleiku.

Central Intelligence Agency.
The primary function of the U.S.
Central Intelligence Agency
(CIA),which was established in
1947, is to give the president
accurate, apolitical intelligence
about the rest of the world. U.S.
intelligence operations in

Indochina began in 1943 when
the CIA's World War II predecessor, the Office of Strategic
Services, rescued downed U.S.
aviators in the Japanese-occu-
pied French colonies and
cooperated with the communist-
led Viet Minh to harass and
overthrow the Japanese. In
Vietnam, Cambodia, and Laos
the CIA was heavily involved in
intelligence-gathering and clandestine activities. The U.S.
intelligence effort in Vietnam,
Cambodia, and Laos was the
largest in any one area since
World War II. By the end of the
Vietnam War, covert operations
far surpassed the agency's intelligence-gathering efforts.

During the Eisenhower
administration, the CIA provided
accurate intelligence, especially
following France's defeat at Dien
Bien Phu. The Saigon Military
Mission, a CIA offshoot headed
by Col. Edward G. Lansdale in
1954, aided Ngo Dinh Diem in
establishing control of South
Vietnam. The CIA was not
directly involved in the 1963
coup that toppled Diem,
although one agent, Lucien
Conein, was the liaison between
U.S. embassy personnel, U.S. officials in Washington, and the
Vietnamese plotters.

President Lyndon Johnson
distrusted CIA intelligence and
its views on how to win the
"hearts and minds" of the
Vietnamese people. To counter
assassinations and intimidation
by Viet Cong guerrillas, the CIA
organized South Vietnamese

teams to use similar methods. One such effort was the Phoenix program (*Phuong Hoang*), organized in 1967 by the Office of Civil Operations and Revolutionary Development Support (CORDS). The program, although not directly run by the CIA, was linked to it by the American public when it was made public in 1973.

See also: Adams, Sam; Agency for International Development; Air America; Bush, George; Civil Operations and Revolutionary Development Support; Civilian Irregular Defense Groups; Colby, William; Conein, Lucien; Cooper, Chester; Dulles, Allen; Helms, Richard M.; Huston Plan; Komer, Robert W.; Kong Le; Lansdale, Edward G.; Montagnards; Office of Strategic Services; Pathet Lao; Phoenix Program; Phoumi Nosavan; Provincial Reconnaissance Units; Rheault, Robert; Richardson, John H.; Schlesinger, James R.; Search and Rescue; Sihanouk, Norodom; Smith, Walter Bedell; Special Forces, ARVN; Stilwell, Richard G.; Tran Thien Khiem; Tran Van Don; Truong Dinh Dzu; Vang Pao; Watergate.

Central Office for South Vietnam (COSVN). COSVN originated in 1961 when the southern and central branches of the Lao Dong Party (Vietnam Workers) merged. The group's designation was the Central Committee Directorate for the South. An advance element of the Communist Party's Central Committee, COSVN's purpose was to direct the Viet Cong guerrillas in the South. COSVN was first headed by Nguyen Van Linh, who had spent most of his career in the South. Nguyen Chi Thanh, a northerner, assumed command in 1964. COSVN was a mobile leadership group, but U.S. military leaders believed it had a fixed headquarters that could be located and destroyed, crippling the communist war effort in the South. U.S. strategists, who believed COSVN was located in Laos and later in Cambodia, launched several operations to destroy it, beginning with Operation Junction City in 1967. Two years later, Gen. Creighton Abrams requested a short "surgical" B-52 strike in Cambodia where he believed COSVN was located. In 1970, President Nixon authorized an incursion into Cambodia with the purpose of destroying COSVN. The U.S. military never succeeded in locating or destroying it.

See also: Cambodian Incursion; Fishhook; Menu, Operation; Nguyen Van Linh; People's Liberation Armed Forces; Pham Hung; Phnom Penh; Tran Van Tra.

Chae Myung-Shin. Commanding general of the first Republic of Korea troops that arrived in Vietnam in 1965.

See also: Korea, Republic of.

Champa. Ancient kingdom located in the southeastern coastal region of southern Vietnam between the Red River and Mekong Deltas, dating from the 2nd century and inhabited by the Cham, a Malay-speaking people ethnically distinct from the Vietnamese who had been converted to Islam. Until it was absorbed into Vietnam in the 17th century, there were periodic conflicts between Champa and Vietnam and the border shifted in response to the vicissitudes of the relationship. The Cham occasionally seized the Vietnamese capital of Thang Long (Hanoi), while Vietnamese armies sometimes penetrated deep into Cham territory. In the 14th century the Cham kings became vassals of Vietnam.

Chaos, Operation. Code name for a covert CIA actions against elements of the antiwar movement begun in 1967 by President Johnson and continued during the Nixon administration. Chaos included penetration of antiwar groups and provocation of acts of violence against antiwar groups in the U.S., a violation of the CIA charter. Chaos was terminated in 1972; it was made public in 1973.

See also: Central Intelligence Agency.

Chapelle, Georgette Meyer (Dickey) (1918–1965), journalist. Chapelle, a freelance war correspondent, covered WWII and the Korean and Vietnam Wars. She became the first and only U.S. woman correspondent killed in Vietnam when she stepped on a land mine during a Marine Corps operation near Chu Lai.

Chapman, Leonard Fielding Jr. (1913–), U.S. Marine Corps commandant, 1968–1971. Chapman served as commandant while U.S. forces were withdrawn from Southeast Asia under the policy of Vietnamization. As commandant, Chapman maintained the corps' strict standards on drugs and discipline matters, even as other military services relaxed disciplinary regulations. In 1968 Chapman initiated programs to improve race relations in the corps. Chapman retired as commandant on 31 December 1971.

See also: Krulak, Victor; Walt, Lewis W.

Charner, Léonard Victor Joseph (1797–1869), French admiral who commanded French forces in the Far East and led a 70-ship armada that conquered Saigon for France on 1 July 1861.

Chea Sim (1932–), hard-line Cambodian communist leader who in 1991 replaced Heng Samrin as party secretary of the Vietnamese-backed communist government. A few days later he agreed to share power with other factions in Cambodia, including the Khmer Rouge. Elected president of Cambodia's National Assembly in October 1993.

See also: Heng Samrin.

Checkpoint and Snatch. U.S. Army tactic to surprise Viet Cong soldiers and their supporters by conducting surprise roadblocks to inspect traffic on roads frequented by insurgents.

Chemical Warfare. Technically and legally the U.S. did not wage chemical warfare in Vietnam. However, the U.S. did use non-lethal riot control agents (RCAs) and herbicides.

The first herbicides were sprayed by the U.S. Air Force to deny the enemy cover and destroy rice crops in December 1961. Operational flights to deliver defoliants began in January 1962, under the code name Operation Ranch Hand, and continued until January 1971. Crop-destruction missions flown by the Vietnamese air force began in October 1962. During the peak year of 1967, Ranch Hand involved 6,847 sorties, used 4.8 million gallons of herbicide, defoliated 1.2 million acres, and destroyed 60,000 hectares (148,000 acres) of crops.

RCAs were originally developed for use by domestic police to incapacitate victims temporarily by suddenly causing crying, vomiting, coughing, sneezing, and combinations of these symptoms. During 1963–1964 the U.S. Army procured about 180 tons of CS powder, a powerful tear agent, for use in Southeast Asia. As with herbicides, CS was used sparingly and cautiously at first, but soon became routine and widespread. CS was first used in early 1964. In February 1965, the Military Assistance Command, Vietnam (MACV) authorized defensive-only use of RCAs. In February 1966 the

Pentagon authorized use of RCAs to force the enemy out of shelters just before bombing raids. RCAs were used to defend perimeters, counter ambushes, prepare landing zones, and restrict terrain. Man-portable flamethrowers were used by both sides, though infrequently. North Vietnamese soldiers used Soviet-made flamethrowers. U.S. Chemical Corps soldiers used rocket-powered flash flamethrowers equipped with jellied gasoline called napalm beginning in 1969.

See also: Agent Blue; Agent Orange; Agent White; Herbicides; Napalm; Ranch Hand, Operation.

Chen Geng. China's Vice Minister of Defense who led a 1950 Chinese military advisory mission that worked with Ho Chi Minh's Viet Minh forces in the war against the French.

Chennault, Anna (1925–), Chinese-born wife of "Flying Tigers" General Claire Chennault; friend and Washington, D.C., contact of South Vietnamese president Nguyen Van Thieu. Working with U.S. presidential candidate Richard M. Nixon's representatives, Chennault boosted Nixon's electoral chances in the 1968 U.S. presidential campaign when she successfully urged South Vietnamese President Nguyen Van Thieu to delay committing to and attending the Paris peace talks.

See also: Bui Diem.

Cherry, Fred (1928–), retired U.S. Air Force colonel. Cherry, an F-105 fighter-bomber pilot, was shot down over North Vietnam in October 1965 and held as a prisoner of war until February 1973. He was the senior African-American officer held prisoner by the North Vietnamese.

Chicago Eight. *See* Chicago Seven

Chicago Seven. The eight men who were indicted for conspiring and traveling over state lines to incite rioting among antiwar demonstrators at the August 1968 Democratic National Convention in Chicago. These men were David Dellinger, Tom Hayden, Rennie Davis, Abbie Hoffman, Jerry Rubin, Lee Weiner, John Froines, and Bobby Seale.

Their trial began in September 1969 and was marked by outbursts as the defendants and defense attorneys William Kuntsler and Leonard Weinglass sparred with Federal Judge Julius Hoffman. In November, Seale's case was severed from the others, leaving the "Chicago Seven." In February 1970, Weiner and Froines were acquitted. The others were convicted. The convictions were overturned on appeal because of the inappropriate behavior of Judge Hoffman and prosecutors.

See also: Davis, Rennard Cordon (Rennie); Dellinger, David; Froines, John; Hayden, Tom; Hoffman, Abbie; Kuntsler, William; Rubin, Jerry; Seale, Bobby; Weiner, Lee; Weinglass, Leonard.

Chieu Hoi (Open Arms) Program. A 1963–1973 amnesty program that encouraged nearly 160,000 Viet Cong to desert and rally to the South Vietnamese government. Some joined the ARVN and served as Kit Carson scouts with U.S. Army units. Although more than 11,000 weapons were turned in, most analysts believe the program failed because many Chieu Hoi later returned to the Viet Cong.

China, People's Republic of (PRC). As Vietnam's northern neighbor and one of the two largest socialist countries after World War II, the People's Republic of China (PRC) provided significant support to the Vietnamese communists after 1949.

In 1950 the PRC became the first country to recognize Ho Chi Minh's Democratic Republic of Vietnam (DRV). After Ho's secret visit to Beijing in January 1950, the PRC sent a military advisory mission, a training, and a political advisory group of administrative experts to the DRV. Armed with weapons from China, the Vietnamese won the battle at Dien Bien Phu in 1954. In 1954, Chinese Premier Zhou Enlai led the effort by the PRC, the Soviet Union, and the DRV at the Geneva Conference to arrange the French withdrawal from Indochina.

The PRC became the first country to recognize the National

Liberation Front (NLF) in South Vietnam, and supplied most of the weapons for the insurgents. The PRC also helped build a transport line to South Vietnam through Cambodia and a secret port on Hainan Island to ship supplies.

In response to U.S. escalation of the Vietnam War in February 1965, the PRC considered aggression against the DRV as aggression against China. In April 1965 the PRC and the DRV signed an agreement to send Chinese air defense, engineering, railroad, and support troops to assist North Vietnam. The PRC claimed that a total of 320,000 Chinese troops served in Vietnam between January 1965 and July 1970, and that more than 1,000 died on Vietnamese soil. Military aid from China accounted for approximately 70 percent of the total military aid to North Vietnam. The total value of PRC aid between 1949 and 1979 was estimated at $20 billion. When the U.S. and the PRC began to improve relations in 1971, the PRC endorsed a DRV peace plan to end the Vietnam War. Still, Chinese aid to North Vietnam continued in large quantities even after the Paris peace accords were signed in 1973.

After the end of the Vietnam War, Chinese-Vietnamese relations deteriorated rapidly because of Vietnam's invasion of Cambodia and territorial disputes between Vietnam and the PRC. In 1979, Deng Xiaoping and other post-Mao Chinese leaders launched a short, punitive border war. The conflict was inconclusive. After a summit of the two countries' new leaders in Beijing in 1991, relations between China and Vietnam were normalized.

See also: DeSoto Missions; Détente; Dien Bien Phu; Easter Offensive; Geneva Conference, 1954; Haiphong; Ho Chi Minh; India; Kennan, George; Khmer Rouge; Kissinger, Henry; Korean War; Lao Dong; Le Duan; Normalization; People's Army of Vietnam; Rolling Thunder, Operation; Rules of Engagement; Rusk, (David) Dean; Viet Minh; Vo Nguyen Giap; Zhou Enlai.

China, Republic of (Taiwan). In 1956 Ngo Dinh Diem dissolved a centuries-old form of self-government by Chinese nationals in South Vietnam and barred foreign nationals from engaging in key areas of the economy. Taiwan retaliated by placing an embargo on rice exports and refusing to lend money to South Vietnam. In the 1960s Taiwan sought a role in the Vietnam War to increase its legitimacy and enhance its status with the U.S. The U.S., fearing retaliation by the People's Republic of China, kept Taiwan's involvement to a minimum. In 1964 and 1965 the Republic of China Military Assistance Advisory Group, Vietnam came to South Vietnam to assist with political warfare, medical work, the refugee situation, agriculture, and engineering. Taiwan provided $3 million to South Vietnam between 1964 and 1970 and donated 5,000 tons of rice.

See also: Free World.

Chu Lai. Coastal city in Quang Tin Province in north-central Vietnam. During the American War Chu Lai was headquarters of several units, including the First U.S. Marine Division and the U.S. Army Americal Division.

Church, Frank (1924–1984), U.S. senator (D-Idaho), 1957–1981; chairman, Senate Intelligence Committee, 1975–1976. An outspoken liberal, Sen. Frank Church turned against the Vietnam War in 1965. He cosponsored the Cooper-Church amendment in 1970 to prohibit deployment of U.S. ground forces in Cambodia, and the Case-Church amendment in 1973, to cut off funding for all U.S. military activity in Vietnam. Church's investigation of U.S. intelligence agencies in the mid 1970s revealed rampant abuses in the wake of the Vietnam War. After a strong run for the presidency in 1976, Church lost his bid for reelection to the Senate in 1980.

See also: Case-Church Amendment; Cooper, John Sherman; Cooper-Church Amendment.

Churchill, Winston (1874–1965), British Prime Minister (1940–1945, 1951–1955). Churchill met with President Dwight Eisenhower in the spring of 1954 at the urging of Lyndon Johnson and other U.S. senators who were concerned about the U.S. coming to the aid of the French at Dien Bien Phu. Churchill refused to be drawn into the fray, and the White House shelved plans to take military action.

See also: Dien Bien Phu.

CIA. *See* Central Intelligence Agency

Cimmeron, Operation. U.S. Marine operation in the spring of 1967 that repelled NVA attacks along the DMZ.

CINCPAC. *See* Commander-in-Chief, Pacific

CINCPACFLT. *See* Commander in Chief, U.S. Pacific Fleet

Civil Guard (CG). The official name for the various South Vietnamese Regional Forces that served as supplements to the South Vietnamese Army. Created in 1956 by President Ngo Dinh Diem, the Civil Guard was supposed to be a full-time, regional force operating in company-size (approximately 150-man) units in South Vietnam's 44 provinces. However, only one third reported for duty, while the remaining two thirds pursued other activities assigned by the province chiefs who controlled them. In 1964 the Civil Guard was renamed the Regional Forces (RF).

See also: Regional/Popular Forces.

Civilian Irregular Defense Groups (CIDGs). A program designed to protect South Vietnam's western border in the Central Highlands, based on work by Col. Gilbert B. Layton of the Central Intelligence Agency, who began training local self-defense units of Montagnard tribesmen in 1961. U.S. Army Special Forces took over the program in 1963, reorganizing village defense units into Civilian Irregular Defense Groups (CIDGs) under Operation Switchback. CIDGs conducted border surveillance from isolated mountain camps and defended against Viet Cong guerrilla infiltration or North Vietnamese Army attack. The tribesmen received salaries, medical care, and development aid. About forty thousand tribesmen joined the CIDGs, which were reorganized into mobile-strike or "Mike Force" battalions in 1965 so the camps could support each other when attacked. When the American Special Forces withdrew under Vietnamization in 1970–1971, the Saigon regime incorporated the CIDGs into the Army of the Republic of Vietnam.

See also: Central Highlands; Central Intelligence Agency; Layton, Gilbert B.; Montagnards; Special Forces, U.S. Army; Switchback, Operation.

Civil Operations and Revolutionary Development Support (CORDS). Organized by MACV Deputy Commander Robert Komer in 1967, the CORDS program brought together U.S. military, State Department, AID, USIA, and CIA pacification experts into one program. CORDS teams worked throughout South Vietnam, helping the Regional/Popular Forces and instituting programs that won Vietnamese peasants to the South Vietnamese government's cause and destroyed support for the Viet Cong. The CORDS program was de-emphasized following the 1968 Tet Offensive.

See also: Colby, William; Komer, Robert W.; Vann, John Paul.

Civil Rights Movement. In mid-1965, as the escalation of the war accelerated, some civil rights leaders became concerned about the effect of the war on President Johnson's Great Society programs and on the civil rights movement. In the summer of 1965 Rev. James Bevel, a close associate of Martin Luther King Jr., called for an alliance between the civil rights movement and the antiwar movement.

As American casualties mounted in 1966, the antiwar movement gained strength and the civil rights movement became more intimately involved with it. Civil rights leaders, especially Martin Luther King, Jr., noticed that African-American casualties in Vietnam were higher than their percentage in the American population, and that African American men were more likely to be drafted than whites, more likely to be assigned to infantry platoons, and more likely to enter combat.

Early in 1967, King formally linked the civil rights and antiwar movements, arguing that the Vietnam War was destroying the civil rights and antipoverty movements in the U.S. and creating an African American bloodbath on the other side of the world.

See also: Bevel, James, Rev.; Brown, H. Rap; Carmichael, Stokely; King, Martin Luther Jr.

Clark, Ramsey (1927–), deputy assistant attorney general, U.S. Department of Justice, 1965–1967; attorney general, 1967–1969. Clark, a peace advocate, resisted policies to repress the antiwar movement, despite pressure from the administration and Congress. As acting attorney general in 1966, Clark opposed a Selective Service System proposal to induct draft resisters quickly into military service in Vietnam. He allowed large, potentially violent demonstrations—including the 1967 March on the Pentagon—rather than repress such protests under his authority to prevent civil disorders.

In 1968, under pressure from the administration, Clark indicted several prominent antiwar figures, including Dr. Benjamin Spock and the Reverend William Sloan Coffin, for conspiracy to violate draft laws. The subsequent trial, despite a guilty verdict, helped promote the peace movement by giving a public forum to its most articulate activists. After successful appeals by the defendants, the Justice Department dropped the charges. After leaving office in 1969, Clark joined the antiwar movement.

See also: Justice, Department of.

Clay, Cassius. *See* Ali, Muhammad

Claymore Mines. The Claymore mine is an antipersonnel mine designed to emit a fan-shaped spray of fragments about three feet above the ground when detonated. These mines were carried by infantry troops and were commonly used by U.S. forces during the Vietnam War to defend static positions. Viet Cong forces who captured Claymores used them for booby traps.

Clay v. U.S. *See* Ali, Muhammad

Clear and Hold. A strategy emphasizing population security in South Vietnam over battle attrition of North Vietnamese and Viet Cong forces. British counterinsurgency expert Sir Robert Thompson first recommended clear-and-hold tactics in 1961. Static defense of villages cleared of North Vietnamese or Viet Cong troops, he said, would deprive the Viet Cong of their power base. Rather than chase insurgents in the jungle, U.S. forces should defend populated areas, where government officials and aid workers could operate safely. U.S. commanders relegated such pacification chores to South Vietnamese forces, concentrating instead on pursuing the enemy. Search-and-destroy remained the object of three out of four U.S. ground combat missions until 1968. U.S. Marines practiced clear-and-hold tactics in I Corps with Combined Action Platoons from 1966 to 1971.

See also: Combined Action Program; Search-and-Destroy; Thompson, Robert G. K.

Cleaver, (Leroy) Eldridge (1935–1998), a leader of the militant Black Panther Party. Cleaver, with other black-power advocates such as H. Rap Brown, Stokely Carmichael, and Bobby Seale, was critical of the nonviolent civil disobedience tactics of Martin Luther King Jr., and supported the radical wing of the antiwar movement. While in exile in Algeria in August 1970, Cleaver made two broadcasts over Radio Hanoi aimed at black servicemen in Vietnam, extolling the cause of the North Vietnamese.

See also: Civil Rights Movement.

Cleland, Joseph Maxwell (1942–), captain, U.S. Army, 1967–1968; head of the Veterans Administration (VA), 1977–1981. A highly decorated triple amputee who was wounded in action near Khe Sanh, Max Cleland became the first Vietnam veteran to head the VA. He vowed to stop the agency from treating Vietnam veterans as "social misfits." Cleland expanded counseling services, opened drug and alcohol treatment centers,

and helped organize Vietnam Veterans Week in 1979. He was less successful at expanding GI Bill benefits, and continued the VA's official policy of denying most Agent Orange disability claims. Cleland was elected to the U.S. Senate from Georgia in 1996.

Clergy and Laity Concerned About Vietnam (CALCAV). An ad hoc committee formed in October 1965 by antiwar American clergymen composed largely of liberal Protestants with some Jewish and Roman Catholic members. CALCAV was a moderate, mainstream, national organization. Using peaceful methods, CALCAV advanced a moral critique of the war. Some members later turned to more extreme measures of arson and vandalism.

See also: Berrigan Brothers; Coffin, William Sloane; King, Martin Luther Jr.; McCarthy, Eugene J.

Clifford, Clark (1906–), adviser to President Johnson; secretary of defense, 1968–1969. Clifford first participated in Vietnam policy in 1965 when President Johnson debated sending combat troops. Clifford joined Undersecretary of State George Ball as one of the few Johnson advisers arguing against such escalation. He felt the war might be unwinnable and questioned Vietnam's strategic importance.

After the combat troop deployment, Clifford supported the effort, believing that the U.S.

should take all steps to insure quick victory. In 1966 and 1967, Clifford, bolstered by optimistic briefings by U.S. military officials, advised against bombing halts, which he thought would be viewed by North Vietnam as a sign of weakness. As one of the "wise men," Clifford supported further escalation and urged Johnson to stay the course.

In 1968 Johnson appointed Clifford Secretary of Defense. When the military requested 206,000 additional troops after the Tet Offensive, Clifford became convinced that the U.S. should withdraw its forces from Vietnam, and tried to persuade Johnson of such a course. Knowing that many of the "wise men" also had changed their views, Clifford scheduled a historic meeting between the group and Johnson. Nearly all the "wise men" shared Clifford's conviction that disengagement was the best policy. Johnson felt betrayed by Clifford but was deeply affected by Clifford and his other long-time advisers' belief in the war's futility. Shortly after the meeting Johnson denied the military's request for more troops and stunned the nation with his decision not to seek a second term. Clifford spent the last months of Johnson's presidency laying the groundwork for U.S. withdrawal and Vietnamization.

See also: Hoopes, Townsend; McPherson, Harry; Read, Benjamin; Thompson, Robert G. K.; Vietnamization; Warnke, Paul C.; Wise Men.

Clinton, Bill (1946–), governor of Arkansas, 1979–1981, 1983–1992, president of the U.S., 1993– . The turmoil of the Vietnam War era reemerged as an issue during Bill (William Jefferson) Clinton's 1992 presidential campaign and early administration. Before the New Hampshire primary, the media obtained a letter he wrote in 1969 to Arkansas draft officials in which Clinton expressed opposition to the war. Clinton's opponents attempted to use his record to impugn the candidate's honesty and character, but polling showed that the issue was not a decisive factor for most voters.

In the late 1960s, Clinton played a minor role organizing antiwar demonstrations as an Oxford University student in England. Clinton received a draft induction notice while at Oxford in 1968. He obtained a temporary deferment from Arkansas draft officials. In the fall of 1969, after committing to join the Reserve Officers' Training Corps, he put himself up for the draft. Clinton received a high lottery number, assuring he would not be called into service.

Clinton's draft record affected his presidency. He had strained relations with the armed forces, exacerbated in part by some military officials' resentment of the president's activities in the 1960s. Clinton ended the 19-year trade embargo on Vietnam on 3 February 1994. On 11 July 1995 he announced the establishment of full diplomatic relations with Vietnam.

See also: Embargo.

Close Quarters (1977), well-regarded autobiographical Vietnam War novel by Larry Heinemann.

See also: Heinemann, Larry; *Paco's Story.*

Cluster Bomb. An assembly of smaller bombs dropped from the air. After a cluster bomb is released its subunits—usually fragmentation or incendiary bombs—separate and fall individually, broadening the area of impact. A U.S. innovation during the Vietnam War, the weapon was used mainly against personnel, but antitank and fuel-air (which create exploding concussive gaseous clouds) varieties were also deployed.

See also: International War Crimes Tribunal.

Coalition Government. During the Paris Peace talks in 1968 the North Vietnamese would not accept anything less than a U.S. withdrawal and a coalition government, terms the U.S. was not prepared to agree to. President Johnson made it clear to South Vietnamese Premier Thieu that he would not recognize the National Liberation Front nor accept a coalition government.

Coast Guard, U.S. In May 1965 President Johnson ordered U.S. Coast Guard patrol boats to conduct coastal surveillance and interdiction along South Vietnam's 1,950 kilometers (1,200 miles) of coastline. They joined U.S. and South Vietnamese units of the Coastal Surveillance Force in Operation Market Time, which closed down the sea infiltration route from North Vietnam. U.S. Coast Guard units patrolled the entire South Vietnamese coast from bases in Da Nang, Qui Nhon, Nha Trang, Vung Tan, and An Thoi. They confiscated hundreds of tons of supplies, performed six thousand fire support missions, and provided port security, explosives handling, sea rescue, navigation, and training. Coast Guardsmen in Vietnam suffered 7 killed, 53 wounded, and 1 missing in action. As part of Vietnamization in 1971, the Coast Guard turned over all patrol boats and four cutters to South Vietnam.

See also: Appendix B, "Order of Battle, U.S."

Cochinchina. The name used by the French to describe the southern region of Vietnam during the period of French colonial rule of Indochina. The area, which includes the Mekong Delta and the city of Saigon, was divided between the Champa and Khmer kingdoms for centuries until it was occupied by the Vietnamese in 1471. France took over Cochinchina in 1862; it became part of Vietnam in 1949.

See also: Annam; France; Saigon; Tonkin.

Coffin, William Sloane
(1924–), chaplain, Yale
University, 1958–1975. A leading
opponent of the Vietnam War,
Coffin was an important founding member of the group that
became Clergy and Laity
Concerned About Vietnam
(CALCAV). He was convicted
with Dr. Benjamin Spock in 1968
for conspiring to encourage resistance to Selective Service laws,
though the verdict was reversed
on appeal and charges against
both men were later dropped.

See also: Clark, Ramsey;
Clergy and Laity Concerned
About Vietnam; New Mobe.

Cogny, Rene (1904–1968),
French Army general who
helped plan the defense of Dien
Bien Phu.

See also: Dien Bien Phu.

Cointelpro. Code name for an
FBI operation targeting student
radicals in the antiwar movement begun in 1967, at President
Johnson's request. The operation
consisted of two main components: disrupting from the inside
and intimidating from the outside. Agents of the FBI and
agents of the CIA went undercover and infiltrated various
antiwar groups. This program,
which was continued and
expanded under President
Richard Nixon, sought to keep
the movement off guard and
upset its activities.

Colby, William (1920–1996),
station chief, Central Intelligence
Agency (CIA), Saigon,
1959–1962; deputy director, Civil
Operations and Revolutionary
Development Support (CORDS),
1968; director, the Phoenix program, 1969; director, CIA,
1973–1976. Colby arrived in
Vietnam in 1959, and served as
Saigon station chief until 1962.
He remained involved with the
Vietnam War until 1975 as Chief
of the CIA's Far East Division
and Director of the CIA.

Colby strongly supported
President Ngo Dinh Diem, while
urging Diem to curb his authori-
tarianism. Colby worked with
Diem's brother Nhu to conceive
the Strategic Hamlet program.
He considered the 1963 coup
against Diem a grave error that
led to the U.S. defeat.

Colby opposed the use of massive military force, which he felt
alienated the Vietnamese people.
He believed in pacification and
the use of Vietnamese civilian
defense forces, aided by the CIA
and Green Berets. Colby took
over the Phoenix program from
Robert Komer. He denied charges
that the Phoenix program was
involved assassinations for personal vendettas. He and the
Phoenix program became a focal
point for the antiwar movement's
opposition to the conflict.

During his tenure as director
of the CIA from 1973 to 1976
Colby revealed to a Senate committee the extensive illegal
activities of the CIA's proprietary
corporations, such as Air
America and other CIA illegal
actions during the war. He was
pressured by President Ford to
resign in 1976.

See also: Accelerated Pacification Campaign; Central Intelligence Agency; Phoenix Program.

Cold War. The worldwide rivalry that began after World War II between the U.S. and the Soviet Union and their allies. The Cold War had a strong impact on American support for France in the First Indochina War (1945–1954) and on American prosecution of its war in Vietnam beginning shortly after the French defeat at Dien Bien Phu. Presidents from Harry Truman to Gerald Ford directed interventionist policies in Vietnam in an attempt to contain communist expansionism in Southeast Asia. Congress acquiesced because it deferred to presidents in the realm of foreign policy throughout the Cold War and because it shared the anticommunist ideology of the day. The Indochina wars, like the Korean War, became part of the Cold War, with free nations including the U.S., Australia, South Korea, New Zealand and the Philippines supporting one side and communist nations, including the Soviet Union and China, the other.

See also: Congress, U.S.; Eisenhower, Dwight D.; Flexible Response; Geneva Conference, 1961–1962; Kennan, George; Rusk, (David) Dean; Taylor-Rostow Report; U.S. Information Service.

Collège Hau Bo. A French school of administration taught by French schoolteachers appointed by the French governor of the colony of Annam. Among its students was Ngo Dinh Diem, who would go on to become prime minister and president of the Republic of Vietnam. Diem enrolled in the school after graduating from a Catholic secondary school in Hue.

College Unrest. *See* Jackson State College; Kent State University; New Mobe; Students for a Democratic Society; Teach-Ins; University of Wisconsin Bombing

Collins, James Lawton Jr. (1917–), general, U.S. Army; special assistant to the Commander, Military Assistance Command, Vietnam (COMUS-MACV),1965–1966; senior adviser to South Vietnam's Regional/Popular Forces (RF/PF), 1964–1965. Gen. William Westmoreland made Collins his personal representative responsible for coordinating allied operations with South Vietnam's Joint General Staff and other allies in May 1965. Collins harshly criticized the ARVN officer corps for corruption and incompetence.

Collins, Joseph Lawton (1896–1987), general, U.S. Army; special representative to South Vietnam, 1954–1955. Known as "Lightning Joe" in World War II, Gen. J. Lawton Collins was sent to South Vietnam by President Eisenhower in November 1954 to assess the situation and to set up a military training program for President Diem's army. Collins recommended reducing U.S. support because of Diem's refusal to institute democratic reforms. Collins said that Diem could not prevent the country from falling under communist control. This advice went unheeded in Washington, and General Collins was recalled in May 1955.

Colson, Charles (1931–), special counsel to President Nixon, 1969–1973. Colson coordinated a series of "dirty tricks" tied to the Watergate scandal, including ordering the forgery of a State Department cable linking the Diem assassination with President Kennedy and writing a newspaper ad that claimed to be a citizens' group effort in support of the May 1972 mining of Haiphong Harbor. On 3 June 1974, Colson pled guilty to obstructing justice in connection with the administration's prosecution of Daniel Ellsburg for releasing the Pentagon Papers. He was sentenced to serve one to three years in prison and pay a $5,000 fine.

See also: Pentagon Papers; Watergate.

Combat Infantryman Badge (CIB). Badge awarded U.S. Army personnel actively engaged in ground combat.

Combined Action Program (CAP). Developed as part of the III Marine Amphibious Force's (III MAF) strategy of counter-guerrilla operations and control of the rural population, CAP paired squads of U.S. Marines with platoons of Popular Forces (PF), the government-sponsored Vietnamese village militia. Begun in August 1965, CAP produced more than one hundred Combined Action platoons in the coastal lowlands of South Vietnam's five northern provinces. At maximum strength in 1968–1969 some 2,500 Marines took part in CAP. After reaching a high of 114 platoons in 1970, CAP declined as III MAF withdrew. U.S. Marines suffered approximately 1,000 dead and wounded. CAP efforts such as medical help for the villagers, small-scale construction, and other civic action activities were passed to other agencies, largely Vietnamese. The last civil affairs group and Combined Action company disbanded in May 1971.

See also: Clear and Hold; Regional/Popular Forces.

COMECON. The communist common market, which the Democratic Republic of Vietnam joined in June 1978, thus launching a massive economic integration with the Soviet Union.

Coming Home (1978), award-winning Hal Ashby film, the first Hollywood movie with a positively portrayed Vietnam veteran as the main character.

Comintern (Communist International). The association of communist parties founded in 1919 with the goal of promoting world revolution. Also known as the Third International, the Comintern was dominated by the Soviet Union. One of its agents was the Vietnamese revolutionary Nguyen Ai Quoq, who would take the name Ho Chi Minh in 1942. In 1923 Ho Chi Minh was invited to Moscow to work at the Comintern headquarters. The following year he was posted to the Comintern mission in Canton, with instructions to form a Marxist-Leninist revolutionary organization in French Indochina. He formed the Vietnamese Communist Party in 1925. That group later became the Indochinese Communist Party, which included factions in Cambodia and Laos and followed orders from the Comintern.

See also: Ho Chi Minh; Indochinese Communist Party.

Commander, U.S. Military Assistance Command, Vietnam (COMUSMACV).

The title of the head of the American military effort in Vietnam from 1962–1973. Beginning with the establishment of the U.S. Military Assistance Command, Vietnam on 8 February 1962, the MACV commanders were: U.S. Army Gens. Paul D. Harkins (1962–1964), William C. Westmoreland (1964–1968), Creighton W. Abrams (1968–1972), Frederick C. Weyand (1972–1973).

See also: Abrams, Creighton W. Jr.; Harkins, Paul D.; Military Assistance Command, Vietnam; Westmoreland, William C.; Weyand, Frederick C.

Commander, U.S. Naval Forces, Vietnam (COMNAVFORV).

The naval subordinate of the commander of USMACV, known as the Chief of the Navy Section, Military Assistance Advisory Group, Vietnam from August 1950 to May 1964; the Chief of the Naval Advisory Group, Vietnam, from May 1964 to April 1966; and the Chief of the Naval Advisory Group/Commander of Naval Forces, Vietnam from April 1966 to March 1973.

Commander-in-Chief, Pacific (CINCPAC).

During the Vietnam War, the office of Commander-in-Chief, Pacific, was held by four U.S. Navy admirals: Harry D. Felt, Ulysses S. G. Sharp, John S. McCain Jr., and Noel A. M. Gayler. They directed U.S. ground, air, and sea forces in the Pacific Command, which covered 220 million square kilometers (85 million square miles) from Alaska to the Indian Ocean, and included the entire Southeast Asian area of operations. During the Vietnam War, the commander of the U.S. Military Assistance Command, Vietnam (COMUSMACV) in Saigon reported to CINCPAC in Honolulu, who in turn reported to the Joint Chiefs of Staff in Washington.

See also: Felt, Harry D.; Gayler, Noel; McCain, John S. Jr.; Military Assistance Command, Vietnam; Rolling Thunder, Operation; Sharp, Ulysses S. Grant Jr.

Commander-in-Chief, U.S. Pacific Fleet (CINCPACFLT).

During the Vietnam War, the Commander-in-Chief, U.S. Pacific Fleet received his orders from the Commander-in-Chief, U.S. Pacific Command. The admirals who commanded the U.S. Pacific Fleet during the Vietnam War were: John H. Sides (1960–1963), Ulysses S. G. Sharp (1963–1964), Thomas H. Moorer (1964–1965), Roy L. Johnson (1965–1967), John J. Hyland (1967–1970), Bernard A. Clarey (1970–1973) and Maurice F. Weisner (1973–1976).

Commanding General, III Marine Amphibious Force (III MAV).

The head of the chief U.S. Marine Corps unit in Vietnam. III MAV was formed in May 1965 with headquarters at Da Nang. The unit departed Vietnam in April 1971. III MAV's commanders were U.S. Marine Gens. William R. Collins (May to June 1965), Lewis W. Walt (June 1965 to February 1966), Keith B. McCutcheon (February to March 1966), Lewis W. Walt (March 1966 to June 1967), Robert E. Cushman, Jr. (June 1967 to March 1969), Herman Nickerson, Jr. (March 1969 to March 1970), Donn J. Robertson (December 1970 to April 1971).

See also: Cushman, Robert E. Jr., Walt, Lewis W.

Commando Hunt, Operation.

Code name for U.S. air interdiction efforts against the Ho Chi Minh Trail, 1968–1973. Commando Hunt included five semiannual campaigns during the dry, northeast monsoon season, roughly October through April. B-52 Arc Light strikes were used for disruptive effect. Fighter bombers and AC-130 Spectre gunships hunted trucks and troops with targeting information from air-dropped seismic and acoustic sensors. Commando Hunt exacted a heavy toll on troops and supplies but did not halt the supply and reinforcement of People's Army of Vietnam forces in the South.

See also: Arc Light, Operation; Barrier Concept; Ho Chi Minh Trail.

Commercial-Import Program (CIP).

A program used by the U.S. to direct billions of dollars into South Vietnam from the late 1950s through the early 1970s. The U.S. financed Vietnamese importers through the Agency for International Development (AID). The importers ordered foreign goods through the CIP, paying for them in South Vietnamese piasters. That money then went into a fund at the National Bank of Vietnam, which the South Vietnamese government used to finance development projects and cover operating expenses.

The CIP enabled South Vietnam's economy to survive the first years after independence and the program achieved some success covering South Vietnam's foreign exchange deficit and holding inflation in check. But extensive patronage and corruption prevented it from successfully promoting basic economic development.

See also: Agency for International Development; National Bank of Vietnam.

Committee for the Re-election of the President (CREEP).

The group headed by U.S. Attorney General John Mitchell that spearheaded President Nixon's 1972 re-election effort. Mitchell and other committee members later were implicated in Watergate-related "dirty tricks," including the June 1972 break-in at Democratic National Committee headquarters at the Watergate Hotel.

See also: Mitchell, John N.; Watergate.

Commonwealth Peace Mission.

An effort to end hostilities in Vietnam headed by British Prime Minister Harold Wilson in June 1965 and supported by South Vietnam and the U.S. Wilson's mission failed because the DRV, the Soviet Union, and the People's Republic of China refused to receive it.

See also: Wilson, (James) Harold.

Communism.

The political philosophy first espoused by Karl Marx and Friedrich Engels in 1848 based on common property or equal distribution of wealth. In Vietnam, the communist movement emerged from nationalist agitation against French colonial rule in the 1920s. Marxist ideas became familiar to Vietnamese workers and intellectuals living in France during and after WWI and gradually penetrated into Vietnam during the years immediately following the war. The founder of Vietnamese communism was Ho Chi Minh. He was a founding member of the French Communist Party, the founder of the Vietnamese Communist Party in 1925, and later, founder of the Indochinese Communist Party (ICP).

Ho Chi Minh's brand of communism often appealed to peasants who had been heavily taxed or denied land by the colonialists and their Vietnamese collaborators. When the southern Vietnamese communist group, the National Liberation Front, called for higher wages for workers and civil servants and redistribution of rice-growing lands, it found many supporters in the cities and the countryside. The communists were popular because, in general, they behaved better than the South Vietnamese government officials. They typically treated villagers with respect, did not loot, and made themselves part of the community. And they pointed out that the South Vietnamese government that asked for the people's loyalty was totally dependent on the U.S. for sustenance.

See also: Comintern; Communist Party, Vietnamese; Ho Chi Minh.

Communist International. *See* Comintern

Communist Party, Chinese.
See Zhou Enlai

Communist Party, French.
Founded in 1920, the French
Communist Party was, in the
late 1940s and early 1950s, a
strong opponent of what it called
France's "dirty war" against the
communist-led insurgents in
Vietnam. The Vietnamese communist leader, Ho Chi Minh, had
been a founding member of the
French Communist Party.

See also: Ho Chi Minh.

**Communist Party,
Vietnamese.** Formed by Ho Chi
Minh in 1925, the Vietnamese
Communist Party led an abortive
peasant rebellion against French
colonial rule in Nghe An and Ha
Tinh provinces in 1930. Brutally
suppressed in the aftermath of
that rebellion, the party in 1935
nonetheless adopted guidelines
for the future organization of
armed forces on the Soviet
model, and led the fight against
the French that culminated in
the 1954 French defeat at Dien
Bien Phu. In early 1959, Ho Chi
Minh began infiltrating the
South with anti-Diem southerners who had come north in 1954.
Their mission was to begin an
armed struggle against the
South Vietnamese government
and its U.S. sponsors. The following year saw the formation of
the National Liberation Front
(NLF), an organization made up
of dissatisfied peasants and former religious cultists formed
around a Communist Party core.
Diem derisively called the front

the Viet Cong, or "Vietnamese
Commies." The NLF joined the
North Vietnamese Army in the
war against South Vietnam and,
beginning in the early 1960s, the
U.S. The Communist Party,
known from 1951 to 1976 as the
Vietnam Worker's Party, claimed
525,000 members in 1960; in
1975, just prior to the victory
over South Vietnam, membership
stood at 1.2 million in a nation of
25 million.

See also: All for the Brotherly
South Campaign; Comintern;
Communism; Ho Chi Minh; Land
Reform.

**Communist Party of
Kampuchea (CPK).** *See* Khmer
Rouge

COMNAVFORV. *See*
Commander, U.S. Naval Forces,
Vietnam

Company. Basic U.S. Army and
Marine unit designation below
battalion. A company is commanded by a captain and most
often is divided into two or more
platoons. Companies vary in size
and mission. Artillery companies
are known as batteries; cavalry
companies are called troops.

See also: Platoon; Appendix B,
"Order of Battle, U.S."

COMUSMACV. *See*
Commander, U.S. Military
Assistance Command, Vietnam

Conein, Lucien (1919–1998),
French-born officer in the Office
of Strategic Services (OSS); CIA

agent in Vietnam. Conein, an expert in demolition and guerrilla tactics, fought the Japanese in northern Vietnam in 1945. He returned to Vietnam to organize covert operations against the communists in North Vietnam in 1954 under Edward Lansdale's Saigon Military Mission. He went to Saigon in 1962 as an adviser to the South Vietnamese Ministry of the Interior and in 1963 aided the coup that ousted Ngo Dinh Diem.

See also: Central Intelligence Agency; Ngo Dinh Diem; Saigon Military Mission.

Confucianism. The system of thought and belief based on the teachings of the sixth century B.C. Chinese philosopher Confucius. His teachings emphasize ancestor worship and study of the past as the source of wisdom and power, and hold that the state is an extension of the family. The Chinese introduced Confucianism to Vietnam when they annexed the region in 111 B.C. Although Buddhism remained the dominant popular religion, Confucianism became the basis for politics, government, and formal education in Vietnam. The French replaced Vietnam's Confucian mandarin political leaders in the nineteenth century, but Confucianism remained a vibrant part of Vietnamese society.

See also: Hoa Hao.

Cong Hoa (Republican) Youth. A sociopolitical organization formed by South Vietnamese President Diem in the early 1960s to participate in massive pro-government demonstrations. Its members were recruited and trained by Col. Le Quang Tung, and Dr. Tran Kim Tuyen, the head of the South Vietnamese secret police. At its height in 1963 the group had nearly 1 million adolescents in 43 chapters nationwide. The Cong Hoa's largest unit (6,000 members) was in Saigon, and it, in conjunction with Madame Nhu's Women's Solidarity Movement, whose members were young women aged 12 to 25 years, acted as the eyes and ears of the government in the streets.

See also: Ngo Dien Diem; Women's Solidarity League, Vietnam.

Congress, U.S. Beginning in the 1950s, Congress acquiesced to American presidents' Vietnam policies because it deferred to the president in foreign policy during the Cold War, and because it shared the anticommunist ideology of the day.

President Johnson, former Senate majority leader, secured passage of congressional authorization to use military force to protect South Vietnam's independence and to repel attacks on American military units with the August 1964 Tonkin Gulf Resolution. His main allies were Senators J. William Fulbright and Richard B. Russell. Only Senators Wayne L. Morse and Ernest Gruening voted against the resolution. For the next several years, a bipartisan majority, reflecting the public's mood, supported President Johnson's war policies. Led by Fulbright, who regretted his earlier support, members of the Senate Foreign Relations Committee expressed growing skepticism during public hearings in February 1966. Senate Majority Leader Mike Mansfield, Morse, and Frank Church, among others, challenged Johnson's war policymaking, but with little success.

During the Nixon administration antiwar feelings became more pronounced in the Senate than they had been during the Johnson years. The Senate supported legislation favoring the withdrawal of all U.S. troops from Vietnam in exchange for North Vietnam's return of U.S. prisoners, repealed the Gulf of Tonkin Resolution and passed the Cooper-Church Amendment, which required the president to remove the troops he had sent to Cambodia by 30 June 1970. A substantial minority embraced the bipartisan McGovern-Hatfield Amendment, designed to force the president to withdraw all U.S. troops from Vietnam by the end of 1971. Nixon retained the loyalty of a more prowar House. His ability to control Congress lasted until after his victory in the 1972 election, when Congress, frustrated with the stalled peace talks in Paris, began to legislate an end to the war.

After the January 1973 withdrawal of U.S. troops from Vietnam, Congress hoped to end all U.S. military activity in the region, especially after North Vietnam returned the U.S. prisoners of war. Congress forced Nixon to end the bombing of Cambodia by 15 August 1973, marking a crucial turning point in executive-legislative relations bearing on the Vietnam War. By the summer of 1973, abundant evidence from the Pentagon Papers and the *New York Times* exposé of the secret bombing campaigns in Cambodia and Laos proved that the Nixon administration had deliberately falsified statistics, data, and reports to Congress to hide the extent of questionable U.S. military activity in Vietnam, Cambodia and Laos. In July, Congress responded by formulating the War Powers Resolution, which required the president to report to Congress within 48 hours if he committed U.S. troops to a foreign conflict or if he "substantially" increased the number of combat troops in a foreign country. Unless Congress approved the president's action within 60 days, the commitment would have to be terminated. Congress passed the War Powers Resolution, which survived a Nixon veto, in November 1973.

President Gerald Ford asked Congress to authorize a substantial aid package for the faltering South Vietnamese government in 1974, but Congress refused, reducing considerably the amount Ford believed necessary to keep South Vietnam viable.

See also: Cooper-Church Amendment; Gulf of Tonkin

Resolution; POW/MIA
Controversy; Truman, Harry S;
War Powers Resolution;
Appendix E, "Gulf of Tonkin
Resolution."

**Congressional Medal of
Honor.** *See* Medal of Honor

**Congress of Industrial
Organizations (CIO).** *See*
Goldberg, Arthur J.

Conscientious Objectors.
Traditionally, conscientious objection required a rejection of war
on specific religious doctrinal
grounds. In 1965 the Supreme
Court decided that religion did
not have to be church-based to be
grounds for conscientious objection. In 1970 the Court ruled
that objections based on moral,
ethical, or general religious
beliefs were as valid as those
originating in specific creeds. In
other Vietnam War–
related cases, however, the Court
refused to widen conscientious
objection. In 1971 the Court
denied conscientious objector status to those who objected not to
all wars, but specifically to the
Vietnam War. Not all conscientious objectors refused military
service. Those who agreed to
serve were given non-combat
jobs such as clerks and medics.
In 1966 just over 6 per 100
inductions received conscientious
objector status from their draft
boards. By 1970 the rate had
increased to more than 25 per
100. Concientious objectors generally were required by their
draft boards to perform two

years of civilian humanitarian
service.

See also: Supreme Court, U.S.

Con Son. Island located 80 kilometers (50 miles) off the coast of
Vinh Binh province. Originally a
French colonial prison, Con Son
Island was used by South
Vietnam in the late 1960s and
1970s to jail political prisoners,
Viet Cong guerrillas, and North
Vietnamese POWs. It became a
center of controversy in 1970
when a visiting U.S. congressional delegation found prisoners
living in inhumane conditions.
Some were confined in "tiger
cages," small cement cells in
which they were chained and
unable to move their legs.

See also: Atrocities; Binh
Xuyen; Le Duan; Pham Van
Dong; Tiger Cages.

Containment, Policy of.
Formulated by U.S. diplomat and
historian George Kennan in an
article in the July 1947 issue of
Foreign Affairs magazine (written
under the pseudonym "X").
Kennan's ideas became the foundation for U.S. foreign policy for
four decades. Containment,
which was intended to prevent
the spread of communism, was
grounded in the belief that the
Soviet Union, and later the
People's Republic of China,
would aggressively try to foster
communism throughout the
world. The policy of containment
held that the U.S. and its
Western allies must use all
means necessary, including
military force, to prevent the

Soviet Union and China from building communist empires that would threaten democratic nations and U.S. economic interests. Kennan revised the policy in the late 1950s, arguing that containment was not relevant to the situation in Vietnam.

See also: Kennan, George.

Con Thien. Village in Quang Tri province, on the South Vietnamese side of the demilitarized zone (DMZ). A U.S. Marine outpost in Con Thien was attacked by North Vietnamese Army (NVA) forces in September 1967, in a month-long pre-Tet-Offensive siege. The NVA troops, equipped with new Soviet weapons, bombarded the fire base. The Marines, aided by U.S. air, naval, and artillery support, successfully defended the base. The battle distracted U.S. attention from South Vietnamese cities, which were about to be attacked in the surprise Tet Offensive.

See also: Tet Offensive.

Convoy of Tears. A term used by journalists to describe the withdrawal of the Army of the Republic of Vietnam (ARVN) and civilian refugees from the Central Highlands in 1975 in which thousands died from starvation and as a result of NVA or ARVN shellfire.

See also: Pleiku.

Cooper, Chester (1917–), Central Intelligence Agency (CIA) analyst, 1958–1964; senior member, U.S. National Security Council, 1964–1967; member, Institute for Defense Analysis, 1967. In 1965, as a member of the National Security Council, Cooper questioned the ability of the U.S. to win a guerrilla war. In 1966 Cooper supported Operation Marigold, a diplomatic mission led by Polish diplomat Janusz Lewandowski, to negotiate with Hanoi. Cooper and Averell Harriman suggested a halt to the bombing of Hanoi. Robert McNamara agreed, but Dean Rusk and Walt Rostow opposed the request, and President Johnson refused to halt the bombing. Cooper later worked on Operation Sunflower, an abortive British diplomatic effort to encourage the Soviet Union to pressure the Democratic Republic of Vietnam (DRV) to compromise.

See also: American Friends of Vietnam; Marigold, Operation; Sunflower, Operation.

Cooper, John Sherman (1901–1991), U.S. senator (R-Ky.), 1957–1973. Cooper doubted the wisdom of the Vietnam War by 1964, though he voted for the Gulf of Tonkin Resolution. A critic of U.S. involvement in Vietnam from the late 1960s on, Cooper unsuccessfully cosponsored the Cooper-Church Amendment with Frank Church. The amendment, a response to the 1970 Cambodian incursion, called for the termination of funds for all military operations in Cambodia if U.S. troops were not withdrawn.

See also: Cooper-Church Amendment.

Cooperativization Program. A Democratic Republic of Vietnam program first announced in 1977 but not stressed until mid-1978 because of the need to gather material and human resources to fight the war against the Khmer Rouge in Cambodia. One aim of the program was to make land more productive through mass mobilization for land reclamation and irrigation. The collectiviza- tion efforts backfired, however, and caused the agricultural sec- tor to stagnate and government food procurement to decrease.

Cooper-Church Amendment. Following the U.S.-Army of the Republic of Vietnam incursion into Cambodia in May 1970, Republican U.S. Sen. John Sherman Cooper of Kentucky and Democratic Sen. Frank Church of Idaho drew up an amendment to a defense appro- priations bill that required the president to remove all U.S. troops from Cambodia by 30 June 1970. Congress adopted a modified version of the Cooper- Church Amendment in December 1970 that prohibited the presi- dent from committing U.S. ground forces to combat in Laos and Thailand.

See also: Church, Frank; Cooper, John Sherman.

Coordinated Studies Group. A group that included CIA, Agency for International

Development, and U.S. Special Forces personnel, which armed and assisted Montagnard tribes, such as the Sre and Rhade, in the Central Highlands.

Coppola, Francis Ford (1939–), film director. Coppola directed the award-winning Vietnam War film, *Apocaplyse Now* (1979), and the Vietnam War–themed *Gardens of Stone* (1987).

CORDS. *See* Civil Operations and Revolutionary Development Support

Corps Tactical Zones (CTZs). The U.S. military divided South Vietnam into four Corps Tactical Zones, numbered I, II, III and IV. The I Corps (pronounced "eye corps") Tactical Zone consisted of the five northern provinces of South Vietnam. The II Corps Tactical Zone was situated in the Central Highlands and central coastlands, with headquarters in Pleiku. The III Corps Zone con- sisted of Saigon and its surrounding area to the north, and IV Corps was made up of the Mekong Delta region south of Saigon.

COSVN. *See* Central Office for South Vietnam

Counterinsurgency. Counterinsurgency, or unconven- tional counterguerrilla warfare, appealed to U.S. strategic plan- ners in the early 1960s as an appropriate response to Soviet support for guerrilla-based wars of national liberation in the developing world. The theory was that guerrilla wars required a new approach that emphasized winning the allegiance of civilians over defeating enemy forces in battle. President Kennedy strongly encouraged counterinsurgency, creating the U.S. Army Special Forces to fill the counterinsurgency role.

Under titles such as "population security" and "pacification," counterinsurgency became the "other war" in Vietnam—a vast American outpouring of agricultural experts, doctors, teachers, engineers, CIA agents, and civil advisers dedicated to overcoming the Viet Cong infrastructure and winning "the hearts and minds" of the Vietnamese people. Counterinsurgency efforts came under one command with the formation of Civil Operations and Revolutionary Development Support (CORDS) in 1967, headed by Robert W. Komer.

See also: Civil Operations and Revolutionary Development Support; Hilsman, Roger; Lansdale, Edward G.; Malaysia; McNamara, Robert; Pacification; Taylor, Maxwell D.; Thompson, Robert G. K.; U.S. Information Service; Westmoreland, William C.

Courts Martial, U.S. Military forces in Vietnam were subject to courts martial under the Uniform Code of Military Justice (UCMJ). In 1968 Congress passed a new UCMJ that guaranteed legal counsel before a court-martial.

See also: Uniform Code of Military Justice.

COWIN Report. In early 1971, a U.S. Army task force investigated whether Gen. William Westmoreland was personally culpable for war crimes. Its report, called the "Conduct of the War in Vietnam" (COWIN), found no basis for Westmoreland's guilt.

See also: Westmoreland, William C.

Cox, Archibald (1912–), Harvard Law professor appointed special prosecutor to investigate the Watergate scandal. Cox was fired by President Nixon in what was called the "Saturday night massacre" in October 1973 which, led to the resignations of Attorney General Elliot Richardson and Assistant Attorney General William Ruckleshaus.

See also: Saturday Night Massacre; Watergate.

C-Rations. Boxed meals, consisting of canned and packaged food, issued to U.S. military personnel when no kitchen facilities are available.

Credibility Gap. A phrase used during the Johnson and Nixon administrations referring to the disparity between official pronouncements on the Vietnam War and actual policy and events. Reporter David Wise first wrote of a "credibility gap" in the *New York Herald Tribune* in 1965.

See also: Pentagon Papers.

CREEP. *See* Committee for the Re-election of the President

Crimp, Operation. January 1966 operation in the heavily forested Ho Bo Woods north of Saigon in which elements of the U.S. Army's 1st Infantry Division, 173rd Airborne Brigade and the 1st Royal Australian Regiment discovered the Cu Chi tunnels. The operation helped prepare for the subsequent establishment of the 25th Infantry Division base camp at Cu Chi.

See also: Tunnels.

Cronkite, Walter (1916–), CBS Evening News anchor, 1954–1981. Because Cronkite was a respected and influential newsman, his coverage of the Vietnam War greatly concerned the Johnson and Nixon administrations. Cronkite was cautiously optimistic about the war until the 1968 Tet Offensive, when he traveled to Saigon. In a special report on 27 February 1968, Cronkite concluded: "It seems now more certain than ever that the bloody experience of Vietnam is to end in stalemate." Sensing that Cronkite accurately reflected public opinion, Johnson reportedly remarked, "If I have lost Walter Cronkite, I have lost Mr. Average Citizen."

CTZ. *See* Corps Tactical Zones

Cu Chi. Located about 25 miles northwest of Saigon, Cu Chi was the home of the U.S. 25th Infantry Division's base camp. It was also an area heavily infiltrated by the Viet Cong. Just north of the camp was a large Viet Cong underground tunnel complex.

See also: Tunnels.

Cuong De, Prince (1882–1957), Vietnamese prince directly descended from the Emperor Gia Long who was not permitted by the French to become Vietnam's emperor. He was forced into exile in Japan and elsewhere where he tried to form a nationalist movement to overthrow French colonial rule. Revered by Vietnamese nationalists, Cuong De died in exile.

Cushman, Robert E. Jr. (1914–1985), commander of III Marine Amphibious Force, 1967–1969; Central Intelligence Agency (CIA) deputy director, 1969–1972. During his tour in Vietnam Cushman oversaw the defense of Khe Sanh, the battle for Hue, and the I Corps counteroffensive against the Tet Offensive. As deputy director of the CIA, he became briefly enmeshed in allegations of CIA authorization of the burglary of Daniel Ellsberg's office but was never formally charged. Cushman served as Marine Corps commandant from 1972 until his retirement in 1975, during which time he acted to end voluntary racial segregation in U.S. Marine facilities.

See also: Marines, U.S.

Cuu Nuoc (National Salvation). A newspaper distributed by the Viet Minh, and later the Viet Cong, in South Vietnam.

Dai Viet Party. Non-communist nationalist party formed in Hanoi in 1939. During WWII the party tried to work with the Japanese for an independent Vietnam. After the war, the Dai Viet Party was outlawed in North Vietnam. In the south, it remained a minority opposition party.

Dak Pek. A hamlet on Highway 14 in the Central Highlands of South Vietnam, 12 kilometers east of the Laotian border and the site of a U.S. Special Forces camp.

See also: Central Highlands.

Dak Seang. A village in the Central Highlands 15 kilometers northwest of Dak To, and the site of a U.S. Special Forces and South Vietnamese Civilian Irregular Defense Group camp. Located along a known North Vietnamese Army (NVA) and Viet Cong infiltration route, the camp was attacked unsuccessfully by the NVA in April 1970.

Dak To. Jungle region in the western Central Highlands near the Laotian and Cambodian borders and the site of a 1965 U.S. Special Forces camp. In October to November 1967, the North

Vietnamese Army launched a direct attack on elements of the U.S. 4th Infantry Division and 173rd Airborne Brigade there in a pre–Tet Offensive battle. In a battle that included heavy bombardment by U.S. B-52s, the NVA lost some 1,600 men.

See also: Central Highlands; Tet Offensive.

Da Lat. Central Highlands city founded by the French as a resort in 1897 due to its temperate climate. Little fighting took place during the war in Da Lat, which is populated by Montagnards and other hill tribespeople.

Da Lat Military Academy. The Vietnamese equivalent of West Point, the Da Lat Military Academy was founded by the French and trained many officers in the Army of the Republic of Vietnam. Nguyen Van Thieu, South Vietnam's president from 1967–1975, graduated from the academy as an infantry lieutenant in 1949.

Daley, Richard J. (1902–1976), mayor of Chicago, 1955–1976. The powerful Democratic Mayor Daley ordered the Chicago police to quell the large demonstrations that were held during the Democratic National Convention in 1968. As a result, downtown Chicago became the scene of what was later called a "police riot" when officers violently attacked demonstrators with dogs, horses, and billy clubs.

See also: Democratic Convention, 1968.

Da Nang. South Vietnamese city, capital of Quang Nam province. The most important port in the Central Lowlands of Vietnam, Da Nang was the second largest urban area in South Vietnam in 1967 with a population of 143,910. During the Vietnam War Da Nang was a magnet for rural peasants who fled their villages for the city. By 1970, the city's population reached 450,000. As a result of the decrease in food production in the countryside and the official corruption that hampered the delivery of food and medicine from the United States, the uprooted rural population lived at little more than subsistence level in makeshift camps on the outskirts of the city

To protect its air base at Da Nang, the United States landed two battalions of Marines on 8 March 1965, beginning the U.S. commitment of ground forces in Vietnam. Da Nang was also the site of the headquarters of the Army of the Republic of Vietnam's I Corps and its 3d Division. A year later, Da Nang was the scene of the 1966 Buddhist "Struggle Movement" against Prime Minister Nguyen Cao Ky's government. When ARVN troops sided with the Buddhists, Ky declared the city under communist control (despite the presence of U.S. Marines stationed in Da Nang) and sent one thousand South Vietnamese marines to crush the uprising. In 1968, Da Nang was attacked by North Vietnamese Army (NVA) and Viet Cong forces during the Tet Offensive.

During the NVA's final offensive in 1975, Da Nang fell within a matter of days. The city's defenses quickly disintegrated and the defending army and civilians fled in a retreat under heavy crossfire between the ARVN and the NVA. Da Nang was later a heavily used port for the exodus of Vietnamese boat people.

See also: Nguyen Chanh Thi; Seabees; Search and Rescue; Teach-Ins.

Dang Cong San Viet Nam. *See* Vietnamese Communist Party

Dang Lao Dong Viet Nam. *See* Lao Dong

Daniel Boone, Operations. Code name for 1967–1968 covert operations in which squads of U.S. and South Vietnamese Army Special Forces, dressed as peasants or in unrecognizable uniforms, went into Cambodia to gather intelligence or to sabotage communist installations at the southern end of the Ho Chi Minh Trail, despite U.S. law forbidding operations in countries not at war with the United States. The information gathered on these raids led to the 1969 secret bombing of Cambodia, Operation Menu, and to the 1970 invasion of Cambodia. The missions were renamed Salem House in 1968 and Thot Not three years later.

See also: Cambodian Incursion; Menu, Operation.

Dau Tranh (struggle). Vietnamese communist military and political strategy adopted in the 1930s combining Marxist, Leninist, Maoist, and Vietnamese doctrines.

See also: Communism.

Davidson, Carl (1943–), a leader of the Students for a Democratic Society, the radical antiwar group. During what was called "Stop the Draft Week" in October 1967, Davidson advocated tearing down and burning military induction centers "if necessary."

See also: Students for a Democratic Society.

Davidson, Phillip B. (1915–), a 1939 graduate of the U.S. Military Academy at West Point, Lt. Gen. Davidson served in WWII, Korea and Vietnam, where he was the chief intelligence officer for MACV commanders Gens. William Westmoreland and Creighton Abrams. A former associate professor of military history at West Point, Gen. Davidson is the author of *Vietnam at War: The History: 1946-1975* (1988) and *Secrets of the Vietnam War* (1990).

Davis, Rennard Cordon (Rennie) (1940–), a leader in several radical groups, including Students for a Democratic Society, the Economic Research and Action Project, and the May Day Tribe. In 1968 Davis was a leader of the demonstrations at the Democratic National Convention in Chicago. Along with seven others Davis was charged with conspiracy to cause a riot. He was acquitted of conspiracy, but found guilty of rioting, a conviction that was overturned on appeal.

See also: Chicago Seven; Daley, Richard J.

Day, George E. (1925–), U.S. Air Force forward air control pilot, shot down over North Vietnam and held prisoner from August 1967 to March 1973. During his three-war military career, Day, who retired as a colonel, was the recipient of forty combat decorations and awards, including the Medal of Honor for heroism while held prisoner in Hanoi, which was presented to him by President Ford on March 4, 1976.

See also: Medal of Honor.

DCI. *See* Director of Central Intelligence

Dean, John Gunther (1926–), U.S. ambassador to Cambodia, 1974–1975. A career diplomat, Dean also spent two years in the U.S. embassy in Laos (1972–1974). Dean's attempts to achieve a negotiated settlement of the war in Cambodia failed, partly because of conflicts with Secretary of State Henry Kissinger. As the Khmer Rouge prevailed over the U.S.-supported Lon Nol government in April 1975, Dean supervised the evacuation of U.S. personnel from Cambodia.

See also: Cambodia.

Dear America: Letters Home from Vietnam (1987). Film documentary directed by Bill

Couturie in which actors read excerpts from letters sent from Vietnam by those who fought in the war. Based on the 1985 book edited by Bernard Edelman.

Declaration of Conscience against the War in Vietnam.
The first public statement endorsing draft resistance to protest the increasing number of U.S. military advisers being sent to Vietnam. The declaration was issued in October 1964 by A. J. Muste, a veteran antiwar activist and the head of the Fellowship of Reconciliation, an influential pacifist organization established in 1914 during WWI.

See also: Muste, A. J.

Decoux, Jean (1884–1963),
governor general of French Indochina under the Vichy government, 1940–1945. A vice admiral and commander in chief of French naval forces in the Far East, Decoux took over as governor general soon after Germany invaded France in 1940. He was forced to sign a convention granting Japanese troops the right to station troops in Vietnam. The Japanese allowed the French colonial administration to remain in place, and Decoux instituted some political and social reforms, including allowing Vietnamese to have jobs in the French civil service. Near the end of the war Decoux abandoned the Vichy government and joined Gen. Charles DeGaulle's Free French forces fighting the Japanese. He was arrested by the Japanese on March 9, 1945,

when they assumed complete control over Indochina, and later that year was imprisoned by France for two years for collaborating with Japan.

See also: France; Japan.

Deer Hunter, The (1978).
Award-winning film directed by Michael Cimino about three Pennsylvania men whose lives are changed drastically by their service in the Vietnam War.

Deer Teams.
Code name for U.S. Office of Strategic Services (OSS) groups that helped support the Vietminh against Japan in 1945.

See also: Office of Strategic Services; Patti, Archimedes L. A.

Defense, Department of.
Created by the National Security Act of 1947, which unified the War and Navy departments, the U.S. Department of Defense (DoD) is made up of all of the military service branches. The U.S. Army, Navy, Air Force, and Marines maintain separate staffs under their individual service chiefs, who report to the chairman of the Joint Chiefs of Staff. He, in turn, reports to the secretary of defense, who reports to the president and is part of the cabinet.

During the Vietnam War presidential directives were relayed through the secretary of defense to the Commander-in-Chief, Pacific, bypassing the JCS. Secretary of Defense Robert McNamara (1961–1968) generally distrusted the advice and information he received from the military. He created the civilian Office of Systems Analysis within the Defense Department to provide independent estimates. He staffed the office with young college graduates and RAND Corporation experts skilled in the advanced management techniques of systems analysis and operations research. The personnel in this office were known as "McNamara's Whiz Kids." While he was MACV commander, Westmoreland deeply resented civilian experts in the Defense Department, but the civilian experts were often more realistic about the progress of the war. Cost-benefit analysis of military troop requests suggested that the United States was failing massively by 1967. Secretary of Defense Clark Clifford (1968–1969) commissioned more civilian studies that recommended disengagement and shifting the combat burden to South Vietnam. Military commanders, including JCS Chairman Gen. Earle Wheeler, CINCPAC Adm. Ulysses S. Grant Sharp, and General Westmoreland, called for more troops and more bombing as the price of victory in Vietnam. Civilian opponents of escalation in DoD, such as Assistant Secretary of Defense Paul Warnke and Deputy Secretary of Defense Paul Nitze, helped influence President Johnson to seek negotiations and not increase troop levels. When President Nixon stepped up the U.S. war effort by invading Cambodia in 1970 and bombing

North Vietnam in 1972, he issued orders through the JCS with specific instructions not to inform Secretary of Defense Melvin Laird (1969–1973), critic of escalation.

See also: Clifford, Clark; Gelb, Leslie H.; Hoopes, Townsend; Joint Chiefs of Staff; Laird, Melvin R.; McNamara, Robert; Nitze, Paul H.; Rusk, (David) Dean; Vance, Cyrus R.; Warnke, Paul C.

Defense Intelligence Agency (DIA). The Pentagon agency established in 1961 by Sec. of Defense Robert S. McNamara that collects and evaluates military-related intelligence. During the Vietnam War the DIA was one of several intelligence agencies, including those of the individual branches of the military and the CIA, that advised policymakers in Washington. After the war, the DIA became the clearinghouse for information pertaining to Americans listed as missing in action in the war.

See also: Central Intelligence Agency; POW/MIA Controversy.

Defense Reorganization Act (1958). A law that removed the Joint Chiefs of Staff from direct operational control over troops (the chain of command). Vietnam was the first war fought under this revised command system in which the JCS reported directly to the secretary of defense and issued orders in his name.

See also: Joint Chiefs of Staff.

Defoliation. The U.S. Air Force aerial defoliation program in Vietnam was designed to deny cover to the enemy and to destroy the enemy's rice crops. The program was carried out in Operation Ranch Hand, which sprayed some 19 million gallons of herbicides (primarily Agent Orange) over 2.5 million hectares (6 million acres) in South Vietnam from January 1962 to February 1971, and 400,000 gallons over 66,000 hectares (163,000 acres) in Laos from December 1965 to September 1969.

See also: Agent Orange; Chemical Warfare; Ranch Hand, Operation.

De Gaulle, Charles. *See* Gaulle, Charles de.

Delaware, Operation. Joint U.S. Army/Army of the Republic Vietnam operation in April and May 1968, in which elements of the U.S. 1st Cavalry Division, 196th Light Infantry Brigade, 101st Airborne Division, 3rd ARVN Airborne Task Force and the ARVN 1st Division engaged Viet Cong and North Vietnamese Army forces in the A Shau Valley along the Laotian border. Code-named Operation Lam Son 216 by the ARVN, the month-long fighting resulting in many casualties on both sides, including heavy American helicopter losses.

Dellinger, David (1915–), labor and community organizer and radical pacifist who was a leader

in the Vietnam antiwar movement. Dellinger, a leader of the pacifist War Resisters League, began lobbying against American participation in Vietnam in 1963. He helped organize the Assembly of Unrepresented People in 1965, which sponsored acts of civil disobedience against the war. Dellinger co-chaired the Spring Mobilization to End the War in Vietnam in 1967 and in 1968 was involved in the demonstrations at the Democratic National Convention in Chicago. He was among eight leaders of the demonstrations indicted for conspiring and traveling over state lines to incite rioting. Dellinger was acquitted of conspiracy, but found guilty of rioting, a conviction that was overturned on appeal.

See also: Chicago Seven; Davis, Rennard Cordon (Rennie); Democratic National Convention, 1968.

Del Vecchio, John (1948–), author of Vietnam War–related novels: *The 13th Valley* (1982), *For the Sake of All Living Things* (1990), and *Carry Me Home* (1995). Del Vecchio served as a combat correspondent with the U.S. Army's 101st Airborne Division in Vietnam in 1970–1971.

See also: 13th Valley, The.

Demilitarized Zone (DMZ). At the 1954 Geneva Conference, the country of Vietnam was created from the former colony of French Indochina. It was divided into north and south along the Ben Hai River near the 17th parallel until national elections could be held. A 10-kilometer-wide (6-mile) buffer zone from which both sides agreed to withhold military forces surrounded this demarcation line. This demilitarized zone (DMZ) became the de facto border between North and South Vietnam. During the war the North Vietnamese Army (NVA) and Viet Cong units took refuge in the DMZ from U.S. planes and artillery. In response, the United States constructed a series of fire support bases along Route 9 just south of the DMZ in 1966–1967. From these positions U.S. artillery reached enemy troops in the DMZ, and the NVA frequently attacked to suppress the shelling. NVA armor attacked and broke through the DMZ in the Easter Offensive of 1972, and again in the Spring Offensive in 1975.

See also: Barrier Concept; Con Thien; Easter Offensive; Khe Sanh; Quang Tri; Tet Offensive.

DeMille, Nelson (1942–), novelist. Several DeMille best-sellers, including *Word of Honor* (1985), *The General's Daughter* (1993), *Spencerville* (1994) and *Plum Island* (1997), have strong Vietnam War themes. DeMille served as a U.S. Army 1st Cavalry Division lieutenant in Vietnam in 1967–1968.

Democratic National Convention, 1968. The 1968 Democratic National Convention took place in Chicago on 24–29

August. Ten thousand antiwar protesters gathered, and police and National Guard troops were-mobilized to insure order. In addition, U.S. military intelligence services and undercover Central Intelligence Agency (CIA) agents infiltrated the crowd, even though the CIA is prohibited by law from operating inside the United States. On 28 August the demonstration erupted into violence when police and National Guard forces tried to prevent the protesters from marching on the International Amphitheater, where the convention met. The police used clubs, rifle butts, and tear gas; the demonstrators responded with rocks and bottles. Hundreds of arrests resulted, but thousands of other protesters rallied the next day at Grant Park. That meeting also resulted in violence when law officers prevented a group led by comedian and activist Dick Gregory from marching to his house on the South Side. The demonstrators hurled objects at the police and troops, who retaliated with tear gas and beatings.

Inside the convention, the Democrats wrestled with the party platform on the war. Vice President Hubert Humphrey, the leading candidate for the party's presidential nomination, drafted a compromise that called for an end to U.S. air strikes against North Vietnam and for shifting more responsibility to the South Vietnamese. Outgoing President Johnson objected, believing that the platform would undercut his war policies. Humphrey scrapped his compromise and, the convention adopted the Johnson plank by a narrow margin.

See also: Chicago Seven; Democratic Party, U.S.; Humphrey, Hubert H.; McCarthy, Eugene J.

Democratic Party, U.S.

Presidents John F. Kennedy and Lyndon B. Johnson and many in the Democratic establishment were strongly influenced by accusations that Democratic President Harry S. Truman had "lost" China to the communists. They believed they had to make a stand in Vietnam to prevent another loss. Fear of attacks from conservatives held sway over the Democrats' Vietnam policies as much as did their belief in the domino theory and containment. As the Vietnam War escalated, more liberal Democrats opposed the war because it disrupted the Great Society social agenda, and because they considered involvement in Vietnam contrary to U.S. interests, if not immoral. Many blue-collar and rural Democrats felt alienated from the antiwar and civil rights movements, which they associated with the Democratic left wing. The strains heightened during the 1968 Democratic presidential primaries and exploded at the national convention in Chicago. Robert F. Kennedy and Eugene J. McCarthy embodied the hopes of the antiwar Democrats. Hubert Humphrey became the standard bearer for the adminis-

tration's Vietnam policies. Republican Richard Nixon appealed to blue-collar Democrats with his themes of law and order and promises of an "honorable" settlement in Vietnam. This strategy worked again in 1972 against George McGovern, as the Democrats' more liberal elements dominated the party.

See also: Democratic National Convention, 1968; Domino Theory; Great Society; Watergate.

Democratic Republic of Vietnam (DRV). *See* Vietnam, Democratic Republic of.

Denton, Jeremiah (1924–),

U.S. Navy pilot; U.S. Senator (R-Ala.), 1981–1987. Denton was shot down over Hanoi in July 1965 and spent seven years in North Vietnamese prisons.

See also: Prisoners of War.

Deputy Chief, Joint U.S. Military Assistance Advisory Group Thailand (DEPCHIEF).

Established in Bangkok in October 1962 by Major Gen. Reuben H. Tucker, III. After he withdrew his U.S. Military Assistance Group Laos from that nation, the DEPCHIEF coordinated support for the U.S.-led secret war in Laos. This clandestine unit provided the Royal Lao military with military equipment and training, and operated under the control and authority of the U.S. Ambassador to Laos.

See also: Laos; Thailand.

DePuy, William E. (1919–1992), major general, U.S. Army; chief of operations, Military Assistance Command, Vietnam (MACV), 1964–1966; commanding general, U.S. Army First Infantry Division, 1966–1969; assistant army vice chief of staff, 1969–1973. Gen. William Depuy devised the search-and-destroy strategy that pursued victory in Vietnam with "more bombs, more shells, more napalm," as he put it, "until the other side cracks and gives up." After the war, Depuy helped devise the army's new "Airland Battle" doctrine, which prevailed in the Persian Gulf War.

See also: Search-and-Destroy.

DEROS (Date Eligible to Return from Overseas). Military acronym for the date U.S. service personnel finished their Vietnam War tours of duty. For U.S. Army, Air Force, and Navy personnel the date was one year after they entered the country; for Marines, it was 13 months after they began their Vietnam tours.

Desertion. The U.S. military defined desertion as being "absent with the intention to remain away permanently." From 1965–1973 some 500,000 U.S. military desertion incidents were reported. Of these deserters 93,250 remained away longer than 30 days. Few of the U.S. deserters deserted from the field of battle or from Vietnam; 20,000 Americans deserted after they had finished their Vietnam tours of duty. During the Vietnam War, desertion rates reached an all-time high of 73.5 out of 1,000 soldiers in 1971, a 400 percent increase over the 1966 rate of desertion. In contrast, only 25 out of 1,000 soldiers deserted annually during the Korean War. Vietnam War deserters, in general, were younger than their fellow soldiers, poorly educated, and from low-income backgrounds. Of Army deserters 75 percent were white, but an African-American serviceman was twice as likely to desert. Navy deserters also were overwhelmingly white, while Air Force deserters tended to be African-American and better educated. Soldiers were motivated to desert for a variety of reasons, including personal issues, family and financial problems, and antiwar sentiments. Many deserters, for example, cited difficulties with military life to explain their actions. The combination of desertion and the far more numerous absent without leave (AWOL) incidents cost the military about one million man-years of military service, almost half the total number of man-years spent by U.S. troops in Vietnam during the war.

The 83,135 deserters who either returned or were found received less-than-honorable discharges. Such discharges are not "dishonorable;" they are simply considered "bad paper." The approximately 9,000 deserters who evaded authorities were technically fugitives.

The clemency and amnesty policies of Presidents Gerald Ford and Jimmy Carter did little to improve the situation of deserters. Ford's program grouped together draft resisters and military deserters, offering both "clemency discharges" in return for two years of alternative service. The Carter administration gave blanket pardons to resisters, while demanding that deserters apply in person for a review and possible discharge upgrade. Due to these stringent requirements, application levels were low. Only 19 percent and 9 percent of those eligible applied for the Ford and Carter programs respectively. As a result, the vast majority of deserters continue to be denied veterans' education and medical benefits.

In contrast to U.S. servicemen in Vietnam, Vietnamese deserters, from the Army of the Republic of Vietnam (ARVN), from the National Liberation Front (NLF), or from the North Vietnamese Army (NVA), could take refuge easily in the densely populated areas of South Vietnam. Between 1965 and 1972, the Republic of Vietnam Armed Forces (RVNAF) lost about 120,000 servicemen annually todesertion. The ARVN sustained the greatest losses, with soldiers deserting at 2.5 times the overall RVNAF rate. South Vietnamese cited primarily low pay, homesickness, military corruption, and dangerous fighting, rather than political reasons, as motivations for desertion. Defection to the

North Vietnamese Army or Viet Cong was rare. Desertion rates from the Viet Cong and NVA averaged about 20,000 per year between 1967 and 1971. The ARVN Rangers, some of South Vietnam's best troops, were composed almost exclusively of NLF and NVA defectors. *See also:* Amnesty; Discipline, U.S. Military; Ho Chi Minh Campaign.

De Silva, Peer. (1917–), Central Intelligence Agency (CIA) station chief, Saigon, 1963–1965; special assistant for Vietnam affairs to the director of central intelligence, 1965–1966. De Silva, a veteran Office of Strategic Services (OSS) and CIA intelligence officer, worked closely with U.S. Ambassador Henry Cabot Lodge to establish ties with the new South Vietnamese regime following the November 1963 assassination of President Ngo Dinh Diem.

See also: Central Intelligence Agency.

DeSoto Missions. Code name for covert operations against the People's Republic of China, North Korea, North Vietnam, and the Soviet Union conducted by U.S. Navy intelligence-gathering destroyers in international waters beginning in the 1950s. In early 1964, President Johnson authorized covert operations against North Vietnam that included DeSoto missions. The DeSoto missions gathered information about North Vietnamese radar, charted and photographed the coast, monitored ship traffic, and recorded radio communications. A DeSoto mission, carried out by the destroyer *Maddox* on 2 August 1964, sparked the Gulf of Tonkin incident.

See also: Gulf of Tonkin Incident; Gulf of Tonkin Resolution; OPLAN 34A; Appendix E, "Gulf of Tonkin Resolution."

Détente. A French word meaning lessening of tension, *détente* is often used to denote the period 1967–1976 when the United States and the Soviet Union sought to de-escalate the cold war. President Johnson pursued détente when the U.S. war in Vietnam became too costly, hoping that reducing tensions with the Soviet Union would help the United States extricate itself from Vietnam.The Soviets needed economic assistance and were willing to negotiate to a point, but not about Southeast Asia. Détente stalled until 1972, when President Nixon proposed economic aid to the Soviet Union. At the same time, he opened talks with the People's Republic of China (PRC), exploiting the Sino-Soviet split to pressure the Soviets into negotiating in good faith at the Strategic Arms Limitation Talks and hoping to enlist the PRC's leverage with NorthVietnam. Just before Nixon's May 1972 trip to Moscow, the North Vietnamese launched the Easter Offensive.While Nixon hoped to secure Soviet and Chinese

cooperation in Southeast Asia, he believed that if the United States did not achieve "peace with honor," it wouldlose credibility and détente would fail. Therefore, despite fears that the Soviets might cancel the meeting if the United States launched a bombing campaign, Nixon responded to the offensive with Operation Linebacker. The Soviets and the Chinese responded to the bombing with only mild protests, and the North Vietnamese offensive ground to a halt.

See also: Linebacker and Linebacker II, Operations.

Development Loan Fund. A predecessor to the U.S. State Department's Agency for International Development, which came into being as a result of the Foreign Assistance Act of 1961. Taking over the functions of the International Cooperation Administration and the Development Loan Fund, AID became the principal U.S. agency responsible for the design and implementation of nonmilitary U.S. development and assistance programs in Vietnam.

See also: Agency for International Development.

Dewey, A. Peter (1917–1945), the first American serviceman killed in Vietnam. Dewey, a U.S. Army Lieutenant Colonel working for the Office of Strategic Services (OSS), the predecessor of the CIA, was in Saigon in 1945 helping Americans who had been imprisoned by Japan during WWII. On September 26, 1945, Dewey was killed by Vietminh machine-gun fire while driving a jeep near OSS headquarters in Saigon.

See also: Office of Strategic Services.

Dewey Canyon, Operation. A nearly two-month combat action in January and March 1969 undertaken by the U.S. 9th Marine Regiment in the A Shau Valley along the Laotian border designed to cut North Vietnamese Army supply lines from Laos. A second operation, Dewey Canyon II, took place in the same area in January 1971.

See also: A Shau Valley.

DGER (Direction Générale des études et Recherche). A French intelligence agency, the counterpart to the American Office of Strategic Services, which operated in French Indochina until 1954.

Dien Bien Phu. The site in northwestern Vietnam near the Laotian border where some 50,000 Viet Minh forces, led by Gen. Vo Nguyen Giap, overran the French garrison manned by some 15,000 troops on 7 May 1954 after a two-month siege. The Viet Minh victory ended the eight-year Indochina War and brought about France's withdrawal from Indochina in July 1954, an event that signaled the end of French colonialism in Asia.

The encounter at Dien Bien Phu took shape in late 1953. In November, French paratroopers occupied a small outpost along a 16-kilometer-long (10-mile) river valley near Laos. Gen. Henri Navarre, the French commander, hoped that such an aggressively positioned air head would disrupt the Viet Minh's rear operations and thwart raids into Laos. The Viet Minh forces surrounded the garrison during the winter. General Giap had purposely sent forces into Laos to overextend the French forces, and the isolated garrison provided him with an opportunity to strike a significant blow against the French.

Military scholars credit the Viet Minh's success in the siege to their formidable logistical preparations. Because of the inaccessibility of the valley, French command expected a minimal assault on the base. The Viet Minh, however, mounted an extraordinary supply effort, supporting an eventual fifty thousand troops of the People's Army of Vietnam (PAVN) around Dien Bien Phu. "[H]undreds of thousands of men and women," as Giap noted, built new roads and transported food and war materiel. Laborers carried an estimated 250 heavy weapons, including 105 mm artillery and 37 mm antiaircraft weapons, through the rugged terrain.

The extensive artillery, unexpected by the French, proved decisive during the battle. The French outpost depended on air transport for resupply, performed largely by an overtaxed fleet of U.S. C-47 transports. The Viet Minh's Chinese-supplied artillery, dug into the hills around Dien Bien Phu, disabled the French airstrip a few weeks into the siege, and subsequent Viet Minh antiaircraft fire hampered crucial airdrops, effectively strangling the garrison.

The Viet Minh attack on Dien Bien Phu began on 13 March 1954. The fifteen thousand defenders included some French soldiers, but most were Foreign Legion, Vietnamese, North African, and Tai Montagnard forces. The garrison's defenses consisted of a central fortified area about 2,700 meters (3,000 yards) in diameter surrounding an airstrip and a former village. Limited supplies forced the garrison to dig earthen fortifications rather than construct more sturdy defenses. Giap initially attacked three defense outposts about 1.5 kilometers (1 mile) north of the central perimeter. An artillery barrage and human wave attacks captured the compounds within a week, though with heavy PAVN casualties. For subsequent attacks, the Viet Minh dug trenches so they could approach the French perimeter less dangerously.

Inside the fortress, increasing resupply problems produced shortages and horrific conditions, particularly for casualties. By May only 3,000 effective troops, desperately low on ammunition, defended the central fortifications. The PAVN overran the fort on 7 May. An estimated 2,200 of the French garrison died in the siege, and 6,500 were taken prisoner. The Viet Minh suffered an estimated 23,000 casualties with 8,000 fatalities.

After the French realized the precarious situation of their forces in late March, the government asked President Eisenhower for U.S. air strikes to relieve the siege. Some administration figures favored intervention, including Secretary of State John Foster Dulles and Vice President Richard Nixon. Others expressed skepticism of such a raid's effectiveness and, led by Gen. Matthew Ridgeway, warned that intervention would draw U.S. ground forces into a protracted conflict. Congressional leaders, including Lyndon B. Johnson, also opposed air strikes. Later in April, Eisenhower expressed support for air raids if joined by Great Britain, but the British declined, sealing the fate of the garrison. After the fall of Dien Bien Phu the ruling French coalition fell, and a new government, led by Pierre Mendès-France, agreed to negotiate a withdrawal from Indochina.

The military success of the Viet Minh, however, did not transfer into a decisive political victory. The Geneva peace accords, concluded in July 1954, partitioned Vietnam at the 17th parallel with a vague promise for future national elections. The Viet Minh's allies, the People's Republic of China (PRC) and the Soviet Union, pressured them to accept the compromise peace terms. The PRC feared a unified Vietnamese power to the south, while the Soviet Union sought French support for European initiatives. The diplomatic failure, or the "betrayal," as the Vietnamese communists termed it, prepared the way for the next war.

See also: Bidault, Georges; Castries, Christian de; Eden, Anthony; Ely, Paul; Laniel, Joseph; Navarre, Henri; Ngo Dinh Diem; Radford, Arthur W.; Ridgway, Matthew B.; Truman, Harry S; Twining, Nathan F.; Van Tien Dung; Vo Nguyen Giap.

Dikes. For two thousand years the Vietnamese people have constructed an elaborate network of dikes, dams, and ditches for irrigation and flood control. The most extensive system of dikes was in the Red River Delta, a densely populated region of 3,000 square kilometers (1,800 square miles) that was the "rice bowl" of North Vietnam during the war. In 1966, Assistant Secretary of Defense John McNaughton proposed bombing the dikes to trigger floods and pressure the North Vietnamese government to negotiate. U.S. strategic bombing doctrine, however, preferred industrial targets, and President Johnson feared a propaganda backlash if he induced famine. With few exceptions, U.S. pilots had strict orders to avoid bombing the Red River dikes, which then became favored sites for North Vietnamese antiaircraft batteries.

See also: Red River (Song Hong) Delta.

Dillon, C. Douglas (1909–), U.S. Ambassador to France, 1953–1957; U.S. Secretary of the Treasury, 1961–1965. While serving as U.S. Ambassador in Paris in 1954 Dillon met with French leaders and forwarded their requests to Washington for U.S. assistance at the siege of Dien Bien Phu.

See also: Dien Bien Phu.

Dinh Diem Ngo. *See* Ngo Dinh Diem

Director of Central Intelligence (DCI). The head of the nation's main intelligence and counterintelligence agency. The DCIs during the Vietnam War were: John A. McCone (1961–1965), Adm. William F. Raborn (1965), Richard M. Helms (1965–1973), James R. Schlesinger (1973) and William E. Colby (1973–1976).

See also: Central Intelligence Agency.

Discipline, People's Army of Vietnam. Both the People's Army of Vietnam, known as the North Vietnamese Army (NVA), and Viet Cong emphasized political indoctrination in military discipline. The military, advised by Communist Party officials, addressed personnel problems with forced "education" designed to rehabilitate individuals for return to the war effort. On a unit level, self-criticism sessions among commanders and soldiers assessed individuals' performance and fostered coordinated, disciplined conduct. Serious personnel problems such as lax combat duty, desertion, and theft brought incarceration. Disciplined soldiers faced manual labor in camps, accompanied by educational programs that stressed personal sacrifice and commitment to national and Communist Party goals. NVA and Viet Cong security forces dealt harshly with crimes considered more serious, such as defecting while armed or performing espionage.

The PAVN and Viet Cong emphasis on ideological indoctrination reflected the Communist Party's concern with maintaining influence over the armed forces. Party elites feared the growth of an autonomous military during the wars for independence, and they established an institutional presence in the armed forces that included overseeing morale and military discipline matters. Political officers accompanied fighting units, though their uncertain advisory role often created tension with commanders. Military officers who offended political officers or who performed their duties poorly faced a purge from the party and an end to career advancement.

Discipline, Republic of Vietnam Armed Forces. The Republic of Vietnam Armed Forces (RVNAF) maintained a system of regular military and smaller field courts to try military discipline cases. After 1966, a military judicial police operated throughout South Vietnam. Infractions by RVNAF personnel, such as treating superiors with disrespect, dereliction of duty, or desertion, brought various punishments. Sentences included demotion, fieldwork assignment, or incarceration at the notoriously harsh RVNAF military prisons.

The RVNAF military discipline apparatus faced massive desertion of enlisted personnel during the war, estimated to have averaged about 120,000 per year between 1965 and 1972. Factors such as inadequate pay and food, inattentive commanders, and the unpopularity of the government fueled desertion rates. The RVNAF initiated several programs to improve soldiers' morale, including increasing compensation and developing support activities. The RVNAF established field military courts to speed the processing of desertion cases, and increased punishment (the death penalty for third-time deserters). These policies failed to stem desertions, however, as soldiers continued to return to villages or blend into urban areas around Saigon with relative ease.

Discipline, U.S. Armed Forces. Discipline problems increased significantly among U.S. forces in Vietnam after 1967. Some soldiers openly challenged authorities and customs. Malingering became widespread. "Short-timer's fever," a neglect or refusal to perform assigned tasks, was common as soldiers neared the end of their tours in Vietnam. Drug use became so common late in the war that officers and senior noncommissioned officers often ignored it. Desertion, defined as being absent without leave (AWOL) for more than 30 days, increased despite reluctance to report men as deserters: 27,000 in 1967; 29,234 in 1968; 56,608 in 1969; 65,643 in 1970. About 800 soldiers fled to other countries, notably Sweden.

Deliberate errors in paperwork and other procedures sabotaged efficient administration. "Fragging"—violent attacks on superiors—alarmed the Pentagon as reported incidents increased from 96 incidents in 1969 to 363 in 1970. There were also organized, explicit challenges to U.S. military authority.

Most military leaders associated discipline with basic military capability: discipline was vital to unit cohesion, which in turn was crucial to combat effectiveness. Commitment to tasks assigned differed sharply between "lifers"—career soldiers—and first-time enlisters and draftees. Lifers were more likely to push troops to achieve a mission, even if only to achieve promotion. Scrutiny of the factors underlying the decline in discipline revealed real dilemmas for the post–Vietnam War military. The values of career soldiers and conscripts conflicted. Unhappiness with the army and their particular military occupational

specialty (MOS) motivated those who went AWOL. Most had used drugs before entering the army. Dissenters, however, were different; they were disproportionately college-educated and from wealthier regions of the country. African-Americans dissented at about the same ratio in which they were found in the army as a whole—11 percent. The self-interest of service members reflected dominant values but contradicted the sacrifice that military duties could demand. Many of the sources of discontent within the U.S. military disappeared upon the withdrawal of U.S. troops from Vietnam and the creation of the All-Volunteer Force.

Those who saw the decline in discipline as revealing causes of the U.S. failure in Vietnam fell into two camps. The first saw problems stemming from a social liberalism that undercut strong military authority. In 1968 Congress passed a new Uniform Code of Military Justice (UCMJ) that guaranteed legal counsel before a court-martial. In June 1969 the Supreme Court, reversing the conviction of a sergeant for raping a civilian, restricted a court-martial to service-connected matters. Field commanders and senior NCOs were frustrated and confused when U.S. government officials set aside or reduced approved sentences, especially in highly publicized cases. The leaders of the U.S. Army warned commanders not to press cases that would make the chain of command look foolish. Those in the second group, including many with long military service, believed that the disciplinary decline reflected a grievous decline in the quality of leadership, including at the highest levels.

By the end of the war, the army had found ways to diffuse dissent. Command information programs, soldiers' councils, and chaplain and psychiatric services formed networks that addressed key concerns. The armed forces struck a balance between standards of discipline and dissent. Most of the military learned to accept dissent and understood that discipline did not require tyranny. The military also found ways to convey to most of its members that military support of national goals requires greater limits on individuality than is otherwise demanded in American society.

See also: Amnesty; Desertion.

Dispatches (1978). Book of Vietnam War reporting by Michael Herr that is regarded as an evocative journalistic rendering of the war as experienced by U.S. infantrymen.

See also: Herr, Michael.

Distinguished Service Cross. The second highest U.S. Army award for bravery.

See also: Medal of Honor; Navy Cross.

Division. Administrative and tactical military unit of some 20,000 troops usually commanded by a major general divided into regiments or brigades. Seven entire U.S. Army and two U.S. Marine divisions fought in the Vietnam War. The South Vietnamese Army (ARVN) had eleven divisions; the North Vietnamese Army (NVA) had twenty-one.

See also: Army of the Republic of Vietnam; Army, U.S.; People's Army of Vietnam.

Dixie Station. The staging area in the South China Sea southwest of Cam Ranh Bay that was used by the U.S. Navy's Seventh Fleet aircraft carriers beginning in 1965.

See also: Aircraft carriers; Yankee Station.

DMZ. *See* Demilitarized Zone

Doan Van Quang (1923–), commanding general of the Luc Luong Dac Biet, South Vietnamese Special Forces from 1964–1970.

See also: Special Forces, ARVN.

Dobrynin, Anatoly (1919–), Soviet ambassador to the United States, 1962–1986. Dobrynin negotiated with Henry Kissinger and President Nixon to establish ground rules for the Brezhnev-Nixon summit in 1969. Dobrynin told Nixon and Kissinger that the Soviets wanted to pursue improved relations with the United States separate from the Vietnam issue. Dobrynin rejected the Kissinger-Nixon policy of linking a U.S.-USSR nuclear arms reduction agreement to Soviet cooperation in pushing the Democratic Republic of Vietnam for a peace settlement.

See also: Détente; Kissinger, Henry.

Dog Soldiers (1974). Literary novel by Robert Stone with a strong Vietnam War theme, winner of the National Book Award for fiction.

Dohrn, Bernardine (1942–), a former member of Students for a Democratic Society, who left that group in 1969 to help found a small, violent, Marxist antiwar group called the Weathermen. She was placed on the FBI's "Ten Most Wanted" list for terrorist activities in 1970, went underground and surrendered to authorities in 1981.

See also: Weathermen.

Doi Moi (Renovation) Policy. In 1986, with the Democratic Republic of Vietnam's economy in a virtual state of collapse, new party leader General Secretary Nguyen Van Linh launched a program known as *doi moi,* or "renovation," embracing economic reforms roughly parallel to those in Mikhail Gorbachev's Soviet Union and Deng Xiaoping's China.

See also: Nguyen Van Linh.

Domino Theory. A political theory that the collapse of one country in a region to communism would lead to the collapse of the remaining countries in the region—like falling dominoes. The theory originated with the Truman Doctrine in 1947 when U.S. officials worried about communist activity in Greece and Turkey. After China's "loss" to communism in 1949, U.S. policymakers applied the theory to Korea in 1950. Truman and his successor, President Dwight D. Eisenhower, used the domino theory to justify U.S. aid for the French in Indochina. They believed that a communist victory in Vietnam would lead to a communist takeover of countries from Laos to the Philippines to India. Eisenhower first spoke of the "falling domino principle" at a 7 April 1954 press conference. The domino theory also served as the underpinning for the Vietnam policies of Presidents John F. Kennedy, Lyndon B. Johnson and Richard M. Nixon.

Johnson invoked it to defend the presence of U.S. military advisers in Vietnam. Gen. Maxwell Taylor, chairman of the Joint Chiefs of Staff (JCS), encouraged Kennedy to increase U.S. military involvement, arguing: "If Vietnam goes, it will be exceedingly difficult, if not impossible, to hold Southeast Asia." As the war dragged on and the United States became entangled in a web of rapid escalation, the domino theory was repeatedly invoked to justify new troop requests.

See also: Malaysia; Ten-Pin Theory; Truman Doctrine.

Do Muoi (1916–), Vietnamese communist leader. Do Muoi joined the Vietnamese Communist Party in the late 1930s. He took part in the 1954 Geneva Conference, served as minister of domestic trade in the Democratic Republic of Vietnam, and held a series of high positions after 1975 in the Socialist Republic of Vietnam, including prime minister and general secretary.

See also: Vietnamese Communist Party.

Dong, Pham Van. *See* Pham Van Dong

Dong Ha. Now the capital of Quang Tri Province, located less than 20 kilometers south of the Demilitarized Zone. During the Vietnam War Dong Ha was the site of a large U.S. Army and Marine logistics and combat base and, later, a South Vietnamese military base.

Dong Khe. A small, isolated, but strategic French mountain outpost in northern Vietnam, Dong Khe was attacked by five Chinese-trained Vietminh light battalions on 26 May 1950, in the Vietminh's first major offensive of the Indochina war. Two days later the Vietminh won a complete victory inflicting a humiliating loss on the French.

Dong Son Culture. A prehistoric Indochinese culture named for a village in northern Vietnam in the Red River Delta. Dong Son was an advanced Bronze Age civilization, known as the kingdom of Van Lang, that emerged in the early seventh century B.C. Among other things, the Dong Son people were known for their bronze and iron works, great stone monuments, and for the introduction of rice cultivation into the region. Most of the culture disappeared after China conquered the region in the second century B.C.

Dong Xoai. South Vietnamese town in Phuoc Long province, 83 kilometers (50 miles) north of Saigon. Site of a South Vietnamese government military headquarters and of a U.S. Special Forces camp. Dong Xoai was attacked on 10 June 1965 by Viet Cong troops, who were turned back with the aid of Army of the Republic of Vietnam (ARVN) and U.S. air strikes. On 12 June the Viet Cong made a second attack and decimated ARVN forces.

See also: Seabees.

Donovan, William J. (1883–1959), director, Office of Strategic Services (OSS), 1942–1945. As WW II neared its end, Maj. Gen. "Wild Bill" Donovan dispatched a U.S. OSS team to French Indochina to rescue downed aviators and provide intelligence about Japanese forces in the region. Ho Chi Minh had asked the United States to support Vietnamese independence. The OSS mission, which worked with the Viet Minh against the Japanese, was the first U.S. involvement in

Vietnam. Donovan served as U.S. ambassador to Thailand in 1953–1954.

See also: Office of Strategic Services.

Dooley, Thomas A. (1927–1961), U.S. physician, author. Dooley went to North Vietnam in 1954 as a U.S. Navy doctor to help refugees fleeing south before the communist takeover. In 1955 he went back to Vietnam and, later, to Laos to do volunteer medical work. He became a U.S. folk hero following the April 1956 publication of excerpts of his book, *Deliver Us From Evil,* in condensed form by *Reader's Digest.*

Douglas, Paul (1892–1976), U.S. Senator (D-Ill.) whose strong backing of President Johnson's Vietnam policies lost him the support of liberals in the 1966 election. In 1967, Douglas formed the Citizens Committee for Peace with Freedom in Vietnam, a non-partisan group that urged continued support of Johnson's war aims. Former Presidents Harry S Truman and Dwight D. Eisenhower served as the committee's honorary chairmen. The group continued to support the Vietnam War policies of President Nixon.

Douglas, William O. (1898–1980), U.S. Supreme Court Justice who in 1970 urged his colleagues to rule on the legality of the Vietnam War during the court's deliberations over the constitutionality of a Massachusetts law that allowed men in that state to refuse to serve in Vietnam because Congress had not declared war. The court refused to hear the case. In August 1970 Douglas, in response to the appeal of a law suit, ordered that U.S. bombing be halted in Cambodia, an action that was overruled by Justice Thurgood Marshall.

See also: Supreme Court, U.S.

Doumer, Paul (1857–1932), French governor general, Indochinese Union, 1897–1902. Doumer set up state monopolies in the newly formed French Indochinese Union and established colony-wide administrative offices.

See also: French Indochinese Union.

Doves. *See* Hawks and Doves

Dow Chemical Company. The manufacturer of napalm, Agent Orange, and the heavy plastic bags used to ship home the bodies of Americans killed in Vietnam. Antiwar protesters began picketing Dow offices in 1966 and disrupting Dow recruiters on college campuses in 1967. Later, Dow facilities in California, Michigan, and Washington, DC, were picketed and attacked. In February 1967, students at the University of Wisconsin–Madison protested when Dow recruiters tried to interview job applicants on campus. Similar protests against Dow recruitment, often organized by Students for a

Democratic Society, occurred on many college campuses.

See also: Agent Orange; Napalm; Students for a Democratic Society.

Dowd, Douglas (1919–), a Cornell University professor who was one of the main organizers of the New Mobilization Committee to End the War in Vietnam (New Mobe) antiwar group in 1966. He stayed active in the moderate wing of the antiwar movement through the early 1970s.

Downs, Frederick (1944–), writer, Veterans Administration official. Downs, who served as a U.S. Army 4th Infantry Division lieutenant in Vietnam in 1967–1968, is the author of three critically praised nonfiction books: *The Killing Zone: My Life in the Vietnam War* (1978), *Aftermath: A Soldier's Return From Vietnam* (1984), and *No Longer Enemies, Not Yet Friends: An American Soldier Returns to Vietnam* (1991).

Draft. *See* Selective Service

Dragon Lady. *See* Ngo Dinh Nhu (Madame Nhu)

Drug Trafficking. When heroin use among U.S. soldiers in South Vietnam expanded in 1969–1970, its source was the subject of a great deal of speculation. Gradually, U.S. intelligence work exposed the trafficking syndicates among America's Indochina allies. Significantly, these same

investigations failed to detect any sign of communist involvement in drug trafficking.

Opium was a venerable vice in Indochina, but heroin, a chemical derivative, was a recent development. For nearly a century, the French colonial administration had permitted opium smoking, which provided as much as 16 percent of all tax revenues. In 1930, for example, French Indochina licensed 3,500 opium dens to supply the colony's 125,200 registered smokers. Under pressure from the United Nations, however, the French government abolished its opium monopoly in 1950. Instead of eradicating the vice, the French military transferred the drug trade informally to its intelligence service, whose commanders used it to finance their covert operations against the communist Viet Minh. Although localized opium trading continued after the end of the Indochina War in 1954, largescale heroin trafficking did not start until 1969, when a complex of seven laboratories opened in the Golden Triangle—a mountain region where Burma, Thailand, and Laos converge. Since the early 1950s, the region's drug merchants had been producing both smoking opium and crude, granular heroin to service addicts in cities such as Bangkok and Hong Kong. Starting in 1969–1970, however, these syndicates used their opium supplies to manufacture pure, powdery heroin for U.S. troops fighting in South

Vietnam. Although these remote laboratories were operated by criminal chemists from Hong Kong, their principals were all U.S. allies—notably the Nationalist Chinese irregulars based in northern Thailand and the commander in chief of the Royal Lao Army, Gen. Ouane Rattikone.

In a June 1971 report on these laboratories, the Central Intelligence Agency (CIA) noted that their establishment "appears to be due to the sudden increase in demand by a large and relatively affluent market in South Vietnam"—U.S. troops. Allied military forces in Laos played a key role in the Indochina drug traffic. General Ouane owned the region's largest heroin laboratory, which processed, under its distinctive "Double U-O Globe Brand" label, some 100 kilograms per day of raw opium into heroin for export to U.S. soldiers in South Vietnam. While General Ouane used the troops and aircraft of the Royal Lao Army to transport his heroin, local commanders of the CIA's secret army, a force of some 30,000 Hmong highlanders, relied upon the agency's resources to market their opium. Hmong farmers harvested their traditional crop of raw opium for sale to the new heroin refineries, and the CIA's contract airline, Air America, allowed the Hmong commanders, albeit on an informal basis, to transport opium on its aircraft.

In a 1972 investigation of the agency's Vientiane station, the CIA's inspector general explained the predicament of its covert-action operatives: "The past involvement of many of these [Lao Army] officers in drugs is well known, and the continued participation of many is suspected; yet their goodwill . . . considerably facilitates the military activities of Agency-supported irregulars."

Once the raw opium was processed into powdery heroin in the Golden Triangle's laboratories, elements within South Vietnam's ruling military factions secured the bulk of their heroin supplies through contacts in Laos. The structure of this traffic was exposed in 1970–1971 when seizures and subsequent investigations uncovered official involvement in South Vietnam's heroin trade. Even before the last GIs had left, criminal exporters began shipping heroin to the United States. By November 1972, the U.S. Bureau of Narcotics estimated that the Southeast Asia share of the heroin supply in the United States had increased from 5 to 30 percent.

See also: Air America; Drug Use, U.S. Military.

Drug Use, U.S. Military. As with U.S. troops in all previous American wars, the troops sent to South Vietnam indulged in regular alcohol abuse without arousing significant controversy. When great numbers began using marijuana after 1968, the military command reacted rigorously. As marijuana gave way to widespread heroin use, the military became concerned about the combat effectiveness of its forces, and the public was aroused by the threat that addiction posed.

During the first three years of combat operations in Vietnam, most U.S. forces engaged in offensive operations that left little time for recreation of any sort. The military encouraged off-duty alcohol consumption by licensing service clubs on its rear-area bases and distributing beer to troops in the field. It was not until March 1972 that the Defense Department classified alcoholism as a treatable illness and launched a serious program to identify alcoholics in the services.

As the U.S. combat role wound down after 1969, illicit drugs became a persistent problem. In 1969, a Defense Department study reported that 25 percent of U.S. soldiers in Vietnam were using marijuana occasionally or frequently. By then, many units suffered an informal division between "the juicers," prowar career officers and noncommissioned officers (NCOs) who drank alcohol in their clubs, and "the heads," low-ranking enlisted personnel who were often antiwar or ambiguous about the war and who indulged in illegal drugs, particularly marijuana.

Disturbed by reports of widespread use, the military launched an aggressive campaign against marijuana use in Vietnam. At the operation's peak in 1969, military police were arresting soldiers for marijuana possession at the rate of 1,000 per week. The military's suppression of marijuana use, however, inadvertently created a market for powdery highgrade heroin, which began appearing for sale in Saigon, so pure that it could be smoked in an ordinary cigarette without any trace odor. In mid-1970, heroin addiction spread rapidly through the ranks of the 450,000 strong U.S. military forces in South Vietnam. In May and June, the Army had revived its antimarijuana campaign with a renewed burst of arrests and seizures that eliminated market competition for the incoming heroin. At all major U.S. military bases and social clubs, tiny plastic vials of 96 percent pure heroin became readily available for sale to U.S. soldiers for only $2.00 or $3.00 a dose. Subsequent survey research discovered an epidemic level of heroin use in the ranks. In September 1970, Army medical officers questioned 3,103 soldiers of the Americal Division and found that 11.9 percent had used heroin since their arrival in Vietnam. In November, an Army engineer battalion in the Mekong Delta reported that 14 percent of its troops were regular heroin users. In 1972, the White House Office for Drug Abuse Prevention interviewed 900 enlisted men who had returned from Vietnam in September 1971, the peak of the epidemic, and found that 44 percent had tried opiates while in Vietnam and 20 percent regarded themselves as having been "addicted." The full extent of the problem was not revealed until 1974 when the Office for Drug Abuse Prevention published surveys indicating that 34 percent of U.S. troops in Vietnam had "commonly used" heroin. On the whole, the army's attempts at education and eradication did little to stem the spread of addiction. In June 1971, the military required all GIs to pass a drug urinalysis test before boarding their flights home. By 1973, the Defense Department was collecting 4 million urine specimens annually for worldwide screening of all U.S. troops in thirteen drug-testing laboratories. At the start of the Vietnam heroin epidemic in 1970, there was great concern that veterans would return home with lasting heroin habits. But by 1974 it was clear that drug use in the war zone was largely a situational response to combat stress.

See also: Discipline, U.S. Armed Forces.

Duck Hook. Code name for contingency plan to escalate the Vietnam War drastically drawn up by National Security adviser Henry Kissinger in the summer of 1969. The plan, which included mining Haiphong Harbor and bombing North Vietnam, was not implemented.

See also: Kissinger, Henry.

Dudman, Richard (1918–), *St. Louis Post-Dispatch* correspondent taken captive with two other journalists, Elizabeth Pond of the *Christian Science Monitor* and Michael Morrow of the *Dispatch*

News Service International, by Khmer Rouge guerrillas in Cambodia while covering the U.S.-ARVN invasion in May 1970. They were released 40 days later. In 1963 Dudman had written that U.S. forces in Vietnam were "spraying the land with poison" herbicides.

See also: Agent Orange.

Duggins, George C. (1942–), veterans advocate. Duggins served two tours in Vietnam with the U.S. Army Security Agency. He became president of Vietnam Veterans of America in January 1997. He is believed to be the first African-American to head a national U.S. veterans' service organization.

See also: Vietnam Veterans of America.

Dulles, Allen (1893–1969), director, Central Intelligence Agency, 1953–1961, brother of John Foster Dulles. A supporter of Ngo Dinh Diem, Dulles urged President Dwight D. Eisenhower to bolster Diem's government during its first years. He approved the first CIA mission, under U.S. Air Force Major Edward G. Lansdale, that went into South Vietnam 1 June 1954. Dulles also supported Diem's blocking of the 1955 elections because of his belief that Ho Chi Minh would win.

See also: Central Intelligence Agency; Lansdale, Edward G.

Dulles, John Foster (1888–1959), U.S. secretary of

state, 1953–1959. Dulles regarded the Viet Minh as an
instrument of communist aggression and argued that the fall of
Indochina would lead to the loss
of Southeast Asia with disastrous consequences for the U.S.
Yet, Dulles was reluctant to commit U.S. combat troops to
Southeast Asia, believing that
France should bear that burden.
Dulles reluctantly participated
in the 1954 Geneva Conference
and tried to secure a settlement.
Later that year, Dulles negotiated the Southeast Asia Treaty
Organization (SEATO) treaty. He
enthusiastically supported Ngo
Dinh Diem, encouraging him
to accept U.S. military advisers
and aid.

See also: Bidault, Georges;
Dien Bien Phu; Domino Theory;
Faure, Edgar; Geneva
Conference (1961–1962);
Southeast Asia Treaty
Organization; Smith, Walter
Bedell.

Duncan, Patrick Sheane
(1947–), screenwriter, director.
Duncan wrote and directed *84
Charlie MoPic* (1989), a Vietnam
War combat film widely regarded
as the most realistic of its genre.
Duncan, who served with the
173rd Airborne Brigade in
Vietnam in 1968–1969, wrote
and directed several episodes of
the award-winning HBO *Vietnam
War Stories* series.

See also: 84 Charlie MoPic.

Dung, Van Tien. *See* Van Tien
Dung

Duong Quynh Hoa (1930–), a
founder of the National
Liberation Front. Duong Quynh
Hoa attended medical school in
Paris in the 1950s, where she
joined the French Communist
Party. After returning to Saigon,
she worked covertly to undermine President Diem's regime
while practicing medicine. In
1968, she was secretly appointed
health minister of the Viet
Cong's Provisional Revolutionary
Government in South Vietnam.
She went into hiding after the
Tet Offensive and traveled
abroad on propaganda missions.
After the war, Duong Quynh Hoa
ran a children's hospital in Ho
Chi Minh City and became a
prominent critic of the communist government.

See also: National Liberation
Front.

Duong Van Minh (1916–1997),
general, Army of the Republic of
Vietnam (ARVN); chairman,
Revolutionary Military Council,
1963–1964; president of South
Vietnam, 1975. Known as "Big
Minh" because of his size, Gen.
Minh received military training
in France, and then commanded
Saigon's colonial garrison in the
Indochina War. He chaired the
Revolutionary Military Council
that overthrew South
Vietnamese President Ngo Dinh
Diem on 1 November 1963. Minh
briefly held power until his fac-
tion was overthrown on 30
January 1964. Minh went into
exile for four years. He ran
unsuccessful campaigns for pres-
ident of South Vietnam in 1966

and 1971. As the North Vietnamese Army (NVA) closed in on Saigon in April 1975, President Thieu resigned in favor of Vice President Tran Van Huong, who appointed Minh as president on 28 April. Two days later NVA forces took the presidential palace. Minh officially surrendered and was arrested. Imprisoned in reeducation camps, Minh emigrated to France in 1983.

See also: Ho Chi Minh Campaign; Le Nguyen Khang; Military Revolutionary Council; Ngo Dinh Diem; Nguyen Cao Ky; Nguyen Chanh Thi; Nguyen Khanh; Nguyen Van Thieu; Tran Van Huong.

Durbrow, Elbridge
(1903–1997), U.S. ambassador to South Vietnam, 1957–1961. President Eisenhower appointed Durbrow, a career foreign service officer, U.S. envoy to Saigon. Durbrow sharply criticized corruption and nepotism in President Diem's government. Clashing often with U.S. military advisers, Durbrow blamed repression for driving the South Vietnamese people to support the Viet Cong. Durbrow reluctantly backed Diem in the failed coup of 1960 but continued pressing him to build popular support with reforms and elections. President Kennedy sent Frederick Nolting to replace Durbrow in 1961.

See also: Williams, Samuel T.

Dustoff. A nickname for U.S. medevac helicopters.

See also: Aeromedical evacuation; Helicopters.

Duy Tan (1899–1945), the emperor of Vietnam from 1907–1916. Duy Tan, who was born Vinh San, was the son of Vietnamese Emperor Thanh Thai, who was deposed by the French. At age of eight, Duy Tan was put on the throne by the French to act as a puppet leader. He was dethroned by the French in 1916 because of his support for Vietnamese nationalists, and forced into exile. Duy Tan served with the Free French Army in Europe during WWII, earning high honors for bravery. He was killed in a plane crash on 26 December 1945.

Dye, Dale (1944–), actor, film consultant, author. Dye, who served with the U.S. Marine Corps in Vietnam in 1965 and 1967–1970, is regarded as the most accomplished movie military technical adviser for his work in films such as *Platoon, 84 Charlie MoPic, Born on the Fourth of July,* and *Heaven and Earth.*

Dye Marker, Operation. Sec. of Defense Robert S. McNamara's idea to build a barrier of barbed wire, mines and sensors on a strip of 11.6 kilometers (8 miles) along the Demilitarized Zone which became known as McNamara's Line or McNamara's Wall. The operation began in April 1967 but was suspended soon after and never completed.

See also: McNamara's Line.

Eagle Pull, Operation. Code name for 12 April 1975 U.S. Marine Corps helicopter operation that evacuated U.S., Cambodian, and other foreign personnel from Cambodia before the Khmer Rouge takeover.

Easter Offensive. The massive North Vietnamese attack launched 30 March 1972 designed to achieve a conventional military victory. Some 120,000 troops, backed by armor and artillery, struck South Vietnam on three fronts when U.S. troop strength was down to less than 100,000, of which only 5,000 were combat troops. The opening offensive began in I Corps, the northern five provinces of South Vietnam. At noon on 30 March the North Vietnamese Army (NVA) attacked the arc of South Vietnamese firebases along the demilitarized zone (DMZ) and the western border with Laos, raining artillery rounds on the surprised defenders. The 308th NVA Division plus two independent regiments moved south of the DMZ along the sandy coastal plains between the sea and Highway 1. They assaulted the "Alpha group" of firebases, known as the Ring of Steel, arranged in a loose arc just south of the DMZ. From the west, the 304th NVA Division,

including an armored regiment, rolled out of Laos along Highway 9, past Khe Sanh, and into the Quang Tri River Valley.

Realizing the seriousness of the situation, on 1 April Brig. Gen. Vu Van Giai, commander of the 3d ARVN Division, ordered his troops to withdraw and reorganize south of the Cua Viet River. The following morning South Vietnamese armor held off NVA tanks attempting to cross the river at Dong Ha, but some of the North Vietnamese crossed at the Cam Lo bridge, about 11 kilometers (7 miles) west.

Although natural barriers slowed the NVA assault from the north, the western approaches were completely exposed. Camp Carroll, a South Vietnamese base located halfway between the Laotian border and the coast, was strategic for both sides. For the South Vietnamese, its large artillery component was crucial because its 175mm guns could provide support fire at ranges up to 32 kilometers (20 miles). For the NVA, Camp Carroll was the strongest obstacle before Quang Tri City. On 2 April Camp Carroll surrendered, and later that day, ARVN troops abandoned Mai Loc, its last western base, allowing the NVA almost unrestricted access to western Quang Tri province north of the Thach Han River.

The North Vietnamese advance slowed for three weeks, but on the morning of 28 April they attacked again, pushing to within about 1.5 kilometers (1 mile) of Quang Tri city. General Giai, with fewer than two thousand troops, intended to abandon the city and consolidate south of the Thach Han River, although this meant conceding most of Quang Tri province to the NVA. Bewildered by conflicting orders, South Vietnamese units splintered and virtually disappeared, abandoning most of the province north of the city. U.S. advisers in Quang Tri called for rescue helicopters, and on 1 May the U.S. Air Force evacuated 132 survivors from Quang Tri, 80 of them U.S. soldiers.

Lt. Gen. Ngo Quang Truong, one of the best officers in the South Vietnamese army, took command of I Corps. His mission was to defend Hue, minimize further losses in northern I Corps, and recapture lost territory. Truong pushed the North Vietnamese from Quang Tri City in September, although much of the province remained in enemy hands.

In II Corps, South Vietnam's central region, the North Vietnamese tried to split South Vietnam from the Central Highlands to the sea. The main objective of the North Vietnamese attack was the Central Highlands. The fighting began in coastal Binh Dinh province, long a stronghold of support for NVA and Viet Cong forces. The attacks in Binh Dinh, which succeeded in capturing several South Vietnamese firebases, was intended as a diversion to draw ARVN troops away from the Central Highlands. General Dzu almost fell into the trap, but John Paul Vann, one of the most experienced and effective advisers of the war, stopped him,

ensuring that the 23d ARVN Division remained in the highlands to defend against the main thrust.

When the NVA realized its diversion had failed, it concentrated on the Central Highlands. During the second week in April elements of the 2d NVA Division attacked two regiments of the 22d ARVN Division at the small town of Tan Canh and nearby Dak To firebase. The South Vietnamese force quickly disintegrated.

Vann faced a deteriorating situation by the end of April. Kontum lay exposed, with less than a single division of defenders. Still, Vann managed to find new troops while dealing with mounting personnel problems. Dzu became increasingly unable to make decisions, and personality conflicts among other South Vietnamese officers and their counterparts hampered progress.

The North Vietnamese inexplicably paused at Tan Canh and Dak To for almost three weeks, allowing the South Vietnamese time to reinforce Kontum. Vann used massive B-52 strikes to hold the NVA at bay and to reduce the strength of its units before they could reach Kontum. On 14 May the North Vietnamese attacked Kontum in force.

With the aid of massive B-52 strikes, the South Vietnamese held Kontum despite heavy losses during a two-week battle. By early June, the NVA had faded away, and South Vietnamese patrols pushed out from the city to eliminate pockets of North Vietnamese resistance. John Paul Vann on 9 June was killed in a helicopter crash.

The third phase of the Easter Offensive occurred just west of Saigon, around the town of An Loc. The area was a good site for a big battle as its open terrain was conducive to conventional warfare and three NVA divisions were stationed just over the border in Cambodia. NVA troops feinted into neighboring Tay Ninh province, hoping to lure the South Vietnamese into believing that was the main attack. NVA armor played a larger role at An Loc than at any other place during the Easter Offensive. NVA tanks entered the city on 13 April, but poor use of infantry in support of the armor, combined with the ARVN's effective use of handheld light antitank weapons (M72 LAWs) hampered the onslaught. By 21 April, the attack had faltered and the North Vietnamese settled into a siege. Despite the danger of annihilation, the 5th ARVN Division commander, Brig. Gen. Le Van Hung, refused to launch offensive operations, relying instead on U.S. air power.

South Vietnamese military officials in Saigon planned to relieve the city by sending the 21st ARVN Division north from the Mekong Delta, but it never arrived. For three weeks the division crept north, often held at bay by much smaller NVA contingents. Although the 21st ARVN Division never reached

An Loc, its slow advance may have turned the tide of battle because it diverted almost a division of NVA troops.

On 11 May the North Vietnamese struck An Loc again. The South Vietnamese held, with large losses on both sides. North Vietnamese strength was spent. Although the NVA attempted limited attacks, the defenders sensed the NVA's weakness and launched a series of cautious counterattacks. South Vietnamese president Nguyen Van Thieu hailed the victory at An Loc as a triumph of democracy over communism, comparing it to the 1954 battle at Dien Bien Phu. The town of An Loc, however, was destroyed and much of the territory surrounding it remained in North Vietnamese hands for the remainder of the war. The area north of An Loc was eventually used as a staging point for the final NVA offensive in 1975.

Both sides claimed victory after the Easter Offensive, but neither gained much. North Vietnam never captured and held a provincial capital, and it did not decisively defeat South Vietnamese Army. Many ARVN units were rendered combat ineffective, and casualties were high (10,000 killed, 33,000 wounded, and 2,000 missing), but U.S. training and resupply brought them back to strength by early 1973.

On the other hand, North Vietnam gained considerable territory along the Laotian and Cambodian borders as well as the area just south of the DMZ. While few people lived in these regions, the ground gained was used to advantage at the Paris negotiating table. Most important, Vietnamization was not conclusively tested because of the massive injection of U.S. air power.

See also: Amphibious Landing Operations; An Loc; Demilitarized Zone; Linebacker and Linebacker II, Operations; Loc Ninh; Vietnamization.

École des Chartes. An elite French archivist school to which Ngo Dinh Nhu, the brother of Ngo Dinh Diem, was the first Vietnamese to be admitted. Nhu graduated from the school with a degree in paleography in 1938 and went to work at the archives of the governor general of Indochina in Hanoi.

Eden, Anthony (1897–1977), British foreign secretary, 1935–1938, 1951–1955; British prime minister, 1955–1957. Together with Soviet Foreign Minister Vyacheslav Molotov, Eden co-chaired the 1954 Geneva Conference, which convened the day after Dien Bien Phu fell to the Viet Minh. Earlier, as Winston Churchill's foreign secretary, he opposed British or U.S. military intervention at Dien Bien Phu.

See also: Geneva Conference, 1954.

Edgerton, Cylde (1944–), novelist. Edgerton, a former U.S. Air Force pilot who served in Southeast Asia in 1970–1971, is the author of seven well-received novels. Several of his books, including *The Floatplane Notebooks* (1988) and *In Memory of Junior* (1992), feature characters who are Vietnam veterans.

Ehrhart, W. D. (William Daniel) (1948–), poet, memoirist, teacher. Ehrhart, who served as a U.S. Marine in Vietnam in 1967–1968, is the author of a well-regarded autobiographical trilogy: *Vietnam-Perkasie: A Combat Marine Memoir* (1983), *Passing Time: Memoir of a Vietnam Veteran Against the War* (1986) and *Busted: A Vietnam Veteran in America* (1995). He is the author of many books of poetry and the editor of two anthologies of Vietnam War–influenced poetry, *Carrying the Darkness: The Poetry of the Vietnam War* (1985) and *Unaccustomed Mercy: Soldier-Poets of the Vietnam War* (1989).

See also: Carrying the Darkness.

Ehrlichman, John (1925–), presidential assistant for domestic affairs, 1969–1973. Ehrlichman in 1969 became one of President Richard Nixon's most powerful aides. He set up the covert group known as the "plumbers," and authorized them to break in to the office of Daniel Ellsberg's psychiatrist to find embarrassing material on Ellsberg, who had leaked the Pentagon Papers to the press. The plumbers later were responsible for the break-in at the Democratic National Committee headquarters at the Watergate office building. Ehrlichman resigned from the White House in 1973. In 1974 he was convicted of conspiracy, perjury and obstruction of justice in connection with the burglaries and subsequent cover-up. He served 18 months in prison.

See also: Plumbers; Watergate.

84 Charlie MoPic (1989). An independently produced, low-budget Vietnam War film widely regarded as the most realistic of its genre. Written and directed by Patrick Sheane Duncan, who served with the 173rd Airborne Brigade in Vietnam in 1968–1969, the movie is a mock documentary told through the lens of an Army cameraman, known as a "MoPic," who follows a reconnaissance squad on a mission into the Central Highlands.

See also: Duncan, Patrick Sheane.

Eisenhower, Dwight D.
(1890–1969), U.S. president (1953–1961). Eisenhower ("Ike") brought to the White House traits honed during an extraordinary military career. He graduated from West Point in 1915, mastered logistics during WWI, established himself as a promising junior officer in the stagnant interwar army, and rose rapidly during WWII, ultimately serving as Allied Supreme Commander in Europe. Afterward he was in quick succession Army Chief of Staff, president of Columbia University, and commander of the

North Atlantic Treaty Organization (NATO). Eisenhower's Indochina policy was based on containing communism. He supported the French with money, arms, and a small contingent of technical personnel. As the French faltered in early 1954, Eisenhower decided not to intervene on a larger scale, even though he believed that if Vietnam fell to communism, other Asian nations might collapse in turn according to the domino theory. Yet Eisenhower had slight faith in the French, who refused to transform their colonial war into a broad anti-communist campaign, and he would not act without British assistance and congressional approval, neither of which was forthcoming.

The Eisenhower administration took the lead in creating the Southeast Asia Treaty Organization (SEATO) to join the non-communist countries together. The United States also used CIA infiltrators to disrupt North Vietnam, and insured Ngo Dinh Diem's consolidation of power in South Vietnam, even though Eisenhower was exasperated by Diem's failure to democratize his regime. After his presidency, Eisenhower publicly supported the Indochina policies of presidents Kennedy and Johnson, but disliked the former's acceptance of a coalition government in Laos and grew increasingly disenchanted with the latter's failure to win the war.

See also: Bidault, Georges; Dien Bien Phu; Domino Theory;

Faure, Edgar; Geneva Conference, 1954; Military Assistance Advisory Group–Vietnam; Radford, Arthur W.; Southeast Asia Treaty Organization.

Eisenhower Doctrine. A pronouncement made by President Dwight D. Eisenhower on 5 January 1958, in which he committed the United States to helping any Middle Eastern nation contain communism. The doctrine echoed that of Eisenhower's predecessor, whose 1948 Truman Doctrine promised American military and economic aid to Greece and Turkey to help those nations fight communist insurgencies.

See also: Truman Doctrine.

Elections, South Vietnam, 1955. The 1954 Geneva Conference included a provision for reunification elections to be held in 1956 throughout Vietnam. The North Vietnamese, U.S. and South Vietnamese governments believed that North Vietnam would win the elections and unify Vietnam under the communist banner. At the end of the conference, the United States declined to endorse the agreements. The French-supported State of Vietnam under Emperor Bao Dai protested the provision for elections and also refused to sign the accords. South Vietnamese president Ngo Dinh Diem said in July 1955 that his government was not bound by the Geneva agreements. Instead, with U.S. support, he proposed a referendum to abolish the Bao Dai monarchy, ratify Diem's presidency, and proclaim a republic. Massive fraud marked the October 1955 elections, which included a heavy police presence at the polls to intimidate voters to vote for Diem as well as unsupervised ballot-counting by Diem's men. Diem recorded a landslide victory with 98.2 percent of the vote.

See also: Geneva Conference, 1954; International Commission for Supervision and Control.

Electronic Counter-Measures (ECM). Electronic devices used mainly in U.S. Air Force and Navy aircraft such as the "Wild Weasel" F-100 and F-105 jet fighters during the Vietnam War to jam defensive radar. ECMs also were used on U.S. Navy vessels patrolling the coasts of Vietnam to detect radar signals.

Electronic Detection Devices. Electronic sensing equipment used by U.S. forces to monitor enemy ground activity. Such devices often were used to pinpoint bombing targets. During the 1965–1968 Operation Rolling Thunder, U.S. aircraft bombed the Ho Chi Minh Trail daily, targeting areas based on information gleaned from electronic detection devices as well as on intelligence gathered by covert teams.

See also: Ho Chi Minh Trail; Rolling Thunder, Operation.

Electronic Espionage. Beginning in 1964 the United States used electronic espionage to monitor North Vietnamese radio communications. Those efforts were carried out on land, in the air with specially equipped C-130 aircraft and on U.S. Navy destroyers patrolling the North Vietnamese coast equipped with mobile electronic espionage facilities known as communications vans. Such electronic espionage was carried out by the destroyer *Maddox* in August 1964 when it reported an attack by North Vietnamese patrol boats in what became known as the Gulf of Tonkin Incident.

See also: Gulf of Tonkin Incident.

Electronic Surveillance.
Electronic surveillance was among the tactics used by the Johnson and Nixon administrations to monitor and destabilize antiwar groups. Carried out by the FBI and by the U.S. Army, electronic surveillance of antiwar groups consisted primarily of covert infiltration and wiretapping.

See also: Wiretaps.

Electronic Warfare Systems.
Electronic sensing, evasion and offensive targeting and tracking equipment used on U.S. aircraft. The systems were operated by an onboard Electronic Warfare Officer. One reason that more than 80 percent of the B-52 Arc Light bombing strikes took place over South Vietnam was concern that the classified onboard electronic warfare systems designed to defeat Soviet radar and surface-to-air missile defenses

might be compromised over North Vietnam.

See also: Arc Light, Operation.

Ellsberg, Daniel (1931–), senior liaison officer, U.S. embassy, South Vietnam, 1965–1966; assistant to the U.S. ambassador to South Vietnam, 1967. A National Security Council operative and one of Secretary of Defense McNamara's "whiz kids," Ellsberg turned from a war supporter to an antiwar activist. Ellsberg, a U.S. Marine Corps veteran, leaked parts of the Pentagon Papers, the classified study of U.S. Vietnam policy he had helped put together, to the *New York Times,* which in June 1971 began publishing excerpts of the classified study of U.S. policy in Vietnam. When the Nixon administration sought an injunction against the newspaper, the Supreme Court upheld the legality of the publications. Ellsberg was charged with conspiracy, theft, and violation of espionage statutes, but his case was dismissed in May 1973 after evidence of government misconduct. That misconduct included government involvement in the burglary of the Los Angeles office of Dr. Lewis Fielding, Ellsberg's psychiatrist.

See also: Fielding, Lewis J.; Pentagon Papers; Plumbers; RAND Corporation; Schlesinger, James R.; Sheehan, Neil; Watergate.

Ely, Paul (1897–1975), commander in chief of French armed forces in Indochina and French High Commissioner in Indochina, 1954–1955. Ely replaced Gen. Henri Navarre early in 1954. On 20 March 1954, Ely came to Washington, D.C., to request U.S. air support for the defense of Dien Bien Phu. During Ely's visit, Adm. Arthur W. Radford, chairman of the Joint Chiefs of Staff (JCS), advocated Operation Vulture, a plan calling for U.S. air strikes against Viet Minh positions. Although the Air Force chief of staff, Gen. Nathan F. Twining, strongly supported the plan, the other members of the JCS opposed it. Ely's request was denied. French forces surrendered Dien Bien Phu on 7 May 1954.

See also: Dien Bien Phu; Navarre, Henri; Radford, Arthur W; Twining, Nathan F.

Élysée Agreement. An 8 March 1949 exchange of letters between former Emperor Bao Dai and French president Vincent Auriol at the Élysée Palace in Paris that paved the way for Bao Dai to return to Vietnam as emperor and head the Associated State of Vietnam within the French Union.

See also: Bao Dai; French Union.

Embargo. In April 1975 after the communist takeover of South Vietnam, the United States extended to all of Vietnam a trade embargo that had been in effect against the Democratic Republic of Vietnam since 1964.

Authorized under the 1917 Trading with the Enemy Act and the 1969 Export Administration Act, four U.S. presidents renewed the embargo annually, leaving it essentially unchanged until 1991. The embargo included a ban on commercial trade and financial transactions between the two countries, a U.S. block on International Monetary Fund (IMF) and World Bank development aid, and a freeze of Vietnam's assets in the United States. Humanitarian aid from private U.S. agencies and small-scale remittances by Vietnamese expatriates to their families was permitted. Together with Cambodia, North Korea, and Cuba, Vietnam faced the United States' most restrictive trade policy through the 1980s. In the late 1980s, Vietnamese policy changes led to improved relations with the United States and a reconsideration of the embargo. In 1989, Vietnam began to move toward a market economy, scaling back state-subsidized industry and centralized planning. Reductions in Soviet foreign aid and the loss of protected Eastern bloc markets drove the new policies. Vietnam withdrew its forces from Cambodia in 1989 and in the early 1990s facilitated efforts to account for Americans still listed as missing in action (MIA). In addition, U.S. companies such as AT&T, Mobil, Caterpillar, and Boeing lobbied on Capitol Hill to allow participation in the Vietnamese market, citing the importance of U.S. economic competitiveness and noting that other countries, most prominently Japan, had begun investment and trade with Vietnam.

In 1991, President Bush lifted the ban on travel to Vietnam and authorized a $1 million aid package, the first official U.S. assistance for the country since 1975. In July 1993, President Clinton ended U.S. opposition to IMF and World Bank aid. After a symbolic Senate vote in support of a new trade policy, President Clinton repealed the embargo on 4 February 1994. Clinton's action did not affect Vietnam's frozen assets in the United States (estimated at $290 million in 1994). The resolution of the issue awaited negotiations over U.S. financial claims within former South Vietnam.

See also: Normalization.

Emerson, Gloria (1930–), journalist, author. Emerson was a *New York Times* correspondent in Vietnam in 1970–1972. Her book, *Winners and Losers* (1978), is a highly praised nonfiction account about the war and its affect on Americans at home. It won the National Book Award for Nonfiction.

See also: Winners and Losers.

Enclave Strategy. An early Vietnam War strategy that called for confining U.S. forces to coastal areas and bases. When the first U.S. combat troops arrived in Vietnam in 1965, Ambassador Maxwell Taylor and Gen. Harold Johnson proposed limiting U.S. forces to 80-kilometer (50-mile) zones around coastal base areas. President Johnson approved this enclave approach in April 1965. U.S. soldiers would thus be spared from fighting in unfamiliar terrain, while their presence would give South Vietnam time to build up its armed forces. The Army of the Republic of Vietnam (ARVN) would subsequently be able to bear the brunt of combat. Almost immediately, Gen. William Westmoreland, MACV commander, and Gen. Earle Wheeler, chairman of the Joint Chiefs of Staff (JCS), pushed for a greater U.S. combat role. Within a few months, U.S. troops left their enclaves and patrolled the hinterlands of South Vietnam and President Johnson sharply dismissed all subsequent suggestions to return to the enclave strategy.

See also: Gavin, James M.; Search-and-Destroy.

Enthoven, Alain (1930–), U.S. assistant secretary of Defense for systems analysis, 1961–1968. Brought to the Pentagon as a McNamara "whiz kid," Enthoven was an economist trained to spot trends in numerical data. As a top aide to Defense Secretary Robert S. McNamara, Enthoven argued against large-scale U.S. combat in Vietnam because he believed the war should be fought primarily through pacification efforts. He also maintained that the North Vietnamese and Viet Cong could control their casualty rates and outlast the Americans until U.S. public opinion forced an end to U.S. participation in the war.

See also: McNamara, Robert.

Erhart, Ludwig (1897–1977), economist and chancellor of the Federal Republic of Germany, 1963–1966. Beginning in 1964, Erhart's West German government, a strong ally of President Johnson, purchased billions of dollars of U.S. military equipment to help finance the U.S. war in Vietnam. Continuing Johnson administration demands to step up payments and rising inflation rates from U.S. and FRG spending embarrassed Erhart's Christian Democratic/Free Democratic Party government and contributed to its collapse in 1966.

Escalation. In July 1965, four months after the first American combat troops arrived in Vietnam, Defense Secretary Robert S. McNamara returned from Saigon warning that South Vietnam might soon collapse. On McNamara's recommendation, President Johnson ordered the immediate deployment of 50,000 additional troops, with 50,000 more to follow later. By the end of 1965 the number of U.S. military personnel in Vietnam stood at 184,300, compared to 23,300 a year earlier. Johnson also expanded the military's role in Vietnam, authorizing Gen. William Westmoreland, the commanding general of American forces, to use combat troops as

he saw fit to strengthen the position of South Vietnamese forces. Johnson also for the first time approved saturation bombing of North Vietnamese strongholds in South Vietnam. This escalation marked the beginning of an open-ended U.S. military commitment to preserve a noncommunist South Vietnam.

See also: Johnson, Lyndon B.; McNamara, Robert; Westmoreland, William C.

European Defense Community (EDC). A 1952 treaty that attempted to create a European army to counter the Soviet Union's growing military force. France conditioned its support for the EDC on U.S. aid for the French war in Indochina. The Eisenhower administration subsequently provided more than $1 billion in loans and grants in 1953 to the French efforts in Indochina. France never ratified the treaty. The EDC gave way to the Western European Unity Treaty in 1955, which set up the Western European Union.

Evans, Diane Carlson (1947–), co-founder and director of the Vietnam Women's Memorial Project, a non-profit group formed in 1984 to build a national memorial honoring American women who served in Vietnam. Evans served as a U.S. Army nurse in Vietnam in 1968–1969. The privately funded memorial—a bronze sculpture of three women helping a wounded male solider—was dedicated on the Mall in Washington, D.C., near the Vietnam Veterans Memorial on Veterans Day, 11 November 1993.

See also: Vietnam Women's Memorial.

Everything We Had (1981). Well-regarded oral history containing the words of 33 Vietnam veterans, edited by Al Santoli who served with the U.S. Army's 25th Infantry Division in Vietnam in 1968–1969.

F-4. Known as the Phantom, the McDonald-Douglas F-4 is a twin-engine, all-weather tactical jet fighter-bomber widely used by the U.S. Marines, Navy and Air Force during the Vietnam War.

F-105 Thunderchief. Single-engine, tactical fighter-bomber widely used by U.S. Air Force in the Vietnam War beginning in 1964.

F-111. U.S. low-altitude, all-weather strike fighter. Conceived by Secretary of Defense Robert McNamara as a multipurpose aircraft, It was produced by the TFX (tactical fighter experimental) program, which was intended to satisfy an Air Force requirement for a Europe-based nuclear strike aircraft and a Navy requirement for a carrier-based, missile-armed, long-range fleet defense interceptor. The multiservice program was to achieve significant savings through a longer production run and common parts inventory; a variable-sweep, "switch-blade" wing, never before used in an operational aircraft, was to satisfy the disparate design requirements. In a controversial decision, McNamara overruled the services and selected General Dynamics rather than Boeing as

contractor because the two General Dynamics versions were closer in design. The Navy F-111B proved badly overweight and was canceled. The Air Force version suffered from developmental problems, culminating in a disastrous premature deployment to Thailand in March 1968 in which three of eight aircraft were lost to unknown causes in 55 missions over North Vietnam. The aircraft's problems were ultimately resolved, and the F-111A proved itself in Operation Line-backer II. Its accurate radar bombing and high subsonic penetration speeds and low-altitude terrain-avoidance radar rendered it effectively immune to antiaircraft defenses. F-111s played a large role in softening up North Vietnamese defenses and were particularly effective in attacking small, targets such as radar sites, SAM sites, and airfields.

See also: Linebacker and Linebacker II, Operations.

FAC. *See* Forward Air Controllers

Fall, Bernard (1926–1967), Austrian-born associate professor at Howard University, Washington, D.C.; internationally known Vietnam War scholar. Fall, a French citizen who first went to Vietnam in 1953, was the author of seven well-regarded books about the French and American wars there, including *Street Without Joy* (1961), *The Two Viet-Nams* (1963), *Viet-Nam Witness: 1953-1966,* (1966), and *Hell in a Very Small Place: The Siege of Dien Bien Phu* (1967). A critic of both French and U.S. policy in Vietnam. Fall was killed by a Viet Cong booby trap in Hue in 1967.

FANK. Acronym for *Forces Armées Nationales Khmères* (Khmer National Armed Forces), the Cambodian national army. In 1970, FANK supported Lon Nol's overthrow of Prince Norodom Sihanouk's government, believing that the new pro-U.S. regime would mean the resumption of U.S. military aid to Cambodia. The Khmer Rouge defeated FANK in 1975.

See also: Cambodia; Khmer Rouge; Lon Nol.

Fan Song Radar. U.S. name for Soviet-made mobile ground radar detection system that provided targeting information for surface-to-air missiles deployed in 1965 by North Vietnam.

See also: Antiaircraft Defenses.

Fassnacht, Robert (1937–1970), a post-graduate researcher at the University of Wisconsin's Army Mathematics Research Center in Madison who was killed on 24 August 1970 by a bomb planted by antiwar extremists. Madison residents Dwight and Karleton Armstrong and University of Wisconsin students David Fine and Leo Burt were arrested in connection with the bombing.

See also: Armstrong, Dwight and Karlton; Burt, Leo; Fassnacht, Robert; Fine, David; University of Wisconsin Bombing.

Fatal Light (1988). A highly regarded, impressionistic novel by Richard Currey, centering on the Vietnam War and postwar experiences of an unidentified Army medic.

Fatherland Front (*Mat Tran To Quoc*). A national front organization established in Hanoi in 1955 to represent all Vietnamese, north and south. The front continued to function in North Vietnam after 1960, but was succeeded in the south by the National Liberation Front (NLF), also known as the Viet Cong. In December 1976 the NLF was merged into the Fatherland Front.

See also: National Liberation Front.

Faure, Edgar (1908–1988), French premier, January 1952–February 1953, February 1955 to January 1956. Born Edgar Sanday, Faure had a decisive confrontation with U.S. Secretary of State John Foster Dulles over the course of Franco-American influence in Vietnam in 1955–1956. The Eisenhower administration's support of Diem caused Faure to break sharply with the Americans. The French subsequently shifted attention to their North African colonies, and abandoned their interest in Vietnam, enabling the United States to embark on its independent course in Vietnam.

See also: Dulles, John Foster.

Faydang, Lo (Phay Dang Lo), anti-French Hmong leader in

Laos who lost out to Touby Lyfoung as district officer in the late 1940s and became a guide and collaborator for the Japanese and Viet Minh. In the 1950s he led a group of Hmong clans into an alliance with the communist Pathet Lao.

See also: Hmong; Laos; Touby Lyfoung.

Federal Bureau of Investigation (FBI). During the Vietnam War Presidents Lyndon Johnson and Richard Nixon used the FBI to undermine and harass domestic critics of the war. Both presidents believed that the antiwar movement was a threat to their Vietnam policies and to domestic stability and that North Vietnam and its allies influenced the movement. FBI director J. Edgar Hoover supported repressive policies against antiwar protestors. In 1967, at Johnson's request, Hoover turned the FBI's attention toward the antiwar movement, particularly groups led by student radicals. Code-named Operation Cointelpro, the FBI's campaign against the antiwar movement was designed to disrupt from the inside and intimidate from the outside. Agents of the FBI and agents of the Central Intelligence Agency (CIA) were directed to go undercover and infiltrate various antiwar groups. This program, which was continued and expanded under President Richard Nixon, sought to keep the movement offguard and upset its activities. The disruptions

included causing conflict within and among antiwar groups. In addition to the undercover program, FBI agents would show up at draft card burnings, rallies, and conventions held by Students for a Democratic Society (SDS), instilling paranoia and fear by their presence. FBI investigators attempted to discover links between movement leaders and the communist governments of North Vietnam, China, and the Soviet Union. These investigations yielded no evidence of a connection. Nixon directed the FBI to tap the phones of administration staff in an effort to uncover and plug leaks. He also tried to enlist the FBI in his illegal Huston Plan, allowing the White House to control the domestic intelligence activities of agencies such as the FBI and CIA, but Hoover refused to do so.

See also: Cointelpro; Hoover, J. Edgar.

Fellowship of Reconciliation (FOR). Established in 1914, the FOR was the most influential pacifist group in Great Britain and the United States. A. J. Muste, a veteran American pacifist, headed the group during the 1950s and early 1960s. In October 1964 the FOR issued the Declaration of Conscience Against the War in Vietnam, the first public statement endorsing draft resistance to protest the increasing number of U.S. military advisers being sent to Vietnam.

See also: Muste, A. J.

Felt, Harry D. (1902–), admiral, U.S. Navy; Commander-in-Chief, Pacific (CINCPAC), 1958–1964. Adm. Harry "Don" Felt succeeded Adm. Felix Stump as CINCPAC in August 1958. More concerned with the communist threats in Korea, Taiwan, and Laos than in Vietnam, Felt recommended against sending U.S. troops to South Vietnam in 1961. He changed his position, and became a vocal supporter of intervention. The first reports of the insurrection against South Vietnamese President Ngo Dinh Diem occurred while Felt was on an official visit to Saigon in November 1963. He rushed out of the presidential palace just prior to the coup. Felt retired and was replaced by Adm. U.S. Grant Sharp Jr. in June 1964.

See also: Commander-in-Chief, Pacific.

Fielding, Lewis J. (1909–), Daniel Ellsberg's psychiatrist, whose office was broken into in September 1971 by White House covert operatives known as the "plumbers" looking for material to discredit Ellsberg, who in June 1971 had leaked the Pentagon Papers to the *New York Times*. White House adviser John Ehrlichman, his aide, Egil Krogh, Jr., White House counsel Charles Colson, Nixon campaign official G. Gordon Liddy, and former CIA operatives Bernard Barker, Felipe DeDiego and Eugenio Martinez pled guilty or were found guilty of perjury or of violating Fielding's rights.

See also: Colson, Charles; Ehrlichman, John; Ellsberg, Daniel; Watergate.

Fields of Fire (1978). Highly acclaimed Vietnam War combat novel by James Webb, a former a U.S. Marine lieutenant in Vietnam.

See also: Webb, James.

Final Offensive. *See* Spring Offensive

Fine, David (1952–), with Karl and Dwight Armstrong and Leo Burt, Fine was responsible for planting the bomb that on 24 August 1970 killed researcher Robert Fassnacht at the Army Mathematics Research Center on the University of Wisconsin Madison campus. The act was intended to protest Vietnam War–related research. Fine, a University of Wisconsin student, fled after the bombing. He was captured by the FBI in California in 1976.

See also: Armstrong, Dwight and Karlton; Army Mathematics Research Center; Burt, Leo; Fassnacht, Robert; University of Wisconsin Bombing.

Fire Brigade Concept. Dominant U.S. ground war strategy employed in 1965–1966 developed by Gen. William Westmoreland. The concept used U.S. Marine and Army ground forces in South Vietnam as reserve/reaction forces in acute situations anywhere in the South. The idea was to move U.S. ground forces into a more offensive military posture during the initial stages of the U.S. military buildup in Vietnam.

See also: Westmoreland, William C.

Fire in the Lake (1972). Acclaimed book, subtitled "The Vietnamese and the Americans in Vietnam," by the foreign correspondent Frances FitzGerald. It examines Vietnamese society and culture and is highly critical of the U.S. war. Winner of the 1973 Pulitzer Prize for General Nonfiction.

Fire Support Bases. Self-contained, U.S. and South Vietnamese helicopter-supplied bases that provided artillery fire to patrolling units and served as bases for infantry operations. Hundreds of fire support bases were established throughout South Vietnam, positioned within range of each another for mutual support and to insure that the fire from at least one base would hit any point within an area of operations. Fire-support guns delivered accurate, concentrated fire even in weather that grounded aircraft.

First Blood (1982). Hollywood film dealing with an alienated, violent Vietnam veteran, John Rambo. In *Rambo: First Blood Part II* (1985), the title character goes back to Vietnam to stage a one-man POW rescue mission. Both extremely popular films were dismissed by critics as cartoonish action melodramas.

See also: Rambo.

First Five-Year and Three-Year Plans. Governmental North Vietnamese industrialization programs in 1958–1960 and 1961–1965 that included nationalizing former French-owned industries and state-directed development of mining enterprises and hydroelectric power. Assisted by large-scale Chinese and Soviet aid, the plans had initial success.

See also: Democratic Republic of Vietnam.

Fishel, Wesley (1919–), political science professor, Michigan State University; head, Michigan State University Vietnam Advisory Group (MSUVAG), 1954–1961; chairman, American Friends of Vietnam. Fishel staunchly backed Ngo Dinh Diem and an anticommunist South Vietnam in the 1950s. He led the MSUVAG, which developed many institutions for the South Vietnamese government. As head of the American Friends of Vietnam, Fishel championed the U.S. military commitment to preserve an independent South Vietnam.

See also: American Friends of Vietnam; Michigan State University Vietnam Advisory Group.

Fisher, Roger (1922–), Harvard Law School professor who proposed building a 100-kilometer (60-mile) anti-infiltration barrier across the demilitarized zone (DMZ) and Laos to interdict the Ho Chi Minh Trail.

See also: Barrier Concept; Ho Chi Minh Trail.

Fishhook. A small strip of land in Cambodia's Mondolkiri province on the South Vietnamese border. The Fishhook area, 160 kilometers (100 miles) northwest of Saigon, was a large supply base and sanctuary for the Viet Cong . President Nixon, believing the Central Office for South Vietnam (COSVN) head-quarters of the Viet Cong was located there, ordered secret bombing of the Fishhook and other Cambodian sanctuaries in 1969–1970. Operation Total Victory, the assault on the Fishhook by U.S. and Army of the Republic of Vietnam (ARVN) troops, was part of the invasion of Cambodia in May 1970. The invaders found deserted bunkers and tons of supplies, but few sol-diers and no command post.

See also: Cambodian Incursion; Central Office for South Vietnam.

FitzGerald, Frances (1940–), journalist, author. FitzGerald covered the Vietnam War as a free-lance journalist beginning in 1966. Her book, *Fire in the Lake: The Vietnamese and the Americans* (1975) won a Pulitzer Prize.

See also: Fire in the Lake.

Five O'Clock Follies. Nickname for the daily U.S. Information Agency press brief-ings on the progress of the war. Every day at 4:45 P.M., the U.S. Military Assistance Command Office of Information (MACOI) conducted official briefings for U.S. and foreign journalists in Saigon. After 1966, the briefings were held at the Joint U.S. Public Affairs Office (JUSPAO) auditorium and directed by U.S. Information Agency officer Barry Zorthian. Military setbacks and operations by South Vietnamese forces received scant mention, while Viet Cong guerrilla and North Vietnamese losses were exaggerated. Following the 1968 Tet Offensive reporters lost faith in official pronounce-ments, and derided the JUSPAO briefing as the "Five O'Clock Follies."

See also: Zorthian, Barry.

Flaming Dart, Operation. The successor to Operation Pierce Arrow, Flaming Dart was the code name for February 1965 U.S. retaliatory air raids against North Vietnam. Triggered by the 6 February mortar attack on the U.S. base at Pleiku, Flaming Dart was launched on 7 and 8 February from attack carriers *Coral Sea* and *Hancock* against barracks and port facilities in southern North Vietnam. Flaming Dart II was a response to the 10 February bombing of U.S. billets in Qui Nhon.

See also: Pierce Arrow, Operation; Pleiku; RAND Corporation.

Fleet Marine Force Pacific. *See* Krulak, Victor.

Flexible Response. A Cold War–era strategic doctrine

founded on the principle that the U.S. should equip its armed forces to allow it to match any act of aggression from a communist nation with a reciprocal level of violence. The idea was promulgated by retired U.S. Army Gen. Maxwell Taylor in his book, *The Uncertain Trumpet* (1959). Taylor suggested that a flexible response strategy should replace President Eisenhower's "New Look" defense policy of threatening massive nuclear retaliation in response to any threat from communist nations. Taylor cautioned that excessive reliance on air power and nuclear weapons left the United States unprepared to fight communism around the world. As he stated, "massive retaliation could offer only two choices: the initiation of general nuclear war or compromise and retreat." Instead, Taylor maintained that the United States should develop "a capability to react across the entire spectrum of possible challenges," from nuclear war to counterinsurgency operations. President Kennedy embraced flexible response and named Taylor his special military representative in 1961. Vietnam became a test of Kennedy's promise of the doctrine.

See also: Taylor, Maxwell D.

Fonda, Jane (1937–), actress; antiwar activist. Fonda spoke at many antiwar rallies beginning in 1969, and earned the enmity of war supporters and the nickname "Hanoi Jane" after a controversial trip to Hanoi in July 1972, during which she broadcast an appeal over Hanoi radio urging U.S. pilots to stop bombing North Vietnam.

See also: Hawks and Doves; Teach-Ins.

Fontainebleau Conference. A failed French-Vietnamese conference held at Fontainebleau on 6 July 1946 during which no agreement was reached on Vietnam's role within the French Union. Before the conference began, French high commissioner Georges Thierry d'Argenlieu undercut the Viet Minh by recognizing a French puppet state, led by former emperor Bao Dai. This action caused the Viet Minh to doubt French sincerity, and they left the meetings. Ho Chi Minh remained in France, however, to work out a modus vivendi with the French, thus salvaging something with which to placate the more extreme elements in the Viet Minh.

See also: Argenlieu, Georges Thierry D'; Bidault, Georges; French Union; Gaulle, Charles de.

Food for Peace. A U.S. government aid program that provided some $1.3 billion in American farm surplus food to South Vietnam from 1958–1975. Half the food was rice, formerly South Vietnam's major export. Cotton, wheat, tobacco, and milk also were sent in the program.

FOR. *See* Fellowship of Reconciliation

Forces Armées Nationales Khmères (FANK). *See* FANK

Ford, Gerald R. Jr. (1913–), member, U.S. House of Representatives (R-Mich.), 1949–1973; U.S. vice president, 1973–1974; U.S. president, 1974–1977. Ford, a pro–World War II isolationist turned Cold War internationalist, presided over the final U.S. withdrawal from Vietnam.

He graduated from the University of Michigan and Yale Law School, where he was active in a group that later formed the nucleus of the America First Committee, the foremost nonintervention organization on the eve of U.S. entry into World War II. Moved by his service as a naval gunnery officer during the war, he converted to internationalism, defeated an isolationist incumbent in the Republican primary, and was elected to the U.S. House in 1948. A moderate Republican, Ford opposed most expansion of the welfare state and endorsed the liberation of Eastern Europe from Soviet rule. As House Minority Leader and Vice President, Ford supported President Nixon's pursuit of détente with the Soviet Union, rapprochement with the People's Republic of China, and Vietnamization of the Vietnam War.

After succeeding Nixon in 1974, Ford offered amnesty to draft evaders who performed alternative service. He also tried to bolster the sagging Cambodian and South Vietnamese governments. Congress appropriated less than half of the $2 billion in aid for South Vietnam that Ford requested for fiscal year 1975. This decision, Ford said, gravely impaired the chances of survival for South Vietnam.

Facing major North Vietnamese and Khmer Rouge offensives in early 1975, Ford used discretionary funds to bring some two thousand South Vietnamese orphans to the United States in Operation Babylift and made two unsuccessful efforts to secure emergency military assistance for the South Vietnamese government.

In May 1975 Ford responded with military action when Cambodia seized the U.S. merchant ship *Mayaguez*. He ordered air strikes on Cambodian bases and a rescue mission that cost the lives of 41 Americans even as the *Mayaguez* crow was being released.

See also: Amnesty; Baby Lift, Operation; Kissinger, Henry; *Mayaguez* Incident; Weyand, Frederick C.

Ford Foundation. The charitable foundation that provided significant funding for the RAND Corporation, the federally funded think tank that produced hundreds of reports during the Vietnam War that influenced U.S. policy.

See also: RAND Corporation.

Foreign Assistance Act, 1961. The law that established the U.S. Agency for International Development, the State Department unit that was the principal U.S. agency responsible for designing and implementing nonmilitary U.S. development and assistance programs in Vietnam and elsewhere around the world.

See also: Agency for International Development.

Foreign Relations Committee. U.S. Senate Committee with jurisdiction over legislation on foreign affairs, including economic and military assistance programs. During the Vietnam War, the committee's chairman, Sen. J. William Fulbright (D-Ark.), became an outspoken opponent of the war. Fulbright led a series of committee public hearings in February 1966 that served as a sounding board for criticism of the Johnson administration's handling of the war effort.

See also: Congress, U.S.; Fulbright, J. William.

Forrestal, Michael (1927–1989), National Security Council aide, 1962–1965. Forrestal visited Vietnam with State Department official Roger Hilsman at President Kennedy's request in January 1963. Their report presented a mixed assessment of the war, predicting a prolonged conflict but did not recommend major policy changes. On 24 August 1963,

Forrestal, Averell Harriman, George Ball, and Hilsman sent a cable to Ambas-sador Henry Cabot Lodge signaling the U.S. government's willingness to abandon South Vietnam's President Ngo Dinh Diem, an action that led to Diem's overthrow.

See also: Hilsman, Roger.

Forrestal, USS. U.S. Navy aircraft carrier deployed in the South China Sea on Yankee Station. On 29 July 1967, five days after arriving at Yankee Station, a rocket accidentally touched off on the *Forrestal's* deck. In the resulting explosions and 18-hour fire 135 crewmen were killed and 62 were injured. Twenty-one aircraft were destroyed and 42 were damaged in the worst U.S. naval disaster in a combat zone since WWII. The *Forrestal* was taken out of action for seven months of repairs and did not return to Yankee Station.

See also: Aircraft carriers.

Fortas, Abe (1910–1982), U.S. Supreme Court Justice, 1965–1969. A friend and unofficial adviser to President Johnson, Fortas played a significant behind-the-scenes role formulating Vietnam policy. Fortas strongly endorsed Johnson's escalation of the war and supported further troop commitments after other advisers counseled de-escalation and withdrawal.

See also: Wise Men.

Fort Hood Three. Three U.S. soldiers—Private Dennis Mora, Private First Class James Johnson, and Private David Samas—who refused orders to go to Vietnam after completing basic training at Fort Hood, Texas, in June 1966. They were court-martialed and served two years in prison. The antiwar movement widely publicized the case.

Fort Polk. U.S. Army base in Louisiana reactivated during the Vietnam War to provide advanced training for infantrymen. Weather conditions at Fort Polk's "Tigerland" were similar to those in South Vietnam.

Fortunate Son (1991). Autobiography of Lewis B. Puller, Jr.; winner of the 1992 Pulitzer Prize for Biography or Autobiography. Puller, the son of legendary U.S. Marine Corps Gen. Lewis B. "Chesty" Puller, was severely wounded while serving as a U.S. Marine lieutenant in Vietnam in 1968. His book focuses on his war and postwar experiences and his relationship with his father.

Forward Air Controllers (FACs). U.S. Air Force airborne forward air controllers directed air strikes from low-flying, low-speed, propeller-driven light aircraft such as the Cessna 0-1 Bird Dog. FACs also participated in search and rescue missions, visual reconnaissance, escort and cover missions for convoys. They were a major feature of the war in Indochina, especially along the Ho Chi Minh Trail, and in northern Laos.

Four-Party Joint Military Commission. The Four-Party Joint Military Commission was created by the Paris Peace Accords of 1973. It included representatives from North Vietnam, the Provisional Revolutionary Government (formerly the National Liberation Front), South Vietnam, and the United States. From January to March 1973, the commission oversaw the pullout of more than fifty thousand U.S., Australian, New Zealand and South Korean troops from South Vietnam; arranged the return of prisoners-of-war; and tried unsuccessfully to preserve the cease-fire. It was replaced on 29 March 1973 by the Four-Party Joint Military Team, with the same membership, which attempted in vain to resolve the issue of soldiers who were still listed as missing in action.

See also: International Commission for Supervision and Control; Paris Accords; Summers, Harry G. Jr.

Fragging. Military slang for killing unpopular NCOs and officers, derived from the practice of rolling fragmentation grenades into the tents of sleeping officers deemed incompetent or overzealous. Fragging peaked in 1970–1971, a period of widespread demoralization among U.S. troops. According to the Pentagon, 788 probable explosive-device fragging assaults took place in Vietnam between 1969 and 1972, resulting in 86 dead and 714 wounded. Many more suspected fraggings were not investigated for lack of evidence.

See also: Ticket Punching.

Fragments (1984). A highly praised literary novel by Jack Fuller that follows a U.S. Army draftee to Vietnam and explores his readjustment problems after returning home.

See also: Fuller, Jack.

France. France established missionary and trade organizations in Vietnam in 1664 and consolidated its control throughout the eighteenth and nineteenth centuries. The French referred to the southern part of Vietnam, including the Mekong Delta and Saigon, as Cochinchina; the central third as Annam; and the northernmost section, including Hanoi, as Tonkin. In 1859 France conquered the Mekong Delta and in 1862 gained control of southern Vietnam (Cochinchina). Between 1863 and 1893, France added northern Vietnam (Tonkin), and central Vietnam (Annam), Laos, and Cambodia as protectorates and in 1887 attempted to centralize control over the region by establishing the Union of Indochina under a single governor general. French control was decentralized; the French administered Cochinchina directly and the other areas indirectly, through Vietnamese political institutions. The French levied taxes; controlled trade in rice, opium, and alcohol; confiscated land; and forced some peasants into labor on rubber plantations and in mines.

Armed resistance to French rule began in the 1930s. In an attempt to legitimize its control of the region, France in 1932 permitted the former emperor of Annam, Bao Dai, to return from France and assume governmental power in Vietnam. However, as with other indigenous leaders whose rule was reinstated by France, he was primarily a puppet. The Popular Front government in France was lenient toward the colony, but after its 1938 demise the French increased their repression of the independence movement. When France fell to Germany in 1940, it signed a treaty allowing Japan to use military facilities in northern Vietnam. The French continued to administer the Japanese-controlled government. The Viet Minh–led independence movement resisted the French and Japanese. In March 1945 the Japanese abolished French rule in the name of Asian nationalism and offered Bao Dai limited independence. Soon, however, the Japanese themselves had surrendered to the Allies. After Japan's surrender, the French, with British and U.S. acquiescence, returned to Indochina.

In 1945 Ho Chi Minh declared Vietnam's independence and entered into negotiations with the French. In a 6 March 1946 treaty, France recognized Vietnam as a free state and

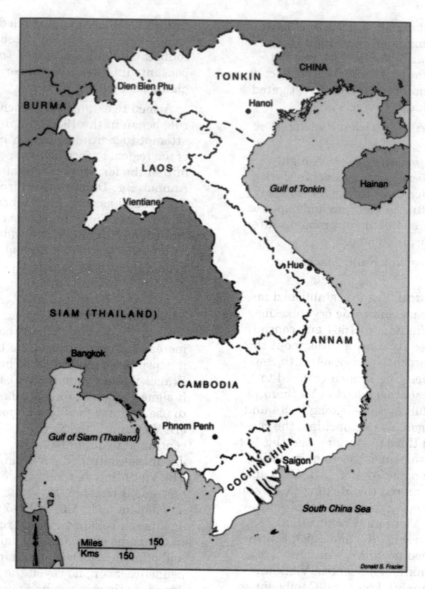

Vietnam agreed to join the Indochinese Federation. This agreement was merely a truce as the two sides solidified their forces. War broke out in November 1946 with French attacks on Hanoi and Haiphong; the Viet Minh responded on 19 December with attacks on French barracks and residences.

From 1946 to 1954 France engaged in a protracted struggle to retain Vietnam. It installed a government under Emperor Bao Dai so that it could conclude a settlement with anticommunist Vietnamese; Bao Dai, however, made many of the same demands for independence as had Ho Chi Minh. France finally convinced

Bao Dai to assume leadership of an anticommunist Vietnam in 1949 with only nominal independence from France.

The military struggle from 1947 to 1950 was marked by Viet Minh caution and refusal to engage in large-scale direct combat with the French. General Etienne Valluy began a campaign in 1947 to wipe out the Viet Minh but underestimated their strength and popular support. The French army of 30,000 could not penetrate mountainous and remote areas. French generals, beginning with Gen. Jean de Lattre de Tassigny in 1950, repeatedly requested the formation of a Vietnamese National Army, but this army never successfully freed the French expeditionary forces from their losing battle with the Viet Minh. Under Gen. Vo Nguyen Giap, the Viet Minh mounted repeated offensives beginning in 1952, culminating in the decisive battle and French defeat at Dien Bien Phu in March 1954. The 1954 Geneva Conference formalized the French withdrawal from northern Vietnam, although they remained in the South until March 1956, when their last troops departed after South Vietnamese President Diem expelled them. During the 1960s France opposed U.S. involvement.

See also: Annam; Bao Dai; Bay Vien; Binh Xuyen; Cambodia; China, People's Republic of; Cochinchina; Da Nang; Dien Bien Phu; Eisenhower, Dwight D.; European Defense Community; Franco–Viet Minh War; Geneva Conference, 1954; Giap, Vo Nguyen; Haiphong; Hanoi; Hmong; Hoa Hao; Ho Chi Minh; Land Reform; Laniel, Joseph; Laos; Pathet Lao; People's Army of Vietnam; Rusk (David) Dean; Sihanouk, Norodom; Ten-Pin Theory; Tonkin; United Nations; Viet Minh; Vietnamese National Army.

Francis Marion, Operation. Code name for a series of eight battles fought by the U.S. 4th Infantry Division against the North Vietnamese Army in the Ia Drang Valley from April to October 1967. The operation was incorporated into Operation MacArthur.

Franco–Viet Minh War. The war that broke out between France, the colonial ruler of Vietnam, and Ho Chi Minh's communist Viet Minh at the end of 1946, also known as the First Indochina War and the French Indochina War. France tried to undercut the nationalist Viet Minh by forming a puppet Vietnamese government under former emperor Bao Dai. After 1949 the Viet Minh received support from China. The United States began to provide military assistance to the French in 1950. As the war turned into a stalemate on the battlefield, French public support for the war steadily weakened. In the spring of 1954, France agreed to discuss a peace settlement at Geneva. Negotiations opened on

7 May, immediately after the Viet Minh achieved a major victory by overrunning the French base at Dien Bien Phu, in the far northwest. The July Geneva Agreement provided for a cease-fire and the creation of the communist-controlled Democratic Republic of Vietnam in the north and the French-supported Bao Dai government in the south. The agreement established an International Control Commission composed of representatives from Canada, India, and Poland to enforce it. A declaration drafted at Geneva and approved by all attending countries except the Bao Dai government and the United States called for national elections in the two zones in 1956 to create a united Vietnamese government. Those elections were never held.

See also: Dien Bien Phu; France; Geneva Conference, 1954; Viet Minh; Vo Nguyen Giap.

Freedom Birds. Nickname given by U.S. soldiers to the leased commercial passenger airplanes that took them home from Vietnam. This quick return to the United States contributed to the development of Post-traumatic Stress Disorder in some returning soldiers by depriving them of a transitional period between the combat zone and civilian life.

Freedom Train, Operation. One of the heaviest bombing campaigns of the war, Operation Freedom Train began in April 1972 in response to the North Vietnamese Army's Easter Offensive. It consisted of U.S. Air Force, Navy and Marine strikes against North Vietnamese Army targets in South Vietnam. The operation was renamed Linebacker I in May 1972.

See also: Easter Offensive; Linebacker and Linebacker II, Operations.

Free-Fire Zones (FFZs). Areas in South Vietnam authorized for unrestricted U.S. attacks on North Vietnamese or Viet Cong forces. Free-fire zones were designed in the early 1960s to coordinate combat operations and minimize civilian injury. Province chiefs, appointed by the South Vietnamese government, authorized free-fire zones if National Liberation Front (NLF) forces were believed to control an area and civilians were not likely to be present. In practice, often without regard for the presence of civilians, South Vietnamese officials gave routine clearance at U.S. request. The U.S. military initially established free-fire zones during the early 1960s to authorize firepower around protected villages in the Strategic Hamlet program. In 1964, the military expanded their use, and they became a vital aspect of the strategy to direct massive firepower against the NLF insurgency. After 1965, the Pentagon renamed the zones "specific strike zones," largely in response to negative connotations of indiscriminate bombing that "free-fire zones" carried. The U.S. military's extensive use of the zones drew heated criticism from the antiwar movement.

See also: Ben Suc; Bui Phat; Rules of Engagement; Tunnels.

Free World. Term used to refer to the group of countries that assisted South Vietnam from 1959 to 1975. Along with the United States, six nations provided military aid: Australia, New Zealand, the Philippines, the Republic of China (Taiwan), the Republic of Korea (South Korea), and Thailand. More than thirty other nations sent technical and economic aid through the Free World Assistance Program, including Argentina, Belgium, Brazil, Canada, Costa Rica, Denmark, Ecuador, the Federal Republic of Germany, France, Greece, Guatemala, Honduras, Iran, Ireland, Israel, Italy, Japan, Liberia, Luxembourg, Malaysia, Morocco, the Netherlands, Norway, Pakistan, Spain, South Africa, Switzerland, Tunisia, Turkey, the United Kingdom, Uruguay, and Venezuela.

Free World Assistance Program. Program under which some thirty nations provided technical and economic aid to South Vietnam from 1959–1975.

See also: Free World.

Free World Military Assistance Policy Council. A military working agreement signed in 1966 by the U.S. Military Assistance Command, Vietnam (MACV), and the Republic of China (Taiwan) Military Assistance Advisory Group, Vietnam under which the handful of troops from the Republic of China in Vietnam were supervised by the Free World Military Assistance Policy Council under the direct command of a military commander designated by the Republic of China.

See also: China, Republic of (Taiwan).

French, Albert (1944–), novelist, memoirist. French, a Pittsburgh native, served with U.S. Marines in Vietnam in 1965–1966. He is the author of the African-American-themed novels, *Billy* (1993), *Holly* (1995), and the highly praised *Patches of Fire* (1997), a Vietnam War memoir.

French Communist Party *(Parti Communiste Française)*. Founded on 30 December 1920 by leftists in the French Socialist Party. One of its founding members was a Vietnamese nationalist exile, Ho Chi Minh. The party, which was part of France's first post–World War II government, looked with favor upon Ho Chi Minh's nationalist aspirations for Vietnam, but agreed with prevailing French opinion that Vietnam and the rest of Indochina should remain in the French colonial empire. More nationalistic than ideological, French communist party leaders focused their attention on domestic matters after 1954.

See also: Communism; Ho Chi Minh.

French Expeditionary Corps. The French military force that came to Indochina in the early 1880s and thereafter constituted the French colonial military presence. The corps was defeated by Japan in 1940, rearmed by the British in 1945, and fought the communist Viet Minh beginning in 1946. During that 1946–1954 war the French Expeditionary Force was made up of French nationals, European volunteers and soldiers from France's colonies in Asia and Africa. At its peak in 1954 the corps had some 178,000 troops.

See also: French Union Forces.

French Indochinese Union. Created in 1887 by France as a centralized governing body with a governor general to rule over the separate French Indochinese states of Cochinchina, Annam, Tonkin, and Cambodia. The Union was dissolved less than a year later and the Indochinese states reverted to their previous colonial status.

See also: Annam; Cochinchina; Tonkin.

French Union (*Union Française*). The political entity established in 1946 to oversee French colonies around the world, including those in Indochina. It was superceded in 1958 by the French Community (*La Communaute*).

French Union Forces. The armed force made up primarily of Vietnamese that, together with the French Expeditionary Corps (FEC), fought the Indochina War against the Viet Minh from 1946–1954. At its peak in 1954 the French Union Forces numbered more some 517,000, including 178,000 FEC troops.

See also: Franco–Viet Minh War; French Expeditionary Corps.

Frequent Wind, Operation. The 29–30 April 1975 U.S. Navy evacuation of some 2,100 U.S. embassy and military personnel and South Vietnamese civilians from Saigon before the North Vietnamese entered the city. Nearly 80,000 other Vietnamese escaped from Saigon on South Vietnamese Air Force aircraft and by boat during the same period.

Friendly Fire. The term for combat deaths or wounds accidentally caused by friendly forces. Estimates of casualties from friendly fire in the Vietnam War range from 2 percent to between 15 and 20 percent.

Friendly fire is a common aspect of battle in all wars. Friendly fire is caused by what military commanders refer to as the "fog of war," the confusion caused by smoke and noise from guns and artillery, faulty communications between troops and artillery and air forces, and the tension and fear of the combatants.

Friendly fire casualties most often result from artillery-to-ground, air-to-ground, and ground-to-ground fire. In Vietnam, casualties resulting from accidents in the first two categories most often were caused by the dense jungle fighting conditions and errors in calling in coordinates for artillery or air strikes. In Dak To in 1967, for example, 42 U.S. paratroopers were killed and 45 wounded when U.S. Air Force jets mistakenly bombed their position. Ground-to-ground friendly fire in Vietnam resulted from the war's pattern of guerrilla warfare. Marked by night patrols, ambushes, and a "shoot first" survival mentality, this type of ground combat often created confusion and sometimes led to attacks on friendly troops.

See also: Fragging.

Friendly Fire (1976). Book by C. D. B. Bryan that tells the story of the 1 March 1970 death in Vietnam of U.S. Army Sgt. Michael Mullin, who was killed by friendly fire. The highly praised book, which examines the incident in Vietnam and its impact on the Mullin family, was the basis for a 1979 ABC-TV television film of the same name.

See also: Bryan, C. D. B.

Friends Committee on National Legislation.
American Quaker pacifist group that cautioned against U.S.

involvement in the French war in Vietnam in 1954 when the Eisenhower administration was considered U.S. military intervention.

Friends of Vietnam. *See* American Friends of Vietnam

Froines, John (1941–), antiwar activist who was one of the eight men indicted in Federal court for conspiring and traveling over state lines to incite rioting at the 1968 Democratic National Convention in Chicago. Froines and Lee Weiner were acquitted in the 1970 "Chicago Seven" trial.

See also: Chicago Seven; Davis, Rennard Cordon (Rennie); Dellinger, David; Hayden, Tom; Hoffman, Abbie; Kuntsler, William; Rubin, Jerry; Seale, Bobby; Weiner, Lee; Weinglass, Leonard.

Front Unifié pour la Lutte des Races Opprimées (FULRO). The United Front for the Liberation of Oppressed Races (FULRO) was an anti-Vietnamese separatist group made up of Montagnards, Chams and Khmers. FULRO staged several uprisings against the South Vietnamese government in 1964–1965. In 1966, the group openly revolted against South Vietnam. FULRO was decimated by 1979, forcing some Montagnards to seek asylum in the United States while others moved their bases into Cambodia.

Fulbright, J. William
(1905–1995), U.S. senator (D-Ark.); chairman, Senate Foreign Relations Committee, 1959–1974. Fulbright supported the U.S. presence in South Vietnam during the Eisenhower and Kennedy administrations because he favored the containment of communism. In August 1964, he was instrumental in congressional passage of the Gulf of Tonkin Resolution, which gave the president legal authority to expand and Americanize the war.

By mid-1965 Fulbright felt the Vietnam War could undermine improved relations with the Soviet Union and precipitate a war with the People's Republic of China. He therefore called for de-escalation and a negotiated settlement and became a major critic of Johnson's policy in Vietnam. In early 1966 Fulbright directed the Senate Foreign Relations Committee in open hearings on the administration's war policy. His book *Arrogance of Power* (1967) helped legitimize domestic opposition to the war.

After Richard Nixon became president, Fulbright continued his staunch opposition to U.S. policy in Vietnam. He saw Vietnamization as an attempt to avoid serious negotiations with North Vietnam. He denounced the April 1970 Cambodian incursion, and worked to enact the Cooper-Church amendment. Fulbright also was a prime participant in the successful congressional fight of 1973 to force Nixon to end the bombing of Cambodia. He helped create a climate in Congress that led to the passage of the War Powers Resolution of 1973, a direct challenge to the power of the president to commit troops to military action without the consent of Congress.

See also: Congress, U.S.; Cooper-Church Amendment; Foreign Relations Committee; Gulf of Tonkin Resolution; Hawks and Doves; War Powers Resolution; Appendix E, "Gulf of Tonkin Resolution."

Fuller, Jack (1946–), newspaper publisher; newspaper editor; novelist. Fuller served as a U.S. Army correspondent in Vietnam in 1969–1970. He won the 1986 Pulitzer Prize for editorial writing at the *Chicago Tribune*. Fuller later became that newspaper's editor and its publisher, and is the author of five novels, including *Fragments* (1984), a well-received literary novel of the Vietnam War and its aftermath.

See also: Fragments.

Full Metal Jacket (1987).
Critically acclaimed film produced, directed and co-written by Stanley Kubrick. Based on the Gustav Hasford novel, *The Short-Timers*, *Full Metal Jacket* follows several U.S. Marines from boot camp into Vietnam, culminating at the Battle of Hue during the 1968 Tet Offensive.

See also: Short Timers, The.

FULRO. See *Front Unifié pour la Lutte des Races Opprimées*

See also: Arnett, Peter; Associated Press.

Gabeler, Pierce G. (1922–1998), Central Intelligence Agency (CIA) administrator. Gabeler, a WWII naval aviator, directed Air America, the CIA's special air operations in Laos from the late 1960s to the early 1970s.

See also: Air America; Laos.

Galbraith, John Kenneth (1908–), economist; U.S. ambassador to India, 1961–1963. Galbraith, a key adviser to President John F. Kennedy, lobbied against U.S. involvement, arguing that the South Vietnamese government was corrupt and that South Vietnam lacked the strategic or economic importance to justify U.S. military involvement. He gave similar advice to President Johnson.

See also: Vietnam Moratorium Committee.

Gallagher, Wes (1911–1997), Associated Press managing editor, personnel head and president in New York from the early 1960s through the end of the Vietnam War. Gallagher was known for encouraging his Vietnam War correspondents, including Peter Arnett, to report the war aggressively.

Gallieni, Joseph-Simon (1849–1916), French governor-general in Indochina, 1892–1896. Gen. Gallieni suppressed nationalist movements in Vietnam and worked to win over the populace through limited social, economic and political reforms.

Game Warden, Operation. U.S. Navy brown-water program begun in December 1965 that sought to interdict the Viet Cong guerrillas' use of intercoastal and interior waterways, especially in the Mekong Delta. The operation was conducted by Task Force 116, also known as the Riverine Assault Force.

See also: Mobile Riverine Force; Navy, U.S.; SEALs; Task Force 116.

Gardens of Stone (1987). Film directed by Francis Ford Coppola, based on the 1983 Nicholas Proffitt novel dealing with a U.S. Army burial unit in Arlington National Cemetery. The film centers on an enlisted man's quest to fight in Vietnam.

Garwood, Robert R. (1946–), former prisoner of war. Garwood, a U.S. Marine Corps jeep driver, was taken prisoner in September 1965 in Quang Nam Province. On 21 March 1979 he became the last U.S. prisoner of war to be released. In a 1980 Marine Corps court martial he was convicted of collaborating with the enemy as a POW.

Gaulle, Charles de
(1890–1970), Free French leader,
1940–1945; first president, Fifth
Republic, 1958–1969. During
WWII and in 1946 de Gaulle
supported continued French control of Indochina, advocating
military force wherever necessary to retain the overseas
territories he believed were
indispensable to the legitimacy
of France as a world power. As
French president in the 1960s,
de Gaulle warned Presidents
Kennedy and Johnson to avoid
entangling the United States in
Vietnam. He called for neutrality
for Southeast Asia, proposing
that the United States, the
Soviet Union, France, and China
stay out of the region. To implement this plan, de Gaulle, on 23
July 1964, called for a conference
of the same order and including
the same participants as the
Geneva conference of 1954.

See also: Argenlieu, Georges
Thierry D'; Leclerc, Jacques
Philippe.

Gavin, James M. (1907–1990),
lieutenant general, U.S. Army;
ambassador to France,
1961–1963. A heavily decorated
WWII hero who retired in 1957,
Gen. Gavin became a sharp critic
of U.S. involvement in Vietnam
soon after U.S. combat troops
arrived there in 1965. He
denounced the war as wasteful
and without purpose, and predicted a "tragedy" for the United
States after touring South
Vietnam in 1967.

See also: Enclave Strategy.

Gayler, Noel (1915–), admiral,
U.S. Navy; Commander-in-Chief,
Pacific (CINCPAC), 1972–1976.
An ace Navy fighter pilot in
WWII, Adm. Gayler headed the
National Security Agency before
being named CINCPAC in
September 1972. He planned
Operation Frequent Wind, the
April 1975 helicopter evacuation
of Americans and South
Vietnamese from Saigon. Gayler
repeatedly tried to persuade
Ambassador Graham Martin to
implement the plan, but afraid of
touching off panic in the city,
Martin demurred until it was
almost too late. Gayler commanded the operation on 29–30
April 1975. In just eighteen
hours, over six thousand people
were flown to safety aboard U.S.
ships offshore. Gayler ended the
evacuation when the U.S.
embassy became "a bottomless
pit of refugees," leaving many
behind.

See also: Commander-in-Chief,
Pacific; Frequent Wind,
Operation.

Gelb, Leslie H. (1937–), deputy
director of Defense Department
policy planning staff, 1967–1968.
In June 1967 Secretary of
Defense Robert McNamara
asked Gelb to write a history of
U.S. policy and involvement in
Vietnam. He and 35 others
worked for 18 months to produce
the 7,000-plus page history,
which became known as the
Pentagon Papers.

See also: Pentagon Papers.

Geneva and Hague Conventions. Series of international conferences beginning in 1864 that established laws for war, particularly with regard to treatment of prisoners. During the Vietnam War U.S. forces generally treated prisoners in conformity with the Geneva and Hague conventions. The South Vietnamese and South Koreans, who were not under U.S. command, frequently did not, nor did the North Vietnamese nor the National Liberation Front.

See also: Chemical Warfare; Tiger Cages.

Geneva Conference, 1954. On 8 May 1954, the day after the French defeat at Dien Bien Phu, representatives of the People's Republic of China (PRC), France, Great Britain, the Soviet Union, U.S., Cambodia, Laos, the State of Vietnam, and the Viet Minh met in Geneva, Switzerland to decide the political fate of Indochina.

The Viet Minh, who controlled most of Vietnam, wanted the total withdrawal of French forces and the establishment of an independent government led by Ho Chi Minh. The French hoped to retain influence in the south, but could no longer pursue the war. U.S. Secretary of State John Foster Dulles told the U.S. delegation to participate only as an "interested nation."

After two months of negotiating, the delegates reached an agreement. On 21 July 1954 France and the Viet Minh agreed to a temporary partition of Vietnam along the seventeenth parallel and a cease-fire. The accords also provided for the peaceful withdrawal of French troops from the north and Viet Minh troops from the south, prohibited the introduction of new forces and the establishment of foreign military bases, and restricted future military alliances. The agreement established a cease-fire and the removal of forces from Cambodia and Laos, and prohibited those countries from entering into military alliances or permitting foreign bases on their soil. To unify Vietnam, the agreement provided for free elections in North and South Vietnam in 1956, supervised by an International Control Commission (ICC).

France, Great Britain, the PRC, and the Soviet Union endorsed the accords. The Viet Minh did not sign them, nor did Ngo Dinh Diem, who became prime minister of the State of Vietnam. Dulles instructed the U.S. delegation not to sign, but the Eisenhower administration pledged to abide by the Geneva agreement.

See also: Bui Phat; Catholics; Da Nang; Demilitarized Zone; Dien Bien Phu; Dulles, John Foster; Eden, Anthony; Elections, South Vietnam 1955; Group 559; International Commission for Supervision and Control; Knowland, William F.; Laniel, Joseph; Le Duan; Mendès-France, Pierre; Molotov,

Vyacheslav M.; National Security Council; Ngo Dinh Luyen; Refugees; Smith, Walter Bedell; Southeast Asia Treaty Organization; Vietnam, Republic of; Viet Minh; Vo Nguyen Giap; Zhou Enlai.

Geneva Conference, 1961–1962. An international conference that met to try to resolve the Laotian civil war fought by the Soviet-backed Pathet Lao and the U.S.-backed Royal Lao government. The conference convened in Geneva in May with representatives of the major powers, members of the International Control Commission (ICC), and representatives of the nations of mainland Southeast Asia. On 23 July 1962, the delegates signed the Declaration on the Neutrality of Laos, which called for the withdrawal of foreign forces from Laos and reconciliation among the Lao factions. The United States complied, but the North Vietnamese, who never admitted the presence of North Vietnamese Army (NVA) troops in Laos, did not. The Pathet Lao opposed international inspection and enforcement of neutralization, thus enabling NVA forces to cross freely into the communist-held areas of Laos, including the Ho Chi Minh Trail.

See also: Harriman, W. Averell; Laos; Pathet Lao.

Germany, Federal Republic of (FRG). The Federal Republic of Germany officially supported U.S. policy in Vietnam. Its government provided economic and humanitarian aid to South Vietnam, averaging $7.5 million annually between 1966 and 1973, and including more than two hundred medical and technical personnel. Beginning in 1964, Chancellor Ludwig Erhart, a strong ally of President Johnson, agreed to purchase billions of dollars of U.S. military equipment to help finance U.S. policy. Continuing Johnson administration demands to step up payments and rising inflation rates from U.S. and FRG spending embarrassed Erhart's Christian Democratic/Free Democratic Party government and contributed to its collapse in 1966. U.S. preoccupation with Vietnam facilitated Chancellor Willy Brandt's 1969–1970 Ostpolitik diplomacy involving recognition of Eastern European states and normalization of ties with the USSR, which brought about renewed German influence in Europe.

The Vietnam War attracted increasing opposition from the German public during the late 1960s. Some U.S. soldiers stationed at German bases began antiwar agitation. A network of U.S. Army deserters formed Resist inside the Army (RITA), which staged demonstrations and published antiwar material throughout Europe. Starting in 1970, disgruntled U.S. soldiers sabotaged and firebombed U.S. Army property, protesting against the war and oppressive base conditions. The violence, sometimes led by black militants, peaked in mid 1971 and drew alarmed responses from military command. The United States moved to discharge many low-ranking soldiers in 1972 and staged a crackdown the following year.

See also: Erhardt, Ludwig; Free World; Resisters Inside the Army.

Gia Long (1762–1820), founding emperor of the Nguyen Dynasty. Born Nguyen Phuc Anh, Gia Long was the last surviving member of the Nguyen Lords, who had ruled southern Vietnam for two centuries. With the help of French bishop Pigneau de Behaine and French mercenaries he overthrew the Tay Son Dynasty in 1802 and took control of Vietnam from Hanoi to Saigon. Gia Long allowed French missionaries to remain in Vietnam, but did not convert to Christianity. Under his reign the imperial capital was moved to Hue and the empire's name changed from Dai Viet to Viet Nam. He was succeeded by his son, Chi Dam, who took the dynastic name Emperor Minh Mang.

See also: Béhaine, Pigneau de.

Giap, Vo Nguyen. *See* Vo Nguyen Giap

Gibbons, William Conrad (1927–), historian, author. Gibbons, a former U.S. foreign

policy specialist at the Library of Congress's Congressional Research Service, is the author of the highly acclaimed five-volume work, *The U.S. Government and the Vietnam War: Executive and Legislative Roles and Relationships* (1986–1998), a highly detailed study commissioned by the U.S. Senate Foreign Relations Committee in 1978.

Gio Linh. One of four U.S. Marine fire bases just south of the DMZ. Gio Linh was under constant threat from the North Vietnamese Army beginning in the summer of 1966.

See also: Con Thien; Demilitarized Zone; Dong Ha.

Glasser, Ronald J. (1940–), major, U.S. Army Medical Corps. Drafted into the Army, Dr. Glasser was assigned to an Army hospital in Japan in September 1968. His well-received memoir, *365 Days* (1971), deals with his experiences treating severely wounded soldiers evacuated from Vietnam.

Going After Cacciato (1978). National Book Award–winning novel by Tim O'Brien. A surrealistic tale of a U.S. Army draftee who decides to leave Vietnam and walk to Paris, along with his entire platoon. O'Brien served as an infantrymen with the 198th Light Infantry Brigade in Vietnam.

See also: O'Brien, Tim.

Goldberg, Arthur J.
(1908–1990), secretary of labor,
1961–1962; associate justice of
the Supreme Court, 1962–1965;
ambassador to the United
Nations (UN), 1965–1968. As
U.S. ambassador to the UN
Goldberg favored a halt to U.S.
bombing and a negotiated withdrawal, but his position forced
him to defend official U.S. policy.
By the start of 1968, Goldberg
realized that he was being
ignored by President Johnson.
He resigned as UN ambassador
in July and entered private life.
In 1970 he was an unsuccessful
candidate for governor of New
York, endorsing antiwar protests
and claiming to have always
favored de-escalation and a negotiated settlement.

See also: Wise Men.

Golden Triangle. Opium-poppy
growing mountainous region of
Southeast Asia, where the borders of Burma, Thailand, Laos
and China's Yunnan Province
meet. Large-scale heroin trafficking began in the region in 1969,
when a complex of seven laboratories opened. Some of the heroin
made its way to Vietnam where
by the middle of 1970, heroin
addiction spread rapidly through
the ranks of the U.S. military
forces.

See also: Drug Trafficking;
Drug Use, U.S. Military.

Goldman, Eric F. (1915–),
Princeton University historian;
Johnson administration "cultural
ambassador," 1963–1966.

Goldman organized the White
House Festival of the Arts in
1965 to enable President
Johnson to mingle with the
nation's artistic community. The
event angered and embarrassed
Johnson when several antiwar
artists boycotted it and others
used the occasion to criticize the
government's Vietnam policy.

See also: Johnson, Lyndon B.

Goldwater, Barry (1909–1998),
U.S. senator (R-Ariz.),
1953–1965, 1969–1987; 1964
Republican presidential nominee. During World War II, he
flew cargo planes in the Asian
theater and thereafter joined the
U.S. Air Force Reserve, retiring
as a general in 1967. After serving on the Phoenix city council,
he was elected to the Senate in
the Eisenhower landslide of
1952. By 1960, Goldwater had
emerged as the national leader
of a growing conservative movement that united cultural
traditionalists, economic libertar-
ians, and fervent anti-
communists. Along with most of
his followers, Goldwater lacked
the skepticism toward military
intervention abroad that had
characterized earlier, so-called
isolationist conservatism. In
1963 and early 1964, Goldwater,
a leading conservative, cited
Johnson administration policy in
Vietnam as an example of U.S.
failure to seek "total victory" over
communism. He called for
expanding the war into North
Vietnam and spoke of using
nuclear weapons to defoliate
infiltration routes. During the

1964 presidential campaign he and President Johnson privately agreed to say little about Vietnam. Although Vietnam was not central to the campaign, Goldwater's earlier advocacy of escalation contributed to his overwhelming defeat. Out of office during the next four years, he spoke out in favor of total conventional war in Vietnam instead of incremental escalation. Elected to the Senate again in 1968 Goldwater urged President Nixon to carry the war to North Vietnam, assailed liberals for promoting new isolationism that strengthened the North Vietnamese during peace talks, opposed amnesty for "draft dodgers," and insisted that the war was lost "at home."

See also: Gulf of Tonkin Resolution; Rules of Engagement; Appendix E, "Gulf of Tonkin Resolution."

Goodacre, Glenna (1939–), New Mexico artist whose 2,000-pound, 6-foot-8-inch bronze statue of three women nurses attending a wounded U.S. soldier is the centerpiece of the Vietnam Women's Memorial, dedicated near the Vietnam Veterans Memorial in Washington, D.C., 11 November 1993.

See also: Evans, Diane Carlson; Vietnam Women's Memorial.

Good Morning, Vietnam (1987). Film directed by Barry Levinson, starring Robin Williams as a U.S. Army radio disc jockey in Saigon. A comedy, the film also deals with the main character's fight against the military hierarchy.

Goodpaster, Andrew J. (1915–), U.S. Army general. Goodpaster served as the deputy to U.S. Military Assistance Command, Vietnam commander Creighton Abrams from 1968–1969 and then became Supreme Allied Commander in Europe. He served in that position, often facing hostility from U.S. allies because of the continuing war in Vietnam, until 1974.

Good Scent From a Strange Mountain (1992). Robert Olen Butler's collection of short stories, each of which tells the story of a Vietnamese expatriate living in Louisiana. Winner of the Pulitzer Prize for fiction. Butler served as a U.S. Army intelligence specialist in Vietnam.

See also: Butler, Robert Olen.

Go Tell the Spartans (1978). Film directed by Ted Post dealing with the disastrous experiences of U.S. military advisers in Vietnam in 1964. Praised by reviewers as a prophetic early Vietnam War film.

Goulding, Phil G. (1921–1998), chief Defense Department spokesman, 1967–1969. Goulding, a WWII Navy veteran, was a journalist before joining the Pentagon in 1965. During the height of the Vietnam War,

Goulding unknowingly misled reporters about the war's progress. He wrote *Confirm or Deny: Informing the People on National Security* (1970).

Gracey, Douglas (1894–1964), British major general; commander of British Expeditionary Forces, Indochina, 1945–1946. Sent to Southern Vietnam in September 1945 to disarm the Japanese, General Gracey refused Ho Chi Minh's request to turn civil and military control over to his fledgling government, and, instead, returned power to the French in Saigon. Gracey led French and British troops against Viet Minh forces in the Mekong Delta and was made an honorary French citizen. He left Vietnam in January 1946.

See also: Great Britain; Ho Chi Minh.

Graham, Donald E. (1945–), publisher, *Washington Post* (1979–); chairman of the board, Washington Post Company (1993–). Graham, a 1966 Harvard University graduate, was drafted into the U.S. Army and served as an information specialist with the 1st Cavalry Division in Vietnam in 1967–1968.

Grant, Zalin B. (1941–), journalist, author. Grant served as a U.S. Army intelligence officer in Vietnam. He reported from Vietnam for *Time* magazine from 1965–1967 and was the *New Republic's* Southeast Asia correspondent in 1968. His Vietnam

War books include *Survivors* (1975) and *Facing the Phoenix* (1991).

Gravel, Mike (1930–), U.S. senator (D-Alaska), 1969–1981. Gravel, a vocal critic of the Vietnam War, read from the Pentagon Papers in the U.S. Senate Subcommittee on Buildings and Grounds, which he chaired, on 29 June 1971. He later published his own edition of the papers. The incident led to a Supreme Court case, *Gravel v. U.S.,* in which the court held that the speech and debate clause of the Constitution, which protects legislative activity from prosecution, protected Senator Gravel's disclosure of the Pentagon Papers.

See also: Pentagon Papers.

Gray, Amlin (1947–), playwright. Gray, who served with the U.S. Army in Vietnam, is the author of highly regarded surrealistic, farcical play, *How I Got That Story,* in which a newspaper reporter tells the story of the Vietnam War.

Great Britain. After disarming the Japanese in Indochina at the end of WWII, Great Britain helped reestablish French power in Indochina and then withdrew in 1946. During the 1954 French crisis at Dien Bien Phu, President Dwight D. Eisenhower requested British support for a U.S. air strike to aid the French forces, but Prime Minister Winston Churchill refused the request. Great Britain co-chaired the 1954 Geneva Conference and supported the political division of Vietnam at the 17th parallel. Until 1962, the British government openly opposed U.S. military intervention in Vietnam. From 1962 to 1968 Britain provided only moral support for the U.S. effort. Prime Minister Harold Wilson, in power from 1964 to 1970, prevented formal British participation in the war and did not contribute war materiel.

Although both the Labour and Conservative parties supported the bombing of the Democratic Republic of Vietnam (DRV) following the Gulf of Tonkin incident, Wilson privately opposed continuation of the bombing and advocated a negotiated settlement. Great Britain supported the United States in part because it needed U.S. financial help to stabilize the British currency. Thus, in March 1965 Great Britain did not join the International Control Commission's condemnation of the U.S. bombing of the DRV. By December, however, Wilson strongly opposed such bombing and conveyed his position to President Lyndon B. Johnson. Great Britain attempted peace missions in 1965, 1966, and 1968, all of which failed. The student movement in Britain opposed the Vietnam War and British complicity in the late 1960s. The government supported President Nixon's Vietnamization policy, the mining of North Vietnamese ports, and the continued bombing of the

Democratic Republic of Vietnam. It refused to condemn the 1970 invasion of Cambodia despite sharp criticism in Parliament, pushing instead for a new Geneva convention.

See also: Dien Bien Phu; Free World; Geneva Conference, 1954; Geneva and Hague Conventions; International Reaction; Wilson, Harold.

Great Society. President Lyndon Johnson's plan, much of which became law, to lift millions of Americans out of poverty and provide housing, health care, education, and equal opportunity to all. Johnson, faced with being blamed by conservatives for the "loss" of Vietnam to communism, felt bound to preserve an anticommunist South Vietnam. He believed that the support he would gain from his anticommunist stance on Vietnam would carry over into support for the passage of the Great Society programs. As the Vietnam War escalated, its costs skyrocketed, threatening the funding for domestic programs. Johnson's congressional allies and supporters who had fought for the Great Society turned against him because of the war. The war so consumed Johnson that he had little time or energy for his domestic agenda.

See also: Fulbright, J. William; Johnson, Lyndon B.

Green Berets. *See* Special Forces, U.S. Army

Green Berets, The (1968). Film directed by and starring John Wayne based on the 1965 novel by Robin Moore. The only big Hollywood film about Vietnam produced during the war, *The Green Berets* resembles WWII U.S. war films in its entirely positive portrayal of the American war effort and completely negative depiction of the enemy.

Greene, Graham (1904–1991), British novelist whose 1955 novel, *The Quiet American*, which deals with American CIA agents and State Department officials in Vietnam in the early 1950s, is widely regarded as the seminal work of Vietnam War literature.

See also: Quiet American, The.

Greene, Wallace M. Jr. (1907–), U.S. Marine Corps commandant, 1964–1968. Greene strongly supported John F. Kennedy's policy in Vietnam. In May 1965, he advocated an increased combat role for the U.S. Marines. Greene subsequently maintained an optimistic view of U.S. prospects in Vietnam, despite his prediction that pacification would take approximately 10 years to accomplish. He retired in January 1968, just before the Tet Offensive.

See also: Combined Action Program.

Gritz, James G. "Bo" (1940–), retired U.S. Army Special Forces Lieutenant Colonel who led a privately sponsored two-week expedition into Laos in February 1983 searching for American Vietnam War POWs. The unsuccessful mission was criticized by State and Defense Department officials and the National League of Families of American Prisoners and Missing in Southeast Asia.

See also: POW/MIA Controversy.

Groom, Winston (1944–), novelist. Groom, who served as a U.S. Army 4th Infantry Division lieutenant in Vietnam, is the author of the Vietnam War novel, *Better Times Than These* (1978). His comic novel, *Forrest Gump* (1986), centering on a character awarded the Medal of Honor for heroism in Vietnam, was made into a popular 1994 film.

Groupements Administratifs Mobiles Opérationnels (GAMOS). Early 1950s pacification teams made up of civilians and military forces aimed at securing popular support as French control of Vietnam began to weaken. On 1 January 1953, a new entity, the Regional Forces and Provincial Forces (RF/PF), was added to help the GAMOS teams.

See also: France; Pacification; Regional/Popular Forces.

Group 559. In May 1959, while claiming to respect the Geneva Conference ban on intervention, North Vietnam created a secret army logistical unit code-named Group 559 to supply Viet Cong forces in the South. Under Maj.

Vo Bam, a few hundred engineers and laborers began construction of the Ho Chi Minh Trail in Laos. By 1960, tons of arms, ammunition, supplies, and trained cadres flowed along the trail into South Vietnam. Bam commanded five thousand troops and a regiment of engineers by 1963. Members of Group 559 carried heavy loads on foot, bicycle, and truck. When U.S. bombing of the trail began in 1965, Group 559 was reorganized under direct authority of North Vietnam's Communist Central Committee and commanded by Gen. Phan Trong Tue.

See also: Ho Chi Minh Trail.

Gruening, Ernest (1887–1974), U.S. senator (D-Alaska), 1959–1969. An early critic of U.S. involvement in Vietnam, Gruening and Sen. Wayne L. Morse cast the only votes against the Gulf of Tonkin Resolution in 1964. Gruening subsequently criticized the war from the Senate floor, in public appearances, and in the media. Beginning in May 1965, he voted against every military appropriations bill. Partly because of his position on the war, Gruening was defeated by Mike Gravel in the 1968 Democratic Senate primary.

See also: Gravel, Mike; Gulf of Tonkin Resolution; Morse, Wayne L; Appendix E, "Gulf of Tonkin Resolution."

Guam Conference. A largely symbolic meeting in March 1967 between President Lyndon Johnson and the South Vietnamese. Johnson sought to demonstrate the continuing U.S. commitment to an independent, anticommunist South Vietnam. During the conference Johnson pressed South Vietnam for a greater effort on its pacification program, while the South Vietnamese requested increased U.S. military commitment.

Gulf of Tonkin Incident. Actions that took place on 2 and 4 August 1964 in the Gulf of Tonkin off the North Vietnamese coast. On 2 August, the U.S. destroyer *Maddox*, engaged in a secret, intelligence-gathering DeSoto mission, reported that it was fired on by North Vietnamese torpedo boats in international waters. On 4 August the Maddox and another U.S. destroyer, the *C. Turner Joy*, reported a second attack. U.S. Navy commanders told Secretary of Defense Robert McNamara that unreliable radio and sonar contacts made it difficult for them to confirm the attacks. President Johnson nevertheless ordered retaliatory air strikes against North Vietnamese torpedo boat bases and oil storage depots. The incident led to congressional passage of the Gulf of Tonkin Resolution, giving President Johnson the authority to wage war in Vietnam.

See also: DeSoto Missions; Gulf of Tonkin Resolution; Appendix E, "Gulf of Tonkin Resolution."

Gulf of Tonkin Resolution.
Congressional resolution submitted by the Johnson administration on 5 August 1964 in the wake of the 2 and 4 August Tonkin Gulf incidents in which two U.S. destroyers reported that they were fired upon by North Vietnamese boats in international waters in the Gulf of Tonkin. The resolution, which when passed would have the force of law, authorized the president to take "all necessary measures to repel any armed attacks against the forces of the United States and to prevent further aggression" in Vietnam. Congress approved the resolution, which gave Johnson broad authority to conduct the war in Vietnam, on 7 August. The only dissenting votes were cast by Senators Wayne L. Morse of Oregon and Ernest Gruening of Alaska. During the process, Johnson did not inform Congress about the circumstances of the incidents or of the covert operations the U.S. vessels had been conducting. In 1970 Congress repealed the Gulf of Tonkin Resolution following the Nixon administration's incursion into Cambodia.

See also: Bundy, William P.; Fulbright, J. William; Gruening, Ernest; Gulf of Tonkin Incident; Morse, Wayne L.; War Powers Resolution; Appendix E, "Gulf of Tonkin Resolution."

H-13 Helicopter. *See* OH-13 Helicopter

H-21 Helicopter. *See* CH-21 Helicopter

HH-3 Helicopter. U.S. Air Force and Coast Guard long-range helicopter known as the "Jolly Green Giant." The Sikorsky HH-3 was used as a rescue and transport helicopter in Vietnam beginning in 1965. The Air Force versions were known as the CH-3A and CH-3E; the Coast Guard's was designated the HH-3E.

See also: Helicopters.

Habib, Philip (1920–1992), Foreign Service officer, 1949–1987; counselor for political affairs, U.S. embassy in Saigon, 1965–1967. In 1967 Habib led a State Department task force to examine Vietnam policy. Believing that the Saigon government could not survive without U.S. military support, Habib advocated a bombing halt and peace negotiations. In 1968 Habib was the highest ranking career diplomat on the U.S. negotiating team at the Paris peace talks. When Henry Cabot Lodge and Lawrence Walsh resigned in November 1969 Habib became acting head of the delegation. Nixon replaced him with David Bruce in July 1970.

See also: Paris Peace Accords; Appendix F, "Paris Peace Accords."

Hackworth, David H. (1931–), lieutenant colonel, U.S. Army. One of the Army's most highly decorated officers when he retired in 1971, Hackworth spent four years in Vietnam. After coming home, he appeared on ABC-TV's "Issues and Answers" and attacked his fellow officers for their ticket-punching careerism and for wasting lives in pursuit of combat honors so they could get promoted. He subsequently retired from the military and moved to Australia. Hackworth told his life story in a memoir, *About Face* (1989).

Haig, Alexander M. (1924–), general, U.S. Army. Haig served in Vietnam and was wounded in 1966 while commanding the 1st Battalion, 26th Infantry, 1st Infantry Division, and later received the Distinguished Service Cross after the battle of Ap Gu. Haig became Henry Kissinger's military assistant at the National Security Council in 1971 and U.S. Army vice chief of staff in 1973. Nixon appointed him White House chief of staff in April 1973. Nixon used Haig to persuade President Thieu to accept the Paris accords.

See also: Nixon, Richard M.

Hainan Island. Island in the South China Sea, part of the People's Republic of China. Hainan Island was the site during the Vietnam War of a secret port used to ship supplies to communist forces in Vietnam.

See also: People's Republic of China.

Haiphong. The primary port and a major industrial center in North Vietnam. The city stands along the Cua Cam River, some 48 kilometers (30 miles) inland from the Gulf of Tonkin. Railroads, rivers, and roads connect the city to Hanoi, 112 kilometers (70 miles) to the northwest. During the colonial period, the French developed the city as a seaport and railroad hub, and promoted industry using nearby coal and zinc mines.

The Hanoi-Haiphong corridor was an economic center for the Democratic Republic of Vietnam (DRV) during the Vietnam War. Extensive aid from the Soviet Union and the People's Republic of China (PRC) developed heavy industryin the region, including a railyard and shipyard, phosphate plant, fish cannery, cement factory, and electric power plant. The city was the second largest in the DRV, with a population in 1960 of 369,000.

Haiphong was the site of extensive military hostilities beginning in World War II. In 1943, the Allies bombed the city, which was occupied by the Japanese. In 1946 the French navy, after a dispute with the DRV over authority in Haiphong, opened fire on the native section of the city. The French naval bombardment, known as the Haiphong Incident, killed more than one thousand civilians and

precipitated the slide toward war between the French and Viet Minh forces. Haiphong was a pivotal distribution hub for Soviet military aid. The U.S. military pressed for air strikes in the area and for operations to close the harbor. In September 1967, as part of Operation Rolling Thunder, President Johnson authorized air raids to disrupt transportation routes around the city. In April 1972 President Nixon allowed extensive bombing of military installations and storage areas in Haiphong. Following North Vietnam's Easter Offensive, Nixon approved the mining of Haiphong harbor on 8 May, an operation long advocated by the U.S. military. Later in 1972, Nixon ordered massive bombing of the Hanoi-Haiphong corridor. During the "Christmas bombings" of 18–29 December, U.S. planes dropped seventeen thousand tons of ordnance.Nixon ordered the strikes to pressure the DRV to negotiate accords formalizing U.S. withdrawal. After the signing of the Paris accords, the U.S. Navy helped clear the harbor of mines to reopen the port.

See also: Rolling Thunder, Operation.

Hai Van Pass. Winding mountain pass in north central Vietnam at the boundary between Quang Nam and Thua Tien Provinces that once formed the north-south divide between Annam and Champa. During the Vietnam War, Route 1, which runs through the Hai Van Pass, was the main U.S. supply route in northern South Vietnam.

See also: Demilitarized Zone.

Halberstam, David (1934–), *New York Times* Vietnam correspondent, 1962–1964. Halberstam came to Vietnam in 1962 believing in the basic aims of the American effort. He soon began questioning U.S. optimism for the authoritarian South Vietnamese regime. Halberstam's reporting of problems in the Army of the Republic of Vietnam and the success of the Viet Cong forces in the Mekong Delta earned the ire of Kennedy administration officials. Halberstam won a Pulitzer Prize for his reporting. He went on to write a Vietnam War novel, *One Very Hot Day* (1967), and three nonfiction books on the war, including *The Best and the Brightest* (1972), an acclaimed examination of the Kennedy and Johnson Vietnam War policy making.

Haldeman, Joe (1943–), science-fiction novelist, author of more than twenty novels and short stories, including the award-winning novel, *The Forever War* (1975), and the Vietnam War–influenced *War Year* (1972) and *1968* (1995). Haldeman served as a U.S. Army combat engineer attached to the 4th Infantry Division in Vietnam in 1968.

Halperin, Morton (1938–), deputy assistant secretary of defense, 1966–1969; senior official, National Security Council (NSC), 1969–1970. Halperin resigned from the NSC to protest the 1970 invasion of Cambodia. From 1969 to 1971, President Nixon and Henry Kissinger ordered 24-hour wire surveillance of Halperin's home as part of a campaign to investigate leaks from the White House. Halperin sued the government in 1972 over the wiretapping. After a 20-year legal suit, he received a letter of apology from Kissinger.

See also: Kissinger, Henry.

Hamblen, Donald N. (1932–), former U.S. Marine sergeant. Hamblen, whose left leg was amputated following a 1962 parachute jumping accident, served a 30-month Vietnam War tour beginning in 1965 with the covert Studies and Observation Group (SOG). He is believed to be the only U.S. Marine ever to serve in combat with a prosthesis.

Hamburger Hill. Term coined by U.S. soldiers for Ap Bia Mountain, the site of bloody fighting in the A Shau Valley near the Laotian border. In a 10-day battle in May 1969, the 101st Airborne Division successfully overtook a well-fortified North Vietnamese Army (NVA) position on the mountain. The U.S. Air Force delivered more than one million pounds of napalm and other ordnance to support the operation. The battle culminated with brutal bunker-to-bunker fighting. Fifty-six U.S.

soldiers were killed, 420 were wounded; NVA losses were estimated at 505. The U.S. forces abandoned the hill soon after the fighting, and the North Vietnamese retook the position a month later.

See also: Ap Bia.

Hamburger Hill (1987). Vietnam war combat film directed by John Irvin that takes a fictional look at the 1969 battle of the same name. The film is notable for its unusually brutal, realistic depiction of combat.

Hamlet Evaluation Survey (HES). Computerized system developed in 1967 by Robert W. Komer's Civil Operations and Revolutionary Development Support (CORDS) pacification group designed to keep track of the loyalty of all villages in South Vietnam.

See also: Civil Operations and Revolutionary Development Support; Komer, Robert W.; Pacification.

Hammer and Anvil. Military tactic often used by U.S., South Vietnamese and Korean forces in Vietnam. In a typical hammer-and-anvil operation, infantry units would be inserted into an upland valley to seek out and drive opposing forces toward the coast, where other forces would block their path. The inserted forces would be the hammer and the coastal plain and the natural barrier formed by the sea the anvil or killing zone.

H & I Fire. *See* Harassment-and-Interdiction Fire

Hanoi. Northern Vietnamese city, capital of French protectorate of Tonkin (1884–1887), of French Indochina (1887–1946), of Democratic Republic of Vietnam (1954–1976), of Socialist Republic of Vietnam (1976–). Located 120 kilometers (70 miles) inland from the South China Sea at the center of the Red River Delta, with a metropolitan population of about 2.6 million, Hanoi is one of Vietnam's oldest cities. It first became a capital in the eleventh century A.D. French troops took the city in 1883, and French cultural influence had a lasting impact on Hanoi's architecture and ambiance. Hanoi was the home of Vietnamese nationalist resistance to France beginning in the 1920s. Ho Chi Minh proclaimed Vietnam's independence in Hanoi in 1945, and the Indochina War started there one year later. Viet Minh forces reentered Hanoi in triumph when the French departed in 1954. As the main industrial center and railroad hub of North Vietnam, Hanoi underwent periodic U.S. bombing after 1966. The heaviest came during Operation Rolling Thunder in 1967 and Operations Linebacker and Linebacker II in 1972.

The United States did not target nonmilitary installations such as schools, homes, and hospitals, but these nonetheless sustained considerable damage from accidental bomb strikes.

About 1,300 people died in the Christmas bombings of December 1972, when U.S. warplanes dropped 17,000 tons of bombs on Hanoi in 12 days. Hanoi's wartime residents withstood air raids, drills, rationing, and shortages as well as "revolutionary zeal" campaigns, forced labor in underground factories, and compulsory evacuation to the countryside. Hanoi was not subjected, however, to the kind of saturation bombing that was inflicted on German and Japanese cities in World War II.

See also: Antiaircraft Defenses; Ho Chi Minh; Lao Dong; Linebacker and Linebacker II, Operations; Red River (Song Hong) Delta; Socialist Republic of Vietnam; Viet Minh; Vietnam, Democratic Republic of.

Hanoi-Haiphong Corridor. A Democratic Republic of Vietnam economic center during the Vietnam War. Extensive aid from the Soviet Union and the People's Republic of China developed heavy industry in the region, including a rail yard and shipyard, phosphate plant, fish cannery, cement factory, and electric power plant.

See also: Haiphong; Hanoi.

Hanoi Hannah. The U.S. troops' nickname for Trinh Thi Ngo, a Vietnamese woman who broadcast propaganda over Radio Hanoi in English into South Vietnam beginning in 1965 to try to destroy morale among U.S. soldiers.

Hanoi Hilton. U.S. POW nickname for Hoa Lo prison, the former French colonial jail near the center of Hanoi. It was the most renowned of the North Vietnamese prisons that together housed more than seven hundred U.S. prisoners of war (POWs) between 1964 and 1973.

After the unsuccessful U.S. raid on the Son Tay prison complex in 1970, North Vietnam concentrated its U.S. POWs in the Hanoi The North Vietnamese insisted that the Hoa Lo captives were political internees rather than POWs, and therefore were not covered by the Geneva Conventions. As a result, conditions at Hoa Lo were horrendous, and prisoners were punished for anything that their captors considered a breach of rules. Torture and other forms of physical and mental abuse were used routinely.

See also: POW/MIA Controversy.

Harassment-and-Interdiction Fire (H&I). The term for U.S. bombing and artillery shelling of probable concentrations of communist forces without direct observation of targeted sites. H&I fire was designed to maximize the use of available firepower for disrupting suspected enemy operations. A procedure for coordinating heavy weaponry in the U.S. military's rules of engagement, H&I fire required clearance from South Vietnamese officials, which was usually given on a routine basis.

Because of its indiscriminate nature, the United States authorized H&I bombing or shelling mostly in remote areas.In 1966, nearly two-thirds of the total tonnage of U.S. ordnance consisted of H&I fire, much of which involved B-52 carpet bombing. Despite the massive amount of delivered firepower, H&I attacks had a negligible effect on North Vietnamese and Viet Cong resources while causing considerable civilian destruction and injury.

Hardhats. Officially known as the National Hard Hats of America, the Hardhats were a group of construction workers who organized to support the Vietnam War during the Nixon administration. The Hardhats conducted counter-demonstrations during antiwar protests, sometimes clashing violently with opponents of the war. On 8 May 1970, 200 New York City construction workers attacked student demonstrators protesting the invasion of Cambodia, injuring 70.

Harkins, Paul D. (1904–1984), general, U.S. Army; MACV commander, 1962–1964. A cavalry officer and Gen. George Patton's protégé in World War II, Paul Harkins was the U.S. Eighth Army chief of staff in Korea, where he also commanded two infantry divisions. President Kennedy named Harkins the first commander of the U.S. Military Assistance Command, Vietnam (COMUSMACV) on

13 February 1962. For two years he sent positive reports to Washington, D.C., about President Diem's government and the war, encouraging President Kennedy and his advisers to believe that victory was imminent. Harkins severely disciplined subordinates who criticized Diem, and tailored the itineraries of visiting dignitaries to hide uncomplimentary facts. He countered any pressure on Diem to liberalize his regime, promising continued U.S. support. Kennedy sent independent fact-finding missions to circumvent Harkins, who was replaced by his subordinate, General William Westmoreland, on 20 June 1964.

See also: Military Assistance Command, Vietnam (MACV); Taylor-McNamara Report.

Harriman, W. Averell (1891–1986), assistant U.S. secretary of state for Far Eastern affairs, 1961–1963; undersecretary of state for political affairs, 1963–1965; ambassador-at-large, with responsibility for Southeast Asia, 1965–1969. Harriman consistently opposed a military solution in Vietnam, believing that a permanent settlement could be reached only through political and diplomatic means.

As chief U.S. representative at the 1962 Geneva Conference, Harriman negotiated a neutrality agreement for Laos. With the widening commitment to Vietnam, Harriman expressed doubts about the ability of President Ngo Dinh Diem to survive, warned that the United States should not stake its prestige on events in Vietnam, and urged a diplomatic settlement of Vietnam followed by a U.S. withdrawal. He became increasingly critical of South Vietnam's President Ngo Dinh Diem, and in 1963 helped set in motion the coup against Diem. In 1968, Harriman, one of the "wise men," advised Johnson to deescalate in Vietnam. The president subsequently named Harriman to head the U.S. delegation at the Paris peace talks. Harriman urged a compromise with the North Vietnamese, but Johnson rejected his proposal. In 1969, Henry Cabot Lodge replaced him. Later that year Harriman endorsed the 15 October Moratorium antiwar protest.

See also: Cooper, Chester; Forrestal, Michael; Geneva Conference, 1961–1962; Hilsman, Roger; Ngo Dinh Diem; Paris Accords; Vietnam Moratorium Committee; Xuan Thuy.

Harold E. Holt, USS. U.S. Navy frigate stationed near the Philippines in May 1975 to help Vietnamese boat people. The *USS Harold E. Holt* landed a boarding party on 15 May 1975 on the *SS Mayaguez*, a U.S. container ship that had been seized off the Cambodian coast three days earlier. The boarding party found the ship abandoned.

See also: Mayaguez Incident.

Hasford, Gustav (1947–1993), novelist. Hasford served as a U.S. Marine journalist in Vietnam in 1967–1968. His Vietnam War novel, *The Short-Timers* (1978), was the basis for the acclaimed film *Full Metal Jacket* (1987).

See also: Full Metal Jacket.

Hastings, Operation. July 1966 battle between a joint U.S. Marine–South Vietnamese Army force and a North Vietnamese Army division in the Song Ngan Valley in I Corps.

Hatfield, Mark O. (1922–), U.S. Senator (R-Ore.), 1967– . Hatfield was a leading antiwar Senator during the Vietnam War. He co-sponsored an amendment in 1970 to cut off funds for the U.S. war effort.

See also: Hatfield-McGovern Amendment; Senate, U.S.

Hatfield-McGovern Amendment. Legislation sponsored by prominent antiwar U.S. Sens. Mark Hatfield (R-Ore.) and George McGovern (D-S.D.). Following the U.S. incursion into Cambodia in 1970, the amendment would have cut off funds for the Vietnam War after 31 December 1970 and withdrawn all U.S. forces from Vietnam. The amendment was rejected by the U.S. Senate in 1970 and in 1971 when the cut-off date was changed to 31 December 1971.

See also: Congress, U.S.; McGovern, George.

Hathcock, Carlos J. II (1942–), U.S. Marine sergeant. Hathcock, a U.S. Marine sniper, in two Vietnam tours of duty was credited with 300 kills, 93 of them confirmed, more than any other sniper in Marine Corps history.

Hauteclocque, Philippe de.
See Leclerc, Jacques Philippe

Hawk, David (1945–),

a former theology student and campaign worker for Sen. Eugene McCarthy. Hawk was one of the organizers of the Vietnam Moratorium Committee (VMC) in the spring of 1969. The VMC was a moderate antiwar group whose aim was to arrange a monthly nationwide protests against U.S. involvement in Vietnam.

See also: Vietnam Moratorium Committee.

Hawks and Doves.

Labels referring to supporters and opponents of U.S. involvement in Vietnam. The labels were used in the mid 1960s to differentiate between groups of government policymakers who differed in their war views and to underscore divisions within the Johnson administration and Congress. More broadly, the labels identified segments of the American public. Generally, a dove favored ending the U.S. role in Vietnam, and a hawk was determined to see the United States win the conflict at all costs.

In the early stages of U.S. intervention, few officials opposed administration policy, and President Johnson was concerned primarily about hawks— Republicans and conservative Democrats—who would attack him if he "lost" South Vietnam to the communists. By mid 1967, however, the dove and hawk factions within the administration were discernible.

The dove faction included George Ball and Averell Harriman at the State Department and Secretary of Defense Robert McNamara and his aides Paul Warnke, Townsend Hoopes, and John McNaughton. In addition to the Joint Chiefs of Staff (JCS), the hawk ranks included Secretary of State Dean Rusk, national security adviser Walt Rostow, and the leadership of the Central Intelligence Agency (CIA).

Hawks and doves were also clearly defined in Congress, with dove Sen. J. William Fulbright of the Foreign Relations Committee and hawk Sen. John C. Stennis of the Armed Services Committee taking the lead for their respective positions. The hawks in the administration and Congress subscribed to the domino theory and believed that the United States could not afford to lose in Vietnam. The doves, in turn, did not think that Vietnam was strategically significant and questioned whether the United States could win the war. Initially, the doves did not advocate disengagement but sought to block further troop deployments and pushed for a bombing halt. The Tet Offensive of 1968 caused most doves to support an end to U.S. involvement. Hawks reacted to the Tet Offensive by calling for more troops and bombing campaigns against North Vietnam.

After Richard Nixon took office, hawks in Congress pressed him to take aggressive action against North Vietnam if the Paris peace talks proved unproductive. The doves attacked Nixon's policies and called for a complete withdrawal of U.S. troops by late 1970. When Nixon ordered the mining of Haiphong harbor and increased bombing of North Vietnam in 1972, congressional doves reacted angrily, introducing resolutions designed to end U.S. participation in the war. Their most notable victory came in November 1973, when, over Nixon's veto, Congress successfully passed the War Powers Resolution, which limited the president's ability to carry out military action without congressional approval.

Hayden, Tom (1940–), antiwar activist; a founder and the first leader of Students for a Democratic Society (SDS). Hayden went to North Vietnam in 1965 and 1967 with other antiwar activists. He was arrested for helping lead the antiwar demonstrations at the 1968 Democratic National Convention in Chicago, and became one of the "Chicago Seven" charged, and later acquitted of, conspiracy. Hayden and his future wife Jane Fonda led the "Free the Army" campaign which held meetings at sites near military installations to influence U.S. military

personnel to question the Vietnam War.

See also: Chicago Seven; Fonda, Jane; Students for a Democratic Society.

Hayes, Anna Mae (1920–), U.S. Army general, chief, U.S. Army Nurse Corps, 1967–1971. A veteran of WWII and the Korean War, Hayes and Elizabeth Hoisington on 11 June 1970 became the first women in the U.S. armed services to attain the rank of general.

See also: Hoisington, Elizabeth P.; Women, U.S. Military.

Hayslip, Le Ly (1950–), Vietnamese author. Hayslip, born Phung Thi Le Ly, is the author of two well-received books, *When Heaven and Earth Changed Places* (1989) and *Child of War, Woman of Peace* (1993). The books tell Hayslip's life story, beginning with her childhood in a peasant family in a village outside Da Nang in the 1950s and ending with her move to the United States. The books were the basis for the Oliver Stone film, *Heaven and Earth* (1994).

Headquarters 333. Covert Royal Thai military unit that worked with U.S. intelligence on military and intelligence-collection activities in Laos. Beginning in 1962, Headquarters 333 recruited, trained and oversaw the battalions of Thai troops who fought clandestinely in Laos.

See also: Laos; Thailand.

Hearts and Minds. Phrase used to describe U.S. pacification efforts to win the allegiance of the South Vietnamese people to their government.

See also: Pacification.

Hearts and Minds (1973). Documentary film strongly critical of U.S. Vietnam War–making policy directed by Peter Davis. The film won the 1974 Academy Award for best documentary feature.

Heath, Donald (1894–1981), U.S. ambassador to Vietnam, Cambodia, and Laos, 1952–1954. A career Foreign Service officer, Heath became the first U.S. ambassador to Vietnam when the U.S. legation became an embassy. Stationed in Saigon, he also served as ambassador to Laos and Cambodia. Heath was sympathetic to the French and advocated a strong French role in Vietnam with minimal U.S. involvement. Despite early misgivings, Heath became a supporter of Ngo Dinh Diem and helped discourage a coup attempt by Gen. Nguyen Van Hinh in 1954. Gen. J. Lawton Collins replaced Heath in 1954.

See also: Ngo Dinh Diem; Nguyen Van Hinh.

Heaven and Earth (1993). Film directed by Oliver Stone that looks at the Vietnam War and its aftermath through the eyes of a Vietnamese woman. Based on Le Ly Hayslip's *When Heaven and Earth Changed Places* (1989)

and *Child of War, Woman of Peace* (1993).

See also: Hayslip, Le Ly; Stone, Oliver.

Heinemann, Larry (1944–), novelist. Heinemann, who served with the U.S. Army's 25th Infantry Division in Vietnam, is the author of two highly regarded Vietnam War novels, the autobiographical *Close Quarters* (1977), and *Paco's Story* (1986), which won the National Book Award for Fiction.

Helicopters. Rotary-winged, vertical takeoff and landing aircraft that came of age in U.S. hands as machines capable of combat. U.S. forces used helicopters to conduct rescues behind enemy lines in WWII and the Korean War; the French in Algeria and U.S. Marines in Korea used helicopters as battlefield transports; and the British conducted a helicopter assault in the 1956 Suez invasion. These, however, were small-scale operations, and the most important previous military use of helicopters was in evacuating U.S. battlefield casualties in Korea. Helicopters were used for a wide variety of tasks previously performed by other means: infantry assault, fire support, reconnaissance, and logistic support of troops in the field.

The first combat use of U.S. helicopters in Vietnam came in December 1961 and April 1962 when piston-engine Army H-21s and Marine H-34s were

employed in assault operations with Army of the Republic of Vietnam (ARVN) troops. The U.S. Army was by far the largest user of helicopters and fielded entire airmobile divisions with heli- copter transport, reconnaissance, and fire support organic to the division. Most notable was the 1st Cavalry Division (Airmobile). U.S. helicopters were last used in Vietnam in the evacuation of Saigon by U.S. Marine and Air Force helicopters on 29–30 April 1975.

The most important helicopter used in Vietnam was the tur- bine-engine UH-1 Huey, whose silhouette and rotor noise became symbols of the war. Modified Hueys carrying turret- ed machine guns, 40 mm grenade launchers, and rockets entered service in early 1962, and the AH-1G Cobra, which entered service in 1966, was the first helicopter gunship designed from the outset as such. Huey- equipped U.S. Army aeromedical evacuation (medevac) units res- cued tens of thousands of U.S., ARVN, and communist wounded under fire. The Marines used H-34s and CH-46s for the same purpose. Heavy-lift Army CH-54 "flying cranes," CH47s, and Marine CH-53s were used to transport artillery pieces and heavy loads of ammunition using external cargo slings. Army H-13 and OH-6 light observation heli- copters were the eyes of the U.S. infantry in the field. The Air Force used HH-3Es and HH-53s, refueled in flight by HC-130

tankers, to rescue downed avia- tors deep in communist-held territory. The Navy used carrier- based SH-3As for the same purpose.

See also: Aeromedical Evacuation; UH-1 Helicopter.

Helms, Richard M. (1913–), director, Central Intelligence Agency (CIA), 1966–1972. Helms served with the Office of Strategic Services (OSS) during WWII and worked his way up through the CIA to become the first career officer appointed Director of Central Intelligence (DCI). As CIA director during most of the Vietnam War, Helms often had to provide two presi- dents gloomy assessments of the war's progress. Still, Helms served as director longer than any other man, with the excep- tion of Allen Dulles. During the Johnson administration, Helms was at the center of a debate in 1966 over the appropriate level of U.S. bombing and the number of troops the United States should commit. Helms's position remained consistent throughout the war. The bombing, he believed, had not worked, neither breaking the resolve of the North Vietnamese, nor disrupting their supply lines to the south. In the late stages of the war, Helms came under attack from critics protesting covert CIA operations in Southeast Asia.During the Nixon administration, Nixon pressured Helms into involving the CIA in Watergate; the director first agreed, but then disengaged the CIA from the cover-up. Helms believed that Nixon's personal use of the CIA made it vulnerable to congressional attack. President Nixon dismissed Helms in November 1972.

See also: Central Intelligence Agency.

Heng Samrin (1934–), president, Khmer People's Revolutionary Council, 1979–1991; general secretary, People's Revolutionary Party of Kampuchea, 1981–1991. A communist since 1959, Heng Samrin rose to political commissar and deputy commander of Cambodia's Eastern Zone under the Khmer Rouge. In 1978, after an unsuccessful coup attempt against Cambodian Khmer Rouge leader Pol Pot, he fled to Vietnam and took charge of refugee Cambodians opposed to the Khmer Rouge. Samrin was named president of the People's Republic of Kampuchea when Vietnam occupied Cambodia in January 1979. He became general secretary two years later. Samrin ended the Khmer Rouge reign of terror, cultivated close ties with Moscow, and attempted economic reforms. After Vietnam's withdrawal from Cambodia in 1989, few countries recognized Samrin's regime. In 1991, Samrin was replaced as party secretary by Chea Sim. Prince Sihanouk returned from exile to replace Samrin as president in November 1991.

See also: Khmer Rouge; Sihanouk, Norodom.

Herbert, Anthony B. (1930–), lieutenant colonel, U.S. Army. In 1971 Herbert, a heavily decorated paratrooper, charged that his superior officers in Vietnam suppressed evidence of U.S. war crimes and harassed him into retirement. His claims were not confirmed, however, and CBS's television program *Sixty Minutes* later found that Herbert was relieved of command in 1969 because superiors considered him violently overzealous and unfit to be an Army officer. Herbert's resulting libel suit against CBS News was dismissed in 1986.

Herbicides. *See* Agent Orange; Chemical Warfare; Ranch Hand, Operation

Herr, Michael (1940–), journalist, author. Herr covered the Vietnam War in 1967 as a freelance correspondent for *Esquire* magazine. His book, *Dispatches* (1978), is regarded as an evocative journalistic rendering of the war as experienced by U.S. infantrymen.

Hersh, Seymour (1937–), journalist; winner of Pulitzer Prize for reporting the My Lai massacre. Hersh's report in 1969 was one factor that led to a lengthy U.S. Army investigation of the incident. Writing for the *New York Times* in 1974, Hersh exposed the Central Intelligence Agency's illegal domestic surveillance of opponents of the Vietnam War.

See also: My Lai.

Hershey, Lewis B.
(1893–1977), director of the
Selective Service System,
1948–1969. General Hershey
advocated using deferments and
exceptions. Rather than draft
men randomly from all walks of
life, Hershey preferred "chan-
nelling" them with "pressurized
guidance." He encouraged local
draft boards to threaten antiwar
college students with the induction by stripping away their
educational deferments.

See also: Selective Service.

Hickory II, Operation. May
1967 operation in which elements of the 3rd, 4th and 9th
U.S. Marine regiments engaged
in fierce fighting with several
North Vietnamese Army regiments just south of the DMZ.

See also: Demilitarized Zone;
Marines, U.S.

Higgins, Marguerite
(1920–1966), journalist. Higgins,
a *New York Herald Tribune* correspondent, won a Pulitzer Prize
for her coverage of the Korean
War. She went to Vietnam in the
early 1960s and was an outspoken proponent of the regime of
Ngo Dinh Diem and U.S. involvement in the fight against the
Viet Cong.

Hilsman, Roger (1919–), director, U.S. Department of State,
Bureau of Intelligence and
Research, 1961–1963; assistant
secretary of state for Far Eastern
affairs, 1963–1964. Hilsman
influenced U.S. counterinsurgency programs in Vietnam in

the early 1960s. He argued for
building popular support and iso-
lating the Viet Cong through the
Strategic Hamlet program.

In late 1962, Kennedy sent
Hilsman and Michael Forrestal
to Vietnam on a fact-finding mission. The resulting Hilsman-
Forrestal Report expressed reservations about U.S. policy in
Vietnam, but concluded that it
essentially was sound. Following
South Vietnamese President Ngo
Dinh Diem's repression of
Buddhists in 1963, Hilsman recommended that Kennedy
encourage a coup against Diem.
Together with Forrestal and W.
Averell Harriman, Hilsman prepared a cable instructing
Ambassador Henry Cabot Lodge
to warn Diem that he had to
reform or lose U.S. support. The
cable also instructed Lodge to
inform a group of South
Vietnamese Army generals that
the United States would not continue to support Diem if he
refused to cooperate. Hilsman
remained briefly as assistant
secretary of state in the Johnson
administration, although never
as an insider. He resigned in
early 1964.

See also: Forrestal, Michael;
Strategic Hamlet Program.

Hilsman-Forrestal Report.
1963 report by assistant secre-
tary of State for Far Eastern
Affairs Roger Hilsman and
National Security Council aide
Michael Forrestal on their
Vietnam fact-finding trip. The
report, commissioned by
President Kennedy, questioned

the stability of Ngo Dinh Diem's regime and expressed reservations about U.S. policy in Vietnam, but concluded that it essentially was sound.

See also: Forrestal, Michael; Hilsman, Roger; Ngo Dinh Diem.

Hmong. A migratory, highland Lao tribe. After the French seized Laos in the 1890s, the Hmong achieved an accommodation with the colonial administration punctuated by countless small conflicts and one major anticolonial revolt in 1919–1921. During WWII several Hmong clans took up arms to aid the French.

After the French withdrawal, the U.S. Central Intelligence Agency (CIA) recruited Touby Lyfoung's Hmong clans to fight the Pathet Lao communist guerrillas. By 1961, the CIA had 18 U.S. agents working with 9,000 Hmong. Their leader was Vang Pao, a Hmong officer who used the CIA's arms and air support to recruit Hmong villagers into a secret army of 30,000. When the Vietnam War spilled into Laos after 1965, the Hmong helped recover downed U.S. pilots, blocked communist offensives, and guarded radar that guided the bombing of North Vietnam. After 1968, Gen. Vang Pao converted his Hmong partisans from guerrillas into ground troops, and—backed by CIA air logistics and U.S. Air Force bombing— fought communist forces on the Plain of Jars. In 1974, the last CIA operatives left Laos. A year later, as the Pathet Lao took power, Gen. Vang Pao and a thousand of his loyalists fled in a limited U.S. airlift. In postwar Laos, conflicts erupted between the Hmong and the new socialist government, eventually forcing some 100,000 to flee into Thai refugee camps. In the late 1970s, Hmong families began migrating to the United States from the Thai camps.

See also: Air America; Pathet Lao; Vang Pao.

Hoa, Duong Quynh. *See* Duong Quynh Hoa

Hoa Hao. A Buddhist sect in South Vietnam founded by Huynh Phu So, a reformist Buddhist, in 1919. So, a faith healer, was regarded as a prophet by his followers. He based the sect on internal faith and simple prayers rather than on elaborate rituals. In the 1940s, the French arrested So and committed him to an insane asylum. During WWII, the Japanese freed So and armed the Hoa Hao. The sect turned anti-communist after the Viet Minh assassinated So in 1947, and split into three rival factions, all of which opposed Ngo Dinh Diem's pro-Catholic, anti-Buddhist regime. Sect leaders joined the Binh Xuyen and Cao Dai armies in opposition to Diem, who defeated them in 1955. The Hoa Hao sect was further crushed in 1956 when Ba Cut, one of its leaders, was publicly guillotined.

See also: Ba Cut; Binh Xuyen; Cao Dai; Duong Van Minh; Huynh Phu So.

Hoa Lo Prison. *See* Hanoi Hilton

Hoang Duc Nha (1941–), minister of information, Republic of Vietnam, 1973–1974. A cousin of President Thieu, Nha accompanied Thieu during meetings with Henry Kissinger in late 1972 concerning conditions for U.S. withdrawal. Nha advised Thieu to reject the peace agreement arranged between Kissinger and Le Duc Tho because it kept a North Vietnamese presence in the South. After the war, Nha escaped to the United States.

See also: Nguyen Van Thieu.

Hoang Xuan Lam (1928–), South Vietnamese Army general. Gen. Hoang Xuan Lam coordinated the massive 1971 South Vietnamese Army Operation Lam Son 719, in which his troops, with American artillery support, crossed into Laos to raid the Ho Chi Minh Trail. South Vietnamese President Nguyen Van Thieu then put General Lam in charge of all South Vietnamese troops in I Corps. He was relieved of that post following the 1972 North Vietnamese Easter Offensive.

See also: Easter Offensive; Lam Son 719.

Hobart. Royal Australian Navy guided missile destroyer that joined U.S. Navy vessels in the South China Sea off the coast of central Vietnam near Chu Lai on 31 March 1967.

See also: Australia.

Ho Chi Minh (1890–1969). The founder of the Vietnamese Communist Party (1930) and the first president of the Democratic Republic of Vietnam (1945–1969), the father of the Vietnamese revolution and the most influential political figure in modern Vietnam. Ho Chi Minh was born Nguyen That Thanh in a small village in central Vietnam. His father was a Confucian scholar who had served as an official in the Vietnamese imperial bureaucracy but resigned to protest French occupation of his country. Ho Chi Minh was educated at the prestigious National Academy *(Quoc Hoc)* in Hue. In Paris at the end of WWI he became involved in socialist political circles. Using the name Nguyen Ai Quoc (Nguyen the Patriot), he co-wrote a petition to the Allied leaders at Versailles to demand self-determination for those under colonial rule. The petition was ignored.

Ho joined the French Communist Party at its founding congress in 1920. In 1923 he went to Moscow to work at the headquarters of the Communist International (Comintern). The next year he went to Canton to form a Marxist-Leninist revolutionary organization in French Indochina. Ho formed the Vietnamese Revolutionary Youth League in 1925 as a training ground for a future communist party. In 1930, he presided over a meeting in Hong Kong which brought several factions into a single Vietnamese Communist Party, later renamed the Indochinese Communist Party (ICP). In May 1941, under Ho Chi Minh's guidance, the ICP announced the formation of a broad nationalist alliance, the League for the Independence of Vietnam (Viet Minh). The new group downplayed ideology and emphasized anti-imperialism and land reform.

During WWII, Ho Chi Minh shuttled between Vietnam and China to build support for the movement. Ho also worked with U.S. military units in south China. In August 1945, when Japan surrendered, the Viet Minh occupied Hanoi and declared the formation of the Democratic Republic of Vietnam (DRV). He adopted the pseudonym Ho Chi Minh ("He Who Enlightens") and became president of the new republic. During the fall of 1946 Ho Chi Minh sought to avoid hostilities, but differences between the Vietnamese and the French could not be resolved. In mid December, Viet Minh units attacked French installations and residential areas in Hanoi and the first Indochina conflict began.

During the war against the French, Ho Chi Minh played an active part in policy formulation, while Gen. Vo Nguyen Giap was chief military strategist. Ho was

a symbol of national resistance and was primarily responsible for dealings with the Soviet Union and the People's Republic of China. After the 1954 French defeat, Ho Chi Minh played an active part in formulating policy in the DRV. After the mid-1960s, his role in decision making, due to failing health, was primarily ceremonial. He died in September 1969.

See also: Comintern; Communism; Democratic Republic of Vietnam; French Communist Party; Indochinese Communist Party; Viet Minh; Vietnamese Communist Party; Vo Nguyen Giap.

Ho Chi Minh Campaign. North Vietnam's name, to honor the father of the Vietnamese revolution, for the final offensive launched 9 April 1975 against South Vietnam that began with the shelling of Xuan Loc, 65 kilometers (40 miles) east of Saigon. It ended as North Vietnamese tanks rolled into Saigon on the morning of 30 April 1975.

Ho Chi Minh City. See Saigon

Ho Chi Minh Trail. The North Vietnamese infiltration and supply route into the South Vietnamese Central Highlands through Laos and Cambodia. The trail, an intricate network of jungle paths not visible from the air, was used during the wars against French and the United States. In 1964 the North Vietnamese began upgrading the

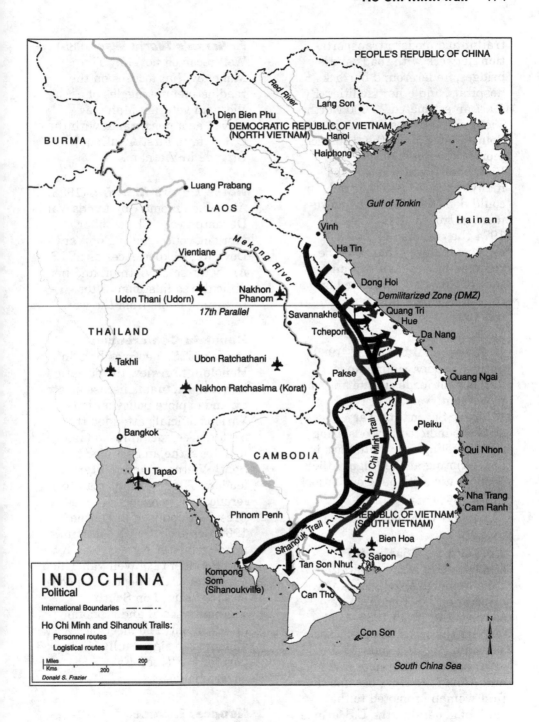

trail into a modern transportation network with roads and bridges, underground barracks, hospitals, and other facilities. By 1967 an estimated 20,000 North Vietnamese troops moved into South Vietnam via the trail each month. U.S. and South Vietnamese forces attempted many times to close the trail, but could do little to slow the movement of troops or supplies. By 1974 the trail had become a modern highway that could be traveled by car, with rest and service areas and protected by considerable antiaircraft weapons.

Hoffmann, Abbie (1936–1989), antiwar leader. Hoffmann, a flamboyant leader in the antiwar movement, was one of the "Chicago Seven" antiwar activists indicted for conspiring and traveling over state lines to incite rioting at the August 1968 Democratic National Convention in Chicago.

See also: Chicago Seven.

Hoisington, Elizabeth P. (1920–), U.S. Army general. Hoisington, a WWII veteran, was director of the Women's Army Corps (WAC) from 1966–1971, leading the corps throughout the Vietnam War. In a joint 11 June 1970 promotion ceremony she and Anna Mae Hays became the first woman promoted to the rank of general in the U.S. armed forces.

See also: Hayes, Anna Mae; Women, U.S. Military.

Hollaran's World War (1985). Well-received novel by Tim Mahoney that focuses on the readjustment struggles of a Vietnam veteran. Mahoney served as a mortarman with the U.S. Army's First Aviation Brigade in Vietnam.

Home Before Morning (1983). Acclaimed memoir by Lynda Van Devanter, with Christopher Morgan, concentrating on Van Devanter's experiences as a U.S. Army nurse in Vietnam and her difficult readjustment after returning home from the war.

Honolulu Conferences. A series of U.S. meetings held in Honolulu to review the situation in South Vietnam, discuss strategy, and explore policy options. Various officials attended the conferences, including cabinet members, the ambassador to South Vietnam, and military leaders. The most important conference was convened by President Johnson in February 1966. Johnson, South Vietnam's prime minister Nguyen Cao Ky, and President Nguyen Van Thieu joined the U.S. officials. The conference focused on South Vietnam's social and economic development. The meeting appeared to signal full U.S. support for the Thieu-Ky government.

Hoopes, Townsend (1922–), deputy assistant secretary of defense for international security affairs, 1965–1967; undersecretary of the U.S. Air Force

1967–1969. Hoopes was a leader of a Pentagon faction that opposed escalation of the Vietnam War. In a 1965 memo to Assistant Secretary of Defense John McNaughton, Hoopes wrote that continued bombing of North Vietnam would be counterproductive and advised against sending combat troops. By 1967, Hoopes and several other key officials, frustrated by the continuing escalation, sought to end the war and influenced Secretary of Defense McNamara and his successor, Clark Clifford, to change their views.

See also: Defense, Department of.

Hoover, J. Edgar (1895–1972), director of Federal Bureau of Investigation (FBI), 1924–1972. Hoover supported repressive policies against antiwar activists, including those in Congress. Beginning in 1967, Hoover, at President Lyndon Johnson's request, turned the FBI's attention toward the antiwar movement, particularly groups led by student radicals.

See also: Federal Bureau of Investigation; Huston Plan.

Ho Tung Mau (1896–1951), Vietnamese communist leader. A founding member of the Indochinese Communist Party and close associate of Ho Chi Minh, Ho Tung Mau was imprisoned by the French from 1931 to 1945.

See also: Indochinese Communist Party.

House, Edward M. (1858–1938), close adviser to President Woodrow Wilson. House was President Wilson's most trusted foreign affairs aide. At the 1919 Paris Peace Conference in Versailles following WWI, he and other allied leaders turned down a petition written by Ho Chi Minh calling for self-determination in French Indochina. Ho helped found the French Communist Party the following year.

See also: Ho Chi Minh; World War I.

House Committee to Study the Problem of U.S. Servicemen Missing in Action in Southeast Asia. *See* Montgomery Committee

Hou Yuon, popular Cambodian independent Marxist politician elected to the National Assembly in the 1960s. Hou Yuon disagreed with Pol Pot and the Khmer Rouge and disappeared after their takeover of Cambodia in April 1975.

See also: Cambodia; Khmer Rouge.

How I Got That Story (1979). Surrealistic, farcical play, by Vietnam veteran Amlin Gray, in which a newspaper reporter tells the story of the Vietnam War.

See also: Gray, Amlin.

Howitzers. Comparatively short-barreled cannons used primarily to fire shells at high elevation angles. The most widely used U.S. howitzers in Vietnam were the 105mm, 155mm and self-propelled 8-inch guns. The 105mm and 155mm howitzers could be towed by helicopters and lifted into landing zones within range of combat units. Among the howitzers used by the North Vietnamese Army were the Soviet-made towed D20 152mm howitzer; the D30 towed 122mm howitzer, which fired shells to a range of 15,300 meters; and the M1938 towed 122mm howitzer.

Hue. South Vietnam's third-largest city, 75 kilometers (45 miles) south of the demilitarized zone in Thua Thien province. An old imperial capital and considered Vietnam's most beautiful city, Hue was the scene of widespread protests against President Diem in May 1963 and against President Ky in March 1966. The protests were harshly suppressed. During the 1968 Tet Offensive, the North Vietnamese Army (NVA) and Viet Cong captured the city and held it for 25 days. Communist agents went house to house arresting some 2,800 civil servants, religious leaders, soldiers, educators, and anyone with American connections. They were executed. In the fight by U.S. Marines and ARVN troops to retake Hue, much of the city was destroyed, including the ancient inner city called the Citadel. The city fell to North Vietnam's Spring Offensive in March 1975.

See also: Atrocities; Buddhists; Cushman, Robert E. Jr.;

Ngo Dinh Thuc; Tet Offensive; Tri Quang.

Huey Helicopters. *See* UH-1 Helicopter

Hull, Cordell (1871–1955), U.S. representative (D-Tenn.), 1907–1921; 1923–1931, U.S. senator (D-Tenn.), 1931–1933, U.S. secretary of state, 1933–1944. Along with President Franklin D. Roosevelt, Secretary of State Hull tried, without success in 1943 and 1944 to influence Britain and France to grant independence to their colonies, including Vietnam, following the conclusion of WWII.

See also: Roosevelt, Franklin D.; Teheran Conference; Yalta Conference.

Humphrey, Hubert H. (1911–1978), U.S. Senator (D-Minn.), 1948–1964, 1970–1978; vice president, 1964–1968; Democratic presidential nominee, 1968. Humphrey did not play a large role in the formulation of Vietnam policy as vice president. In the early 1960s Humphrey favored providing only military training and supplies to South Vietnam. In 1964 he supported the Gulf of Tonkin Resolution. As vice president, Humphrey at first opposed escalation of the conflict and argued against bombing North Vietnam. Humphrey did not participate in the Johnson administration decision to commit combat troops, but publicly defended Johnson's policies. At the Democratic

Convention in Chicago, Humphrey proposed a halt in the bombing and an increase in South Vietnam's participation in the combat. Johnson disagreed, and convinced Humphrey to support a plank that mirrored administration policies. One week before the election, Humphrey called for a bombing halt, gradual U.S. disengagement, and a negotiated settlement. After failing in his quest for the presidency, Humphrey returned to the Senate where he generally avoided involvement with the Vietnam issue.

See also: Democratic National Convention, 1968; Democratic Party, U.S.; McCarthy, Eugene J.

Hun Sen (1951–), a commander of the Khmer Rouge army, Hun Sen defected to Vietnam in 1977. He became Cambodia's prime minister in 1985 and proceeded with liberalization. After 1993 UN-organized elections, he was named second prime minister in a coalition with the Sihanouk party.

See also: Cambodia; Khmer Rouge.

Hunt, E. Howard (1918–), a former Central Intelligence Agency operative, Hunt was a consultant to Nixon White House aide Charles Colson. Hunt, the leader of the "plumbers," pled guilty to all charges against him in the Watergate break-in trial.

See also: Colson, Charles; Plumbers; Watergate.

Hunter-Killer Team. Term for two U.S. Army helicopters, a light observation OH-6 Loach and an AH-1G Cobra gun ship, flying in tandem to uncover and attack enemy ground forces.

See also: OH-6 Helicopter.

Huong, Tran Van. *See* Tran Van Huong

Huston Plan. Designed with President Richard Nixon's knowledge by White House aide Tom Charles Huston, the Huston plan gave the White House control over the domestic intelligence activities of the Federal Bureau of Investigation (FBI), the Central Intelligence Agency (CIA), and U.S. Army intelligence. It authorized warrantless telephone taps, the opening of mail, break-ins, and other activities designed to harass and intimidate the antiwar movement. The illegal and unconstitutional plan was blocked by objections from FBI director J. Edgar Hoover in a 1970 meeting with Nixon and top government officials.

See also: Federal Bureau of Investigation; Hoover, J. Edgar; Justice, Department of; Nixon, Richard M.; Watergate.

Huynh Phu So (1919–1947), founder of the Hoa Hao reformist Buddhist sect. Huynh Phu So declared himself a holy man in 1939, and thereafter was regarded as a prophet by his followers mainly in the villages of the lower Mekong River Delta.

Huynh Phu So was assasinated by the Viet Minh in April 1947.

See also: Hoa Hao.

Huynh Tan Phat (1913–), a southerner, Huynh Tan Phat became active in the Indochinese Communist Party in the 1940s. He was jailed for his opposition to the regime of Ngo Dinh Diem in the early 1960s. After his release, Huynh Tan Phat joined the National Liberation Front. He became secretary general and in 1969 was chosen prime minister of the Provisional Revolutionary Government.

See also: Indochinese Communist Party; National Liberation Front; Provisional Revolutionary Government.

Ia Drang. In November 1965, U.S. soldiers engaged regulars of the People's Army of Vietnam (PAVN) in a fierce four-day battle near the Drang River in the Central Highlands. The combat marked the first large military engagement between the armies. The U.S. Army's 1st Cavalry Division (Airmobile) inflicted heavy casualties on the North Vietnamese (estimated at over 2,500), though the United States lost 234 dead and nearly 300 wounded. While signaling the onset of a destructive ground war in Vietnam, the battle at Ia Drang also proved a crucial test of the armies' combat tactics.

On 14 November 1965, the 1st Battalion, 7th Cavalry, helicoptered into the Ia Drang valley 23 kilometers (14 miles) west of Plei Me. The 450-man unit pursued suspected North Vietnamese forces hidden in the mountainous area near the Laotian border. They landed within a few miles of two PAVN regiments with several thousand troops. A vicious battle ensued, in which U.S. soldiers desperately defended a perimeter only about 270 meters (300 yards) across. The PAVN nearly overran the U.S. position in a series of flanking operations, but the battalion held its position over the next 72 hours. U.S. troops fought courageously, led by Lt. Col. Harold Moore and many Korean War veterans who served as non-commissioned officers. Critical to the battle was the well-coordinated array of heavy U.S. firepower, which included aerial rocket artillery helicopters, attack aircraft, and B-52 bombers. By 16 November, the PAVN forces had withdrawn from the withering U.S. attack, but they suffered further casualties from Army of the Republic of Vietnam (ARVN) battalions helicoptered across their line of retreat. On 17 November, however, PAVN forces that had just arrived from Laos overran the 2d Battalion, 7th Cavalry, as it traveled on foot near the battle site, killing 155 U.S. soldiers.

The Ia Drang campaign was a preview of the tactics of U.S. ground forces in the war. The engagement represented the first time helicopters ferried large units into combat, a historically unprecedented battle scheme that would become the standard for U.S. forces in Vietnam. Even more crucial, the success of the main confrontation at the Ia Drang committed the United States to a "war of attrition," with its key instruments of search-and-destroy missions. As the United States expanded its forces, U.S. generals sought to repeat the Ia Drang engagement, where a search-and-destroy operation located PAVN or Viet Cong soldiers and, with superior weaponry and massive firepower, inflicted devastating casualties on North Vietnamese forces. North Vietnamese commanders drew their own lessons from the

Ia Drang. After the battle the PAVN forces generally did not fight head on against U.S. forces and rarely took the bait of ensuing search-and-destroy missions. When they did engage U.S. troops, the PAVN troops approached as closely as possible to the perimeter of U.S. forces, as soldiers did in attacks at the Ia Drang, to minimize their vulnerability to U.S. firepower.

The battle also set off high-level debates in North Vietnam concerning military strategy for defeating U.S. forces. Some North Vietnamese commanders, led by General Vo Nguyen Giap, called for increased emphasis on guerrilla operations, citing the failure of conventional campaigns at the Ia Drang. These heated debates were not fully resolved until 1967, when the North largely abandoned conventional warfare in the Tet Offensive.

See also: Arc Light, Operation; Attrition Strategy; Helicopters; Search-and-Destroy.

ICP. *See* Indochinese Communist Party

ICSC. *See* International Commission for Supervision and Control

Ieng, Sary. Radical communist Khmer Rouge Cambodian leader. Born Kim Trang, Ieng Sary was a brother-in-law and close associate of Saloth Sar (Pol Pot). Ieng Sary helped coordinate the Khmer Rouge 1975–1979 Cambodian holocaust.

See also: Cambodia; Khmer Rouge; Pol Pot.

If I Die in a Combat Zone (1973). Critically acclaimed, stylized Vietnam War memoir by the literary novelist Tim O'Brien, who served with the 198th Light Infantry Brigade in Vietnam in 1969–1970.

See also: Going After Cacciato; O'Brien, Tim.

In Country (1989). Film directed by Norman Jewison based on the highly praised 1985 novel of the same name by Bobbie Ann Mason. The film and book tell the story of a teenage girl and her quest in the mid-1980s to find out about her father who was killed in Vietnam before she was born.

India. Officially a nonaligned nation, India did not join the Southeast Asia Treaty Organization (SEATO), even though the United States regarded that nation as a "domino" threatened by Asian communism. India's own struggle against colonialism made it generally sympathetic to the Democratic Republic of Vietnam (DRV), but its conflicts with the DRV's ally, the People's Republic of China, caused India to tone down its support.

Public opinion in India supported the Vietnamese against the French and, throughout the 1960s, favored U.S. withdrawal. India joined the International Commission for Supervision and

Control (ICSC) after the 1954 Geneva Conference. Because it was nonaligned, India chaired the ICSC and provided the vast majority of its personnel. By the mid 1960s the divisions within the ICSC were clear, with India generally siding with Poland against Canada; India withdrew from the ICSC in 1973. Within hours of the April 1975 fall of Saigon, India recognized the new revolutionary government.

See also: Domino Theory; International Control Commission.

Indochina (Indochine). The name given by France in the 19th century to its Southeast Asian colonies in Vietnam, Cambodia and Laos. The name referred to the mingling of Indian and Chinese cultures in the region.

See also: French Indochinese Union.

Indochina War. A term that refers to the war of Vietnamese independence against French colonial rule from the end of WWII to 1954.

See also: Dien Bien Phu; Franco–Viet Minh War; Ho Chi Minh; Mendès-France, Pierre; Pham Hung; Pham Van Dong; Sainteny, Jean; Salan, Raoul; Van Tien Dung; Vo Nguyen Giap; Viet Minh; Xuan Thuy.

Indochinese Communist Party (ICP). Organized in February 1930 as the Vietnamese Communist Party, the group changed its name to the Indochinese Communist Party (ICP) in October 1930. The name change, ordered by the Comintern, brought Cambodian and Lao radicals into the group. The ICP was the primary political organization that opposed French colonial rule. In 1941, the party formed the League for the Independence of Vietnam, or Viet Minh. In August 1945 the Viet Minh declared the establishment of an independent Democratic Republic of Vietnam (DRV) under Ho Chi Minh. Soon after, the DRV began fighting the French for control of the country. The ICP changed its name to the Vietnamese Workers' Party in 1951.

See also: Ho Chi Minh; Lao Dong; Le Duan; Le Duc Tho; Pham Hung; Truong Chinh; Xuan Thuy.

Indonesia. In 1947 Indonesia issued a joint appeal with the Democratic Republic of Vietnam (DRV) to the United Nations requesting recognition of their post-colonial independence. Although the United States considered Indonesia threatened by the spread of communism, Indonesia, like India, did not join the Southeast Asia Treaty Organization and remained officially nonaligned. Under President Sukarno, Indonesia was critical of the U.S. war effort in Vietnam, but a bloody counter-coup in 1965 pushed the country more toward the United States under President Suharto. Indonesia replaced India on the 1973 International Commission for Control and Supervision.

See also: International Commission for Control and Supervision; Southeast Asia Treaty Organization.

In Pharaoh's Army (1994). A revealing, literary memoir by Tobias Wolff, in which the former U.S. Army Special Forces soldier and acclaimed short-story writer described his tour of duty in Vietnam.

See also: Wolff, Tobias.

In Retrospect (1995). Controversial book in which former Defense Secretary Robert S. McNamara for the first time explained his actions as he directed the U.S. war in Vietnam from 1961–1968.

See also: McNamara, Robert.

Institute for Defense Analyses (IDA). Federally funded research and development center that conducts research for the Department of Defense. During the Vietnam War, IDA work was carried out at several U.S. universities, including Columbia University. Under pressure from the radical group, Students for a Democratic Society (SDS), Columbia agreed to cut its ties to the IDA in 1968.

See also: Students for a Democratic Society.

Insurgency. *See* Pacification

Intelligence Coordination and Exploitation (ICEX). Central Intelligence Agency (CIA) program begun in July 1967 to gather intelligence on the Viet Cong. The first serious U.S. program designed to neutralize the Viet Cong, ICEX was renamed the Phoenix Program in July 1968.

See also: Pacification; Phoenix Program.

International Commission for Supervision and Control (ICSC). The International Commission for Supervision and Control, also known as the International Control Commission (ICC) and later the International Commission for Control and Supervision (ICCS), was established by the 1954 Geneva Conference. Comprising three nations not directly involved in the military conflict—Canada, India, and Poland—the ICSC's mission was to supervise the cease-fire and political reunification of Vietnam and the 1956 elections, which never took place. The ICSC used mobile teams to investigate alleged treaty violations and established committees to evaluate the findings. Its broad mandate, combined with a lack of substantial enforcement powers and the requirement of unanimity on most issues, limited the commission's influence, particularly after the French withdrawal. The ICSC published eleven interim reports from 1954 through 1961 and three special reports from 1962 through 1965.

These reports were increasingly pessimistic and criticized both sides for violating the Geneva agreement. Its 1962 special report was particularly critical of the Democratic Republic of Vietnam (DRV) for aggressive actions and of the military alliance between South Vietnam and the United States.

The ICSC members were divided along ideological lines. Canada supported the United States and South Vietnam. Poland supported the Soviet Union and the DRV, and India tried to remain nonaligned, although it was generally more sympathetic toward the DRV. The 1965 special report, for example, included a majority report condemning the U.S. bombing and a Canadian minority report justifying it. An additional problem facing the ICSC was that it did not report to a political body, such as the United Nations. Instead, it directed its recommendations only toward the largely defunct Geneva Conference and toward the parties themselves. The ICSC's activities declined in the late 1960s.

The Paris Peace Accords of 1973 reconstituted the ICSC as the International Commission for Control and Supervision (ICCS), in which Hungary replaced Poland and Indonesia replaced India. Either the Four-Party Joint Military Commission or the Two-Party Joint Military Commission could request investigations of accord violations. Like its predecessor, the ICCS

had no enforcement power; it merely reported its findings to all four parties to the Paris agreement, which were then supposed to resolve the conflict. Canada remained a member for a few months, withdrawing because it believed Hungary was undermining the ICCS's work. The commission became irrelevant after the North Vietnamese military victory in 1975.

See also: Canada; Gevena Conference, 1961–1962; Great Britain; India; Indonesia; Paris Accords; Poland.

International Control Commission (ICC). *See* International Commission for Supervision and Control

International Cooperation Administration. A pre-1961 predecessor of the U.S. Agency for International Development (AID), the main U.S. agency that designed and implemented non-military U.S. development and assistance programs during the Vietnam War.

See also: Agency for International Development.

International Days of Protest. Antiwar demonstrations held 15–16 October 1965 in dozens of cities in the United States, Europe and Asia. The largest U.S. events were held in Berkeley, Calif., and New York City. The protest was the first sponsored by the National Coordinating Committee to End the War in Vietnam.

International Federation of Christian Workers. Catholic labor organization. Ngo Dinh Nhu, the brother of South Vietnamese President Ngo Dinh Diem, first gained prominence in 1953 as an organizer of the Vietnamese Federation of Christian Workers, which was affiliated with the International Federation of Christian Workers.

See also: Ngo Dinh Nhu.

International Monetary Fund (IMF). International organization that promotes world trade. In April 1975, after the communist takeover of South Vietnam, the United States extended to all of Vietnam a trade embargo that had been in effect against the Democratic Republic of Vietnam since 1964. The embargo included a U.S. block on International Monetary Fund (IMF) development aid.

See also: Embargo.

International Reaction. In responding to the war in Vietnam, the world's nations were divided into three camps: capitalist countries sympathetic to the United States, socialist countries sympathetic to the Democratic Republic of Vietnam (DRV), and countries that remained nonaligned. The United States and South Vietnam had six official allies: Australia, New Zealand, the Philippines, the Republic of China (Taiwan), the Republic of Korea (South Korea), and

Thailand. Thirty-two additional countries provided nonmilitary aid to South Vietnam. Many traditional U.S. allies, including Great Britain, France, and West Germany, expressed reservations about the U.S. policy. The bombing of the DRV, the mining of its ports, and the invasion of Cambodia were watershed events in stimulating opposition among citizens of allied nations.

All socialist countries opposed the U.S. presence in Vietnam, but were not united in their positions. The Soviet Union in the mid 1960s sought peaceful coexistence with the United States and, while continuing to provide military aid to the North Vietnamese, also acted as intermediary in several failed peace missions. The People's Republic of China (PRC), threatened by Soviet power, especially following the 1968 Soviet invasion of Czechoslovakia and subsequent attacks on the PRC's borders, refused to cooperate with Soviet policies in North Vietnam. Nonaligned countries such as India remained officially neutral but generally called for a negotiated peace between the National Liberation Front and the South Vietnamese. The PRC viewed the National Liberation Front (NLF) and communist movements in neighboring countries as a counter to U.S. imperialism and supported them with material aid. The United Nations was not officially involved in the conflict, and did not succeed in fostering a resolution to the conflict because of the strongly divided camps.

International Rescue Committee. An American-sponsored, nonsectarian, volunteer organization formed in 1942 to aid refugees from Nazi Germany. The committee first worked in Vietnam after the division of the country in 1954, providing emergency aid to some 900,000 Vietnamese who fled the north to relocate in the south. After 1964, the committee organized assistance for the millions of refugees in South Vietnam displaced by the U.S. escalation of the war. After the fall of South Vietnam in 1975, the committee helped with the final evacuation of Vietnamese refugees and their resettlement in the United States.

International War Crimes Tribunal. Also known as the Russell tribunal, the International War Crimes Tribunal met in 1967 under the direction of the Bertrand Russell Peace Foundation. Russell, the British philosopher and mathematician, was a longtime pacifist who opposed U.S. involvement in Vietnam. The tribunal declared that American treatment of prisoners and the use of weapons such as napalm and cluster bombs against civilians constituted war crimes. The testimony and findings were published by Russell in the book *Against the Crime of Silence* but had little impact on U.S. policy.

See also: Russell, Bertrand.

Iron Triangle. A large Viet Cong guerrilla base located 32 kilometers (20 miles) northwest of Saigon, formed by the junction of the Saigon and Thi Tinh rivers between the villages of Ben Suc and Ben Cat. This heavily forested area concealed a vast underground tunnel complex containing 130 square kilometers (50 square miles) of barracks, supply dumps, hospitals, and weapons factories. Operations Cedar Falls and Junction City attacked the area in January and February 1967 with bombs, shells, napalm, explosives, bulldozers, and 32,000 troops. Hundreds of tons of enemy supplies were captured, but most of the guerrillas escaped to Cambodia. The Iron Triangle served as the staging base for attacks on Saigon during the 1968 Tet Offensive. The Iron Triangle's underground bases were neutralized with delayed-fuse bombs dropped by B-52s in 1970.

See also: Ben Suc; Cedar Falls, Operation; Junction City, Operation; Tunnels.

Irving, Operation. Search-and-destroy operation carried out by elements of the U.S. 1st Cavalry Division and Republic of Korea troops in October 1966 in Binh Dinh Province.

See also: Search-and-Destroy.

Isaacs, Arnold R. (1941–), journalist, author. Isaacs covered the Vietnam War for the *Baltimore Sun* from 1972–1975.

He is the author of the acclaimed *Without Honor: Defeat in Vietnam and Cambodia* (1983) and *Vietnam Shadows: The War, Its Ghosts, and Its Legacy* (1997).

Jacknife (1989). Film directed by David Jones that won praise for its non-sensationalist portrayal of the emotional problems of Vietnam veterans.

Jackson State College. On 14 May 1970, following several days of protests over the Vietnam War, racism, and local issues, police killed two students and wounded twelve others at Jackson State College in Mississippi. The police claimed they fired in response to an alleged sniper.

See also: Cambodian Incursion.

James, Daniel, Jr. (Chappie), (1920–1978), U.S. Air Force general; commander, North American Air Defense Command, 1975–1978. The first African-American to achieve four-star rank in the U.S. military, James flew 78 combat F-4 fighter missions into North Vietnam with the 8th U.S. Air Force Tactical Wing from 1966–1967.

See also: Air Force, U.S.

Japan. During WWII Japan occupied Indochina (1940–1945), imposed de facto rule through the nominal control of French authorities, and exploited the Vietnamese. The Viet Minh resisted the occupation and proclaimed independence for Vietnam in 1945. Following the successful Chinese communist revolution in 1949, U.S. attention focused on Vietnam. The United States sought to contain the spread of communism and emerging nationalism and to provide a market to assist economic recovery in Japan.

In a 1960 security treaty with the United States, Japan pledged to support U.S. policy in Vietnam, allowing the United States to use its bases to take military actions if the Far East were endangered. Although not an official participant in the Vietnam War, Japan (and Okinawa) played a key role channeling U.S. military personnel and supplies to Vietnam. Japan hosted approximately 100,000 military-related Americans, along with some 50,000 troops in Okinawa, and provided a dozen large bases and more than 130 other military facilities. Meanwhile, Japan's rapid economic growth during this period offered an alternative noncommunist model for Southeast Asia.

Japan benefited greatly from the war. Between 1966 and 1971, the United States spent more than $150 billion for the war effort, of which at least $5 billion was spent in Japan for military procurement. U.S. military personnel in Japan and Okinawa consumed Japanese goods and used Japanese services, to the benefit of the Japanese economy. Taking advantage of U.S. military protection, Japan spent less than 1 percent of its gross national product (GNP) on defense, devoting its efforts to domestic economic growth.

Worldwide inflation during the war also strengthened Japanese international competitiveness. In addition, as the United States sent military and economic aid to other Asian countries to fend off communism, these countries in turn purchased goods from Japan. Consequently, the Japanese economy experienced an annual growth rate of approximately 10 percent during the Vietnam War. An antiwar movement developed among student groups, opposition political parties, and labor unions, but it had little impact on Japanese foreign policy.

See also: Free World.

Japan–U.S. Security Treaty

(1960). Security treaty in which Japan agreed to allow U.S. forces to use Japanese territory. During the Vietnam War, the U.S. Seventh Fleet had its home port at Yokosuka, U.S. Air Force units used Tachikawa and Yokota Air Bases and the U.S. Army had logistical bases and hospitals near Tokyo.

See also: Japan.

Jason Studies. Secret reports commissioned by Defense Secretary Robert S. McNamara in 1966 and 1967 through the Washington, D.C.–based think tank, the Institute for Defense Analysis. The studies looked at the effectiveness of the U.S. bombing campaigns in North Vietnam and concluded that they had no effect in reducing North Vietnam's military capability or political will to continue the war.

See also: Institute for Defense Analyses; McNamara, Robert; Rolling Thunder, Operation.

Javits, Jacob K. (1904–1986), U.S. Senator (R-N.Y.), 1947–1981. Javits, a liberal, was one of his party's leading Vietnam War critics.

See also: Senate, U.S.

JCS. *See* Joint Chiefs of Staff

JGS. *See* Joint General Staff

Johns Hopkins Speech.

Speech by President Lyndon B. Johnson delivered 7 April 1965 at Johns Hopkins University in Baltimore in which he stated that the U. S. was willing to take part in "unconditional discussions" about the prospect of peace in Vietnam and proposed a massive, billion-dollar U.S. economic development program for all of Vietnam.

The administration correctly believed that North Vietnam would not respond to this initiative because it was not accompanied by a pause in the U.S. bombing of North Vietnam and because Johnson offered no other tangible concessions. The speech represented the first significant example of the expanding antiwar movement's impact on U.S. foreign policy during the war.

See also: Johnson, Lyndon B.

Johnson, Harold K.

(1912–1983), general, U.S. Army; U.S. Army chief of staff, 1964–1968. Survivor of the

Bataan Death March and three year's imprisonment by The Japanese in WWII, Johnson was chosen over 43 more senior generals to replace Gen. Earle Wheeler as Army chief of staff on 3 July 1964. President Johnson sent him on a fact-finding trip to South Vietnam in March 1965. Doubtful that bombing could win the war, General Johnson recommended sending the first U.S. combat troops, but came to regret his decision. Johnson retired and was replaced by Gen. William Westmoreland in 1968.

See also: Enclave Strategy; Special Forces, U.S. Army.

Johnson, James. *See* Fort Hood Three

Johnson, Lyndon B.
(1908–1973), U S. representative (D-Tex.), 1937–1949; U.S. senator (D-Tex.), 1949–1961; Senate minority leader, 1953–1955; Senate majority leader, 1955–1961; vice president, 1961–1963; president, 1963–1969. As the U.S. Senate minority leader in 1954 Johnson helped persuade President Eisenhower not to intervene in the French Indochina war. In 1961, as vice president, Johnson traveled to Vietnam at President Kennedy's request to assure the government of Ngo Dinh Diem that the U. S. intended to protect South Vietnam from a communist takeover. Johnson promised Diem technical and financial aid and military supplies and hinted at the possibility of sending U.S. combat troops. The latter proposal was only a gesture at that time, although the Kennedy administration stepped up other aid to South Vietnam, including an increase in the number of military advisers from 700 to 10,300.

Against Johnson's advice, the Kennedy administration endorsed a military coup that toppled Diem's government and took his life. Three weeks later, on 22 November 1963, the assassination of John Kennedy shifted the burden of responsibility far Vietnam to Johnson.

At the start of his presidency Johnson was fearful that a communist victory would open the rest of Southeast Asia to communist control, embolden the Soviet Union and China to take actions that could lead to world war, and give the Republicans a point of attack against his administration. He determined in November 1963 not to "lose" South Vietnam. In following this policy, Johnson believed he was continuing Kennedy's intentions. Kennedy had remarked to various advisers in the last months of his life about getting out of Vietnam after the 1964 presidential election and had given indications of this shift by ordering one thousand troops home from Vietnam by the end of 1963. Despite this, Johnson had good reason to think that Kennedy would not have pulled out of Vietnam as long as there was a substantial risk of a communist takeover.

During 1964, Johnson's principal concerns were his

presidential election campaign and the implementation of his Great Society domestic reform program. Fearing that a U.S. military buildup in Vietnam would jeopardize the election and his domestic agenda, Johnson promised that he would not send combat troops to Vietnam. At the same time he increased the number of advisers to 23,300 and increased economic assistance by $50 million.

On the night of 4 August 1964, two U.S. destroyers operating off the North Vietnamese coast in the Gulf of Tonkin reported that they were under attack. Though he lacked conclusive evidence of an actual attack, Johnson nevertheless ordered retaliatory air strikes against North Vietnamese torpedo boat bases and oil storage depots. Moreover, Johnson asked Congress for a resolution that would allow him to repel future armed attacks and to prevent further aggression. The Gulf of Tonkin Resolution, which won nearly unanimous congressional approval, stood as a symbol of national support far Johnson's foreign policy in Vietnam. Toward the end of 1964, Johnson's advisers devised a plan to intensify air attacks gradually and to avert a collapse in South Vietnam. In November 1964, when a Viet Cong attack on a U.S. air base killed four servicemen, Johnson did not retaliate. But three months later, with Buddhist and student protests threatening to topple the South Vietnamese government and with North Vietnamese Army units entering South Vietnam, Johnson made further plans for an air assault on North Vietnam.

After Viet Cong forces killed nine Americans on 6 February 1965 at Pleiku, Johnson ordered Operation Rolling Thunder, a sustained bombing campaign against North Vietnam. During the initial bombing campaign, Johnson maintained tight personal control over the war effort. Following the Pleiku incident, Westmoreland requested and Johnson approved the dispatch of two U.S. Marine battalions to protect the U.S. air base at Da Nang from Viet Cong attacks. Shortly after the first Marines arrived, Johnson conferred with Secretary McNamara, Gen. Maxwell Taylor, and the Joint Chiefs of Staff in Honolulu. They agreed to send an additional 40,000 troops. Although this decision marked a major shift in policy, the president discouraged congressional and public debate on the issue. Johnson feared that a formal declaration of war might trigger a Soviet or Chinese response.

In July 1965, Secretary McNamara returned from Saigon with the warning that South Vietnam might soon collapse. In July 1965 Johnson ordered the immediate deployment of 50,000 additional troops, with 50,000 more to follow later. Johnson also expanded their role, authorizing Westmoreland to use combat troops as he saw fit to strengthen the position of South Vietnamese forces. In addition, for the first time, Johnson approved saturation bombing of North Vietnamese strongholds in South Vietnam.

In early 1966 Johnson and South Vietnamese premier Nguyen Cao Ky met in Honolulu and agreed to a series of reforms designed to strengthen the South Vietnamese government. Through the Revolutionary Development Program, Johnson hoped to improve the standard of living of the South Vietnamese people, win greater support for U.S. military operations from the South Vietnamese, and undermine Viet Cong programs in rural areas. In Jane 1966, Johnson approved General Westmoreland's request for a total of 431,000 troops. At the end of 1967, some 485,600 U.S. troops were in Vietnam.

In December 1966, to counter growing domestic and international pressures for peace talks, Johnson halted the bombing campaign and sent Ambassador Averell Harriman and Vice President Hubert Humphrey on missions to say that the United States was ready for negotiations. When North Vietnamese president Ho Chi Minh demanded a permanent halt to bombing as a condition of talks, Johnson refused. Instead, he resumed the bombing of North Vietnam. In 1967 Johnson came under increasing criticism at home and abroad for his handling of the war. Unwilling to unleash unrestrained use of U.S. power or to compromise the U.S. commitment to a noncommunist South

Vietnam, Johnson was caught in the middle between "hawks" demanding further escalation and "doves" urging withdrawal from what they considered a Vietnamese civil war. Within his own administration, Johnson tried to balance conflicting points of view. He rejected the military's call for 200,000 more troops and mobilization of U.S. reserves, but at the same time he refused to back Secretary McNamara's proposals to halt the bombing, place a ceiling on U.S. troop levels, and limit ground operations. Although Johnson publicly expressed confidence in his decisions, he was privately tormented by the growing domestic tensions over the war. Johnson, who was personally involved in the war's day-to-day operations, radically altered his view of the war following the 1968 Tet Offensive. He rejected General Westmoreland's proposal to send 200,000 additional troops to Vietnam. Instead, he accepted Defense Secretary Clark Clifford's recommendation that the U. S. limit its forces in Vietnam and that the South Vietnamese do more of the fighting. On 31 March he announced that the bombing of North Vietnam would be reduced, that the United States was ready for peace talks, and that he would not run again for president.

Despite the start of formal peace talks in Paris later that year, the Johnson administration, like the North Vietnamese government, was unwilling to compromise on its goals with respect to the future of South Vietnam. During the talks, Johnson and his civilian advisers ordered military escalation to bolster their negotiating position, but that strategy had little effect on the continuing stalemate in Vietnam.

See also: Abrams, Creighton W. Jr.; Acheson, Dean; Ball, George W.; Bundy, McGeorge; Central Intelligence Agency; Clifford, Clark; Détente; Domino Theory; Enclave Strategy; Fortas, Abe; Great Society; Guam Conference; Gulf of Tonkin Resolution; Honolulu Conferences; Humphrey, Hubert H.; Johns Hopkins Speech; Joint Chiefs of Staff; King, Martin Luther Jr.; McNamara, Robert; McPherson, Harry; Philippines; Pleiku; Ridgway, Matthew B.; Rolling Thunder, Operation; Rostow, Walt Whitman; Rules of Engagement; Rusk, (David) Dean; Search-and-Destroy; Taylor, Maxwell D.; Tet Offensive; Westmoreland, William C.; Wheeler, Earle G.; Wise Men; Appendix E, "Gulf of Tonkin Resolution."

Johnson, U. Alexis

(1908–1997), U.S. Foreign Service officer, 1935–1977; deputy ambassador to South Vietnam in Saigon, 1964–1965. Johnson acted as the coordinator for the U.S. delegation to the Geneva Conference of 1954. He helped shape the State Department's Vietnam policies during the Eisenhower, Kennedy, and Johnson administrations.

See also: Geneva Conference, 1954.

Joint Casualty Resolution Center (JCRC).

U.S. military group set up in 1973 in Thailand to work for the accounting of U.S. prisoners of war and missing in action in Southeast Asia during the Vietnam War. In 1991 the JCRC was replaced by the Pentagon's Joint Task Force/Full Accounting (JTF/FA), which set up field offices in Hanoi, Vientiene, Laos; and Phnom Penh, Cambodia.

See also: POW/MIA Controversy.

Joint Chiefs of Staff (JCS).

Created by the National Security Act of 1947, the U.S. Joint Chiefs of Staff comprise the Army chief of staff, the Air Force chief of staff, the chief of naval operations, and the commandant of the Marine Corps, along with a nonvoting chairman. The JCS advises the president on military matters and is responsible for strategic planning and review of significant logistical and personnel requirements of the armed forces. Since the Defense Reorganization Act of 1958 removed the JCS from direct operational control over troops (the chain of command),they report directly to the secretary of defense and issue orders in his name.

During the Vietnam War, the JCS had six chairmen and thirty different members. Many retired in frustration, feeling ignored or manipulated by civilian leaders. Interservice rivalry and bureaucratic intransigence during the war often obstructed the flow of information between U.S. and South Vietnamese officials. Presidents Kennedy, Johnson, and Nixon often distrusted advice they received from the JCS. The JCS consistently advocated increased bombing of North Vietnam, greater U.S. troop commitments, and more aggressive tactics regardless of the costs. In August 1965, the JCS officially recognized U.S. objectives in Vietnam: keep China out of the war, end North Vietnam's support for insurgency, and expand the authority of South Vietnam's government throughout the South. The recommended means for achieving these political ends were entirely military: interdict communist supply routes, destroy communist forces, and improve the Army of the Republic of Vietnam (ARVN). Pacifying the countryside or rallying the people to support their government did not interest the generals.

See also: Bradley, Omar N.; Brown, George S.; Defense, Department of; Ely, Paul; Joint General Staff; Khe Sanh; Krulak, Victor; Military Assistance Command, Vietnam; Rules of Engagement; Search-and-Destroy; SIGMA; Wheeler, Earle G.

Joint General Staff (JGS).
South Vietnam's counterpart to the U.S. Joint Chiefs of Staff. The Joint General Staff included the branch commanders of the Republic of Vietnam Armed Forces (RVNAF): the Army of the Republic of Vietnam (ARVN), the Republic of Vietnam Air Force (VNAF), and the Vietnamese Navy (VNN), which included the Vietnamese Marine Corps (VNMC). The JGS also had deputy chiefs of staff (all ARVN officers) for personnel, logistics, political warfare, and operations. Unlike the JCS, the JGS had direct operational control over troops. Gen. William Westmoreland deluged the JGS with memos, advice, and personal emissaries. Considerable prodding was required to induce the JGS to enact military reforms, and when they acted, the JGS usually transferred incompetent commanders. Yet the United States never demanded a complete overhaul for fear it would be too risky and too indicative of American control.

See also: Republic of Vietnam Armed Forces.

Joint Liaison Detachment, 4802d. CIA unit that worked closely with the Royal Thai government in the "secret" war in Laos to provide operational and training advisers and to oversee specialized covert operations.

See also: Laos; Thailand.

Joint Military Commissions.
See International Commission for Supervision and Control

Joint U.S. Public Affairs Office (JUSPAO). U.S. Information Service agency created in 1965 in Saigon and put in charge both of relations with the news media and psychological warfare operations. Beginning in 1966, the daily official press briefings by the U.S. Military Assistance Command Office of Information were directed by JUSPAO head Barry Zorthian. The briefings came to be known by correspondents as "The Five O'Clock Follies."

See also: Five O'Clock Follies; Zorthian, Barry.

Jones, David C. (1921–), general, U.S. Air Force; vice commander, Seventh Air Force, 1969; commander, Second Air Force, 1969–1971. A flight instructor in WWII and a bomber pilot in the Korean War. As vice commander and director of operations of the Seventh Air Force in Vietnam in 1969, Jones helped plan the secret bombing of Cambodia and kept it concealed from Congress. Promoted to full general in 1971, he left Vietnam to command U.S. Air Forces in Europe. He succeeded Gen. George Brown as U.S. Air Force chief of staff in 1974, and as chairman of the Joint Chiefs of Staff in 197S. Jones retired in 1982.

See also: Air Force, U.S.

Junction City, Operation. Large 22-battalion, joint U.S.-ARVN operation in the Iron Triangle area of Tay Ninh Province February to May 1967 designed to find and destroy the Viet Cong's Central Office for South Vietnam (COSVN).

See also: Ben Suc; Central Office for South Vietnam; Iron Triangle.

Jungle boots. Specially constructed leather and nylon boots issued to U.S. Army and Marine troops in Vietnam.

Just, Ward (1935–), former Vietnam War correspondent who used the war as a theme in his fiction, including the literary novels, *Stringer* (1974), and *The American Blues* (1984).

Justice, Department of. From 1965 to 1973, the U.S. Department of Justice confronted growing dissent and social unrest resulting from the Vietnam War. The agency's response reflected the different outlooks of its Democratic and Republican attorneys general under the Johnson and Nixon administrations.

President Johnson's attorneys general generally pursued restrained policies toward antiwar activities. President Nixon's officials tended toward more repressive measures. Despite differences, however, the department's policies displayed continuities over the course of the war. Both prosecuted high-profile antiwar figures and under both administrations the department maintained electronic surveillance of antiwar groups and infiltrated these organizations.

During the Johnson administration, the Federal Bureau of Investigation (FBI), the investigatory arm of the department, launched the COINTELPRO program of infiltration and disinformation of New Left activities, which continued through the Nixon era. The department similarly established intelligence surveillance of domestic antiwar groups beginning in the mid-1960s. Carried out by the FBI as well as by the U.S. Army, this campaign consisted primarily of covert infiltration and wiretapping. As protests escalated in 1965, the department stepped up its activities, driven initially by concern over Communist Party infiltration of the antiwar movement. After the weekend of the International Days of Protests (15–16 October 1965), Attorney General Nicholas Katzenbach promised President Johnson a nationwide investigation of the antiwar movement. Citing statutes criminalizing interference with the draft and federal sedition laws, Katzenbach hinted that prosecutions might be forthcoming. Nevertheless, neither Katzenbach nor his successor, Ramsey Clark, agreed to carry out a prosecutorial witch-hunt. The department's prosecution record against draft resisters from 1965 to 1966 was almost nil, as it refused to equate antiwar dissent with treason or sedition.

Publicly, the administration upheld dissent as a right. For example, Clark chose not to prevent large-scale protests at the March on the Pentagon in 1967 and at the Democratic convention in 1968, despite having received intelligence that protesters intended to provoke clashes with police.

Under John Mitchell, the new attorney general in the Nixon administration, the Justice Department pursued a more confrontational policy toward antiwar activities. In 1971, Assistant Attorney General William H. Rehnquist supported the suspension of normal arrest procedures to facilitate the detention of twelve thousand protesters in Washington, D.C. In 1970, the White House proposed the Huston Plan for an interagency working group to practice a wide range of undermining activities such as mail openings, burglaries, wiretapping, break-ins, and infiltrations. The FBI balked at this riot of governmental illegality. Attorney General John Mitchell sought to bypass the Fourth Amendment with an appeal to an overarching exercise of presidential defense of national security. The Supreme Court rejected this argument.

See also: Federal Bureau of Investigation; Huston Plan.

Kalsu, James R. (1945–1970), U.S. Army captain. Kalsu, who served with the 101st Airborne Division's 11th Artillery, was killed by enemy mortar fire in Vietnam on 21 July 1970. Kalsu, who played football with the Buffalo Bills in 1968–1969, is believed to be the only former U.S. professional football player killed in the Vietnam War.

Kampuchea. *See* Cambodia

Karlin, Wayne (1945–), novelist, essayist, and editor whose work, including his highly praised novel, *Lost Armies* (1988), is strongly influenced by his service as a U.S. Marine in Vietnam.

Karnow, Stanley (1925–), journalist, author. Karnow covered the Vietnam War for *Time* magazine and the *Washington Post*. His acclaimed book, *Vietnam: A History* (1983), won the Pulitzer Prize and was the basis for the 13-part PBS documentary, *Vietnam: A Television History* (1983).

See also: Vietnam: A Television History.

Kattenburg, Paul (1922–), U.S. foreign service officer. An expert on Vietnam, Kattenburg in August 1963 recommended that the United States end its commitment to the defense of South Vietnam.

See also: State, Department of.

Katzenbach, Nicholas (1922–), U.S. attorney general, 1965–1966; undersecretary of state, 1966–1969. Katzenbach supported the war effort. As attorney general in 1965, Katzenbach promised to investigate those who protested the draft. As undersecretary of state, Katzenbach testified before the Senate Foreign Relations Committee in 1967, offering a broad interpretation of presidential power to start military action, arguing that the Gulf of Tonkin Resolution gave the president the authority to prosecute the Vietnam War as he saw fit. In 1973 Katzenbach charged that President Nixon had exceeded his constitutional powers, and supported the War Powers Resolution.

See also: Gulf of Tonkin Resolution; Justice, Department of; Appendix E, "Gulf of Tonkin Resolution."

Kaysone, Phomvihan (1920–1992), member of the Indochina Communist Party (ICP) who helped create the Pathet Lao communist insurgents. When the Lao People's Democratic Republic was declared on 2 December 1975, Kaysone Phomvihan became secretary of the Lao People's Revolutionary Party *(Phak Pasason Pativat Lao)* and prime minister. In 1991 Phomvihan took charge of the nation until his death in December 1992.

See also: Laos; Pathet Lao.

Kelley, Paul X. (1929–), U.S. Marine Corps general, commandant of the Marines, 1983–1987. Kelley commanded a 4th Marine battalion in Vietnam in 1965–1966, and in 1970 became commander of the 1st Marine Division.

See also: Marines, U.S.

Kelly, Francis J. (1919–1998), U.S. Army colonel; commander, U.S. Army Special Forces in Vietnam (June 1966 to June 1967). Kelly developed the Mobile Guerilla Force concept, Special Forces–led operations that included South Vietnamese soldiers and Civilian Irregular Defense Group personnel.

See also: Civilian Irregular Defense Groups; Special Forces, U.S.

Kennan, George (1904–), State Department official at the U.S. embassy in Moscow, 1933–1935, 1944–1946; director of State Department policy planning, 1947; ambassador to the Soviet Union, 1942; ambassador to Yugoslavia, 1961–1963. Kennan formulated the policy of containment in 1947 that became the foundation for U.S. foreign policy for four decades.

Containment, intended to prevent the spread of communism, was grounded in the belief that the Soviet Union and the People's Republic of China would aggressively try to foster communism throughout the world. The policy held that the United States and its allies should use all means necessary, including military force, to prevent the USSR and PRC from building communist empires that would threaten democratic nations and U.S. economic interests. In many articles and speeches Kennan, intellectual father of U.S. Cold War policy, criticized U.S. involvement in Vietnam, arguing that Vietnam had no strategic or economic significance and stating that he opposed the military effort. Kennan insisted that any further escalation would seriously reduce the chances for détente with the Soviet Union and China, imperiling relations that were far more important to U.S. interests than the future of Vietnam.

See also: Containment, Policy of; Fulbright, J. William.

Kennedy, Edward M. (1932–), U.S. senator (D-Mass.), 1962– . During his first six years in office, Kennedy, the brother of President John F. Kennedy, focused primarily on domestic issues. He offered limited support to President Johnson's Vietnam policy in January 1966 by not opposing the bombing of North Vietnam.

Kennedy visited South Vietnam in 1965 and in 1967 began to criticize America's the war. Kennedy became openly outspoken against the war in Vietnam after the assassination of his brother, Robert, on 4 June 1968. On 21 August Kennedy outlined a four-point plan to end the war. This plan included an end to the bombing of North Vietnam, negotiations with North Vietnam to remove all foreign troops from South Vietnam, formation of a government in South Vietnam that could survive a U.S. departure, and a decrease in the U.S. military presence to begin in 1968. Along with Senators Eugene J. McCarthy (D-Minn.) and George McGovern (D-S. Dak.), Kennedy sponsored a similar plank at the 1968 Democratic convention, but the delegates voted against it. Kennedy continued as a vocal opponent of President Nixon's war policy. He denounced the battle for Ap Bia (Hamburger Hill), gave a speech at the Boston protest of 100,000 people in the 1969 moratorium, criticized Nixon's apparent lack of a timetable for ending the war, and sharply condemned the invasion of Cambodia. In 1970 Kennedy demanded a withdrawal from Cambodia and Vietnam, and by 1973 he fully opposed the war in Vietnam.

See also: Congress, U.S.

Kennedy, John F. (1917–1963), U.S. representative (D-Mass.), 1947–1953; U.S. senator (D-Mass.), 1953–1960; U.S. president, 1961–1963. Vietnam, for Kennedy, was a symbol of America's commitment to contain communist advances in the developing world. As early as 1956, then-Senator Kennedy called South Vietnam "the cornerstone of the Free World in Southeast Asia," characterizing that struggling young nation as "a test of American responsibility and determination."

In the spring of 1961 Kennedy sought a negotiated settlement of the Laotian civil war, a decision that led to communist participation in a coalition government. The Laos compromise undermined the prospects for a similar compromise in Vietnam. Acutely conscious of images, Kennedy determined to avoid any additional Cold War defeats or retreats. In May 1961 he authorized a modest increase in the number of advisers attached to the U.S. Military Assistance Advisory Group (MAAG) in Vietnam, and sent 400 members of U.S. Special Forces to Vietnam to help train the South Vietnamese military. By the end of 1961, more than 3,000 U.S. military advisers were in Vietnam. The number grew to 11,300 a year later. That modest increase in U.S. support, however, did little to ease the problems facing South Vietnamese Premier Ngo Dinh Diem. In September 1961 Diem urgently requested a significant increase in U.S. economic assistance. Kennedy dispatched his military adviser Gen. Maxwell D. Taylor and National Security Council aide Walt W. Rostow to Saigon to provide him with a firsthand report.

The Taylor-Rostow assessment recommended the immediate dispatch of an 8,000-man logistical task force as a minimal step to insure the survival of the Saigon regime, with the caveat that more drastic measures might be required in the near future. During the administration's extended deliberations about the Taylor-Rostow report, several advisers, including the Joint Chiefs of Staff (JCS), urged the dispatch of regular combat troops while others urge d the president to seek a negotiated settlement similar to that concluded in Laos. Kennedy rejected the combat force option. He also staunchly opposed any neutralization scheme as a potentially dangerous sign of American weakness. Instead, the president chose a middle course, opting to increase the number of U.S. advisers and the volume of U.S. aid in the hopes that those steps would bolster the South Vietnamese government sufficiently to preclude the need for regular U.S. combat units.

His middle course brought greater U.S. influence to bear on the conduct of military operations in Vietnam. United States equipment and expertise lent valuable assistance to the counterinsurgency campaign of the South Vietnamese army. Upon the urging of U.S. advisers, Diem's government also inaugurated the strategic hamlet program to separate and protect the peasantry from the Viet Cong guerrillas and their North Vietnamese allies. This military-political progress soon proved illusory.

Viet Cong forces had by early 1963 adapted effectively to the widespread use of helicopters by the South Vietnamese and U.S. armed forces, largely neutralizing that tactical innovation. The strategic hamlet program also faced severe limitations. With the local Self-Defense Corps and Provincial Civil Guard units of the Diem government increasingly unwilling to engage large and determined Viet Cong forces, government control over the strategic hamlets steadily eroded.

In the spring and summer of 1963 a series of demonstrations against South Vietnamese President Ngo Dinh Diem's dictatorial rule was led by Buddhists, students, and other disaffected groups. Diem's heavy-handed response to those protests, capped by brutal government-sanctioned raids on Buddhist pagodas in August, brought South Vietnamese society to the brink of chaos. Even more alarming were the indications that Diem was seriously considering opening negotiations with the Viet Cong. A consensus soon developed among the president, most of his top national security aides in Washington, and U.S. Ambassador Henry Cabot Lodge in Saigon that Diem posed a fundamental obstacle to U.S. policy objectives in Vietnam. In August 1963 Kennedy authorized Lodge to cooperate with South Vietnamese officers plotting a coup against Diem. On 1 November 1963, the military seized power, in the process murdering Diem and his brother, Ngo Dinh Nhu. Three weeks later Kennedy was assassinated.

See also: American Friends of Vietnam; Ball, George W.; Bowles, Chester; Buddhists; Bundy, McGeorge; Catholics; Central Intelligence Agency; Domino Theory; Flexible Response; Halberstam, David; Harkins, Paul D.; Hilsman, Roger; Joint Chiefs of Staff; Military Assistance Command, Vietnam; McNamara, Robert; Ngo Dinh Diem; Pentagon Papers; Project 100,000; Ranch Hand, Operation; Rostow, Walt Whitman; Rusk, (David) Dean; Special Forces, U.S.; Taylor, Maxwell D.; Taylor-McNamara Report; Wheeler, Earle G.

Kennedy, Robert F, (1925–1968), U.S. attorney general, 1961–1964; U.S. senator (D-N.Y.), 1964–1968. Robert F. Kennedy moved from unconditional support for President John F. Kennedy's Vietnam policies to strong criticism of their continuation in the late 1960s. After his brother's assassination in 1963, Robert Kennedy remained in Johnson's cabinet as attorney general for several months. He resigned in 1964 and was elected to the U.S. Senate from New York. During the domestic debate over Vietnam policy in 1965, Kennedy supported Johnson, voting in May for a supplemental appropriations bill. At the same time, in his first major Senate speech on Vietnam, Kennedy articulated three possible policies that the United States could pursue: withdrawal, military escalation, or "honorable negotiations."

During the 1965 debate over Vietnam, Kennedy supported President Johnson. On 19 February 1966 Kennedy broke with the Johnson administration, calling for a coalition government in South Vietnam, yet he dismissed any suggestion of a U.S. withdrawal. On 2 March 1967 he blamed himself and his brother John F. Kennedy for having pursued the wrong policy in Vietnam, and continued his attacks on U.S. policy throughout 1967. In the campaign for the 1968 Democratic nomination Kennedy made the war the central issue, repeatedly advocating a negotiated solution. He was assassinated on 5 June 1968 in Los Angeles after winning the California primary.

See also: Schlesinger, Arthur M. Jr.

Kent State University. President Nixon's 30 April 1970 televised announcement that troops had invaded Cambodia to attack North Vietnamese and Viet Cong bases prompted student protests across the United States. Students at Kent State University in Ohio staged a demonstration that degenerated into a riot on 1 May. On 2 May, protesting students burned down the campus Reserve Officers' Training Corps (ROTC) building. In response, Governor James Rhodes called in the National Guard.

At midday on 4 May, students gathered to protest the Cambodian invasion and the presence of the National Guard on campus. National Guard soldiers moved in with tear gas to disperse the crowd and encountered heckling and rock throwing. Without warning, some of the soldiers fired upon the students, killing four and wounding at least nine. The Kent State shootings provoked protests on other college campuses. Hun-dreds of schools closed as a result. A grand jury exonerated the National Guard soldiers; 25 protesters were indicted. Three were convicted of minor misdemeanors; all other charges were dropped or resulted in acquittals.

See also: Cambodian Incursion.

Kentucky, Operation. One of several 1967 U.S. Marine Corps engagements against North Vietnamese Army units just below the Demilitarized Zone.

See also: Demilitarized Zone; Marines, U.S.

Kerrey, Joseph R. (Bob), (1943–), governor of Nebraska, 1983–1987; U.S. senator (D-Neb.), 1989– . Kerrey, who served as a U.S. Navy SEAL lieutenant in Vietnam, was awarded the Medal of Honor for his actions while leading a 14 March 1969 night assault near Nha Trang Bay during which he was severely wounded.

See also: Medal of Honor.

Kerry, John F. (1943–), U.S. senator, (D-Mass.), 1985– . Kerry, who served as a U.S. Navy lieutenant in Vietnam, was a founding member of the antiwar

group, Vietnam Veterans Against the War in 1971.

See also: Vietnam Veterans Against the War.

Kha. *See* Lao Theung

Khai Dinh (1884–1925), emperor of Vietnam, 1916–1925. Khai Dinh had little power as emperor over French-ruled Vietnam. He was succeeded by his son, Bao Dai.

See also: Bao Dai.

Kham Duc. Site of a U.S. Special Forces camp 50 miles south of Da Nang, near the Laotian border, evacuated under intense Viet Cong and North Vietnamese Army attack in May 1968.

Khang, Le Nguyen. *See* Le Nguyen Khang

Khanh, Nguyen. *See* Nguyen Khanh

Khe Sanh. A Marine Corps base in northwestern South Vietnam, some 10 kilometers (6 miles) from the Laotian border and about 23 kilometers (14 miles) south of the DMZ. Khe Sanh was surrounded by tall, tree-canopied hills, some more than 1,000 meters (3,000 feet) in elevation. Khe Sanh overlooked Route 9, the main eastward entryway from Laos into South Vietnam's northern coastal region.

In August 1962, the Military Assistance Command, Vietnam (MACV), established a U.S.

Army Special Forces camp for border surveillance near Khe Sanh. In the summer of 1966 Gen. William Westmoreland, concerned over possible North Vietnamese infiltration, ordered the Marines to set up a base there. The garrison was reinforced to regimental strength in the spring of 1967. From 24 April through 12 May 1967, the Marines engaged North Vietnamese regulars for a series of strategic hills, retaining them after heavy casualties on both sides. By the end of 1967, U.S. intelligence indicated that elements of three North Vietnamese Army (NVA) divisions were in the Khe Sanh sector. Since the late summer or early fall, NVA forces had successfully cut Route 9 and the only means of resupply for the base was by air. The U.S. command reinforced Khe Sanh and by 24 January 1968, the 26th Marines' commander, Col. David E. Lownds, had one artillery and four infantry battalions under his operational control. With small detachments from the other services and the approximately 300-man South Vietnamese 37th ARVN Ranger battalion, the Khe Sanh defenders numbered more than 6,000 troops.

Fearful of a debacle similar to that of the French at Dien Bien Phu in 1954, President Lyndon B. Johnson sought guarantees from Westmoreland and the Joint Chiefs of Staff (JCS) that Khe Sanh would not be overrun. They reassured him that given the U.S. artillery and air support

available to the Marines at Khe Sanh, the base could be defended indefinitely. On 21 January, forewarned by an NVA defector, the Marine outpost on Hill 861 beat back a determined assault by NVA infantry. While their ground forces were unable to capture any Marine positions, North Vietnamese artillery, which included Soviet-made 152mm howitzers firing from positions in Laos, scored a direct hit on a Marine ammunition supply point, destroying about 1,500 tons of high explosive. Marine casualties for the day were 14 dead and 43 wounded. While the enemy launched occasional battalion-size ground attacks on exposed Marine positions, North Vietnamese forces confined most of their activity to small probing assaults and artillery, mortar, and rocket bombardment. Throughout the Tet Offensive launched shortly before the siege, the situation at Khe Sanh remained much the same. The heaviest loss to U.S. forces occurred on 25 February, when the North Vietnamese ambushed a Marine platoon, inflicting 48 casualties. Four nights later, on 29 February, NVA forces attempted to breach the South Vietnamese Ranger battalion's perimeter, but were repulsed with heavy losses when caught in the open by artillery fire and a B-52 Arc Light strike. Westmoreland began an all-out air assault including both tactical aircraft and B-52 bombers, code-named Operation Niagara, against North Vietnamese troop positions. B-52s and U.S. tactical aircraft dropped thousands of tons of high explosives on North Vietnamese positions and U.S. Air Force and Marine transport aircraft brought in food and ammunition. Although enemy antiaircraft fire and artillery kept large Marine and Air Force transports from landing at the exposed Khe Sanh airfield, the Air Force devised several sophisticated parachute drop techniques to keep the base resupplied. Using seismic and acoustic sensors closely coordinated with U.S. artillery and aviation, the 6,000 Marines at Khe Sanh held the enemy at bay until the northeast monsoon weather broke and reinforcements arrived. On 15 April, in Operation Pegasus, a relieving task force of combined Army-Marine and South Vietnamese Army forces, under the 1st Cavalry Division, broke through and lifted the siege. General Westmoreland vetoed initial plans to raze the base, but after he relinquished command of MACV in June, his successor, Gen. Creighton W. Abrams, ordered the abandonment of Khe Sanh. On 5 July the Marines officially closed the base.

See also: Arc Light, Operation; Barrier Concept; Cleland, Joseph Maxwell; Johnson, Lyndon B.; Niagara, Operation; Tet Offensive.

Khiem, Tran Thien. *See* Tran Thien Khiem

Khieu Samphan (1932–), Cambodian communist leader.

Khieu Samphan joined the Khmer Rouge communist insurgents in 1967. He became commander in chief of the Khmer Rouge High Command in 1973 and headed the communist Cambodian state from 1976–1979.

See also: Cambodia; Khmer Rouge.

Khmer Kampuchea Kron (KKK). Armed force of ethnic Cambodians living in the Mekong Delta that fought the South Vietnamese government for the return of Khmer land in the mid-1950s. In the 1960s many Khmer Kampuchea Kron fought the Viet Cong and North Vietnamese in U.S.-supported Civilian Irregular Defense Group units.

See also: Civilian Irregular Defense Groups.

Khmer People. The ancient ancestors of the modern-day Cambodians. From the 10th to the 15th centuries the Khmer were the dominant power in Southeast Asia, ruling all of modern Cambodia and parts of Vietnam, Laos, Thailand, Burma and the Malay Peninsula. The most famous Khmer cultural achievement was construction of Angkor Wat, a mammoth temple complex, in the 12th century.

See also: Angkor Wat; Cambodia.

Khmer Rouge. The French term Prince Sihanouk coined in the 1960s to describe Cambodia's communist-led dissidents. The Communist Party of Kampuchea (CPK) grew out of the anti-French independence movement and was linked to Vietnam's communists. Its early leadership was rural, Buddhist-educated, and moderate, but by 1963, Pol Pot's younger group of urban, Paris-educated, anti-Vietnamese radicals had taken over the standing committee of the CPK Central Committee.

In the early 1970s, the Khmer Rouge, allied with North Vietnam in a war against the U.S.-backed Lon Nol government, murdered nearly one thousand Vietnam-trained Cambodian communists. The purges accelerated during the U.S. aerial bombardment of 1973. In the three years after its 1975 victory over Lon Nol, the Khmer Rouge killed as many as two million Cambodians in a holocaust that became known as "The Killing Fields." Targets of the Khmer Rouge included those allied with Sihanouk, moderate indigenous communists, and such independent Marxists as Hou Yuon, a popular Paris-educated intellectual who disagreed with Pol Pot.

The Khmer Rouge's activities following its 1975 victory over Lon Nol demonstrated the anti-urban sentiment that dominated the Khmer Rouge leadership. Khmer Rouge forces quickly emptied the cities of their 2 million inhabitants, who were forced to labor in rural areas. Rural peasants initially supported the Khmer Rouge, but they too were soon forced into a life of unpaid collective labor. Rights to land, freedom of religion, and family life were prohibited; couples were separated, and youths were drafted into the work force, army, or militia. Many peasant children were trained to spy on their parents and to kill suspected "enemies" such as former city dwellers, "CIA" and "KGB" agents, and alleged malingerers.

The Khmer Rouge also targeted ethnic minorities, who were removed from their homes and massacred, starved, or worked to death. Most victims of the Khmer Rouge, however, were members of the majority Khmer population. On 10 May 1978, Phnom Penh radio broadcast a call not only to "exterminate the 50 million Vietnamese" but also to "purify the masses of the people" of Cambodia. The moderate Cambodian communists in the Eastern Zone rebelled two weeks later. Pol Pot's Khmer Rouge armies were unable to crush the rebellion quickly, but branded the 1.5 million easterners "Khmer bodies with Vietnamese minds." Between 100,000 and 250,000 were exterminated in six months, bringing the death toll in four years of Khmer Rouge rule to 1 .5 million.

On 7 January 1979, the army of the Socialist Republic of Vietnam (SRV) captured Phnom Penh, drove the remaining Khmer Rouge into Thailand, and ended the holocaust. Former Khmer Rouge Hun Sen, who had defected to Vietnam in 1977, established a new regime. Sen became prime minister in 1985 and proceeded with liberalization. Pol Pot's Khmer Rouge army of 10,000 troops, assisted by the People's Republic of China, posed a threat on the western border until Pol Pot's death in 1998. The few remaining Khmer Rouge and their families then went into exile in Thailand.

See also: Cambodia; Dean, John Gunther; FANK; Ford, Gerald R. Jr.; Heng Samrin; Hun Sen; Lon Nol; Phnom Penh; Pol Pot; Sihanouk, Norodom; Thailand; United Nations.

Khmer Serei (Free Khmer). Strongly anti-communist Cambodian paramilitary group backed by the United States, South Vietnam, and Thailand. Based in South Vietnam, the group, headed by Son Ngoc Thanh, unsuccessfully tried to overthrow the regime of Prince Norodom Sihanouk beginning in the late 1950s.

See also: Cambodia; Sihanouk, Norodom.

Khrushchev, Nikita (1894–1971), secretary general of the Soviet Communist Party and leader of the USSR, 1958–1964. Khrushchev provided only lukewarm support to North Vietnam and the Viet Cong during the U.S. war. Anxious to improve relations with the West, Khrushchev pressured the North Vietnamese to negotiate with the United States in exchange for Soviet military aid. Ho Chi Minh distrusted him and welcomed the more hard-line Leonid Brezhnev, who succeeded Khrushchev.

See also: Brezhnev, Leonid; Union of Soviet Socialist Republics.

KIA. *See* Killed in Action

Killed in Action (KIA). U.S. military terminology for service personnel who lose their lives during a war. In the Vietnam War, 47,244 American military personnel were killed in action. An additional 10,446 service personnel died as a result of accidents and disease in Vietnam. The names of all of those who died are engraved on the Vietnam Veterans Memorial in Washington, D.C.

See also: Vietnam Veterans Memorial.

Killing Fields, The (1984). Acclaimed Hollywood film about the Cambodian holocaust directed by Roland Jaffe.

Killing Zone, The (1978). Critically praised Vietnam War memoir by Frederick Downs based on his experiences as a U.S. Army 4th Infantry Division lieutenant in Vietnam.

Kim, Le Van. *See* Le Van Kim

King, Coretta Scott (1927–), The widow of civil rights leader Martin Luther King, Jr., Coretta Scott King led a candlelight vigil in Washington, D.C., during the 15 October 1969 Vietnam

Moratorium Day antiwar demonstration.

See also: King, Martin Luther Jr.; Vietnam Moratorium Committee.

King, Martin Luther Jr. (1929–1968), civil rights leader; cochairman of Clergy and Laity Concerned About Vietnam, 1966–1968. King first broke with the Johnson administration over the Vietnam War in July 1965 in a controversial speech opposing escalation and calling for a negotiated settlement. King's speech provoked harsh criticism from several quarters. President Johnson, recently allied with King to gain the passage of the Civil Rights Act of 1964 and the Voting Rights Act of 1965, felt betrayed by King's criticism of his Vietnam policy. The *New York Times* and other influential papers chastised King for linking the civil rights and antiwar movements, and the National Association for the Advancement of Colored People (NAACP) passed a resolution calling such linkage a "serious tactical mistake." Set back by such disapproval, King maintained a low profile on the war for the next year, but by late 1966 he decided he could no longer remain silent and became cochairman of Clergy and Laity Concerned About Vietnam.

King based his opposition to the Vietnam War on his belief in nonviolence, his concern about the war's cost and its effect on the Great Society, and the racial implications of the war as it became apparent that a disproportionate number of young black men were fighting and dying in Vietnam. King's criticism of the war became increasingly forceful throughout 1967. He explicitly aligned the civil rights movement with the antiwar movement, renewed his call for civil disobedience, and urged young men to seek conscientious objector status.

See also: African-Americans; Great Society; Hawks and Doves.

Kingfisher, Operation. U.S. Third Marine Division operation in July to September 1967 against North Vietnamese Army units along the Demilitarized Zone supported by artillery, naval gunfire support, and air strikes.

See also: Demilitarized Zone.

Kingpin, Operation. Code name for the joint U.S. Army–Air Force raid on 21 November 1970 on the Son Tay prison camp outside Hanoi, the largest and most celebrated U.S. prisoner-of-war (POW) Vietnam War rescue effort. No U.S. prisoners were found at the camp.

See also: POW/MIA Controversy; Son Tay Raid.

Kinnard, Harry W. Jr. (1915–), U.S. Army general. Gen. Kinnard was the commander of the 11th Air Assault Division, which he took to Vietnam in 1965 under its new name, the 1st Cavalry Division (Airmobile).

See also: Helicopters.

Kissinger, Henry (1923–), national security adviser, 1969–1975; secretary of state, 1973–1977. Henry Kissinger played a prominent role in setting U.S. policy in the Vietnam War in the Johnson, Ford, and Nixon administrations. He first undertook negotiations regarding Vietnam on behalf of the Johnson administration while a Harvard professor in 1967. Kissinger observed the Paris peace talks' preliminary public negotiations in May 1968, reporting to the Democratic and Republican presidential nominees, Hubert Humphrey and Richard Nixon.

In the summer of 1969 Kissinger returned to Paris to start secret negotiations with representatives of North Vietnam. These so-called back-channel talks, initially conducted without the knowledge of the official U.S. delegation to the peace negotiations, soon became the real venue for discussion. In three years of negotiations Kissinger offered to separate the military aspects from the political aspects of the war, a significant weakening of U.S. support for the South Vietnamese government. To balance that concession to the north, Kissinger sought to have the Soviet Union and the PRC, two communist countries whose relations with the United States had warmed, put pressure on the DRV. Neither the USSR nor the PRC, however, was willing or able to exert the sort of influence that Kissinger wanted.

From 1969 until the end of the war Kissinger directed often-secret negotiations over the future of Vietnam and advised Nixon and Ford about the military conduct of the war. Kissinger supported the policy of Vietnamization. Inside the government, he backed Nixon's escalations: the 1969 bombing of Cambodia and the 1970 invasion of that country; the 1971 raid into Laos; and the bombing of North Vietnam in May and December 1972. On 27 January 1973 Kissinger and North Vietnamese negotiator Le Duc Tho signed a peace agreement that called for a cease fire, the withdrawal of U.S. troops and the exchange of POWs. In September 1973, he received the Nobel Peace prize jointly with Le Duc Tho. In early 1975 the war resumed in earnest, and Kissinger urged President Ford to reenter the fighting. Ford refused to resume bombing or send in U.S. combat troops.

See also: Bunker, Ellsworth; Cambodian Incursion; Dobrynin, Anatoly; Ford, Gerald R.; Hoang Duc Nha; Laird, Melvin R.; Lake, Anthony W.; Le Duc Tho; National Security Council; Nixon, Richard M.; Paris Accords; San Antonio Formula; Schlesinger, James R.; Union of Soviet Socialist Republics; Watergate.

Kit Carson Scouts. Former Viet Cong and North Vietnamese Army soldiers who deserted their units and served as scouts with the U.S. military in Vietnam.

See also: Chieu Hoi (Open Arms) Program.

Kitty Hawk, USS. U.S. Navy aircraft carrier first deployed off the South Vietnamese coast in 1964.

See also: Aircraft Carriers; Navy, U.S.

Kleindienst, Richard (1923–), Attorney General of the United States, June 1972 to April 1973. In 1969, as Deputy Attorney General, Kleindienst led an effort to prosecute all violations of the law by members of the radical antiwar movement.

See also: Justice, Department of.

Knowland, William F. (1908–1974), U.S. senator (R-Calif.), 1945–1959; Senate majority leader, 1953–1955; minority leader, 1955–1959. Knowland, a leader of the "China lobby," consistently urged greater U.S. involvement in opposing communism in China, Korea, and Vietnam. He labeled the Geneva accords of 1954 a communist victory, and he was an important congressional supporter of South Vietnamese President Ngo Dinh Diem.

See also: Congress, U.S.

Koh Tang. Island off the Cambodian coast. On 15 May 1975 U.S. Marines stormed the island after receiving intelligence reports that the crew of the merchant ship *Mayaguez* was being held there. Eighteen Marines were killed in the rescue attempt. The *Mayaguez* crew at the time was adrift in a fishing boat.

See also: Harold E. Holt, USS; *Mayaguez* Incident.

Komer, Robert W. (1922–), deputy commander, U.S. Military Assistance Command, Vietnam (MACV), 1967–1968. A senior CIA analyst, Komer was deputy national security adviser when President Johnson named him special assistant for pacification in 1966. Sent to Saigon with ambassadorial rank a year later, Komer headed Civil Operations and Revolutionary Development Support (CORDS), taking charge of diverse counterinsurgency programs operated by the military, the State Department, the U.S. Agency for International Development, and the CIA. Komer sent thousands of pacification teams into every district of South Vietnam with orders to root out the Viet Cong infrastructure. CORDS lavished U.S. aid on friendly villages while hostile areas were forcibly evacuated to deprive Viet Cong forces of support. Komer's computerized Hamlet Evaluation Survey (HES) showed that the number of Viet Cong guerrillas was steadily decreasing—right up to the Tet Offensive. He initiated the controversial multi-faceted effort to eliminate the Viet Cong infrastructure, known as the Phoenix program, which led to assassinations of 20,000 Viet Cong suspects after his departure in 1968.

See also: Abrams, Creighton W. Jr.; Counterinsurgency; Cao Van Vien; Pacification; Phoenix Program.

Kompong Som. Cambodian city that was the target of four punitive U.S. air strikes following the 12 May 1975 Cambodian seizure of the U.S. merchant ship Magayguez.

See also: Ford, Gerald R.; *Mayaguez* Incident.

Komunyakaa, Yusef (1947–), poet whose work is influenced by his service of as a U.S. Army journalist in Vietnam. Komunyakaa's *Neon Vernacular* won the 1994 Pulitzer Prize for Poetry and the Kingsley Tufts Poetry Award.

Kong Le (c. 1934–), Laotian army captain. Kong Le led the August 1960 coup that overthrew a pro-U.S. regime and returned Prince Souvanna Phouma to the head of government. Le's coup alarmed U.S. policymakers, who feared the spread of communism in Southeast Asia. By December, rightist Laotian forces supported by the U.S. Central Intelligence Agency defeated Kong Le's troops and retook the capital city of Vientiane.

See also: Laos; Souvanna Phouma.

Kontum. Vietnamese city in the Central Highlands some 50 km north of Pleiku, primarily inhab- ited by ethnic minority groups. During the Vietnam War, Kontum was nearly destroyed by B-52 bombing and heavy fighting during 1972 North Vietnamese Army Easter Offensive.

See also: Central Highlands; Easter Offensive.

Korea, Republic of. The Republic of Korea (South Korea) sent large numbers of combat troops to Vietnam, a level second only to that of South Vietnam and of the United States. It did so in order to cement the South Korean alliance with the United States and thus help maintain the U.S. security presence in Asia.

The Republic of Korea deployed its first troops (known as ROKs) early in 1965 in conjunction with the arrival of the first U.S. combat troops. The Republic of Korea Military Assistance Group, Vietnam arrived in March 1965. Based in Bien Hoa province, it consisted of engineer, medical support, construction support, and security. In November 1965 South Korea sent its Capital Infantry Division and 2d Marine Brigade to provide security for Cam Ranh Bay and Qui Nhon. Approximately 20,000 South Koreans served in Vietnam under Gen. Chae Myung-Shin during 1965, a number that more than doubled to 45,000 in 1966. South Korea deployed the 9th ROK Division in September and October 1966, and in 1967, it sent a marine battalion.

The issue of command of Korean troops remained sensitive throughout the first few years of South Korea's involvement. Koreans served under the Free World Military Assistance Policy Council, but in 1965, as a result of the South Korean reputation for brutality, they operated under special South Vietnamese restrictions—restrictions placed on no other Free World force. They were forbidden to fire unless attacked and forbidden to move outside specified areas. South Korea consequently demanded that its troops serve only under U.S. command.

South Korea was particularly interested in keeping its casualties at a low level and consequently relied on extensive preparation and the use of what the United States viewed as excessive U.S. air support. South Korean ROKs engaged primarily in small unit operations. Troop deployment reached a high of 50,000 in 1968 and continued at approximately 48,000 during the following two years. As the United States reduced its troop levels in 1971, South Korea agreed to keep its Capital and 9th Infantry divisions in Vietnam until March 1973.

See also: Domino Theory; Four-Party Joint Military Commission; Free World; International Reaction.

Korean War. The first application of the policy of containment in Asia, the Korean War served as a model for some U.S. policymakers during the Vietnam War.

In Korea, the United States sought to contain Chinese-backed communist North Korea north of the thirty-eighth parallel to preserve a non-communist, democratic South Korea.

The Korean War began in 1950 and ended in a stalemate in July 1953. The experience showed the difficulties of fighting a land war in Asia. It also contributed to the U.S. decision to enter the Vietnam conflict. The People's Republic of China's support of North Korea and later North Vietnam caused the United States to view events in Vietnam as communist expansionism rather than as an anticolonial or a nationalist movement. United States intervention had allowed South Korea to remain a separate, anticommunist state, the same goal the U.S. government had for South Vietnam, convincing U.S. policymakers that a favorable outcome could be achieved. The French secured U.S. aid for their struggle in Vietnam by emphasizing the similarities between the two conflicts. U.S. policymakers saw both wars as fights against communist expansion. President Lyndon Johnson invoked the stalemate in Korea as justification for an expanded effort in Vietnam.

See also: Casualties; Helicopters; Ridgway, Matthew B.

Koster, Samuel (1920–), U.S. Army major general, commanding general of Americal Division, 1968. General Koster was indicted for offenses connected with the cover-up of the My Lai massacre. Charges against him were dismissed, but the Army reduced him in rank and issued a letter of censure, effectively terminating his military career.

See also: My Lai.

Kosygin, Alexei (1904–1980), prime minister of the Soviet Union, 1964–1980. Kosygin traveled to Hanoi in early 1965 to press North Vietnam for negotiations with the United States as a condition of Soviet aid. U.S. bombing of North Vietnam ended Kosygin's trip and hardened his position on the conflict. Kosygin dropped the requirement for negotiations and approved unconditional Soviet military aid. Two years later, Kosygin informed British Prime Minister Harold Wilson that the Soviet Union was ready to pressure North Vietnam once again to come to the negotiating table.

See also: Great Britain; Khrushchev, Nikita; Union of Soviet Socialist Republics.

Kovic, Ron (1946–), former U.S. Marine severely wounded in Vietnam whose 1976 war and post-war memoir, *Born on the Fourth of July*, was the basis for the Oliver Stone film of the same name.

Krepinevich, Andrew (1950–), U.S. military officer and military strategist. In his 1986 book, *The Army and Vietnam*, Krepinevich argued that the U.S. military attrition strategy of conventional warfare was ill-suited in Vietnam and that the military should have concentrated on counterinsurgency measures.

See also: Attrition Strategy; Counterinsurgency.

Krogh, Egil (Bud) Jr. (1939–), aide to Nixon White House chief domestic adviser John Ehrlichman. Krogh headed the White House "plumbers," and planned the burglary of Daniel Ellsberg's psychiatrist's office. In January 1974 he was sentenced to six months in prison for his role in the burglary.

See also: Plumbers; Watergate.

Krulak, Victor (1913–), lieutenant general, U.S. Marine Corps. A 1934 Naval Academy graduate, Krulak had a distinguished combat record in WWII and the Korean War. Major General Krulak served as special assistant for counterinsurgency and special activities for the Joint Chiefs of Staff from February 1962 until January 1964. As such he was responsible for the development of counterinsurgency doctrine and policy, especially as it applied to Vietnam. Promoted to lieutenant general, Krulak commanded the Fleet Marine Force until his retirement in June 1968. In this capacity, he was responsible for the readiness and organization of all Marine units in the Pacific, including Vietnam. Although not in the operational chain of command, Krulak strongly influenced Marine strategy in

South Vietnam's northern provinces. With his emphasis on pacification, he was a strong dissenting voice to the search-and-destroy tactics and attrition strategy pursued by operational commander, Gen. William C. Westmoreland.

See also: Attrition Strategy; Search-and-Destroy; Westmoreland, William C.

Kuntsler, William (1921–1995), attorney well known for his antiwar activism. Kunstler was the defense attorney in the highly publicized Catonsville Nine and Chicago Seven trials.

See also: Berrigan, Daniel; Berrigan, Philip; Berrigan Brothers; Chicago Seven.

Kuomintang. Political party that ruled China from 1928–1949. After Japan surrendered at the end of WWII, Kuomintang troops occupied northern Vietnam beginning in September 1945. The Chinese troops left Vietnam in March 1946 after signing a treaty with France in which the French relinquished all extra-territorial rights to China.

See also: People's Republic of China; Japan.

Ky, Nguyen Cao. *See* Nguyen Cao Ky

Lac Long Quan (Dragon Lord of Lac), mythological
Vietnamese figure considered the founder of Vietnamese civilization. According to legend, Lac Long Quan, a lord of the sea, came to the Red River Delta in northern Vietnam to defeat evil spirits and to bring advanced civilization to the people. His marriage to Au Co, the wife of a lord of the mountains, produced one hundred sons, the ancestors of the Vietnamese race.

See also: Red River (Song Hong) Delta.

Laird, Melvin R. (1922–), sec-
retary of defense, 1969–1973. Daring WWII, Laird served aboard the USS *Maddox*—the same destroyer involved in the Tonkin Gulf incident. Laird pushed for timely disengagement from Vietnam. After visiting South Vietnam twice in 1969–1970, Laird urged President Nixon "to initiate the removal from Southeast Asia of some U.S. military personnel," and warned that victory was impossible "considering the restrictions with which we are compelled to operate." Laird popularized the term "Vietnamization" to describe shifting the burden of fighting from the United States to South

Vietnam. Realizing that abandoning an ally would be as politically untenable as further escalation, Laird portrayed Vietnamization as "a crucial test of the Nixon Doctrine," which relied on regional powers armed by the United States to preserve international stability. Laird also devised the term protective reaction to describe the newly cautious combat posture of U.S. forces in Vietnam, which was designed to minimize casualties by replacing search-and-destroy tactics. He advocated lower draft calls, faster troop withdrawals and reduction of U.S. war expenditures. Laird was also the first U.S. official to condemn North Vietnam publicly for mistreating U.S. prisoners of war.

Laird wielded considerable clout early in the Nixon administration, but due to disagreements with Henry Kissinger and the President over Vietnam policy, he later was not always informed of White House decisions. Laird opposed the secret bombing of Cambodia and the 1972 "Christmas" bombing of North Vietnam. He resigned in March 1973.

See also: Abrams, Creighton W. Jr.; Cambodian Incursion; Kissinger, Henry; Menu, Operation; Vietnamization.

Lake, Anthony W. (1939–),
vice consul in Saigon, 1964–1965; special assistant to national security adviser Henry Kissinger, 1969–1970. Lake resigned in 1970 to protest the invasion of Cambodia. Initially a strong supporter of the war, Lake grew skeptical about the possibility of victory, and urged a

negotiated settlement. Kissinger ordered wire surveillance of his home two weeks after Lake's resignation. In 1989, Kissinger apologized for the action.

See also: Cambodian Incursion.

Lam Son 719. Operation Lam Son 719, a crucial test of Vietnamization, began 18 February 1971. U.S. forces provided air and artillery support for 16,000 elite Army of the Republic of Vietnam (ARVN) troops who crossed into Laos to raid the Ho Chi Minh Trail. All sustained heavy losses: more than 8,000 ARVN and 1,460 American casualties, along with 100 helicopters and 150 tanks left behind in the withdrawal. The North Vietnamese lost nearly 20,000 soldiers and enough equipment to set back the planned Easter Offensive until 1972. President Nixon declared the operation a success because the NVA suffered 20,000 casualties.

See also: Ho Chi Minh Trail; Vietnamization.

Landing Zone (LZ). U.S. military term for helicopter landing zone, usually in remote areas in South Vietnam. Many LZ's were given code names, such as the First Cavalry Division's LZ X-Ray in the 1965 Ia Drang Battle.

Land Reform. In predominantly rural Vietnam, the land policies of both North and South Vietnamese governments were crucial tools in acquiring

political support. The land reform schemes of the North Vietnamese Democratic Republic of Vietnam (DRV) and the South Vietnamese National Liberation Front (NFL) generally promoted the welfare of poorer and mid-level peasants. The South Vietnamese Republic of Vietnam (RVN) until the late 1960s favored wealthy landlords.

In 1946 as war erupted with the French, the communist-led Viet Minh began policies to mobilize peasants in support of the nationalist movement. In the late 1940s, the Viet Minh enforced a 25-percent rent reduction and redistributed the land of colonials and pro-French Vietnamese to the peasants. The policy particularly benefited peasants in the south, where 500,000 received the property of pro-French landlords. Communist Party elites wavered initially on whether to pursue confrontational policies against pro-Viet Minh landlords.

In 1953, the communist-led Viet Minh began a campaign to eradicate the rich peasant landlord classes. Built on Maoist doctrine, the policy entailed massive land redistribution to poor and mid-level peasants. After initial success, the party accelerated the program in 1955, which led to extensive conflict within the countryside. Violence against landlords intensified, and many poor peasants faced imprisonment by abusive local tribunals. A People's Army of Vietnam (PAVN) division suppressed a peasant uprising in

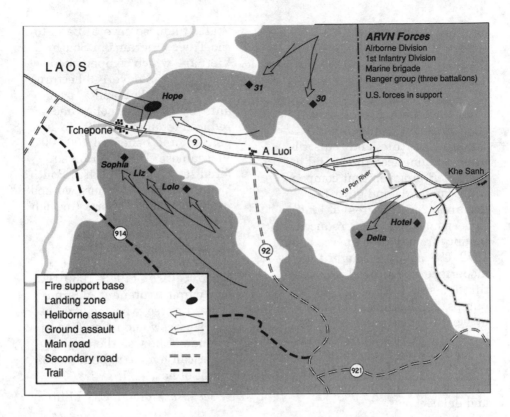

LAOS

ARVN Forces
Airborne Division
1st Infantry Division
Marine brigade
Ranger group (three battalions)

U.S. forces in support

Hope

♦ 31

♦ 30

Tchepone

9

A Luoi

Sophia

Liz ♦

Lolo ♦

Xe Pon River

Khe Sanh

914

Hotel ♦

♦ Delta

92

Fire support base	♦
Landing zone	⬮
Heliborne assault	⇐
Ground assault	⇦
Main road	═══
Secondary road	═ ═ ═
Trail	▬ ▬ ▬

921

Operation Lam Son 719, 8 February to 9 April 1971.

Nghe An, Ho Chi Minh's home province. An estimated 30,000–100,000 died in the turmoil before the government ended the program in 1956.

Beginning in 1958, the DRV tried to collectivize agriculture by organizing peasants into large producer cooperatives. They also sought to increase production by implementing crop diversification and collective water technology such as canal building. Surplus output, they hoped, would help finance industrialization projects. The collectivization effort achieved considerable success; by 1960, 86 percent of peasants were in cooperatives. Water programs also improved

productivity, although farming remained nonmechanized. By 1959, production of staple crops such as rice, corn, and potatoes had increased to 5.79 million metric tons, a 47-percent increase from 1955.

The Republic of Vietnam sponsored land policies largely favorable to landlords, as Ngo Dinh Diem had allied his government with this powerful group. The 1955 program established a moderate rent limit of 25 percent of crops. The policy, however, angered many peasants, who had paid no rent under the Viet Minh. A later ordinance promoted moderate redistribution and some limits on large landholdings. But Diem's vice president, Nguyen Ngoc Tho, a wealthy landlord, oversaw the program and enforced only minor reforms.

In 1969 the U.S. pressured RVN President Nguyen Van Thieu to institute land redistribution and financed the "Land to the Tiller" program that compensated landlords and gave 1–3 hectares (2.5–7.4 acres) of land to peasants. The policy reduced tenancy from 60 to 34 percent in 1972. U.S. advisers sought to modernize agricultural practices through seed technology, water pumps, and fertilizer purchased by wealthy peasants and landlords. The expected production boom, however, never materialized. South Vietnamese elites thwarted reform through fraud and delay.

Also in the South, NLF land reforms varied across regions under its control. The insurgents generally pursued egalitarian policies that benefited poorer peasants, which resulted in decreased rural support for the RVN government. In a similar pattern to the DRV's land reform, the NLF did not challenge the landlord class until after 1963, when it had consolidated its political and military position. By 1964, an estimated 1.5 million hectares (3.8 million acres) of land had been redistributed by NLF policies.

See also: Ngo Dinh Diem; Nguyen Van Thieu; Viet Minh.

Land-to-the-Tiller Program. Beginning in 1969, the United

States financed several Land-to-the-Tiller programs in South Vietnam, which compensated landlords and gave 1–3 hectares (2.5–7.4 acres) of land to peasants. By 1972, the policy had reduced tenancy from 60 to 34 percent, and benefited 400,000 Vietnamese. The program suffered setbacks when large South Vietnamese land owners worked to thwart reform efforts through fraud and delay.

See also: Land Reform.

Lane, Sharon (1943–1969), U.S. Army first lieutenant. Sharon Lane, a nurse, was one of eight U.S. servicewomen who died in Vietnam. She was the only American female to be killed as a result of hostile fire.

See also: Women, U.S. Military.

Langlais, Pierre Charles (1909–), French Army colonel. Langlais, one of France's most respected soldiers, commanded the French 2nd Airborne Battle Group at Dien Bien Phu.

See also: Dien Bien Phu.

Lang Son. City in northern Vietnam and the site of a September 1940 battle in which the Japanese overran a French outpost and an October 1950 battle in which French forces were soundly defeated by the Viet Minh.

See also: Lattre de Tassigny, Jean de.

Lang Vei. Site of a U.S. Special Forces camp near the South

Vietnamese-Lao border, about 14 kilometers (9 miles) southwest of the Khe Sanh base. On 7 February 1968 a North Vietnamese division equipped with Soviet-made light tanks overran the camp, which was defended by some 350 Montagnards and 24 U.S. advisers. Almost 300 of the Lang Vei garrison were killed, wounded, or missing, including 10 U.S. Special Forces soldiers killed or missing and 13 wounded. The event marked the beginning of the siege of Khe Sanh.

See also: Khe Sanh.

Laniel, Joseph (1889–1975), prime minister, French Fourth Republic, June 1953 to June 1954. In June 1953 Laniel's government promised a measure of independence for the Associated States, France's new name for its Indochinese colonies, and endorsed the Navarre Plan, Gen. Henri Navarre's design to subdue the Viet Minh. After Navarre's defeat at Dien Bien Phu, Laniel began negotiations to end the war, but his government was wracked with insurmountable internal divisions. Pierre Mendès-France replaced him, and with widespread public support, successfully concluded the Geneva peace agreement in 1954.

See also: Bidault, Georges; Navarre, Henri; Navarre Plan.

Lansdale, Edward G.
(1908–1987), major general, U.S. Air Force; assistant air attaché, U.S. embassy in Saigon, 1954–1956; special assistant to the U.S. ambassador, 1965–1968. Gen. Edward Lansdale was the model for Alden Pyle in Graham Greene's *The Quiet American* (1955) and for Edwin Hillendale in William Lederer and Eugene Berdick's *The Ugly American* (1958).

A former advertising man, Lansdale served with the Office of Strategic Services (OSS) in WWII. Working for the Central Intelligence Agency (CIA) from the time of its inception until 1956, he served with the CIA in the Philippines before arriving in South Vietnam on 1 June 1954. His mission was to encourage emigration from North Vietnam and to shore up the South Vietnamese government. Lansdale helped organize the departure of nearly one million Catholic refugees from the north as the communists took over. Diem won an election with Lansdale's help, and followed his advice in crushing rival sects before Lansdale left in 1956.

From 1957 to 1963 Lansdale served as the deputy director of the Pentagon's Office of Special Operations. President Kennedy sent Lansdale back to South Vietnam in 1961, and Lansdale recommended continued aid for Diem. In 1965, Lansdale returned to Saigon as special assistant to the U.S. ambassador. He tried to reorient the U.S. war effort toward counterinsurgency and pacification, but Lansdale's advice went unheeded and he returned to the United States in 1968.

See also: Central Intelligence Agency; Cao Dai; Elections, South Vietnam, 1955; Hoa Hao; Ngo Dinh Diem; *Quiet American, The; Ugly American, The.*

Lao Dong. The Lao Dong Party (formally, *Dang Lao Dong Viet Nam*, usually translated into English as the Vietnamese Workers' Party, or VWP) was created in February 1951 at a national congress held in Tuyen Quang, north of Hanoi. Nearly 160 delegates, representing 500,000 members, attended the congress. The VWP was the descendant of the Indochinese Communist Party (ICP), created in 1930. The ICP was formally dissolved in November 1945 by Ho Chi Minh to deflect suspicion about the communist nature of his new Democratic Republic of Vietnam (DRV), established in September 1945 in Hanoi. The ICP continued to exist as a clandestine organization directing the war against the French. It resurfaced as the Lao Dong Party in 1951. The new name indicated that party leaders were placing primary emphasis on national reunification rather than on socialism.

During the next quarter of a century, the VWP was the leading political party in the DRV and the guiding force in the struggle for the reunification of North and South Vietnam into a single country under a socialist system. Its organizational principles and its program were Marxist-Leninist. In the late 1950s it took steps to transform the DRV into a socialist society. That process, delayed by the resumption of revolutionary war in the South, resumed after the fall of Saigon in 1975.

In December 1976, at its Fourth National Congress, the VWP was renamed the Vietnamese Communist Party (*Dang Cong San Viet Nam*). The more than one thousand delegates at the congress represented some 1.5 million party members.

See also: Central Office for South Vietnam; Communism; Ho Chi Minh; Indochinese Communist Party.

Lao Issara (Free Laos). Government formed by a group of prominent non-communist Lao nationalists including Prince Souvanna Phouma and Prince Souphanouvong led by their older brother, Prince Phetsarath, in October 1945 to fight against the re-imposition of French colonial rule after WWII. The princes fled to Thailand when the French regained control of Laos in September 1946; the Lao Issara was dissolved in 1949.

See also: Laos; Souvanna Phouma; Souphanouvong.

Lao Lum. Lao ethnic group, a subgroup of a Thai people who originated in southern China and settled in the lowland areas of Laos along the Mekong River. The Lao Lum (valley or lowland Lao) are the country's largest single ethnic group and have dominated commerce, government, and trade. The royal family and most of the ruling elite during the Vietnam War were Lao Lum.

See also: Laos.

Lao Nation. *See* Pathet Lao

Lao Patriotic Front *(Neo Lao Hak Sat).* Covert political arm of the Pathet Lao communist guerrillas formed in January 1956 by the exiled Prince Souphanouvong in northern Vietnam.

See also: Pathet Lao.

Lao People's Democratic Republic. Established on 2 December 1975 when the Lao monarchy was abolished by the Pathet Lao communists. Prince Souphanouvong became head of state of the communist regime closely aligned with the Democratic Republic of Vietnam; Kaysone Phomvihane was appointed secretary of the Lao People's Revolutionary Party and prime minister.

See also: Kaysone, Phomvihane; Pathet Lao; Souphanouvong.

Lao People's Liberation Army *(Kongthap Potpoi Pasason Lao).* The Pathet Lao's military wing, the Lao People's Liberation Army (LPLA), grew from 5,000 in 1956 to nearly 50,000 by 1970. Heavily sup-ported by North Vietnam, the LPLA was made up of dissident Lao nationals, aspiring communists, highland tribesmen, and deserters from Souvanna Phouma's Royal Lao Army. The LPLA's greatest accomplishment was its assistance in building and maintaining the Lao segments of the Ho Chi Minh Trail, and a labyrinth of supply bases, underground field hospitals, and staging depots where North Vietnamese Army and LPLA forces regrouped and retrained.

See also: Ho Chi Minh Trail; Pathet Lao.

Lao People's Revolutionary Party (LPRP). Communist party created at Sam Neua on 22 March 1955. Sometimes referred to as the People's Party of Laos *(Phak Pasason Lao),* the LPRP's covert political wing was the Lao Patriotic Front.

See also: Kaysone, Phomvihane; Souphanouvong.

Laos. Until December 1975, Laos was ruled by a line of monarchs dating back more than six centuries to the ancient Lao kingdom of Lan Xang (Million Elephants). A mountainous and landlocked country (approximately 236,800 square kilometers, 91,428 square miles), Laos has a population of about 4 million. There are dozens of ethnic groups, in four primary divisions: the Lao Loam (lowland Lao), the Lao Tai (tribal Tai), the Lao Theung (mountainside Lao), and the Lao Sung (mountaintop Lao). The Lao Loam, predominantly

Theravadan Buddhists, are the largest single group and have dominated commerce, government, and trade. The royal family and all but a few of the ruling elite during the Vietnam War were Lao Loam. The Lao Tai and Lao Theung are animists who practice subsistence farming in the upland valleys and on the mountainsides. Believed to have been the original inhabitants of Laos, the Lao Theung are sometimes referred to as the Kha, or "slave" people of Laos. The Lao Sung, also animists, traditionally have been called by outsiders the Meo (alternate spelling Miao), or "cat" people. The Lao Sung consider this term pejorative and today most people refer to them as the Hmong. Adept at raising opium poppies as a cash crop, the Hmong have a long tradition of self-sufficiency and fierce armed resistance to outside authority. During the Vietnam War the Hmong of northeastern Laos were sought after as guerrilla fighters by both the communist Pathet Lao/North Vietnamese alliance and the Royal Lao/American partnership.

In the late 19th century, France, already in control of Vietnam and Cambodia, pressured the Lao monarchy to accede to French domination. This sovereignty continued, except during the Japanese occupation of Indochina during WWII, until 1947, when France granted Laos limited independence and the country became a constitutional monarchy within the French Union. In 1953 Laos gained complete independence, but political factors battered the kingdom. The Pathet Lao (Lao Nation), a small communist movement nominally headed by Prince Souphanouvong, had fought alongside the Viet Minh communist forces of Ho Chi Minh, who recognized the strategic importance of the borders Laos shared with Cambodia, China, Thailand, and Vietnam. Viet Minh units also conducted large-scale military operations in Laos against French and Royal Lao government forces.

The 1954 Geneva agreements created a Lao coalition government, but the Pathet Lao quit the coalition and, with assistance from North Vietnam, recommenced their insurrection. The Pathet Lao and neutralist factions engaged in a loose state of conflict with the royal government until 1962 when, following another international conference at Geneva, the Lao factions agreed to stop fighting and formed a coalition government headed by Prince Souvanna Phouma. The coalition failed, and within a year the Pathet Lao had again allied with North Vietnam to effect an armed takeover of Laos. Despite many attempts by the Lao to settle their political differences, the kingdom remained embroiled in political and military strife.

The technically neutral kingdom of Laos, home of much of the Ho Chi Minh Trail, became a critical conduit for troops and materiel supporting communist operations in South Vietnam and

Cambodia. The United States and its Lao and South Vietnamese allies conducted a "secret war" against the Pathet Lao and North Vietnamese in Laos in which the United States recruited Hmong tribesmen as guerrilla fighters under Gen. Vang Pao. Air America, Inc., the CIA's proprietary airline, played a vital role in Laos by supplying and moving conventional and guerrilla troops, undertaking clandestine reconnaissance missions and search-and-rescue operations for downed aviators.

By August 1975 the Pathet Lao gained control of the central government. A complete communist takeover occurred on 2 December 1975 when the Lao monarchy was abolished and the Lao People's Democratic Republic was established.

See also: Air America; Barrier Concept; Central Intelligence Agency; Geneva Conference, 1954; Geneva Conference 1961–1962; Hmong; Ho Chi Minh Trail; Kennedy, John F.; Kissinger, Henry; Kong Le; Lam Son 719; Pathet Lao; Phoumi Nosavan; Refugees; Souphanouvong; Souvanna Phouma; Special Forces, ARVN; Special Forces, U.S. Army; Thailand.

Lao Seri (Free Lao). A small band of Lao nationalists led by Prince Phetsarath, who in August 1945 proclaimed a neutralist buffer zone around the kingdom of Luang Prabang following Japan's capitulation in the region. The Lao Seri became the anti-French Lao Issara (Free Lao) government two months later.

See also: Lao Issara.

Lao Sung (Mountaintop Lao). Known by outsiders as the Meo, (the Lao Sung ethnic group consider this term pejorative). They are referred to today as the Hmong. During the Vietnam War the Hmong of northeastern Laos were sought after as guerrilla fighters by both the communist Pathet Lao/North Vietnamese alliance and the Royal Lao/U.S. partnership.

See also: Hmong.

Lao Tai (Higher Valley Lao). A Lao ethnic group sometimes called the tribal Tai. The Lao Tai live mainly in the upland river valleys and plateaus of Laos.

Lao Theung (Mountainside Lao). The Lao Theung are a rice growing Lao ethnic group who live on mountain slopes. Believed to have been the original inhabitants of Laos, the Lao Theung sometimes are referred to as the *Kha*, or "slave" people of Laos.

Laotian Fragments (1974). Acclaimed literary novel by John Clark Pratt that tells the story of a forward air controller in Laos. Pratt served as a U.S. Air Force pilot and historian in Southeast Asia during the Vietnam War.

See also: Pratt, John Clark.

Lattre de Tassigny, Jean de (1889–1952), French high

commissioner and commander in chief in Vietnam, 1950–1952. De Lattre assumed political and military responsibility in the wake of humiliating French losses to the Viet Minh in the fall of 1950. Instructed by the French government to revitalize the war effort, de Lattre predicted victory within fifteen months of his arrival. The French armed forces responded by defeating a large Viet Minh offensive in the Red River Delta in 1951. De Lattre's son, a French Army lieutenant, was killed at the battle of Nam Dinh; General de Lattre died of liver cancer in January 1952.

See also: France; Vietnamese National Army.

Lavelle, John D. (1916–1979), U.S. Air Force general; commander, Seventh Air Force, Saigon, 1971–1972. Gen. Lavelle was relieved of his command in the fall of 1972 for authorizing illegal air strikes on North Vietnamese air defense installations.

See also: Air Force, U.S.

Law for the Protection of Morality. South Vietnamese statute pushed through the National Assembly by Ngo Dinh Nhu (Madame Ngu) in the early 1960s. The law, among other things, outlawed polygamy, divorce, dancing, beauty contests, gambling, fortune-telling, cock-fighting, contraceptive use, marital infidelity, and prostitution

See also: Ngo Dinh Nhu (Madame Nhu).

Layton, Gilbert B. (1911–1996), CIA officer; chief, Combined Studies Division, Military Assistance and Advisory Group (MAAG), Vietnam, 1960–1964. Layton, a U.S. Army colonel, began training local self-defense units of Montagnard tribesmen in 1961 to protect South Vietnam's western border in the remote Central Highlands in what became known as the Civilian Irregular Defense Group (CIDG) program.

See also: Civilian Irregular Defense Groups.

Lea, Operation. Code name for large French Army operation in the fall of 1947 that tried unsuccessfully to capture Viet Minh headquarters in northern Vietnam.

See also: Franco–Viet Minh War.

League for the Independence of Vietnam. The formal name for the Viet Minh, the organization formed by Ho Chi Minh in 1941, also known as the Front for the Independence of Vietnam.

See also: Ho Chi Minh; Viet Minh.

League of Wives of American Vietnam POWs. Organization founded in San Diego in 1967 by four wives of American POWS, including Sybil Stockdale, the wife of naval aviator Adm. James B. Stockdale, the highest-ranking U.S. prisoner held by North Vietnam. The organization was a support group that worked to bring public attention to North Vietnam's treatment of American POWs. Sybil Stockdale founded a similar nationwide group, the National League of Families of American Prisoners and Missing in Southeast Asia, in 1969.

See also: National League of Families of American Prisoners and Missing in Southeast Asia; POW/MIA Controversy; Stockdale, James B.

Leclerc, Jacques Philippe (1902–1947), French military commander in Indochina, 1945–1946. "Jacques Philippe Leclerc" was the nom de guerre that Philippe de Hauteclocque adopted as a leader of the Resistance in France during WWII. Assigned to command French forces in Indochina, Leclerc defeated the Viet Minh in southern Vietnam in 1945. He returned to Indochina on a fact-finding mission in 1946–1947, and recommended a political solution. Following that controversial message, he resigned. He died in a 1947 plane crash.

See also: Franco–Viet Minh War.

Le Duan (1908–1986), founding member, Indochinese Communist Party (ICP); general secretary of Vietnamese Workers' Party (VWP) and Vietnamese Communist Party, 1957–1986. Le Duan joined Ho Chi Minh's Revolutionary Youth League in 1928 and became a founding member of the Indochinese Communist Party. In 1950 or 1951 be became the party's leading representative in the southern provinces, remaining in the South after the 1954 Geneva agreement as secretary of the party's regional committee. He returned to Hanoi in 1956 and under his guidance the VWP unrelentingly pursued victory in the South. After the Vietnam War, Le Duan served as general secretary of the VWP (renamed the Vietnamese Communist Party in December 1976) until his death in June 1986.

See also: Indochinese Communist Party; Vo Nguyen Giap.

Le Duc Tho (1911–1990), born Phan Dinh Khai; secret negotiator for North Vietnam at the Paris peace talks, 1969–1973. Le Duc Tho helped found the Indochina Communist Party in 1930. Ho Chi Minh placed Tho in charge of southern Viet Minh resistance to the French in the 1950s. He supervised the war in the south from hidden jungle bases in the 1960s. In 1968 Le Duc Tho became the real force behind the scenes at the Paris Peace talks in secret meetings with U.S. negotiator Henry Kissinger.

Tho stonewalled for years with unconditional demands for U.S. withdrawal and South Vietnamese President Nguyen Van Thieu's resignation. A tentative agreement that allowed Thieu to remain in office was reached in October 1972, but both sides grew intransigent and President Nixon subsequently ordered the heaviest bombing of the war. Tho and Kissinger signed the final peace accords on 25 January 1973. Co-recipient of the Nobel Peace Prize, Tho declined the award.

After the Paris agreement, Tho secretly returned to South Vietnam, where he joined Gen. Van Tien Dung in planning the Final Offensive of April 1975. Tho oversaw the Vietnamese invasion of Cambodia before resigning from the politburo in 1986.

See also: Hoang Duc Nha; Ho Chi Minh Campaign; Kissinger, Henry; Paris Accords; Sainteny, Jean; Xuan Thuy.

LeMay, Curtis (1906–1990), U.S. Air Force chief of staff, 1961–1965; George Wallace's vice presidential candidate, 1968. General LeMay believed that air power could achieve most military aims. In late 1963 he advocated a massive bombing campaign against North Vietnam. He gained notoriety with his remark in a 1965 book that the United States should "bomb them [the North Vietnamese] back to the Stone Age."

See also: Air Force, U.S.; SIGMA.

Lemnitzer, Lyman (1899–1988), general, U.S. Army, commander in chief, Far East Command, 1955–1957; U.S. Army chief of staff, 1959–1960; chairman, Joint Chiefs of Staff, 1960–1962. Lyman Lemnitzer planned the first U.S. Military Assistance Advisory Group (MAAG) in Saigon, commanded the 7th Infantry Division in the Korean War, and supervised the rearming of Japan, gaining many years of military experience in Asia. As chairman of the Joint Chiefs of Staff, Lemnitzer toured South Vietnam in May 1961, and was unimpressed by the threat from Viet Cong guerrillas. The real danger, he believed, was a full-scale Korea-style invasion from the north. General Lemnitzer warned that Americans could not fight guerrilla wars, advising against intervention in Laos with anything less than 140,000 men and a willingness to use nuclear weapons. Lemnitzer's views clashed with President Kennedy's enthusiasm for limited war and counterinsurgency. Kennedy sent him to command NATO in 1962, and Lemnitzer retired in 1969.

See also: Military Assistance Advisory Group, Vietnam.

Lemon, Peter C. (1950–), former U.S. Army infantryman. Lemon, who was awarded the Medal of Honor for his actions in a battle in April 1970, is the only Canadian-born recipient of the highest U.S. military honor in the Vietnam War.

Le Nguyen Khang, brigadier general, South Vietnamese armed forces; longest serving commandant of South Vietnam's marine corps. Born in Son Tay province, North Vietnam, Khang fled south after the Geneva accords of 1954. The first Vietnamese to graduate from the U.S. Marine Corps' Amphibious Warfare School, Khang was instrumental in the development of South Vietnam's Marine Brigade (later a division).

A favorite of Diem, Khang did not participate in the coup that unseated Diem in 1963. The new government of Gen. Duong Van Minh, fearing his influence in the Army of the Republic of Vietnam (ARVN), reassigned Khang to the Philippines in December 1963 as South Vietnam's military attaché. In February 1964 Gen. Nguyen Khanh, who toppled the Minh government, reinstated Khang to his former duties. Khang's competence and popularity among his troops, plus his carefully cultivated political connections, paved the way for new appointments. In 1968, in addition to his marine duties, Khang was commander of the Capital Military District, military governor of Saigon, commander of III Corps Tactical Zone (CTZ), governor-delegate for III CTZ, and a member of the National Leadership Committee. He relocated to the United States after South Vietnam collapsed on 30 April 1975.

See also: Nguyen Cao Ky; Nguyen Van Thieu.

Lens, Sidney. *See* New Mobe

Le Quang Tung (1918–1963), Special Forces ARVN colonel; commander of Can Loa party in South Vietnam during the regime of Ngo Dinh Diem. In August 1963, Le Quang Tung, under orders from Ngo Dinh Nhu, led a secret police raid on the Buddhist Xa Loi pagoda in Saigon in which more than 30 monks were killed. Le Quang Tung was killed in the November 1963 coup that overthrew the Diem regime.

See also: Can Loa; Ngo Dinh Nhu.

Le Thanh Nghi (1915–), Vietnamese communist leader. Le Thanh Nghi joined the Indochinese Communist Party in the late 1930s, took part in the August 1945 revolution and became an economics specialist in the Democratic Republic of Vietnam (DRV) government from 1946 to the early 1980s.

See also: Indochinese Communist Party.

Le Thanh Tong (1441–1497), fourth emperor of the Later Le Dynasty. Le Thanh Tong, who ruled from 1460–1497, consolidated Vietnam's central government administration, streamlined its civil service, and instituted a penal code. He also consolidated the territory of the Vietnamese state, while expanding steadily southward and reducing rival Champa to the status of a vassal.

See also: Champa.

Letourneau, Jean (1927–),
French minister of overseas territories. In 1953, Letourneau
devised a plan for the war
against the Viet Minh in
Vietnam. His idea was to secure
the south with Vietnamese forces
and then win a decisive battle in
the north, all to be accomplished
by 1955.

See also: Navarre Plan.

Le Van Bang (1947–),
Vietnamese diplomat. A career
diplomat and former ambassador
to the United Nations, Le Van
Bang was named the first
ambassador of the Socialist
Republic of Vietnam to the
United States in May 1997.

Le Van Hung, Army of the
Republic of Vietnam (ARVN)
brigadier general; commander,
5th ARVN Division, 1971–1972.
During the 1972 North
Vietnamese Army Easter
Offensive Le Van Hung refused
to launch offensive operations,
relying instead on U.S. air power.
President Nguyen Van Thieu
replaced him as division commander and Hung became
deputy III Corps commander.

See also: Easter Offensive.

Le Van Kim (1918–), general,
Army of the Republic of Vietnam
(ARVN). Born in Vietnam and
raised in France, Gen. Le Van
Kim was the top Vietnamese
aide to Adm. Georges
d'Argenlieu, French high commissioner of Indochina. Kim
represented Vietnam's colonial

army at Geneva in 1954.
President Diem appointed Kim
of South Vietnam's military
academy, but then fired him in
1960. Kim joined Duong Van
Minh and Tran Van Don in the
coup that killed South Vietnam's
President Ngo Dinh Diem in
November 1963. He briefly
became foreign minister and
chief of staff, but within days he
and Don were arrested in
Nguyen Khanh's coup of January
1964. Khanh accused them of
conspiring with the French to
create a neutral government in
Vietnam. After a show trial, Kim
was cleared and resumed command of the military academy.
He retired in 1965.

See also: Ngo Dinh Diem.

Le Van Vien. *See* Bay Vien

Levie, Howard S. (1907–), U.S.
Army judge advocate,
1942–1963; professor of law
emeritus, Washington University,
St. Louis. A scholar of international law, Levie wrote
extensively during the Vietnam
War about the treatment and
repatriation of prisoners of war
and against U.S. use of tear gas,
napalm, and defoliants.

Levy, Howard B. (1937–),
physician, captain, U.S. Army. In
1967, after a long and widely
publicized court-martial, Levy
was convicted for refusing to
train Special Forces medics
bound for Vietnam and for
speaking out against U.S.
involvement in the Vietnam War

to U.S. soldiers. He served 27 months in prison before the Supreme Court ordered him released on bail in August 1969.

Lewandowski, Janusz (1931–), Polish diplomat. Lewandowski led Operation Marigold, a failed 1966 attempt to set up U.S.–North Vietnamese peace talks.

See also: Poland; Marigold, Operation.

Liberation Armed Forces of South Vietnam. *See* People's Liberation Armed Forces

Liddy, G. Gordon (1930–), general counsel, Committee to Re-elect the President. Liddy was convicted of conspiracy in the break-ins at Daniel Ellsberg's psychiatrist's office and the Watergate headquarters of the Democratic National Committee.

See also: Pentagon Papers; Plumbers; Watergate.

Lien Doi Nguoi Nhai. South Vietnamese underwater demolition teams/frogmen, similar to the U.S. Navy SEALs.

See also: Provincial Reconnaissance Units.

Lin, Maya Ying (1959–), architect who designed the Vietnam Veterans Memorial in Washington, D.C. Maya Lin was a 21-year-old architecture student at Yale University when she submitted the winning design as part of a class in funereal architecture.

See also: Vietnam Veterans Memorial.

Linebacker and Linebacker II, Operations. Two U.S. bombing campaigns, 10 May to 23 October (Linebacker) and 18–29 December 1972, (Linebacker II) against North Vietnam ordered by President Richard Nixon, were instrumental in bringing the Paris peace negotiations to a conclusion.

Ordered in response to the 30 March 1972 Easter Offensive, Linebacker was a resumption of the strategic bombing of North Vietnam, which had been discontinued since the cancellation of Operation Rolling Thunder. Linebacker's objectives were to halt the invasion of South Vietnam by cutting the North Vietnamese Army's lines of supply and to force North Vietnam to resume peace negotiations. Commanders were given wide latitude to achieve those goals. Air power was employed with full intensity from the outset; military commanders exercised full control of tactics and targeting within broad White House guidelines. B-52s were used extensively against North Vietnamese targets; precision-guided munitions (PGMs), notably laser-guided bombs, were available in quantity; and categories of targets previously off limits were attacked, notably airfields and Haiphong harbor, which was mined by Naval aircraft.

The operational burden of Linebacker was borne by B-52s and by U.S. Air Force F-4 Phantom tactical fighter units and two-seater F-105G Thunderchief "Wild Weasel" surface-to-air missile (SAM) suppression aircraft based in South Vietnam and Thailand, and by U.S. Navy carrier-based F-4 Phantom, F-8 Crusader, A-6 Intruder, and A-7 Corsair fighter and attack squadrons. U.S. Air Force F-111s were also redeployed to Southeast Asia in September 1972.

Linebacker was preceded by a massive redeployment of U.S. airpower and featured wide-ranging strikes on transportation, power-generation and petroleum production and storage targets and included mining harbors and rivers. Strikes were supported by attacks on airfields and SAM sites, chaff corridors (clouds of thin strips of aluminum foil), and radar jamming to block North Vietnamese radars, F-105G SAM-suppression patrols, and antiMiG combat air patrols. By mid-October, with war materiel depleted, the North's transportation net a shambles, and PAVN forces in the South feeling the pinch, North Vietnam communicated its readiness to negotiate, and Linebacker was terminated.

Linebacker II, the so-called "Christmas bombings," was Nixon's response to diplomatic intransigence by the North Vietnamese. It centered on B-52 attacks in the Hanoi and Haiphong areas. Strategic Air Command (SAC) headquarters dictated B-52 tactics. B-52 losses to SAMs were heavy and fell disproportionately on Guam-based B-52Gs, which had less capable electronics countermeasures suites. An aircrew mutiny protesting the rigid tactics resulted and made its point: B-52 raids were scaled back, but later resumed with full fury—and more intelligent tactics—after a two-day Christmas standdown.

The attacks wreaked havoc on North Vietnam's economic and military infrastructure, forcing the North Vietnamese back to the peace table. Of a total of 206 B-52s deployed during Linebacker II, 15 were shot down by SAMs, 9 during the first three days. Despite the intensity of the attacks and over 20,000 tons of bombs dropped, the North Vietnamese claimed only 1,318 civilians killed.

See also: Antiaircraft Defenses; B-52; Détente; F-111; Haiphong; Hanoi; Moorer, Thomas H.; Nixon, Richard M.; Rolling Thunder, Operation; Surface-to-Air Missiles; Vogt, John W. Jr.

Lionheads, The (1972). Highly praised Vietnam War novel by Josiah Bunting that focuses on the actions of U.S. infantry officers. Bunting served with the U.S. Army's 9th Infantry Division in Vietnam.

Lippmann, Walter (1889–1974), Pulitzer Prize–winner and influential syndicated columnist for the *New York Herald Tribune.*

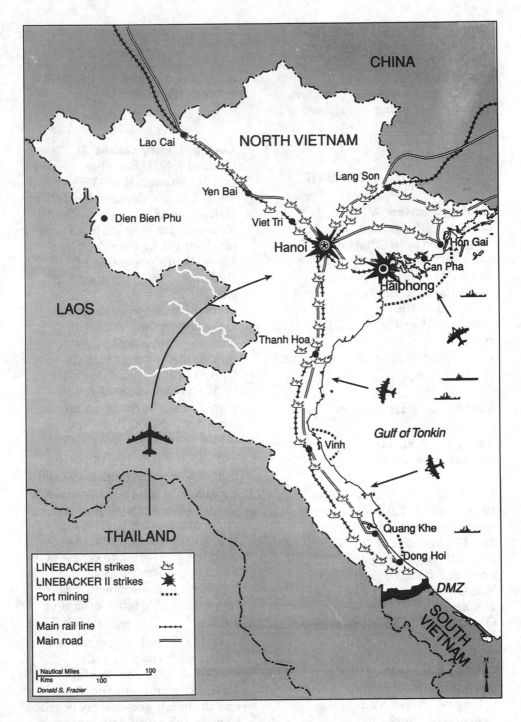

Linebacker and Linebacker II. *May–December 1972. In Operation Linebacker, U.S. Air Force air strikes combined with U.S. Navy 7th Fleet carrier strikes and aerial mining of North Vietnamese ports severely hampered North Vietnam's ability to resupply its invasion forces in the South. During Linebacker II, in 729 sorties B-52s dropped approximately 14,000 tons of bombs on targets within Hanoi and Haiphong. Though denounced as "terror bombing," considering the weight fo explosives expended, these massive strikes resulted in remarkably few civilian casualties; the North Vietnamese claimed to have sustained only between 1,300 and 1,600 casualties.*

Lippmann's opposition to escalating the war and his support for a negotiated settlement antagonized President Johnson. Johnson had courted Lippmann at the outset of his presidency, but reacted bitterly when Lippmann criticized his Vietnam policy in 1966.

See also: Johnson, Lyndon B.

Liteky, Charles J. (1931–), U.S. Army 199th Light Infantry Brigade battalion chaplain awarded the Medal of Honor for rescuing twenty wounded soldiers during a jungle firefight on 6 December 1967 in Bien Hoa province. After the war, Liteky resigned from the priesthood and the military and became a peace activist.

Loaches. *See* Helicopters

Loan, Nguyen Ngoc. *See* Nguyen Ngoc Loan

Loc Ninh. South Vietnamese town, capital of Binh Long province, near Cambodian border, 117 kilometers (70 miles) north of Saigon. In one of the pre–Tet Offensive border battles, Viet Cong forces attacked the U.S. outpost at Loc Ninh on 29 October 1967. During ferocious fighting, U.S. forces inflicted heavy casualties on the Viet Cong and drove them back. During the 1972 Easter Offensive , North Vietnamese Army (NVA) forces battled U.S. defenders successfully for the town on 4–6 April. Loc Ninh sub-

sequently served as one of the NVA's main headquarters and communications centers, and was a key staging area for the 1975 Spring Offensive.

See also: Tet Offensive.

Lodge, Henry Cabot Jr. (1902–1985), U.S. ambassador to South Vietnam, 1963–1966. In 1963, Lodge succeeded Frederick Nolting as ambassador to South Vietnam, arriving during a crisis precipitated by President Ngo Dinh Diem's repression of Buddhists. Lodge notified U.S. officials in Washington that a group of army generals sought U.S. support for a coup. In October he was authorized to inform the generals that the United States would do nothing to "thwart a change of government." On 1 November, they ousted and killed Diem and his brother, Nhu.

Lodge resigned in 1964 for a tentative run in the presidential election. He returned to Saigon as ambassador the following June. Attempting to revitalize U.S. pacification efforts, Lodge outlined a program to create popular support for the South Vietnamese government in the countryside. He left Vietnam in 1966.

Lodge served as one of the "wise men" who met with Lyndon Johnson on 25 March 1968. Lodge recommended an end to search-and-destroy operations in the south and suggested that U.S. troops be used as a shield to protect South

Vietnamese society. In early 1969, President Richard Nixon designated Lodge titular head of the U.S. delegation to the Paris Peace talks.

See also: Buddhists; Forrestal, Michael; Harkins, Paul D.; Hilsman, Roger; Ngo Dinh Diem; Ngo Dinh Nhu; Nguyen Cao Ky; State, Department of; Taylor-McNamara Report; Wise Men.

Lo Guibo (1911–), Chinese political administrative expert sent by China to aid Ho Chi Minh in 1950 as part of a Chinese team that included a military advisory mission under Gen. Wei Guoqing and a training team led by Vice Minister of Defense Chen Geng.

See also: China; Viet Minh.

Loi Phong, Operation (Thunder Hurricane). May 1972 South Vietnamese Army operation led by Gen. Ngo Quang Truong following the North Vietnamese Army's Easter Offensive. By mid-September the ARVN reestablished its positions in northern South Vietnam under General Truong's leadership.

See also: Easter Offensive; Ngo Quang Truong.

Long An. Province immediately south of Saigon at the gateway to the Mekong Delta. During the Vietnam War the U.S. 25th Infantry Division, the ARVN 25th Division, and other military and paramilitary forces were stationed in the province.

See also: Pacification; Mekong River and Delta.

Long Binh. Large U.S. military logistical and headquarters complex located just outside the city of Bien Hoa, about 32 kilometers (20 miles) north of Saigon. Headquarters of the U.S. Army, Vietnam (USARV), the First Logistical Command, the II Field Force, Vietnam, and III ARVN Corps. The base supported surgical hospitals, restaurants, swimming pools, and movie theaters, among other facilities, with associated military equipment and support personnel. Long Binh served as a transit base where U.S. troops waited for transport while leaving and coming into the country. The complex also included a U.S. Army jail known derisively as LBJ. On 29 August 1968 several hundred prisoners, almost all of them African-Americans, rioted at the prison, the first widely publicized incident of the racial strife within the U.S. forces in Vietnam. Viet Cong forces unsuccessfully attacked Long Binh in 1968 as part of the Tet Offensive and later in 1969.

See also: Ho Chi Minh Campaign.

Long Range Reconnaissance Patrols (LRRPs). U.S. Army units, sometimes called "Lurps," that went on long, intelligence-gathering missions deep into enemy territory.

Lon Nol (1913–1985), general, Cambodian army; prime minister,

Cambodia, 1966–1967, 1969, 1970–1972; president, Khmer Republic, 1972–1975. Lon Nol, a pro-monarchist, authoritarian general in the Cambodian army, was born in Tay Ninh, Vietnam, was French-educated, and rose to power by preventing a coup against Sihanouk in 1959. He opposed Viet Cong infiltration into eastern Cambodia in the late 1960s.

Dissatisfied with Prince Sihanouk's neutrality, the United States encouraged a military coup against him in 1970 and supported Lon Nol's seizure of power. Lon Nol was nonetheless surprised by the U.S. invasion of Cambodia, announced on 30 April 1970. He tolerated extensive U.S. bombing, which lasted throughout the next five years, in return for large amounts of military and economic aid.

His poorly led forces suffered a string of defeats by the communist Khmer Rouge and by the North Vietnamese Army, and popular discontent against his regime mounted. By late 1972 North Vietnamese artillery, tank, and infantry attacks had broken Lon Nol's forces. Henry Kissinger attempted to persuade the Khmer Rouge to negotiate with Lon Nol, but they refused.

After the United States signed the Paris peace accords with Vietnam on 30 January 1973, Lon Nol demanded that the Vietnamese communists withdraw from Cambodia, surrender their arms, and allow Cambodian government forces to occupy previously held communist territory. These demands were not supported by the United States. After U.S. military involvement in Vietnam ended in 1973, U.S. forces continued to drop more than 257,000 tons of bombs in support of Lon Nol's forces in Cambodia. Lon Nol escaped to Indonesia before the 17 April 1975 Khmer Rouge takeover.

See also: Cambodia; Dean, John Gunther; FANK; Khmer Rouge; Pol Pot; Sihanouk, Norodom.

Lowenstein, Allard K.
(1929–1980), U.S. Representative (D-N.Y.), 1969–1971. A liberal, antiwar activist, Lowenstein was a leader among the Democrats who worked against President Lyndon's 1968 bid for the Democratic presidential nomination.

See also: Johnson, Lyndon B.; McCarthy, Eugene J.

Lownds, David E. (1921–), U.S. Marine colonel who commanded the Marine base at Khe Sanh.

See also: Khe Sanh.

Lucas, Jim G. (1914–1970), journalist. Lucas, a WWII U.S. Marine Corps combat correspondent, covered the Korean War and the French Indochina War for Scripps Howard. He served as the U.S. Embassy spokesman in Saigon in the early 1960s.

Luce, Henry R. (1898–1967), publisher. Luce's publications, especially *Time* magazine, strongly supported the U.S. military effort in Vietnam, reflecting Luce's strong anti-communism.

Luc Luong Dac Biet (LLDB). *See* Special Forces, ARVN

Lyautey, Louis Hubert-Gonzalve (1854–1934), French statesman, soldier; minister of war, 1916–1917. Lyautey, an ardent colonialist, helped suppress the first Vietnamese nationalist movement in 1915 led by Annamese emperor Duy Tan.

See also: France; Gallieni, Joseph-Simon.

Lycéum Pellerin. Catholic secondary school in Hue attended by Ngo Dinh Diem.

Lynd, Staughton (1929–), antiwar movement activist. Lynd, a Yale University history professor, helped found the Student Nonviolent Coordinating Committee (SNCC) in 1962.

M-16 Rifle. Automatic rifle used as the basic infantry weapon for U.S. troops in Vietnam beginning in 1967. It succeeded the heavier M-14 rifle that had been in use since 1959.

M-42 Duster Tank. *See* Tanks

M-48A3 Patton Tank. *See* Tanks

M-60 Machine Gun. Standard light machine gun used by U.S. forces in the Vietnam War. The M-60 fired at a rate of 600 rounds per minute and could be used mounted on a tripod or fired with a folded bipod on its barrel.

M-79 Grenade Launcher. Widely used U.S. infantry weapon. The single-shot, single-barred M-70 fired several different types of rounds, including a 40mm grenade cartridge.

M-113 Armored Personnel Carrier. *See* Tanks

MAAG-L. *See* Military Assistance Advisory Group–Laos

MAAG-V. *See* Military Assistance Advisory Group–Vietnam

MacArthur, Operation. October to November 1967 operation against the North Vietnamese Army (NVA) around Dak To in the Central Highlands involving elements of the U.S. Army 4th Infantry Division and 173rd Airborne Brigade and the ARVN 42nd Infantry Regiment. In a battle that included heavy B-52 bombardment, the NVA lost some 1,600 men.

See also: Dak To.

MACTHAI. Military Assistance Command Thailand.

See also: Thailand.

MACV. *See* Military Assistance Command, Vietnam

Madame Nhu. *See* Ngo Dinh Nhu (Madame Nhu)

***Maddox*, USS.** U.S. Navy destroyer that reported an attack by North Vietnamese torpedo boats in the Gulf of Tonkin on 2 August 1964, sparking the Gulf of Tonkin incident.

See also: DeSoto Missions; Gulf of Tonkin Incident; Appendix E, "Gulf of Tonkin Resolution."

Madman Strategy. During his 1968 campaign, Richard Nixon told aides that if the North Vietnamese believed that he would do anything to end the Vietnam War, including using nuclear weapons, then they would settle the war. Nixon borrowed the tactic from Dwight Eisenhower, who used it during the Korean War. No nuclear weapons were used, but Nixon believed that massive bombing of the North eventually led to the signing of the Paris accords.

See also: Nixon, Richard M.

Mailer, Norman (1923–), American author, antiwar activist. Mailer was a frequent speaker at antiwar rallies and demonstrations. He wrote *Why Are We in Vietnam?* (1967), an antiwar novel, and *The Armies of the Night* (1968), about the October 1967 march on the Pentagon, which won the Pulitzer Prize for general nonfiction and the National Book Award for Arts and Letters.

See also: Hawks and Doves.

Malaysia. The Federation of Malaya was a British protectorate until 1957, when it became an independent state in the British Commonwealth. It joined the former British colony of Borneo to form the Federation of Malaysia in 1963. A communist insurrection, led by Malaya's Chinese population, began in 1946 and lasted sporadically until 1963. This long conflict marked Malayasia as a potential "domino" and served as a model of guerrilla warfare for Western powers. Sir Robert Thompson, a British administrator in Malayasia, developed a successful counterinsurgency program that later formed the basis for South Vietnam's Strategic Hamlet program.

Malaysia's official involvement in the Vietnam War was limited to training and providing equipment to South Vietnam. In 1964,

Malaysia began training some three thousand South Vietnamese military and police officers in Malaysia and provided counterinsurgency equipment such as transport vehicles. Despite the relatively small amount of material support Malaysia gave to the South Vietnamese, the war nonetheless elicited popular opposition, even among anticommunists; demonstrations in several cities erupted in the late 1960s.

See also: Domino Theory; Strategic Hamlet Program; Thompson, Robert G. K.

Manila Conference. Conference held 24–25 October 1966 that included representatives from Australia, New Zealand, the Philippines, South Korea, South Vietnam, Thailand, and the United States. The conference, attended by President Lyndon B. Johnson and South Vietnamese Prime Minister Nguyen Cao Ky, was called by Philippine president Ferdinand Marcos to review the war and nonmilitary development programs and to consider the region's future. The delegates issued a series of statements dealing with peace, security, and an end to hunger, illiteracy, and disease. One statement set forth the conditions under which U.S. and allied troops would withdraw from South Vietnam.

See also: Marcos, Ferdinand.

Manila Pact. Official name for the agreement signed

8 September 1954 and ratified by the U.S. Congress 19 February 1955 creating the Southeast Asia Treaty Organization (SEATO). That regional defense group included the Australia, New Zealand, Pakistan, the Philippines, and Thailand, in addition to the western powers France, Great Britain, and the United States.

See also: SEATO.

Manor, Leroy J. (1921–), U.S. Air Force general. Gen. Manor was overall task force commander of the Son Tay Raid to rescue POWs.

See also: Son Tay Raid.

Mansfield, Mike (1903–), U.S. representative (D-Mont.), 1943–1953; U.S. senator (D-Mont.), 1953–1977; Senate majority leader, 1961–1977. A Catholic with an interest in Asian history, Mansfield was an important early supporter of Ngo Dinh Diem and of the U.S. commitment to South Vietnam. By 1965, however, after several visits to Vietnam, he concluded that the South Vietnamese government enjoyed little popular support and that military action in Vietnam was doomed to failure. As the war continued, Mansfield supported legislation to counter the precedent established by the Gulf of Tonkin Resolution and to reassert Congress's war powers. In 1969, he called for a cease-fire, and in June 1971, he sponsored an amendment to the Selective Service bill that required the withdrawal of U.S. troops within nine months. The amendment failed to pass in the House, but a provision was substituted that urged President Nixon to set a firm date for U.S. troop withdrawal; this was the first time Congress went on record in support of the withdrawal of troops from Vietnam.

See also: Catholics; Ngo Dinh Diem.

Mao Zedong (1893–1976), leader, Chinese Communist Party, 1935–1976; chairman, Central Committee of the Party, 1945–1976; president, People's Republic of China, 1949–1959. Throughout most of the 1960s, Mao challenged the Soviet Union's Vietnam policy and advised the Vietnamese communists to insist on armed struggle to overthrow South Vietnam by force rather than to negotiate with the United States. He advocated protracted guerrilla war, or "peoples war," based on his own revolutionary experience.

Vietnamese leaders drew heavily on Maoist concepts of guerrilla war. Ho Chi Minh and Vo Nguyen Giap made significant changes to Maoist doctrine to adapt it to the Vietnamese circumstances. The Vietnamese leaders placed less emphasis than Mao on self-reliance as opposed to external aid, rural areas as opposed to cities, guerilla war versus armed uprisings, and the preeminence of human beings and political actions over weapons and technological skills. With these modifications, Vietnamese communist leaders benefitted greatly from Mao's strategic ideas, including the three devices prescribed by Maoist doctrines as necessary for the triumph of the revolution: the party (whose role is to provide leadership for the revolution), the army (a tool to seize state power), and the united front (a means to win the support of the people).

See also: China, People's Republic of; Ho Chi Minh; Vo Nguyen Giap.

March on the Pentagon

(1967). Antiwar demonstration on 21 October 1967 in Washington, D.C., that attracted between 50,000 and 100,000 people. After a rally at the Lincoln Memorial, demonstrators marched to the Pentagon, where U.S. Army troops kept them from entering the building.

See also: Clark, Ramsey; Mailer, Norman.

March on Washington (1969).

Antiwar demonstration on 15 November 1969 sponsored by the Vietnam Moratorium Committee in Washington, D.C., in which more than 250,000 people marched along Pennsylvania Avenue to a rally at the Washington Monument.

See also: Brown, Sam; Vietnam Moratorium Committee.

Marcos, Ferdinand (1917–1989),

Philippine president (1965–1986) who supported the U.S. effort in Vietnam. In 1966,

Marcos hosted the Manila Conference to review the war and development team programs with U.S. officials. That same year he sent 2,000 Filipino combat engineers to Vietnam. As student and nationalist opposition to Philippine involvement intensified, Marcos withdrew the forces in October 1969.

See also: Free World; Manila Conference; Philippines.

Marigold, Operation.

A failed diplomatic mission led by Polish diplomat Janusz Lewandowski, to set up U.S. negotiations with Hanoi in 1966.

See also: Cooper, Chester; Lewandowski, Janusz.

Marine Amphibious Units (MAU).

In 1975, as part of Operation Frequent Wind, the U.S. Navy's Seventh Fleet amphibious forces, known as Marine Amphibious Units, evacuated the last U.S. personnel and several South Vietnamese officials and their families from Saigon before the North Vietnamese entered the city.

See also: Frequent Wind, Operation.

Marine Detachment, Advisory Team One.

Group of U.S. Marine Corps radio intelligence experts and infantry that deployed along the Laotian border in Quang Tri province beginning in June 1964.

Marines, U.S.

The Vietnam War was the Marines' longest

war (seven years of major engagements) and its bloodiest. The war cost the corps 101,574 casualties, 4,000 more than it suffered in WWII. Marine combat deaths in Vietnam numbered 13,073 with an additional 1,748 deaths from all other causes in the war zone. More U.S. Marines served during the Vietnam War than during WWII, 794,000 compared with 669,100. In 1968 more Marines (85,755) were fighting in Vietnam than landed on either Iwo Jima or Okinawa. At its wartime peak strength in 1969 the Marine Corps numbered 314,917, only 170,000 short of its WWII strength.

Marine Corps participation in the Vietnam War followed the general pattern of the entire U.S. military commitment. The first period began in the waning days of the Franco–Viet Minh war and ended with the arrival of the 9th Marine Expeditionary Brigade at Da Nang in March 1965. The first Marine adviser in Vietnam arrived in August 1954 to organize a Vietnamese riverine assault force that evolved into the Marine Corps of the Republic of Vietnam. As the Vietnamese Marine Corps grew from two battalions to a 6,000-man brigade in 1962, the number of U.S. Marines assigned as advisers also climbed. To support the direct use of U.S. aircraft and helicopters in the war, a Marine radio intelligence detachment of 42 deployed in January 1962 to the Central Highlands as part of a larger U.S. Army communications unit. This commitment

expanded in April with the arrival of a marine transport helicopter squadron in the Mekong Delta region.

From its first combat operation in April 1962, the marine helicopter task force moved to the I Corps Tactical Zone (the five northern provinces of South Vietnam) in September, where it set up its base at the Da Nang airfield. Because the Marines already had advance elements in I Corps, Gen. Wallace M. Green Jr., commandant of the corps, and Lt. Gen. Victor H. Krulak, commander of Fleet Marine Force Pacific, sent more Marines to northern South Vietnam when the United States began ground combat operations in 1965. The real offensive mission, however, went to the 1st Marine Aircraft Wing, assigned to participate in the U.S. air war. The first ground units from the 3d Marine Division assumed security duties around Da Nang, Phu Bai, Chu Lai, and Qui Nhon.

The command in I Corps became the III Marine Amphibious Force (III MAF), commanded by Lt. Gen. Lewis W. Walt. General Walt mixed conventional multi-battalion operations with small-unit pacification and civic action. He also instituted a program to place marine squads in villages with Vietnamese militiamen, which was labeled the Combined Action Program (CAP). III MAF received substantial U.S. Navy and civilian engineering support to supplement its own five engineer battalions. Reinforced by the 1st Marine Division, which arrived from California in early 1966, III MAF followed a dual operational approach worked out by Greene, Krulak, and Walt. Large-unit offensive operations in the rugged back-country or along the coastline were conducted only when the Marines could use helicopter assaults and close air support; the emphasis instead would be on pacification operations among the coastal population.

From the first significant battles along the DMZ, which began in the summer of 1966, the 3d Marine Division fought in places such as Khe Sanh, The Rockpile, Con Thien, Cam Lo, Gio Linh, and Dong Ha. In many ways the war along the DMZ resembled warfare on the western front in WWI and in Korea. 111 MAF operations became a combination of big battles with the NVA along the northern and western approaches to Quang Tri province, supplemented by offensive operations into the western mountains and pacification activities conducted by the 1st Marine Division.

At the western flank of the DMZ, the combat base at Khe Sanh became a focus of national attention in the United States when, in late 1967, two NVA divisions closed around the Marine regiment that held the base and the commanding hills to the north. In March 1968, the Vietnamese withdrew after suffering approximately 10,000 casualties. The Khe Sanh force lost 205 killed in action and 800 wounded.

The Tet Offensive January 1965) forced II MAF into battles with NVA forces to throw back attacks around Da Nang, and three Marine battalions fought with Army of the Republic of Vietnam (ARVN) forces to recapture the ancient citadel of the city of Hue. In the summer of 1969, III MAF received orders to leave Vietnam as part of President Richard Nixon's Vietnamization program. For the next two years the Marines withdrew from Vietnam. Even after the 1st Marine Division and the 1st Marine Aircraft Wing completed their withdrawals in the summer of 1971, U.S. Marine advisers remained with the Vietnamese marines. When the Cambodian and Vietnamese armed forces collapsed in 1975, a Marine expeditionary brigade conducted rescue and evacuation operations in both Phnom Penh and Saigon. The last two Marines killed in Vietnam died during operations at the Tan Son Nhut military compound outside Saigon on 29 April 1975.

See also: Amphibious Landing Operations; Casualties; Chapman, Leonard Fielding Jr.; Combined Action Program; Cushman, Robert E. Jr.; Da Nang; Greene, Wallace M. Jr.; Hue; Khe Sanh; Krulak, Victor; Walt, Lewis W.

Market Garden, Operation.
Effort by U.S. Navy coastal and river surveillance forces and U.S. Coast Guard cutters to prevent

Viet Cong infiltration from the sea and along inland water passages.

See also: Coast Guard, U.S.; Navy, U.S.

Market Time, Operation. Code name for U.S. Navy and Coast Guard operations that began in March 1965 designed to help the South Vietnamese Navy limit North Vietnamese infiltration of weapons and supplies into South Vietnam from the South China Sea.

See also: Coast Guard, U.S.; Navy, U.S.

MARS (Military Amateur Radio Services). Network of ham radio operators in the United States and Vietnam that allowed troops to make relayed two-way radio telephone calls from the war zone.

Marshall, S.L.A. (1900–1977), U.S. Army general, military historian. Brigadier General Marshall, a veteran of WWI and WWII, is best known for his eyewitness military history books about WWII and the Korean and Vietnam Wars, including *Men Against Fire* (1947).

Marshall, Thurgood (1908–1993), U.S. Supreme Court Justice, 1967–1993. Justice Thurgood Marshall supported the rights of some draft resisters, but did not support draft resistance if it was brazen and openly contemptuous of the procedures regulated by the

Selective Service System. In June 1973 he rejected an appeal that would have halted U.S. bombing in Cambodia.

See also: Supreme Court, U.S.

Marshall Plan. The program developed by U.S. Secretary of State George C. Marshall in 1947 that provided millions of dollars in economic assistance to Western European states judged most essential to the economic recovery of the noncommunist world and most vulnerable to Soviet subversion.

See also: Domino Theory.

Martin, Graham A. (1912–1990), U.S. ambassador to South Vietnam, 1973–1975. Martin was U.S. ambassador to Thailand (1963–1967) and Italy (1969–1973) before President Nixon appointed him the last U.S. envoy to South Vietnam. Arriving in Saigon after the Paris accords had been signed, Martin concentrated on shoring up South Vietnamese faith in President Nixon's support and on lobbying Congress for increased military aid. Martin defended President Thieu against pressure to resign or negotiate with the communists. He also sent optimistic reports on the military situation to his superiors, delaying the realization that the war was lost.

To avoid creating panic during North Vietnam's Spring Offensive in April 1975, Martin declined to implement contingency plans for an orderly

U.S. departure from Saigon. The last-minute helicopter evacuation of 29–30 April 1975 left behind piles of classified documents and thousands of South Vietnamese supporters of the U.S.-backed government, who were ruthlessly treated by the victorious communists. Martin himself was among the last Americans to leave Saigon. He served as special assistant to Secretary of State Henry Kissinger before retirement in 1977.

See also: Gayler, Noel; Nguyen Van Thieu.

M*A*S*H (1970). Popular film directed by Robert Altman, set in the Korean War. The movie's darkly comic antiwar tone reflected contemporary anti–Vietnam War sentiment. The long running (1972–1983) *M*A*S*H* television series also contained attitudes and actions that conjured up visions of Vietnam.

Mason, Bobbie Ann (1940–), novelist, short story writer. Mason's well-regarded novel, *In Country* (1985), tells the story of a teenage girl and her quest in the mid-1980s to find out about her father who was killed in Vietnam before she was born.

See also: In Country.

Mason, Robert (1946–), U.S. Army warrant officer. Mason's memoir of his 1965–1966 tour of Vietnam, *Chickenhawk* (1983), is a revealing look at the war from the point of view of U.S. helicopter pilots.

Mat Tran Dan Toc Giai Phong Mien Nam. *See* National Liberation Front

Mat Tran To Quoc. *See* Fatherland Front

MAU. *See* Marines, U.S.

Mayaguez Incident. On 12 May 1975, the *Mayaguez*, a U.S.-registered container ship operating in the Gulf of Thailand near the Cambodian coast, was seized by Cambodian troops. President Gerald R. Ford ordered a military rescue, but action was hampered by a lack of knowledge about the crew's location and by confusion stemming from the involvement of multiple branches of the U.S. armed forces.

U.S. intelligence determined that the ship was being held off the coast of the Cambodian island of Koh Tang, and the rescue of the ship and crew was initiated on 15 May 1975. The USS *Holt* landed a boarding party on the *Mayaguez;* they found the ship abandoned. At the same time, U.S. Marines were landed by Air Force helicopters on Koh Tang Island off the Cambodian coast. Eighteen Marines were killed and fifty wounded in the operation. Later in the day, the U.S. destroyer *Wilson* picked up the *Mayaguez's* crew, which was adrift at sea aboard a fishing boat. President Ford ordered four punitive air strikes against military targets on the Cambodian mainland near Kompong Som; two strikes were carried out.

See also: Ford, Gerald R.

Mayday Tribe. A group of mostly young antiwar activists that attempted to shut down the U.S. government from 3 May through 5 May 1971. Rennie Davis, a former leader of Students for a Democratic Society (SDS), led the group. They planned to use nonviolent direct action, blocking bridges and street intersections, to interrupt traffic in Washington, D.C., and disrupt normal federal government activity. City police, backed by federal troops, stopped the protest with mass arrests. More than twelve thousand people were arrested.

See also: Davis, Rennard Cordon (Rennie).

McCain, John S. Jr.
(1911–1981), admiral, U.S. Navy; Commander-in-Chief, Pacific (CINCPAC). A highly decorated submarine commander in WWII, Adm. John McCain, Jr., was the first admiral's son to become a full admiral himself. He held important Navy staffposts, including that of top congressional lobbyist, and he commanded amphibious landings in the Dominican Republic in 1968–1972. McCain succeeded Adm. Ulysses S. Grant Sharp as CINCPAC on 31 July 1968. He long advocated mining Haiphong harbor, which President Nixon approved in May 1972. McCain also called for increased bombing of Hanoi even though his son, a U.S. Navy aviator, was held prisoner there.

See also: Commander-in-Chief, Pacific; McCain, John S. III.

McCain, John S. III (1936–), lieutenant commander, U.S. Navy. The son and grandson of full admirals, Lt. Cmdr. John McCain III was a naval aviator aboard the USS *Forrestal* in the Vietnam War. Shot down over Hanoi on 26 October 1967, he suffered three broken limbs and was beaten and stabbed by angry mobs on the ground. McCain was denied medical attention and tortured for over three years in solitary confinement. Released with other prisoners of war in 1973, McCain resumed his U.S. Navy career before retiring in 1981. He was elected as a Republican U.S. representative from Arizona in 1982 and U.S. senator in 1986.

See also: McCain, John S. Jr.

McCarthy, Eugene J. (1916–), U.S. senator (D-Minn.), 1959–1971; member, Senate Foreign Relations Committee. After graduating from St. John's College in Minnesota, serving in Army intelligence, and teaching high school and college, McCarthy was elected in 1948 to the House of Representatives, where he criticized Cold War anticommunist hysteria and helped to found the liberal Democratic Study Group. He moved to the Senate in 1958, attracted national attention with an eloquent nominating speech for Adlai Stevenson in 1960, and was widely mentioned as a vice presidential prospect in 1964.

In January 1966, he joined 14 other senators in urging the continuation of a bombing pause. In 1966 and 1967 McCarthy spoke often against the Vietnam War in Congress and under the auspices of college groups and Clergy and Laity Concerned About Vietnam (CALCAV). He ran for president in 1968 on a strong antiwar platform and many college students rallied to his cause. After the Tet Offensive, McCarthy won 42 percent of the Democratic vote in the New Hampshire primary, but lost the nomination to Vice President Hubert H. Humphrey. Humphrey and the Democratic National Convention rejected McCarthy's proposals for a bombing halt and negotiations to establish a coalition government in South Vietnam. McCarthy retired from the Senate in 1971.

See also: Democratic Party, U.S.; Humphrey, Hubert H.; Johnson, Lyndon B.

McCloy, John (1895–1989), banker, civilian adviser to President Johnson. A firm adherent of the domino theory, McCloy told President Johnson in 1965 that Vietnam should be a "test case" for the U.S. policy of containment. In the crucial "wise men" meeting on 25 March 1968, however, McCloy joined the majority in backing deescalation and the end of U.S. involvement in Vietnam.

See also: Wise Men.

McCone, John (1902–1991), director, Central Intelligence Agency (CIA), 1961–1965. President Kennedy appointed McCone, a conservative Republican millionaire, director of the CIA in September 1961. McCone believed that to be successful in Vietnam the United States should commit sufficient troops and resources to gain victory. A supporter of Ngo Dinh Diem, McCone opposed the 1963 coup against the South Vietnamese president. In September 1964, following the Gulf of Tonkin incident, McCone reported that the prospects for a stable government in South Vietnam remained slim and opposed counterstrikes against North Vietnam. McCone's influence in the Johnson administration subsequently declined, and he resigned in 1965.

See also: Central Intelligence Agency; SIGMA.

McConnell, John P. (1908–1986), general, U.S. Air Force; chief of staff, 1965–1969. McConnell served as air adviser in India and China before he was named U.S. Air Force chief of staff in January. During the Vietnam War, McConnell consistently advocated heavier bombing of a greater number of targets in North Vietnam. McConnell believed that ground forces alone could not defeat the enemy, but concentrated air power could. He insisted that the Air Force could play a decisive role in limited wars through "strategic persuasion," but political restrictions on the exercise of air power in Vietnam left him frustrated. McConnell retired in 1969.

See also: Air Force, U.S.

McGarr, Lionel C. (1904–), U.S. Army general; head, U.S. Military Assistance Advisory Group–Vietnam (MAAG-V), 1960–1962. McGarr led an expansion of MAAG advisory activities, including an increase in the number of U.S. advisers helping South Vietnamese units in the field.

See also: Military Assistance Advisory Group–Vietnam.

McGovern, George (1922–), U.S. Representative (D-S.Dak.), 1957–1963; U.S. senator, 1963–1981; 1972 Democratic Party presidential nominee. McGovern was a decorated bomber pilot during WWII. An early critic of the Cold War, he was a delegate to the left-of-center Progressive Party convention in 1948. McGovern was elected to the House of Representatives from South Dakota in 1956, served President Kennedy as director of Food for Peace, and won a Senate seat in 1962.

McGovern was opposed to the Eisenhower Doctrine, which committed the United States to containment of communism in the Middle East. In 1964 McGovern reluctantly voted for the Gulf of Tonkin Resolution. Starting in early 1965 he steadily criticized U.S. participation in

what he believed to be a Vietnamese civil war. By 1970 he favored phased U.S. withdrawal from Vietnam and a congressional cutoff of funds. As the Democratic nominee in 1972, McGovern hoped to defeat President Richard Nixon by combining opposition to the war with a domestic reform agenda. His campaign was unsuccessful. After losing overwhelmingly to Nixon, McGovern in 1974 won reelection to the Senate, where he remained a critic of Cold War premises and prospective military interventions.

See also: Democratic Party.

McGovern-Hatfield Amendment. Legislation sponsored by prominent antiwar U.S. Sens. Mark Hatfield (R-Ore.) and George McGovern (D-S. Dak.) following the U.S. incursion into Cambodia in 1970. The amendment would have cut off funds for the Vietnam War after 31 December 1970 and withdrawn all U.S. forces from Vietnam. It was rejected by the U.S. Senate in 1970 and in 1971 when the cut-off date was changed to 31 December 1971.

See also: Congress, U.S.; Hatfield-McGovern Amendment; McGovern, George.

McNamara, Robert (1916–), U.S. secretary of defense, 1961–1968. The longest-serving Pentagon chief since World War II, McNamara headed the Defense Department under presidents John F. Kennedy and

Lyndon B. Johnson from January 1961 through February 1968—the period of deepening U.S. involvement in the Vietnam War. As defense secretary, McNamara shaped U.S. policy in Vietnam more than any other individual during these crucial years. His gradual disenchantment with the war and disillusionment over Vietnam led to his departure from the Pentagon in a state of near emotional exhaustion. McNamara put great faith in empiricism. He approached the Vietnam War—as he did all issues— through a study of facts and figures, believing that objective analysis promised a solution to this and every problem.

Viewing the struggle in these terms, McNamara reasoned that the United States could prevail in Vietnam through its superior values and by committing its superior resources effectively—in this case, economic, political, and military support for the noncommunist South Vietnamese regime in its counterinsurgency war against the Viet Cong guerrillas aided by North Vietnam. He promoted this view throughout President Kennedy's years in office as he assumed greater day-to-day responsibility for the issue.

After McNamara maintained his public optimism that the Viet Cong and the North Vietnamese could be forced to abandon their war against the U.S.-backed South Vietnamese regime. But McNamara began voicing private doubts to President Johnson about South Vietnam's political

future. Because he still feared the international and domestic consequences of disengagement, McNamara continued to advocate steps to save the situation, including the sustained bombing of North Vietnam in February 1965 and U.S. combat troop deployments in July 1965.

By the fall of 1965 McNamara started to doubt the effectiveness of U.S. military operations—particularly air strikes against the North—and the likelihood of achieving a military solution in Vietnam at acceptable cost or risk. He pressed for construction of an anti-infiltration barrier system, which critics dubbed the "McNamara Line," and favored periodic bombing halts as an impetus to negotiations.

In 1966, McNamara's confidence eroded further. The war's increasing destructiveness, rising casualties, mounting infiltration of troops from the North despite U.S. bombing, and U.S. troop increases that failed to produce large communist losses deepened his anxiety, as did the growing disenchantment of his key aide, John T. McNaughton. In 1967 McNamara proposed limiting the bombing of the North; capping U.S. troop deployments; lowering political objectives; and shifting war-fighting responsibility back to the South Vietnamese.

President Johnson reacted coolly to McNamara's proposals, and lost confidence in his secretary of defense. McNamara, exhausted and burdened by a costly and inconclusive war, commissioned the Pentagon Papers to enable future scholars to understand how and why things went wrong. Recognizing his deteriorating relationship with Johnson and increasingly at odds with the president, McNamara accepted Johnson's offer to resign and left the Pentagon in 1968 to become head of the World Bank. McNamara remained silent about Vietnam until 1995 when he published his memoir on the war, *In Retrospect.*

See also: Barrier Concept; Defense, Department of; Enthoven, Alain; Gelb, Leslie H.; Hawks and Doves; Johnson, Lyndon B.; Kennedy, John F.; Krulak, Victor; Pentagon Papers; Project 100,000; RAND Corporation; Rolling Thunder, Operation; Taylor, Maxwell D.; Taylor-McNamara Report.

McNamara Line. *See* Barrier Concept

McNaughton, John T. (1921–1967), assistant secretary of defense for international security affairs, 1964–1967. McNaughton strongly influenced Secretary of Defense Robert McNamara's Vietnam policy throughout McNamara's tenure.

In 1964, after Congress passed the Gulf of Tonkin Resolution, McNaughton advocated increased U.S. military involvement and endorsed bombing of North Vietnam. He supported the introduction of combat troops and convinced Secretary of Defense McNamara to support the troop requests of the Joint Chiefs of Staff (JCS).

By late 1966 McNaughton believed that the United States was primarily fighting to avoid defeat and humiliation, not because progress was being made in the war effort. As the American public became increasingly divided, McNaughton lost faith in the U.S. effort in Vietnam. Involved in many aspects of the military effort, from strategic bombing planning to troop deployments, McNaughton was frustrated with the lack of military progress he saw. Further, by late 1966 he revised his earlier position that a communist Vietnam would threaten U.S. interests in Asia, from India to the Philippines to Korea. The domino theory, he now believed, did not apply to the Vietnam situation, and the loss of Vietnam would therefore be of no grave consequence for the United States.

McNaughton's change of view affected McNamara who, in turn, resisted further troop requests and called for disengagement before President Johnson forced him out of the Defense Department. McNaughton, his wife, and one of his sons were killed in a plane crash in July 1967.

See also: Dikes; Hawks and Doves; Hoopes, Townsend; McNamara, Robert; Pentagon Papers; SIGMA.

McPherson, Harry (1929–), deputy secretary for international affairs, Defense Department, 1963–1964; White House special counsel and principal speechwriter, 1965–1969. McPherson turned against the war after the 1968 Tet Offensive and worked with Defense Secretary Clark Clifford to influence Johnson to deescalate. In March 1968, McPherson drafted a presidential speech calling for an end to the bombing of North Vietnam; Johnson accepted the draft and added to it a statement of his decision not to seek a second presidential term.

See also: Clifford, Clark.

Meany, George (1894–1980), president of the American Federation of Labor–Congress of Industrial Organizations (AFL-CIO), 1955–1979. Meany, a staunch anticommunist, vigorously supported the Vietnam policies of Presidents Kennedy and Johnson. During the 1972 presidential campaign, Meany refused to endorse either the pro-labor, antiwar George McGovern or Richard Nixon. After the election, Meany backed Nixon's Vietnamization plan. In 1974, in a television appearance, Meany said that he had been wrong to support the war.

Medal of Honor. The highest and most respected U.S. military decoration. Awarded by the president "in the name of the Congress of the United States," the medal often is erroneously called the Congressional Medal of Honor. Established during the Civil War as a decoration for the U.S. Navy and Marine Corps in 1861 and for the U.S. Army

in 1862, the medal honors extraordinary bravery and valor in battle.

For their actions in the Vietnam War, 239 military personnel received the Medal of Honor, with 155 Army, 57 Marine Corps, 15 Navy, and 12 Air Force recipients. This was a higher proportion of awards to total military participants than in World War II. Capt. Roger Donlon received the first Medal of Honor for the Vietnam War from President Lyndon B. Johnson on 5 December 1964; prisoners of war Rear Adm. James Stockdale, Col. George Day, and Capt. Lance J. Sijan (who died in captivity) received the medals of the war from President Gerald R. Ford in 1976. Presidents Johnson and Nixon regularly held public ceremonies to award the medal, using the occasions as opportunities to spark support for the war.

See also: Kerrey, Joseph R. (Bob); Oliver, Milton Lee III; Pitts, Riley L.; Sijan, Lance J.; Stockdale, James B.

Medevac. See Aeromedical Evacuation

Medical Support, People's Army of Vietnam. Compared with those of the United States, the North Vietnamese People's Army of Vietnam (PAVN) had crude medical facilities. Casualties were moved by foot, boat, or, occasionally, vehicle. The North Vietnamese medical operations received considerable resources and maintained force levels despite staggering, ongoing losses. A medical brigade accompanied each division and built field hospitals, often in underground tunnels to protect against U.S. air power or artillery. The North Vietnamese established larger medical facilities away from combat areas, such as hospitals with extensive underground operating rooms situated along the Ho Chi Minh Trail.

North Vietnamese medical personnel resorted frequently to limb amputations for the treatment of combat casualties. They often found unorthodox sources for surgical material. In their treatments, medical personnel often combined formal Western medical treatment procedures with traditional Asian herbal techniques. North Vietnamese soldiers typically suffered from malnourishment. In 1965, the daily combat ration of a PAVN soldier consisted of rice (250 g, 8.75 oz) and vegetables (300 g, 10.5 oz). If available, supplementary foods were issued to all soldiers based on strict rationing. These infrequent extras, however, did not meet the basic nutritional standard required of combat troops. Therefore foraging was a necessity, and most fauna were targeted, including snakes, monkeys, tigers, wild dogs, and elephants.

North Vietnamese soldiers also faced health problems associated with prolonged exposure to jungle conditions. Snake bites and, more critically, malaria

were constant problems. The North Vietnamese manufactured many antibiotics and other medicines and purchased items on the black market. They also received medical supplies from Eastern bloc countries as well as from neutral European nations.

Medical Support, People's Liberation Armed Forces. The PLAF (commonly known as the Viet Cong) developed a crude but effective medical care system. First aid cadre members, usually women, maintained medical stations at combat hamlets within sympathetic territory. Medical personnel, often informally trained, accompanied small fighting groups; medical contingents were incorporated into larger units. Viet Cong personnel utilized a combination of indigenous, Asian medical treatments and Western medical procedures. The Viet Cong forces created elaborate facilities, occasionally staffed with doctors from the North, at fixed installations throughout South Vietnam, often in underground tunnels.

The Viet Cong guerrillas obtained much of their medical supplies from North Vietnam or international sources. They also acquired medical material from the South Vietnamese army through raids or illicit purchases from corrupt officials. Viet Cong forces also occasionally abducted South Vietnamese doctors temporarily for treatment of prominent National Liberation Front (NLF) officials.

Medical Support, Republic of Vietnam Armed Forces. Although subsidized and overseen by the United States, the Republic of Vietnam Armed Forces' (RVNAF) medical operations were largely inadequate. Poor quality of medical care contributed to high desertion rates and poor morale. At the height of the war, the RVNAF maintained several dozen military hospitals and a few convalescent centers. In general, South Vietnamese personnel treated South Vietnamese wounded; the U.S. supervised operations and provided nearly all medical supplies. U.S. Army helicopters performed combat casualty evacuations until late in the war, because the ARVN did not have an air command and the South Vietnam Air Force (VNAF) was reluctant to commit resources to assist ground troops. Chronic shortages of medical personnel, supplies, and facilities undermined RVNAF medical operations during the war. The RVNAF did not establish a nursing corps until 1971. Medical facilities were also inadequate for extensive combat casualties. In 1968, the South Vietnamese military had 21,000 hospital beds, yet the ARVN averaged 16,595 casualties per month in that year. In 1975, the RVNAF surgeon general reported that 548 of 865 essential medical drugs were unavailable, contributing to a rise in death-from-injury rates above 10 percent.

The South Vietnamese government's ministry of health maintained a network of provincial hospitals for civilians throughout the country. These facilities were often meager, though after 1965 the United States committed military medical personnel to staff clinics.

Medical Support, U.S. The U.S. Army and Navy modified their medical operations for the Vietnam War, creating a system in which hospitals supported geographic areas, regardless of the units operating within them. Coupled with the ability of helicopters to move patients long distances rapidly, this concept made mobile large facilities unnecessary.

Military hospitals replaced field equipment with permanent, more sophisticated technology. Buildings on concrete slabs replaced tents. As a result, the wounded under U.S. care were treated in clean, comfortable surroundings in which medical personnel rarely wanted for equipment or supplies. The U.S. military relied critically upon helicopter evacuation to support its medical operations. The U.S. Army deployed its first helicopter ambulance units during the Korean War, and in the Vietnam conflict, medical evacuations by helicopter, or "dustoffs," became the norm. Helicopter evacuation teams carried critically wounded soldiers directly to military hospitals. The Army Medical Service adapted the UH-1 "Huey," developed initially as an evacuation helicopter, to become its first effective air

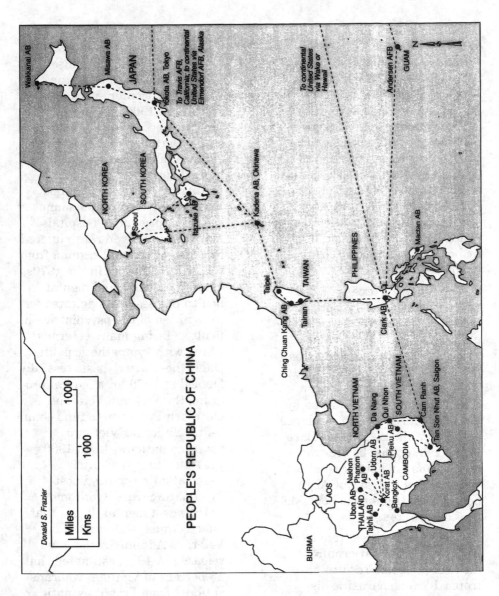

ambulance. Beginning in April 1966 the 44th Medical Brigade operated most Army medical helicopters. At the height of the war, the brigade controlled 116 air ambulances that transported casualties to the several dozen army hospitals in South Vietnam. In the Central Highlands the 1st Cavalry Division and the 101st Airborne Division maintained their own evacuation helicopters. The U.S. Navy, which oversaw medical services for U.S. Marines in the I Corps Tactical Zone in northern South Vietnam, similarly relied on helicopters to transport casualties to large, sophisticated facilities. Navy and Marine helicopters moved the wounded to either the 600-bed Navy hospital in Da Nang or to the hospital ships USS *Repose* and USS *Sanctuary.* Smaller battalion and regimental aid stations treated less severe casualties and provided routine services for Marines in the tactical zone. Navy medical detachments also supported Marine and Navy coastal and riverine operations, such as campaigns in the Mekong Delta beginning in 1967. More extensive casualties in these operations were transported by helicopter to nearby Army hospitals.

The U.S. Air Force provided additional medical support, transporting severe casualties by plane to hospitals in Asia and the U.S. Soldiers requiring treatment unavailable in Vietnam (or if recovery would take longer than sixty days) were moved by modified USAF transport planes, usually to Clark Air Force Base in the Philippines before transfer. Serious Air Force casualties were treated at Navy or Army hospitals or transported outside the combat area.

Besides casualties from combat, the U.S. military confronted medical problems resulting from tropical fevers, parasitic diseases, and, most critically, malaria. Early in the war, the Military Assistance Command, Vietnam (MACV), established malaria control procedures. During the war, the United States also committed medical resources to civic programs for the South Vietnamese. The U.S. Agency for International Development funded the construction of many hospitals and several hundred medical dispensaries. The military also integrated civilian casualties into the helicopter evacuation system. In 1966, military personnel increased medical and dental care programs for civilians, often establishing clinics in rural villages. During lulls in combat, U.S. Army physicians trained Vietnamese medical personnel or served in provincial hospitals. Many Vietnam veterans suffered lingering emotional trauma from the war. Beginning in the 1970s, veteran activists and mental health professionals agitated for recognition of the psychiatric difficulties facing many veterans. Allied with sympathetic politicians, these activists successfully lobbied in 1979 for a federal program, the Vietnam Veterans Outreach Program, to fund counseling clinics far Vietnam veterans nationwide. In 1980, the American Psychiatric Association recognized post-Traumatic Stress Syndrome (PTSS) as a mental illness that affected many veterans. A Veterans Administration study, released in 1988, estimated that 15 percent of Vietnam veterans suffered from Post-Traumatic Stress Disorder (PTSD).

See also: Aeromedical Evacuation; Agency for International Development; Nurses; Post-traumatic Stress Disorder.

Medina, Ernest (1936–), U.S. Army captain; commander, Charlie Company, 11th Infantry

Brigade, 23rd Infantry (Americal) Division, 1966–1968. Charged in 1970 with murdering 102 Vietnamese civilians, in the 16 March 1968 My Lai massacre, Medina was acquitted in a U.S. Army court martial.

See also: My Lai.

Medium Cool (1969). Film directed by Haskell Wexler set in Chicago amid the turbulent anti-war demonstrations at the 1968 Democratic National Convention done in an experimental, *cinema-verité* style.

Mekong River and Delta. The Mekong River originates in China and runs into southern Vietnam where it forms the Mekong Delta and empties into the South China Sea. A fertile region laced with canals and irrigation ditches, it constitutes about one quarter of the total area of South Vietnam, although the delta was home to 40 percent of the population in 1963. Travel in the region is difficult, except by boat or helicopter, because the terrain consists largely of water, mud, and tropical foliage. To combat these conditions, the French, during their colonial rule, constructed a road system and expanded the canal system, which played a vital role in the Vietnamese and Cambodian economies.

As early as 1954, pro-independence guerrillas established bases in the delta, where the thick jungles provided cover. South Vietnamese government pacification programs, with U.S. Marine assistance, reduced Viet Cong guerrilla activity by 1964. In 1962 the Diem government created a series of strategic farming hamlets throughout the region to isolate peasant farmers from Viet Cong guerrillas. These hamlets were extremely unpopular with the Vietnamese people because the program uprooted them from the lands their ancestors had inhabited for centuries. Regional support for the South Vietnamese government dwindled as a result of this spreading discontent.

During the 1968 Tet Offensive, much of the fighting occurred in the delta, and the North Vietnam–backed guerrillas expected the peasants to rise against Diem's government. Instead, because the guerrilla-initiated fighting caused further disruption and suffering for the people, their support for the South Vietnamese government increased.

Most of the fighting during the 1972 North Vietnamese Easter Offensive occurred outside the delta region. President Nguyen Van Thieu was forced to move South Vietnamese army units out of the delta to combat North Vietnamese troops in other areas; Viet Cong guerrillas quickly filled the vacuum left by the redeployment.

By the summer of 1973, North Vietnam controlled enough of South Vietnam to begin construction of a large highway from Quang Tri province to the delta. When completed, the highway enabled the North Vietnamese to move large-scale weaponry and troops into position for an attack on Saigon. The delta highway was an important route in the 1975 Spring Offensive.

See also: Amphibious Landing Operations; Ben Tre; Provincial Reconnaissance Units; SEALs; Zumwalt, Elmo R. Jr.

Mendenhall, Joseph (1920–), U.S. Foreign Service officer, 1946–1975. President Kennedy sent Mendenhall, who had been counselor for public affairs at the U.S. Embassy in Saigon, and Gen. Victor Krulak to Vietnam on a four-day investigative trip in September 1963. Mendenhall, the director of the State Department's Far East planning office, reported that the Diem government could not win the war. Krulak concluded that South Vietnam was winning the war. These conflicting reports reflected the split over Vietnam policy among the president's advisers.

See also: Krulak, Victor.

Mendès-France, Pierre (1907–1982), French prime minister, June 1954 to February 1955; foreign minister, 1954–1955. Elected premier 18 June 1954, following the French loss at Dien Bien Phu, Mendès-France promised to end France's involvement in Indochina within thirty days. He met his deadline by helping secure a settlement at the Geneva Conference. Last-minute negotiations among Mendès-France,

Pham Van Dong, Zhou Enlai, and Vyacheslav Molotov broke the conference deadlock; the latter two abandoned communist unity with the Viet Minh to pursue their respective geopolitical goals. Zhou and Molotov pressured Pham Van Dong to retreat from the strong positions won by the Viet Minh on the battlefield and to accept partition and late elections. Mendès-France extricated France militarily from a lost war and won much for France by negotiation, while denying the Viet Minh the victor's spoils.

See also: Dien Bien Phu; European Defense Community; Geneva Conference, 1954.

Menu, Operation. Code name for President Nixon's 1969–1973 secret bombing of Cambodia intended to destroy communist Vietnamese sanctuaries. The Menu raids reflected Nixon's policy of covering the withdrawal of U.S. ground forces with sharp military escalations. Nixon determined to keep secret the extension of Arc Light strikes to then-neutral Cambodia. "Breakfast" was launched on 18 March 1969; "Lunch," "Dinner," "Snack," "Supper," and "Dessert" followed over the next fourteen months. Menu operations amounted to 3,630 B-52 sorties and more than 100,000 tons of bombs, and resulted in substantial Cambodian civilian loss of life. The targets were all within 8 kilometers (5 miles) of the border. After the May 1970 ground invasion of Cambodia, Menu bombings continued openly until

Congress cut off funds for Cambodian operations in August 1973.

See also: B-52; Cambodia; Cambodian Incursion; Central Office for South Vietnam; Daniel Boone, Operation; Jones, David C.

Meo. *See* Hmong

Messmer, Pierre (1916–), French government official. Messmer was sent to Hanoi to reclaim French authority in Indochina in August 1945, but was prevented from doing so by Ho Chi Minh's Viet Minh government, which had declared the independence of Vietnam.

See also: Franco–Viet Minh War.

Meyer, Edward C. (1928–), U.S. Army general; Army Chief of Staff, 1979–1983. Meyer served two tours with the 1st U.S. Cavalry Division in Vietnam, in 1965–1966 and 1969–1970. He was in charge of the Army when many post–Vietnam War modernization reforms were implemented.

See also: Army, U.S.

MIA. *See* Missing in Action

Miao. *See* Hmong; Lao Sung

Michigan, University of. At the University of Michigan in Ann Arbor several faculty members organized the first Vietnam War "teach-in"—patterned after the 1960s civil rights "sit-ins"— on 24 March 1965. More than 3,500 students attended the teach-in during which faculty members discussed the nature of the war. The teach-in idea soon spread to college campuses nationwide.

See also: Teach-Ins.

Michigan State University Vietnam Advisory Group (MSUVAG). An advisory group of scholars and public administration experts created to make recommendations for U.S. policy and to help the South Vietnamese government set up democratic institutions. Supported by the U.S. Operations Mission, a government relief organization, MSUVAG was led by Michigan State professor Wesley Fishel and operated under the auspices of the university. The group worked from 1954 to 1961 to train Vietnamese civil servants and set up an internal security force of civil guard and police units in South Vietnam.

MSUVAG had difficulties overcoming South Vietnam's authoritarian style of government. President Ngo Dinh Diem believed the civil guard should be a heavily armed auxiliary military unit, whereas the American advisers pressed for a more traditional police force with light weapons. Outfitted with nightsticks and whistles, the guard was unprepared to deal with guerrillas armed with machine guns and grenades.

Conflicts between the South Vietnamese government and the MSUVAG reached a boiling point in 1961 when several returning advisers wrote articles in the American media highly critical of Diem, who subsequently ordered the MSUVAG contract dissolved.

See also: Central Intelligence Agency; Fishel, Wesley; Regional/ Popular Forces.

Midway Island Conference. Conference on 8 June 1969 in which President Nixon and his national security adviser, Henry Kissinger, met for six hours with Nixon's South Vietnamese counterpart, Nguyen Van Thieu, and his Special Assistant for Foreign Affairs, Nguyen Phu Duc. The agenda included the Paris peace talks, the battlefield situation, and South Vietnam assuming a larger share of the fighting. After the meeting, Nixon announced the first withdrawal of U.S. troops and the start of Vietnamization, a policy he had already settled upon privately, despite objections from Thieu and General Creighton Abrams, commander of U.S. forces in Vietnam.

See also: Vietnamization.

MiG. Soviet-built military jet fighter aircraft used by the North Vietnamese for air defense during the American war.

See also: Union of Soviet Socialist Republics.

Military Airlift Command. *See* Military Air Transport Service

Military Air Transport Service (MATS). U.S. Air Force globe-circling transport fleet formed in 1948. MATS was redesignated the Military Airlift Command (MAC) in January 1966. MATS and MAC transport aircraft were in wide use in Vietnam during the American war. In Operation Eagle Thrust, a fleet of MAC C-141s carried more than 10,000 101st Airborne Division troops and some 5,000 tons of equipment directly from Ft. Campbell, Kentucky, to Bien Hoa Air Base in South Vietnam in November 1967.

See also: Air Force, U.S.

Military Assistance Advisory Group-Indochina (MAAG-I). Military unit created by President Truman in September 1950 to oversee U.S. military assistance to the French, who were fighting to retain their colonial empire in Indochina. MAAG-I was replaced by the Military Assistance Advisory Group–Vietnam (MAAG-V) in November 1955.

See also: Military Assistance Advisory Group–Vietnam; O'Daniel, John W.

Military Assistance Advisory Group-Laos (MAAG-L). Created by President Kennedy 19 April 1961 to manage U.S. military assistance to Laos. MAAG-L replaced the U.S. State Department's Program Evaluations Office, which had been operating in Laos since December 1955. MAAG-L was withdrawn on 7 October 1962 under terms of the 1962 Geneva Conference.

See also: Geneva Conference, 1961–1962.

Military Assistance Advisory Group Vietnam (MAAG-V).

On 1 November 1955 the Military Assistance Advisory Group–Vietnam (MAAG-V) was activated in Saigon to direct U.S. military advisory efforts in South Vietnam. Primarily concerned with the development of the Army of the Republic of South Vietnam (ARVN), MAAG-V advisers organized and trained ARVN soldiers in the image of the U.S. Army. They focused on preparing to repel a conventional invasion by communist North Vietnam.

MAAG-V replaced the Military Assistance Advisory Group–Indochina (MAAG-I), which had been created in 1950 to funnel military aid to the French. MAAG-V was commanded by Lt. Gen. Samuel T. Williams, Lt. Gen. Lionel C. McGarr, and Lt. Gen. Charles J. Timmes. Early in 1962, the Kennedy administration established the Military Assistance Command, Vietnam (MACV), to oversee logistical and operational support for the South Vietnamese military. MAAG-V continued to operate as an independent entity, but its overall importance declined. It was deactivated 15 May 1964.

See also: Agroville Program; Kennedy, John F.; Military

Assistance Command, Vietnam; Pacification; Regional/Popular Forces; Williams, Samuel T.

Military Assistance Command, Vietnam (MACV).

Activated on 8 February 1962, the Military Assistance Command, Vietnam became responsible for directing U.S. military units being deployed to provide the South Vietnamese with logistical and operational support. General Paul D. Harkins was its first commanding officer (COMUSMACV). MACV's authority extended to most U.S. military operations in South Vietnam, including air operations along both sides of the demilitarized zone (DMz).

Although MACV was a joint service headquarters with responsibility for a specific battle zone, the Pentagon did not declare MACV a full-fledged theater command, and placed its operational jurisdiction under very tight restrictions. COMUSMACV reported to the commander-in-chief, Pacific (CINCPAC), who received his orders from the Joint Chiefs of Staff. The senior military officer in South Vietnam, therefore, was not directly responsible to the top U.S. military and political leadership, but to CINCPAC. The U.S. secretary of defense ordered CINCPAC to forward all MACV communications to the Pentagon.

MACV operated under strict geographic limitations as well. For example, military operations in North Vietnam and Laos, which had a significant impact on the military situation in South Vietnam, were technically outside the geographic boundaries of the COMUSMACV's authority. Special permission was required from Washington for such operations, and CINCPAC generally conducted them through other subordinate commands. The continued independent existence of the Military Assistance Advisory Group–Vietnam (MAAG-V), for more than two years after the creation of MACV also complicated the command situation.

General Harkins was replaced in June 1964 by General William D. Westmoreland. The most significant change came in May 1964 with the abolishment of MAAG-V and the transfer of its functions to MACV. The task of advising and training the Army of the Republic of Vietnam (ARVN) then became MACV's responsibility. Responsibility for ARVN's development was dispersed among the MACV headquarters staff and senior advisers in each of the corps tactical zones. In an effort to centralize MACV control further, General Westmoreland did not establish a U.S. Army field headquarters in South Vietnam. He ignored the Korean War experience in which the Eighth Army focused exclusively on the ground war and operated under the direction of a separate theater headquarters. Westmoreland wanted MACV to serve as both a joint service and a field army headquarters with a single stuff handling all military issues.

In addition to holding the title of COMUSMACV, he became commanding general, U.S. Army, Vietnam (USARV), as well. This command arrangement broadened MACV's area of responsibility to include field operations, assistance and advisory efforts, various politico-military issues, and many other activities. Westmoreland was replaced by General Creighton W. Abrams in July 1968. General Freerick C. Weyand succeeded Abrams as COMUSMACV in June 1972. MACV directed the U.S. war effort until it was dissolved on 29 March 1973.

See also: Abrams, Creighton W. Jr.; Commander-in-Chief, Pacific; DePuy, William E.; Harkins, Paul D.; Komer, Robert W.; Military Assistance Advisory Command–Vietnam; Pacification; Rules of Engagement; Stilwell, Richard G.; Westmoreland, William C.; Weyand, Frederick C.

Military Payment Certificates (MPC). Scrip given to U.S. military personnel in Vietnam. The certificates were issued instead of dollars to try to prevent U.S. currency from being sold on the South Vietnamese black market.

Military Police (MPs). U.S. military police began operating in Vietnam in September 1962. During the war, military police from the Army, Navy, Air Force, and Marines were used for law enforcement, as sentries (some with dogs), escort guards and for physical security operations.

Military Revolutionary Council (MRC). The junta that governed South Vietnam after the assassination of President Diem in November 1963. The MRC declared itself noncommunist, rather than anticommunist and sought an eventual reconciliation with the Democratic Republic of Vietnam (DRV) and the National Liberation Front (NLF). The MRC freed jailed Buddhists in an effort to build domestic political support and opposed the U.S. bombing of the DRV and the entry of U.S. personnel into villages.

The MRC was short lived. A pro-U.S. faction within the MRC, led by Gen. Nguyen Khanh, helped depose Gen. Duong Van Minh, who headed the junta, in January 1964.

See also: Duong Van Minh; Ngo Dinh Diem; Nguyen Khanh; Nguyen Van Thieu; Tran Van Huong.

Military Sealift Command (MSC). U.S. Navy command that shipped 95 percent of the vehicles, ammunition, fuel, equipment, and other military supplies to the ports of South Vietnam to support the U.S. war effort.

See also: Navy, U.S.

Miller, William, U.S. Army colonel; senior adviser, 5th Army of the Republic of Vietnam (ARVN) Division. During the 1972 North Vietnamese Army (NVA) Easter Offensive, NVA troops tried to lure the South Vietnamese into believing that Tay Ninh was the main attack. Col. William Miller correctly predicted that An Loc was the real target.

See also: An Loc; Easter Offensive.

Mine Warfare, Land. The military forces in the Vietnam War relied heavily upon land mines. U.S. ground forces widely used the small, powerful M18A1 Claymore mine. When detonated by trip wire or hand-held device, the Claymore exploded, firing several hundred steel balls in a cone-shaped spiral with a devastating impact up to 50 meters (55 yards). The U.S. military used Claymores to protect air and fire bases. Army and Marine units deployed the mine to defend positions or to ambush Viet Cong and North Vietnamese troops.

The U.S. military also used aircraft-delivered mines to close enemy supply routes in southern Laos along the Ho Chi Minh Trail. In operations over Laos beginning in 1967, U.S. Air Force attack aircraft, and later Hercules transport planes, dropped gravel mines designed to disable vehicles.

North Vietnamese and Viet Cong forces used land mines effectively against U.S. ground operations. Along with booby traps, mines served as effective weapons against U.S. soldiers on patrols and sweeps. Mines accounted for approximately 75 percent of the losses of U.S.

tanks and armored personnel carriers during the war. The North Vietnamese and Viet Cong troops often deployed Claymore-style mines manufactured in the North or in the People's Republic of China, though they also used recovered U.S. mines. In addition, they constructed mines with undetonated bombs from U.S. air raids and artillery.

See also: Claymore Mines.

Mine Warfare, Naval. Viet Cong guerrillas repeatedly mined the Saigon harbor and river channel, in addition to other rivers, and the U.S. Navy aided the South Vietnamese Navy with regular mine sweeps beginning in 1961. The U.S. and South Vietnamese military leadership gave priority to the interdiction of North Vietnamese supplies to Viet Cong forces in the south. To that end, the U.S. Navy proposed as early as 1961 a naval blockade and aerial mining of North Vietnamese ports, especially Haiphong harbor, and continued to urge the adoption of this tactic throughout the war. The Kennedy and Johnson administrations both rejected these proposals, first because the United States was not officially at war with North Vietnam and, later, because Johnson feared that such strong measures against North Vietnam would provoke overt conflict with the People's Republic of China (PRC) and a wider war. In 1972, President Nixon ordered the mining of Haiphong harbor as part of the U.S. response to

North Vietnam's Easter Offensive. The administration's goals were to stabilize the military situation in the south, bring about a cease-fire, and force the North Vietnamese into peace negotiations.

See also: Haiphong.

Minh, Duong Van. *See* Duong Van Minh

Missiles. *See* Surface-to-Air Missiles

Missing in Action. *See* POW/MIA Controversy

Miss Saigon. Long-running pop musical, an adaptation of *Madama Butterfly* set in Vietnam during the American war, written by lyricist Alain Boublil and composer Claude-Michel Schonberg that opened in London in 1989 and on Broadway in 1991.

Mitchell, John N. (1913–1988), U.S. attorney general, 1969–1972; chairman, Committee for the Reelection of the President (derogatorily known as CREEP), 1972. Mitchell pushed the Justice Department to initiate many conspiracy trials against antiwar groups such as Vietnam Veterans Against the War and the Chicago Eight. Mitchell also pursued draft evaders and deserters, directed the Federal Bureau of Investigation to infiltrate and disrupt antiwar groups, and ordered massive numbers of illegal wiretaps. His suit to block publication of the Pentagon Papers was rejected by the U.S. Supreme Court. In 1975 Mitchell was convicted for his role in Watergate and subsequently served nineteen months in prison.

See also: Justice, Department of; Watergate.

Mobile Riverine Force (MRF).
An Army-Navy Mobile task force established in June 1967 made up of the 9th U.S. Army Division's Riverine Forces and the Navy's Task Force 117. The MRF's main goal was to stop the Viet Cong from moving supplies and personnel on junks in the Mekong Delta. The MRF was turned over to the South Vietnamese Army in 1971.

See also: Navy, U.S.

Moffat, Abbott Low (1901–),
U.S. foreign service officer; chief, State Department Division of Southeast Asian Affairs, 1945–1947. Moffat urged the United States not to help France regain its Indochinese colonies after WWII and predicted a long, bloody war if France refused to allow independence for Vietnam, Cambodia and Laos.

See also: State, Department of.

Mohr, Charles H. (1929–1989),
journalist. Mohr covered the Vietnam War for *Time* magazine and the *New York Times*. He was awarded a bronze star for helping rescue a U.S. Marine under fire in 1965.

Molotov, Vyacheslav M.
(1890–1984), commissar for foreign affairs, USSR, 1939–1949, 1953–1956. Molotov, with British prime minister Anthony Eden, co-chaired the 1954 Geneva Conference, which negotiated the cessation of hostilities for the Franco–Viet Minh War. Along with the representative from China, the other major communist power, Molotov pressured the Viet Minh to accept unfavorable peace terms despite their military victory against the French. The Viet Minh were forced to accept partition of the country and did not gain international recognition for their communist allies in Cambodia and Laos.

See also: Eden, Anthony; Geneva Convention, 1954; Mendès-France, Pierre; Union of Soviet Socialist Republics.

Momyer, William W. (1916–),
general, U.S. Air Force; commander, Seventh Air Force, and deputy commander, U.S. Military Assistance Command, Vietnam (MACV), 1966–1968. An ace fighter pilot in WWII, "Spike" Momyer succeeded Gen. Joseph H. Moore as commander of the Seventh Air Force in Vietnam in July 1966. Gen. Momyer directed extensive bombing campaigns against North Vietnam during Operation Rolling Thunder and in South Vietnam during Operation Niagara. He opposed target restrictions and said that bombing halts signaled U.S. weakness and lack of resolve. After the war Momyer wrote

that victory could have been attained with "airpower applied in full strength against the heart of North Vietnam." He left Vietnam to lead the Tactical Air Command in August 1968 and retired in 1973.

See also: Niagara, Operation; Rolling Thunder, Operation.

Monsoon. Semiannual periods of heavy rain and inclement weather that dominate the climate and agricultural economy of Southeast Asia. Throughout history, monsoons have determined the timing and often the outcome of military operations. The southwest monsoon, which lasts from about mid-May to mid-October, drenches the entire region with heavy rain, with the exception of the coastal strip of central Vietnam east of the Annamite Mountains. It inundates the Mekong Delta and Southeast Asia west of the Annamite Mountains before moving into the Tonkin Highlands and the Red River Delta. The southwest monsoon renders unimproved roads impassable. The northeast monsoon occupies the balance of the year save for a month or so of unsettled weather at each end. It reverses the wet/dry cycle over the area, bringing clear skies and dry weather to Thailand, Laos, and the Mekong Delta, but depositing rain on the Red River Delta and the coastal strip of Vietnam south to Nha Trang between mid-September and mid- to late December. Both monsoons feature poor flying

weather in which visual bombing is often impossible.

Weather favorable to military campaigns is generally limited to the relatively dry mid-October to mid-May "winter-spring" period. In the Vietnam War, communist forces launched virtually all of their major offensives during this period. U.S. decision-makers were insensitive to the weather. Many large bombing campaigns took place during wet monsoons, including Rolling Thunder and Linebacker II Operations.

See also: Dikes; Linebacker and Linebacker II, Operations; Rolling Thunder, Operation.

Montagnards. Name given by the French to 33 tribes, estimated at 800,000 to 1 million people, living in the southern half of the Annamite mountain range. Ethnically distinct from the Vietnamese, the Montagnards never considered themselves Vietnamese. They rejected Vietnamese political authority, which led to centuries of Vietnamese discrimination against them. The National Liberation Front (NLF) and the Army of the Republic of Vietnam (ARVN) sought Montagnard support during the Vietnam War. In the early 1960s the Montagnards made up much of the Civilian Irregular Defense Groups (CIDG), organized by the Central Intelligence Agency (CIA) in conjunction with U.S. Special Forces. The Montagnards cooperated with U.S. advisers and welcomed them as an alternative to the

Vietnamese. ARVN forces continued to alienate the Montagnards by taking their animals and destroying their crops and houses. In response, Montagnards organized into the *Front Unifié pour la Lutte des Races Opprimées* (FULRO), which by 1966 was in open revolt against South Vietnam. By 1971 large numbers of Montagnards had defected from the ARVN. In March 1975, Montagnards did not report to ARVN officials the movements of North Vietnamese troops around Ban Me Thuot, thus contributing to the North Vietnamese and victory. Some 200,000 Montagnards died during the Vietnam War, and 85 percent were displaced from their homes. After 1975 many continued their fight against the Vietnamese. FULRO was decimated by 1979.

See also: Central Highlands; Central Intelligence Agency; Civilian Irregular Defense Forces; FULRO; Herbicides; Khe Sanh; Special Forces, ARVN; Special Forces, U.S. Army.

Montgomery Committee.
Officially titled the House Select Committee to Study the Problem of United States Servicemen Missing in Action in Southeast Asia, the Montgomery Committee was known by the name of its chairman, Rep. G. V. "Sunny" Montgomery (D-Miss.). Established on 11 September 1975, the committee was formed to determine if any Americans listed as prisoners of war or missing in action were being held by the Vietnamese government. After fifteen months of investigation, the committee concluded that no Americans were "being held alive as prisoners in Indochina, or elsewhere, as a result of the war in Indochina." The committee conceded that some deserters probably remained in Southeast Asia. The National League of Families of American Prisoners and Missing in Southeast Asia denounced the committee and its conclusions and increased its own political activities and demands for Vietnamese accountability. The committee was terminated on 3 January 1977.

See also: POW/MIA Controversy.

Moore, Harold G. (1922–), U.S. Army Lieutenant General. As a lieutenant colonel, Harold Moore commanded the 1st Cavalry Division's 1st Battalion, 7th Cavalry in Vietnam in the November 1965 battle of the Ia Drang valley. He is the co-author, with Joseph L. Galloway, of *We Were Soldiers Once and Young: Ia Drang: The Battle that Changed the War in Vietnam* (1992), a highly praised account of that significant battle.

See also: Ia Drang.

Moorer, Thomas H. (1912–), admiral, U.S. Navy; commander in chief, Pacific Fleet, 1960–1965; chief of naval operations, 1967–1970; chairman, Joint Chiefs of Staff, 1970–1974. As chairman of the Joint Chiefs of

Staff, Moorer planned the mining of Haiphong harbor and the Vietnamization policy, and, after peace talks broke down in December 1972, Operation Linebacker II, which dropped over 36,000 tons of bombs on Hanoi. After retiring in 1974, Moorer said the U.S. should have invaded North Vietnam.

See also: Haiphong; Linebacker and Linebacker II, Operations; Vietnamization.

Mora, Dennis, U.S. Army private. Mora, Private First Class James Johnson, and Private David Samas refused to go to Vietnam after completing basic training at Fort Hood, Texas, in June 1966. The men, called the "Fort Hood Three," were court-martialed and served two years in prison.

See also: Fort Hood Three.

Moratorium Day. Antiwar demonstrations held 15 October 1969 sponsored by the Vietnam Moratorium Committee and the New Mobilization Committee to End the War in Vietnam. Large rallies were held in Boston, New York City, and Washington, D.C.

See also: Brown, Sam; New Mobe.

Morse, Wayne L. (1900–1974), U.S. senator (D-Ore.), 1945–1969. Morse, a former Republican, was an early, outspoken opponent of U.S. participation in the Vietnam War. He and Sen. Ernest Gruening cast the only votes against the Gulf of Tonkin

Resolution in 1964, arguing that it violated the Constitution. Three years later, Morse unsuccessfully fought to repeal the resolution. Divisions among Oregon Democrats over the war and local issues led to Morse's defeat for reelection in 1968.

See also: Gulf of Tonkin Resolution; Appendix E, "Gulf of Tonkin Resolution."

Moscow Summit (1972). May 1972 meeting between President Richard M. Nixon and Soviet leader Leonid Brezhnev. Just before the summit North Vietnam launched its Easter Offensive. Despite fears that the Soviets might cancel the meeting, Nixon ordered the large-scale Operation Linebacker bombing campaign. The Soviets and the Chinese responded to the U.S. bombing with only mild protests. The summit, during which the leaders discussed Vietnam and strategic arms limitations, took place as scheduled.

See also: Easter Offensive; Linebacker and Linebacker II, Operations; Strategic Arms Limitations Talks.

Moyers, Bill (1934–), journalist, public official; special assistant to the president, 1964–1965; presidential press secretary, 1965–1967. As President Lyndon Johnson's special assistant and press secretary, Moyers strongly supported Johnson's Vietnam War policies.

See also: Johnson, Lyndon B.

MRF. *See* Mobile Riverine Force

MSUVAG. *See* Michigan State University Vietnam Advisory Group

Muller, Robert O. "Bobby"
(1945–), U.S. Marine lieutenant. Muller, a veterans' advocate who was severely wounded in Vietnam, in 1978 was the founder of Vietnam Veterans of America (VVA), the only congressionally chartered U.S. veterans service organization devoted exclusively to Vietnam-era veterans and their families. Muller was VVA's president until 1991.

See also: Veterans, American; Vietnam Veterans of America.

Munich Analogy. An analogy drawn by U.S. policymakers referring to British prime minister Neville Chamberlin's September 1938 attempt to appease Adolf Hitler on the eve of WWII by ceding the Sudetenland region of Czechoslovakia. Presidents John F. Kennedy and Lyndon Johnson and their advisers, civilian and military, were strongly affected by the events of WWII. Their foreign policy philosophies were grounded in the lessons of that war and then shaped by containment policy and the domino theory. The Munich analogy convinced Kennedy and Johnson and their advisers that if they allowed North Vietnam to take over the South, North Vietnam's aggression would turn toward Cambodia and Laos and other noncommunist Southeast Asian nations. The Munich analogy also affected the U.S. negotiations with the North Vietnamese, influencing the United States to take a hard line in the peace talks.

Murphy, Robert D.
(1894–1978), Foreign Service officer, 1921–1959. Murphy was a member of Lyndon Johnson's informal group of senior foreign policy advisers called "the wise men." At meetings of the group in 1967 and 1968, Murphy persistently advocated vigorous pursuit of the Vietnam War despite growing pessimism among Johnson's advisers and the public.

See also: Wise Men.

Mus, Paul (1902–1969), French Southeast Asian scholar. Mus, a French citizen who grew up in Hanoi, studied Southeast Asian history in Paris and in Vietnam. In 1946 he negotiated unsuccessfully with Ho Chi Minh on behalf of the French government to end the Franco–Viet Minh war. He then left Vietnam and became a one of the most respected western scholars of modern Vietnamese history at Yale University.

See also: Franco–Viet Minh War.

Muste, A. J. (1885–1967), influential American radical pacifist leader from the 1940s through the 1960s. Muste, a minister in the Dutch Reformed Church, began speaking out against the Vietnam War in 1964, and was a leading antiwar activist until his death in 1967. He conducted private peace missions to South and North Vietnam in 1966 and 1967.

My Lai. Hamlet in Quang Ngai province, South Vietnam, one of several in Song My village. On 16 March 1968, during what was supposed to be a routine search-and-destroy mission in My Lai, soldiers of Company C, 1st Battalion, 20th Infantry, of the 23d Infantry (Americal) Division killed between 175 and 400 unresisting, unarmed Vietnamese men, women, and children, committed several rapes, and engaged in destruction of dwellings, livestock, and other property.

The causes of this atrocity were various. They included weak company and platoon leadership, inadequate training and lack of combat experience among the troops, and hatred of the Vietnamese because of recent booby trap casualties inflicted on U.S. soldiers in the area. Intelligence and planning for the operation were also inadequate. The men of Company C had been told that an enemy local force battalion was occupying the hamlet and that no civilians would be present; they received no instructions for dealing with civilians if encountered.

Some U.S. troops refused to participate in the massacre. The pilot of one supporting helicopter,

Hugh C. Thompson Jr., and his crew, Lawrence Colburn and Glenn U. Andreotta, protected a group of Vietnamese by threatening their would-be killers with machine guns and stopping the massacre.

The responsible officers, from Capt. Ernest Medina of Company C through the division commander, Maj. Gen. Samuel Koster, took no corrective or punitive measures, although they either observed during the action or learned subsequently from reports that the operation had gone terribly wrong. By omission and commission, they suppressed reports of the incident and submitted false or misleading accounts to higher headquarters.

The crime came to light early in 1969 through a letter from a Vietnam veteran, Ronald Ridenhour, to the chairman of the House Armed Services Committee. Informed of the allegations, Secretary of the Army Stanley Resor and Chief of Staff General William Westmoreland began an army investigation. An Army investigation determined that a major atrocity had occurred and secured sufficient evidence to begin indictments, the first of which was of Lt. William Calley, whose platoon had done much of the killing. In November 1969 Seymour Hersh, a free-lance investigative reporter, published the first full story of the massacre. Hersh's articles set off an outcry in the media and by the public. As the controversy expanded, the army appointed a special board, headed by Lt. Gen. William R. Peers, that looked into the Americal Division's cover-up of the incident. The investigation led to indictments against 25 officers and enlisted men on various charges—13, including Calley, for war crimes and 12, including General Koster, for offenses connected with the cover-up. Of these, only Lt. Calley was convicted by military court-martial of murder and sentenced to life imprisonment. The secretary of the army reduced the sentence to ten years, and Calley was paroled in November 1974.

Charges against General Koster were dismissed, but the Army reduced him in rank and issued a letter of censure, effectively terminating his military career. The other My Lai cases ended either in acquittals or in the dropping of charges on various technicalities. In response to the My Lai incident, the service intensified its training of all its personnel in the law of war and military professional ethics.

See also: Atrocities; Calley, William L. Jr.; Hersh, Seymour; Medina, Ernest.

My Tho. Mekong Delta city, capital of Dinh Tuong province, located some 76 kilometers southwest of Saigon. It was the site of a large U.S. Army base during the Vietnam War.

See also: Mekong River and Delta.

Nam (1981). Oral history book edited by Mark Baker, containing testimony by Vietnam veterans about every aspect of their military service.

Nam Bo. Vietnamese name for southern provinces of Vietnam.

See also: Cochinchina; Republic of Vietnam.

Nam Dong. Site of a Civilian Irregular Defense Group (CIDG) camp in north central Thua Thien province nearly overrun by Viet Cong troops on 6 July 1964.

See also: Civilian Irregular Defense Groups.

Nam Ky Uprising. Unsuccessful anti-colonial revolt begun by Indochinese Communist Party's Cochin China branch in 1940. The uprising was put down by French troops.

See also: Indochinese Communist Party.

Nam Viet. Ancient Chinese kingdom located in what is now northern Vietnam and southern China. The name was restored at the beginning of the Ngo Dynasty in the 10th century A.D.

See also: Ngo Quyen.

Napalm. Gasoline-based compound that burns at about 2,000 degrees Fahrenheit. In Vietnam, U.S. forces used napalm, mostly in aerial bombs, for defoliation, tactical bombing, and, most commonly, close air support against North Vietnamese and Viet Cong forces.

Napalm kills by burning or by asphyxiation; its burning causes massive deoxygenation and produces lethal amounts of carbon monoxide. While an effective weapon, napalm is indiscriminate, and it will burn anyone it contacts. In Vietnam, civilian casualties occurred despite restrictive rules of engagement, reports of which caused public concern about the cruelty of napalm use. As early as 1966, protesters picketed the New York offices of the main napalm manufacturer, the Dow Chemical Company, calling for a production halt. Later, Dow facilities in California, Michigan, and Washington, D.C., were picketed or even attacked. In February 1967, students at the University of Wisconsin—Madison protested when Dow recruiters tried to interview job applicants on campus. Similar protests against Dow recruitment, often organized by the Students for a Democratic Society (SDS), occurred on many college campuses in the next year. Despite the public outcry against it, napalm continued to be used throughout the war.

See also: Catonsville Nine; Hamburger Hill; International War Crimes Tribunal; Levie, Howard S.; Rules of Engagement.

Napoleon III (Charles-Louis-Napoleon Bonaparte),

(1808–1873), president, Second French Republic, 1850–1852; emperor of France, 1852–1871. During Napoleon III's reign as emperor, Cambodia accepted status as a French protectorate, Cochinchina was conquered, and a French exploratory mission along the upper Mekong River opened new possibilities for colonizing northern Vietnam.

Na San. French stronghold 125 miles (200 km) west of Hanoi, the site of a ferocious battle between nine French battalions and two People's Army of Vietnam (PAVN) regiments 23–30 November 1952.

See also: Franco–Viet Minh War.

National Academy (*Quoc Hoc*).

Prestigious secondary school run by French administrators dating from 1896 in Hue where Ho Chi Minh, Ngo Dinh Diem, and many other prominent Vietnamese were educated.

National Assembly Law 10/59.

A 6 May 1959 South Vietnamese government measure that stiffened penalties for those with communist affiliations and provided for special military tribunals to try the accused. The law was aimed at more than communists, since it suppressed dissenters in general. In 1956, by presidential order, anyone "deemed dangerous to the safety the state" could be arrested.

Armed with Law 10/59 and supplemental decrees, South Vietnamese President Ngo Dinh Diem expanded the military courts and wielded state-of-emergency powers to suspend the application of laws. By the time of Diem's death in 1963, more than 75,000 people had been jailed, the majority of whom were neither communists nor procommunists.

See also: Ngo Dinh Diem.

National Bank of Vietnam.

North Vietnam's official state monopoly on revenue, currency, and foreign aid. Established by the Viet Minh in 1951, the bank issued bank notes called *dong,* for which all North Vietnamese had to exchange their money in 1954. Private businesses in North Vietnam paid heavy taxes and interest on National Bank loans; state enterprises received subsidies. All foreign currency and business profits were deposited with the National Bank after 1960. Within five years, 95 percent of North Vietnam's economy was state-owned.

In South Vietnam, President Ngo Dinh Diem created his own National Bank of Vietnam in 1955. Local merchants paid national currency called *piasters* into the bank's "counterpart fund" for U.S. imports. U.S. foreign aid dollars then bought the goods and shipped them to South Vietnam under the Commercial Import Program, which channeled $1.9 billion in economic aid to South Vietnam by 1964. Most of the imports were luxury consumer goods that contributed little to economic development. In 1975, after the fall of Saigon, the North Vietnamese bank assumed control of South Vietnam's economy by requiring residents to exchange their *piasters* for *dong*.

National Committee for Peace and Freedom in Vietnam. A bipartisan group of U.S. legislators and private citizens formed in 1967 with the encouragement of Johnson administration officials. The organization, headed by Illinois Democratic Sen. Paul Douglas, strongly endorsed U.S. activities in Vietnam.

See also: Douglas, Paul.

National Committee for Sane Nuclear Policy (SANE). Moderate group founded in 1957 to support a nuclear test ban treaty and nuclear disarmament. Many activists opposed to the war in Vietnam were members of SANE.

National Coordinating Committee to End the War in Vietnam. Umbrella group of 33 organizations formed in August 1965 to organize national demonstrations against the war in Vietnam.

National Council of Reconciliation and Concord. The 1973 Paris Peace Accords established a council to administer elections and promote the implementation of the peace agreement in Vietnam. The tripartite council, which included representatives from the Democratic Republic of Vietnam, the Republic of Vietnam, and the Provisional Revolutionary Government of South Vietnam, was the center of great contention throughout the peace process. The council never was effectively organized; the military resolution of the war made it irrelevant.

See also: Paris Peace Accords; Provisional Revolutionary Government; Appendix F, "Paris Peace Accords."

National Defense Council (NDC), Vietnam. The branch of the Democratic Republic of Vietnam (DRV) responsible for military administration. Until 1980 the DRV president served as supreme commander of the armed forces and president of the NDC. After 1980 the chairman of the Council of State headed the NDC.

See also: Peoples Army of Vietnam.

National Front for the Liberation of South Vietnam. *See* National Liberation Front

National Guard. Reserve branch of U.S. military, with units under the jurisdiction of the Department of Defense and each state's governor. Members serve four to six months on active duty for training, plus yearly summer camp and monthly unit meetings for six years. During the Vietnam War, joining the National Guard was a virtual guarantee against being sent to the war zone; only a handful of units were called to active duty and sent to Vietnam.

See also: Kent State University; Selective Service.

National Hardhats of America. *See* Hardhats

National League of Families of American Prisoners and Missing in Southeast Asia. Washington, D.C.–based organization founded in 1969 made up of family members of Vietnam War MIAs and POWs and returned POWs. The group works for the release of all prisoners of war, the accounting of the missing and repatriation of remains from Southeast Asia.

See also: League of Wives of American Vietnam POWs; POW/MIA Controversy.

National Liberation Front (NLF). *Mat Tran Dan Toc Giai Phong Mien Nam,* the National Front for the Liberation of South Vietnam, was created at a secret meeting in South Vietnam on 31 December 1960. It was designed as a broad national front organization to attract support in South Vietnam to overthrow the government of Ngo Dinh Diem and to reunify the country under communist rule. The NLF was the successor of the Fatherland Front (*Mat Tran To Quoc*), a national front that had been established in Hanoi in 1955. Another ancestor of the NLF was the League for the Independence of Vietnam, popularly known as the Viet Minh Front, which had been established in May 1941. Like the Viet Minh Front, the NLF disguised the communist character of its leadership.

The organizational structure of the NLF was similar to that of the Viet Minh Front. At the apex was an elected central committee and a presidium. The chairman of the presidium was Nguyen Huu Tho, a lawyer who had been involved in resistance activities since the late 1940s. Similar committees existed at the provincial and district levels. At the heart of the NLF were the functional liberation associations, grassroots organizations designed to appeal to specific constituencies such as peasants, workers, women, students, writers and artists, and the ethnic and religious minorities. Such associations served as the initial contact point between the NLF leadership and the masses and provided a vehicle for channeling local aspirations into mobilizing support for the programs of the movement. Talented and dedicated members of such organizations could then be enlisted into higher levels of the NLF, into the People's Liberation Armed Forces (PLAF, popularly known in the West as the Viet Cong), or into the People's Revolutionary Party, a branch in the South of the Vietnam Workers' Party. The NLF continued to exist as a non-governmental national front until the end of the war. The NLF suffered heavy losses during the final years of the Vietnam War, and in December 1976 was merged into the Fatherland Front, its counterpart in the North.

See also: Fatherland Front; People's Liberation Armed Forces; Provisional Revolutionary Government; Viet Minh.

National Police. South Vietnam's police force, consisting of two subsections: the Special Branch—the intelligence branch—and the Field Force—the paramilitary component that worked with army units in hamlets and villages.

See also: Phoenix Program.

National Revolutionary Movement. *See* Can Lao

National Security Act (1947). Law creating the Department of Defense (unifying the War and Navy departments), the Joint Chiefs of Staff (JCS), the National Security Council, and the Central Intelligence Agency (CIA).

See also: Central Intelligence Agency; Defense, Department of; Joint Chiefs of Staff; National Security Council.

National Security Action Memorandum (NSAM) 263. Issued 11 October 1963 by the National Security Council,

NSAM 263 outlined a plan to withdraw one thousand U.S. military advisers from South Vietnam by December 1963, with all remaining forces to be withdrawn by late 1965, when the communist insurgency was expected to be fully suppressed. After President Kennedy's death, President Johnson reiterated this policy in NSAM 273.

See also: Kennedy, John F.

National Security Action Memorandum (NSAM) 288. NSAM 288 was drafted by national security adviser McGeorge Bundy in March 1964, prior to the Tonkin Gulf incidents and Resolution. The document called for increased U.S. military and economic aid for South Vietnam to put the Army of the Republic of Vietnam in a position to fight Viet Cong and North Vietnamese Army forces effectively and established the U.S. commitment to a non-communist South Vietnam. NSAM 288 also advocated increased bombing of strategic targets in North Vietnam in retaliation for Viet Cong guerrilla attacks in the South. Bundy argued for a congressional resolution supporting such actions to ensure an independent, anticommunist South Vietnam.

See also: Bundy, McGeorge; Gulf of Tonkin Incident; Appendix E, "Gulf of Tonkin Resolution."

National Security Adviser. *See* National Security Council

National Security Council (NSC).

Established by the National Security Act of 1947, the National Security Council (NSC) evaluates intelligence and advises the president on the integration of foreign and military policy. The NSC is composed of the president, the vice president, and the secretaries of State and Defense, with the director of central intelligence (DCI) and the Joint Chiefs of Staff (JCS) acting as statutory advisers. The NSC staff also includes the assistant to the president for national security affairs, known as the national security adviser.

The NSC played an important role in the formation of U.S. policy in Vietnam. Beginning in 1949, the council warned of the possibility of communism sweeping Southeast Asia. In 1952, it issued a formal statement of U.S. objectives in Indochina, emphasizing support of the French against the Viet Minh. Following the 1954 Geneva Conference, the council recommended U.S. efforts to weaken the communist-dominated Viet Minh and support the creation of a non-communist South Vietnam.

Although the NSC's influence declined under Presidents Kennedy and Johnson, national security advisers McGeorge Bundy and Walt Rostow remained among the closest and most influential presidential counselors. In 1969, President Richard Nixon and his national security adviser Henry Kissinger revitalized the NSC as a policy-making body.

See also: Bundy, McGeorge; Cambodian Incursion; Cooper, Chester; Halperin, Morton; Kissinger, Henry; Rostow, Walt W.

National Security Council (NSC) Policy Paper 48/2.

Issued 30 December 1949 by the National Security Council, and approved by President Harry S. Truman, NSC 48/2 pledged U.S. political, economic, and military help to help Asian governments fight communism. Should Southeast Asia fall to communism, NSC 48/2 warned, "we shall have suffered a major political rout the repercussions of which will be felt throughout the rest of the world." The paper was the first U.S. government document setting forth an official, presidentially approved policy for blocking communism in Asia, including Indochina.

National Union for Independence and Peace.

Organization formed by Ngo Dinh Nhu in 1953 to support a new government planned for South Vietnam to be headed by his brother, Ngo Dinh Diem. The union, composed of diverse religious groups and political leaders, lobbied against former emperor Bao Dai and the French and promoted Diem's cause in September 1953.

See also: Ngo Dinh Diem; Ngo Dinh Nhu.

NATO. *See* North Atlantic Treaty Organization

Natsios, Nicholas A. (1920–),
U.S. intelligence officer. Natsios
served with the Office of
Strategic Services during WWII
and with the Central Intelligence
Agency's clandestine service
after the war. He was CIA station chief in Saigon from
1956–1960.

See also: Central Intelligence
Agency.

**Naval Forces, Vietnam (NAV-
FORV).** Command created 1
April 1966 to control U.S. Navy
and Coast Guard activities in
Vietnamese coastal waters and
rivers. Outside Vietnamese territorial waters, Navy activities
came under the Commander in
Chief, Pacific (CINCPAC).

See also: Navy, U.S.

Navarre, Henri (1898–1983),
French commander in chief,
Combined Forces, Indochina,
1953–1954. A career soldier,
Navarre shared the colonial
"military background of his post–
World War II peers" service in
Syria and French Morocco in the
1920s and 1930s. He also distinguished himself as a Resistance
leader from 1943 to 1945, earning a promotion to brigadier
general. In 1953 Navarre was
named to replace Raoul Salan as
commander in chief of French
forces in Vietnam. Navarre was
optimistic in public, forecasting
victory. Navarre's forces were
defeated in Vietnam at Dien
Bien Phu.

See also: Castries, Christian
de; Dien Bien Phu; French Union

Forces; Laniel, Joseph; Navarre
Plan.

Navarre Plan. The July 1953
blueprint for French victory in
Indochina, designed to assure
U.S. military aid. The imperative
to produce the Navarre plan
stemmed from U.S. insistence in
March 1953 that the French
design a proposal to win the war
within 24 months. Jean
Letourneau, France's minister of
overseas territories, improvised a
quick scheme: secure the south
with Vietnamese forces and then
win a decisive battle in the
north, all to be accomplished by
1955.

In early May 1953, the French
government responded to
increasing U.S. demands for
aggressive war-making by
appointing Gen. Henri Navarre
commander of French forces in
Vietnam. Drawn up by Gen.
Navarre, the plan proposed an
enlarged Vietnamese National
Army of at least 200,000 men, all
of whom would benefit from a
new training program especially
established for this army of
nationals. The overall strength
of the anti–Viet Minh effort
would be reinforced by the addition of nine battalions of French
regulars.

Strategically, the plan called
for concentrating existing French
forces and moving against the
Viet Minh stronghold in the Red
River Delta area. In September
1953 the United States agreed to
supply $385 million in military
assistance. General Navarre was

forced to abandon the scheme in the fall of 1953 when Gen. Vo Nguyen Giap's offensive opened simultaneously on many fronts in central and southern Laos.

See also: Laniel, Joseph; Navarre, Henri.

NAVFORV. *See* Naval Forces, Vietnam

Navy, Republic of Vietnam. The naval component of the South Vietnamese Armed Forces (SVNAF). The navy, supported by the U.S. Navy, had some 42,000 personnel and 1,500 vessels in 1973 when U.S. combat troops were withdrawn. That included U.S.- and Norwegian-built fast patrol boats, former U.S. Coast Guard cutters, and minesweepers.

See also: Republic of Vietnam, Armed Forces.

Navy, U.S. During the Vietnam War, the Hawaii-based Commander-in-Chief, U.S. Pacific Command (CINCPAC) controlled the Navy's carrier and other forces involved in combat operations outside South Vietnam. The Saigon-headquartered Commander, U.S. Military Assistance Command, Vietnam (COMUSMACV), a U.S. Army general, controlled the operations of the U.S. Navy's coastal, river, SEAL, advisory, and logistical units in South Vietnam. Seventh Fleet aircraft carriers operated from Yankee Station in the Gulf of Tonkin and, for a time, at Dixie Station southeast

of Cam Ranh Bay. Carrier squadrons carried out day and night bombing of targets in Laos, North Vietnam, and Cambodia. The air campaigns cost the Navy 881 pilots and other aircrew killed and captured and 900 aircraft.

The battleship *New Jersey,* and many cruisers, destroyers, and other surface vessels that steamed off North Vietnam rained high-explosive shells on targets in North Vietnam. These ships also ranged the 1,900-kilometer (1,200 mile) littoral of South Vietnam bombarding NVA and Viet Cong troops, fortifications, and supply caches. The U.S. Navy-Marine Corps amphibious teams launched large-scale assaults, smaller combat raids, and intelligence forays along the coast between the Gulf of Thailand in the south and the Demilitarized Zone in the north. U.S. Naval Forces, Vietnam (NAVFORV), command craft patrolled the thousands of rivers, canals, and other waterways in South Vietnam, primarily in the Mekong Delta.

An Army-Navy Mobile Riverine Force (MRF) was a mainstay of the allied inland effort. Employing destroyers, mine warfare ships, Coast Guard cutters, gunboats, patrol vessels, shore-based aircraft, and high-powered radar, U.S. and allied naval forces mounted Operation Market Time to limit North Vietnamese seaborne infiltration of supplies into South Vietnam. The merchant ships of the

Navy's Military Sealift Command delivered 95 percent of the vehicles, ammunition, fuel, equipment, and other military supplies that entered the ports of South Vietnam. Navy Seabee construction units built enormous logistic support bases at Da Nang and Saigon. Of the 1,842,000 Navy men and women who served in Southeast Asia, 2,600 were killed and 10,000 were wounded.

See also: Casualties; Coast Guard, U.S.; Commander-in-Chief, Pacific; Defense Department of; DeSoto Missions; Gulf of Tonkin Incident; Gulf of Tonkin Resolution; Linebacker and Linebacker II, Operations; Naval Forces, Vietnam; Mobile Riverine Forces; Philippines; *Pueblo* Incident; Rolling Thunder, Operation; Seabees; SEALs; Women, U.S. Military; Appendix E, "Gulf of Tonkin Resolution."

Navy Cross. The second highest U.S. Navy and Marine Corps award for bravery.

See also: Distinguished Service Cross.

Negroponte, John D. (1938–), U.S. foreign service officer; National Security Council (NSC) aide. Negroponte was the Vietnam specialist on the Nixon administration NSC. He served as a deputy to NSC adviser Henry Kissinger at the Paris Peace talks.

See also: National Security Council; Paris Accords.

New Economic Zones (NEZs). Program administered by the North Vietnamese Army begun after the war in which some one million people, including many South Vietnamese veterans and their families, were sent to rural areas (the NEZs) to cultivate fallow lands. Many died of malaria and other diseases; others returned to the cities after their supplies ran out.

See also: Democratic Republic of Vietnam.

New Jersey, USS. As part of two-year Operation Sea Dragon, begun in October 1966, the battleship *New Jersey* joined many other cruisers, destroyers, and other surface vessels that steamed off North Vietnam, raining high-explosive shells on North Vietnam's roads, bridges, railway lines, radar sites, artillery batteries, and coastal defenses. From its September 1968 deployment in the South China Sea to its March 1969 withdrawal, the *New Jersey* fired some 12 million pounds of ordnance.

See also: Navy, U.S.

New Left. Sociologist C. Wright Mills termed the leftist youth movement that emerged in the early 1960s the "new left" to differentiate it from the "old left" Marxists and socialists of the 1930s. The new left was disillusioned with both Soviet communism and the West and viewed the established left as excessively focused on international affairs. Members of the new left, largely affluent middle-class urban and suburban college students, were cynical about the American culture of their 1950s childhoods and were inspired by the civil rights movement to become politically active.

The movement included such groups as Students for a Democratic Society (SDS), the Revolutionary Youth Movement, the Progressive Labor Party, and the Worker-Student Alliance. In the mid 1960s the new left turned its attentions to the Vietnam War. Disagreements on tactics led to a split within the movement. Militancy increased and some, such as the Revolutionary Youth Movement, advocated violence, while many others took part in peaceful demonstrations and community activism.

See also: Students for a Democratic Society.

New Mobe. A coalition, the New Mobilization Committee to End the War in Vietnam, formed in July 1969 by antiwar activists including Benjamin Spock, William Sloane Coffin, and David Dellinger. The New Mobe sponsored the largest protest in U.S. history on 15 November 1969 when an estimated 700,000 people in Washington, D.C., and 250,000 in San Francisco marched to protest the war. After that demonstration, New Mobe organizers returned to their churches, unions, and party work.

See also: Chicago Seven; Kent State University; Vietnam Moratorium Committee.

Newport. U.S.-built deep-water port near Saigon built in 1967.

New Standards Men. Name given to those who came into the U.S. military under the 1966–1971 Project 100,000 program, which brought in a large number of men who would have been rejected for service because of their low scores on military aptitude tests.

See also: Project 100,000.

New Zealand. In 1964, New Zealand sent twenty engineers and medical personnel to Vietnam. In 1965 and 1967 New Zealand replaced them with combat troops, who worked with the Australian Task Force in Phuoc Tuy Province.

Although New Zealand's political parties sharply disagreed over the war, New Zealand maintained its troop strength of about one thousand from 1967 to 1969. In 1966 the New Zealand government augmented its artillery forces and medical team in Qui Nhon. After lengthy discussions with the U.S. Military Assistance Command, Vietnam (MACV), New Zealand sent another medical team, two rifle companies, and a platoon of New Zealand Special Air Services personnel to South Vietnam in 1967. The two rifle companies joined Australians to form an ANZAC battalion. New Zealand began to withdraw its troops in 1970, and withdrew all combat troops in 1971.

See also: Australia; Four-Party Joint Military Commission; Free World; International Reaction; Manila Conference.

Nghe An. Province in central Vietnam in which Ho Chi Minh was born. Nghe An was the site of a 1930 attack by French forces against communist-led demonstrators. In 1955, a peasant uprising took place in Nghe An province against North Vietnam's land reform program. It was suppressed by a People's Army of Vietnam division.

See also: Ho Chi Minh; Land Reform.

Ngo Ba Thanh, South Vietnamese women's rights activist. Ngo Ba Thanh was president of the Women's Movement for the Right to Life, which was organized 25 July 1970. Her group worked for women's rights and against war and lobbied for the withdrawal of U.S. troops and a new coalition government to represent the Vietnamese people.

See also: Women, Vietnamese.

Ngo Dinh Can (d.1964), administrator of Hue and environs. After his younger brother, Ngo Dinh Diem, came to power in 1954, Ngo Dinh Can controlled the northern provinces around Hue. Although he never held an official post, his family ties permitted him to direct the shipping and cinnamon trade in the region. He controlled a private police force whose aim was to kill those with ties to the Viet Cong. He was the only family member to advocate conciliation during Diem's 1963 Buddhist crisis. After Diem's fall in 1963, Can was tried and executed in a public square in Saigon.

See also: Ngo Dinh Diem.

Ngo Dinh Diem (1901–1963), prime minister and president, Republic of Vietnam, 1954–1963. Ngo Dinh Diem was born in Hue to a family that had been converted to Catholicism as early as the seventeenth century. His grandparents had been poor peasants and fishermen in the province of Quang Binh. But at the time of his birth, Ngo Dinh Diem's father, Ngo Dinh Kha, had become a high mandarin at court, thanks to the French colonial conquest that had helped Christian Vietnamese climb quickly up the ladder of success.

Third in a family of eight children, Diem attended Le Lyceum Pellerin, a Catholic secondary school in Hue. After graduating, Diem enrolled in the French school of administration, Collège Hau Bo. Diem became minister of the interior under Emperor Bao Dai in 1933, but resigned to protest French colonial rule. Diem's anti-communist and anti-French attitude thereafter made him appear as a credible nationalist figure to many in Vietnam and in the West. In the eyes of others, however, his nationalist credentials had been tarnished by his willingness to work with the Japanese.

Diem's nationalist stature was reestablished when Diem refused an offer of a high position in Ho Chi Minh's government in late 1945, partly because he regarded the Viet Minh as ultimately responsible for the assassination of his brother Ngo Dinh Khoi, governor of Ouang Ngai province.

From 1950 to 1954 Diem lived in Europe and the United States. During a stay at a Catholic seminary in New Jersey, he met many American religious and political leaders, including Francis Cardinal Spellman and Senators John F. Kennedy and Mike Mansfield. After the May 1954 French surrender at Dien Bien Phu, the United States pressured Emperor Bao Dai to appoint Diem prime minister in June 1954. On 7 July Diem returned to Saigon to take over the government. In 1955 he made his family the core of the political structure. Diem's brother, Ngo Dinh Can, ran the northern provinces around Hue. Bishop Ngo Dinh Thuc, Diem's older brother, ran the Catholic Church, which was composed largely of northern refugees who gave the regime its only appearance of mass support.

In a country that was more than 90 percent non-Catholic, the majority of high officials in the government were members of the Church. Another brother, Ngo Dinh Nhu, was Diem's chief political adviser and, by 1956, the creator and chief of the Can Lao party, which also served as a secret police. Membership in the party was a prerequisite for advancement to higher posts in the administration and military. Nhu and his wife exercised enormous influence over Diem and power over the government and the country.

In an effort to consolidate power and stabilize the regime, Diem mounted a repressive campaign against all potential political opposition in the urban area and a merciless pacification program against the countryside. As part of pacification, Diem instituted a land reform program that in effect allowed landlords to reclaim lands the revolution had parceled out to the peasants and to collect land rents for as many years back as the landlords could claim. With the help of U.S. and British experts, in 1959 Diem began a wholesale resettlement program that forced the resident population into so-called agrovilles—and later on, strategic hamlets—in an effort to weed out the communists and control the population.

After the insurrection of January 1960 in Ben Tre, which resulted in the takeover of nearly the entire province by former Viet Minh cadres and caused a chain reaction throughout the Mekong Delta, North Vietnam approved the shift to armed struggle in the South. With North Vietnam's blessing, on 20 December some twenty organizations, opposed to the United States and the Diem regime, merged with the former southern Viet Minh revolutionaries into the National Front for Liberation (NLF), whose program included the overthrow of the Diem regime. From then on the NLF dealt the Diem regime repeated military and pacification setbacks and the urban opposition created such turmoil and instability that the United States became convinced that Diem was no longer equal to his task.

When South Vietnamese troops killed nine Buddhist protesters in Hue on 8 May 1963, tensions between Diem and the United States reached a crisis. By mid-June the United States threatened to break with Diem over the issue of Buddhist repression. In October 1963, the U.S. ambassador, Henry Cabot Lodge, secretly informed a group of South Vietnamese military officers plotting a coup against Diem that the U.S. government would not oppose a change in leadership. On 2 November 1963, Diem and his brother were ousted and murdered, and Duong Van Minh became the leader of South Vietnam.

See also: American Friends of Vietnam; Army of the Republic of Vietnam; Bao Dai; Binh Xuyen; Buddhists; Can Lao; Catholics; Conein, Lucien; Dulles, John Foster; Duong Van Minh; Eisenhower, Dwight D.; Elections, South Vietnam, 1955; Geneva Conference, 1954; Harkins, Paul D.; Harriman, W. Averell; Hilsman, Roger; Hoa Hao; Johnson, Lyndon B.; Kennedy, John F.; Land Reform; Lansdale, Edward G.; Lodge, Henry Cabot, Jr.; Michigan State University Vietnam Advisory Group; Military Revolutionary Council; National Assembly Law 10/59; Ngo Dinh Nhu; Nolting, Frederick E.; Regional/Popular Forces; Tran Thien Khiem; Tran Van Don; Tri Quang; Vietnam, Republic of.

Ngo Dinh Kha, father of Ngo Dinh Diem. Descended from a Vietnamese noble family that converted to Catholicism in the 17th century, Ngo Dinh Kha was a high mandarin at the imperial court in Hue of the Emperor Thanh Thai. He resigned after the French deposed the emperor in 1907.

See also: Ngo Dinh Diem.

Ngo Dinh Khoi (d.1945), Ngo Dinh Diem's older brother who was governor of Quang Ngai province. He was assassinated by the Viet Minh in 1945.

See also: Ngo Dinh Diem.

Ngo Dinh Luyen, South Vietnam's ambassador to Great Britain, early 1960s. Luyen, the youngest brother of Ngo Dinh Diem, served in Emperor Bao Dai's delegation to the 1954 Geneva Conference. He was in England during the 1963 coup that toppled the Diem government.

Ngo Dinh Nhu (1910–1963), chief adviser to Ngo Dinh Diem;

head of the Can Lao party. Ngo Dinh Nhu, Ngo Dinh Diem's immediate younger brother. He was the first Vietnamese admitted to the elite French archivist school, the École des Charles. Graduating with a degree of paleography at the age of 28, he worked at the archives of the governor general of Indochina in Hanoi from 1938 to 1943. In 1943, he became chief of the archive of the French Residence in Hue.

Nhu first gained prominence in 1953 as an organizer of the Vietnamese Federation of Christian Workers, which was modeled after Frances Force Ouvrière and affiliated with the International Federation of Christian Workers. His real talent, however, was behind-the-scenes political manipulations, which manifested itself in the summer of 1953 when he organized the National Union for Independence and Peace in support of a new government to be headed by his brother.

After Diem gained power in 1954, Nhu served as the Diem regime's ideologue and directed the secret and police services in his capacity as his brother's chief political adviser and minister of the Interior. Nhu wielded enormous power, partly because he also headed the Can Lao party (Can Lao Nhan Vi Cach Mang Dang, or Revolutionary Personalist Diligent Labor party), which he created in 1956 along with the uniformed Republic Youth and Special Forces.

The Can Lao party was a combination of private political machine and mafia, and membership in it was a prerequisite for advancement to higher posts in the government and the military. Nhu used the Can Lao to obtain intelligence on suspect members of the government, military officers, and private citizens; and he allowed it to take over much of the criminal activity in South Vietnam in order to expand its coffers. Nhu's Republic Youth and Special Forces, meanwhile, were used for popular control and for repression.

Nhu discreetly explored the possibility of a political settlement with the National Liberation Front (NLF) and the Democratic Republic of Vietnam (DRV) in the spring of 1963 in the face of mounting opposition to the regime. In August 1963, he ordered elite U.S.-trained troops to raid pagodas throughout South Vietnam, expelling and arresting resident monks who protested the regime's policies. Vietnamese of all political persuasions were appalled. U.S. officials repeatedly told Diem that Nhu and his wife had to be removed, but Diem refused. Nhu was assassinated, along with his brother, in the 2 November coup that overthrew the Diem government.

See also: Binh Xuyen; Buddhists; Can Lao Party; Colby, William; Lodge, Henry Cabot Jr.; Ngo Dinh Diem; Ngo Dinh Nhu (Madame Nhu); Richardson, John H.; Special Forces, ARVN.

Ngo Dinh Nhu (Madame Nhu) (1924–), wife of Ngo Dinh Nhu; surrogate first lady of the Diem regime. Madame Nhu was born into an upper-class family whose grandfathers on both sides had been high court mandarins. Madame Nhu, born Tran Le Xuan, married Ngo Dinh Nhu in 1943 and converted from Buddhism to Catholicism.

She wielded enormous power under the Diem regime, due to her influence on Diem and her husband, Diem's most trusted adviser and chief of the nation's security forces. Madame Nhu organized and headed an anticommunist paramilitary organization, the Vietnamese Women's Solidarity Movement and used it to lobby the various branches of the government. She was able, for example, to push through the National Assembly the Family Code and the Law for the Protection of Morality, which, among other things, outlawed polygamy, divorce, dancing, beauty contests, gambling, fortune-telling, cockfighting, use of contraceptives, marital infidelity, and prostitution. Her outspokenness caused American officials to pressure Diem to send her and her husband abroad. Diem steadfastly refused. She was traveling in the United States when her husband and Diem were assassinated on 2 November 1963, and went into exile in Rome.

See also: Ngo Dinh Diem; Ngo Dinh Nhu; Women's Solidarity League, Vietnamese.

Ngo Dinh Thuc (1897–1984), Roman Catholic archbishop of Hue. As eldest male in the Ngo family, Thuc exercised formidable influence in the regime of his brother, Ngo Dinh Diem. An anticommunist and nationalist Catholic priest, and later archbishop of Hue, Thuc served as a liaison to South Vietnam's 1.2-million-member Catholic community. Diem lobbied for Thuc's appointment as archbishop of Saigon, but the Vatican refused because it would appear as a public endorsement by the Vatican of Diem's government. Archbishop Thuc was in Rome at the time Diem was overthrown. He died in the United States in 1984.

See also: Catholics; Ngo Dinh Diem.

Ngo Dzu (1926–), ARVN Lt. Gen.; II Corps commander. Ngo Dzu worked closely with his American counterpart, John Paul Vann, during the 1972 North Vietnamese Easter Offensive.

See also: Easter Offensive; Vann, John Paul.

Ngo Quang Truong (1929–), lieutenant general, Army of the Republic of Vietnam (ARVN); commander, I Corps Tactical Zone (CTZ), 1972–1975; commander, IV CTZ, 1970–1972. General Truong was widely regarded as one of the most competent commanders in the ARVN, possibly its best field officer. In May 1972 Truong was sent to Hue to replace Gen. Hoang Xuan Lam. Truong regained lost territory and saved the ARVN's reputation. Much of his success was also based on unlimited U.S. air support and the fact that North Vietnamese units were overextended and undersupplied. General Truong relocated to the United States after South Vietnam collapsed on 30 April 1975.

See also: Army of the Republic of Vietnam; Easter Offensive.

Ngo Quyen (897–944 A.D.), a prefect of a province in Chinese-controlled northern Vietnam, Ngo Quyen led an uprising against the Chinese in 938–939. After his victory, Ngo Quyen created the first Vietnamese independent kingdom, Nam Viet, and the first Vietnamese dynasty, the Ngo.

See also: Nam Viet.

Nguyen. Vietnamese dynasty that ruled southern Vietnam in the 17th and 18th centuries and all of Vietnam beginning in 1802 under Emperor Gia Long. The dynasty ended when Emperor Bao Dai was deposed in South Vietnam in 1955.

See also: Bao Dai; Gia Long.

Nguyen Ai Quoc. *See* Ho Chi Minh

Nguyen Binh (d.1951), born Nguyen Phuong Thao, Nguyen Binh commanded Viet Minh forces in southern Vietnam from 1945 until he was killed in an ambush in 1951.

Nguyen Cao Ky (1930–), prime minister, Republic of Vietnam, 1965–1967; vice president, 1967–1971. Nguyen Cao Ky was born in Son Tay province, northwest of Hanoi. After graduation from junior high school he joined the French air force as a corporal. A short tour of training in France and a French wife helped him rise quickly through the ranks.

Although officially only vice air marshall during the November 1963 coup against Diem, the absence of the air force chief and the personal loyalty of the men toward him gave Ky effective control of the air force and considerable leverage over other military leaders. In January 1964 Ky joined Gen. Nguyen Khanh in a coup against Duong Van Minh's government. In February, Ky was appointed head of the air force. After General Khanh purportedly sought secret negotiations with the National Liberation Front (NLF), in February 1965, Gen. Maxwell Taylor and Gen. William Westmoreland relied on Ky to urge the Armed Forces Council to remove Khanh from his position of commander in chief. On 24 February Khanh left South Vietnam as "roving ambassador."

In June 1965 Ky joined with Gen. Nguyen Van Thieu and Gen. Nguyen Chanh Thi to oust South Vietnamese Premier Phan

Huy Quat, and with U.S. backing, Ky became the new prime minister. The U.S. mission judged that among the triumvirate Ky, a nominal Buddhist, would be the safest bet to be the new prime minister.

Ironically, Ky became the most effective destroyer of the Buddhists. On 3 April 1966, with the approval of both Ambassador Henry Cabot Lodge and General Westmoreland, Ky announced that the Buddhist movement had fallen into communist hands and requested U.S. aid in shuttling loyal troops to Da Nang. In early May, Ky flew troops in and launched his attack. Aided by U.S. Marines, Ky brutally crushed the Buddhists and their supporters. In June, Ky turned against the city of Hue and, once more succeeded in ending that opposition. Remnants of the movement in Saigon were similarly crushed.

In 1967 Ky effectively used his protégés, including Gen. Nguyen Ngoc Loan, head of South Vietnam's police and intelligence services, and Gen. Le Nguyen Khang, commander of the 3d Army Division, to rig the presidential election and intimidate the National Assembly into ratifying the results that allowed him and Thieu to become vice president and president, respectively.

Relations between Ky and Thieu deteriorated after the 1968 Tet Offensive. Ky retired from politics in 1971. He fled Vietnam for the United States just before the collapse of Saigon in April 1975.

See also: Buddhists; Da Nang; Guam Conference; Honolulu Conferences; Lodge, Henry Cabot Jr.; Nguyen Chanh Thi; Nguyen Ngoc Loan; Nguyen Van Thieu; Taylor, Maxwell D.; Tri Quang; Vietnam, Republic of.

Nguyen Chanh Thi (1923–), general, Army of the Republic of Vietnam (ARVN). Col. Nguyen Chanh Thi helped President Diem subdue the Binh Xuyen gangsters in 1955. He led rebel paratroopers in an abortive coup against Diem in 1960, and went into exile in Cambodia. In 1964, Thi joined the Young Turks, who overthrew Duong Van Minh's Military Revolutionary Council. Numerous coups ensued until U.S. ambassador Maxwell Taylor called Thi and other top generals together in December 1964. Taylor offered to send more U.S. troops and start bombing North Vietnam if the generals would stabilize the Saigon government and institute democratic reforms. But a few days later, Thi helped stage yet another coup.

Thi rose to virtual warlord status in Central Vietnam until President Nguyen Cao Ky tried to relieve him in March 1966. Thi and the Buddhist leader Tri Quang then led a major revolt among Buddhists and students opposed to the Saigon regime. Thi's loyal troops joined the Struggle Movement, as it was called, and manned barricades in defiance of Ky. They denounced the United States and demanded elections to restore civilian government. Hundreds of Thi's followers perished in Danang when Ky's government forces defeated Thi in May and Thi was arrested and exiled to the U. S.

See also: Nguyen Cao Ky; Tri Quang; Young Turks.

Nguyen Chi Thanh (1914–1967), People's Army of Vietnam general, commander of operations in South Vietnam, 1965–1967. Second in importance only to Gen. Vo Nguyen Giap in the wars against France and the United States, General Thanh took control of the Central Office of South Vietnam in 1965. He sought a quick victory using conventional tactics, and his forces sustained heavy losses when U.S. troops were deployed in 1965–1966. Gen. Giap opposed Thanh's use of conventional methods. When Thanh was killed in a U.S. bombing raid in July 1967, the North Vietnamese switched to an emphasis on guerrilla operations.

See also: Central Office for South Vietnam; Vo Nguyen Giap.

Nguyen Co Thach (1928–1998), North Vietnamese negotiator in the Paris peace talks; foreign minister of the Socialist Republic of Vietnam (SRV), 1980–1991. Thach, leader of the liberal wing of the Vietnamese Communist Party, was an aide to Le Duc Tho in the secret peace talks in Paris in 1968 and played a leading role in the 1973 Paris

peace accords. He sought to normalize relations with the United States after the war. His efforts were, however, unsuccessful: the United States rejected the SRV's demand for war reparations and opposed the 1977 Vietnamese invasion of Cambodia.

See also: Paris Accords.

Nguyen Don, People's Army of Vietnam (PAVN) major general who headed the Central Office of South Vietnam and Region Five military commission in the early 1960s.

See also: Central Office of South Vietnam; People's Army of Vietnam.

Nguyen Duy Trinh (1910–1985), Vietnamese communist leader; foreign minister, Democratic Republic of Vietnam, 1965–1980. Nguyen Duy Trinh, a member of the Indochinese Communist Party, began fighting French colonialism in the late 1920s. He directed communist party activities in central Vietnam during the war against France. After 1954, he held a series of high-level positions in Hanoi.

See also: Indochinese Communist Party.

Nguyen Hai Than (1879–1955), Vietnamese nationalist leader. Nguyen Hai Than worked to overthrew French colonial rule in Vietnam and in China, where he fought during WWII with the noncommunist Vietnamese Revolutionary League. After the war he briefly was vice president of Ho Chi Minh's Democratic Republic of Vietnam, but resigned in protest because of the communists' controlling influence.

Nguyen Hue Campaign. *See* Easter Offensive

Nguyen Huu Tho (1910–), chairman, National Liberation Front (NLF), 1960–1976. A French-trained Saigon lawyer, Tho was active in the anti-French movement and was later jailed by the Diem government. He became chairman of the NLF when it was formed in December 1960. A noncommunist, Tho was chosen for his broad public appeal, but was a figurehead without significant power.

See also: National Liberation Front.

Nguyen Khanh (1927–), general, Army of the Republic of Vietnam (ARVN); prime minister, South Vietnam, 1964–1965; president, South Vietnam, 1965. At age 16 Khanh ran away from his wealthy, well-connected family and joined the Viet Minh and fought the French for a year before he was dismissed for poor discipline. Khanh then switched sides, attended a French officers' school, and led colonial troops against the Viet Minh.

As deputy chief of staff, Khanh joined the coup that killed President Diem in November 1963. Two months later, Khanh led the Young Turk faction of officers who overthrew Duong Van Minh. Khanh then named himself prime minister. Khanh never won over his own people, and he alarmed U.S. advisers by jeopardizing the war effort with repeated attempts to establish a dictatorship. His purging of the ARVN officer corps turned Khanh's fellow generals against him while stepped-up draft calls angered the populace.

Amid rising protests against his rule, Khanh used the Tonkin Gulf incident to proclaim a state of emergency on 7 August 1964. He proclaimed himself president, but angry mobs in Saigon forced him to resign on 25 August. Khanh returned to power on 27 August as a member of the Provisional Leadership Committee, which reappointed him prime minister on 3 September. He foiled a coup attempt by Catholic officers on 13 September, and appointed a civilian council to draw up a new constitution. Tran Van Huong was named prime minister of the new government on 4 November, but Khanh retained supreme command of the military. He led the Armed Forces Council in yet another coup on 20 December.

Ambassador Maxwell Taylor then suspended U.S. military aid in hopes of forcing Khanh to resign, but a month later, Khanh dismissed the rest of the Armed Forces Council and assumed dictatorial powers. Khanh's supporters, Gen. Nguyen Van Thieu, Gen. Nguyen Van Cao, and Air Marshal Nguyen Cao Ky deposed him on 21 February 1965. Khanh left the next day to become South Vietnam's "roving ambassador." He spent the rest of the war in France. After the war he moved to the United States.

See also: Buddhists; Military Revolutionary Council; Nguyen Cao Ky; Nguyen Van Thieu; Phan Huy Quat.

Nguyen Luong Bang (1904–), founding member of the Indochinese Communist Party; Democratic Republic of Vietnam ambassador to the Soviet Union, 1952–1956.

Nguyen Ngoc Loan (1932–1998), general, Army of the Republic of Vietnam (ARVN); chief of South Vietnam's national police. As Saigon's chief of police in 1966 Loan helped eliminate South Vietnamese president Nguyen Cao Ky's opponents in Da Nang. He performed so well that he was assigned to crush the dissident Buddhist movement in Hue several months later. Loan's performance earned him a promotion to general and to chief of South Vietnam's national police. During the 1968 Tet Offensive, an Associated Press photograph of Loan executing a Viet Cong suspect in Saigon was widely circulated in the United States. In 1975, Loan fled to the United States.

See also: Nguyen Cao Ky; Nguyen Van Thieu; Tet Offensive.

Nguyen Ngoc Tho, South Vietnam's vice president under Ngo Dinh Diem. Nguyen Ngoc Tho, a Buddhist who oversaw Diem's land reform program, became disenchanted with Diem and joined the generals who overthrew him in November 1963.

See also: Land Reform; Ngo Dinh Diem.

Nguyen Sinh Sac, the father of Ho Chi Minh. Nguyen Sinh Sac was a Confucian scholar who had served as an official in the Vietnamese imperial bureaucracy in Hue but resigned in protest against French occupation of his country in 1884. He left his family and roamed the country as a teacher and medicine man.

See also: Ho Chi Minh.

Nguyen Thai Hoc (1902–1930), founder of Vietnamese Nationalist Party (VNQDD). Nguyen Thai Hoc was arrested and executed by the French following the VNQDD insurrection in northern Vietnam in 1930.

See also: Vietnamese Nationalist Party.

Nguyen That Thanh. *See* Ho Chi Minh

Nguyen Thi Binh (1927–), minister of foreign affairs, People's Revolutionary Government (PRG), chief delegate, National Liberation Front (NLF) at Paris peace talks, 1969–1973. Born near Saigon, Madame Binh was a granddaughter of the patriot Phan Chau Trinh, advocate of Vietnamese independence in the 1920s.

From a civil servant's family, French-educated, Madame Binh joined the revolution against the French as a schoolgirl and participated in the August 1945 Revolution, becoming a leader of student-intellectual resistance. In 1950 she was arrested for participating in a Saigon demonstration against U.S. aid to France and was jailed from 1951 to 1954. After the Geneva Conference in 1954, she returned to political activism and married, but she kept her husband's name secret to protect him from the police.

A vigorous opponent of U.S. intervention in the Vietnam War, Binh was elected to the NLF central committee and served as vice president of the South Vietnam Women's Union for Liberation. She led many delegations abroad for both. Binh was named foreign minister of the PRG, which she represented at the Paris peace talks, ranking second only to Le Duc Tho. In 1975, Madame Binh became minister of education in the Socialist Republic of Vietnam (SRV), one of the highest positions to be held by a member of the PRG and the highest held by a woman. She continued to work for peace and served in the National Assembly. She participated in dialogues on normalization of U.S.-SRV relations in 1991 and 1992. In 1993

she was elected vice president of Vietnam, a largely symbolic office.

See also: Provisional Revolutionary Government.

Nguyen Thi Dinh (1920–1992), leading revolutionary leader in southern Vietnam, 1940s–1975. Dinh joined the revolution against the French while in her teens. She was jailed from 1940 to 1943, but helped lead an insurrection that seized power in her native Ben Tre in 1945. In 1960 she led an uprising of women in Ben Tre province, which enabled the Viet Cong to seize power there. In 1965 she was appointed deputy commander of the South Vietnam Liberation Armed Forces, the highest ranking combat position held by a woman during the war.

See also: Ben Tre.

Nguyen Thi Minh Khai (1910–1941), leading member, Indochinese Communist Party (ICP). Nguyen Thi Minh Khai joined the ICP in the early 1930s and reportedly was briefly married to Ho Chi Minh. In 1935 she became secretary of the ICP municipal committee in Saigon. Captured by the French in 1940, she was executed a year later.

See also: Ho Chi Minh; Indochinese Communist Party.

Nguyen Van Hinh, South Vietnamese Army general; chief of staff, Vietnamese National Army (VNA), 1951–1954. Nguyen

Van Hinh, a French army officer and French citizen, was named VNA chief when it was formed by the French. He led an aborted coup against South Vietnamese President Ngo Dinh Diem in the summer of 1954.

See also: Vietnamese National Army.

Nguyen Van Linh (1915–1998), Vietnamese communist party official, director, Central Office for South Vietnam (COSVN), 1961–1964; communist party general secretary, 1986–1991. Born Nguyen Van Cuc, Nguyen Van Linh led the communist insurgency in South Vietnam during the American war, and was an architect of the 1968 Tet Offensive. In 1986 he launched a program known as *doi moi,* or "renovation," embracing economic reforms.

See also: Central Office for South Vietnam; Tet Offensive.

Nguyen Van Thieu (1923–), president, Republic of Vietnam, 1967–1973. During the coup against South Vietnamese President Ngo Dinh Diem in 1963, Colonel Thieu led a division of troops against the presidential palace. Thieu then became a member of Gen. Duong Van Minh's ruling Military Revolutionary Council. He and other Young Turks aided Maj. Gen. Nguyen Khanh in the 20 January 1964 coup against Minh. Thieu was appointed deputy prime minister and minister of defense on 14 February

1965. In June, he became chief of state and chairman of the military junta, the National Leadership Committee, and Gen. Nguyen Cao Ky was installed as prime minister.

In 1966, the junta selected Thieu as the official candidate and forced Ky to join Thieu as vice presidential nominee in the 1967 presidential election. On 1 October combat police surrounded the National Assembly and Gen. Le Nguyen Khang brought the 3d Infantry Division into Saigon. The next day, Gen. Nguyen Ngoc Loan, head of the national police and security forces, walked into the National Assembly with armed guards and watched until the deputies agreed to ratify Thieu and Ky as the "legitimate" president and vice president of the Second Republic. Thieu was reelected president without opposition in 1971.

During the post-Paris agreement period of 1973–1975 Thieu persistently ordered attacks on the areas controlled by the Provisional Revolutionary Government (PRG) and suppressed any alternative elements in a publicly stated effort to prevent the formation of a coalition government as stipulated by the Paris accords. Lavish U.S. military aid, dispatched by President Nixon as part of his Vietnamization strategy, encouraged Thieu's stance. The military attacks coupled with Thieu's "economic blockade" of the countryside so disrupted food

production and economic activities that, according to reports by
Saigon deputies and Catholic
priests, up to 60 percent of the
population in the central
provinces was reduced to eating
bark, cacti, banana roots, and the
bulbs of wild grass by mid 1974.
The suffering inflicted upon the
general population made the
Thieu regime so unpopular that
when PRG and Democratic
Republic of Vietnam (DRV)
forces launched the Ho Chi Minh
Offensive in spring 1975, one
province after another fell with
hardly a fight. On 21 April 1975,
with the North Vietnamese Army
closing in on Saigon, Thieu gave
a three-hour radio and television
address, denouncing the United
States for signing the Paris
agreement. Five days later,
Thieu flew into exile in a U.S.
transport.

See also: Army of the Republic
of Vietnam; Berger, Samuel D.;
Bunker, Ellsworth; Cao Van Vien;
Chennault, Anna; Duong Van
Minh; Guam Conference; Haig,
Alexander M.; Hoang Duc Nha;
Ho Chi Minh Campaign;
Honolulu Conferences; Kissinger,
Henry; Martin, Graham A.;
Midway Island Conference;
Nguyen Cao Ky; Nguyen Khanh;
Nixon, Richard M.; Pacification;
Paris Accords; Tiger Cages; Tran
Thien Khiem; Tran Van Don;
Vietnam, Republic of;
Vietnamization; Xuan Thuy;
Young Turks.

Nha, Hoang Duc. See Hoang
Duc Nha

Nhu, Madame. See Ngo Dinh
Nhu (Madame Nhu)

Nhu, Ngo Dinh. See Ngo
Dinh Nhu

Niagara, Operation. Code
name for the 18 January to 31
March 1968 bombing of the
People's Army of Vietnam
(PAVN) forces besieging the U.S.
Marine base at Khe Sanh. The
intensive bombing was a combined Air Force, Navy, and
Marine effort under Seventh Air
Force commander Gen. William
Momyer. Under the "single man-
ager" concept, Gen. William
Westmoreland gave Momyer
direct authority over all U.S. air
force and naval air strikes used
in the defense of Khe Sanh; the
Marines, however, retained control over their own close support
sorties. The PAVN divisions were
decimated by the more than
100,000 tons of bombs dropped,
which included B-52 Arc Light
strikes as close as 900 meters
(3,000 feet) from defending
forces.

See also: Arc Light; B-52; Khe
Sanh; Momyer, William W.

Ninh Thuan Province.
Province in central Vietnam,
south of Nha Trang, birthplace of
South Vietnamese President
Nguyen Van Thieu.

See also: Nguyen Van Thieu.

Nitze, Paul H. (1907–), assistant secretary of defense for
international affairs, 1961–1963;

secretary of the Navy,
1963–1967; deputy secretary of
defense, 1967–1969. A protégé of
Dean Acheson in the 1940s,
Nitze held many key government
posts in the Roosevelt and
Truman administrations. He was
instrumental in creating the
North Atlantic Treaty
Organization (NATO), the
Marshall Plan, and the containment policy. President Kennedy
brought Nitze back into government service in 1961 after Nitze
chaired the Kennedy campaign
task force on national defense.

Nitze was the only high-level
dissenter from the Kennedy
administration's policy to commit
ground troops to Vietnam in
1962. As President Johnson's secretary of the Navy at the peak of
the Vietnam War, Nitze was one
of the most prominent opponents
of escalation within the administration. He helped to draft the
San Antonio Formula, which
offered to halt bombing in
exchange for negotiations in
1967. He served on the Ad Hoc
Task Force on Vietnam in 1968,
dissenting from its recommendation that President Johnson call
up the reserves and send more
troops to Vietnam.

See also: Defense, Department of.

Nixon, Richard M.

(1913–1994), U.S. vice president,
1953–1961; president,
1969–1974. Richard M. Nixon
played a prominent role in setting U.S. policy toward Vietnam
from 1953 to 1974. As

Eisenhower's vice president, he
advocated deeper U.S. involvement in the Vietnam War. Out of
office from 1961 to 1968, Nixon
supported forceful U.S. military
intervention. During the 1968
presidential campaign Nixon
assailed the Johnson administration for letting the war grind on
indefinitely without a clear victory. As president, his Vietnamization policy gradually withdrew
U.S. ground forces and turned
more of the conduct of the war
over to the Army of the Republic
of Vietnam (ARVN), at the same
time ordering more intensive
bombing of North Vietnam. In
May 1970 he ordered the invasion of Cambodia to demonstrate
continued U.S. support for the
South Vietnamese as the withdrawal went forward. The move
triggered some of the most intensive antiwar demonstrations of
the Vietnam era. Worried that
critics of his Vietnam policy
might jeopardize his foreign policy, Nixon authorized a series of
illegal actions against dissenters.
After the *New York Times* published the Pentagon Papers,
White House officials created the
"plumbers," secret operatives
who would plug such leaks. Their
work included the 1972 break-in
at the Democratic National
Committee headquarters in the
Watergate office building. Nixon
and his national security adviser
Henry Kissinger directed negotiations with the North
Vietnamese and the National
Liberation Front, leading to the
Paris peace agreement of
January 1973, which ended

direct U.S. involvement in the war. Despite the Paris accords, the cease-fire did not hold. The North Vietnamese triumphed in Vietnam less than eight months after Nixon had resigned the presidency on 9 August 1974.

An ardent anticommunist member of the House of Representatives and the Senate from 1947 to 1953, Nixon became one of the most forceful advocates of direct U.S. involvement in the war in Vietnam. During the Dien Bien Phu crisis of April 1954, he consistently recommended deeper U.S. military involvement than President Eisenhower wanted to provide. He advocated U.S. air strikes, including possibly the use of tactical nuclear weapons, to relieve the embattled French, and later suggested introducing U.S. forces into the war should the French pull out.

The Vietnam War played a significant role in Nixon's successful 1968 presidential campaign. After his inauguration as president, Nixon tried to make the war seem less important to Americans. His strategy for doing so involved pressing forward with Vietnami-zation, a policy developed at the end of the Johnson administration of turning the ground fighting over to the South Vietnamese. In the summer of 1969 Nixon announced a gradual reduction in the number of U.S. ground troops, promising to lower the level by 25,000 by the end of the year. He also announced a new policy for the United States to follow toward Vietnam-style conflicts after the Vietnam War ended. Quickly characterized by journalists as the Nixon Doctrine, this formula promised U.S. equipment, munitions, and training, but not troops or pilots, to governments threatened by domestic communist insurrections.

At the same time Nixon expanded the air war. In spring of 1969 he acceded to the perennial requests from the Joint Chiefs of Staff for bombing of Cambodia to stop infiltration along the Ho Chi Minh Trail. Until the middle of 1970, B-52s flew more than 3,600 sorties and dropped more than 100,000 tons of explosives over Cambodia. The air raids were kept secret. In the fall of 1969. Nixon authorized White House aides to infiltrate antiwar groups and disrupt their activities. In March 1970 Nixon announced that an additional 150,000 troops would return home by the end of the year. But the antiwar movement revived in the spring after Nixon ordered the invasion of Cambodia. The publication of the Pentagon Papers by the *New York Times* in June 1971 reinforced Nixon's belief that public discussion of Vietnam could threaten his chances for reelection in 1972. Immediately after the publication of the Pentagon Papers, White House officials created the "plumbers" unit of secret operatives who would plug leaks of government documents.

Meanwhile the Paris peace talks continued along two tracks. Publicly, Ambassador David Bruce met weekly with counterparts from the Democratic Republic of Vietnam (DRV) and the National Liberation Front (NLF). However, the more significant work at Paris occurred in secret meetings, begun in August 1969, between Henry Kissinger, Nixon's national security adviser, and two negotiators from North Vietnam, Xuan Thuy and Le Duc Tho.

In 1971 Nixon and Kissinger adopted a strategy of threatening the North with more ferocious bombing, while at the same time demanding that the South make greater concessions. In March, 120,000 North Vietnamese troops launched the full-scale Easter Offensive invasion of the south. The military situation deteriorated until 8 May, when Nixon ordered the largest U.S. escalation of the war since 1968. Peace talks finally moved forward in August 1972. President Thieu felt betrayed and refused to go along with the agreement before the election, just as he had done in 1968. Over the next two months, Nixon and Kissinger cajoled and threatened South Vietnamese leaders to drop their objections. Should the South Vietnamese government acquiesce, however, Washington promised increased military aid, including the resumption of direct U.S. involvement in the event of a breakdown of the cease-fire. In December Nixon ordered massive B-52 bombings of North Vietnam in Operation Linebacker. For twelve days, beginning on December 22 U.S. planes dropped 36,000 tons of explosives over the North, more bombs than in the period from 1969 to 1971.

In early January 1973, the South Vietnamese government announced that it had dropped its objections to the October formula and North Vietnam offered to return to the bargaining table at Paris. Nixon ordered the cessation of Linebacker II and Kissinger and Le Duc Tho made a few minor changes to their earlier agreement. On 27 January they signed the Paris accords, bringing a cease-fire to Vietnam and an end to direct U.S. military involvement.

The cease-fire lasted barely two years, and South Vietnam was conquered in April 1975.

See also: Agnew, Spiro T.; Brezhnev, Leonid; Bunker, Ellsworth; Cambodian Incursion; Détente; Ellsberg, Daniel; Federal Bureau of Investigation; Ford, Gerald R. Jr.; Haig, Alexander M.; Haiphong; Hawks and Doves; Huston Plan; Joint Chiefs of Staff; Katzenbach, Nicholas; Kissinger, Henry; Laird, Melvin R.; Linebacker and Linebacker II, Operations; Madman Strategy; Midway Island Conference; Moorer, Thomas H.; National Security Council; Paris Peace Accords; Pentagon Papers; POW/MIA Controversy; Republican Party, U.S.; Richardson, Elliot; Schlesinger, James R.; "Silent

Majority" Speech; Vietnami-
zation; War Powers Resolution;
Watergate; Appendix F, "Paris
Peace Accords."

Nixon Doctrine. International
relations policy announced by
President Richard M. Nixon 25
July 1969 in Guam. The policy
held that the United States
would support threatened allies,
but rely on them to "assume the
primary responsibility of providing the manpower for defense."
Under that doctrine in Vietnam,
U.S. forces turned over combat
operations to the Army of the
Republic of Vietnam (ARVN) and
began an intensified training of
ARVN soldiers through the
Vietnamization program.

See also: Vietnamization.

NLF. *See* National Liberation
Front

Nolting, Frederick E.
(1911–1989), U.S. ambassador to
South Vietnam, 1961–1963.
Nolting believed that President
Diem's anti-communism made
him worthy of unqualified U.S.
support despite his repressive
rule. Diem promised democratic
reforms in exchange for more
U.S. advisers, whose numbers
increased from 2,000 to 16,000
during Nolting's tenure. The
reforms never materialized, but
Nolting continued to praise
Diem. When Nolting left South
Vietnam in August 1963, Diem
sent troops on raids against
Buddhist temples only days after
assuring Nolting he would

respect Buddhist rights. Nolting's
devotion to Diem never wavered.
He left government service in
disgust over the U.S.-approved
coup that killed Diem in
November 1963.

See also: Buddhists; Ngo Dinh
Diem.

Normalization. The United
States spurned the Democratic
Republic of Vietnam's (DRV's)
request for normal relations in
1975 to protest the DRV's violations of the Paris agreements and
because of questions about the
2,238 Americans listed as missing in action (MIA). President
Ford demanded a full accounting
of MIAs, vetoed Vietnam's entry
into the United Nations, and
imposed a trade embargo. In
1978, President Carter allowed
Vietnam to join the UN. Vietnam
dropped demands for U.S. reparations in 1979. But the American
public's sympathy for families of
MIAs and for Vietnamese
refugees kept pressure on the
U.S. government to delay normalization of relations between the
two nations. Official hostility
intensified when the United
States renewed ties with the
People's Republic of China while
the DRV joined the Soviet trade
bloc and invited the Soviet Union
to establish military bases in
Vietnam.

Progress on normalization
stopped when the DRV invaded
Cambodia in 1979. In the 1980s,
the Reagan administration
refused to normalize relations as
long as the DRV occupied

Cambodia and withheld MIA
information. During the U.S.
trade embargo, the DRV became
one of the world's poorest countries while the Soviet military
presence grew. The DRV sporadically returned remains of dead
Americans and permitted investigation of wartime crash sites.
In 1988, the U.S. allowed private
charitable donations to Vietnam,
and the DRV loosened emigration restrictions. The trade
embargo continued, however, and
when Soviet aid ended in
1989–1990, the DRV's already
weak economy collapsed. The
DRV withdrew its troops from
Cambodia and began high-level
talks with the U.S. government.

In April 1991, the Bush
administration announced that
the United States would move
toward lifting the trade embargo
if the DRV complied with the
U.N. peace plan for Cambodia
and provided "the fullest possible
accounting" of MIAs. President
Bush allowed sales of food and
medicine and permitted U.S.
companies to sign contracts and
open offices in Vietnam in 1992.
President-elect Bill Clinton
vowed to deny normalization if
the DRV withheld MIA information, and despite expanding
investments in Vietnam by
Japanese and European companies, the U.S. trade embargo
remained in place.

On 3 February 1994,
President Clinton ended the
trade embargo, citing satisfactory
Vietnamese cooperation in locating MIAs. On 28 January 1995,
the U. S. and the DRV agreed to
exchange diplomats. The United
States formally recognized
Vietnam on 11 July 1995.

See also: POW/MIA
Controversy.

Norman, Michael (1947–),
journalist, author. In Norman's
highly praised book, *These Good
Men* (1989), the author, a former
Marine, tracked down members
of the platoon he served with in
Vietnam in 1968.

**North Atlantic Treaty
Organization (NATO).** Defense
agreement implemented 4 April
1949 by the United States,
Canada, and most western
European nations to contain
communist expansion in Europe.
The Southeast Asia Treaty
Organization (SEATO) was mod-
eled on NATO.

See also: Cold War; Southeast
Asia Treaty Organization.

**North Korea (Democratic
People's Republic of Korea).**
See Korean War

North Vietnam. *See* Vietnam,
Democratic Republic of

**North Vietnamese Army
(NVA).** *See* People's Army of
Vietnam

Nuclear Weapons. The United
States, the only nuclear-capable
country directly engaged in the
Vietnam War, never deployed
nuclear weapons, but considered
using them in 1954 to assist the

French at Dien Bien Phu; in the mid 1960s for tactical purposes; and in 1968 while planning the defense of Khe Sanh. President Nixon also reportedly considered the use of nuclear weapons several times.

See also: B-52; Bidault, Georges; Brezhnev, Leonid; Dien Bien Phu; Eisenhower, Dwight D.; Flexible Response; Goldwater, Barry; Khe Sanh; Madman Strategy; Radford, Arthur W.; Taylor, Maxwell D.

Nui Ba Dinh (Black Virgin Mountain). Mountain located north of Tay Ninh city, some 80 kilometers northwest of Saigon, used by the North Vietnamese Army and Viet Cong as a base area during the Vietnam War.

Nung. Vietnamese ethnic minority group living primarily in northern Vietnam. Many of the northern Nung were early supporters of the Viet Minh. Some Nung living in the Central Highlands fought for South Vietnam against the Viet Cong during the American war.

See also: Civilian Irregular Defense Forces.

Nurses. Some eighty percent of the American women who served in Vietnam were U.S. military nurses. The majority were U.S. Army nurses; all nurses were volunteers. Eight female military nurses died in Vietnam; one nurse, U.S. Army Lt. Sharon Lane, was killed by hostile fire.

See also: Lane, Sharon; Women, U.S. Military.

NVA. *See* North Vietnamese Army

O

Oakland Army Base. Main departure point for U.S. troops being shipped as replacements from the United States to Vietnam, 1966–1973.

O'Brien, Tim (1946–), novelist. O'Brien, who served with the 198th Light Infantry Brigade in Vietnam in 1969–1970, uses the Vietnam War as the main theme in much of his critically acclaimed literary work. That includes the novels *Going After Cacciato* (1978), which won the National Book Award; *The Things They Carried* (1990); *In the Lake of the Woods* (1994); and his stylized war memoir, *If I Die in a Combat Zone* (1973).

See also: Going After Cacciato; If I Die in a Combat Zone.

O'Daniel, John W.
(1894–1975), lieutenant general, U.S. Army; chief of U.S. Military Assistance Advisory Group–Indochina (MAAG-I), 1954–1956. Lt. Gen. John "Iron Mike" O'Daniel had trained South Korea's army and was U.S. Army commander in the Pacific when he was sent to Vietnam by President Eisenhower to assess French military needs in 1953. A year later, O'Daniel returned to head the first U.S. MAAG in Indochina. He expressed

confidence that the French and, later, President Diem, would win against the communists. He trained South Vietnam's military to repel a Korea-style conventional invasion, but not to counter a guerrilla war. O'Daniel departed Vietnam in October 1955, retired, and was the first chairman of the American Friends of Vietnam, a private advocacy group. He resigned that position in September 1963.

See also: Ngo Dinh Diem; Salan, Raoul.

Office for Drug Abuse Prevention, White House.
Nixon administration office that, among other things, studied drug use among U.S. military personnel in Vietnam. In 1972, the office found that 44 percent of 900 enlisted men surveyed after they returned from Vietnam in September 1971 had tried opiates in Vietnam and 20 percent regarded themselves as addicted. In 1974 the office published surveys indicating that 34 percent of U.S. troops in Vietnam had "commonly used" heroin.

See also: Drug Trafficking; Drug Use, U.S. Military.

Office of Civil Operations (OCO). Interim U.S. pacification program begun following the October 1966 Manila Conference. In 1967 OCO was succeeded by the Civil Operations and Revolutionary Development Support (CORDS) program.

See also: Civil Operations and Revolutionary Development Support.

Office of Strategic Services (OSS). Established in 1942, the

Office of Strategic Services (OSS) was the precursor to the Central Intelligence Agency (CIA). Headed by William J. Donovan, the organization collected intelligence, disseminated propaganda, conducted paramilitary operations, and supported resistance groups.

The OSS involved itself in Indochina near the end of WWII, using Ho Chi Minh's Viet Minh to help rescue downed U.S. airmen. The OSS sent an advisory team to help the Viet Minh in northern Vietnam against the Japanese in early 1945. Supplying the Viet Minh with rifles, mortars, and ammunition, the team trained them to use the weapons and taught them how to train other partisans. Hoping to enlist the United States against the reestablishment of French rule over Vietnam, Ho Chi Minh received OSS officers warmly and earned an official appointment as OSS Agent 19. Many OSS officers favored self-rule for the Vietnamese. Maj. Archimedes Patti, an OSS officer, helped Ho draft his declaration of independence. Lt. Col. A. Peter Dewey, an OSS operative, became the first American casualty in Vietnam when he was killed in an ambush in Saigon in September 1945.

See also: Central Intelligence Agency; Colby, William; Conein, Lucien; Deer Teams; Dewey, A. Peter; Donovan, William J.; Helms, Richard M.; Lansdale, Edward G.; Patti, Archimedes L. A.

Office of Systems Analysis. Pentagon unit created by Secretary of Defense Robert McNamara in 1961 and headed by a civilian, Alain Enthoven. The office provided McNamara with quantitative analyses of defense issues, including those relating to the Vietnam War. McNamara staffed the office with young college graduates and RAND Corporation experts skilled in the advanced management techniques of systems analysis and operations research.

See also: Enthoven, Alain; McNamara, Robert; RAND Corporation.

Ogborn, Charlton, Jr. (1911–), U.S. State Department foreign service officer. Ogburn, held a series of positions in the State Department's Division of Southeast Asian Affairs and Far Eastern Bureau in the late forties and early fifties. He spoke out against helping the French in Indochina and favored using U.S. military and economic aid to support a non-communist alternative to the Vietminh.

See also: State Department, U.S.

OH-6 Helicopter. U.S. Army small light observation helicopters—known as "loaches" from the acronym LOH—were built by Hughes Aircraft and were used in Vietnam beginning in 1967 primarily for scouting and surveillance.

See also: Helicopters.

OH-13 Helicopter. The Bell Helicopter Company's small, light OH-13, known as the "Sioux," was used in Vietnam for short-range scouting.

See also: Helicopters.

OH-23 Helicopter. U.S. Army three-seat light scout observation helicopter known as the "raven," manufactured by Hiller Aircraft, featuring a large plexiglass cockpit similar to the OH-13.

See also: Helicopters.

Okinawa. Large Japanese island in the East China Sea. During the Vietnam War Okinawa was the home of several U.S. Marine Corps, Army, Navy and Air Force units and served as a logistical support for U.S. troops in Vietnam.

See also: Japan.

Olds, Robin (1922–), U.S. Air Force general; commandant of cadets, U.S. Air Force Academy, 1967–1973. Olds was head of the 8th Tactical Fighter Wing in Thailand in 1966–1967. He flew more than 100 F-4 fighter missions over North Vietnam.

See also: Air Force, U.S.

Oliver, Milton Lee III (1946–1965), U.S. Army private first class awarded the Medal of Honor posthumously after he smothered a Viet Cong grenade on 22 October 1965 while serving with the 173rd Airborne Brigade near Phu Cong in the Iron Triangle. In the summer of 1966 the city of Chicago named a 10½-acre park on Lake Michigan after Olive, one of the first U.S. memorials to honor a Vietnam veteran. The city subsequently named a junior college and a portion of the McCormick Place Convention Center in honor the Chicago native.

Operations. Ground, naval and air battle actions, thousands of which took place during the Vietnam War. U.S. and South Vietnamese operations were given code names. In this volume operations are listed alphabetically under the code name.

Opium. Narcotic drug derived from the opium poppy widely grown in the mountainous Golden Triangle region of Southeast Asia, where the borders of Burma, Thailand, Laos and China's Yunnan Province meet. During the Vietnam War opium and its refined product, heroin, were transported down the Ho Chi Minh Trail into Vietnam and was easily available inexpensively to U.S. troops.

See also: Air America; Drug Trafficking; Drug Use, U.S. Military; Golden Triangle.

OPLAN 34A (Operation Plan 34A). Early 1964 U.S. clandestine warfare operation in which U.S. PT boats ferried South Vietnamese commandos into North Vietnam to destroy coastal targets.

See also: DeSoto Missions.

Oregon, Task Force. U.S. Army task force formed in February 1967, made up of elements of the 101st Airborne Division, 196th Light Infantry Brigade, and 25th Infantry Division. Oregon's job was to replace Marine Corps units in southern I Corps. In September the task force was redesignated the 23rd Infantry Division, also known as the Americal Division.

See also: Army, U.S.; Appendix B, "Order of Battle, U.S. Military."

Oriskany, USS. U.S. aircraft carrier first sent to patrol the South China Sea in November 1963. The *Oriskany* was stationed in the South China Sea's Yankee Station for seven deployments of up to nine months each from 1965–1972. During the carrier's Vietnam combat deployments 81 of its sailors were killed, 109 of its aircraft were lost, and 18 fliers were captured.

See also: Aircraft Carriers; Yankee Station.

OSS. *See* Office of Strategic Services

Ouane Rattikone (d.1975), Lao Army general; commander in chief, Royal Lao Army, 1965–1975. General Ouane reputedly was Laos's largest opium trafficker and owned Southeast Asia's largest heroin laboratory. He used the troops and aircraft of the Royal Lao Army to transport his heroin into South Vietnam. Gen. Ouane was executed following the May 1975 communist takeover of Laos.

See also: Drug Trafficking; Drug Use, U.S. Military; Opium.

Oudone Sananikone (1921–1984), Major general, Royal Lao Army. After WWII, Oudone Sananikone was active in Lao independence movements with Prince Souphanouvong. He was the last commanding officer of the Royal Lao Army before its 8 May 1975 surrender to the Pathet Lao.

See also: Pathet Lao; Souphanouvong.

P-38. Small, government-issued metal can opener widely used by U.S. military personnel in Vietnam, primarily to open C-Ration cans.

Pacific Air Forces (PACAF).

Air Force command with headquarters at Hickam Air Force Base, Hawaii, that during the Vietnam War planned, conducted and coordinated U.S. air operations in the Pacific and Asian theaters.

See also: Strategic Air Command; Tactical Air Command.

Pacification.

The process by which a government extends its influence into an area beset by insurgency. Pacification includes programs to distribute food and medical supplies to poor villagers and reforms such as land redistribution. Since guerrillas resist such efforts, the core of pacification is bringing security to the countryside.

The Viet Cong followed the Maoist model of guerrilla war, establishing secret political cadres in the countryside and forming front organizations. Fundamental to this system was the intimidation and assassination of government officials.

Between 1956 and the introduction of U.S. combat troops in 1965, the Viet Cong penetrated virtually every level of Vietnamese rural life. The earliest pacification program established with American advice was the 1959 Agroville program, launched by the U.S. Military Assistance and Advisory Group–Vietnam and the South Vietnamese government, in which communities were built by the government as a means of protection from the insurgents. Peasants, however, resented being uprooted and being forced to build the Agrovilles themselves in exchange for vague promises of schools, farm aid, and land. In 1960, peasant resistance and insurgent attacks led to the program's abandonment.

In 1961, the government launched the Strategic Hamlet program, in which villages were surrounded by barbed wire and other defenses and the villagers were armed and trained in basic defense. Hamlets were to be transformed into "antiguerrilla bastions" and thereby to confront the Viet Cong guerrillas with a network of fortified hamlets. Unlike the Agroville program, strategic hamlets received better government support, though they remained unpopular with the peasants. By the end of 1962, 3,235 strategic hamlets were built, leading South Vietnamese officials to claim that 34 percent of the population lived under government control.

A series of crises in 1963 led to the dissolution of the strategic hamlets and the development of a new pacification system. Buddhist uprisings in Da Nang and Hue, as well as a series of debilitating coups, turned attention away from the countryside and focused on the population centers, which were traditionally threats to the power structure in South Vietnam. As Saigon looked inward the Viet Cong guerrillas again infiltrated the countryside.

Not until President Lyndon Johnson personally intervened was the issue of implementing a single pacification strategy undertaken. Johnson viewed pacification as a counterbalance to Gen. William C. Westmoreland's military emphasis. In February 1966 the South Vietnamese agreed to place special emphasis on pacification, most notable was the creation of mobile 59-man teams called Revolutionary Development Cadres. These teams were charged with improving the lives of rural villagers.

The Revolutionary Development (RD) program was the first step in a hands-on pacification program. In 1967 Robert Komer was put in charge of the pacification program known as Civil Operations and Revolutionary Development Support (CORDS). The placement of CORDS within the military chain of command demonstrated that U.S. planners had come to recognize that no matter how successful big-unit operations were, they would never solve the war in the countryside as long as the Viet Cong had influence there. They also learned that U.S. economic and social programs had to be better

coordinated with U.S. and South Vietnamese military efforts; and that no pacification program could succeed without providing permanent security within the villages.

Security was a thorny issue for pacification officials, particularly when the North Vietnamese Army (NVA) forces and Viet Cong guerrillas could bring overwhelming conventional force to bear, as exemplified by the 1968 Tet Offensive. Although Viet Cong forces eliminated much of the government's limited control in the countryside, it cost the Viet Cong thousands of its political and military cadres when they attacked the better-defended urban targets. The Viet Cong never fully recovered from the massive casualties, making it difficult for them ever again to dominate the countryside. In addition, the ferocity of the Tet Offensive convinced the South Vietnamese government that pacification needed to be made a top priority.

In August Komer received the backing of the new MACV commander, Gen. Creighton Abrams, for a revamped pacification campaign closely coordinated with U.S. military operations. Under William Colby, the CORDS Accelerated Pacification Program began in November 1968 working with the existing South Vietnamese rural militia, the Regional Forces and Popular Forces. APC was intended to improve existing security in contested hamlets throughout South

Vietnam by coordinating military operations and pacification teams, and to deny the Viet Cong guerrillas their traditional access to the countryside. By the end of the campaign, 1,100 formerly contested hamlets were considered secure, and communist control reportedly dropped from 17 percent to 12 percent. The RF/PF allowed villagers to enlist in units from their own villages and kept men close to their families. Although not always militarily effective, the RF/PF kept pressure on the Viet Cong and provided a constant security presence within the villages. Colby also helped form the People's Self-Defense Force, an informal militia designed to give the government an armed presence in even the most remote villages.

The most controversial, and one of the most important, programs of pacification was the Phoenix program, which began in July 1968. Operated through the Agency for International Development (AID) with manpower supplied by the South Vietnamese, the program involved detaining and questioning individuals who were identified as Viet Cong. Colby said that 20,587 deaths had been recorded in connection with the program, although he staunchly denied charges that Phoenix was an assassination program. In 1973 the U.S. military departed Vietnam, leaving pacification to the South Vietnamese. But the war had changed since North Vietnam's Easter Offensive of 1972, and pacification was no longer paramount.

See also: Agroville Program; Central Intelligence Agency; Civilian Irregular Defense Groups; Colby, William; Counterinsurgency; Komer, Robert W.; Krulak, Victor; Mekong River and Delta; Phoenix Program; Porter, William J.; Provincial Reconnaissance Units; Regional/Popular Forces; Special Forces; Strategic Hamlet Program; Viet Cong Infrastructure; Vietnamization; Walt, Lewis W.; Westmoreland, William C.

Pacific Command (PACOM).
Located in Honolulu, PACOM was a unified (U.S. Army, Navy, Air Force) command during the Vietnam War covering the area from Alaska to the Indian Ocean including the Southeast Asian area of operations. The PACOM commander-in-chief (CINCPAC) reported through the Joint Chiefs of Staff to the Secretary of Defense.

See also: Commander-in-Chief, Pacific.

Paco's Story (1986). Highly regarded literary novel by Larry Heinemann about a Vietnam veteran suffering physically and mentally from his war wounds. Winner of the National Book Award for fiction.

See also: Close Quarters; Heinemann, Larry.

Page, Tim (1944–), British photojournalist. Page made his professional reputation covering the civil war in Laos in the early 1960s and the American War in Vietnam in the late 1960s and early 1970s for United Press International, the Associated Press, *Paris Match* and *Time-Life*.

Palmer, Bruce Jr. (1913–), commanding general II Field Force, Vietnam, 1967–1968; vice chief of staff, U.S. Army, 1968–1972; chief of staff, U.S. Army, 1972–1974. In his book *The 25-Year War* (1984) Palmer blamed U.S. political leaders for not adequately mobilizing public support and for establishing ambiguous combat goals. Senior U.S. military leaders, he said, even though they recognized U.S. strategy was not working, failed to make their realization clear to the president and the secretary of defense.

See also: Civilian Irregular Defense Groups; Free-Fire Zones; Joint Chiefs of Staff.

Paris Peace Accords. After nearly five years of negotiations, the United States and North Vietnam signed the Paris peace accords on 25 January 1973. Essentially the same agreement had been reached three months earlier, but intransigence over details and South Vietnam's refusal to cooperate delayed the treaty. In December 1972, President Nixon ordered the heaviest bombing of the war to intimidate North Vietnam and to reassure South Vietnam. A week of talks between Henry Kissinger and North Vietnam's Le Duc Tho resulted in a cease-fire under international supervision and North Vietnam's retaining control over large areas of the south. The U. S. gained time to withdraw its troops and obtain the release of prisoners of war. South Vietnam received promises from North Vietnam not to invade and U.S. promises of reintervention if the agreement broke down. Tho and Kissinger jointly received the Nobel Peace Prize, which Tho declined. After two years, North Vietnam broke the Paris accords with a massive conventional invasion that ended the war in 1975.

See also: Bunker, Ellsworth; Canada; Four-Party Joint Military Commission; Ho Chi Minh Campaign; International Commission for Supervision and Control; Kissinger, Henry; Le Duc Tho; National Council of Reconciliation and Concord; Nixon, Richard M.; Pham Van Dong; POW/MIA Controversy.

Paris Accords (1991). Multinational peace agreement signed in Paris in October establishing a Supreme National Council for Cambodia made up of members of three coalition political parties, including the Khmer Rouge, and the ruling party of the State of Cambodia.

See also: Khmer Rouge; Pol Pot.

Parrot's Beak. Region of mostly uninhabited jungle in southeastern Cambodia, jutting into southern Vietnam 65 kilometers (40 miles) west of Saigon. The Parrot's Beak was an area in which Cambodian Prince Norodom Sihanouk permitted Vietnamese communist forces to establish base camps, beginning in 1965. U.S. military commanders conducted illicit clandestine operations in the area until February 1969 when President Nixon ordered the Operation Menu bombing of the Parrot's Beak.

See also: Cambodia; Menu, Operation.

Patches of Fire (1997). Novelistically written Vietnam War memoir by former Marine Albert French that illuminates the war and postwar experiences of an African-American veteran.

See also: French, Albert.

Pathet Lao (Lao Nation). A generic term first coined in 1950 to describe Lao nationalists agitating against French colonial rule. The Pathet Lao was largely created by Prince Souphanouvong, a member of the royal family, and Kaysone Phomvihan, a member of the Indochinese Communist Party (ICP). Both men had observed the modest rise of the Lao Seri (Free Lao), a small band of nationalist sympathizers led by Prince Phetsarath, who in August 1945 had proclaimed a neutralist buffer zone around the kingdom of Luang Prabang following Japan's capitulation in the region. Phetsarath's activities resulted in censure by the monarch and Phetsarath's loss of rank, but, undeterred, he created

a rebel government called the Lao Issara (Free Lao) two months later, which stimulated Souphanouvong's and Phomvihan's nationalist sympathies. In August 1950, Souphanouvong created a new front based on Marxist-Leninist concepts. For the next five years Lao cadres were organized, trained, and supplied by the Viet Minh. The withdrawal of all French forces from Indochina by 1955 gave the Pathet Lao room to maneuver.

Pathet Lao (PL) cadres established cells and people's action committees identical to those used by the Viet Minh. The party's political platform focused on social and agricultural reforms, eradication of the corruption of business groups, and the expulsion of Western interests in Laos. In 1957 Souphanouvong, in conjunction with his half brother, Prince Souvanna Phouma, attempted to create a new coalition government, which was contested in an election by representatives from all political parties. The conservatives, led by Souvanna Phouma and Prime Minister Phoumi Sanaikone, were alarmed by the election's results: PL cadres seemed to have won 13 of 21 eligible seats even though all parties were guilty of ballot stuffing and electioneering characterized by excessive graft and corruption. A reconciliation was attempted, but failed when Sanaikone arrested PL leaders and attempted to disarm 1,500 LPLA troops monitoring the election at Vientiane. The LPLA troops escaped, and the PL withdrew to jungle sanctuaries.

In 1957 the U.S. government, absorbed with the Cold War, identified the PL as a communist menace and exerted pressure on Souvanna Phouma to nullify his half brother's growing influence. Despite enormous U.S. aid, Souvanna Phouma failed to censure or placate all interest groups. The United States proceeded to sponsor an alternative army of Lao and Thai forces led by Gen. Phoumi Nosavan, which toppled Souvanna Phouma in 1959 and attempted to destroy the Pathet Lao. By December 1960, two regimes existed: Souvanna Phouma's neutralist government set up headquarters in the Plain of Jars; an alternative right-wing faction, led by Nosavan, remained in Vientiane. The Pathet Lao again withdrew to its mountain sanctuaries. Within a year Souphanouvong and Souvanna Phouma joined forces against Nosavan, which sparked the Laotian crisis of 1961. The Geneva Convention of 1962 reinstated Phouma and gave the Pathet Lao a minor voice in government, which prompted the United States to expand its covert operations in Laos, especially against Pathet Lao forces.

The Lao People's Liberation Army (Kongthap Potpoi Pasason Lao), the Pathet Lao's military wing, grew from 5,000 in 1956 to nearly 50,000 by 1970. Soldiers, like political cadres, were trained and equipped by the Viet Minh between 1950 and 1954; after that, the People's Army of Vietnam (PAVN) assumed sole patronage of LPLA activities. PAVN officers often criticized the LPLA for its lack of aggressiveness, but overall their relationship was harmonious. The LPLA's greatest contribution was its assistance in building and maintaining the Laotian segments of the Ho Chi Minh Trail, plus a labyrinth of supply bases, underground field hospitals, and staging depots where PAVN-LPLA forces regrouped and retrained.

As the Vietnam War intensified after 1965, the United States embarked on one of the most secret covert operations in contemporary military history. Operation Barrel Roll, conceived in 1964 and designed to destroy the Ho Chi Minh Trail and PAVN-LPLA bases, intensified to a point at which thousands of hectares of Laotian soil were laid waste by U.S. bombers. Alternatively, the Central Intelligence Agency (CIA) funded a 40,000-strong Meo-Hmong army, led by General Vang Pao, which attacked and harassed PAVN-LPLA units at every opportunity in order to disrupt the Ho Chi Minh Trail.

A cease-fire was proclaimed in February 1973, but the covert war continued through April 1975. By then the Pathet Lao dominated Laos's coalition government. Phouma's RLA surrendered to the Pathet Lao on 8 May 1975, one week after the collapse of Saigon. On

2 December 1975, the Lao People's Democratic Republic was declared: Souphanouvong emerged as president, and Kaysone Phomvihane was appointed secretary of the Lao People's Revolutionary Party (Phak Pasason Pativat Lao) and prime minister.

See also: Geneva Conference, 1961–1962; Hmong; Laos; Souphanouvong; Souvanna Phouma.

Pathfinders. U.S. Army combat aircraft-control crews known as the black hats because of the black baseball caps they wore. Pathfinders were landed by helicopter or parachuted into territory held by North Vietnamese or Viet Cong forces to direct air traffic. They played a pivotal role in the Vietnam War, with responsibility for coordinating aircraft flights, identifying drop and landing zones for helicopters, assisting in navigation, and targeting and coordinating artillery fire and aircraft bombardment.

Path of Revolution in the South (1956). Pamphlet urging the overthrow of the Saigon regime written by Le Duan, then secretary of the communist party's Central Office for South Vietnam (COSVN).

See also: Central Office for South Vietnam; Le Duan.

Patrol Boat, River (PBR). Compact, fast, maneuverable, heavily armed U.S. Navy river craft built by United

Boatbuilders introduced into Vietnam in March 1966.

See also: Navy, U.S.

Patti, Archimedes L. A., OSS and CIA agent; chief, OSS Secret Intelligence Operations for Indochina, 1945. Patti and other U.S. OSS operatives worked closely with Ho Chi Minh in 1945 in their common fight against the Japanese. Patti chronicled that experience in his well-received book, *Why Vietnam? Prelude to America's Albatross* (1980).

See also: Deer Teams; Office of Strategic Services.

Patton, George S. (1923–), U.S. Army general. The son of legendary WWI and WWII Gen. George S. Patton, Jr., the younger Patton served three tours in Vietnam. He commanded the 11th Armored Cavalry, the "Blackhorse Regiment," in 1968–1969.

See also: Appendix B, "Order of Battle, U.S. Military."

Paul Revere, Operation. Code name for U.S. Army operations against the North Vietnamese Army in May 1966 in the Central Highlands near the Cambodian border involving elements of the 4th Infantry Division, 25th Infantry Division and 1st Cavalry Division.

Paul VI (1897–1978), born Giovanni Battista Montini; pope, Roman Catholic Church, 1963–1978. Paul VI was an important spokesman for world peace, social reform, and human rights. He consistently pressed for a cease-fire and for negotiations to end the conflict in Vietnam.

PAVN. *See* People's Army of Vietnam

Peace with Honor. Phrase used by President Richard M. Nixon to describe his goal of withdrawing from Vietnam under conditions that did not resemble an American defeat. Republicans used the phrase in the 1972 presidential campaign to contrast Nixon's Vietnam strategy with that of the strident antiwar Democratic nominee George McGovern.

See also: Nixon, Richard M.; Vietnamization.

Pearson, Lester (1897–1972), Canadian prime minister, 1963–1968. Initially Pearson supported U.S. entry into the war, but in 1965 called for a cease-fire and a suspension of U.S. bombing. Pearson approved Canadian diplomatic missions to Hanoi in June 1964 and March 1966. The first informed North Vietnam of the U.S. intention to escalate the war, and the second, not fully supported by the United States, sought an opening for negotiations.

See also: Canada.

Peasant Problem, The (1938). Study written by Vietnamese communist leaders Vo Nguyen Giap and Truong Chinh that became a key work for Viet Minh planning on agriculture.

See also: Truong Chinh; Vo Nguyen Giap.

Peers, William R. (1914–1984), U.S. Army lieutenant general. Peers, who commanded the Army's 4th Infantry Division and the First Field Force in Vietnam, headed a special Army board to investigate the Americal Division's cover-up of the My Lai massacre. The board's strongly worded 225-page report, known as the Peers Report, led to court martial charges against twelve Army participants.

See also: My Lai.

Pegasus, Operation. Code name for 1–15 April 1968 operation in which a combined U.S. Army-Marine and South Vietnamese Army task force, under the 1st Cavalry Division, broke through North Vietnamese lines and lifted the siege of Khe Sanh.

See also: Khe Sanh.

Pennsylvania, Operation. Code name for secret talks held in the summer and fall of 1967 with representatives of North Vietnam by two French citizens, Herbert Marcovich and Raymond Aubrac, and then Harvard University government professor Henry Kissinger on behalf of the Johnson administration. The talks did not lead to formal U.S.–North Vietnamese negotiations.

See also: Kissinger, Henry.

Pentagon Papers. A 7,000-page document chronicling U.S. actions in Vietnam from 1945–1968 written secretly by three dozen Pentagon aides between 1967 and 1969 at the instruction of Secretary of Defense Robert McNamara. Thirty-six Defense Department aides, including Daniel Ellsberg and Leslie Gelb, worked on the 47-volume archive, which chronicled U.S. actions in Vietnam from 1945 to 1968. The Pentagon Papers included official statements and unofficial Defense Department memos. They did not include White House memoranda.

Daniel Ellsberg, who had served as an aide to McGeorge Bundy and John McNaughton, secretly copied the Pentagon Papers, and in February 1971 he turned them over to *New York Times* reporter Neil Sheehan. The *Times* began publication on 13 June 1971. The Justice Department obtained a temporary court order against the *Times,* but the Supreme Court, citing the First Amendment, ruled that the *Times* had the constitutional right to publish the documents. The day before the Supreme Court order, Ellsberg was indicted for his role in leaking the papers. The Nixon administration organized the "Plumbers," a secret White House group, to investigate and discredit Ellsberg. In 1972 they broke into the office of Ellsberg's psychiatrist, Dr. Lewis Fielding, looking for damaging information.

In 1973 Ellsberg's case was declared a mistrial because of the Plumbers' activities, and the indictment was dropped. The Pentagon Papers were significant both in exposing government policy and in prompting the Plumbers break-in, a harbinger for the Watergate scandal.

See also: Ellsberg, Daniel; Gelb, Leslie H.; Gravel, Mike; McNamara, Robert; Mitchell, John N.; Nixon, Richard M.; Plumbers; Richardson, Elliot; Schlesinger, James R.; Sheehan, Neil; Watergate.

People's Action Teams. Small South Vietnamese Army political teams, developed in 1965 by ARVN Major Nguyen Be, often made up of young peasants, sent into villages to reactivate local government and services. By 1967, the U.S. CIA was training team members for use throughout all of South Vietnam.

See also: Central Intelligence Agency; Pacification; Regional/Popular Forces.

People's Anti-Corruption Movement. South Vietnamese protest group formed in 1974 by a Catholic priest, Father Tran Huu Thanh, who strongly denounced the government of President Nguyen Van Thieu. Father Thanh charged President Thieu with "undermining the nationalist cause for his own financial gain" and accused him of protecting the heroin trade.

See also: Nguyen Van Theiu.

People's Army of Vietnam (PAVN).

The People's Army of Vietnam was best known to Americans during the Vietnam War as the North Vietnamese Army. It was made up of a main force of regular troops, a regional force of full-time troops responsible for territorial security and support of the main force, and a self-defense force of part-time militia in the villages.

The PAVN's official history claims antecedents in the "self-defense teams" *(doi tu ve)* organized by Communist Party members during the abortive peasant rebellion in Nghe An and Ha Tinh provinces in 1930. In 1935 the party adopted guidelines for the future organization of armed forces on the Soviet model. Following Japan's 1940 occupation of Indochina, Vietnamese communists organized a guerrilla movement in the mountains in northern Vietnam in May 1941 and named it the *Viet Nam Doc Lap Dong Minh* (Vietnam Independence League), or Viet Minh for short. On 22 December 1944 the party formed the Vietnam Propaganda and Liberation Unit under Vo Nguyen Giap. The unit combined with other bands to form the Vietnam Liberation Army in May 1945. The Liberation Army's ranks grew to a few thousand by the August (1945) Revolution, after which it was renamed the National Defense Army and, in 1950, the People's Army of Vietnam. On the eve of war with France in December 1946, the total force was about 100,000

troops. By 1950, the main force alone had 130,000 troops and manufactured its own recoilless rifles and mortars. Although most of the manpower came from the poor peasantry, the sons of middle and higher peasant families could better afford the absence from home, knew how to read, and so tended to fill the cadre ranks. Officers came at first from among the handful of party members who had attended short courses in the People's Republic of China (PRC) or had gained experience in the Liberation Army before the August Revolution. All top-ranked commanders such as Giap were party members who had begun their revolutionary careers as political activists; none of them were military professionals.

The PAVN operated in small units until the late 1940s. The first division, the 308th, was commissioned in August 1949 in Viet Bac, near the border with the PRC. A second, the 304th, emerged in northern central Vietnam in March 1950. The commander in chief's office was divided into a general staff, political directorate, and supply directorate. Four more divisions, bringing the total to six (four in the northern provinces, two in the center), took shape by late 1952.

China set up training centers for the PAVN at six locations on its side of the border, and the volume of Chinese material assistance increased slowly to 1,500 tons per month at the

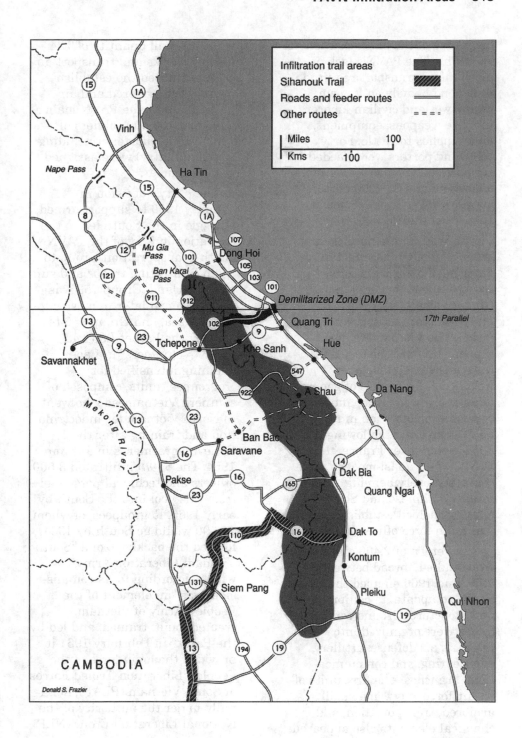

Infiltration trail areas
Sihanouk Trail
Roads and feeder routes
Other routes

Miles 100
Kms 100

(15) (1A)

Vinh

Nape Pass

Ha Tin

(15)

(8)

(1A)

(12) Mu Gia Pass

(107)

Dong Hoi

(105)

(101)

Ban Karai Pass

(103)

(121)

(101)

(911) (912)

Demilitarized Zone (DMZ)

(13)

(102)

17th Parallel

(23) Tchepone

(9)

Quang Tri

(9)

Khe Sanh

Hue

Savannakhet

(547)

(922)

A Shau

Da Nang

Mekong River

(13)

(23)

Ban Bac

Saravane

(1)

(16)

(14)

Dak Bia

Pakse

(16)

(165)

(23)

Quang Ngai

(110)

(16)

Dak To

Kontum

(131)

Siem Pang

Pleiku

Qui Nhon

CAMBODIA

(13)

(194)

(19)

(19)

Donald S. Frazier

beginning of the battle of Dien Bien Phu. The PAVN's lack of mechanized transport required it to depend heavily on its own manpower and civilian laborers to move weapons, equipment, and supplies to battle. Forty thousand porters were needed to support one division on a simple operation, and 260,000 porters supplied PAVN siege forces at Dien Bien Phu.

The Vietnamese mimicked a great deal of Chinese tactical doctrine and organizational structure, but they had to adapt Chinese strategy to Vietnam's much smaller territory and population. The Vietnamese also tapped their own history and that of the Soviet October Revolution for models of general offensive and uprising and the coordination of action in rural and urban areas. Following the 1954 victory over France, the PAVN was a quasi-modern force composed overwhelmingly of infantry. Chinese and Soviet advisers helped establish a central main force officers' academy.

The return of 2,400 officers who studied abroad between 1955 and 1960 enabled the PAVN to update its equipment and structure. Ground combat forces were organized into infantry, air defense, artillery, engineering, and communications branches. The first units of an air force, navy, and small armored, transportation, and chemical elements also appeared. Both the Soviet Union and the PRC supplied assistance, in

which a small quantity of T34 medium tanks and transport aircraft facilitated the establishment of the armored and air units. In 1960, the PAVN main force had 160,000 soldiers of which three-quarters (including 93,000 infantry) were assigned to ground combat.

The party's decision in January 1959 to support armed struggle in the South led to the formation in May of the PAVN 559th Transportation Group to begin infiltrating troops and supplies overland. Group 759 was commissioned later to move supplies by sea, and Group 959 to support the Pathet Lao and PAVN "volunteers" in Laos. Training intensified for "regroupee" units, composed of southern Vietnamese who went to North Vietnam for indoctrination and training after the Geneva agreements in autumn 1954. The *559th* infiltrated 3,500 officers and technical personnel from this pool into the South by early 1960. Regroupees, of whom 44,000 would go South by 1964, formed the backbone of a "South Vietnam Liberation Army," which, according to its commission, was "an element of the People's Army of Vietnam, created, built, trained, and led by the Party." In February 1961 it provided the main force of the People's Liberation Armed Forces of South Vietnam (PLAF), nominally under the authority of the National Liberation Front (NLF).

The first whole unit of northern-born PAVN regulars entered

the South in 1964. The PAVN contributed to the 1968 Tet Offensive by drawing U.S. forces out of the lowlands with diversionary attacks at Khe Sanh and other points just south of the DMZ. With few exceptions PAVN forces stayed out of the cities.

The main factors laying the basis for an expanded PAVN role, however, were a massive influx of Soviet T-54 tanks, armed personnel carriers, 57mm antiaircraft batteries, SA-7 hand-held surface-to-air missiles (SAMs), 130mm long-range field artillery, and the reduction of U.S. forces. The expansion of conventional capability allowed the PAVN to organize fifteen infantry divisions of about 12,000 men each, while U.S. withdrawal lowered the risk of maneuvering in large units.

Five PAVN divisions, each with integral artillery, tank, anti-aircraft, and missile units, spearheaded frontal assaults on South Vietnamese positions in spring 1972. The attacking forces seized all former U.S. Marine bases just south of the DMZ, occupied the capital of Quang Tri province, and overran a number of South Vietnamese outposts in the Central Highlands and Mekong Delta. The PAVN launched its final offensive of the war in January 1975. Total main forces by then numbered 685,000 organized into 24 divisions, a separate artillery command of 10 regiments, 10 independent infantry regiments, 15 SAM regiments, and 40 antiaircraft

regiments. It was the overextension of South Vietnamese forces that allowed the PAVN to concentrate overwhelming might against exposed positions and caused the disintegration of South Vietnamese forces that ended the war on 30 April 1975.

Material inferiority was the main justification for the PAVN's extensive use of sappers *(dac conk)*, or specialists in the use of explosives to breach defenses, sabotage airfields, mine roads and waterways, lead assaults, and conduct clandestine operations in cities and towns.

Until the U.S. withdrawal in 1973, the PAVN was forced to devote a large part of its resources to the defense of the "strategic rear" in the North. It had to organize civilian support of the war effort and to train local militia of forces of around two million, or 10 percent of the population. Naval, air force, and air defense commands were components of the PAVN and subordinate to its general staff. The main effort went into constructing the world's densest defense network of radar-directed SAMs and antiaircraft guns ranging in size from 37mm to 100mm. The latter weapons accounted for most of the U.S. aircraft shot down over the North.

PAVN intervention in Cambodia in December 1978 to remove the Khmer Rouge government by force provoked a punitive strike across Vietnam's northern border by Chinese forces in February to March 1979. The PAVN force level in the early 1980s peaked at 1.2 million, making it the world's fourth largest army. But the ongoing economic crisis, a program of domestic reform adopted in 1986, and declining Soviet military assistance (terminated in 1991) forced cuts in spending, undermined morale, and led to the demobilization of 600,000 soldiers, including 200,000 officers, specialists, and workers in defense industries.

See also: Bui Tin; Cambodia; Casualties; Central Office for South Vietnam; Dien Bien Phu; Discipline, People's Army of Vietnam; Group 559; Ho Chi Minh Campaign; Ho Chi Minh Trail; Ia Drang; National Liberation Front; People's Liberation Armed Forces; Pike, Douglas; Tet Offensive; Van Tien Dung; Viet Minh; Vietnam, Democratic Republic of; Vo Nguyen Giap.

People's Front in the Struggle for Peace. Formed on 7 October 1970 in South Vietnam, the group included many civic organizations that called for U.S. withdrawal from Vietnam.

People's Liberation Armed Forces (PLAF). Popularly known as the Viet Cong, the PLAF was the military arm of the National Liberation Front (NLF). Formally established in early 1961, the PLAF was created after the North

Vietnamese decision to escalate the level of armed struggle in South Vietnam. Like its antecedent, the Viet Minh, the PLAF had regular forces (operating under the Central Office for South Vietnam), full-time guerrillas, and a part-time self-defense militia. During the early and mid 1960s, the PLAF grew rapidly. Some of its leading cadres and officers were infiltrated from North Vietnam to the South along the Ho Chi Minh Trail. Beginning in the early 1960s, the PLAF launched hit-and-run attacks on government installations, military outposts, convoys, strategic hamlets, and district towns throughout South Vietnam. Its most celebrated victory was at the village of Ap Bac in January 1963.

After the 1965 introduction of U.S. combat troops, the PLAF's role was gradually superseded by regular forces of the People's Army of Vietnam (PAVN), which bore the brunt of the fighting with U.S. troops. PLAF units were most commonly used against lightly armed South Vietnamese units. The PLAF assumed the primary role in the 1968 Tet Offensive and suffered over 30,000 casualties. The PLAF, which had some 200,000 troops on the eve of Tet, declined as a major factor on the battlefield for the remainder of the war. It played little role in the 1975 offensive that led to the fall of South Vietnam. After the war, PLAF units were disbanded or integrated with the PAVN.

See also: Central Office for South Vietnam; National Liberation Front; People's Army of Vietnam; Viet Cong; Viet Minh.

People's Party of Laos (Phak Pasason Lao). *See* Lao People's Revolutionary Party

People's Republic of China (PRC). *See* China, People's Republic of

People's Revolutionary Party of Vietnam. A branch of the Democratic Republic of Vietnam's Marxist-Leninist Vietnam Workers' Party (VWP) set up in South Vietnam in 1962 under the Central Office of South Vietnam (COSVN). It merged with the VWP in 1976 to form the new Vietnamese Communist Party.

See also: Central Office of South Vietnam.

People's Self-Defense Force (PSDF). National program begun in South Vietnam in 1968 in which men and women in villages too old or too young to serve in the armed forces were required to perform part-time self-defense jobs, such as guard duty. Created by William Colby of the CIA and the South Vietnamese government, the PSDF included some 400,000 villagers by 1970.

See also: Central Intelligence Agency; Colby, William; Pacification; Regional/Popular Forces.

Perfume River (Song Huong). The river that flows through the city of Hue in central Vietnam, a prime shipping channel patrolled by U.S. riverine forces during the Vietnam War.

See also: Hue.

Perot, H. Ross (1930–), businessman; activist on behalf of U.S. prisoners of war (POWs). Between 1969 and 1973, Perot sought to publicize the plight of U.S. prisoners in Vietnam. He attempted to deliver Christmas presents and conducted meetings with North Vietnamese officials, offering to rebuild schools and clinics in exchange for the release of POWs. After 1973 he contended that the federal government knowingly left POWs behind in Vietnam. Perot's running mate in his unsuccessful 1992 independent presidential campaign was former POW Adm. James B. Stockdale, who was awarded the Medal of Honor for his resistance to years of torture in Hoa Lo prison.

See also: POW/MIA Controversy; Stockdale, James B.

Pershing, Operation. Code name for 1967–1968 operations by the U.S. Army's 1st Cavalry Division against the Viet Cong and North Vietnamese Army in the coastal plain of Binh Dinh province.

Pershing, Richard W. (1942–1968), U.S. Army 2nd lieutenant, the grandson of famed WWI U.S. Army Gen. John J. "Black Jack"

Pershing, killed in action in Vietnam while serving with the 101st Airborne Division near Hue.

Personalist Labor Party. *See* Can Lao

Peterson, Douglas (Pete) (1935–), U.S. Representative, D-Fla. (1991–1997); U.S. Ambassador to Vietnam (1997–). Peterson, a U.S. Air Force pilot, was shot down over North Vietnam in September 1966 and held as a prisoner of war until March 1973. In 1997, he became the first U.S. ambassador to the Socialist Republic of Vietnam following the normalization of relations between the two countries in 1995.

Pham Conq Tac (d.1955), pope of the Cao Dai religious sect in South Vietnam, 1935–1955. Under Pham Conq Tac's leadership the Cao Dai became more actively involved in politics and social issues.

See also: Cao Dai.

Pham Hung (1912–1988), chief, Central Office of South Vietnam (COSVN), 1967–1975; deputy premier, Democratic Republic of Vietnam (DRV), 1976–1980; interior minister, DRV, 1980–1986; premier, DRV, 1987–1988. Born Pham Van Thien, Pham Hung was expelled from school at age 16 for anti-French agitation. He joined the newly formed Indochinese Communist party in 1930. A protégé of Pham Van Dong's, in 1956 he became the highest-ranking party official from southern Vietnam elected to the politburo. Nine years later, Hung secretly returned to South Vietnam to take charge of the Viet Cong insurgency. As COSVN commander he oversaw the Tet Offensive in 1968 and served as political commissar for Gen. Van Tien Dung's 1975 Spring Offensive.

See also: Central Office of South Vietnam; Pham Van Dong; Ho Chi Minh Campaign.

Pham Van Dong (1906–), premier, Vietnam, 1955–1975; premier, Socialist Republic of Vietnam, 1975–1986. Pham Van Dong, a mandarin's son, attended the finest French colonial schools and was a classmate of Ngo Dinh Diem, future president of South Vietnam. Dong entered the University of Hanoi in 1925, organized a student strike against the French, and fled to China to join the Indochina Communist Party in 1930. Sent back to Vietnam, Dong spent six years in the Con Son prison before resuming his exile in China in 1939.

With Ho Chi Minh, he co-founded the Viet Minh and helped organize resistance to Japan in WWII, becoming finance minister after the war. During the Indochina War, Dong commanded Viet Minh forces in his home province of Quang Ngai. Ho named him foreign minister and sent him to the 1954 Geneva Conference. A year later, Dong became North Vietnam's first premier. He guided the communist takeover of North Vietnam's economy in the 1950s and gradually assumed more power as Ho faded from view in the 1960s.

After Ho's death in 1969, Dong took charge of the American War. Bowing to pressure from Moscow, he accepted a cease-fire and U.S. withdrawal in 1973, but resumed the war in 1974 in violation of the Paris peace accords. Dong approved the April 1975 final North Vietnamese Offensive and supervised the communist takeover of the south where 400,000 people were sent to "reeducation" camps. In 1981, Dong was forced to introduce capitalist incentives, especially in the south. He resigned the premiership in December 1986.

See also: China, People's Republic of; Geneva Conference, 1954; Ho Chi Minh; Mendès-France, Pierre; Pham Hung; Viet Minh; Zhou Enlai.

Pham Van Phu (1929–1975), South Vietnamese Army general. Gen. Pham Van Phu, who had commanded the Vietnamese Special Forces, as the Army of the Republic of Vietnam (ARVN) 1st Division commander in March 1975 led the disastrous ARVN retreat from the Central Highlands. He killed himself in Saigon on 30 April.

See also: Army of the Republic of Vietnam; Ho Chi Minh Campaign.

Phan Boi Chau (1867–1940), anti-colonial leader, sometimes called Vietnam's first modern nationalist. Phan Boi Chau began working against French colonialism in 1903, forming revolutionary organizations and writing patriotic tracts. He was arrested by the French in Shanghai in 1925 and imprisoned in Hanoi. He died in 1940 under house arrest in Hue.

Phan Chu Trinh (1872–1926), began advocating French reforms in Vietnam in 1906. He was jailed for anti-colonial activities in 1908, and exiled to France for seventeen years. His grand daughter, Nguyen Thi Binh, became a National Liberation Front leader.

See also: Nguyen Thi Binh.

Phan Dinh Khai. *See* Le Duc Tho

Phan Dinh Phung (1847–1895), Vietnamese resistance leader. Phan Dinh Phung, who served in the Vietnamese imperial court, led a rebellion in Ha Tinh Province in 1885 against French colonial rule. The revolt lasted until his death in 1895.

Phan Huy Quat (1901–1975), prime minister, South Vietnam, 1965. A physician from Hanoi, Quat had brief U.S. support as a possible replacement for President Ngo Dinh Diem in 1955. A longtime nationalist, Quat formed a fragile government at the request of Gen. Nguyen Khanh during the chaotic months from February to June 1965. His government fell to a military coup led by Air Marshal

Nguyen Cao Ky. Quat was executed by the communists in 1975.

See also: Nguyen Cao Ky; Nguyen Khanh; Nguyen Van Thieu.

Phan Khac Suu, Republic of Vietnam chief of state, September 1964 to June 1965. Phan Khac Suu, an agricultural engineer and member of the Cao Dai sect, was chosen by Gen. Nguyen Khanh as chief of state after Khanh overthrew the Military Revolutionary Council in January 1964.

See also: Nguyen Khanh.

Phan Trong Tue (1919–), North Vietnamese Army general. When U.S. bombing of the Ho Chi Minh Trail began in 1965, Group 559, the NVA logistical unit in charge of operations along the trail was reorganized as a special military zone under direct authority of North Vietnam's Communist Central Committee and commanded by Gen. Phan Trong Tue.

See also: Group 559; Ho Chi Minh Trail.

Phay Dang, anti-French, anti-U.S. Hmong leader in Laos who collaborated with the Japanese during WWII and with the Viet Minh after the war and became a leader in the communist Pathet Lao.

See also: Hmong; Pathet Lao.

Phetsarath, Prince, viceroy of Laos. A small band of nationalist sympathizers led by Prince Phetsarath in August 1945 proclaimed a neutralist national government opposed to reimposition of French colonial rule in Laos. Phetsarath's activities resulted in censure by the monarch. In October he formed a rebel government called the Lao Issara (Free Laos) to fight against the French with his two younger brothers, Prince Souvanna Phouma and Prince Souphanouvong. All three were forced into exile in Thailand in September 1946.

See also: Lao Issara; Souphanouvong; Souvanna Phouma.

Philippines. Throughout the Vietnam War, the Philippines was a strategic rear area that provided critical logistical, medical evacuation, and recreational support for the U.S. war effort. Most important were the U.S. Navy base at Subic Bay and the U.S. Air Force base at Clark Field.

The Republic of the Philippines was a staunch supporter of the U.S. position in Vietnam. After 1965, when the United States intervened directly in Vietnam, the Philippines provided significant support for the war effort. The U.S. Thirteenth Air Force based at Clark Field, north of Manila, used its Philippine facilities to support the bombing campaigns against North Vietnam. Similarly, the U.S. Seventh Fleet operating in the Tonkin Gulf had its home port at Subic Bay. The Philippines also provided all U.S. forces in Vietnam with a nearby site for logistic support, medical evacuation, and recreation. As a signatory of the Southeast Asia Treaty Organization (SEATO) in 1955, the Philippine government firmly supported U.S. policy in Vietnam from the outset. In 1966, Philippine president Ferdinand Marcos sent 2,000 Filipino combat engineers in February 1966. Reluctant to commit troops, Marcos agreed only after considerable diplomatic pressure by the United States, and even then negotiated privately for special payments totaling $39 million. In addition to this subsidy, Marcos won lucrative contracts for Filipino firms as third-country nationals providing civilian support services into Vietnam. In October 1966, Marcos hosted a Manila summit of all allied nations fighting in Vietnam, an ambitious diplomatic overture that fell flat. As student and nationalist opposition to Philippine involvement intensified, Marcos withdrew Filipino forces in October 1969.

See also: Free World; Manila Conference; Marcos, Ferdinand.

Phnom Penh. Capital of Cambodia. Phnom Penh escaped the direct effects of the Vietnam War, although the secret U.S. bombing of the Cambodia-Vietnam border area forced refugees into the city or into the ranks of the Khmer Rouge. By 1970 civil war was widespread, the result of the overthrow of

Prince Sihanouk, his replacement by Lon Nol, and the increase in the numbers of the Khmer Rouge. The war widened as U.S. and Army of the Republic of Vietnam (ARVN) forces invaded in pursuit of North Vietnamese and Viet Cong troops and the Central Office for South Vietnam (COSVN), the communist command post for operations in South Vietnam. After U.S. forces left, the Vietnamese soldiers continued to fight.

Phnom Penh was besieged by the Khmer Rouge in April 1975. With the defeat of the Lon Nol regime on 17 April, the Khmer Rouge ordered the evacuation of the population. Thousands died of starvation, malnourishment, and lack of medical care as they were resettled in the countryside. Intellectuals, doctors, and other professionals were systematically killed by the Khmer Rouge, and many others were separated from family members. Phnom Penh became a virtual ghost town. On 7 January 1979 forces of the Socialist Republic of Vietnam captured Phnom Penh and gradually began restoring services in the city. The city returned to a semblance of its former elegance when a truce was signed in 1991 between the factions of the civil war. By 1993 the long war seemed ended; foreign capital financed the rebuilding of hotels and restaurants, and tourism began again.

See also: Cambodia; Khmer Rouge; Pol Pot.

Phoenix Program (Phung Hoang). The most controversial, and one of the most important, programs of pacification was the Phoenix program, which began in July 1968. Phoenix was designed to counter the most basic aspect of an insurgency—the political underground, known as the Viet Cong Infrastructure (VCI). As long as a viable infrastructure existed, the insurgency could not be defeated. Phoenix was designed to coordinate intelligence gathering as well as paramilitary efforts aimed at rooting out the VCI. It decentralized its command process by placing most of the responsibility in the provinces and districts. This included building intelligence-gathering and interrogation centers in regions where the Viet Cong operated. Phoenix established a reporting system of files and dossiers on suspects and concentrated on "neutralizing"—capturing, converting, or killing— members of the Viet Cong Infrastructure. The system established rules by which suspected VCI could be tried and imprisoned. Phoenix emphasized the police, rather than the armed forces, as the main operational arm of the program.

In addition to the RF/PF, these included the National Police and the Provincial Reconnaissance Units (PRU). The RF/PF were territorial forces recruited from local areas and used as civil guard units. Part of their responsibilities included reacting to information sent from the District Intelligence and Operations Coordinating Center (DIOCC; PIOCC at the provincial level). The National Police included two subsections, the Police Special Branch (PSB—the intelligence branch) and the National Police Field Force (NPFF—the paramilitary component). The PRU, a largely CIA-operated paramilitary unit, were considered the best "action arm" available to the Phoenix program, and most of the stories that came out of Vietnam about brutality and assassination pointed to the PRU.

Established in 1966, the PRU never numbered more than 4,000 throughout South Vietnam, and its members were charged with other missions besides the Phoenix program. Each DIOCC was led by a Vietnamese Phung Hoang chief, who was aided by a U.S. Phoenix adviser. The Phoenix adviser had no authority to order operations; his only input was advice. The DIOCC was answerable to the district chief who in turn reported to the province chief.

DIOCC personnel compiled intelligence on VCI in the district and made blacklists that included all the available data on members of the VCI. An accusation brought against a suspected member had to be accompanied by at least three separate reports of communist activities to corroborate the other evidence. When the whereabouts of a person on the blacklist was discovered, an operation was planned, and one of the groups—RF/PF, PRU, or

NPFF—went to capture the target. After capture, the prisoner was taken to the DIOCC and interrogated. The prisoner was then sent to the province center for further interrogation and trial. If the evidence against the suspect was strong enough, he or she was sentenced.

The South Vietnamese and U.S. advisory sides of the program were beset by problems and criticism throughout its existence. Under the Phoenix program countless political cadres were identified and captured or killed. But some officials used Phoenix to settle old scores and many operations netted innocent people. By the end of 1972 neutralization figures for Phoenix were 81,740, with 26,369 prisoners

See also: Agency for International Development; Air America; Central Intelligence Agency; Colby, William; Komer, Robert W.; Pacification; Provincial Reconnaissance Units; Regional/ Popular Forces; Special Forces, ARVN.

Phoui Sanaikone, pro-Western Lao government leader; prime minister, 1958–1960. Phoui Sanaikone succeeded Prince Souvanna Phouma as prime minister. His government was overthrown in a military coup in January 1960.

See also: Laos; Pathet Lao.

Phoumi Nosavan (1920–1985), deputy prime minister of Laos, minister of defense, chief of the Lao general staff. General Nosavan rose to power via the U.S. Central Intelligence Agency–supported Committee for Defense of National Interests. Despite considerable U.S. aid in the late 1950s, Phoumi was unable to develop an effective national army.

See also: Laos; Pathet Lao.

Phu Bai. City in central Vietnam, 8 kilometers south of Hue, that was the home of Camp Eagle, the headquarters of the U.S. Army's 101st Airborne Division beginning in 1968.

Phung Hoang. *See* Phoenix Program

Phuoc Binh. Capital of Phuoc Long Province in the Central Highlands 125 kilometers north of Saigon near the Cambodian border. Rocketed frequently by the North Vietnamese Army and the Viet Cong, the city was known as "rocket alley" during the Vietnam War. Also known as Song Be, Phuoc Binh was the scene of heavy fighting in May 1965 and October 1967, and was the first provincial capital to fall to the North Vietnamese in the spring 1975 Ho Chi Minh Campaign.

See also: Ho Chi Minh Campaign.

Phuoc Long. Province in the Central Highlands of South Vietnam from which the North Vietnamese Army launched the Ho Chi Minh Campaign.

See also: Dong Xoai; Phuoc Binh.

Pierce Arrow, Operation. Code name for a 5 August 1964 retaliatory air raid against North Vietnam. The first U.S. air attack on North Vietnam, Pierce Arrow came in response to the Gulf of Tonkin incidents. Aircraft from the U.S. carriers *Ticonderoga* and *Constellation* attacked torpedo boat bases and petroleum storage facilities in southern North Vietnam. Four aircraft were lost, one pilot killed, and one, Lt. (jg) Everett Alvarez, became the first U.S. prisoner of war in North Vietnam.

See also: Alvarez, Everett Jr., Lt. (jg); Flaming Dart, Operation; Gulf of Tonkin Incident; Appendix E, "Gulf of Tonkin Resolution."

Pignon, Leon (1908–1976), French colonial official; high commissioner, Indochina, 1948–1950. Pignon was an ardent colonialist and a strong anti-communist. During his tenure, the colonial Associated State of Vietnam was formed with Emperor Bao Dai as its chief of state to fight the communist Viet Minh.

See also: Associated State of Vietnam; Bao Dai.

Pike, Douglas (1924–), U.S. Foreign Service officer, 1958–1982; expert on Vietnamese communism. Pike spent considerable time in Saigon and Washington, D.C., advising policymakers on the communists' insurgency. His books on the People's Army of Vietnam (PAVN) and the Viet Cong (NLF) stress the tactic of close coordination of military struggle *(dau tranh vu trang)* and political action *(dau tranh chinh tri).* He credits North Vietnamese propaganda and political activities for the success of the U.S. antiwar movement. In 1982 Pike became director of the Indochina Studies Program at the University of California, Berkeley. He was named associate director of The Vietnam Center at Texas Tech University in 1997.

Pitts, Riley L. (1937–), U.S. Army captain. Pitts, a 25th Infantry Division company commander, was awarded the Medal of Honor posthumously for heroism during a 1967 Viet Cong firefight. He was the first African-American officer to receive the Medal of Honor during the Vietnam War.

Platoon (1986). Realistic, controversial, award-winning Vietnam War combat film written and directed by former infantryman Oliver Stone.

See also: Stone, Oliver.

Pleiku. Capital of Pleiku province in the Central Highlands. Pleiku City was the site of a small French garrison during the Indochina War. During the Vietnam War, the city was the headquarters of the South Vietnamese Army's II Corps. After 1965, with the arrival of U.S. troops, Pleiku became an important U.S. command center. On the morning of 7 February 1965, the Viet Cong attacked the U.S. helicopter base and army barracks in Pleiku, killing eight Americans and destroying ten aircraft. The attack, and another on Qui Nhon, provided the Johnson administration with the rationale to begin air strikes against North Vietnam, codenamed Operation Flaming Dart. Johnson quickly upgraded the strikes into the sustained bombing campaign Rolling Thunder.

In 1975, during the North Vietnamese Spring Offensive, President Nguyen Van Thieu of South Vietnam ordered regular army troops withdrawn from the Central Highlands, including Pleiku. Military commanders did not inform civilian officials, and when the panicked population fled, the ensuing chaos and attacks by the North Vietnamese Army upon the line of retreat turned the withdrawal into a rout. Part of the "Convoy of Tears," the retreat signaled the beginning of the collapse of the Army of the Republic of Vietnam.

See also: Arc Light, Operation; Central Highlands; Flaming Dart, Operation; Rolling Thunder, Operation.

Plumbers. Name of the secret group formed in 1971 authorized to use legal or illegal methods to plug leaks to the press within President Nixon's administration. The Plumbers were led by White House aides David Young—who gave the group its comical name—and Egil "Bud" Krogh, and it operated under the supervision of White House Counsel John Ehrlichman; its operatives included key Watergate figures E. Howard Hunt and G. Gordon Liddy.

The Plumbers were formed to investigate Daniel Ellsberg and the Pentagon Papers leak. After publication of the papers in June 1971, the Plumbers installed dozens of illegal wiretaps on the phones of administration staff and in September 1971 broke into the office of Ellsberg's psychiatrist, Dr. Lewis Fielding, to find material to discredit Ellsberg. Ehrlichman and several of the Plumbers pled guilty or were found guilty of perjury or of violating Fielding's rights. The Plumbers' activities were included as part of the impeachment articles charging President Nixon with "abuse of power" and thus contributed to the downfall of his presidency.

See also: Ehrlichman, John; Ellsberg, Daniel; Fielding, Lewis J.; Pentagon Papers; Richardson, Elliot; Watergate.

Poilane Coffee Plantation. Located near the village of Khe Sanh, the plantation was established in 1926 by a Frenchman, Eugene Poilane. The Japanese burned the plantation's trees in 1945. The Viet Minh did the same in 1953. Poilane was killed by the Viet Cong in 1964. His family was evacuated from the plantation during the 1968 North Vietnamese siege at Khe Sanh. Felix Poilane, Eugene Poilane's son, died in a 13 April 1968 plane crash trying to return to Khe Sanh to check on the plantation's trees.

See also: Khe Sanh.

Poland. A member of the International Control Commission, Poland generally supported the Democratic Republic of Vietnam (DRV). Its delegate, Janusz Lewandowski, participated in the June 1966 negotiations that resulted in the DRV dropping its demand that South Vietnam become a neutral state and that the United States withdraw all its troops. Poland agreed to host a DRV-U.S. meeting in Warsaw in November 1966, but North Vietnam canceled the meeting in December when President Johnson refused to halt U.S. bombing of the DRV.

See also: International Commission for Supervision and Control.

Polgar, Thomas (1922–), OSS and CIA intelligence officer. Polgar, a Hungarian-born, naturalized U.S. citizen, was the CIA's station chief in Saigon at the time of the U.S. evacuation in 1975.

See also: Central Intelligence Agency; Martin, Graham A.

Pol Pot (1928–1998), head of the Khmer Rouge; prime minister, Democratic Kampuchea (Cambodia), 1976–1979. Pol Pot ("the original Cambodian") was born Saloth Sar in Kompong Thom province, Cambodia. His parents were landowners and had royal connections. Sar was sent to Phnom Penh at the age of six to join his brother Loth Suong, who worked in the palace as an administrator. Sar's upbringing was strict, and he was isolated from Cambodia's vernacular culture. In 1948, he received a scholarship to study radio electricity in Paris, where he joined the Cambodian section of the French Communist Party. His scholarship ended after he failed his course three years in a row, and he arrived home in January 1953, just after King Sihanouk had declared martial law to suppress Cambodia's independence movement, which was becoming radicalized in response to French colonial repression.

In 1953 Sar joined the Cambodian and Vietnamese communists. Following independence in 1954, Sar rose within the Cambodian communist movement, becoming party leader in 1962. He believed that under his rule Cambodia would recover its pro-Buddhist glory by rebuilding the powerful economy of the medieval Angkor kingdom and regaining ancient territory from Vietnam and Thailand. Pol Pot's group treasured the Cambodian "race," not individuals, and believed that impurities included the foreign-educated (himself and his colleagues excepted) and "hereditary enemies," especially Vietnamese. To return

Cambodians to their imagined origins, Pol Pot saw the need for war and for secrecy as "the basis of the revolution." In 1966 he began planning an uprising against the Cambodian ruler, Prince Sihanouk.

In 1975, after defeating Lon Nol, the U.S.-backed general who overthrew Sihanouk in a 1970 coup, Pol Pot became prime minister. A true nationalist chauvinist, Pol Pot could not see Cambodia living in peace with its neighbors in a community of nations. He shared the traditional Khmer elite's racism and grandiose designs on "lost territories." Raids on Laos, Thailand, and Vietnam began simultaneously in 1977.

He imposed policies that resulted in a holocaust against his own countrymen in which some 1.5 million Cambodians died. His identity as Saloth Sar was realized in late 1978, when his brother, Loth Suong, recognized him in a poster. Two months later the Pol Pot regime was overthrown by the invading army of the Socialist Republic of Vietnam.

See also: Cambodia; Heng Samrin; Khmer Rouge; Lon Nol; Sihanouk, Norodom.

Popeye Project. Covert U.S. military cloud-seeding operation begun in September 1966. Later known as Project Compatriot, the objective was to try to extend the rainy season in Laos to cause flooding and hamper North Vietnamese supply efforts along the Ho Chi Minh Trail.

Porter, William J. (1914–1988), U.S. deputy ambassador to South Vietnam; delegate to the Paris peace talks. For eighteen months beginning in 1965, Porter was responsible for coordinating the pacification programs of U.S. government agencies in South Vietnam. Porter also served as an adviser to Lyndon B. Johnson and as a delegate to the Paris peace talks.

See also: Pacification.

Port Huron Statement. July 1962 manifesto, issued by Tom Hayden and other Students for a Democratic Society (SDS) members following discussions at a retreat in Port Huron, Michigan. The document explained the SDS leaders' views on ending the Cold War and improving and increasing democracy in the United States.

See also: Hayden, Tom; Students for a Democratic Society.

Post-Traumatic Stress Disorder (PTSD). A condition marked by feelings of anxiety, depression, thoughts of suicide, recurring nightmares, and sudden outbursts of violence. Traumatic events such as natural disasters and accidents can trigger PTSD. It is common among combat veterans of all wars. Several unique aspects of the Vietnam War contributed to greater incidence of PTSD among American veterans. They included the one-year tour of duty; the uncertain and unpredictable nature of guerrilla combat; the war's moral ambiguities and controversies at home; and the treatment veterans received upon returning home. Many veterans felt unable to talk about Vietnam, and they often vividly reexperienced traumatic combat memories when they heard a helicopter or a car backfire. It has been estimated that between 500,000 and 650,000 Vietnam veterans, about one-fifth of those who served, have had PTSD. The U.S. Department of Veterans Affairs was slow to recognize and treat the condition.

See also: Veterans, American.

Potsdam Conference. Meeting of allied WWII leaders held 17 July to 2 August 1945 in Potsdam, Germany. At the conference the leaders authorized the creation of two occupation zones for post-WWII Vietnam: A Chinese zone north of the sixteenth parallel and a British zone south of it. The leaders sent Nationalist Chinese troops to take the Japanese surrender in the north, and British troops to do the same in the southern zone.

Poulo Condore Prisons *See* Con Son

POW. *See* Prisoners of War

Powell, Colin (1937–), U.S. Army general; national security adviser, 1987–1989; chairman, Joint Chiefs of Staff, 1989–1993. Powell, who oversaw the Persian

Gulf War, served two Vietnam War tours: in 1962–1963 as an adviser with an Army of the Republic of Vietnam (ARVN) battalion, and in 1968–1969 as a battalion officer with the Americal Division.

POW/MIA Controversy. More than two decades after U.S. troops withdrew from Vietnam the issue of Americans still listed as prisoners of war (POWs) or missing in action (MIAs) remained controversial. A 1991 public opinion poll indicated that more than 70 percent of Americans believed that POWs were left behind and were still being held captive.

In March 1973, 591 POWs were released and the Nixon administration maintained that all American POWs were returned. However, MIA family members, Vietnam veterans, and others did not accept that conclusion and formed support groups, including the National League of Families of American Prisoners and Missing in Southeast Asia, to lobby for further efforts on the POW issue. Nearly 80,000 troops were unaccounted for after WWII, and more than 8,000 after the Korean War. Of the 2,273 troops in Vietnam listed as unaccounted for, half are known to have died, but their bodies were not recovered. These were primarily aviators who were shot down in remote jungle areas and were not seen parachuting to safety. The remaining missing, 1,172 men, were lumped into a POW/MIA category, even though the POW designation had formerly been used only for known prisoners and even though in nearly all cases the missing men were believed to have been killed, although their deaths were not witnessed.

An investigation in 1975–1976 by the House Select Committee on Missing Persons in Southeast Asia concluded that "no Americans are still being held alive as prisoners in Indochina, or elsewhere, as a result of the war in Indochina." Despite that pronouncement, the POW/MIA issue persisted. Live sightings reports of U.S. POWs from Vietnamese refugees in the early 1980s prompted President Reagan to triple the budget of the Defense Intelligence Agency. The Reagan and Bush administrations publicly operated on the assumption that at least some Americans were held captive. That policy was the main barrier to normalizing relations with Vietnam, which, since 1973, had insisted that all POWs had been released. Vietnam at first refused to provide detailed information on MIAs, but in 1992 began new efforts to cooperate in resolving the MIA question. In response, the Clinton administration took the first steps that led to U.S. formal recognition of Vietnam on 11 July 1995.

See also: Four-Party Joint Military Commission; Montgomery Committee; Normalization; Paris Peace Accords; Reagan, Ronald; Appendix F, "Paris Peace Accords."

POW/MIA Interagency Working Group (IAG). White-House based unit set up in 1980 to set U.S. policy on POW/MIA matters made up of representatives of the Joint Chiefs of Staff, State Department, National Security Council, the National League of Families, and the Secretary of Defense's International Security Affairs office.

See also: POW/MIA Controversy.

Prairie, Operation. Code name for August 1966 to March 1967 3rd Marine Division combat activities against the North Vietnamese Army just below the Demilitarized Zone (DMZ).

See also: Demilitarized Zone.

Pratt, John Clark (1932–), novelist, university professor. Clark, a Colorado State University professor of English, is the author of several books on the war, including the literary novel, *Laotian Fragments* (1974), and the acclaimed non-fiction book, *Vietnam Voices: Perspectives on the War Years, 1941–1982* (1984). Pratt served as a U.S. Air Force pilot and historian in Southeast Asia during the Vietnam War.

See also: Laotian Fragments.

PRC. *See* China, People's Republic of

Prisoners of War. *See* Con Son; Hanoi Hilton; Montgomery Committee; Perot, H. Ross;

POW/MIA Controversy; Son Tay Raid; Stockdale, James B.

Progressive Forces Alliance.
A political party in South Vietnam established in 1954 opposed to President Ngo Dinh Diem's authoritarian rule.

See also: Cao Dai; Lansdale, Edward G.

Progressive Party. Short-lived U.S. dissident political party formed by Henry A. Wallace in 1947. The party was oriented toward foreign affairs, and advocated improved relations with the Soviet Union. Sen. George McGovern (D-S.Dak.), the antiwar 1972 Democratic presidential nominee, was a delegate to the Progressive Party's 1948 convention.

See also: McGovern, George.

Project 100,000. A controversial plan announced 23 August 1966 by Defense Secretary Robert S. McNamara to provide remedial training within the U.S. military to men with poor academic skills, with the goal of better equipping them as members of society. As a part of the plan, the armed services accepted a large number of men who would have been rejected for service because of their low scores on military aptitude tests. Project 100,000 went into effect in October 1966 and lasted until December 1971, when Congress ended quotas based on aptitude-test-scores.

U.S. political leaders had shown interest in military

remedial training as a form of social engineering from the end of WWII on. In 1945 the Truman administration proposed a universal military training program intended to correct both physical and educational shortcomings among America's young men. In 1963, President Kennedy again suggested using the military to provide remedial training to disadvantaged men, charging the Task Force on Manpower Conservation, among its other duties, to examine the military's experience with "special training units for illiterates." In the summer of 1966 McNamara learned that for over a decade the Marine Corps had used part of its normal training funds to run Special Training Branches at its recruit training camps, providing remedial training to those recruits who required it. McNamara realized that by expanding this program to all services, the military could provide remedial training to men with low scores without congressional authorization.

On 23 August 1966 Secretary McNamara announced Project 100,000, declaring that the military would "salvage tens of thousands of these men each year, first to productive military careers and later for productive roles in society." The armed forces would take 40,000 disadvantaged youths the first year and 100,000 every year thereafter. The armed forces accepted roughly 354,000 men under the Project 100,000 guidelines; most had low scores on military aptitude tests. Some 37 percent were African American. Three-quarters served in the Army or Marine Corps. Just over a third received ground combat assignments. Nearly 2,100 died in the Vietnam War.

See also: McNamara, Robert; New Standards Men.

Project Agile, Operation. Code name for the Pentagon's Advanced Project Agency, which was commissioned to develop counterinsurgency techniques. In 1961, the group studied the use of herbicide operations in Vietnam.

See also: Chemical Warfare.

Prostitution. Prostitution was officially illegal in South Vietnam but, when Saigon fell in 1975, approximately 400,000 Vietnamese women worked as prostitutes. Women had worked as prostitutes under the French regime also, but the increase in the number of U.S. troops and the refugee problem dramatically increased prostitution in South Vietnam. The majority were in Saigon, although many worked in the other major cities. Never viewed merely as an economic activity, prostitution meant severe and permanent ostracism from Vietnamese society. Women often combined their sexual services for U.S. soldiers with domestic services. Prostitution was closely associated with sexually transmitted diseases and drug addiction. North Vietnam banned prostitution after reunification, but many cities continued

to have high numbers of prostitutes.

See also: Veterans, Vietnamese.

Provincial Intelligence and Operations Coordinating Center (PIOCC). *See* Pacification

Provincial Civil Guard. *See* Regional/Popular Forces

Provincial Reconnaissance Units (PRUs). The enforcement branch of Phoenix program, the largest and most controversial program aimed at eliminating the Viet Cong Infrastructure (VCI). Originally called Counter-Terror Units in 1965, PRUs obtained their new name one year later. Their basic mission was to destroy the VCI by sabotage, kidnapping, and assassination. The Central Intelligence Agency (CIA) funded the program.

PRU members were Vietnamese mercenaries who performed any duty for a price. They were paid 15,000 piasters monthly, or nearly four times the equivalent wage of a private in the Army of the Republic of Vietnam (ARVN). Bounties also existed: 10,000 plasters (US $85) per prisoner. In 1969, PRU strength was approximately 4,454 men. The force was organized into 18-man units; each unit had 3 teams of 6 men each. A minority of South Vietnamese volunteered for PRU service. The majority of the PRU's members were murderers, rapists, extortionists, and social outcasts from local jails who were given the option of PRU duties in lieu of life imprisonment. Many were Viet Cong or North Vietnamese defectors who rallied under the *Chieu Hoi* (Open Arms) program. Once recruited, this colorful assortment of men underwent basic training at My Tho, the PRU headquarters in the Mekong Delta, supervised by U.S. military and intelligence personnel.

PRU teams often worked with Military Assistance Command, Vietnam–Studies and Observations Group (MACV-SOG), U.S. Navy SEAL teams, or South Vietnam's *Lien Doi Nguoi Nhai* (underwater demolition teams/frogmen), usually at night. Although there were reports of widespread inefficiency and corruption within the Phoenix program, high-ranking North Vietnamese and Viet Cong officials interviewed after the war stated that the program was highly effective and that it severely damaged the VCI.

See also: Chieu Hoi (Open Arms) Program; Pacification; Phoenix Program; Viet Cong Infrastructure.

Provisional Leadership Committee. Group of South Vietnamese military leaders including Gen. Nguyen Khanh that seized power on 27 August 1964. The committee appointed Gen. Khanh prime minister on 3 September.

See also: Nguyen Khanh.

Provisional Revolutionary Government (PRG). The Provisional Revolutionary Government was established at a June 1969 congress convened near the border of Cambodia and South Vietnam to supersede the National Liberation Front (NLF) in the South. The PRG was created by the North Vietnamese government to provide a legal alternative to the Republic of Vietnam in the peace talks. Huynh Tan Phat was chosen as chairman of the organization, and Madame Nguyen Thi Binh was named foreign minister. The PRG was recognized as the legal government of South Vietnam by the Democratic Republic of Vietnam (DRV) and several other socialist countries, and it participated in the Paris negotiations. The PRG was one of the four signatories of the Paris agreement. After the fall of Saigon in 1975 the PRG was rapidly brushed aside and in early July 1976 North and South Vietnam were reunited into the Socialist Republic of Vietnam.

See also: Duong Quynh Hoa; Four-Party Joint Military Commission; National Liberation Front; Nguyen Van Thieu; Paris Accords; Tran Van Tra.

Psychological Operations (PsyOps). The first U.S. psyops efforts began in 1954 led by the CIA's Edward Lansdale to encourage Catholics to emigrate from North to South Vietnam and to shore up the South Vietnamese government. After 1965, U.S. psyops were run by the Joint U.S. Public Affairs Office (JUSPAO), an arm of the U.S. Information Service, and the Psychological Operations Directorate of the Military Assistance Command, Vietnam (MACV). The operations involved spreading anti-communist leaflets and other printed material and broadcasting similar radio messages. North Vietnam had a similar program aimed at breaking the will of U.S. troops that included the propaganda broadcasts of Hanoi Hannah in English over Radio Hanoi.

See also: Joint U.S. Public Affairs Office; Hanoi Hannah; Lansdale, Edward G.

PTSD. *See* Post-Traumatic Stress Disorder

Public Opinion, American. The Vietnam War's excessive length, its lack of clear progress toward victory, and the accompanying domestic turmoil contributed to a failure by the U.S. government to sustain supportive public opinion. In the war's early stages, before U.S. combat troops were deployed, few Americans had an opinion on Vietnam. By late 1964 many viewed North Vietnam as a puppet of the People's Republic of China and supported active assistance for South Vietnam. In 1965 polls indicated that a majority of Americans favored bombing North Vietnam and sending U.S. combat troops. A majority believed the Vietnam conflict would result in a U.S. victory or, at worst, in a

stalemate as in Korea. Such supportive poll numbers are typical of the "rally 'round the flag" phenomenon that occurs when a president takes military action as commander in chief. By mid 1966, three-fourths of the public expected that the war would be long.

A 1966 Gallup poll found that 35 percent viewed U.S. involvement as a mistake. That figure grew to 48 percent in 1967 and to 52 percent in 1969. Although a majority of Americans opposed U.S. involvement by 1969, there was little consensus about what action to take. In 1971, 61 percent called U.S. involvement a mistake and 58 percent said they believed the war was immoral. In 1972 and 1973 public opinion polls indicated support for President Richard M. Nixon's Vietnamization policy and for peace negotiations. When the last U.S. troops were withdrawn, few Americans believed that the United States should have kept fighting. When North Vietnam launched its 1975 Spring Offensive, most Americans opposed increasing military aid to the south or renewing active military involvement.

See also: Cronkite, Walter; Tet Offensive; Tran Do; Watergate.

Pueblo Incident. The USS *Pueblo,* an intelligence-gathering ship, was seized by North Korea on 23 January 1968. Because nearly all available U.S. forces were committed to Vietnam, more than fourteen thousand

U.S. Navy and Air Force reserves were mobilized in case troops had to be sent into North Korea. North Korea claimed that the ship had violated its territorial waters, but the crew and U.S. radio locators placed the ship well outside the 12-mile limit. The incident combined with cold war tensions in Berlin and the Tet Offensive to heighten strains in the Johnson administration. The *Pueblo* crew remained captive until December 1968, when all 82 were released.

Puller, Lewis B. Jr. (1945–1994), former U.S. Marine lieutenant. The son of legendary Marine Corps Gen. Lewis B. "Chesty" Puller, Lewis B. Puller Jr. volunteered for Vietnam and was severely wounded in 1968. His autobiography, *Fortunate Son* (1991), won the Pulitzer Prize for Biography or Autobiography. He committed suicide in 1994.

See also: Fortunate Son.

Punji Stakes. Sharpened bamboo stakes often coated with infection-causing agents buried along jungle trails as booby traps by the Viet Cong.

See also: Booby Traps.

Purple Heart. Medal awarded to U.S. military personnel wounded or killed in action.

Quang Ngai. Province in central Vietnam, some 130 kilometers south of Danang. During the Franco–Viet Minh war, Quang Ngai was a Viet Minh stronghold. During the American war, it was a Viet Cong stronghold. Quang Ngai Province contains the village of Song My, the site of the 1968 My Lai massacre.

See also: My Lai.

Quang Ngu *(National Language).* The Romanized written form of the Vietnamese language invented by 17th century Chinese missionaries, popularized by the French in their Cochin China colony in the 19th century, and widely accepted throughout Vietnam beginning in the 1920s.

Quang Tri. South Vietnamese city, capital of Quang Tri province. As the capital of the province that bordered the demilitarized zone (DMZ) with North Vietnam, Quang Tri was a key point in the northern sector of South Vietnam. The city was attacked by North Vietnamese Army (NVA) forces in April 1972. On 1 May, troops of the Army of the Republic of Vietnam (ARVN) abandoned the city, fleeing with their families and other refugees. Fire from ARVN and NVA forces

and U.S. aircraft and ships resulted in the death of as many as twenty thousand soldiers and civilians. At the end of June, ARVN troops began a counterattack with the aid of U.S. air support, and the city was retaken on 16 September.

See also: Easter Offensive.

Quat, Phan Hay. *See* Phan Huy Quat

Quayle, James D. (Dan) (1947–), U.S representative (R-Ind.), 1977–1981; U.S. senator (R-Ind.), 1981–1989, U.S. vice president, 1989–1993. Quayle served in the Indiana National Guard during the Vietnam War. That fact became the subject of media scrutiny during the 1988 presidential race when reports, which Quayle denied, surfaced that his family used political connections to secure his entry in the National Guard in 1969 so he could avoid serving in Vietnam.

See also: Reserves.

Queen's Cobras. Nickname of a Royal Thai infantry regiment that fought with U.S. forces in 1967–1968.

See also: Thailand.

Quiet American, The (1958). Movie directed by Joseph L. Mankiewicz based on the Graham Greene novel about early U.S. policymaking in Vietnam.

See also: Greene, Graham.

Quiet American, The (1955). Graham Greene's novel about American CIA agents and State

Department officials in Vietnam in the early 1950s, widely regarded as an important work of Vietnam War literature.

See also: Greene, Graham.

Qui Nhon. South Vietnamese coastal city in Binh Dinh province, 677 kilometers (420 miles) north of Saigon. Beginning in August 1965, the U.S. military used Qui Nhon as a large supply base and transportation terminal, eventually providing support service for some 100,000 troops. The bombing of U.S. enlisted personnel's quarters at Qui Nhon on 10 February 1965 led to retaliatory U.S. naval air strikes of North Vietnam, code-named Flaming Dart II. Qui Nhon was one of five coastal surveillance centers supporting Operation Market Time, the U.S. naval interdiction of seaborne infiltration of supplies and personnel from North Vietnam to South Vietnam.

See also: Flaming Dart, Operation; Market Time, Operation.

RAAF. *See* Royal Australian Air Force

Rabe, David (1940–), playwright. Rabe, who served with the U.S. Army in Vietnam, is the author of the acclaimed Vietnam-themed trilogy of 1970s plays: *The Basic Training of Pavlo Hummel, Sticks and Bones,* and *Streamers* for which he was awarded Obie, Tony, New York Drama Critics Circle, American Academy of Arts and Letters, and Drama Desk awards.

Rach Ba Rai River. Mekong Delta river located southeast of Saigon, the scene on 15 September 1967 of a bloody battle between elements of the U.S. Mobile Riverine Force and the Viet Cong.

See also: Mekong River and Delta; Mobile Riverine Force.

Racial Epithets, American. In wartime soldiers from all countries have employed derogatory language to dehumanize the enemy. Americans in Vietnam used such racial denunciations as *gooks, dinks, slopes, slants* and *zips* to characterize the Vietnamese.

Radar. Radar was widely used by the North Vietnamese and the United States in the air war in Vietnam. Electronic Countermeasures (ECM) were employed by U.S. Air Force and Navy aircraft jet fighters to jam defensive radar and by U.S. Naval vessels patrolling the coasts of Vietnam to detect radar signals.

See also: Electronic Countermeasures; Menu, Operation.

Radford, Arthur W. (1896–1973), admiral, U.S. Navy; chairman, Joint Chiefs of Staff (JCS), 1953–1957. A veteran of three wars, Adm. Arthur Radford helped devise President Eisenhower's "New Look" defense policy in the 1950s. Radford believed that nuclear weapons coupled with superior U.S. air power would guarantee U.S. security, and that ground forces were practically superfluous in modern warfare. In March 1954 when the French asked for U.S. help during the siege of Dien Bien Phu, Admiral Radford proposed massive U.S. air strikes, possibly including nuclear weapons, against the Viet Minh. President Eisenhower rejected the plan, code named Operation Vulture, after Congress and the European allies refused their support.

See also: Dien Bien Phu; Ely, Paul; Nuclear Weapons; Ridgway, Matthew B.; Twining, Nathan F.; Vulture, Operation.

Rainy Season. *See* Monsoon

Ramadier, Paul (1888–1961), French premier, January to November 1947. Ramadier, a socialist who led a coalition government, dismissed the hardline George d'Argenlieu as French high commissioner for Indochina, and made an unsuccessful attempt to begin negotiations with the Viet Minh.

See also: Argenlieu, George Thierry d'; Mus, Paul.

Rambo. Three popular, action movies featuring John Rambo, an angry, violent Vietnam veteran as the main character: Ted Kotcheff's *First Blood* (1982), George P. Cosmatos's *Rambo: First Blood, Part II* (1985), and Peter Macdonald's *Rambo III* (1988).

Ranch Hand, Operation. U.S. Air Force aerial defoliation program that sprayed some 19 million gallons of herbicides such as Agent Orange and Agent White over 2.5 million hectares (6 million acres) in South Vietnam from January 1962 to February 1971, and 400,000 gallons over 66,000 hectares (163,000 acres) in Laos from December 1965 to September 1969.

The object was to deprive North Vietnamese and Viet Cong forces of cover and concealment and to destroy forests and crops in areas controlled by these forces. The herbicides were based on widely used commercial products, principally Agent Orange and related chlorinated phenoxy acid-based agents with low soil persistence, though persistent picloram-based Agent White comprised about 14 percent of the total.

Although these agents were considered nontoxic to humans and animals except in very large doses, mounting evidence implicated dioxin, an impurity in Agent Orange, as the cause of debilitating illnesses, rashes, tumors, and birth defects. Longterm effects of the spraying have included the destruction of Vietnam's coastal mangrove forests and claims of widespread health problems by Vietnamese authorities and U.S. veterans, who successfully sued the Veterans Administration for recognition of Agent Orange–related disabilities.

See also: Agent Orange; Agent White; Chemical Warfare.

RAND Corporation. Founded in 1948 with grants from the U.S. Air Force and the Ford Foundation, the RAND (Research and Development) Corporation was the first private, nonprofit, federally funded think tank. It conducts classified research on defense and security issues at its headquarters in Santa Monica, California.

RAND helped devise the U.S. strategic doctrine of nuclear deterrence in the 1950s and provided systems analysis experts to carry out Secretary of Defense Robert McNamara's military reforms in the 1960s. During the 1960s RAND concentrated on the Vietnam War, producing hundreds of reports on topics such as South Vietnamese politics, bomb damage assessments, counterinsurgency warfare, and North Vietnam's military command structure. RAND's most famous defense expert was Daniel Ellsberg, who leaked the top-secret Pentagon Papers to the media in 1971.

See also: Defense, Department of; Ellsberg, Daniel; McNamara, Robert; SIGMA; U.S. Information Service.

R&R. U.S. military personnel in Vietnam were eligible to receive morale-boosting rest and recuperation (R&R) leave in Vietnam and outside the war zone. The program provided service personnel with transportation to a "liberty" town in an Asian country friendly to the United States. The U.S. government paid Pan American World Airways some $24 million per year during the war to assist the program. Married personnel frequently met their spouses in Honolulu. Other R&R destinations included Hong Kong, Tokyo, Kuala Lumpur, Manila, Seoul, Singapore, Sydney, and Taipei. The military maintained R&R sites at the beach resort of Vung Tao, about 130 kilometers south of Saigon and at China Beach near Da Nang.

See also: Japan.

Rangers. Soldiers trained in guerrilla warfare tactics. Graduates of the U.S. Army Ranger School at Ft. Benning served in many Army units in Vietnam and as advisers to the South Vietnamese Army (ARVN). The South Vietnamese Army (ARVN) had its own specially trained ranger battalions beginning in the 1960s.

See also: Special Forces, ARVN.

Raye, Martha (1916–1994), U.S. entertainer. Raye, born Margaret Reed, entertained U.S. troops in WWII, Korea, and in Vietnam, where she put on hundreds of shows in remote areas.

Reaction Force. U.S. and South Vietnamese military units designed to reinforce other units that came under attack. Reaction forces were as small as a company and as large as a battalion.

Read, Benjamin (1925–1993), executive secretary and special assistant to Secretary of State Dean Rusk, 1963–1969. A powerful behind-the-scenes influence, Read convinced Rusk in 1968 to support peace negotiations.

See also: Rusk, (David) Dean.

Reagan, Ronald (1911–), governor of California, 1966–1974; U.S. president 1981–1989. Reagan viewed the Vietnam War as a "noble cause" that failed because politicians in Washington did not let the military do its job. Despite an initial conservative isolationist stance, by late 1965 Reagan staunchly supported the war. As California governor, he supported U.S. involvement in Vietnam and condemned those who opposed it. As President, he opposed normalizing relations with Vietnam and spoke often in support of full resolution of the MIA/POW issue.

See also: POW/MIA Controversy.

Rear Echelon. U.S. military term for base camps and other protected areas in Vietnam that generally were safe from enemy attack. The Pentagon did not keep exact statistics, but well over 50 percent of U.S. troops in Vietnam served in rear-echelon areas as clerks, cooks, maintenance personnel and other positions.

Red River (Song Hong) Delta. Large, fertile, rice-growing area in northern Vietnam, the historical homeland of the Vietnamese people. The area, which includes Hanoi, the northern capital, was heavily bombed during the American war, although bombs were not dropped on the many dykes along the delta's banks.

See also: Hanoi; Dikes.

Reeducation Camps. Established after the fall of Saigon in 1975, reeducation camps punished former South Vietnamese citizens and dissident former Viet Cong guerrillas and suppressed political dissent, in the name of indoctrination of communist philosophy and *cai tao* (thought reform). Estimates of the number of people sent to the camps range from 50,000 to more than 350,000.

After the communist takeover of the country, entire classes of South Vietnamese citizens were ordered to report to the camps.

They included former Army of the Republic of Vietnam (ARVN) officers, civil servants, teachers, the native Catholic clergy, journalists, doctors, engineers, political dissidents from North Vietnam, and former Viet Cong guerrillas who had turned against North Vietnam. The time required for reeducation could be a few months, but most were held for three to five years. Some refugees reported that camps operated well into the 1980s.

Most of the reeducation camps were located in the mountains and jungles away from population centers. The reeducation process involved lectures and readings on American imperialism, Vietnamese nationalism, and socialism. The reeducation camps, in addition to punishment for the South Vietnamese, also served as a useful internal security tool. Peasants who were not working hard enough and those people who disagreed with the government could be threatened with being sent to the camps. In addition, the camps held political dissidents from North Vietnam and many former Viet Cong guerrillas—called Hoi Chanh—who had turned against North Vietnam toward the end of the war.

See also: Refugees; Saigon; Veterans, Vietnamese.

Refugees. After the 1954 Geneva accords when the Vietnam was divided, an estimated 80,000 to 120,000 Vietnamese in the South, mainly Viet Minh guerrillas, relocated to the North. More than 900,000 northerners, including an estimated 700,000 Roman Catholics, moved to South Vietnam. By mid-1957, the government of South Vietnam, with the assistance of the United States and private volunteer organizations, had established "refugee villages" for some 605,000 refugees; the remaining 300,000 refugees resettled themselves in both urban and rural areas.

The large number of Catholic refugees from the North created an important anticommunist constituency in the South, which strongly supported the government of Ngo Dinh Diem. Between 1955 and 1963, South Vietnam's Diem government implemented rural resettlement programs, including the Strategic Hamlet program, which displaced 1.3 million Vietnamese from their villages. To achieve primarily political-military aims, such as cutting the links between the Viet Cong guerrillas and South Vietnamese villagers, these programs moved peasants into areas ostensibly controlled and defended by the government of South Vietnam. The vast majority of the peasants were moved involuntarily. These programs failed to achieve their objectives, and were abandoned by 1964; their greatest legacy was the creation of an alienated and resentful relocated population who were insecure in their new homes and villages. Many later joined the flood of refugees fleeing rural Vietnam for the urban areas.

The deployment of U.S. troops and the escalation of the Vietnam War in 1965 intensified the problem of internal refugees. From 1964–1969 some 4 million South Vietnamese were displaced. Most refugees moved into crowded, dismal refugee camps or relocated to urban slums. By 1975 an estimated 12 million South Vietnamese civilians—half the population—had fled or had been displaced or relocated from their homes.

Shortly after the defeat of South Vietnam in 1975, 140,000 Vietnamese with ties to the former government and to the United States left the country. This was followed by about 983,000 refugees, many of whom were ethnic Chinese, who fled to other countries over the next thirteen years. They were joined by tens of thousands who fled from Cambodia and Laos. Refugees who left by sea were called boat people. It is estimated that 10 to 50 percent of the refugees who attempted an ocean passage drowned.

See also: Catholics; Da Nang; Geneva Conference, 1954; Ho Chi Minh Campaign; International Rescue Committee; Saigon; Strategic Hamlet Program; Thailand; United Nations; Veterans, Vietnamese.

Regional/Popular Forces (RF/PF). A two-tiered militia/police force created 1 January 1953 to assist French civilian-military pacification teams called *Les Groupements Administratifs Mobiles*

Opérationnels (GAMOS).
Regional Forces were organized
into 120-man companies of 3 platoons (40 troops each), plus 10
officers. Provincial Forces operated in 40-man platoons
supervised by two noncommissioned officers (NCOs). All RF/PF
units were subordinate to senior
French army officers who shared
responsibilities for their development and deployment with
three French pacification
commissioners appointed by the
French colonial governors of
Annum, Tonkin, and
Cochinchina.

The mission of RF/PF forces—
to assist the French with hamlet
control, supply, and propaganda
via a decentralized militia—was
sound, but it was begun too late
to provide much help to the
French in holding on to their
colonial empire. The RF/PF network (Territorials) was the
largest indigenous army controlled by France; by 1 January
1954, it numbered some 144,150
men, while the Vietnamese
National Army (VNA) numbered
only 123,800 troops.

Following the defeat of the
French at Dien Bien Phu in
1954, the U.S. Military
Assistance Advisory
Group–Vietnam (MAAG-V)
assumed control of the training
and development of the Army of
the Republic of Vietnam (ARVN),
organized out of the VNA.
MAAG-V advisers largely
ignored the former Territorial
network. South Vietnamese
President Ngo Dinh Diem transformed the RF/PF network into a
new unit called the Civil Guard
(CG), responsible only to the
President. In 1956 Diem divided
the Civil Guard in half, creating
a new entity, the People's Self-
Defense Force (PSDF). All
commanders were Diem loyalists
with little, if any, practical military experience. In 1964 the Civil
Guard was renamed the
Regional Forces (RF); the PSDF
became known as the Popular
Forces (PF).

Despite poor pay—an RF
colonel earned US $1,922 per
annum while privates could
expect no more than US $413
per year in 1968—there was
never a lack of volunteers
because service in either branch
allowed volunteers to remain
closer to home, a morale-boosting
consideration not extended to the
ARVN's draftees. In 1968 the
combined strength of the RF
(152,549) and PF (151,945) made
it slightly smaller than the Army
of the Republic of Vietnam's
(ARVN) ten divisions (324,637).
Some RF/PF units refused to
support ARVN forces because of
the ARVN's condescending attitude toward hamlet militias.
After 1967 RF/PF units sometimes helped new pacification
and security groups created or
adapted to destroy the Viet Cong
Infrastructure.

See also: Civil Guard; Collins,
James Lawton Jr.; Combined
Action Program; Pacification;
People's Self-Defense Force;
Veterans, Vietnamese.

Rehnquist, William H.
(1924–), assistant attorney

general, 1969–1971; Associate Justice, U.S. Supreme Court, 1972–1986, Chief Justice, 1986–). In 1971, as a Nixon administration assistant attorney general, Rehnquist supported the suspension of normal arrest procedures to facilitate the detention of twelve thousand antiwar protestors in Washington D.C. In April 1970, at President Nixon's request, Rehnquist drew up a legal justification for the 30 April 1970 U.S.-led Cambodian incursion.

See also: Cambodian Incursion; Justice, Department of.

Reinhardt, G. Frederick (1911–1971), U.S. foreign service officer; U.S. Ambassador to South Vietnam, 1955–1957. Reinhardt was an ardent supporter of the regime of South Vietnamese Prime Minister Ngo Dinh Diem.

See also: Ngo Dinh Diem.

Reorganization Objective Army Division (ROAD). U.S. Army reorganization plan begun in 1961 that restructured divisions into task-organized brigades, a formation adaptable to many types and levels of combat. The new ROAD structured divisions were in place when the U.S. escalated the Vietnam War in 1965.

See also: Army, U.S.

Replacement Center. U.S. military facilities where incoming replacement personnel were processed before being sent to their duty stations. Nearly all

U.S. Army troops in Vietnam were processed at the 90th Replacement Center at Long Binh.

Republican Party, U.S. Nearly all Republican political leaders and officeholders supported U.S. involvement in the Vietnam War. During his 1964 campaign against the conservative Republican Senator Barry Goldwater, President Lyndon Johnson was wary of being accused of being "soft on communism." Goldwater promised to escalate the war drastically if elected. After Johnson's victory and the initial commitment of U.S. troops Republicans in Congress supported further escalation and backed Johnson's requests for more money for the war effort. In the 1968 presidential race Republican candidate Richard Nixon promised an "honorable" peace, implying that the Democrats would "sell out" the South Vietnamese to the communists. In the 1972 campaign, Nixon and his fellow Republicans again campaigned on their policies of "peace with honor" and painted Democratic nominee George McGovern as a dangerous antiwar liberal. As president, Nixon enjoyed broad support from his party in conducting his Vietnam policies, although a few moderate Republicans such as Sens. Jacob Javits (N.Y.) and John Sherman Cooper (Ky.) challenged those policies.

See also: Goldwater, Barry; Laird, Melvin R.; Nixon, Richard M.; Twining, Nathan F.

Republican Youth Movement. *See* Cong Hoa

Republic of China Military Advisory Group, Vietnam (RCMAAGV). In October 1964 the Republic of China Military Advisory Group, Vietnam went to South Vietnam to help with political warfare, medical work, and the refugee situation. By 1965 the group, which never had more than 30 personnel, included agricultural experts and engineers.

See also: China, Republic of (Taiwan); Free World.

Republic of Cochinchina. Also known as the Autonomous Republic of Cochin China. The republic, in southern Vietnam, was set up by French High Commissioner Thierry D'Argenlieu and recognized by France in June 1946 and as a "free state" within the French Indochinese Federation. It was abolished by France in March 1949.

See also: Argenlieu, Georges Thierry D'; Fontainebleau Conference.

Republic of Vietnam (RVN). *See* Vietnam, Republic of

Republic of Vietnam Air Force (VNAF). Air Force component of the Republic of Vietnam Armed Forces (RVNAF).

See also: Joint General Staff; Republic of Vietnam Armed Forces.

Republic of Vietnam Armed Forces (RVNAF). The military entity that included the Army (ARVN), Navy (RVNN), and Air Force (VNAF) of South Vietnam, which was organized, trained, equipped, and supported in the image of its U.S. counterpart. During the American war, the RVNAF suffered some 224,000 killed and more than 1 million wounded, excluding losses in the final, victorious North Vietnamese offensive for which figures are unavailable.

See also: Army of the Republic of Vietnam; Joint General Staff; Regional/Popular Forces.

Reserve Officer Training Corps (ROTC). System in which U.S. military officers are trained while they are college students. Upon graduation, ROTC cadets enter active duty as officers. During the Vietnam War ROTC graduates, graduates of in-service officer training programs, those promoted from enlisted ranks and graduates of the U.S. service academies made up the officer corps of the U.S. military.

Reserves. During the Vietnam War, each branch of the U.S. military had a reserve component, including National Guard units. Reservists served four to six months on active duty for training, plus yearly summer camp and monthly unit meetings for six years. Only a handful of reserve units were called to active duty and sent to Vietnam.

See also: National Guard.

Resisters Inside the Army (RITA). Antiwar group formed in 1967 by U.S. soldiers stationed in Europe.

See also: Discipline, U.S. Armed Forces.

Resor, Stanley R. (1917–), Secretary of the Army, 1965–1971. As Army Secretary during most of the Vietnam War, Resor strongly supported U.S. policy. After being informed in 1969 of allegations about the My Lai massacre, Resor initiated the Army investigation.

See also: My Lai.

Revolutionary Development (RD). South Vietnamese pacification program developed in 1966 that sent specially trained government teams into villages and hamlets to improve security and spur development. In 1969, some 50,000 revolutionary development cadres were at work in some 1,400 villages in South Vietnam. The program was disbanded in 1971.

See also: Pacification.

Revolutionary Development Cadres. *See* Pacification

Revolutionary Personalist Diligent Labor Party. *See* Can Lao

Revolutionary War. *See* Pacification

Revolutionary Youth League. Vietnamese communist revolutionary group, a predecessor of the Indochinese Communist Party, founded in South China in 1925 by Ho Chi Minh.

See also: Ho Chi Minh; Indochinese Communist Party.

Rhade. Known also as the Ede, the Rhade are a tribal minority people of Malayo-Polynesian descent in Vietnam's Central Highlands. During the French and American wars many Rhade joined the *Front Unifié pour la Lutte des Races Opprimées* (FULRO), an anti-Vietnamese separatist group.

See also: Front Unifié pour la Lutte des Races Opprimées; Montagnards.

Rheault, Robert (1925–), commander, U.S. Army Fifth Special Forces Group, May to July 1969. Rheault and six of his officers were indicted for the June 1969 execution of a suspected Viet Cong double agent working for the Special Forces. The Central Intelligence Agency (CIA) refused to release classified information about the case, and it was dropped. Rheault resigned from the Army the same year.

Rhodes, Alexandre de (1591–1660), French Catholic missionary. De Rhodes, a Jesuit, in 1627 was the first Frenchman to visit Vietnam. Before he was expelled from the country in 1630, he had converted some 6,700 Vietnamese to Catholicism. Although he never returned to Vietnam, de Rhodes spent much of the remainder of his life promoting the French missionary effort there.

Rhodes, James A. (1909–), governor of Ohio, 1963–1971, 1975–1983. In response to students staging a demonstration on 1 May 1970 at Kent State University in Ohio, Governor James Rhodes called in the National Guard. On 4 May the National Guard fired into a crowd of protestors, killing four students and wounding nine.

See also: Kent State University.

Richardson, Elliot (1920–), secretary of defense, 1973; attorney general, 1973. Richardson had little influence on Vietnam policy during his four-month tenure as secretary of defense. His time at the Pentagon ended when President Nixon appointed Richardson in April 1973 to the Justice Department after the resignation of Attorney General Richard Kleindienst. Richardson resigned less than six months later after refusing Nixon's order to fire Watergate Special Prosecutor Archibold Cox.

See also: Laird, Melvin R.; Nixon, Richard M.; Schlesinger, James R.; Watergate.

Richardson, John H. (1913– 1998), Central Intelligence Agency (CIA) station chief, Saigon, 1962–1963. Like his predecessor William Colby, Richardson had close ties to the Diem regime, particularly to Ngo Dinh Nhu. Ambassador Henry Cabot Lodge had Richardson recalled on 5 October 1963 primarily because Lodge wanted more power over CIA activities in Vietnam and because of Richardson's links to Nhu. Richardson was succeeded by Peer de Silva.

See also: Central Intelligence Agency; Colby, William.

Ridenhour, Ronald L. (1946–1998). Ridenhour had served in Hawaii with the Americal Division company involved in the My Lai massacre. In Vietnam he heard of the incident from several participants. In 1969, after he came home from Vietnam, Ridenhour wrote a letter to President Nixon, Defense Secretary Laird and to members of Congress. That letter led to the Army's investigation of the massacre.

See also: My Lai.

Ridgway, Matthew B. (1895–1993), general, U.S. Army; U.S. Army chief of staff, 1953–1955. Gen. Matthew Ridgway, who commanded Army combat divisions in WWII and Korea, opposed U.S. intervention in support of the French at Dien Bien Phu and spoke out against sending U.S. troops to Vietnam after the French defeat. As one of the "wise men," Ridgway helped persuade President Johnson to deescalate the Vietnam War in 1968.

See also: Dien Bien Phu; Wise Men.

Rifles. *See* M-16 Rifle

Rigault de Genouilly, Charles
(1807–1873), French admiral. As
a captain, Rigault de Genouilly
took part in an aborted attack on
the Vietnamese port of Tourane
(DaNang) in 1847. In 1858, Vice
Admiral Rigault de Genouilly,
commanding French naval forces
in China and Cochinchina, captured Tourane. He advanced
toward the imperial capital of
Hue but abandoned the effort.
Rigault de Genouilly then sailed
south and occupied the area of
modern-day Saigon on 17
February 1859.

See also: France.

Ring of Steel. Group of South
Vietnamese Army fire bases
arranged in a loose arc just
south of the Demilitarized Zone
that was overrun by the North
Vietnamese Army during the
1972 Easter Offensive.

See also: Demilitarized Zone;
Easter Offensive.

Riot Control Agents (RCA).
See Chemical Warfare

Risner, Robinson (1924–), U.S.
Air Force colonel shot down over
North Vietnam and taken prisoner in September 1965. Risner
was among the first U.S. POWs
released by Hanoi on 12
February 1973.

See also: POW/MIA
Controversy.

Riverine Assault Force. *See*
Mobile Riverine Force

Rivers, L. Mendel (1905–1970),
U.S. representative (D-S.C.),
1940–1970. Rivers, who was
chairman of the House Armed
Services Committee from
1965–1970, supported an all-out
U.S. armed forces war effort in
Vietnam.

See also: Congress, U.S.

ROAD. *See* Reorganization
Objective Army Division

Robb, Charles S. (1939–), for-
mer Marine captain; Governor of
Virginia, 1982–1986; U.S.
Senator (D-Va.), 1989– . Robb,
the son-in-law of President
Lyndon Johnson, served a
1968–1969 tour of duty in
Vietnam.

Rocket Belts. Areas around
South Vietnamese cities and military bases from which Viet Cong
and North Vietnamese Army
units launched a variety of highly
portable artillery rockets.

Rogers, William P. (1913–),
secretary of state, 1969–1973.
During Roger's tenure at the
State Department, Vietnam
policy was formulated by
President Nixon and National
Security Adviser Henry
Kissinger with little input from
Rogers. Rogers strongly opposed
Nixon's bombing and the 1970
invasion of Cambodia, but supported Nixon's Vietnamization
program. In 1973, Kissinger
replaced him as secretary of
state.

See also: Cambodian Incursion;
Kissinger, Henry; State,
Department of.

Rolling Thunder, Operation.
Code name for President Lyndon
Johnson's bombing campaign
against North Vietnam from 2
March 1965 to 31 October 1968.
The campaign was designed by
President Johnson and Secretary
of Defense Robert McNamara to
induce North Vietnam to come to
the negotiating table. The opera-
tion also was used by the Joint
Chiefs of Staff (JCS), the
Commander-in-Chief, Pacific
(CINCPAC), and Air Force and
Navy air commanders as an
interdiction campaign against
communist supply lines; by Gen.
William Westmoreland to justify
additional U.S. ground troops in
South Vietnam for air base security; and by presidential adviser
McGeorge Bandy as a means to
bolster South Vietnamese
resolve.

Most missions were carried
out by U.S. Air Force F-105 and
F-4 tactical fighters based in
South Vietnam and Thailand and
by U.S. Navy-carrier-based F-4,
F-8, A-4, and A-6 fighter and
attack squadrons. Pilots and
weapon systems operators from
these units suffered a disproportionately high share of their
services' combat losses. Of the
655 U.S. military prisoners of
war (POWs) returned by North
Vietnam, 457 were aviators
downed over the North, most
during Rolling Thunder.

Johnson and McNamara
maintained detailed tactical control of the missions, dictating the
numbers and types of aircraft,
kinds of ordnance, timing, and
tactics against specific targets.

Targets were chosen by Johnson,
McNamara, Secretary of State
Dean Rusk, White House press
secretary George Reedy, and the
presidential assistant for nation-
al security affairs (McGeorge
Bundy, later Walt Rostow) at
Tuesday White House luncheons.
The targets chosen came from a
short list selected by
McNamara's staff from among
targets nominated by the
Seventh Air Force and the U.S.
Navy's Task Force-77 (TF-77)
that had been approved by
CINCPAC and the State
Department.

For much of the campaign,
high-value targets such as POL
(petroleum, oil, lubricants) storage facilities, electric power
generation plants, and airfields
were off-limits and many aviators considered the approved
targets hardly worth hitting. The
campaign generated political
controversy when Harrison
Salisbury reported from North

The Bomb Line. *Imposed from the White House,
the "bomb line" was the northernmost limit of
Rolling Thunder bombing operations. As part of a
"slow squeeze" strategy, the area of operations was
extended as the bombing failed to deter the North
Vietnamese. The approximate operational boundaries
as of the end of the months noted are shown. Strikes
were not automatically approved even within these
authorized target areas. Moreover, operations were
strictly forbidden within a 30-nautical-mile buffer zone
along the Chinese border, and restricted and prohibited zones were also established around Hanoi and
Haiphong.*

*Inset: No air strikes were permitted within prohibited
zones unless personally approved by President
Johnson; except for attacks on transportation links,
strikes in restricted zones required Pentagon or White
House approval. Note that the Chinese buffer zone
contracted to 25 nautical miles approximately within
the area shown within the inset. During the 1972
Christmas bombings, the prohibited zones were eliminated and the Hanoi restricted zone was reduced to a
radius of 10 nautical miles. (Map adapted from Barrett
Tillman and John B. Nichols,* On Yankee Station. *Naval
Institute Press, 1987.)*

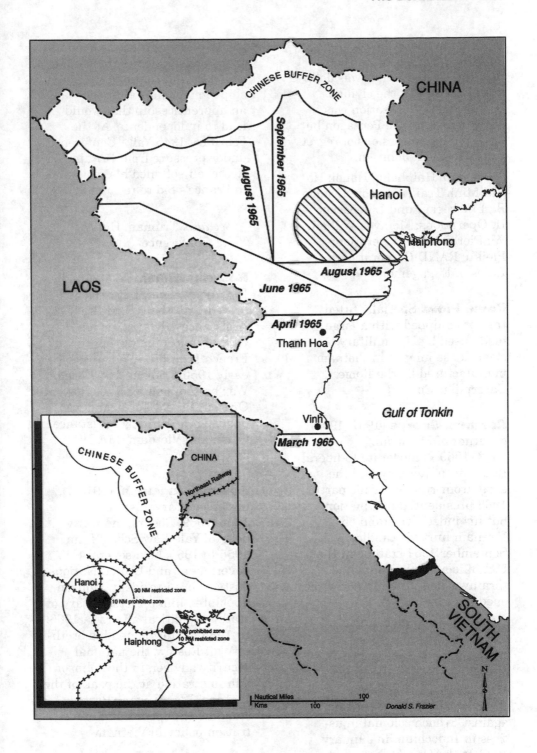

CHINESE BUFFER ZONE

CHINA

September 1965

August 1965

Hanoi

Haiphong

LAOS

August 1965

June 1965

April 1965

Thanh Hoa

Gulf of Tonkin

Vinh

March 1965

SOUTH VIETNAM

CHINESE BUFFER ZONE

CHINA

Northeast Railway

Hanoi

30 NM restricted zone
10 NM prohibited zone

4 NM prohibited zone
10 NM restricted zone

Haiphong

Nautical Miles   100
Kms   100

Donald S. Frazier

N

Vietnam in the *New York Times* on 25 and 27 December 1966 that the United States was deliberately targeting the civilian populace. The accusation was hotly denied by the Pentagon but drew public expressions of regret from President Johnson.

See also: Haiphong; Hanoi; Ho Chi Minh Trail; Johnson, Lyndon B.; Linebacker and Linebacker II, Operations; Momyer, William W.; Pierce Arrow, Operation; Pleiku; RAND Corporation; Rules of Engagement.

Rome Plow. Specially fitted tractor equipped with a large blade used by U.S. military to clear dense jungles in Vietnam manufactured by the Rome Caterpillar Co.

Romney, George (1907–1995), governor of Michigan, 1963–1969. A moderate-to-liberal Republican, Romney was the early front-runner for his party's 1968 presidential nomination, but his indecisive stand on Vietnam hurt his candidacy. A September 1967 statement that U.S. officials in Vietnam had "brainwashed" him further weakened his campaign.

See also: Republican Party, U.S.

Roosevelt, Franklin Delano (1882–1945), U.S. president, 1933–1945. During WWII President Roosevelt spoke out against French colonial injustices in Indochina. In January 1943 at the Casablanca Conference, he vowed not to accept any postwar plan that would permit France to keep its Indochinese colonies. Instead, he called for international trusteeships for colonies after the war: an apprenticeship that would lead to independence. At the February 1945 Yalta Conference, under pressure from Britain, Roosevelt softened his resistance to France's bid to reclaim its colonies.

See also: Truman, Harry S; Yalta Conference.

Rosson, William B. (1918–), U.S. Army general. Rosson served with the U.S. Military Assistance Advisory Group–Indochina during the French Indochina War in the early 1950s. During the Vietnam War he commanded Task Force Oregon, I Field Force, and was deputy U.S. Military Assistance Command Vietnam (MACV) commander.

Rostow, Eugene V. (1913–), undersecretary of state, 1966–1969. Rostow, innovative dean of Yale Law School from 1955 to 1965, held several U.S. government and United Nations posts before President Johnson appointed him undersecretary of state for political affairs in 1966. In 1966 Rostow joined his brother Walt Rostow, the national security adviser, in the Johnson administration at the peak of the Vietnam War. Eugene Rostow steadfastly supported administration policy in Vietnam

Rostow, Walt Whitman (1916–), special assistant for

national security affairs, 1961–1966; national security adviser, 1966–1969. Rostow believed that the U. S. should meet the global challenge of communism with military intervention and economic aid. He accompanied Gen. Maxwell Taylor to Vietnam in October 1961; their report led to the commitment of U.S. ground troops.

Rostow's experience choosing bombing targets in WWII left him supremely confident in U.S. air power. As the Viet Cong insurgency grew, Rostow suggested bombing the north to defeat guerrillas in the south, for he firmly believed that the Viet Cong were controlled from the Democratic Republic of Vietnam. Kennedy rejected the idea, but President Johnson approved it in 1965. When bombing of North Vietnam began in earnest in 1966, Rostow was promoted to national security adviser.

As public opinion turned against the war, President Johnson relied heavily on Rostow's optimism and perseverance. After the 1968 Tet Offensive, Rostow served on the Senior Advisory Group (the "wise men") that reassessed Vietnam policy and recommended against further escalation. Rostow, however, approved military requests for intensifying the bombing, mobilizing the reserves, and sending more troops to Vietnam. Johnson ignored Rostow's advice and stopped escalating the war in March 1968.

See also: Johnson, Lyndon B.; Kennedy, John F.; National

Security Council; Rolling Thunder, Operation; Taylor, Maxwell D.; Taylor-Rostow Report.

Rotation System. *See* Tour of Duty

Route 9. The main eastward entryway from Laos through the Central Highlands into South Vietnam's northern coastal region. During the Vietnam War the North Vietnamese Army waged mobile warfare in the thinly settled areas along Route 9 just south of the Demilitarized Zone.

See also: Central Highlands; Demilitarized Zone.

Rowe, James N. (1938–), U.S Army special forces officer. Rowe was one of the first U.S. soldiers taken prisoner by the Viet Cong. He was captured in October 1963 in the Mekong Delta, and escaped on 31 December 1968.

Royal Australian Air Force (RAAF). Branch of Australian military that participated in the Vietnam War from 1964–1973 with a squadron of B-57 Canberra jet bombers that operated with U.S. Air Force units and a squadron of assault helicopters.

See also: Australia.

Royal Laotian Army (RLA). The Royal Laotian Army was trained by U.S. Special Forces to fight the communist Pathet Lao insurgents and North

Vietnamese Army units in Laos beginning in 1959. The U.S. Central Intelligence Agency supported RLA guerrilla auxiliaries. The RLA surrendered to the Pathet Lao on 8 May 1975.

See also: Laos; Pathet Lao.

Royal Thai Government. *See* Thailand

Rubber. Important agricultural crop in Vietnam from the 1890s to the 1950s. Rubber trees were introduced by the French into the Central Highlands province of Dac Lac in the late 19th century. French-owned rubber plantations accounted for significant exports until the mid-1950s.

Rubin, Jerry (1938–1994), radical antiwar activist. Rubin began organizing antiwar demonstrations in 1965. A founder of the Yippies, he was one of the Chicago Seven indicted for conspiring to incite rioting at the August 1968 Democratic National Convention in Chicago.

See also: Chicago Seven.

Rudd, Mark (1947–), Columbia University student; radical antiwar student leader. From March through May 1968, the Students for a Democratic Society (SDS) chapter at Columbia University, led by Rudd, seized several campus buildings, leading to violent confrontations with the police and a shutdown of the entire campus. Rudd later ran the violent radical group, the Weathermen.

See also: Students for a Democratic Society; Weathermen.

Rules of Engagement (ROEs). The formal authorizations for U.S. ground, air, and naval combat operations in Southeast Asia. The Joint Chiefs of Staff (JCS) and the Military Assistance Command, Vietnam (MACV), formed many ROEs, but the White House exercised final authority in their development. ROEs changed frequently during the war and affected many combat contingencies. They generally worked, however, to prevent geographical expansion of the war and to limit civilian casualties.

The Vietnam War ROEs, especially the Johnson administration's limited war strategy, were controversial. The ROEs established strict territorial limits on U.S. military operations, forbidding ground operations outside South Vietnam (except for the 1970 incursion into Cambodia) and establishing complex restraints on air power in Cambodia, Laos, and North Vietnam. President Lyndon Johnson established the territorial contours of the ROEs in 1965. The strategy and restrictive ROEs reflected administration concern that provocative military activities in the region would trigger a confrontation with the Soviet Union or the People's Republic of China (PRC). Johnson and key advisers judged that carefully directed and contained military power could stem the communist war against South Vietnam.

Government and military leaders also designed extensive ROEs to minimize civilian injury and property loss from U.S. combat operations inside South Vietnam. The directives were seen as crucial to gain South Vietnamese support for U.S. intervention and the anticommunist South Vietnamese government. ROEs also proved inadequate to address the uncertain and volatile environment created by the Viet Cong guerrilla warfare and aggressive U.S. sweeps of rural Vietnam. ROEs called for soldiers to carefully distinguish neutral civilians from Viet Cong forces.

See also: Joint Chiefs of Staff.

Rumor of War, A (1977). Acclaimed, best-selling memoir by Philio Caputo that tells the story of the author's 1965–1966 tour of duty as a U.S. Marine Corps lieutenant in Vietnam.

See also: Caputo, Philip.

Rumsfeld, Donald H. (1932–), U.S. representative (R-Ill.), 1957–1959; secretary of Defense, 1975–1977. Rumsfeld replaced James Schlesinger as secretary of Defense following the end of the Vietnam War.

See also: Defense, Department of.

Rung Sat. Swampy section of the Mekong Delta favored by Viet Cong sappers who disrupted shipping to the port of Saigon.

See also: SEALs.

Rusk, (David) Dean (1909–1994), assistant U.S. secretary of state for Far Eastern affairs, 1950–1952; secretary of state, 1961–1969. A leading foreign policy adviser to presidents John F. Kennedy and Lyndon B. Johnson, Rusk fully supported and helped implement Kennedy's and Johnson's decisions to escalate the U.S. commitment in Vietnam.

A former Rhodes scholar, Rusk served as chief of staff to Gen. Joseph Stilwell in the China-Burma-India theater during WWII. At the end of the war, he joined the State Department, developing expertise in United Nations and East Asian affairs. Rusk proved more sensitive than many of his diplomatic colleagues to the postwar stirrings of Asian nationalism. He played a crucial role, for example, in moving the Truman administration to support Indonesian independence in 1949.

Rusk's post-WWII anticolonial inclinations were tempered by his vigorous anticommunism. As assistant secretary of state for Far Eastern affairs, he supported providing military assistance to the French in Indochina. Rusk believed the Viet Minh were part of a broader communist challenge to Western interests in Asia. As Kennedy's secretary of state, Rusk consistently argued that U.S. global interests required the preservation of a noncommunist South Vietnam. America's treaty obligations under the Southeast Asia Treaty Organization, its prestige as a world power, the credibility of its commitments, and its ability and willingness to deter aggression—all vital issues— were in Rusk's view being tested and challenged in Vietnam. For Rusk there was no debating the ultimate objective of U.S. policy; what he invariably characterized as external communist aggression simply had to be contained, much as the Nazi challenge had had to be quelled in an earlier era. To do so, Rusk favored moderation and gradualism, and advocated the policy of incremental military escalation.

Rusk played a more prominent role in Vietnam War policymaking under President Lyndon Johnson. In 1965 Rusk joined Secretary of Defense Robert S. McNamara and national security adviser McGeorge Bundy to urge Johnson to do whatever was necessary to prevent a North Vietnamese victory.

See also: Ball, George W.; Cooper, Chester; Halberstam, David; Hawks and Doves; Johnson, Lyndon B.; Rolling Thunder, Operation; State, Department of.

Rusk-Thanat Agreement.
1962 U.S.-Thailand pact guaranteeing Thai security against external threats and internal insurgencies. The agreement became the basis for the U.S. military presence in Thailand throughout the Vietnam War.

See also: Thailand.

Russell, Bertrand (1872–1970), British philosopher, logician and pacifist. Russell, an internationally known philosopher and mathematician who won the Nobel Prize for literature in 1950, was a longtime peace activist who opposed U.S. involvement in Vietnam. Russell's International War Crimes Tribunal, also known as the Russell tribunal, met in 1967 and denounced U.S. use of napalm and cluster bombs.

See also: International War Crimes Tribunal; Napalm.

Russell, Richard B. (1897– 1971), U.S. senator (D-Ga.), 1933–1971; chairman, Senate Armed Services Committee, 1951–1969; chairman, Senate Appropriations Committee, 1969–1971. Russell greatly influenced military appropriations and policy. He advised President Eisenhower in 1954 not to intervene militarily to help the French at Dien Bien Phu, and opposed U.S. involvement in Vietnam because he did not consider North Vietnam a threat to U.S. interests. Once U.S. troops were committed, Russell, a close friend of President Johnson, supported the war, although he remained a critic of U.S. strategy and conduct of the war. After the 1968 Tet Offensive, he rejected piecemeal escalation of the ground war and called for full-scale bombing of North Vietnam.

See also: Dien Bien Phu.

Russo, Anthony J. Jr.
(1936–), RAND Corporation
Vietnam analyst, 1964–1968;
antiwar activist. Russo helped
Daniel Ellsberg leak the
Pentagon Papers in 1971. He and
Ellsberg were indicted for the
action in 1972. The charges were
dismissed in 1973.

See also: Ellsberg, Daniel;
Pentagon Papers.

RVNAF. *See* Republic of Vietnam
Armed Forces

SAC. *See* Strategic Air Command

Sadler, Barry (1940–1989), novelist, singer-songwriter. Sadler, a U.S. Army Special Forces sergeant, wrote and sang "The Ballad of the Green Berets," a song that went to the top of the popular music charts in 1965.

See also: "Ballad of the Green Berets, The."

Saigon. The largest city in Indochina; the capital of South Vietnam (1954–1975). Located 75 kilometers (45 miles) from the coast of the South China Sea on the Sai Gon River, Saigon was known as "Paris of the Orient." Adm. Leonard Victor Joseph Charner conquered Saigon for France in 1861. Emperor Tu Duc then ceded the surrounding provinces to form Cochinchina, the first colony of French Indochina. Saigon became a thriving commercial center of the Mekong Delta and the home to rich Vietnamese planters, French aristocrats, and Chinese merchants.

The struggle against French rule in the south began when Saigon workers went on strike in September 1945 following the withdrawal of Japanese occupation forces. French troops, rearmed by the British, assassinated Viet Minh leaders, and in retaliation French settlers were massacred. But the Viet Minh never enjoyed much support in Saigon. Saigon became the capital of South Vietnam when the country was divided in 1954. Saigon's official population of 1.5 million nearly doubled during the war as refugees streamed into the city.

The sudden and gigantic influx of U.S. troops and dollars rapidly transformed the Asian capital into a carnival of Western decadence. Saigon swarmed with thieves, beggars, prostitutes, drug dealers, and black market peddlers. The U.S. war effort flowed through Saigon, the port of entry for 136,000 metric tons (150,000 tons) per month of U.S. cargo. Huge U.S. bases sprawled nearby at Tan Son Nhut, Bien Hoa, and Long Binh. Saigon abounded with offices, apartments, and barracks erected for U.S. personnel. Yet even apart from the pickpockets, Americans were never safe there—notably when Viet Cong guerrillas blew up the U.S. officers' billet at the Brinks Hotel in 1964 and attacked the U.S. embassy in 1968 during the Tet Offensive. After North Vietnamese Army tanks rolled into the city on 30 April 1975, Saigon was renamed Ho Chi Minh City.

See also: Bay Vien; Binh Xuyen; Drug Trafficking; Drug Use, U.S. Military; Ho Chi Minh Campaign; Ho Chi Minh City; Tet Offensive; Tran Van Tra; Marines, U.S.; Vietnam, Republic of.

Saigon Military Mission (SMM). Name given to Central Intelligence Agency-sponsored group of U.S. military personnel under USAF Col. Edward Lansdale that arrived in South Vietnam in 1954 to support the government of President Ngo Dinh Diem and undermine the communist government in North Vietnam.

See also: Central Intelligence Agency; Conein, Lucien; Lansdale, Edward G.

Sainteny, Jean (1907–1978), French commissioner for Annam and Tonkin, 1945–1946. Sainteny represented the French government during negotiations with Ho Chi Minh following WWII. In March 1946 Sainteny and Ho agreed to accords in which France recognized the Democratic Republic of Vietnam as a free state within the French Union. The agreement broke down by December. Sainteny represented France on three later diplomatic missions, including a 1966 peace effort. In 1969, Sainteny brokered correspondence between Nixon administration national security adviser Henry Kissinger and the North Vietnamese leadership. Sainteny also arranged the 1972 secret meetings between Kissinger and Le Duc Tho in Paris.

See also: Ho Chi Minh; Paris Peace Accords; Appendix F, "Paris Peace Accords."

Salan, Raoul (1899–1984), commander in chief, French forces in Indochina, 1952–1953. Salan brought a lifetime of highly decorated military experience to his Vietnam command: he fought in WWI, was wounded in the Levant in 1921, served in Indochina in 1924, and undertook intelligence and subversion operations against the Italians in North Africa in 1942–1943. Salan succeeded General Jean de Lattre de Tassigny in Vietnam in 1952, and chose a defensive strategy for pursuing the Indochina War, a strategy not looked upon with favor by U.S. military leaders. The same year he took command, Salan was forced to withdraw his forces from Hao Binh, an important position southeast of Hanoi. U.S. displeasure with Salan helped bring about his recall in the spring of 1954. He was succeeded by General Henri Navarre.

See also: Lattre de Tassigny, Jean de; Navarre, Henri.

Salem House, Operation. *See* Daniel Boone Operations

Salinger, Pierre (1925–), presidential press secretary, 1961–1963. In 1972 Salinger was sent by Democratic presidential nominee George McGovern to negotiate the release of U.S. prisoners of war with the North Vietnamese.

See also: McGovern, George.

Salibsury, Harrison E. (1908–1992), *New York Times* correspondent who went to North Vietnam in December 1965 and wrote that U.S. planes were bombing civilian targets, a claim government officials denied.

Samas, David, U.S. Army Private David Samas was one of the Fort Hood Three, U.S. soldiers who refused to go to Vietnam in June 1966.

See also: Fort Hood Three.

Sam Houston, Operation. Codename for January 1967 operation by the U.S. Army's 4th Infantry Division against North Vietnamese Army forces in the Central Highlands.

SAMs. *See* Surface-to-Air Missiles

SAM Triangle. Name given by U.S. pilots to the triangular area around Hanoi, Haiphong, and Vinh that contained 60 multiple-launcher surface-to-air missile (SAM) sites in 1966, and more than 150 sites one year later.

See also: Antiaircraft Defenses; Surface-to-Air Missiles.

San Antonio Formula. An August 1967 U.S. government secret offer to stop bombing North Vietnam if the North Vietnamese agreed to enter productive peace negotiations immediately and not take advantage of the cessation. Henry Kissinger, then a private citizen, carried the message to the North Vietnamese. President Lyndon Johnson publicly announced the plan in San Antonio on 29 September and reiterated it 31 March 1968. The North Vietnamese rejected the offer, because it did not promise a concrete role for the National Liberation Front (NLF) in peace negotiations.

See also: Nitze, Paul H.

Sanders, Clinton (1944–), Illinois Drug Abuse Program director of field research, 1970–1971. In 1972 Sanders released a survey that reported that between 60 and 90 percent of lower-ranked U.S. military enlisted men used illicit drugs in Vietnam.

See also: Drug Trafficking; Drug Use, U.S. Military.

Santoli, Al (1949–), oral historian. Santoli, who served with the U.S. Army's 25th Infantry Division in Vietnam in 1969–1970, edited several Vietnam War–related oral histories, including *Everything We Had* (1981).

See also: Everything We Had.

Sappers (Dac Cong). North Vietnamese Army and Viet Cong commandos trained to mine roads and waterways, set booby traps, clear minefields and attack U.S. and South Vietnamese bases most often using satchel charges. Communist forces relied particularly heavily on sappers after 1968 to help conserve other forces. In 1973 sappers were organized into four regiments, 35 battalions, and 2 special groups.

See also: People's Army of Vietnam; Satchel Charges.

SAR. *See* Search and Rescue

Sarraut, Albert (1872–1962), French governor general of Indochina, 1911–1914, 1917–1919. Sarraut instituted political and social reforms, including a new education system.

Satchel Charges. Explosive devices used against U.S. and South Vietnamese forces by Viet Cong and North Vietnamese Army sappers. Typically, satchel charges were thrown at targets such as aircraft, vehicles, bunkers and buildings.

See also: Sappers.

Saturday Night Massacre. Events that took place on 20 October 1973 when President Richard Nixon fired Watergate Special Prosecutor Archibald Cox and Attorney General Elliot L. Richardson. Deputy Attorney General William D. Ruckelshaus resigned rather than carry out the presidential order to fire Cox. The event led to the start of congressional impeachment investigations and the waning of President Nixon's power in all matters, including prosecution of the Vietnam War.

See also: Cox, Archibald; Nixon, Richard M.; Richardson, Elliot L.; Watergate.

Schanberg, Sydney H. (1934–), journalist. Schanberg covered the war in Cambodia from 1970–1975 for the *New York Times*. He won the 1976 Pulitzer Prize for international reporting his Cambodia coverage. The Roland Jaffe film, *The Killing Fields* (1984), was based on his Cambodian reporting. Schanberg's *The Death and Life of Dith Pran* (1985) is his account of the events portrayed in the film.

See also: Cambodia.

Schlesinger, Arthur M. Jr. (1917–), special assistant to the president, 1961–1964. Schlesinger was primarily involved in Latin American, European, and UN issues. He cautiously supported President Kennedy's involvement in South Vietnam, but broke with President Johnson in 1965 and spoke out against the war. Schlesinger's *The Bitter Heritage* (1966) criticized U.S. policy in the war. He later wrote antiwar speeches for Sen. Robert F. Kennedy.

See also: American Friends of Vietnam; Kennedy, Robert F.

Schlesinger, James R. (1929–), director of the Central Intelligence Agency (CIA), 1973; secretary of Defense, 1973–1975. As secretary of defense, Schlesinger, like his predecessor Elliot Richardson and like William Rogers at the State Department, was largely bypassed in Vietnam policy-making by Henry Kissinger. Schlesinger was considered a hard-liner and as secretary of defense made several speeches defending the bombing of Cambodia in 1969–1970. Schlesinger coordinated the May

1975 military response to Cambodia's seizure of the *Mayaguez,* the U.S.-registered container ship. President Ford replaced Schlesinger in the Pentagon with Donald Rumsfeld in November 1975.

See also: Central Intelligence Agency; Ford, Gerald R.; *Mayaguez* Incident.

Schoendorffer, Pierre (1928–), French filmmaker. Shoendorffer's acclaimed documentary, *The Anderson Platoon* (1966), which won the 1967 Academy Award for best documentary feature, follows a U.S. Army platoon led by Lt. Joseph Anderson in the Central Highlands of South Vietnam. His feature film, *Dien Bien Phu* (1992) deals with the epic 1954 French–Viet Minh battle. Shoendorffer was a French Army photographer during the French Indochina War, and was taken prisoner at Dien Bien Phu.

Scholars' Uprising. Also known as the Scholars' Revolt, an 1874–1875 rebellion led by university professors in Ha Tinh and Nghe An provinces protesting French favoritism to Vietnamese Catholic converts. Hundreds of Catholics were killed before the uprising was put down by French imperial troops.

Schwarzkopf, H. Norman (1934–), U.S. Army general; commander of U.S. and allied forces in Operation Desert Storm (1990–1991). Schwarzkopf served

two Vietnam War tours: in 1965–1966 as an adviser to the South Vietnamese Airborne, and in 1969–1970 as an aide to the U.S. Army Vietnam (USARV) chief of staff and as an Americal Division battalion commander.

Scruggs, Jan C. (1950–), rifleman, U.S. Army's 199th Light Infantry Brigade, Vietnam. Scruggs conceived of the idea for a national memorial to Vietnam veterans and organized the group that raised the funds to build the Vietnam Veterans Memorial, dedicated in November 1982 on the Mall in Washington, D.C.

See also: Vietnam Veterans Memorial.

SDS. *See* Students for a Democratic Society

Seabees. Navy construction engineers. Seabees, their name derived from the initials C.B., for Construction Battalion, came to Vietnam in 1954 at the onset of U.S. intervention. Most belonged to the 3d and 32d Naval Construction Regiments with headquarters in Saigon, which moved to Da Nang in 1967. Seabees built port facilities, air strips, fortified camps, roads, bridges, dams, warehouses, barracks, schools, hospitals, and refugee camps. Some of the more notable Seabee projects were the large port at Cam Ranh Bay, the fortified Special Forces camps in the Central Highlands, the 6,000-meter (2,000-foot) Liberty Bridge over the Thu Bon River, and the U.S. Navy hospital at Da Nang.

See also: Navy, U.S.

Seaborn, James B. (1924–), Canadian diplomat. Seaborn was appointed Canada's representative to the International Control Commission (ICSC) in 1964. He tried unsuccessfully to influence North Vietnamese officials to negotiate with the U.S.

See also: Canada; International Commission for Supervision and Control.

Sea Dragon, Operation. Codename for October 1966 to October 1968 U.S. Navy campaign involving cruisers, destroyers and the battleship USS *New Jersey* designed to interdict North Vietnamese supplies.

See also: Navy, U.S.; *New Jersey,* USS.

Seale, Bobby (1936–), Black Panther party leader. Seale, a leading radical civil rights activist, represented the Black Panthers in the antiwar movement. A member of the Chicago Eight, Seale's case was severed from the others, leaving the "Chicago Seven."

See also: Chicago Seven.

SEALORDS (Southeast Asia Lake, Ocean, River, and Delta Strategy). U.S. Navy–South Vietnamese Navy strategy adopted by the commander of U.S. Navy forces in

Vietnam, Vice Admiral Elmo R. Zumwalt Jr. in October 1968. Also known as Task Force 194, SEALORDS lasted until 1972. During that time, U.S. and South Vietnamese river forces established patrol boat barriers along the Cambodian border and penetrated traditional NVA and Viet Cong swampland strongholds forces in the Mekong Delta.

See also: Mekong River and Delta; Navy, U.S.; Zumwalt, Elmo R. Jr.

SEALs. U.S. Navy Sea, Air, Land commandos trained to attack from underwater as frogmen, from small speedboats, from helicopters, by high-altitude parachute drop, or by silent overland infiltration. SEALs first arrived in Vietnam in 1966, reaching a peak strength of about one hundred men in 1968. They typically operated in six-man squads. Most SEALs were attached to Task Force 116, the River Patrol Force stationed in the Mekong Delta and the Rung Sat Special Area.

SEAL missions included night ambushes, reconnaissance patrols, underwater sabotage, and commando raids on Viet Cong guerrilla bases. SEALs took part in Operation Game Warden (1965–1968) and Operation SEALORDS (1968–1969), which cut Viet Cong river supply lines from Cambodia. Some SEALs performed top secret intelligence missions as part of the U.S. Military Assistance Command's Studies

and Observation Group. Forty-
three SEALs were killed in
Vietnam.

See also: Navy, U.S.; Provincial
Reconnaissance Units; Rung Sat.

Seaman, Jonathan O.

(1911–1986), U.S. Army general.
Seaman was commander of the
1st Infantry Division when the
unit was deployed to Vietnam in
late 1965. In March 1966 he took
over command of II Field Force.

Search-and-Clear. *See* Search-
and-Destroy; Clear and Hold

Search-and-Destroy. The tac-
tic of pursuing Viet Cong
guerrillas in the countryside, the
main component of the attrition
strategy that guided U.S. military efforts in the Vietnam War.
U.S. troops aggressively pursued
enemy force concentrations and
sought to initiate battles in
hopes of inflicting decisive losses.
Building a secure ally, bolstering
the government, or protecting
the population were deemed less
important than killing Viet Cong
forces; the former tasks were left
to South Vietnamese forces.

President Johnson approved
the tactic in July 1965 after Gen.
William Westmoreland and the
Joint Chiefs of Staff recommended it. By mid 1967, more
than 80 percent of U.S. battalion-
size operations used search-
and-destroy tactics. Later
renamed "reconnaissance-in-
force" and "pre-emptive
operations," the tactic was used
by U.S. forces until 1969 when

search-and-destroy was turned
over to South Vietnamese troops.

See also: Attrition Strategy;
Bui Phat; Depuy, William E.; Ia
Drang; Krulak, Victor; Laird,
Melvin R.; Taylor, Maxwell D.;
Westmoreland, William C.; Zippo
Squads.

Search and Rescue (SAR).

Operations that rescued more
than 3,800 downed U.S. airmen
from the swamps, jungles, hilltops, and open seas of Southeast
Asia. The U.S. Air Rescue Service
(part of the U.S. Air Force) flew
missions for the French in the
1950s. Official reluctance to
admit growing U.S. involvement
in the war slowed the development of SAR capability. Before
the Third Aerospace Rescue and
Recovery Group was formed in
1966, SAR operations relied on
borrowed helicopters and Central
Intelligence Agency (CIA) contract pilots. SAR units eventually
operated out of air bases at Tan
Son Nhut, Da Nang, and Tuy
Hoa in South Vietnam, and at
Udorn in Thailand. They relied
on long-range helicopters—the
H-3 Jolly Green Giant in 1965
and the HH-53 Super Jolly
Green Giant in 1967, backed up
by F-4 jets, A-1 Skyraiders, and
C-130 transport planes. Navy
ships in the Gulf of Tonkin kept
helicopters on SAR duty around
the clock.

SAR units rescued more than
one-third of downed U.S. airmen,
many of whom were critically
wounded. They officially claimed
3,883 personnel rescued. SAR
personnel sometimes suffered

heavy losses themselves because distress signals from downed pilots also attracted Viet Cong guerrillas, who deployed "flak traps" around crash sites and opened fire on vulnerable rescue helicopters.

See also: Laos; Navy, U.S.; Rolling Thunder, Operation.

SEATO. *See* Southeast Asia Treaty Organization

Secret War. Multi-faceted covert U.S.-led effort in Laos from 1962–1975, directed by the CIA, to support the Royal Lao government against the communist Pathet Lao guerrillas and North Vietnamese Army troops in Laos. The war included aiding the Royal Thai government, arming Lao Hmong tribesmen as guerrilla fighters, operating the CIA's proprietary airline, Air America, providing military assistance to Laos, and using U.S. aircraft to wage an intense, long-term bombing campaign against military targets.

See also: Air America; Central Intelligence Agency; Hmong; Laos; Thailand.

Selective Service. A federal agency that drafted male citizens and residents aged 18 to 26 into the armed forces. During the Vietnam War, if they met certain criteria, draft-age men could avoid induction by qualifying for deferments or exceptions. Gen. Lewis B. Hershey, director of the agency from 1948 to 1969,

advocated using deferments and exceptions.

Hardship deferments would keep families clothed and fed; student deferments would keep young men in college; occupational exemptions would channel them into vital jobs as doctors, engineers, and scientists, or encourage them to join the National Guard, the Coast Guard, or the reserves. When draft calls increased from less than 10,000 to more than 30,000 per month in 1966, the Selective Service became extremely unpopular, and a lightning rod for antiwar protest, much of it directed against the four thousand local draft boards run by part-time unpaid volunteers. Many draft boards used their power of induction to "rehabilitate" nonconformists and "punish" antiwar protesters.

Carefully prepared draftees routinely avoided service by feigning ailments, filing appeals, switching locales, or otherwise bending the rules. Another criticism of the Selective Service was race and class discrimination. Large numbers of lower-income men of all races were drafted because relatively few went to college, escaped to Canada, or landed exempt jobs, and many inherited strong traditions of military service. In 1965–1966, for example, only 2 percent of all draftees were college graduates. Out of 26.8 million draftable men during the Vietnam War years, 2.2 million were inducted by the Selective Service into the

Army and Marines; 8.7 million enlisted voluntarily.

Almost 16 million men avoided military service entirely during the Vietnam War by legal means. Widespread draft evasion, combined with rampant inequality and an unpopular war, discredited General Hershey's Selective Service. Curtis Tarr replaced Hershey in 1969 and introduced a random lottery and sharply curtailed the deferment policy. President Nixon ended the draft completely on 27 January 1973.

See also: Conscientious Objectors; Hershey, Lewis B.; Tarr, Curtis.

Self-Defense Teams (*Doi Tu Ve*). Name given in the 1930s to units used primarily to protect Vietnamese Communist Party meetings and act as bodyguards for leaders.

See also: People's Army of Vietnam.

Senate, U.S. *See* Congress, U.S.

Seventeenth Parallel. Demarcation line between North and South Vietnam set up by the 1954 Geneva Accords. Meant to be temporary, it ran just south of the seventeenth parallel. Eventually a Demilitarized Zone (DMZ) extended three miles (five km) on both sides.

See also: Demilitarized Zone; Geneva Conference, 1954.

Seventh Fleet. U.S. Navy fleet responsible for naval operations in the Western Pacific, including Southeast Asia, from 1965–1973. The fleet included task forces of aircraft carriers, amphibious forces, logistic support, destroyers and cruisers and riverine assault craft.

See also: Aircraft Carriers; Amphibious Landing Operations; Navy, U.S.; Yankee Station.

SH-3 Helicopter. Known as the "Sea King," the Sikorsky SH-3 was used by the U.S. Navy for search and rescue missions.

See also: Helicopters; Search and Rescue.

Shaplen, Robert M. (1917–1988), journalist, author. Shaplen reported from Vietnam for *The New Yorker* beginning in 1962. His books on the war include *The Lost Revolution* (1965) and *Bitter Victory* (1986).

Sharp, Ulysses S. Grant Jr. (1906–), admiral, U.S. Navy; Commander-in-Chief, Pacific (CINCPAC), 1964–1968. Sharp succeeded Adm. Harry Felt as CINCPAC in June 1964. After the Tonkin Gulf incident, President Johnson approved Sharp's plan for immediate retaliatory air strikes, the first U.S. bombing of North Vietnam. Sharp believed the war could be won by keeping pressure on North Vietnam through air attacks, and argued against bombing halts or target restrictions. Sharp retired in 1968. In his 1978 memoir, *Strategy for Defeat,* Sharp wrote that the Vietnam War was lost in

Washington, not on the battlefield.

See also: Binh Gia; CINCPAC; Commander-in-Chief, Pacific.

Sheehan, Neil (1936–), United Press International correspondent and Saigon bureau chief, 1962–1964; *New York Times* reporter. Early in the war, Sheehan exposed problems with the U.S. effort in Vietnam and the corruption of the Diem regime. In 1968, Sheehan broke the story of the large troop request by the Joint Chiefs of Staff following the Tet Offensive. Daniel Ellsberg later leaked the Pentagon Papers to Sheehan, who published them in the *Times.* His book, *A Bright Shining Lie: John Paul Vann and America in Vietnam* (1978), was awarded the Pulitzer Prize and the National Book Award.

See also: Pentagon Papers; Vann, John Paul.

Shields, Marvin G. (1940–1966), U.S. Navy Seabee. In 1966, Seabee construction mechanic third class Shields received the third Vietnam War Medal of Honor—and the U.S. Navy's first. It was awarded posthumously for heroism in defense of the Civilian Irregular Defense Group camp at Dong Xoai on 10 June 1965. Shields is the only Seabee awarded the Medal of Honor.

See also: Medal of Honor; Seabees.

Short-timer. Slang term for a U.S. soldier with relatively little time left on his tour of duty in Vietnam. In previous conflicts, U.S. soldiers were assigned to combat duty for the duration of the war. In the Vietnam War, soldiers served for fixed periods of time: twelve months for Army, Air Force and Navy personnel and thirteen months for Marines. All personnel knew exactly how long they had to serve and the day they were eligible to return home, their "DEROS" date. Short-timers sometimes were relieved of combat duties.

See also: Tour of Duty.

Short-Timers, The (1979). Vietnam War novel by former Marine Gustav Hasford which was the basis for the critically acclaimed Stanley Kubrick film, *Full Metal Jacket* (1987).

See also: Hasford, Gustav; *Full Metal Jacket.*

Shoup, David M. (1904–1983), general, U.S. Marine Corps, commandant of the Marine Corps, 1960–1963, the highest ranking military officer who publicly opposed U.S. participation in the Vietnam War. Shoup entered the Marine Corps as a second lieutenant in July 1926. With pre-WWII service in China and Iceland, then-colonel Shoup commanded the 2d Marines, the spearhead regiment, in the assault on Tarawa in November 1943 and was awarded the Medal of Honor. On 1 January 1960, he became the 22nd commandant of the Marine Corps. While commandant, Shoup counseled against U.S. involvement in

Vietnam but never openly questioned policy. He retired in 1963. In a May 1966 speech he said he believed that all of Southeast Asia was not "worth the life and limb of a single American."

See also: Marines, U.S.

Siam. *See* Thailand

SIGMA. Code name for a series of war games played in the early 1960s to forecast potential outcomes of an expanded U.S. involvement in the conflict in Vietnam. Players included key Johnson administration figures, such as McGeorge Bundy, John T. McNaughton, and generals Curtis LeMay and Earle Wheeler. Conducted by the U.S. Joint Chiefs of Staff, the games were designed and umpired by the RAND Corporation. John McCone controlled the blue team, which represented the United States and the Republic of Vietnam. Maxwell D. Taylor headed the red team, which represented the Democratic Republic of Vietnam (DRV) and the Viet Cong, with William H. Sullivan as his deputy.

SIGMA I, played in late fall 1963, resulted in a clear victory for North Vietnam. Despite the deployment of more than 500,000 U.S. troops, the communists controlled most of South Vietnam and Laos. The game indicated that the DRV could rapidly match U.S. deployments by infiltrating increased numbers of troops into the South and that U.S. bombing of the industrially undeveloped, predominantly rural DRV would have little deterrent effect on the North's policymakers. The game also forecast widespread U.S. domestic unrest.

SIGMA II-64 was played in mid-September 1964 to forecast the impact of a U.S. air offensive against the DRV and essentially confirmed the results of SIGMA I. SIGMA II-65, played in August 1965, confirmed the results of the previous games, predicting that communist guerrilla tactics would pose serious difficulties for U.S. forces and that bombing the DRV would have fundamentally little impact. The games had little influence on U.S. policy.

See also: RAND Corporation.

Sihanouk, Norodom (1922–), king of Cambodia, 1941–1955; premier, Cambodia, 1955–1970; Cambodian head of state, 1993. Sihanouk succeeded his great grandfather, King Sisowath Monivong, in 1941. Sihanouk and his people submitted to first Vichy French and then Japanese rule during World War II. When the Japanese overthrew the Vichy regime in Indochina on 10 March 1945, the French informed Sihanouk that his country was independent. Two days later, the prince proclaimed independence himself. When the French returned after the defeat of the Japanese, they attempted to reassert control by using measures designed to lessen Sihanouk's influence. Sihanouk soon realized that only by championing real independence from

France could he maintain his popularity and power.

The 1954 Geneva Conference proclaimed Cambodia's independence and neutrality and called for free elections. Sihanouk then abdicated his throne in favor of his father to form his own political party, which took as its theme loyalty to monarchy, Buddhism, and nation. Immensely popular among the peasantry, Sihanouk strongly championed neutrality and his continued leadership was assured. Only the communists, the intelligentsia, and politicians excluded from power opposed him.

He won a referendum and became prime minister in March 1955. Sihanouk kept Cambodia out of the Vietnam War until 1969, despite North Vietnamese incursions, the Viet Cong's use of the eastern zone as a sanctuary, U.S. bombing raids, and cross-border operations on both sides. After being ousted in a 1970 army coup, Sihanouk lived in exile in Beijing and allied himself with the communist Khmer Rouge guerrillas. After the 1975 Khmer Rouge takeover, he returned to Cambodia and was placed under house arrest. He was released when Vietnam invaded Cambodia in 1978. Sihanouk served briefly as the symbolic head of state in 1993 following U.N.-supervised elections.

See also: Cambodia; Central Intelligence Agency; FANK; Khmer Rouge; Lon Nol; Parrot's Beak; People's Army of Vietnam; Pol Pot.

Sihanouk Trail. *See* People's Army of Vietnam

Sihanoukville. Cambodian port city on the Gulf of Thailand, also known as Kompong Som. During the Vietnam War, North Vietnam supplied its forces in the South through the port of Sihanoukville and the Ho Chi Minh Trail.

See also: Cambodia; Kompong Som; People's Army of Vietnam.

Sijan, Lance J. (1942–1968), U.S. Air Force Captain. Sijan, who died in captivity in a Hanoi prison, received one of the last Medals of Honor of the Vietnam War from President Gerald R. Ford on 1 March 1976. He was the first graduate of the U.S. Air Force Academy to be awarded the Medal of Honor.

See also: Medal of Honor.

"Silent Majority" Speech. Speech delivered by President Richard Nixon on 3 November 1969. The speech came between the large antiwar protests of 15 October and 15 November. In the speech Nixon vowed to continue the Paris peace negotiations and his Vietnamization policy. He called on "the great silent majority" of Americans to support him and attacked antiwar protesters as cowardly, spoiled students and leftist agitators.

See also: Cambodian Incursion; Nixon, Richard M.

Simons, Arthur D. "Bull."
(1928–1979), U.S. Army Special
Forces colonel. In the early 1960s
Colonel Simons commanded the
covert White Star teams that
advised the Royal Lao Army.
Simons also headed the
November 1970 POW-rescue
attempt, known as the Son Tay
Raid.

See also: Son Tay Raid.

Singlaub, John K. (1921–),
U.S. Army general, commander of
the covert Studies and
Observation Group (SOG) in
Vietnam, 1966–1968.

See also: Studies and
Observation Group.

Sisowath Sirik Matak, a
cousin of Cambodian Prince
Norodom Sihanouk and a pro-
western career civil servant.
Sisowath Sirik Matak spearheaded the March 1970 coup
that ousted Sihanouk and
brought Lon Nol to power.

See also: Lon Nol; Sihanouk,
Norodom.

Sklencar, Marge, antiwar
activist. A member of Students
for a Democratic Society (SDS).
Sklencar was one of the four
organizers of the Vietnam
Moratorium Committee set up to
arrange a nationwide strike to
protest U.S. involvement in
Vietnam.

See also: Vietnam Moratorium
Committee.

Smart Bombs. Weapons with
the ability to direct themselves

to a designated target using
laser beams, television cameras,
computers and infrared detec-
tors. Smart bombs were used
beginning in 1967 in Vietnam to
combat the increasing effectiveness of North Vietnamese
antiaircraft defenses. They were
used extensively over North
Vietnam in Operation
Linebacker II in 1972.

See also: Linebacker and
Linebacker II, Operations.

Smith, Robert C. (1941–),
U.S. representative (R-N.H.),
1985–1991; U.S. senator
(R-N.H.), 1991– . Smith, whose
1965–1967 service in the U.S.
Navy included a year in
Vietnam, has been active in the
POW/MIA issue in Congress.

See also: POW/MIA
Controversy.

Smith, Walter Bedell
(1895–1961), U.S. Army general;
director, Central Intelligence
Agency (CIA), 1950–1953;
undersecretary of state,
1953–1954. Smith, who had
favored supporting France in its
Indochina war, headed the U.S.
delegation to the 1954 Geneva
Conference. Despite Secretary of
State John Foster Dulles's
instructions to play a passive
role, Smith worked behind the
scenes to arrange a settlement
preventing all of Vietnam from
coming under communist control.

See also: Dulles, John Foster;
Geneva Conference, 1954.

SNCC. *See* Student Nonviolent
Coordinating Committee

Snepp, Frank W. (1943–), CIA analyst. Snepp worked as a Central Intelligence Agency analyst at the U.S. Embassy in Saigon in 1969–1971 and 1972–1975. His book, *Decent Interval* (1977), reports on the events leading up to the 1975 North Vietnamese victory.

See also: Central Intelligence Agency.

So, Huynh Phu. *See* Huynh Phu So

Socialist Republic of Vietnam (SRV). *See* Vietnam, Democratic Republic of

Societé des Charbonnages du Tonkin. French buisness syndicate that controlled all coal mining operations in Vietnam in the first half of the twentieth century.

See also: France.

SOG. *See* Studies and Observation Group

Soldier Reports, A (1976). Vietnam War memoir by General William Westmoreland, who served as commanding general of U.S. forces there from 1964–1968.

See also: Westmoreland, William C.

Song Be. South Vietnamese capital of Phuoc Long province, about 80 kilometers (50 miles) north of Saigon, near the Cambodian border. Viet Cong forces attacked and overran the city, a U.S. forces outpost, on 11 May 1965, inflicting severe casualties on U.S. advisers and South Vietnamese troops. The Viet Cong forces withdrew after holding the city overnight. Attacked again by Viet Cong and North Vietnamese Army troops on 27 October 1967, Song Be was successfully defended by South Vietnamese troops with U.S. air support.

See also: Special Forces, U.S.

Song Ben Hai. River running directly south of the seventeenth parallel in north central Vietnam, chosen as the border between North and South Vietnam at the 1954 Geneva Conference.

See also: Demilitarized Zone; Seventeenth Parallel.

Son Ngoc Thanh, Cambodian nationalist leader. Son Ngoc Thanh began working against French colonialism in the 1930s. He was jailed and exiled after WWII. He returned to Cambodia in 1951 and continued to work against French rule and the regime of Prince Norodom Sihanouk. After 1955, he commanded the Khmer Serei paramilitary group that worked unsuccessfully to overthrow Sihanouk.

See also: Cambodia; Khmer Serei.

Son Tay Province. Located in northern Vietnam some 40 km northwest of Hanoi, Son Tay is the birth place of former South

Vietnamese leader Nguyen Cao Ky.

See also: Nguyen Cao Ky.

Son Tay Raid. A joint U.S. Army–Air Force raid on 21 November 1970 on the Son Tay prison camp outside Hanoi. The largest and most celebrated U.S. prisoner-of-war (POW) Vietnam War rescue effort, it was known as Operation Kingpin. Air Force Gen. Leroy J. Manor was overall task force commander and Col. Arthur D. "Bull" Simons took charge of the 56 Special Forces volunteers who made the raid. Despite last-minute intelligence reports that the prisoners had been moved, the operation went ahead on the night of 21 November 1970. Most of the assault force crash-landed and no Americans were found in Son Tay. The raiders killed scores of North Vietnamese troops and returned without losing a single man.

See also: POW/MIA Controversy; Simons, Arthur D. "Bull."

Son Thang. Small hamlet some 20 miles south of Danang. On 19 February 1970, a five-man U.S. Marine patrol entered Son Thang and shot to death sixteen women and children. Four Marines were charged with premeditated murder. Two were convicted; two acquitted in what is believed to be the worst Marine Corps incident of its kind in the Vietnam War.

See also: Marines, U.S.

Souphanouvong (1909–1995), leader of Pathet Lao (Lao Nation) communist movement; first president of the Lao People's Democratic Republic (LPDR), 1975–1986. Prince Souphanouvong was the younger half-brother of Lao prime minister Prince Souvanna Phouma. A leader in the post–WWII Lao Issara (Free Laos) independence movement, the prince became disenchanted with the group's political policies and sought assistance from the Viet Minh. Souphanouvong became a close associate of Ho Chi Minh and a leader in the Viet Minh–supported Pathet Lao after WWII. During the Vietnam War Souphanouvong and other Pathet Lao leaders lived in a cave complex in northeastern Laos. Following the U.S. withdrawal from Vietnam, the prince returned to the Lao capital. In December 1975 the communists established the Lao People's Democratic Republic and Souphanouvong became its first president.

See also: Laos; Pathet Lao; Souvanna Phouma.

Southeast Asia Treaty Organization (SEATO). A NATO-like regional defense system organized by U.S. Secretary of State John Foster Dulles following the 1954 Geneva Conference. SEATO, which came into being 19 February 1955, included Australia, New Zealand, Pakistan, the Philippines, and Thailand, in addition to the western powers France, Great

Britain, and the United States. Taiwan was excluded from the treaty because the treaty's definition of Southeast Asia did not include countries north of 21 degrees, 30 minutes north latitude. The neutral countries of India, Burma, and Indonesia refused to join, and because of restrictions imposed by the Geneva accords, Cambodia, Laos, and South Vietnam could not participate.

The treaty established a council to provide for consultation among the signatories but did not include a unified military command. In the treaty's centerpiece, Article IV, the signatories agreed that in the event of "aggression by means of armed attack in the treaty area against any of the Parties or territory which the Parties by unanimous agreement may hereafter designate," they would "act to meet the common danger." They also agreed that "if the inviolability or the integrity of the territory or the sovereignty or political independence of any Party . . . is threatened . . . other than by armed attack," they would "consult immediately . . . for the common defense." A separate protocol specified Cambodia, Laos, and southern Vietnam as areas vital to the security of the signatories.

In 1964, President Johnson cited the SEATO pact as justification for U.S. military intervention to defend an anticommunist state in South Vietnam following the Gulf of Tonkin incident, even though he never consulted with SEATO allies. In 1969, President Richard Nixon, seeking to bring the war and domestic protest under control, initiated his policy of Vietnamization and denied that membership in SEATO guaranteed a commitment of U.S. troops. In the 1970s, differences appeared among the SEATO countries as they questioned the United States' conduct of the war in Vietnam. These divisions undermined SEATO's effectiveness, and the alliance disbanded in 1977.

See also: Congress, U.S.; Dulles, John Foster; Eisenhower, Dwight D.; Geneva Conference, 1954; Gulf of Tonkin Resolution; Philippines; Thailand; Appendix E, "Gulf of Tonkin Resolution."

South Korea. *See* Korea, Republic of

South Vietnam. *See* Vietnam, Republic of

South Vietnamese Army. *See* Army of the Republic of Vietnam

Southern Provincial Administrative Committee (Uy Ban Hanh Chanh Lam Thoi Nam Bo). Organization formed by key Indochinese Communist Party (ICP) leader Tran Van Giau on 25 August 1945 in Saigon. It was dominated by the ICP and the Viet Minh. On 23 September the group fled Saigon and advocated a guerrilla war, marking the beginning of the war against the French in the South.

See also: Indochinese Communist Party.

Souvanna Phouma (1901–1984), prime minister of Laos, 1951–1954, 1956–1958, August through December 1960, 1962–1975. An older half-brother of Prince Souphanouvong, Souvanna Phouma was head of the wartime Pathet Lao (Lao Nation) communist movement. A proclaimed neutralist for most of his life, Souvanna was often called upon to head the politically fractured government of Laos. His willingness in the 1950s to allow participation in the central government by members of the Pathet Lao led to charges by right-wing Lao officials and the U.S. government that Laos would be taken over by communist agents. After 1962, Souvanna, under pressure from the Lao right wing and the U.S. government, abandoned the Pathet Lao in a coalition government. From 1963 until the 1973 American withdrawal from South Vietnam, Souvanna's government publicly declared a neutral policy with regard to the Vietnam War. In reality the prime minister allowed the United States to conduct bombing and reconnaissance campaigns against communist supply routes in Laos and supported U.S. efforts to use Lao hill tribes in ground and air operations against Pathet Lao and North Vietnamese forces in Laos. Upon the December 1975 communist takeover of Laos,

Souvanna was named special adviser to the president of the Lao People's Democratic Republic.

See also: Geneva Conference, 1961–1962; Hmong; Kong Le; Laos; Pathet Lao; Souphanouvong.

Soviet Union. *See* Union of Soviet Socialist Republics

Special Discharge Review Program. Program begun in 1977 by the Carter administration in which former Vietnam-era military personnel were offered case-by-case reviews of their less-than-honorable discharges and the possibility of discharge upgrades.

See also: Amnesty; Carter, Jimmy.

Special Election Committee. Panel set up by the South Vietnamese National Assembly to investigate irregularities in the 1967 elections in which Nguyen Van Thieu was overwhelmingly elected president. The committee found that 5,105 polling stations experienced procedural and voting violations.

See also: Nguyen Van Thieu.

Special Forces, ARVN. A group of Nung tribal mercenaries, Vietnamese previously trained by French intelligence authorities, defectors from North Vietnam, and volunteers from Ngo Dinh Diem's security guards became the nucleus of the 1st Observation Group (1st O.G.) in February 1956. Funded by the U.S. Military Assistance Program (MAP) and organized by the Central Intelligence Agency (CIA), the 1st O.G.'s primary mission was to reduce North Vietnam's capacity to subvert the South Vietnamese government. Accordingly, some 300 men (20 15-man teams) began training supervised by U.S. Army Special Forces (USASF) and U.S. Ranger advisers at 1st O.G.'s Nha Trang headquarters.

During the next seven years insertion teams of the 77th Group (1st O.G.'s later designation) and a companion unit, the 31st Group, carried out kidnappings, assassinations, intelligence gathering, and sabotage inside Cambodia, Laos, and North Vietnam, usually accompanied by U.S. personnel. Operations inside North Vietnam were generally unsuccessful, and the exact number of personnel lost, killed, or captured north of the 17th Parallel remains obscure. Success rates in Cambodia and Laos were higher.

As Viet Cong activities increased in South Vietnam after 1960, the role of the 77th and 31st groups was altered. From 1960–1963 the special forces spent most of their time performing covert duties within South Vietnam against the National Liberation Front (NLF) and against noncommunist groups to protect the Diem government. On 15 March 1963, the group was renamed the *Luc Luong Dac Biet* (LLDB, South Vietnamese Special Forces). It was accountable only to Diem and his brother Ngo Dinh Nhu. The LLDB, in conjunction with South Vietnam's Central Intelligence Organization (CIO, founded in May 1961 with a staff of 1,400), monitored the activities of the Can Lao Nhan Vi Cach Mang Dang (Revolutionary Personalist Labor Party) and its members. Created by Diem and Nhu in 1954, the Can Lao offered political careers and business connections to Ngo family loyalists, who were carefully investigated before selection. The LLDB's close association with the CIO, secret police, Can Lao, and Cong Hoa Youth made its members a target after the November 1963 coup that resulted in Diem's and Nhu's deaths.

On 1 April 1964 the LLDB was attached to the Army of the Republic of Vietnam's (ARVN) Ranger and Reconnaissance Command as an independent unit. LLDB soldiers participated in many projects, some highly classified, including the Phoenix program, the Civilian Irregular Defense Group network, and covert missions initiated by the Military Assistance Command, Vietnam–Studies and Observations Group. By 1975, all large-scale covert operations by the LLDB ceased.

See also: Civilian Irregular Defense Groups.

Special Forces, South Vietnamese. Set up by Ngo Dinh Nhu in 1960, the 2,000-man

Special Forces military unit was, in essence, a private army for Nhu and his brother, Ngo Dinh Diem. The group took part in the infamous 1963 raids on Buddhist pagodas. Following the November 1963 overthrow of the Diem regime, the Special Forces became a non-political unit in the South Vietnamese Army (ARVN).

See also: Ngo Dinh Diem; Ngo Dinh Nhu; Special Forces, ARVN.

Special Forces, U.S. Army.

Known as the Green Berets, the U.S. Army Special Forces were organized in 1952 to wage guerrilla war and organize resistance behind enemy lines. In the early 1960s, President Kennedy made the Special Forces the centerpiece of his counterinsurgency strategy for combating wars of national liberation in developing countries. Kennedy expanded the Special Forces from 2,500 to 10,000 members and emphasized counterguerilla tactics in their training. At the Special Warfare Center in Ft. Bragg, North Carolina, the Green Berets learned how to beat guerrillas at their own game of unconventional warfare by combining civic action with political subversion and psychological operations.

Their first counterinsurgency mission came in Operation White Star, in which Green Berets trained local militias to resist the communist Pathet Lao in Laos in 1962. Most of the Green Berets who served in Vietnam belonged to the 5th Special Forces Group. Members of the 1st and 7th Special Forces Groups also served. Some were assigned to the U.S. Military Assistance Command's Studies and Observation Group for top-secret intelligence operations, and many helped train the South Vietnamese special forces of *Luc Luong Dac Biet* (LLDB).

Most Green Berets fought a lonely and perilous war from desolate hilltops accessible only by helicopter. They took over a Central Intelligence Agency (CIA) operation that organized Civilian Irregular Defense Groups (CIDGs) among the Montagnard tribesmen of the Central Highlands beginning in 1963. After 1965, mixed teams of Green Berets and LLDB conducted long-range reconnaissance missions into Laos and directed air strikes against the Ho Chi Minh Trail. Seventeen Green Berets were awarded Medals of Honor and 88 received Distinguished Service Crosses in the Vietnam War.

See also: Army, U.S.; Central Highlands; Central Intelligence Agency; Civilian Irregular Defense Groups; Daniel Boone, Operations; Dong Xoai; Kennedy, John F.; Khe Sanh; Montagnards; Son Tay Raid; Special Forces, ARVN; Thailand.

Special Training and Enlistment Program (STEP).

Proposed experimental U.S. Army program, backed by Secretary of Defense Robert S. McNamara, designed to provide special remedial programs to 60,000 inductees with low aptitude scores from 1964–1967. Congress refused to fund the program and it was not implemented. A similar program, Project 100,000, was put into place in 1966.

See also: Project 100,000.

Spellman, Francis Joseph (1889–1967), Roman Catholic archbishop of New York (1939–1967). Cardinal Spellman was an active, influential promoter of the Ngo Dinh Diem regime in South Vietnam. In keeping with the Catholic Church's view of communism as evil and the opinion of some American Catholics that the Cold War was a moral crusade, Spellman consistently supported U.S. military intervention in Vietnam.

See also: Catholics; Ngo Dinh Diem.

Spock, Benjamin M. (1903–1998), author; pediatrician. Dr. Spock's reputation as America's preeminent child care authority earned him a leading role in U.S. domestic opposition to the Vietnam War. He first became known as a peace activist when he joined the National Committee for Sane Nuclear Policy in 1962. As the United States became involved in the Vietnam War, Spock, an active speaker and participant in many protests, tried to unite moderate and radical antiwar groups. He published an antiwar treatise, *Dr. Spock on Vietnam,* in 1968. In January 1968, he was indicted for conspiring to aid and encourage resistance to the draft. He was convicted, but the verdict was overturned on appeal and the charges were eventually dropped.

See also: Clark, Ramsey; Coffin, William Sloane; New Mobe.

Spring Mobilization (Committee) to End the War in Vietnam. A coalition group composed of academics, students, and Old and New Left organizations set up in November 1966 to plan large antiwar demonstrations in New York City and San Francisco. Rev. James Bevell of the Southern Christian Leadership Conference was its director. The group's mass marches held in those cities on 15 April 1967 events were the largest antiwar demonstrations to date.

See also: Bevell, James, Rev.

Spring Offensive. *See* Ho Chi Minh Campaign

Squad. Basic U.S. Army and Marine fighting unit, consisting of eight to ten men divided into two fire teams, commanded by a sergeant.

Squadron. U.S. military designation for an Army battalion-sized cavalry unit or Air Force, Navy or Marine flights of aircraft under the same command.

Stanton, Shelby (1948–), author. Stanton served in Vietnam, Laos, and Thailand with the U.S. Army Special Forces and with the 82nd Airborne Division. He is the author of several well-regarded military histories of the Vietnam War, including *The Rise and Fall of an American Army: U.S. Ground Forces in Vietnam, 1965–1973* (1985).

Starlite, Operation. Code name for August 1965 U.S. Marine operation that defeated the 1st Viet Cong Regiment on the Van Tuong Peninsula just southeast of Chu Lai with ground fire, air strikes and naval gunfire.

See also: Amphibious Landing Operations.

Starlite Scope. Sighting device used by U.S. military in Vietnam that magnified moon and star light enabling night weapons sighting.

State, Department of. U.S. State Department officials often offered advice on the proper course of action for the United States to follow during the Vietnam War. However, the State Department was not the dominant voice in decision making, especially during the period of escalation in the middle 1960s and the negotiations arranging a cease-fire in the early 1970s.

At the end of WWII the War Department persuaded President Harry S. Truman not to follow the advice of Assistant Secretary of State Abbott Low Moffat, who recommended a U.S. overture to Ho Chi Minh. In the late 1940s Foreign Service officers in Southeast Asia recommended that the U.S. government distance itself from France and pursue better relations with Ho. Secretary of State Dean Acheson and other high State Department officials concerned with European affairs overruled them. These higher officials persuaded Truman that maintaining good relations with France at a time of Cold War competition with the Soviet Union took precedence over establishing cordial relations with the Democratic Republic of Vietnam (DRV). Secretary of State John Foster Dulles played a more significant role in supporting the South Vietnamese government of Ngo Dinh Diem.

During the Kennedy administration, Secretary of Defense Robert McNamara overshadowed Secretary of State Dean Rusk in setting policy toward Vietnam. In Saigon, generals Paul Harkins, William Westmoreland, and Creighton Abrams often had more influence than did the U.S. ambassadors. In late spring 1963, the Kennedy administration appointed Henry Cabot Lodge, a prominent Republican, U.S. ambassador to South Vietnam. Lodge's appointment augmented the State Department's influence. In late summer and fall of 1963, Lodge, working with the local CIA chief and staff members of the national security council, helped dissident South Vietnamese generals in two plots to overthrow the Nhu family.

Rusk's State Department became more important in the administration of President Lyndon B. Johnson. From late 1963 until early 1966 both Secretary of State Rusk and Secretary of Defense McNamara agreed that the United States should escalate the war. During these years Rusk saw little room for diplomatic initiatives to end the war, and he did not visit South Vietnam. Johnson, in opposition to Rusk's views, announced on 31 March 1968 that he was stopping the bombing above the nineteenth parallel and opening negotiations with North Vietnam. The influence of the State Department fell to its lowest level during the administration of Richard Nixon.

Department officials David Bruce and Philip Habib conducted the formal talks with North Vietnamese representatives in Paris. Henry Kissinger, the president's national security adviser, undertook the real negotiations that led to the Paris accords of 1973.

See also: Acheson, Dean; Agency for International Development; Dulles, John Foster; Hilsman, Roger; Kissinger, Henry; Rogers, William P.; Rolling Thunder, Operation; Rostow, Walt Whitman; Rusk, (David) Dean; U.S. Information Agency.

Staubach, Roger (1942–), former professional football player. Staubach, a 1965 graduate of the U.S. Naval Academy, served a one-year tour of duty in Vietnam

as a freight terminal officer in Chu Lai. He joined the National Football League Dallas Cowboys in January 1969 after his Navy discharge.

Steel Tiger, Operation. Code name for U.S. air operations beginning in April 1965 over the Ho Chi Minh Trail.

See also: Ho Chi Minh Trail.

Steinbeck, John IV
(1946–1991), U.S. Army broadcast specialist in Vietnam, 1966–1967. The son of the noted novelist, John Steinbeck IV was drafted into the U.S. Army, and served with Armed Forces Radio and Television in Saigon, Qui Nhon and Pleiku. He was best known for his reports on drug use among U.S. troops, the subject of his memoir, *In Touch* (1970).

See also: Drug Trafficking; Drug Use, U.S. Military.

Stevenson, Adlai E. III
(1900–1965), U.S. ambassador to the United Nations, 1961–1965. In 1964 Stevenson discussed with U.N. Secretary General U Thant the prospects for secret U.S.–North Vietnam negotiations. Stevenson passed the information on to Secretary of State Dean Rusk, but the administration did not respond. Although he believed that military intervention should be a last resort, Stevenson consistently defended U.S. policy in Vietnam.

See also: United Nations.

Stennis, John C. (1901–1995), U.S. senator (D-Miss.), 1947–1989; chairman, Senate Armed Service Committee, 1969–1989. Stennis, a conservative Democrat, was one of Capitol Hill's strongest supporters of an all-out military effort in Vietnam.

Sticks and Bones (1972). Award-winning play by David Rabe dealing with an emotionally damaged Vietnam veteran and his family. The second of Rabe's Vietnam trilogy.

See also: Rabe, David.

Stilwell, Richard G. (1917–1991), lieutenant general, U.S. Army; chief of staff, U.S. Military Assistance Command, Vietnam (MACV), 1964–1965. General Stilwell was a respected military intellectual with years of service with the Central Intelligence Agency (CIA) when he went to Saigon in 1963. Gen. Paul Harkins made Stilwell chief of operations in 1963 and promoted him to chief of staff a year later. Stilwell went on to command the XXIV Army Corps in the I Corps Tactical Zone in northern South Vietnam and United Nations forces in Korea before retiring in 1976.

Stockdale, James B. (1923–), vice admiral, U.S. Navy. A wing commander aboard the USS *Oriskany,* Stockdale was shot down on his two-hundredth mission over North Vietnam on 9 September 1965. Hanoi tried to turn Stockdale into a propaganda tool as the highest-ranking prisoner of war (POW), but he defied his captors despite nearly eight years of torture and solitary confinement. Using messages tapped out on prison walls, Stockdale encouraged other POWs to resist. His wife Sybil Stockdale founded the League of Wives of American Vietnam POWs. Promoted after his release in 1973, Stockdale received the Medal of Honor in 1976. He ran for the vice presidency with independent presidential candidate H. Ross Perot in 1992.

See also: Medal of Honor; Perot, H. Ross.

Stockdale, Sybil (1924–), wife of U.S. POW James B. Stockdale, founder of League of Wives of American Vietnam POWs and of the National League of Families of American Prisoners and Missing in Southeast Asia.

See also: POW/MIA Controversy; Stockdale, James B.

Stone, Oliver (1946–), director, screenwriter. Stone wrote and directed three critically acclaimed and controversial Vietnam-War films: *Platoon* (1986), *Born on the Fourth of July* (1989), and *Heaven and Earth* (1994). He served as an infantryman with the U.S. Army's 25th Infantry Division in Vietnam in 1967–1968.

See also: Born on the Fourth of July; *Platoon.*

Stone, Robert (1937–), novelist. Stone's novels, *Dog Soldiers*
(1974), the winner of the
National Book Award for fiction,
and *Outerbridge Reach* (1992) feature characters who are Vietnam
veterans dealing with the emotional aftermath of the war.

See also: Dog Soldiers.

Stop the Draft Week. October
and December 1967 event organized by a group of professors,
authors, clergy and others calling
for resistance to the Vietnam
War and the military draft.
Hundreds of draft cards were
turned in around the country
during the Stop the Draft Week
that began 16 October, which
included a violent confrontation
between police and demonstrators in Oakland, California. A
second Stop the Draft Week took
place during the week of 4–8
December in New York City during which police arrested
hundreds of demonstrators.

See also: Selective Service.

Stout, Mary R. (1944–), former
U.S. Army nurse, veterans advocate. Stout served as a U.S. Army
Nurse Corps lieutenant at the
Second Surgical Hospital in
An Khe and Chu Lai in South
Vietnam in 1966–1967. In 1987
she became the first woman to
head a national U.S. veterans
organization when she was
elected president of Vietnam
Veterans of America. She served
in that capacity until 1991.

See also: Vietnam Veterans of
America.

**Strategic Air Command
(SAC).** U.S. Air Force command
that includes B-52 strategic
bombers that oversaw the
1965–1973 B-52 bombing in the
Vietnam War.

See also: Air Force, U.S.; Arc
Light, Operation; B-52; Menu,
Operation.

**Strategic Arms Limitation
Talks (SALT).** Beginning in
April 1969 President Richard M.
Nixon and his national security
adviser, Henry Kissinger, linked
U.S.-USSR nuclear arms reduc-
tion negotiations to Soviet
cooperation in pushing the
Democratic Republic of Vietnam
for a peace settlement. Nixon
and Soviet leader Leonid
Brezhnev signed the SALT I
agreement on 26 May 1972 in
Moscow.

See also: Brezhnev, Leonid;
Détente; Kissinger, Henry;
Nixon, Richard M.

Strategic Hamlet Program.
Begun in Vietnam in 1962, this
program relocated Vietnamese
villagers into stockaded hamlets
for their better protection, and
was intended to force the North
Vietnamese and Viet Cong to
fight in the open.

See also: Agroville Program;
Free-Fire Zones; Pacification;
Refugees; Rules of Engagement;
Thompson, Robert G. K.

Stratton, Richard A. (1931–),
U.S. Navy pilot shot down over
North Vietnam in January 1967.
As a POW in Hanoi, Stratton

helped publicize systematic torture of U.S. prisoners. He was released on 4 March 1973.

Street Without Joy (*Rue Sans Joie*).

Name given by French troops to a section of Highway 1 between Quang Tri and Tan My, the site of many Viet Minh ambushes during the 1946–1954 French war.

See also: Franco–Viet Minh War.

Struggle Movement.

Term for a series of nationwide protests in South Vietnam led by Buddhist monks and students in 1966 against the governments of Nguyen Cao Ky and Nguyen Van Thieu. Large demmonstrations were held in Hue and Da Nang, in which Struggle Movement supporters called for the resignations of Ky and Thieu, a return to civilian rule and less dependence on the United States. South Vietnamese troops attacked Struggle Movement supporters in May in Da Nang, and ended the resistance in June by seizing control of the Buddhist Institute in Saigon.

See also: Buddhists; Da Nang; Nguyen Cao Ky; Nguyen Chanh Thi.

Student Nonviolent Coordinating Committee (SNCC).

Umbrella radical civil rights group formed in April 1960 comprised mostly of college students who challenged U.S. policy in Vietnam as racist oppression of nonwhite peoples.

See also: African-Americans; Carmichael, Stokely.

Students for a Democratic Society (SDS).

Activist organization founded in 1960 by a group of University of Michigan students concerned with racism, poverty, and social justice. In 1962 Tom Hayden and other SDS leaders issued the Port Huron Statement, outlining their views. SDS sponsored the first anti–Vietnam War march on Washington on 17 April 1965. By that time there were SDS chapters across the country, most on college campuses. At the annual SDS convention delegates debated whether the SDS should focus exclusively on the Vietnam War on a national level or whether local chapters should work independently toward social justice. The majority favored local community organization, a decision that prevented SDS from becoming the leading national voice for youth against the war.

Still, local SDS groups organized against the war, protesting campus visits by administration officials and military research at universities. By 1968 many SDS members became more militant and adopted radical Marxist doctrine. The group fragmented and some broke off to form the terrorist group known as the Weathermen. Although the SDS sponsored another march on Washington in 1969, a year later the split within the movement marked the end of its national profile.

See also: Chicago Seven; Federal Bureau of Investigation; Mayday Tribe; New Left; Teach-Ins; Weathermen.

Studies and Observation Group (SOG). Joint U.S.–South Vietnamese covert group set up in January 1964 by the U.S. Military Assistance Command, Vietnam (MACV). SOG units conducted cross-border missions to disrupt enemy activities, locate downed U.S. pilots, train agents and conduct psychological operations in Laos, Cambodia and North Vietnam. SOG teams were made up of U.S. Army Special Forces, Navy SEALs, Air Force Special Warfare Units, South Vietnamese Special Forces, and Montagnard volunteers.

See also: SEALs; Special Forces, U.S. Army.

Submarines. U.S. submarines, including the USS *Perch,* USS *Tunny* and the USS *Grayback,* transported, launched, and recovered U.S. Navy SEALs, under-water demolition teams, and South Vietnamese marines in covert operations off the coast of Vietnam from 1965–1972.

See also: Navy, U.S.

Sullivan, William H. (1922–), U.S. ambassador to Laos; Foreign Service officer. A career diplomat, Sullivan served as deputy U.S. representative to the 1962 Geneva Conference. In 1964, President Lyndon B. Johnson appointed Sullivan ambassador to Laos. In that position he directed the secret U.S. bombing campaign in Laos. At the Vietnam peace talks in 1972, Sullivan was Henry Kissinger's chief deputy.

See also: Laos; SIGMA.

Sully, François (1927–1971), French journalist. Sully covered the Franco–Vietminh War for *Time* magazine. While serving as Southeast Asia correspondent for *Newsweek* during the American war he was killed in a helicopter crash on 23 February 1971.

Summers, Harry G. Jr. (1932–), retired U.S. Army colonel; instructor, U.S. Army War College; syndicated columnist; editor, *Vietnam* magazine. A leading analyst of the Vietnam War, Summers served two tours of duty in Vietnam, including service with the Four-Party Joint Military Team. In *On Strategy* (1982), Summers criticized the U.S. war of attrition strategy in Vietnam. He argued that the South Vietnamese army should have countered the Viet Cong political insurgency and that the United States should have concentrated on fighting a conventional war against North Vietnam. Summers also criticized the Johnson administration for its failure to summon public support for intervention.

See also: Rules of Engagement.

Sunflower, Operation. Codename for abortive 1967 British diplomatic effort to encourage the Soviet Union to pressure the Democratic Republic of Vietnam to negotiate with the United States.

See also: Cooper, Chester; Wilson, (James) Harold.

Supreme Court, U.S. The nation's highest tribunal dealt with the Vietnam War mainly through cases involving First Amendment rights. The Court also dealt with draft resistance, conscientious objection, and broad governmental claims to national security. The justices consistently refused to decide whether the war, never officially declared, was constitutional. From 1967 to 1974, the Court disapproved of government efforts to punish dissent, limit protest, or, as in the Pentagon Papers case, prevent newspaper publication of embarrassing historical disclosures of the war's origins.

In *Bond v. Floyd* (385 U.S. 116 [1966]), the Court invalidated the Georgia state legislature's refusal to seat a newly elected representative, Julian Bond, because of his antiwar statements. In *Tinker v. Des Moines Independent Community School District* (393 U.S. 503 [1969]) the Court held that school administrators could not infringe on the First Amendment right to symbolic expression, such as when schoolchildren wore black armbands to bear silent witness for peace. Similarly, the Court upheld the rights of an antiwar group in Baltimore against Maryland's public disturbance

law (*Bachellar v. Maryland*, 397 U.S. 564 [1970]), and defended antiwar sentiment, even when expressed in language offensive to many, including the justices themselves *(Cohen v. California*, 403 U.S. 15 [1971]).

When the Nixon administration tried to prevent the *New York Times* and the *Washington Post* from publishing excerpts from the Pentagon Papers, the Defense Department's classified history of the war, the Court rejected on First Amendment grounds the government's national security plea for prior restraint (government authority to prohibit or restrict publication) in *New York Times Co. v. United States* (403 U.S. 713 [1971]).

Similarly, the Court rejected the Nixon administration's national security claims in *United States v. United States District Court for the Eastern District of Michigan* (407 U.S. 297 [1972]). The government argued that the president had "inherent powers" for wiretapping antiwar activities because he needed to defend the nation against "the attempts of domestic organizations to attack and subvert the existing structure of Government." The Court disagreed, holding that that duty was circumscribed in "a manner compatible" with the Constitution.

From 1968 to 1974, the Supreme Court heard several draft resistance cases, and held that the First Amendment did not protect all forms of antiwar expression. In *United States v.*

O'Brien (391 U.S. 367[1968]), Chief Justice Earl Warren declared the government's interest in raising and supporting armies compelling enough to incidentally limit First Amendment freedoms, in this case, the asserted symbolic act of burning a draft card. Justice Thurgood Marshall also did not support draft resistance if it was brazen and openly contemptuous of the procedures regulated by the Selective Service System (*McGee v. United States*, 402 U.S. 479 [1971]). But the Court protected those whom the Selective Service System tried to punish with punitive reclassifications, finding the First Amendment broad enough to defend young men against reprisals for expressing their antiwar defiance (*Gutknecht v. United States*, 396 U.S. 295 [1970]). Still, more often than not the Court refused to interfere judicially with the draft process, specifically in cases where young men sought to challenge their induction through the courts (*Fein v. Selective Service System Local Board No. 7*, 405 U.S. 365 [1972]).

For the Supreme Court, the Vietnam War was best dealt with indirectly, and it sidestepped the war's essential constitutional problem: its undeclared nature. The Supreme Court generally refused to hear constitutional challenges to the war, deferring to the political questions doctrine, which states that questions that involve politics are best left to the political branches of government (the executive and the legislative), and denying these cases the writ of certiorari (an order from a higher court instructing a lower court to forward the record of a case for review). While the war's constitutionality was avoided, the justices found themselves personally embroiled with the war. Justice Abe Fortas operated as a personal adviser to President Johnson. The bombing of Cambodia in 1973 ruffled judicial relations when the justices breached decorum and courtesy in overturning one another's decisions regarding a lower federal court's injunction to halt that bombing (order stayed, *Schlesinger v. Holtzman*, 414 U.S. 1321 [1973], *cert. denied*, 416 U.S. 936 [1973]).

See also: Ali, Muhammad; Conscientious Objectors; Goldberg, Arthur J.; Justice, Department of; Pentagon Papers; War Powers Resolution.

Surface-to-Air Missiles (SAMs).

The SA-2 Guideline, a Soviet-made surface-to-air missile (SAM), appeared in the skies above North Vietnam in 1965. A two stage, supersonic radar-guided missile measuring 10.6 meters (35 feet) long, the SA-2 carried a 130-kilogram (285 pound) warhead and was effective up to 26,000 meters (85,000 feet). North Vietnam fired some 6,000 SAMs before the bombing halt in 1968. When the bombing of North Vietnam resumed in 1972, the United States minimized losses with electronic counter-measures (ECMs) and

"Wild Weasel" aircraft equipped with radar-homing missiles capable of destroying SAM sites on the ground. Nevertheless, SAMs took a heavy toll on B-52 bombers during Operation Linebacker II. After 1972, a new Soviet-made portable SAM, the shoulder-fired, heat-seeking SA-7 Strella (Grail), inflicted heavy losses on low-flying strike aircraft and helicopters.

See also: Air Force, U.S.; Antiaircraft Defenses; Arc Light, Operation; Electronic Countermeasures; F-111; Linebacker and Linebacker II, Operations; People's Army of Vietnam; Rolling Thunder, Operation; Union of Soviet Socialist Republics.

Switchback, Operation. Code name for the 1964 takeover of responsibility of U.S. programs in Vietnam from the Military Assistance Advisory Group Vietnam (MAAG-V) to the Military to the Military Assistance Command, Vietnam (MACV).

See also: Military Assistance Advisory Group–Vietnam; Military Assistance Command, Vietnam.

Tactical Air Command (TAC).
U.S. Air Force command that
manages fighters and fighter-
bombers in support of ground
combat. In the Vietnam War, the
U.S. Air Force TAC included
transportation, supply, fighter
and reconnaissance divisions
based in Vietnam, the
Philippines and Japan.

See also: Momyer, William W.

Taiwan. *See* China, Republic of

Tanks. The U.S. Army and
Marines and the South
Vietnamese Army (Army of the
Republic of Vietnam) made
extensive use of armored vehicles (tanks and armored
personnel carriers) in the
Vietnam War. The North
Vietnamese Army, beginning in
1968, employed T-34, T-54, and
T-59 Soviet-made medium tanks.
The main tank used by U.S. and
ARVN was the diesel-powered
M-48A3 Patton. Also widely used
was the M-42 Duster tank. The
mostly extensively used U.S.
armored vehicle was the M-113
armored personnel carrier. More
than 40,000 M-113s were
deployed in Vietnam.

Tan Son Nhut. Located on the
outskirts of Saigon, Tan Son
Nhut air base was headquarters

of the South Vietnamese Air
Force. Throughout the Vietnam
War, the base handled most of
South Vietnam's commercial and
military air traffic. After 1962, it
served as headquarters for the
U.S. 2d Air Division, which
directed U.S. air operations in
the country. After 1967, Tan Son
Nhut was headquarters of the
Military Assistance Command,
Vietnam (MACV). Prior to the
North Vietnamese takeover of
South Vietnam, MACV head-
quarters was destroyed by the
departing troops on 29 April
1975. The airport today serves
Ho Chi Minh City, formerly
Saigon.

See also: Ho Chi Minh
Campaign; Joint General Staff;
Military Assistance Command,
Vietnam; Search and Rescue
Vietnam.

Taoism. A Chinese-influenced
religion widely practiced in
Vietnam based on spirit worship
and harmony with nature.

Tarr, Curtis (1924–), director,
U.S. Selective Service system,
1970–1972. Tarr introduced
many reforms into the Selective
Service system, including a random lottery.

See also: Selective Service.

Task Force 77. Code name for
the U.S. Navy Seventh Fleet aircraft carriers, destroyers,
cruisers and other vessels operating from Yankee Station and
Dixie Station in the Gulf of
Tonkin and South China Sea.

See also: Aircraft Carriers;
Dixie Station; Navy, U.S.;
Seventh Fleet; Yankee Station.

Task Force 116. Also known as Operation Game Warden and the Riverine Assault Force, Task Force 116 was the code name for U.S. Navy brown-water program begun in December 1965 that sought to interdict the Viet Cong guerrillas' use of intercoastal and interior waterways, especially in the Mekong Delta.

See also: Game Warden, Operation; Navy, U.S.; SEALs.

Task Force 117. Joint U.S. Army-Navy Mobile Riverine Force deployed in early 1967 in the Mekong Delta. The force consisted of two brigades of the U.S. Army 9th Infantry Division operating with U.S. Navy river assault squadrons in the upper Mekong Delta. MACV abolished this force in August 1969.

See also: Amphibious Landing Operations; Mobile Riverine Force.

Task Force on Manpower Conservation. Effort in 1963 to examine the U.S. military's experience with special training units for illiterates.

See also: Project 100,000.

Taxi Driver (1976). Critically acclaimed Martin Scorcese film centering on the title character, a violent, maladjusted Vietnam veteran.

Taylor, Maxwell D.
(1901–1987), U.S. Army general; U.S. Army chief of staff, 1955–1959; chairman, Joint Chiefs of Staff (JCS), 1962–1964;

ambassador to South Vietnam, 1964–1965. Gen. Maxwell Taylor capped a brilliant military career in WWII and Korea by publishing *The Uncertain Trumpet* (1959) upon his retirement. The book cautioned against excessive reliance on nuclear weapons and argued for a limited-war capability that would give U.S. leaders more options for responding to communist aggression.

President Kennedy adopted Taylor's "flexible response" doctrine and named him special military representative. In October 1961, Kennedy sent Taylor, his special military representative, and White House aide Walt Rostow to South Vietnam to assess the military situation. The Taylor-Rostow report downplayed the risks of U.S. intervention and led to Kennedy's commitment of the first U.S. ground troops. Kennedy then brought Taylor back into military service by appointing him chairman of the JCS in 1962.

A leading exponent of counterinsurgency warfare, Taylor believed that the United States had to prevent a communist takeover of South Vietnam. Kennedy sent Taylor to South Vietnam on another fact-finding mission with Secretary of Defense Robert McNamara in September 1963. The Taylor-McNamara report stressed "great progress" in the war, but recommended support for "alternative leadership" in Saigon. President Diem was overthrown a few weeks later.

In 1964, President Johnson sent Taylor to Saigon as U.S. ambassador. While there, Taylor advocated bombing North Vietnam, rather than committing U.S. combat troops. After resigning as ambassador, Taylor became a special White House consultant. He called for more troops and escalated bombing of North Vietnam. Taylor was prominent among the "wise men" who advised Johnson on the war, but he dissented from their recommendation that the United States disengage from Vietnam in 1968.

See also: Domino Theory; Enclave Strategy; Johnson, Lyndon B.; Nguyen Cao Ky; Nguyen Khanh; Nguyen Van Thieu; Rostow, Walt Whitman; SIGMA; Taylor-McNamara Report; Taylor-Rostow Report; Wise Men.

Taylor-McNamara Report.
October 1963 report by Gen. Maxwell Taylor, chairman of the Joint Chiefs of Staff (JCS), and Secretary of Defense Robert McNamara following their 10-day fact-finding mission to South Vietnam. The report found "great progress" in the war against the Viet Cong guerrillas, but cautioned that South Vietnamese President Diem faced a "crisis of confidence." It recommended that the United States encourage "alternative leadership" while pressuring Diem to make his regime more democratic and more effective in fighting the Viet Cong. President Kennedy approved the recommendations.

Diem was overthrown a few weeks later.

See also: Strategic Hamlet Program; McNamara, Robert; Ngo Dinh Diem; Taylor, Maxwell D.

Taylor-Rostow Report.
November 1961 report by presidential aides Maxwell Taylor and Walt Rostow following their fact-finding mission to South Vietnam. The report portrayed the Viet Cong insurgency as part of a global communist threat. The report favored a "hard U.S. commitment on the ground" to shore up the regime of South Vietnam's Ngo Dinh Diem. President Kennedy made the first sizeable commitment of U.S. military advisers in accordance with the Taylor-Rostow recommendations, increasing the number from 600 to 15,000 within one year.

See also: Ball, George W.; Bowles, Chester; McNamara, Robert; Rostow, Walt W.; Taylor, Maxwell D.

Tay Son Rebellion.
Vietnamese peasant uprising begun in 1771 led by three Tay Son brothers against the Nguyen Dynasty. The rebellion succeeded in 1788, ushering in Tay Son rule of Vietnam, which lasted until 1802 when Emperor Gia Long restored Nguyen dynasty rule of the country.

See also: Gia Long.

Tchepone. Town in Laos, a logistical center on the Ho Chi

Minh Trail approximately 40 kilometers (25 miles) from the border with South Vietnam. Tchepone was the objective of the 1971 Army of the Republic of Vietnam's Operation Lam Son 719 raid on the Ho Chi Minh Trail.

See also: Ho Chi Minh Trail; Lam Son 719.

Teach-Ins. The first teach-in took place at the University of Michigan on 24 March 1965. A group of faculty members who opposed increasing U.S. involvement in Vietnam organized the session in response to Lyndon Johnson's ordering of three thousand Marines into Da Nang, the first deployment of U.S. combat troops. The professors debated the war with three thousand students who attended the all-night session. The forum sought to educate people about the conflict rather than to recruit protesters into the antiwar movement, although the process did turn many students against the policies of the Johnson administration.

In May 1965 the State Department launched a "truth team" to visit campuses in the Midwest and counter the teach-ins, but the government officials received hostile responses and had little success. On 15 May 1965, a special radio link connected 122 campuses nationwide for a national teach-in, and participants included both pro- and antiwar speakers. This phenomenon was extended to the military through the "Free the Army"

campaign, led by Tom Hayden (one of the founders of Students for a Democratic Society [SDS]) and Jane Fonda, which modified the teach-in format, using less formal meetings and holding them at sites near military installations so they could more easily include soldiers. Teach-ins continued to be held at various locations until Saigon was taken by the North Vietnamese in 1975.

See also: American Friends of Vietnam.

Teamsters Union. Members of the Teamsters labor union took part in so-called hard hat counter-demonstrations in the early 1970s during Vietnam War protests, sometimes clashing violently with opponents of the war.

See also: Hardhats.

Teheran Conference. December 1943 conference among WWII allied leaders in which U.S. President Franklin D. Roosevelt spoke out strongly against helping France regain its Indochinese colonies.

See also: Roosevelt, Franklin D.; Yalta Conference.

Television. The American war in Vietnam was the first U.S. conflict to be shown extensively on U.S. television news broadcasts. After the war, U.S. television aired many documentaries on the war, including PBS's 13-part *Vietnam: A Television History* (1983) and Home Box Office's *Dear America:*

Letters Home from Vietnam (1987). There also were many made-for-television movies using the Vietnam War as a theme, such as ABC-TV's *Friendly Fire* (1979), *A Rumor of War* (1980), and HBO's *Vietnam War Stories* series (1898–1990). Two prime-time TV series were set in Vietnam during the war: CBS-TV's *Tour of Duty* (1987–1990), and ABC-TV's *China Beach* (1988–1991).

In the 1970s several police and action-adventure shows, including *Hawaii Five-O, Kojak,* and *The Streets of San Francisco,* regularly featured deranged, violent Vietnam veterans intent on bringing the war back home. In the 1980s, television drama series such as *The A-Team, Simon and Simon, Miami Vice,* and *Magnum PI* featured Vietnam veterans as heroic figures, albeit ones who distrusted authority and lived by their own ethical codes.

See also: A Rumor of War; Dear America: Letters Home From Vietnam; Friendly Fire; China Beach; Tour of Duty.

Ten-Pin Theory. Widely embraced by French leaders between 1946 and 1954, the ten-pin theory held that the loss of France's colony in Vietnam would encourage nationalist independence movements in other parts of the French empire such as Algeria. Unlike the image suggested by the domino theory of neat rows of contiguous lands toppling one-by-one in Asia, the ten-pin theory

envisioned a more explosive spreading effect. The effect of toppling one "head pin" country would scatter in random directions, overthrowing French control in noncontiguous lands in all parts of the worldwide French empire—in Africa as well as in Asia.

See also: Domino Theory; France.

Terry, Wallace (1938–) journalist, oral historian. Terry's *Bloods: An Oral History of the Vietnam War by Black Veterans* (1984), a critical and popular success, examines the African-American experience in the Vietnam War in the words of those who fought. Terry was a *Time* magazine Vietnam War correspondent.

See also: Bloods: An Oral History of the Vietnam War by Black Veterans.

Tet (Tet Nhat). The Vietnamese New Year, the most important holiday of the year. Tet is celebrated in Vietnam during the first week of the first month of the lunar calendar, falling between January 19 and February 20. The first night of the new moon is considered the holiday's most important night. The holiday is marked by feasting, setting off fireworks, decorating homes, spending time with one's family, and paying reverence to one's ancestors.

Tet Offensive, 1968. Surprise North Vietnamese Army (NVA) and National Liberation Front

(NLF) attack launched on the Vietnamese New Year, 30–31 January. During the holiday cease-fire, some 84,000 NLF and NVA soldiers attacked South Vietnamese and U.S. military and government installations throughout the country. Most attacking forces failed to penetrate cities, although protracted fighting in Saigon continued for more than a week, and in Hue until early March. The offensive's aim was to topple the South Vietnamese government, but the expected popular uprising did not materialize.

Though a substantial military failure and political miscalculation, the broad offensive shocked the American public, which had been assured that a U.S. victory was imminent. The Tet Offensive convinced many Americans that the war could not be won, setting in motion the process of eventual U.S. withdrawal and tilting public opinion in favor of ending combat intervention.

North Vietnamese military leadership conceived the Tet Offensive to regain the initiative in the war. General Vo Nguyen Giap developed the strategy called the "General Offensive, General Uprising," which coordinated political, military, and diplomatic initiatives. Its crucial aspect entailed attacks on South Vietnamese government and military sites on the Tet holiday to spur defections within the Army of the Republic of Vietnam (ARVN) and a public revolt in the cities. The military replenished NLF guerrilla ranks with

People's Army of Vietnam (PAVN) soldiers and armed the insurgents with improved weaponry, including AK47 rifles and B-40 rocket launchers (obtained from the USSR and China). NLF personnel infiltrated cities and secured weapons caches. Motivational campaigns among soldiers and civilians were begun in the fall of 1967 to prepare for the "total victory."

In summer 1967 General Giap also initiated conventional military campaigns to draw U.S. forces into the interior and thus away from South Vietnam's populated areas, which were generally near the coast. Combined with later operations against the U.S. Marine base at Khe Sanh begun in late 1967, the attacks succeeded in drawing U.S. forces into remote areas. By the Tet holiday, more than half of U.S. combat battalions had been moved into the I Corps Tactical Zone (CTZ) to counter the siege of Khe Sanh. Under the cover of the Tet celebrations—a traditional time for a cease-fire—PAVN and NLF forces massed around cities.

Attacks were initially planned for 30 January, but officials delayed the offensive by 24 hours. Many units did not receive the new orders and fighting began prematurely in 6 cities. By the next night, 27 of South Vietnam's 44 provincial capitals, 5 of 6 autonomous cities, 58 of 245 district towns, and more than 50 hamlets were under fire. The NLF guerrillas exhorted southerners at

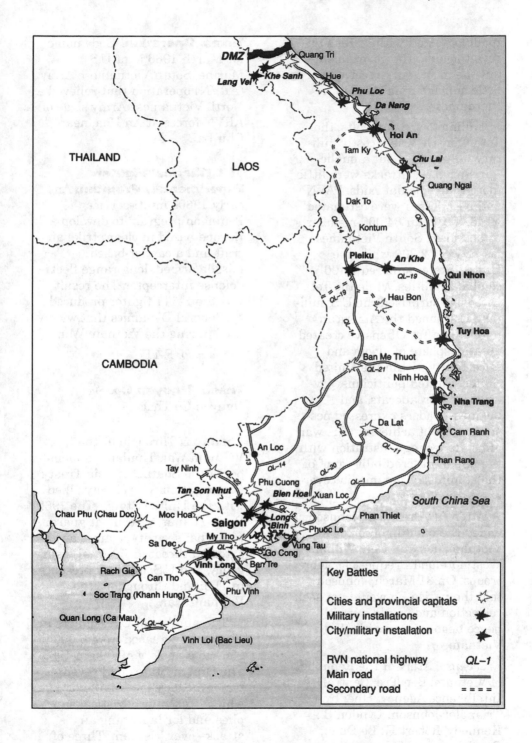

THAILAND

LAOS

DMZ

Quang Tri

Khe Sanh

Lang Vei

Hue

Phu Loc

Da Nang

Hoi An

Tam Ky

Chu Lai

Quang Ngai

Dak To

Kontum

Pleiku

An Khe

Qui Nhon

Hau Bon

QL–19

QL–19

QL–14

CAMBODIA

Tuy Hoa

Ban Me Thuot

QL–21

Ninh Hoa

Nha Trang

Da Lat

Cam Ranh

QL–27

QL–11

Phan Rang

An Loc

QL–13

QL–14

QL–20

QL–1

Tay Ninh

QL–22

Phu Cuong

Tan Son Nhut

Bien Hoa

Xuan Loc

Phan Thiet

South China Sea

Chau Phu (Chau Doc)

Moc Hoa

Saigon

Long Binh

Phuoc Le

Sa Dec

My Tho

QL–4

Go Cong

Vung Tau

Vinh Long

Ben Tre

Rach Gia

Can Tho

Phu Vinh

Soc Trang (Khanh Hung)

Quan Long (Ca Mau)

QL–4

Vinh Loi (Bac Lieu)

Key Battles

Cities and provincial capitals

Military installations

City/military installation

RVN national highway   QL–1

Main road

Secondary road

roadblocks and with leaflets to revolt against the government; but the insurgency received very little support from the South Vietnamese.

Failing to spark revolts, the Tet Offensive was a costly military failure. Without a public uprising, most attacks were little more than suicidal raids. PAVN and NLF losses were estimated at 45,000, of an 84,000-member attack force; South Vietnamese losses were 2,300 while the United States suffered 1,100 combat fatalities.While the Tet Offensive surprised the U.S. military, it stunned the American public. The Tet Offensive created an atmosphere of gloom and uncertainty within the United States. Elected politicians, government bureaucrats, and business leaders expressed pessimism about achieving U.S. war aims. Reflecting frustration with the apparent "credibility gap" of the administration, media coverage turned negative.

After Tet, President Johnson ended the buildup of forces in Vietnam, denying Gen. William Westmoreland's request for more troops. On 31 March, Johnson told the nation he would not seek reelection and would pursue peace negotiations with North Vietnam.

See also: Army of the Republic of Vietnam; Ben Tre; Central Intelligence Agency; Hue; Iron Triangle; Johnson, Lyndon B.; Kennedy, Robert F.; Le Duan; People's Army of Vietnam; Pham Hung; Refugees; Rusk, (David) Dean; Tran Do; Vo Nguyen Giap.

Texas, Operation. Code name for March 1966 joint U.S. Marine, South Vietnamese Army (ARVN) operation that relieved a North Vietnamese Army siege of ARVN forces at An Hoa, near Chu Lai.

TFX (Tactical Fighter Experimental) Program. An early 1960s multi-service Pentagon program to develop a Europe-based nuclear strike aircraft and a carrier-based, missile-armed, long-range fleet defense interceptor. The result was the F-111 fighter produced by General Dynamics that widely used during the Vietnam War.

See also: F-111.

Thach, Nguyen Co. *See* Nguyen Co Thach

Thailand. Throughout the Vietnam War, Thailand, a member of the Southeast Asia Treaty Organization, was closely allied with the United States. The 1962 Rusk-Thanat Agreement guaranteed Thai security against any external threat or internal insurgency, and U.S. military presence in Thailand throughout the Vietnam War.

The number of U.S. soldiers in Thailand increased from 6,000 in 1964 to a peak of 49,000 in 1969. The United States had seven major air bases in Thailand, which it used for logistical supplies and for launching air attacks over Vietnam. Three of these air bases were less than 80 kilometers (50 miles) from the Thai-Laotian borders, and only a

30- to 40-minute flight from Hanoi. The $200-million U Tapao air base, one of the largest in Asia at the time, was built for B-52 operations and was capable of docking about 80 warplanes. There were also many radar and other telecommunication centers, several camps for the U.S. Special Forces, a Central Intelligence Agency (CIA) operation command, and several counterinsurgency training camps.

In 1964, Thailand became the first Asian country to send troops to Vietnam. Three years later it committed its best combat units of 11,000 soldiers to the front lines. The United States paid all expenses for the Thai troops. With U.S. funding, Thailand also took part in the secret war in Laos against the Pathet Lao, the communist Lao insurgency. At its peak, there were some 16,500 Thai and other ethnic "volunteer" soldiers in Laotian territory. The United States provided $936 million in military assistance to the Thai armed forces between 1951 and 1971, nearly 60 percent of Thailand's total military budget. Thailand was flooded with refugees from the Vietnam War from 1975 onward, particularly as a result of the continuing conflict in Cambodia after 1978.

See also: Cambodia; Free World; Hmong; International Reaction; Laos; Manila Conference; Rolling Thunder, Operation; Search and Rescue; Southeast Asia Treaty Organization.

Thanh, Nguyen Chi. *See* Nguyen Chi Thanh

Thanh, Nguyen That. *See* Ho Chi Minh

Thanh Nien. *See* Vietnamese Communist Party

Thanh Thai (1879–1958), Emperor of Vietnam, 1889–1907. Than Thai resented French colonial rule and was deposed by the French for anti-colonial activity in 1907.

That, Ngo Dinh. *See* Ngo Dinh Thuc

Thayer, Operation. Code name for 1966 U.S. 1st Cavalry Division operations against the North Vietnamese Army (PAVN) in the coastal plain of Binh Dinh province.

These Good Men (1989). Book by Michael Norman in which the journalist and former Marine tracked down members of the platoon he served with in Vietnam in 1968

Thi, Nguyen Chanh. *See* Nguyen Chanh Thi

Thich Quang Duc (1907–1963), Buddhist monk. Thich Quang Duc was the first Buddhist monk to immolate himself in public to protest the Diem regime's treatment of the Buddhists. The immolation took place in Saigon on 11 June 1963. It led to months of confrontation between

South Vietnamese police and Buddhists monks.

See also: Buddhists; Ngo Dinh Diem.

Thich Tam Chau, a politically moderate Buddhist leader in the United Buddhist Church in Saigon.

See also: Buddhists; Thich Tri Quang.

Thich Tri Quang (1922–), Buddhist monk; a leading critic of South Vietnamese military governments. Thich Tri Quang sided with the Viet Minh against the French in the 1950s, but broke with the communists, entered a Buddhist monastery, and became the leader of Buddhists in Hue. After General Nguyen Cao Ky defeated Buddhist opposition to his regime in 1966, Tri Quang was placed under house arrest, and Buddhists largely abandoned political activity.

See also: Buddhists; Nguyen Chanh Thi.

Thieu, Nguyen Van. *See* Nguyen Van Thieu

Things They Carried, The (1990). Evocative Vietnam War novel by Tim O'Brien, the former U.S. Army infantryman who won the National Book Award for the surrealistic Vietnam War novel, *Going After Cacciato* (1978).

See also: Going After Cacciato; O'Brien, Tim.

13th Valley, The (1982). Vietnam War combat novel by John M. Del Vecchio, who served as a combat correspondent with the U.S. Army's 101st Airborne Division in Vietnam in 1970–1971.

Thi Thinh River. With the Saigon River, the Thi Thinh River formed the Iron Triangle, the site of a large Viet Cong base, 32 kilometers (20 miles) northwest of Saigon between the villages of Ben Suc and Ben Cat.

See also: Iron Triangle.

Thomas, Norman M. (1884–1968), U.S. Socialist Party leader. Thomas, a charter member of the anti-communist American Friends of Vietnam group, nevertheless was a critic of the repressive policies of South Vietnamese President Ngo Dinh Diem and later became a leading moderate antiwar activist.

See also: American Friends of Vietnam.

Thompson, Hugh C. Jr. (1943–), U.S. Army helicopter pilot. Thompson, a reconnaisance pilot with the 123rd Aviation Battalion aero scouts, and his crew chief, Glenn Andreotta, and door gunner, Lawrence Colburn, intervened during the 16 March 1968 My Lai massacre by landing between U.S. troops and Vietnamese civilians. The crew pointed their machine guns at the soldiers and ended the killing. On 6 March 1998, Thompson, Colburn, and Andreotta (who was later killed in Vietnam) received the Soldier's Medal for their actions at My Lai.

See also: My Lai.

Thompson, Robert G. K. (1916–), British counterinsurgency expert; unofficial adviser to President Nixon. Based on his experience as a colonial administrator in Malaya, Sir Robert G. K. Thompson developed the Strategic Hamlet program. Later in the 1960s Thompson served as key unofficial adviser to President Nixon, endorsing the Vietnamization strategy.

See also: Clear and Hold; Malaysia; Strategic Hamlet Program; Vietnamization.

Thornton, Herbert (1926–), U.S. Army Captain. Thornton, a chemical warfare officer with the U.S. Army's 1st Infantry Division in Vietnam in 1966, specialized in training "Tunnel Rats," soldiers who volunteered to fight in the underground Viet Cong tunnels.

See also: Tunnels.

Thot Not, Operation. *See* Daniel Boone Operations

365 Days (1971). Memoir by Ronald J. Glasser, a U.S. Army Medical Corps physician. The book deals with Glasser's experiences in Japan treating severely wounded soldiers evacuated from Vietnam.

See also: Glasser, Ronald J.

Thua Thien Province. Province in north central Vietnam. Thua Thien contains the former imperial capital of Hue, 75 kilometers (45 miles) south of the former Demilitarized Zone (DMZ), and the A Shau Valley, the main entry point during the Vietnam War of the Ho Chi Minh Trail into South Vietnam.

See also: A Shau Valley; Hue.

Thuc, Ngo Dinh. *See* Ngo Dinh Thuc

Thunder Hurricane. *See* Loi Phong, Operation

Thurmond, Strom (1902–), U.S. Senator (R-S.C.), 1954– . Thurmond, a conservative Republican, strongly supported aggressive U.S. military action in South Vietnam from the early 1960s through the end of the Vietnam War.

Ticket Punching. U.S. military slang referring to careerism in the armed forces. Officers hoping to attain the rank of general needed an "outstanding" mark in their six-month tour of duty in Vietnam. Some officers were more concerned with doing what they believed was necessary to be promoted, to get their "ticket punched," than with leading troops effectively.

See also: Hackworth, David H.

Tiger Cages. Five feet by nine feet cement cells at Con Son prison in South Vietnam. Built by the French in the 1940s, the cages were used in the 1960s by the South Vietnam's Thieu government to hold political prisoners and prisoners of war. The cells were uncovered in a 1970 U.S congressional visit and were subsequently cited by the International Red Cross as a violation of the Geneva Convention.

See also: Atrocities.

Tiger Division. Nickname of Republic of Korea (ROK) Capital Army infantry division that fought in the Vietnam War from September 1965 to March 1973. The division, with headquarters in Qui Nhon, primarily was responsible for security at U.S. bases and along II Corps transportation routes.

See also: Korea, Republic of.

Tiger Hound, Operation. Code-name for U.S. Air Force and Navy air interdiction campaign against the Ho Chi Minh Trail, begun in December 1965. Other aspects of the operation were known as Steel Hound and Commando Hunt.

See also: Air Force, U.S.; Ho Chi Minh Trail.

Tighe, Eugene F. Jr. (1920–1993), U.S. Air Force lieutenant general; director, Defense Intelligence Agency (DIA), 1978–1981. Gen. Tighe headed a 1986 Pentagon POW/MIA panel that concluded that U.S.

prisoners of war were still alive in Southeast Asia.

See also: POW/MIA Controversy.

Toan Thang, Operation (Total Victory). Name given to several South Vietnamese Army (ARVN) operations, including the massive April-May 1968 campaign, launched jointly with U.S. troops, to destroy Viet Cong and North Vietnamese Army units operating around Saigon, and the May 1970 assault on the Fishhook by U.S. and ARVN troops that was part of the invasion of Cambodia.

See also: Cambodian Incursion; Fishhook.

Ton Duc Thang (1888–1980), Vietnamese communist leader; president, Democratic Republic of Vietnam, 1969–1976. Ton Duc Thang joined Ho Chi Minh's communist Revolutionary Youth League in the 1920s and was active in Vietnamese communist party politics for half a century.

See also: Revolutionary Youth League.

Tonkin. Northern section of Vietnam including the city of Hanoi, one of three regions in Vietnam colonized by France in the 19th century.

See also: Annam; Cochinchina; Hanoi.

Tonkin Gulf Incident. *See* Gulf of Tonkin Incident

Tonkin Gulf Resolution. *See* Gulf of Tonkin Resolution;

Appendix E, "Gulf of Tonkin Resolution"

Tonkin Rifles (Régiment de Tirailleurs Tonkinois). Military unit formed by the French in 1883 in Hanoi. Together with the *Régiment de Tirailleurs Annamites* (the Annamite Rifles) in Saigon they helped colonial army units enforce French policies in Vietnam.

See also: Annamite Rifles.

Ton That Dinh (1930–), South Vietnamese Army general. Dinh was one of the Army generals who plotted the overthrow of South Vietnamese President Ngo Dinh Diem in 1963. Dinh lost favor under President Nguyen Khan, commanded an ARVN corps in 1966, and was relieved of his command by President Nguyen Cao Ky when Dinh protested the tactics Ky used to Buddhist-led uprisings in Da Nang, Hue, and Saigon.

See also: Ngo Dinh Diem; Nguyen Cao Ky.

Total Victory, Operation. *See* Toan Thang, Operation

Touby Lyfoung (191?–), leader of a Hmong Lao clan, Touby Lyfoung fought the Viet Minh in Laos in 1952, and joined the French and fought with them at Dien Bien Phu. He remained an anti-communist Hmong leader until the Pathet Lao takeover in 1975.

See also: Hmong; Laos; Pathet Lao; Vang Pao.

Tourane. *See* Da Nang

Tour of Duty. In Vietnam, unlike previous wars, U.S. military personnel served a one-year tour of duty; for U.S. Marines, the tour was thirteen months. Personnel could voluntarily extent their tours of duty.

Tour of Duty (1987–1990). CBS-TV prime-time dramatic series of 58 one-hour episodes that told the story of a group of American soldiers in the Vietnam War.

Tower, John G. (1925–1991), U.S. senator (R-Tex.), 1961–1985. Tower, a conservative Republican, was a strong supporter of the Vietnam War policies of the Johnson and Nixon administrations and an outspoken opponent of the antiwar movement.

Tracers (1980). Award-winning, highly charged play about the Vietnam War's impact on a group of American veterans created by eight Vietnam veterans at Los Angeles's Odyssey Theater. In the initial production the play's creators (John DiFusco, Vincent Caristi, Richard Chaves, Eric E. Emerson, Rick Gallavan, Merlin Marston, Harry Stephens, and Sheldon Lettich) appeared as members of a platoon dramatizing their war and post-war experiences.

Tra, Tran Van. *See* Tran Van Tra

Tran Do (1922–), North Vietnamese Army general.

General Tran Do moved south in 1964 to become deputy commander of National Liberation Front (NLF) and North Vietnamese Army (NVA) forces in South Vietnam. In the mid 1960s, Tran Do increased the number of North Vietnamese commanders, political officers, and technical experts within the NLF to insure the North's oversight and control. An architect of the 1968 Tet Offensive, he later acknowledged that the operation failed in its main goal of igniting uprisings across the South, although it had the unintended result of turning American public opinion against the war.

See also: Tet Offensive.

Tran Dynasty. Series of emperors who took over following the Le Dynasty and ruled Vietnam from 1225–1400. The Tran Dynasty is best known for its ongoing conflicts with the kingdom of Champa, the Khmer state of Angkor, and for repelling an invasion by Kublai Khan's Mongol Army in the 13th century.

Trang Sup. Village in Tay Ninh Province, northeast of Saigon. The headquarters of a South Vietnamese Army regiment, Trang Sup was attacked 26 January 1960 by some two hundred Viet Cong guerrillas who overran the base. Lt. Gen. Samuel Williams, commander of the U.S. Military Assistance Advisory Group-Vietnam (MAAG-V), saw the attack as a severe blow to the prestige of the South Vietnamese Army and an indication of the enemy's ability to stage large-size well-planned attacks. Williams recommended military reforms but did not call for more U.S. troops.

See also: Williams, Samuel T.

Tran Huu Thanh, South Vietnamse activist Catholic priest. In 1974 Father Tran Huu Thanh launched the People's Anti-Corruption Movement with the support of Saigon's Catholic Church. In a series of public manifestos, Father Thanh charged President Nguyen Van Thieu with "undermining the nationalist cause for his own financial gain" and accused him of protecting the heroin traffic.

See also: Nguyen Van Thieu; People's Anti-Corruption Movement.

Tran Le Xuan. *See* Ngo Dinh Nhu (Madame Nhu)

Tran Phu (1904–1931), founding member, Indochinese Communist Party, general secretary, 1930–1931. A teacher, Tran Phu studied communism in Russia from 1927–1930. He died in a French prison the following year.

See also: Indochinese Communist Party.

Tran Thien Khiem (1925–), general, Army of the Republic of Vietnam (ARVN). Gen. Tran Thien Khiem was chief of staff when he helped overthrow President Diem in November 1963. He then held many offices in South Vietnam's government:

defense minister (1964) under Gen. Nguyen Khanh, ambassador to the United States (1965–1968) under President Nguyen Cao Ky, and prime minister (1969–1975) under President Nguyen Van Thieu. Khiem escaped to Taiwan in April 1975, and from there to France.

See also: Ngo Dinh Diem.

Tran Van Don (1917–), South Vietnamese Army general. General Don was one of the four generals who orchestrated the November 1963 coup against Ngo Dinh Diem. As chief of staff for the Army of the Republic of Vietnam (ARVN), Don established the crucial liaison with a U.S. Central Intelligence Agency (CIA) operative through which the generals ascertained U.S. support for the coup. A colleague of President Nguyen Van Thieu, Don served as deputy prime minister, army chief of staff, and roving ambassador during the Thieu administration. He escaped to the United States in 1975.

See also: Ngo Dinh Diem; Nguyen Van Thieu.

Tran Van Giau (1910–), Vietnamese communist leader; historian. Tran Van Giau was the leader of the Indochinese Communist Party in the 1930s until he was imprisoned by the French. After WWII, he led the party in southern Vietnam, but was forced out in 1946. He became a historian, specializing

in the history of the Communist Party and the Vietnamese communist revolution.

See also: Indochinese Communist Party.

Tran Van Hai, South Vietnamese Army brigadier general. The former head of the Army of the Republic of Vietnam Rangers, in May 1968 Tran Van Hai became director of South Vietnam's national police.

Tran Van Huong (1903–), South Vietnamese prime minister, 1964–1965, 1968–1969, 1975; vice president, 1971–1975. Tran Van Huong, the mayor of Saigon, was named prime minister by Gen. Nguyen Khanh in 1964. He served Nguyen Van Thieu as vice president from 1971 through 1975. When Thieu fled Saigon on 25 April 1975, ahead of advancing NVA forces, he appointed Huong president. Huong resigned and in favor of Gen. Duong Van Minh on 28 April, two days before the final collapse of the Republic of Vietnam.

See also: Buddhists; Duong Van Minh; Nguyen Khanh; Nguyen Van Thieu.

Tran Van Tra (1918–1996), military leader of National Liberation Front (NLF); member, Central Committee of Lao Dong Party; lieutenant general, North Vietnamese Army (NVA); chairman, Military Affairs Committee of the Central Office of South Vietnam (COSVN), 1964–1976; minister of defense, Provisional

Military Government (PRG), 1969–1976.

Tran Van Tra fought with the Viet Minh against the French from 1946 to 1954. He became lieutenant general of the NVA in 1961 and commanded the southern half of South Vietnam. From 1964 to 1976, he was chairman of COSVN and coordinated the guerrilla movement against South Vietnam, including the assault on Saigon in the 1968 Tet Offensive. While minister of defense for the Provisional Military Government of South Vietnam, as the NLF was renamed after the Tet Offensive, he advocated a national military campaign in 1974–1975 in order to prevent the Army of the Republic of Vietnam (ARVN) from deploying its forces region by region. His strategy for the final push—in which he served as deputy commander— was an attack on Route 14 across Phuoc Long province and a quick assault on Saigon from five directions. In 1982 Tran Van Tra was purged from the Vietnamese Communist party after publishing a book critical of the North Vietnamese communists.

See also: Central Office of South Vietnam.

Treaty of Friendship and Cooperation. Military alliance signed by the Republic of Vietnam and the Soviet Union on 2 November 1978.

Treaty of Saigon. Peace treaty signed in 1862 by Vietnam and France following a series of French military victories in southern Vietnam. In the treaty Vietnam gave France control of three southern provinces and the right to practice Catholicism there.

Tripartite Electoral Commission. In the 1972 Paris peace talks the United States and North Vietnam agreed to a tripartite electoral commission that would arrange a political settlement after a cease-fire. The commission never was implemented.

See also: Paris Peace Accords; Appendix F, "Paris Peace Accords."

Trip Flare. Small, ground-mounted flare with an attached wire widely used by U.S. forces at night around bases and on ambushes.

Truman, Harry S (1884–1972), U.S. senator (D-Mo.), 1934–1944; vice president, 1944; president, 1944–1952. Truman reversed President Franklin D. Roosevelt's tentative policy of abandoning support for a continued French presence in Indochina. Truman viewed Ho Chi Minh as a communist puppet in the global Cold War and invoked the domino theory and the policy of containment in discussing his Indochina policy. In a 1950 speech announcing the decision to send U.S. troops to Korea, Truman called for aid to the French in Vietnam. Congress appropriated funds for the French war in Indochina, a policy continued by President Eisenhower until the French defeat at Dien Bien Phu in 1954.

Truman's financial commitment to fighting the communists in Vietnam was significant in establishing U.S. interests in the country, but his ideological constructs were even more fundamental. In viewing Ho Chi Minh's forces as communist tools in the Cold War and in his repeated references to containment and the domino theory, Truman established the ideological framework within which the conflict would be viewed for the next two decades. In the 1960s, President Lyndon Johnson made several attempts to persuade Truman to back his Vietnam policies, but Truman would not make any public statement about the war.

See also: Domino Theory; Dulles, John Foster; European Defense Community; Roosevelt, Franklin D.

Truman Doctrine. Foreign affairs policy announced by President Harry S. Truman in a March 1947 speech, committing the United States to the containment of communist expansion in Europe.

See also: Domino Theory; Truman, Harry S.

Trung Sisters. Two sisters, the daughters of a Vietnamese lord and the wives of aristocrats who had been killed by the Chinese, who led a Vietnamese revolt against Chinese rule in the first century AD. The Trung Sisters are revered as patriots who led the fight for Vietnamese independence against foreign rule.

See also: Women, Vietnamese.

Truong Chinh (1907–1988), general secretary, Indochinese Communist party, 1941–1956; president, national assembly, Democratic Republic of Vietnam (DRV), 1960–1976; co-president, DRV, 1981–1987. Born Dang Xuan Khu, Chinh led North Vietnam's pro-Chinese faction. He helped found the Indochinese Communist party in 1930. For the next twenty-six years Chinh ranked second only to Ho Chi Minh on the politburo. In 1956 Chinh resigned as general secretary, but remained the party's top ideologist. Although long opposed to capitalist reforms, Chinh invited the reintroduction of private enterprise when he served again as general secretary in 1986.

See also: Ho Chi Minh; Indochinese Communist Party; Le Duan; Vo Nguyen Giap.

Truong Dinh Dzu, a Saigon lawyer. Dzu ran against Nguyen Van Thieu in South Vietnam's 1967 presidential election. Dzu called for a bombing pause and negotiations with the National Liberation Front. He captured 17 percent of the vote, nearly half of Thieu's total. Angered and embarrassed by Dzu's strong showing, Thieu had Dzu arrested after the election for illegal currency dealings. Dzu was released from prison in 1973.

See also: Nguyen Van Thieu.

Truong Son Mountains.
String of mountains on
Vietnam's western border ending
some 60 miles north of Ho Chi
Minh City (Saigon).

Tu Do Street. A main, heavily
commercialized street in Saigon
called *rue Catinat* by the French,
Tu Do by the South Vietnamese,
and *Duong Tu Do* (Liberty
Street) by the communist government of Vietnam after 1975.

Tu Duc (1829–1883),
Vietnamese emperor. Born
Nguyen Phuoc Hoang Nham, the
Emperor Tu Duc ruled Vietnam
from 1847–1883. During his
reign Admiral Leonard Victor
Joseph Charner conquered
Saigon for France in 1861 and
the next year Tu Duc ceded the
surrounding provinces to form
Cochinchina, the first colony of
French Indochina.

Tunnels. Viet Cong guerrillas
made extensive use of tunnels, a
traditional tactic used against
the French, Japanese, and
Chinese invaders in earlier wars.
South Vietnam contained many
underground guerrilla bases,
built and supplied with forced
labor from nearby villages.

The largest tunnel complexes
were in the Iron Triangle region
and nearby at Cu Chi. Together
these underground installations
contained about 200 kilometers
(125 miles) of tunnels, 1 meter (3
feet) high by 0.75 meters (2.5
feet) wide, dug in dense laterite
clay strata, which set as hard as
concrete. The tunnels zigzagged

to confuse intruders and to isolate the effects of gas or
explosives. Four levels of tunnels
were connected by hidden trap-
doors and tiny air shafts. Viet
Cong fighters spent their days
safely underground and emerged
at night for raids on Saigon or to
attack unsuspecting U.S. and
South Vietnamese troops, often
camped right on top of them.

The U.S. Army's 1st Infantry
Division discovered the Cu Chi
tunnels during Operation Crimp
in January 1966. After taking
casualties for days from invisible
snipers within secured perimeters, the soldiers painstakingly
searched the jungle floor to find
concealed entrances that were
the outer works of the Phy My
Hung tunnel complex. Further
exploration uncovered barracks,
armories, supply dumps, and
hospitals—as well as kitchens,
air-raid shelters, classrooms, conference centers, graveyards,
printing presses, factories, and
holding pens for water buffalo.

The U.S. Army volunteers who
entered these tunnels often surprised resting Viet Cong fighters
and engaged in furious hand-to-
hand combat. They became the
first Tunnel Rats. Gen. William
Westmoreland launched
Operation Cedar Falls to destroy
the Iron Triangle tunnels in
February 1967. More than 30,000
U.S. and South Vietnamese
troops evacuated the local villagers and created a 156-square-
kilometer (60-square-mile) free
fire zone. The area was bombed,
shelled, defoliated, napalmed,
and crushed by bulldozers with

deep-cutting Rome plows. Tons of guerrilla supplies were captured. Despite the operation's success, the underground bases served as the staging ground for guerrilla raids on Saigon in the 1968 Tet Offensive. In 1970, B-52s dropped thousands of delayed-fuse bombs that buried deep in the ground before exploding. The resulting craters drove the Viet Cong out of the Iron Triangle tunnels. In North Vietnam, extensive tunnels were also dug for protection from U.S. bombing raids.

See also: Iron Triangle; Cedar Falls, Operation.

Truong, Ngo Quang. *See* Ngo Quang Truong

Turner Joy, USS. U.S. Navy destroyer that reported being attacked by North Vietnamese torpedo boats in international waters on 4 August 1964 in the Gulf of Tonkin.

See also: Gulf of Tonkin Incident; Appendix E, "Gulf of Tonkin Resolution."

Tuyen Quang. Hamlet located 165 kilometers (60 miles) north of Hanoi in Ha Tuyen Province. The Lao Dong Party (Vietnamese Worker's Party) was created in February 1951 at a national congress held in Tuyen Quang.

See also: Lao Dong.

Tuy Hoa. Small town some 100 kilometers (60 miles) south of Qui Nhon, the capital of Phu Yen province, and the site during the Vietnam War of a large U.S. military base, containing the headquarters of the U.S. Air Force 31st Tactical Fighter Wing.

Twining, Nathan F. (1897–1982), general, U.S. Air Force; chief of staff, 1953–1957; chairman, Joint Chiefs of Staff (JCS), 1957–1960. Twining was the only JCS member to approve Adm. Arthur Radford's 1954 plan for air strikes to save the French at Dien Bien Phu. Twining recommended using one to three small atomic weapons against Viet Minh positions to demonstrate U.S. resolve in fighting communism.

See also: Nuclear Weapons; Dien Bien Phu; Radford, Arthur W.

Two-Party Joint Military Commission. *See* International Commission for Supervision and Control

Ugly American, The (1958). Novel by Eugene Burdick and William J. Lederer. Set in a thinly veiled Vietnam, the book is a Cold War parable of what American political and diplomatic blindness could produce in Southeast Asia. The character, Colonel Edwin Hillendale, is modeled on the CIA's Edward Lansdale.

See also: Burdick, Eugene; Lansdale, Edward G.

Ugly American, The (1963). George England's film adaptation of the novel by Eugene Burdick and William J. Lederer.

UH-1 Helicopter. Known as the "Iroquois" and the "Huey," the turbine-engine Bell UH-1 was the most important helicopter used in the Vietnam War. The first Hueys, the UH-1As, arrived in Vietnam in 1962; they were succeeded by seven other models. Modified Hueys carrying turreted machine guns, 40 mm grenade launchers, and rockets entered service in early 1962. The UH-1D, known as the "Slick," was the Army's main assault helicopter. The Army Medical Service adapted the UH-1 developed initially as an evacuation helicopter, to become its first effective air ambulance.

See also: Helicopters; Medevac.

UH-2 Helicopter. Known as the "Sea Sprite," the Kaman Aerospace UH-2 was used by the U.S. Navy carriers and destroyers at Yankee Station in the Gulf of Tonkin for around-the-clock search-and-rescue missions.

See also: Helicopters.

U Minh Forest. Enormous forested area in An Xuyen and Kieng Giang provinces in the Mekong Delta. During the Vietnam War the U Minh Forest was used as a refuge by the Viet Cong. The waterways were heavily mined and the area was sprayed heavily with Agent Orange.

See also: Mekong River and Delta.

Uniform Code of Military Justice. The U.S. military's justice and legal system. In 1968, during the Vietnam War, Congress passed a new Uniform Code of Military Justice that guaranteed legal counsel before a court-martial.

See also: Atrocities.

Union of Soviet Socialist Republics (USSR). The Soviet Union was, with the People's Republic of China (PRC), the most important military and economic supporter of the Democratic Republic of Vietnam (DRV) during the Vietnam War. Although the Soviet Union had provided military aid to the Viet

Minh in the early 1950s, it chose not to publicize the assistance for fear of jeopardizing the success of diplomatic maneuvers with France and intruding on its ally's (the PRC) special relationship with the DRV. Soviet aid during the Franco–Viet Minh War included trucks, artillery, and communications equipment, estimated to have a total value of $1 billion.

At the 1954 Geneva Conference, the USSR advocated terms relatively favorable to the French and pressured the Viet Minh to accept partition of Vietnam. Considered a betrayal by the DRV, the USSR's actions reportedly reflected an effort to encourage France to forestall the rearming of Germany, a central concern of Soviet foreign policy. In the early 1960s Soviet leader Nikita Khrushchev pursued conciliatory policies with the West on Vietnam, rather than support his ally, the PRC.

Leonid Brezhnev, his successor in 1964 aggressively aided North Vietnam, hoping to counter the PRC's influence in the region. The DRV, with its limited industrial and economic base, depended upon foreign assistance to support its reunification effort, and the Soviet Union provided the military resources to sustain warfare against the South. Shipping most material through Haiphong, the Soviets provided such equipment as high-technology surface-to-air missiles (SAMs), planes, artillery, tanks, fuel, and ammunition. Nearly three thousand military

technicians trained North Vietnamese personnel and maintained advanced equipment. The USSR also provided food, fertilizer, and cement. Total military aid is estimated at $5–8 billion between 1965 and 1975. In the late 1960s, under pressure from the United States, the USSR tried with no success to influence the DRV to pursue peace negotiations. In 1972, the USSR declined to cancel a superpower summit despite the U.S. Christmas bombings of Hanoi and Haiphong and the mining of Haiphong harbor.

After unification in the late 1970s, Vietnam moved firmly into the Soviet Union's political and economic orbit. On 29 June 1978, Vietnam joined the communist common market, COMECON, and launched a massive economic integration with the Soviet Union. Soviet economic aid increased to more than $1 billion annually, financing joint projects in mining, oil and gas, industry, agriculture, and education. The two countries also tightened their military alliance, signing the Treaty of Friendship and Cooperation on 2 November 1978. The close political and economic ties between the countries ended with the collapse of communism in the USSR in 1991.

See also: Brezhnev, Leonid; China, People's Republic of; Détente; Geneva Conference, 1954; Geneva Conference, 1961–1962; Ho Chi Minh; International Reaction; Kennan, George; Kennedy, John F.;

Khrushchev, Nikita; Kissinger, Henry; Kosygin, Alexei; Mao Zedong; Normalization; People's Army of Vietnam; Rules of Engagement.

Union I and Union II, Operations. Code name for April and May 1967 1st U.S. Marine Division combat operations against the Viet Cong and North Vietnamese Army in the Phuoc Ha Valley between Chu Lai and Da Nang.

Uniontown, Operation. Code name for December 1967 to March 1968 U.S. Army 199th Light Infantry Brigade effort to clear Viet Cong forces from Bien Hoa province.

United Buddhist Church of Vietnam. Also known as the United Buddhist Association of Vietnam, the group was a broad-based political organization created in December 1963 in Saigon during the regime of Gen. Duong Van Minh. In March 1966, during the military regime of Nguyen Cao Ky, the group called for elections for a civilian government.

See also: Buddhists; Duong Van Minh; Nguyen Cao Ky.

United Front for the Liberation of Oppressed Races. *See Front Unifié pour la Lutte des Races Opprimées (FULRO)*

United National Front (Mat Tran Guoc Gia Thong Nhut).
Short-lived coalition of pro-Japanese and Trotskyite Vietnamese parties that worked for freedom and independence. Formed in Saigon on 14 August 1945, the front merged with the newly formed Democratic Republic of Vietnam and the Viet Minh ten days later.

United Nations (U.N.). The United Nations did not play a significant role in settling the Vietnamese conflict, primarily because France and the U.S. were members of the U.N. Security Council, and could veto resolutions unfavorable to their positions. The 1954 Geneva peace accords provided no role for the U.N. and neither the Democratic Republic of Vietnam nor the Republic of Vietnam was a U.N. member. As the war intensified in the mid 1960s, the U.N. General Assembly became a forum for heated rhetoric between communist-bloc countries and U.S. supporters. During the war, U.N. Secretary General U Thant made several unsuccessful attempts to start peace negotiations.

The secretary general did, however, successfully challenge certain aspects of U.S. military policy in Vietnam. In the late 1960s, U Thant sought to ban the use of herbicides used to defoliate jungle (Agent Orange and Agent Blue), arguing that the provisions of the 1925 Geneva conventions outlawing chemical warfare applied to the weapons. His pressure, combined with domestic and international criticism, brought about the Nixon administration's renunciation of herbicide use in 1969.

U.N. institutions played a critical role in addressing the dislocation and turmoil caused by the war. U.N. programs facilitated the emigration of several hundred Amerasian children from Vietnam in the mid 1980s. The U.N. high commissioner on refugees also began initiatives to address the problem of the Vietnamese boat people, who left Vietnam in a massive exodus of more than 1.5 million refugees between 1975 and 1992. In 1979, the United Nations established an alternative Orderly Departure Program within Vietnam and in 1982 began patrolling the Gulf of Thailand to protect refugees from piracy.

See also: Cambodia; Chemical Warfare; Goldberg, Arthur J.; Normalization; Paul VI; Geneva Conference, 1954; Stevenson, Adlai E.

United States Army. *See* Army, U.S.

United States Information Agency (USIA). *See* U.S. Information Service

United States Information Service. The overseas component of the United States Information Agency (USIA). Organized in 1953, the USIA was intended to foster a sympathetic understanding of American culture abroad and to build public support for U.S. foreign policy in other nations. The

USIA planned government-sponsored cultural and information activities while the USIS implemented those initiatives. Conceived of during the height of the Cold War, the content of USIA and USIS informational materials was stridently anti-communist; to counter Soviet propaganda, the USIA engaged in a worldwide campaign to explain and justify U.S. policy in Indochina.

In the early 1960s President Lyndon Johnson delegated responsibility for non-military psychological action in Vietnam to the USIA. The USIA set up the Joint U.S. Public Affairs Office (JUSPAO) in Saigon, which directed propaganda at the South Vietnamese people, Viet Cong guerrillas, and the North Vietnamese through radio, leaflet drops, and airborne loud-speakers. By 1967 this counterinsurgency effort involved 12 to 14 percent of all USIA foreign service officers. Throughout the remainder of the Vietnam War, the USIA maintained information centers and libraries, which became the targets of guerrilla attacks.

See also: Five O'Clock Follies; Joint U.S. Public Affairs Office.

United States Marine Corps. *See* Marines, U.S.

United States Navy. *See* Navy, U.S.

United States of America. Beginning in the late 1940s, U.S. leaders committed extensive resources and prestige to create a pro-Western, anticommunist regime in French Indochina. After the 1954 French defeat, the U.S. pursued a policy of economic aid and then military intervention to promote the Republic of Vietnam.

In the late 1940s, the United States supported the policies of Great Britain and France, nations severely weakened by World War II, to revitalize their political and economic interests within Southeast Asia. U.S. leaders also hoped to restore Japan's regional economic influence, which had relied on Indochina's raw materials and markets. The Korean War and the 1949 triumph of the Chinese communists sharpened U.S. determination to contain communist expansionism in Asia and to support the beleaguered French in Indochina. The United States began direct assistance in 1949 and expended $3 billion in military support (nearly 80 percent of the total cost of the conflict) for France's war against the Viet Minh. But when the French military faltered at the siege of Dien Bien Phu in 1954, President Dwight D. Eisenhower rejected French requests for a U.S. military air strike.

After the French withdrawal and the 1954 Geneva Convention, which partitioned Vietnam, the United States extended wide assistance to the newly created Republic of Vietnam in the south. In 1960, North Vietnam lent direct support to the insurgency, now named the National Liberation Front, which ignited open military hostilities. In the face of mounting threats to the South Vietnamese government, President John F. Kennedy authorized the deployment of U.S. military advisers to the region in 1961; by 1963 they numbered sixteen thousand. Faced with the continued weakness of the South Vietnamese government and military successes by the NLF, President Lyndon Johnson committed U.S. combat forces to Vietnam in 1964. Johnson gained nearly unanimous congressional support with the Gulf of Tonkin Resolution in August 1964, which gave him broad authority to expand the war in an effort to curtail communist "aggression." In retaliation for the Gulf of Tonkin incident, the United States bombed North Vietnam in 1964, and after NLF attacks on U.S. military installations, the U.S. ground presence was significantly escalated in July 1965.

In shaping U.S. military policy, President Johnson pursued a strategy of limited war in the region. Confident in U.S. military capability, Johnson sought to limit U.S. intervention both to curtail domestic social costs and to avoid a superpower confrontation. The number of U.S. military personnel in Vietnam increased from 185,000 in December 1965 to 385,000 one year later and peaked at 585,000 in early 1968. The Tet Offensive in January 1968 marked the turning point of U.S. policy in Vietnam and the beginning of U.S. disengagement. In March 1968, the Johnson administration capped U.S. escalation and openly pursued peace negotiations.

In 1969, President Richard Nixon continued U.S. troop withdrawals and inaugurated a policy of Vietnamization, transferring military responsibility to South Vietnam. The 1973 Paris peace accords resulted in the withdrawal of U.S. military forces but allowed North Vietnamese troops to remain in the South. In what would become the longest war in U.S. history, more than 58,000 American died, 23,000 were permanently disabled, and the cost to the U.S. treasury added up to an estimated $170 billion. The North Vietnamese triumph in April 1975 marked a significant setback for U.S. Cold War policy.

The Vietnam War created stark divisions in American society and damaged the domestic economy. The antiwar movement gained increasing grassroots support, evolving to include many religious, labor, and professional groups. Extensive protests occurred at the 1967 March on the Pentagon and during the 1968 Democratic Convention in Chicago. The Tet Offensive, in particular, energized demonstrators and contributed to President Johnson's decision not to run for president in the 1968 election.

The Vietnam War also heightened class tensions in the United States. Of the 2.8 million U.S. personnel in Vietnam, a significant percentage came from working-class or poor backgrounds. The Selective Service provided draft deferments for college students, and many university students effectively manipulated the system to avoid combat duty. The National Guard, especially, served as a refuge for young elites; only 15,000 National Guard troops were called to duty in Vietnam.

U.S. fiscal policies to support Vietnam policy exacerbated larger economic problems arising from Cold War military commitments. Choosing to limit public sacrifice, the Johnson administration ran budget deficits to fund the war and refused to restrain an overheated economy. The defeat forced a broad reconsideration of U.S. diplomatic and military policies and left a bitterness that pervaded American life for years. After the war, U.S. military strategists were determined to avoid another Vietnam quagmire. Twenty years after the fall of Saigon, Americans remained highly suspicious of military actions that would risk U.S. lives and resources.

See also: Congress, U.S.; Geneva Conference, 1954; Geneva Conference, 1961–1962; Manila Conference; Pacification; Paris Peace Accords; Public Opinion, American; Refugees; Republican Party, U.S.; State, Department of; United Nations; Vietnam, Democratic Republic of; Vietnam, Republic of; Appendix F, "Paris Peace Accords."

United We Stand. Lobbying group set up by businessman H. Ross Perot in 1969 that worked to support the Vietnam War, oppose the antiwar movement, and publicize the issue of U.S. servicemen held prisoner by North Vietnam.

See also: Perot, H. Ross.

Unity Congress. Gathering of Vietnamese communist party leaders in February 1930 presided over by Ho Chi Minh in which he brought together differing factions into a single Vietnamese Communist Party.

See also: Vietnamese Communist Party.

University of Wisconsin Bombing. At 3:42 A.M. on 24 August 1970, a bomb blast ripped apart the Army Mathematics Research Center (AMRC) in Sterling Hall at the University of Wisconsin in Madison. Local police were alerted by a phone call just prior to the blast, but did not have enough time to warn the building's occupants. Postgraduate researcher Robert Fassnacht was killed and three others were injured.

The "New Year's Gang" took credit for the bombing, contending that the AMRC research contributed to weapons development for the Vietnam War. The AMRC was in fact funded by a grant from the U.S. Army and devoted half its work to "militarily applicable" research, including determining casualty statistics for various weapons. The bombers were Karl and Dwight Armstrong, two Madison residents, and university students David Fine and Leo Burt. They fled to Canada after the Federal Bureau of Investigation (FBI) launched an extensive manhunt. Between 1972 and 1976 all except Burt were caught. In 1973 Karl Armstrong was tried, convicted, and sentenced to 23 years in prison. His sentence was reduced to 10 years after his younger brother, Dwight, and David Fine pleaded guilty to second- and third-degree murder, respectively, and received 7-year sentences. Burt remains at large.

See also: Armstrong, Dwight and Karleton; Burt, Leo; Fassnacht, Robert; Fine, David; Napalm.

Unknowns, Tomb of the. Section of Arlington National Cemetery honoring unknown soldiers from WWI, WWII, and the Korean and Vietnam Wars. Congress passed a law in 1973 directing the Pentagon to reserve a crypt for an unknown serviceman killed in the Vietnam War. Because only a handful of remains were unidentified and due to pressure from family members of Americans missing in action, it was not until 28 May 1984 that the body of an unknown serviceman was interred. The Pentagon announced in June 1998 that DNA tests confirmed a report that the remains were those of

Michael Joseph Blassie, an Air Force pilot listed as missing in action. In July Blassie's body was disinterred and reburied in his hometown in Missouri.

See also: POW/MIA Controversy.

Urbanization. The movement of tens of thousands of South Vietnamese peasants to cities fleeing combat and air attacks beginning in the late 1960s. More than 90 percent of the population of South Vietnam had lived in the countryside before 1965. By 1972 about 60 percent of the total population had become urbanized.

See also: Refugees.

U.S. Agency for International Development. *See* Agency for International Development

U.S. Air Rescue Service. U.S. Air Force unit widely used in the Korean War that flew missions for the French in Southeast Asia in the 1950s.

See also: Search and Rescue.

U.S. Army Vietnam (USARV). U.S. Army's administrative and logistical command in Vietnam, organized in July 1965 with headquarters first in Saigon and later in Long Binh, renamed USARV/MACV Support Command in 1972. USARV was commanded by its MACV deputy command general.

See also: Long Binh; Military Assistance Command, Vietnam;

Appendix B, "Order of Battle, U.S. Military."

U.S. Congress. *See* Congress, U.S.

U.S. Information Service. *See* U.S. Information Service

U.S. Marine Corps. *See* Marines, U.S.

U.S. Navy. *See* Navy, U.S.

U.S. Operations Mission (USOM). The economic arm of the U.S. Embassy in Saigon. Among its functions, the USOM provided grants to South Vietnamese provinces to undertake pacification programs.

See also: Michigan State University Vietnam Advisory Group.

U.S. Strategic Air Command. *See* Strategic Air Command

USSR. *See* Union of Soviet Socialist Republics

Utah, Operation. Code name for March 1966 joint U.S. Marine–ARVN operations against the North Vietnamese Army just south of Chu Lai in Quang Ngai Province.

U Tapao Royal Thai Air Base. Large air base near Bangkok built for B-52 operations. Beginning in July 1967 U.S. Air Force B-52s flew out of U Tapao on bombing missions over North and South Vietnam. Other U.S. Air Force operations were based at Royal Thai Air Force bases at Korat, U Bon, U Dorn, Nakhan Phanom, and Takhli.

See also: B-52; Thailand.

U Thant (1909–1974), Burmese diplomat; Secretary General, United Nations, 1961–1971. Secretary General U Thant tried to organize peace talks between U.S. and Democratic Republic of Vietnam (DRV) officials in 1964. In 1966 he called for a halt to the bombing of North Vietnam, negotiations that would include the National Liberation Front (NLF), and a reduction in military activities on all sides. In the late 1960s, U Thant sought to ban the use of U.S. herbicides in Vietnam. His pressure helped bring about the Nixon administration's renunciation of herbicide first use in 1969 and led to an April 1972 international treaty outlawing the production of biological weapons.

See also: Chemical Warfare; United Nations.

Vietnam Veterans of America's
Women's Project.

See also: Home Before Morning;
Vietnam Veterans of America;
Women, U.S. Military.

Van Lang. Ancient Vietnamese
kingdom founded by the Lac people in the Red River Delta in the
tenth century B.C.

See also: Red River Delta.

Vang Pao (1929–), Hmong military officer. Vang Pao worked
with the French against the Viet
Minh and then commanded
Hmong troops against the North
Vietnamese and the Pathet Lao.
The Central Intelligence Agency
(CIA) recruited Vang Pao as
leader of the Hmong in 1961. By
mid-decade he led a Hmong
army of 30,000 troops. Ruthless
in his domination of Hmong villagers, Vang Pao used his CIA
connections to make them dependent upon his support for rice
supplies. He withheld shipments
of U.S. aid from villages that
tried to keep their sons from
entering his army. When the
Pathet Lao overran his army in
1975, Vang Pao escaped to the
U. S. with several thousand
Hmong followers, and became a
leader of the expatriate Hmong
community.

See also: Central Intelligence
Agency; Hmong; Laos.

Vann, John Paul (1924–1972),
lieutenant colonel, U.S. Army. As
a senior adviser to the Army of
the Republic of Vietnam (ARVN)
in 1962–1963, John Paul Vann
charged that many ARVN commanders were corrupt,

Vance, Cyrus R. (1917–), U.S.
secretary of the army, 1962–
1963; deputy secretary of
defense, 1964–1967. As an aide
to Secretary of Defense
McNamara, Vance was involved
in the initial decision to send
U.S. combat troops to Vietnam.
By late 1967, following a trip to
Vietnam, Vance's view of the war
changed. He was one of the "wise
men" who, at a pivotal meeting
with Johnson in February 1968,
advocated American disengagement from Vietnam. In May 1968
Vance was named deputy chief
delegate to the Vietnam peace
talks in Paris. As Jimmy Carter's
secretary of state in 1977, Vance
favored normalizing relations
with Vietnam.

See also: Paris Peace Accords;
Wise Men; Appendix F, "Paris
Peace Accords."

Van Devanter, Lynda (1947–),
former U.S. Army nurse; veterans advocate; author. Van
Devanter's acclaimed Vietnam
War memoir, *Home Before
Morning* (1983), relates her experiences as a U.S. Army nurse in
Vietnam and after she came
home from the war. She served
at the 71st Evacuation Hospital
in Pleiku in 1969–1970. In 1979
Van Devanter helped launch

incompetent, and cowardly, accusations that were unpopular with his superiors. Vann retired in 1963. He returned to Saigon as a U.S. Agency for International Development officer in 1965. He became Military Assistance Command, Vietnam (MACV) Civil Operations and Revolutionary Development Support (CORDS) adviser for the area around Saigon. In 1971, Gen. Creighton Abrams appointed Vann, a civilian, to command all U.S. forces in II Corps. Vann died in a helicopter crash near Kontum during the North Vietnamese Army's Easter Offensive in June 1972. He is the subject of Neil Sheehan's award-winning biography, *A Bright Shining Lie* (1988).

See also: Bright Shining Lie, A; Civil Operations and Revolutionary Development Support; Easter Offensive.

Van Tien Dung (1917–), general, People's Army of Vietnam (PAVN); PAVN chief of staff, 1954–1974; PAVN commander in chief, 1974–1980; Socialist Republic of Vietnam defense minister, 1980–1986. Gen. Van Tien Dung was North Vietnam's only high-level communist of peasant origin. He joined the party in 1936, escaped from a French prison in 1944, and fought against the Japanese in WWII. During the Indochina War, Dung rose through the Viet Minh ranks to become Gen. Vo Nguyen Giap's chief of staff during the victorious siege of Dien Bien Phu in 1954. For the next twenty years, Dung's military

reputation in North Vietnam was second only to Giap's. When Dung replaced Giap as PAVN commander in chief in 1974, Giap's guerrilla war gave way to Dung's armored columns and regular infantry. Dung planned North Vietnam's final offensive in 1975, and directed Vietnam's invasion of Cambodia and the border war with China in 1979. He became defense minister in 1980, but was removed during the 1986 politburo shakeup.

See also: Ho Chi Minh Campaign; Le Duc Tho; People's Army of Vietnam; Vo Nguyen Giap.

Van Tuong Peninsula. Small peninsula 18 miles southeast of Chu Lai in Quang Ngai Province. The site in August 1965 of Operation Starlite, a bloody battle between three U.S. Marine Corps battalions and a Viet Cong regiment.

See also: Amphibious Landing Operations; Starlite, Operation.

Varenne, Alexander, governor-general, French Indochina, 1925–1928. A socialist, Varenne established a series of reforms in Vietnam, including giving qualified Indochinese the right to become public servants, protecting peasants against usury by creating a farmers' bank, and developing labor laws.

See also: France.

V.C. *See* Viet Cong

Vessey, John W. Jr. (1923–), U.S. Army general, chairman,

Joint Chiefs of Staff, 1983–1985. In 1987 President Reagan named Gen. Vessey the official U.S. liaison to Vietnam on the MIA issue, a position the retired general held until 1993.

See also: Normalization; POW/MIA Controversy.

Vet Centers. Veterans Administration facilities begun in 1979. The storefront Vet Centers, set up outside VA hospitals, are aimed at Vietnam veterans seeking readjustment counseling and are staffed primarily by Vietnam veteran mental health professionals and para-professinals. The Vet Centers today are open to Vietnam veterans and veterans of subsequent conflicts in Somalia, the Persian Gulf, Panama, Grenada, and Lebanon.

See also: Post-Traumatic Stress Disorder; Veterans Affairs, Department of; Veterans, American

Veterans, American. Because of the many unique aspects of the Vietnam War, American veterans had a postwar experience different from that of veterans of earlier U.S. wars. The challenges the 2.8 million U.S. Vietnam veterans faced included the often cool welcome they received upon return, the general hostile attitude of the public toward the war, and their difficulty making the transition back to civilian life.

Rather than being sent to and from Vietnam as a unit, most troops went on individual one-year tours of duty. This undermined group cohesion and caused feelings of isolation upon return. The Pentagon did not provide comprehensive readjustment programs for returning Vietnam veterans; it was not uncommon for a soldier to be in a jungle firefight one day, and home in the United States the day after that. The GI Bill provided Vietnam veterans with only about half the benefits it had given WWII veterans.

Despite this lack of government support, the majority of Vietnam veterans adjusted without significant problems. However, significant numbers of Vietnam veterans experienced various levels of Post-Traumatic Stress Disorder (PTSD) and difficulties finding jobs. Three decades after the war many veterans continued to deal with homelessness, PTSD, drug and alcohol abuse, as well as Agent Orange–related health problems. They have been assisted by several veterans service organizations, most prominently Vietnam Veterans of America, the nation's only congressionally chartered Vietnam veterans service group.

See also: Agent Orange; Cleland, Joseph Maxwell; Veterans Affairs, Department of; Muller, Robert O.; Post-Traumatic Stress Disorder; Vietnam Veterans of America.

Veterans, Vietnamese. When the Vietnam War ended in 1975 there were at least eight million Vietnamese veterans. With the war's end, the South Vietnamese armed forces disintegrated. The North Vietnamese government disbanded the southern revolutionary National Liberation Front (NLF) forces. Precise figures are unavailable, but in 1993 the Socialist Republic of Vietnam (SRV) disclosed that approximately 3.5 million had been inducted into the northern army and the southern revolutionary forces during the war. Of these, about a half million had been killed and a half million wounded.

In 1975, South Vietnamese government forces included 1.1 million men in the regular army (Army of the Republic of Vietnam, ARVN), nearly 4 million in the Regional and Popular Forces (RF/PF), and at least a half million disabled veterans. According to U.S. statistics, 33 percent of the 145,000 refugees who left Vietnam in 1975 were ARVN or RF/PF veterans.

South Vietnamese veterans who remained in Vietnam after 1975 suffered great hardship. Former South Vietnamese officers considered dangerous by the new regime were among the 100,000 persons incarcerated in reeducation camps created after 1975. Most veterans with families in villages quickly returned to them and reintegrated into village life. Those from the south fared much better than their northern counterparts, many of whom were absent from their villages for nearly the duration of the war. They were given meager subsidies by the central government and the villages. A substantial number of veterans had problems with alcohol or drugs. Many veterans, including former PAVN and NLF soldiers, became "boat people" during the exodus from Vietnam during the late 1970s and early 1980s.

See also: Army of the Republic of Vietnam; National Liberation Front; People's Army of Vietnam; Reeducation Camps; Refugees.

Veterans Affairs, Department of (VA). Known until 1989 as the Veterans Administration, the VA is the federal agency that administers programs benefiting veterans. The VA was slow to recognize Vietnam veterans' needs, including Post-traumatic Stress Disorder (PTSD) and the health problems associated with exposure to Agent Orange. By the 1980s, however, most VA facilities offered special counseling programs and group therapy sessions for veterans with PTSD, including the storefront Vet Centers, staffed primarily by mental health professionals who were Vietnam veterans. The VA did not begin compensating Vietnam veterans for exposure to Agent Orange until 1981.

See also: Agent Orange; Chemical Warfare; Nurses; Post-Traumatic Stress Disorder; Ranch Hand, Operation; Vet Centers.

Vichy France. The French state, July 1940 to September 1944. Japan allowed the German-sponsored Vichy regime to run the French colonial administration in Vietnam after Japan conquered Indochina in 1940.

See also: Decoux, Jean; France.

Vientiane. Capital of Laos, on the east bank of the Mekong River in central Laos.

See also: Laos.

Vientiane Agreement. Known officially as the Agreement on the Restoration of Peace and Reconciliation in Laos, the Vientiane Agreement was signed 21 February 1973 by the Royal Lao government and the Pathet Lao communist insurgents. The agreement ended U.S. bombing in Laos and, once a new Lao coalition government was formed, mandated the expulsion of the CIA-run airline, Air America, and Thai military units fighting the North Vietnamese and Pathet Lao.

See also: Air America; Laos; Pathet Lao; Thailand.

Viet Bac (Northern Vietnam). Vietnamese term for the area between the Red River Delta and the Chinese border. The heavily mountainous region was used by the Viet Minh as its headquarters during WWII and the 1946–1954 Franco–Viet Minh War.

See also: Viet Minh.

Viet Cong. *See* National Liberation Front; People's Liberation Armed Forces; Provisional Revolutionary Government

Viet Cong Infrastructure (VCI). U.S. military and CIA term for the underground political arm of the Viet Cong, the communist insurgents fighting in South Vietnam. The U.S.–South Vietnamese Phoenix Program was designed to destroy the VCI, which was estimated to be 70,000 strong.

See also: Central Intelligence Agency; National Liberation Front; Pacification; Phoenix Program.

Viet Kieu (Overseas Vietnamese). Most of the some 2.5 million Vietnamese living abroad left the country following the 1975 communist victory. About half of the overseas Vietnamese live in the United States. Other countries with large Vietnamese expatriate populations include France, Canada, Australia, and Germany.

See also: Refugees.

Viet Minh. Ho Chi Minh and his communist followers founded the *Viet Nam Doc Lap Dong Minh* (League for Vietnamese Independence) in 1941, inviting all patriots to join and fight French colonial rule. Gen. Vo Nguyen Giap raised an army for the Viet Minh that fought the Japanese during WWII and occupied Hanoi in 1945. In 1946, when the French returned, fighting broke out between Viet Minh and the French, touching off the Franco–Viet Minh War. Ho and Giap withdrew the Viet Minh to mountain strongholds and appealed for broad support by ostensibly disbanding the Communist Party and emphasizing anti-imperialism. New names—*Lien Viet* (United Vietnam Nationalist Front) and *Mat Tran To Quoc Viet Nam* (Vietnam Fatherland Front)—were adopted in the 1950s. But the communists never surrendered control of the Viet Minh. By 1960, southern Viet Minh cadres reorganized as the National Liberation Front, nicknamed the Viet Cong, and began a guerrilla war against South Vietnam.

See also: Argenlieu, George Thierry D'; August Revolution; Bui Tin; Cambodia; Cao Bang; Central Intelligence Agency; Dien Bien Phu; Élysée Agreement; Fontainebleau Conference; France; Franco–Viet Minh War; Geneva Conference, 1954; Ho Chi Minh; Land Reform; League for the Independence of Vietnam; National Liberation Front; Pham Van Dong; Tran Van Tra; Union of Soviet Socialist Republics; Vietnam, Democratic Republic of; Vietnam, Republic of; *Viet Nam Quoc Dan Dang;* Vo Nguyen Giap.

Viet Minh Front. *See* League for the Independence of Vietnam

Vietnam, Associated State of (ASV). *See* Associated State of Vietnam

Vietnam, Democratic Republic of (DRV). In August 1945 the Viet Minh, the communist-led nationalist movement in Vietnam, seized power in Hanoi, Hue, and Saigon. On 2 September, Viet Minh leader Ho Chi Minh declared Vietnam's independence as the Democratic Republic of Vietnam (DRV). Allied and contending Vietnamese political groups challenged the DRV in southern Vietnam. National elections were held by the DRV in January 1946 and a state constitution based on a U.S. and French parliamentary model was promulgated in November. In March 1946, Viet Minh and French negotiators reached accords proposing self-determination for Vietnam within the French Union, but French–Viet Minh hostilities broke out in November 1946, and DRV leaders fled to the mountainous region in northwest Vietnam.

Between 1946 and 1954, the DRV was a skeleton government-in-exile. Real power belonged to the Communist Party, which waged a violent campaign against noncommunist nationalists. After the French defeat, the 1954 Geneva accords partitioned Vietnam at the 17th Parallel. Ho Chi Minh returned to Hanoi and reestablished the Democratic Republic of Vietnam. After assuming state power, the Communist Party organized the economy along socialist lines, including the development of large-scale industry and the collectivization of agriculture. Assisted by large-scale Chinese and Soviet aid, industrialization had initial success. In September 1960, the government committed

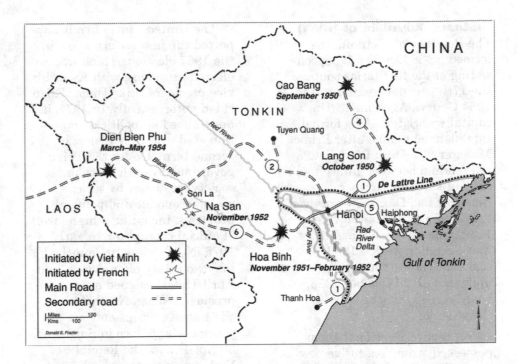

CHINA

Cao Bang
September 1950

TONKIN

Tuyen Quang

Dien Bien Phu
March–May 1954

Red River

Black River

Lang Son
October 1950

De Lattre Line

Son La

LAOS

Na San
November 1952

Hanoi

Haiphong

Red
River
Delta

Hoa Binh
November 1951–February 1952

Day River

Gulf of Tonkin

Thanh Hoa

Initiated by Viet Minh
Initiated by French
Main Road
Secondary road

Miles 100
Kms 100

Donald S. Frazier

the North to a "war of national liberation" in the South, aimed at reunification—a decision that siphoned significant resources away from economic development. Guerrilla warfare in the South, supported by the North, intensified in the early 1960s in its effort to topple the U.S.-supported Republic of Vietnam.

In 1965 the DRV began a ground war against U.S. forces and the South Vietnamese government. In retaliation, the United States launched bombing campaigns against North Vietnam. The DRV defeated the South Vietnamese in April 1975, in a war in which the North suffered more than 800,000 deaths. After the war, the DRV was one of the poorest countries in Asia. In 1975, Vietnam reunited under communist rule, and in April 1976 nationwide elections were held, and the country was officially renamed the Socialist Republic of Vietnam.

See also: Agricultural Reform Tribunals; August Revolution; China, People's Republic of; Embargo; Haiphong; Hanoi; Ho Chi Minh; International Commission for Supervision and Control; Land Reform; Lao Dong; Military Revolutionary Council; Normalization; Paris Peace Accords; People's Army of Vietnam; Pham Hung; Pham Van Dong; Provisional Revolutionary Government; Reeducation Camps; Refugees; Union of Soviet Socialist Republics; Viet Minh; Vietnam, Republic of; Vo Nguyen Giap; Xuan Thuy; Appendix F, "Paris Peace Accords."

Vietnam, Republic of (RVN).
The Republic of Vietnam was
formed on 26 October 1955, consisting of the territories south of
the 17th parallel created by the
1954 Geneva Agreement. The
capital was Saigon. The formal
establishment came after Prime
Minister Ngo Dinh Diem held a
referendum between himself and
chief-of-state and former
Emperor Bao Dai. Diem received
nearly 95 percent of the vote. A
123-member national assembly
was elected in March 1956. A
constitution was formally promulgated on 26 October 1956,
based roughly on the U.S.
Constitution.

In practice, President Diem
possessed strong executive powers, and the National Assembly
became a virtual rubber stamp.
Diem suppressed all dissent to
his rule, communist and noncommunist. He relied almost
exclusively on Catholics and the
affluent landed class for support.
In November 1963 Diem and his
brother Nhu were killed during a
coup, an event that ushered in
an era of political instability as a
series of military governments
replaced each other.

In early 1965, to prevent a
total collapse of the Saigon government, the Johnson administration introduced the first U.S.
combat troops into South
Vietnam. In June, a new group of
"young Turks" took power, led by
two military officers, Nguyen
Cao Ky and Nguyen Van Thieu.
Ky and Thieu consolidated
power and brought a measure of
stability.

The United States firmly supported the new government. In
the 1967 elections Thieu was
elected president, with Ky as his
vice president. Like Diem, Thieu
ruled autocratically. In 1971, he
neutralized all political opposition, and won easy reelection to a
second term. Under the Thieu
government South Vietnamese
society was beset by serious
social, economic and political
problems, including a high level
of official corruption. In early
1975, North Vietnam launched a
major military offensive. In mid-
April Thieu resigned as
president. When North
Vietnamese troops entered the
presidential palace in Saigon on
30 April 1975, the Republic of
Vietnam came to an end.

See also: Bao Dai; Clear and
Hold; Embargo; Fishel, Wesley;
Geneva Conference, 1954; Hoa
Hao; Kennedy, John F.; Land
Reform; Lodge, Henry Cabot Jr.;
Martin, Graham A.; Ngo Dinh
Diem; Nguyen Cao Ky; Nguyen
Khanh; Nguyen Van Thieu;
Pacification; Paris Peace Accords;
Refugees; Regional/Popular
Forces; Seventeenth Parallel;
Special Forces, ARVN;
Vietnamese National Army;
Xuan Loc; Appendix F, "Paris
Peace Accords."

**Vietnam, Socialist Republic
of (SRV).** *See* Vietnam,
Democratic Republic of

**Vietnam: A Television
History** (1983). Thirteen-part
Public Broadcasting Service
television series based on

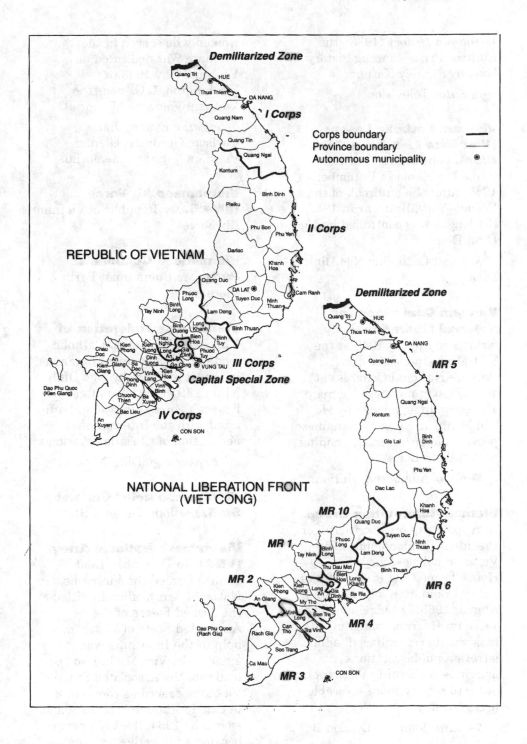

Vietnam: A History (1983), the Pulitzer Prize–winning history book by Stanley Karnow.

See also: Television.

Vietnam Catholic League (*Viet Nam Lien Doan Cong Giao*). Political organization formed in Hanoi in December 1945. After the outbreak of the Franco–Viet Minh war in 1946, the league was controlled by Ngo Dinh Diem.

See also: Catholics; Ngo Dinh Diem.

Vietnam Committee for National Liberation. Body formed 16 August 1945 at the Viet Minh–sponsored first People's National Congress at Tran Trao in northern Vietnam. The committee, headed by Ho Chi Minh, acted as a Vietnamese provisional government pending national elections.

See also: August Revolution.

Vietnam Information Group. In response to press criticism of President Lyndon Johnson's Vietnam policies, the White House formed the Public Affairs Policy Committee for Vietnam in August 1965. Later renamed the Vietnam Information Group, its task was to centralize all administration public relations activities concerning Vietnam in order to receive more favorable press coverage.

See also: Johnson, Lyndon B.

Vietnam Women's Memorial. National memorial to U.S.

women who served in the Vietnam War dedicated on Veterans Day 1993 in Washington, D.C., near the Vietnam Veterans Memorial.

See also: Evans, Diane Carlson; Goodacre, Glenna; Vietnam Veterans Memorial.

Vietnamese Air Force (VNAF). *See* Republic of Vietnam Air Force

Vietnamese Communist Party. *See* Communist Party, Vietnamese

Vietnamese Federation of Christian Workers. Catholic trade-union movement organized in South Vietnam by Ngo Dinh Nhu in 1953 modeled after France's *Force Ouvrière* and affiliated with the International Federation of Christian Workers.

See also: Ngo Dinh Nhu.

Vietnamese Joint General Staff. *See* Joint General Staff

Vietnamese National Army (VNA). In December 1950 France formed the Vietnamese National Army, officially titled the Armed Forces of the Associated State of Vietnam, to help in the Indochina war against the Viet Minh. Bao Dai, leader of the Associated State of Vietnam, served as commander in chief. Although it had 200,000 troops by 1954, the VNA never became an effective fighting force. Following the 1954 Geneva Conference, the VNA became the

Army of the Republic of Vietnam (ARVN).

See also: Army of the Republic of Vietnam; Bao Dai.

Vietnam Nationalist Party.
See Viet Nam Quoc Dan Dang

Vietnamization. U.S. policy, announced by President Nixon on 8 June 1969, that phased out U.S. forces and turned war responsibilities over to the South Vietnamese. Vietnamization, under the direction of Defense Secretary Melvin Laird, included maximizing U.S. military materiel assistance to South Vietnam and intensifying pacification programs. The hope was that South Vietnam could successfully oppose the North Vietnamese and Viet Cong without U.S. support. Vietnamization was based on the declining support for the war among U.S. decision-makers and the American public.

See also: Army of the Republic of Vietnam; Bunker, Ellsworth; Cambodian Incursion; Laird, Melvin R.; Midway Island Conference; Nixon, Richard M.; "Silent Majority" Speech.

Vietnam, Prewar. The territory of prewar Vietnam was shaped like the letter *S* extending along the eastern coast of mainland Southeast Asia from the border with the People's Republic of China (PRC) to the Gulf of Thailand. The country measures more than 1,600 kilometers (1,000 miles) from north to south, while the distance from east to west is often less than 160 kilometers (100 miles). The western border is formed by a string of mountains known to the Vietnamese as the Truong Son, or Central Mountains. Beyond the Truong Son are Vietnam's immediate neighbors, Laos and Cambodia. To the east is the South China Sea.

The entire country is situated approximately within the tropical zone, stretching from 8 degrees to 23 degrees north latitude. It is a region of dense jungles, swamps, and lush rice paddies. In the northern region of the country, the temperature occasionally falls to 10–15°C (50–60°F); in the south the temperature rarely drops below 15°C (60°F), and in the daytime usually averages between 25°C (80°F) and 35°C (95°F).

The modern Socialist Republic of Vietnam is a vastly expanded version of the original Vietnamese state. The historical homeland of the Vietnamese people was in the Red River Delta, surrounding the present-day capital of Hanoi. Calling themselves the "Lac," the early Vietnamese were probably related to Austro-Asiatic-speaking peoples who had been living throughout much of southern China and mainland Southeast Asia since prehistoric times. An advanced Bronze Age civilization, known historically as the kingdom of Van Lang, or in archeological terms the Dong Son era, emerged in the Red River Delta by the early seventh century B.C.

These early peoples were primarily rice farmers ruled by a hereditary aristocracy known as the "Lac lords." Although this embryonic Vietnamese state was originally restricted to the swampy lowland regions of the Red River Delta, it eventually expanded into the neighboring mountains and integrated the peoples there (known to the Vietnamese as the Au) into a new state called Au Lac.

By the third century B.C., the kingdom of Au Lac had become a well-organized state, but at the end of the century Chao T'o, a military commander of the Qin dynasty in China, conquered the state and renamed it Nam Viet, or Southern Viet. The kingdom of Nam Viet was relatively short-lived. In 111 B.C. it fell to the powerful Han Dynasty. The Han placed the Red River Delta under Chinese military jurisdiction and administered the entire area through the indigenous Lac lords. Their occupation aroused resistance from the indigenous aristocracy, and in A.D. 39 a tax rebellion led by the famous Trung sisters broke out. The rebellion was suppressed, but the two sisters would later be revered as patriots who led the fight for Vietnamese independence against foreign rule.

Shaken by the strength of anti-Chinese sentiment among local elites, the Han instituted direct rule over their dependency and placed it under Chinese administration. Chinese officials were posted to the area and the Han assimilated the Vietnamese into the Chinese empire. Over the next several centuries, Chinese institutions and values strongly influenced Vietnamese society. In the tenth century A.D. a local aristocrat, Ngo Quyen, took advantage of the collapse of the Tang Dynasty and declared the independence of a new kingdom called Nam Viet.

In the early 11th century a powerful figure called Ly Thai To emerged through court intrigue and seized power. Making liberal use of Chinese institutions and organizational principles, the Ly Dynasty stabilized the country and ruled it effectively for two hundred years. At the same time, the Ly competed with the neighboring kingdom of Champa along the coast to the south.

The Cham were a Malay-speaking people ethnically distinct from the Vietnamese who had been converted to Islam because of frequent contact with Muslim traders in the area. During the next centuries, periodic conflicts broke out between Champa and Vietnam and the border shifted back and forth in response to the vicissitudes of the relationship.

The Le Dynasty declined in the early 13th century, and in 1225 the Tran, a dynamic new ruling house, replaced it and consolidated the internal development of the Vietnamese state despite ongoing conflicts with the kingdom of Champa. The Tran also clashed repeatedly with the Khmer state of Angkor, then the most powerful kingdom in mainland Southeast Asia. But the primary threat to Tran rule came from the north, where the conquest of China by the Mongols in the late 13th century placed a new and aggressive enemy along the northern border. Under the inspired leadership of the Vietnamese commander Tran Hung Dao, the Vietnamese inflicted a major defeat on the Mongol army, forcing it to withdraw.

Like the Le, the Tran Dynasty lost its vigor in later years, and in the early 15th century a new Chinese dynasty, the Ming, took advantage of court intrigue inside Vietnam and restored Vietnam to Chinese rule. Chinese occupation once again sparked internal resistance, this time under the leadership of Le Loi. After the Chinese withdrawal, Le Loi founded a new dynasty, the Le. The Le further consolidated the territory of the Vietnamese state, while expanding steadily southward and reducing rival Champa to the status of a vassal. Defeated by the Thai in the fifteenth century, the Angkor state rapidly declined and lost territory to the neighboring states of Thailand to the west and Vietnam to the northeast. By 1800 the entire region of the Mekong Delta and the Ca Mau peninsula to the south had been conquered by the Vietnamese.

There was little settlement of Vietnamese into the mountainous Central Highlands, however, an area inhabited by a wide variety of non-Vietnamese tribal peoples. By the end of the sixteenth century, the once powerful state had been reduced to impotence by court intrigue, and rival noble families competed for power and influence. Imperial expansion turned into a disadvantage as the Vietnamese empire divided into two separate administrations, one in the north and one in the south, ruled by two princely families, the Trinh and the Nguyen, respectively.

Direct contact with the West also began in the sixteenth century. During the next century, European merchants and Christian missionaries from several countries established their presence in Vietnam, competing for converts and profits. Although the Portuguese were the first to arrive, the French demonstrated the most sustained interest in the area. By the end of the 17th century the relationship had soured, US Vietnamese officials increasingly feared the effect of Christian influence on Confucian teachings and the tendency of the Europeans to intervene in local politics.

In the 1770s a major peasant revolt led by the so-called Tay Son brothers unseated the Nguyen family in the south and then conquered the north. The Tay Son had revolted in the name of the Le emperor, but following their victory, Nguyen Hue, the leading Tay Son brother, unseated the Le and established his own Nguyen Dynasty. After his death, however, his dynasty rapidly disintegrated, and in 1802 Nguyen Anh, a scion of the princely Nguyen family in the south, defeated the remnants of the Tay Son kingdom and established a new Nguyen Dynasty. As a demonstration of his intention to reunite the country under his authority, he placed his imperial capital in the central Vietnamese city of Hue.

Nguyen Anh had been assisted in seizing power by Pigneau de Béhaine, a French missionary-adventurer who hoped that his aid to Nguyen Anh would restore French influence in the area. By the late 1850s, agitation by mercantile and missionary interests in France for intervention in Vietnam had intensified, spurring the government of Napoleon III to action. Concerned with British advances in Burma and determined to establish a French presence in Southeast Asia, Napoleon ordered a French fleet to launch a naval attack on Da Nang harbor. French troops under the command of Adm. Rigault de Genouilly, advanced toward the imperial capital of Hue but, hampered by local resistance and disease, abandoned the effort. Genouilly then sailed south to the region north of the Mekong Delta, where under new leadership French troops defeated imperial forces and occupied the area of Saigon.

In 1862, a dispirited Emperor Tu Duc, discouraged by the failure of his troops to launch effective resistance, signed the Treaty of Saigon, which ceded three provinces in the south to the French. Two years later, three additional provinces were added, and France transformed its new possessions into the colony of Cochinchina. In 1884 the Vietnamese court signed a treaty granting the French a protectorate over the remaining part of the empire, reducing the Nguyen emperor to a figurehead.

For the remainder of the century, the French consolidated their position, dividing Vietnam into two regions—Tonkin in the north and Annam in the center. Like all industrializing nations, France desired a source of cheap raw materials and markets for its manufactured goods. It found both in Indochina. French official propaganda declared that with the aid of French economic activities, the peoples of Indochina would eventually be brought into the international capitalist marketplace and introduced to modern means of production, transport, and communications.

One element in the French program was the promise to introduce the peoples of Indochina to Western democratic values and attitudes through the introduction of representative institutions and a new educational system. At first, the reaction of many had been to resist French rule while defending traditional institutions. Vietnamese resistance to the French began even before the completion of French conquest, when some members of the traditional civilian and military elite, despite a lack of guidance from the royal court, attempted to organize guerrilla operations in the mountains against foreign-held territory along the coast. At the beginning of the 20th century, a more complex attitude began to take shape, as the desire for self-determination intermingled with admiration for Western culture and a sense of a new world emerging.

Phan Boi Chau, sometimes called Vietnam's first modern nationalist, promoted the idea of violent resistance to be followed by the establishment of a republic on the Western model, but he was driven into exile, captured in China, and eventually returned for trial in Hanoi, where he lived the remainder of his life under house arrest. After World War I, a new wave of anticolonialist ferment arose in the big cities. Ironically, it had been provoked in part by the French themselves, as young graduates of the new Franco-Vietnamese school system, attracted to the allure of European freedom and material affluence, realized that they did not possess such benefits.

During the 1920s, political parties were founded in all three regions of the country. Some, such as the Constitutionalist Party based in Saigon, were essentially reformist in nature, promoting dominion status and a larger role for indigenous elements within the colonial political system. Others, including the Nationalist Party (*Viet Nam Quoc Dan Dang*, VNQDD), sought the eviction of the French by violent means and the

establishment of an independent republic on the capitalist model.

See also: Annam; France; Vietnam, Democratic Republic of; Vietnam, Republic of.

Vietnam Liberation Army. *See* People's Army of Vietnam

Vietnam Moratorium Committee (VMC). In the spring of 1969, antiwar activists Sam Brown, David Hawks, David Mixner, and Marge Sklencar organized the Vietnam Moratorium Committee to arrange a nationwide strike to protest U.S. involvement in Vietnam. The VMC planned to stage a moratorium each month, the first on 15 October, until the United States withdrew from the war.

A moderate organization, the VMC appealed to the mainstream. Supporters included the Americans for Democratic Action (ADA), the Teamsters, the United Auto Workers, Averell Harriman, John Kenneth Galbraith, and 24 U.S. senators, as well as many students across the country. By October, the VMC had an office in Washington, D.C., 31 full-time staffers, and 7,500 field organizers. The 15 October moratorium was the largest nationwide protest in U.S. history. Activities included rallies, teach-ins, and memorial services. The second moratorium coincided with the radical New Mobilization 15 November rallies in Washington and San Francisco. The two groups allied for these protests

despite fundamental differences:
the New Mobe was radical, while
the VMC was moderate to liberal.
The alliance did not last. VMC's
final moratorium came in April
1970; the group disbanded on 19
April 1970.

See also: Brown, Sam; Hawks,
David; New Mobe.

**Vietnam Quoc Dan Dang
(VNQDD).** Also known as the
Vietnamese Nationalist Party,
the organization was founded in
1927 by Vietnamese admirers of
the Chinese nationalist
Kuomintang. Led by Nguyen
Thai Hoc, a teacher in Hanoi, the
VNQDD preached moderniza-
tion, anti-communism, and
resistance to French rule. After a
1930 uprising, Hoc and other
leaders were arrested and executed. When Kuomintang troops
occupied Hanoi in 1945, the
VNQDD briefly held power, but
they were viewed as Chinese
puppets. So, most nationalist
support went to the Viet Minh.
When the French returned to
Vietnam in 1946, most VNQDD
members joined the Viet Minh,
though a few were still active in
South Vietnam in the 1960s.

See also: Ho Chi Minh;
Kuomintang; Nguyen Thai Hoc.

Vietnam Syndrome. Term
referring to the lingering effects
of the Vietnam War on the U.S.
national conscience and specifically to the American public's
reluctance to support military
actions abroad. The syndrome
limited President Jimmy
Carter's options in dealing with
the Iran hostage crisis and prevented President Ronald Reagan
from aggressively aiding the
anti-communist Nicaraguan
Contras. The Persian Gulf War in
1991 somewhat dissipated the
effects of the Vietnam syndrome.

See also: Bush, George; Carter,
Jimmy; Reagan, Ronald;
Weinberger Doctrine.

**Vietnam Veterans Against
the War (VVAW).** Antiwar
group formed in 1967 by six
Vietnam veterans. VVAW, which
had six hundred members in
April 1970, attracted thousands
in the next few years. On 31
January 1971 VVAW held its
Winter Soldier Investigation in
Detroit, during which Vietnam
veterans testified that they had
committed or witnessed acts of
brutality or war crimes. In April
1971 the organization drew
national attention with
Operation Dewey Canyon III, a
week-long encampment in
Washington to protest the war.
VVAW leader John Kerry spoke
against the war at Senate
Foreign Relations Committee
hearings. On 23 April, seven
hundred veterans threw medals
and ribbons over a barricade
onto the Capitol steps. In the
summer of 1972, VVAW demonstrated at the Republican
National Convention in Miami.
As the war ended, the group
called for universal amnesty for
deserters and draft resisters.

See also: Clark, Ramsey; Kerry,
John F.; Mitchell, John N.;
Winter Soldier Investigation.

Vietnam Veterans Leadership Program (VVLP). Begun in 1981 as a federally funded program that encouraged successful Vietnam veterans to work with less successful Vietnam veterans. The program has been privately funded since 1984.

Vietnam Veterans Memorial. The Vietnam Veterans Memorial, popularly known as The Wall, was dedicated on Veterans Day, 13 November 1982, on the Mall in Washington, D.C. The effort to build it began in 1979 when veterans Jan Scruggs, Robert Doubek and John Wheeler established a fund to raise the money for construction. Congress set aside land between the Washington Monument and the Lincoln Memorial for the $5 million memorial, which was paid for entirely by private funds. The memorial's design competition attracted more than 1,400 entries. The guidelines stipulated that the memorial contain the names of all the American dead and not make a political statement. Maya Lin, a 21-year-old Yale architecture student, submitted the winning design: a 150-meter (500-foot) V-shaped wall of polished black granite set into the ground. After objections to the design, authorities agreed to install a statue of three American soldiers near The Wall designed by sculptor Frederick Hart. On Veterans Day in 1993, the Vietnam Women's Memorial was dedicated near the Wall.

See also: Lin, Maya Ying; Scruggs, Jan C.

Vietnam Veterans of America (VVA). The only congressionally chartered U.S. veterans service organization that works exclusively on issues related to Vietnam War–era veterans and their families. VVA was founded by former Marine Robert O. "Bobby" Muller in 1978, and received its congressional charter in 1986.

See also: Muller, Robert O.; Stout, Mary R.; Veterans, American.

Vietnam Veterans' Outreach Program. Federal program signed into law by President Carter 13 July 1979 to fund the national Vet Center program for Vietnam veterans seeking readjustment counseling.

See also: Vet Centers.

Vietnam Workers' Party (VWP). Founded in February 1951 as the successor organization of the Indochinese Communist Party in northern Vietnam. The VWP was the dominant political entity in the Democratic Republic of Vietnam from 1954 to 1976 when it was replaced by the Vietnamese Communist Party.

See also: Indochinese Communist Party; Vietnam, Democratic Republic of.

Village. The main administrative jurisdiction in Vietnam. Two or three villages often are grouped together in communes. Many villages are divided into hamlets.

Vinh. Port city in north central Vietnam, the capital of Nghe An Province, located about halfway between Hue and Hanoi. The city was a center of anti-French rebellion in the 1930s. The site of a large North Vietnamese fuel depot, Vinh was heavily bombed by the United States and South Vietnamese from 1964–1972.

Vinh Long. Province in the Mekong Delta some 145 kilometers southwest of Saigon. The province was briefly captured by the Viet Cong during the 1968 Tet Offensive.

See also: Mekong River and Delta.

Vinh Moc Tunnels. Extensive series of tunnels built in 1966–1968 in the coastal city of Vinh Moc, just north of the Demilitarized Zone, 15 miles north of Dong Ha, used by the Viet Cong and North Vietnamese Army.

See also: Demilitarized Zone; Tunnels.

VNA. *See* Vietnamese National Army

VNAF. *See* Republic of Vietnam Air Force

VNN (Vietnamese Navy). *See* Navy, Republic of Vietnam

VNQDD. *See Viet Nam Quoc Dan Dang*

Vo Bam, People's Army of Vietnam major. In May 1959 Major Vo Bam led a few hundred engineers and laborers into Laos to begin construction of the Ho Chi Minh Trail.

See also: Group 559; Ho Chi Minh Trail.

Vo Chi Cong (1912–), leading Vietnamese communist revolutionary. Vo Chi Cong was an active member of the Indochinese Communist Party in the 1930s. A founding member of the National Liberation Front (Viet Cong), Vo Chi Cong was a leading political cadre in the South during the Vietnam War. After 1976, he held a series of high government posts in the Socialist Republic of Vietnam, including chief of state from 1987–1991.

Vogt, John W., Jr. (1920–), general, U.S. Air Force; commander, Seventh Air Force, 1972–1973. Vogt commanded the U.S. Air Force during some of the heaviest bombing of the Vietnam War. He was in charge of Operation Freedom Train, which blunted the Easter Offensive of the People's Army of Vietnam, and Operations Linebacker and Linebacker II against North Vietnam. Vogt also supervised the U.S. Air Force's withdrawal from South Vietnam in 1973.

See also: Linebacker and Linebacker II, Operations.

Voice of America. U.S. government–funded overseas radio service. The Voice of America began Vietnamese-language broadcasts in September 1950 designed to bolster support for the South Vietnamese government.

Vo Nguyen Giap (1911–), general and commander, People's Army of Vietnam (PAVN), (1946–1972); minister of National Defense (1946–1980). In the 1940s, Giap, Ho Chi Minh's key deputy, organized Viet Minh forces in their war against the French. Born in impoverished Quan Bin province from a family with fervent anti-French sentiments, Giap became an underground member of the Communist Party in his midteens, influenced by the writings of Ho Chi Minh. French authorities imprisoned him for political activities at age sixteen. An excellent student, he entered the country's premier university in Hanoi, where he obtained a bachelor of law degree. At the university, Giap tutored students and studied communism, history, and military strategy. He also began writing political tracts, coauthoring with Truong Chinh in 1938 *The Peasant Problem,* a study that became a key work for Viet Minh planning on agriculture. The next year Giap wrote *The Question of National Liberation in Indochina,* which stressed the importance of protracted war for defeating a powerful foreign adversary.

After the French banned the Communist Party in 1939, Giap fled to China, where he became a key deputy to Ho Chi Minh. He entrusted Giap with the command of the fledgling Viet Minh guerrilla forces, which fought the Japanese occupying Vietnam from 1940 to 1945. During the political vacuum following WWII, the communists seized power in northern Vietnam in the 1945 August Revolution, and Giap became a top figure in the new government, serving as minister of interior in Ho's cabinet and a negotiator with the French in 1946.

During the ensuing Franco–Viet Minh War, Giap shaped the People's Army of Vietnam (PAVN) into a potent fighting force. Giap also began a political indoctrination and education program, credited with developing the highly motivated PAVN soldiers. Giap envisioned the war for independence as a complex, political conflict, a people's war that demanded the nation's total resources and incorporated military, diplomatic, psychological, and economic dimensions.

Giap's historical reputation results from his victory at Dien Bien Phu in May 1954. Using siege tactics, Giap defeated the French with an extraordinary logistical buildup and effective use of well-protected artillery. In the late 1950s and 1960s, Giap remained a key military figure in the Democratic Republic of Vietnam (DRV). As a major land war erupted in the mid 1960s, Giap advocated guerrilla warfare and the advancement of a communist political base in the South. Ho Chi Minh supported aggressive, conventional warfare and ignored Giap's ideas. Giap's tactical concerns were largely validated after PAVN forces suffered extensive defeats to U.S. forces in 1965–1966.

In 1967 Giap designed the Tet Offensive, which collapsed when an expected popular uprising in support of communist forces failed to develop. Between 1968 and 1972, Giap directed the small-unit guerrilla warfare against the U.S. and South Vietnamese troops. He planned the 1972 Easter Offensive, which failed. In 1973, Giap stepped down from direct command of the armed forces. He resigned as minister of defense in 1980 and lost his seat on the politburo in 1982. Despite his waning power, Giap remained popular among the Vietnamese public. In July 1992 he was awarded the Gold Star Order, Vietnam's highest decoration.

See also: Cao Bang; Dien Bien Phu; Easter Offensive; Ho Chi Minh; Navarre Plan; Nguyen Chi Thanh; People's Army of Vietnam; Pham Van Dong; Tet Offensive; Van Tien Dung; Viet Minh; *Viet Nam Quoc Dan Dang.*

Vulture, Operation. Proposed massive U.S. air strikes—possibly including nuclear weapons—against Viet Minh forces surrounding the French at Dien Bien Phu in the spring of 1954. President Eisenhower rejected the plan.

See also: Dien Bien Phu; Eisenhower, Dwight D.; Ely, Paul; Radford, Arthur W.

Vung Tau. Port city in Phuc Tuy Province, 130 kilometers southeast of Saigon, known as Cap St. Jacques during French colonial rule. During the Vietnam War, Vung Tau was a support base for the U.S. Mobile Riverine Force and served as a South Vietnamese R & R center for U.S. troops.

See also: R & R.

Vu Van Giai, South Vietnamese Army (ARVN) general. Gen. Vu Van Giai commanded the ARVN's 3rd Infantry Division during the 1972 North Vietnamese Army Easter Offensive. He was relieved of his command by President Nguyen Van Thieu after a series of battlefield losses.

See also: Easter Offensive.

Vu Van Mau (1914–1998), South Vietnamese Minister of Foreign Affairs, 1955–1963; Prime Minister, 1975. Vu Van Mau resigned in protest over the regime of Ngo Dinh Diem's persecution of the Buddhists. He was named Prime Minister of South Vietnam in the last days before the 30 April 1975 fall of Saigon.

See also: Buddhists; Ngo Dinh Diem.

VVAW. *See* Vietnam Veterans Against the War

VWP. *See* Lao Dong

Wall, The. *See* Vietnam Veterans Memorial

Walt, Lewis W. (1913–1989), general, U.S. Marine Corps. After graduation from Colorado State University, Walt became a Marine Corps second lieutenant in July 1936 and proved an outstanding combat leader in WWII and the Korean War. Lieutenant General Walt commanded the III Marine Amphibious Force in Vietnam from June 1965 until June 1967, with responsibility for the five northern provinces of South Vietnam. He began a balanced strategy of small unit patrolling, large unit operations, and an innovative pacification program using civic action and the U.S. Marine Combined Action Platoons (CAP) operating with local Vietnamese militia. Walt replaced Lt. Gen. Leonard A. Chapman as assistant Marine Corps commandant in January 1968, was promoted to full general in June 1969, and retired in February 1971.

See also: Combined Action Platoons; Krulak, Victor; Marines, U.S.

War Crimes. *See* Atrocities

Warnke, Paul C. (1920–), general counsel, Defense Department, 1966–1967; assistant secretary of defense for international security affairs, 1967–1969. Warnke became one of the Pentagon's leading proponents of de-escalation. When General Westmoreland requested an additional 206,000 troops in 1968, Warnke prepared a critical assessment of Vietnam policy. He argued that more troop deployments would lead to increased casualties and that it was time to reduce U.S. involvement. Warnke's analysis helped sway Defense Secretary Clark Clifford, especially when the Joint Chiefs of Staff failed adequately to address Clifford's concerns about further troop requests and the uncertain length of the war.

See also: Clifford, Clark; Defense, Department of; Enclave Strategy; Hawks and Doves.

War of Attrition. *See* Attrition Strategy

War Powers Resolution. Passed over President Nixon's veto on 7 November 1973, the War Powers Resolution was an attempt to establish congressional coordination with the executive branch over deployment of combat troops abroad. Officially a joint resolution, it has the same legal force as an act of Congress, and often is referred to as the War Powers Act.

The resolution's purpose, as stated in Section 2(a), is to insure that the "collective judgment of both the Congress and the President" be applied to the introduction of U.S. armed forces into hostilities or "situations where imminent involvement in hostilities is clearly indicated by the circumstances." This collective judgment is also to be applied to the continued use of such forces. The resolution mandates that under conditions of undeclared war in which U.S. armed forces are introduced, or when situations threaten hostilities, the president must submit within 48 hours a report to Congress explaining the circumstances necessitating the introduction of U.S. armed forces. Within 60 days the president must terminate use of U.S. military forces unless Congress has declared war, has acted to authorize U.S. armed forces, has extended the 60-day period, or is unable to meet as a result of an armed attack. Although passed before the end of the Vietnam War, the War Powers Resolution was not applied to that conflict.

See also: Congress, U.S.; Fulbright, J. William; Katzenbach, Nicholas; Nixon, Richard M.; Republican Party, U.S.; Vietnam Syndrome.

War Resisters League (WRL). Radical pacifist group founded in the United States in 1923. Under the leadership of David Dellinger, the WRL protested against the expanding U.S. military advisory effort in Vietnam in 1963. At a 16 May 1964 WRL-sponsored demonstration in New York City twelve men burned their draft cards. In December 1964, the WRL organized the first nationwide demonstration against the Vietnam War.

See also: Dellinger, David.

Warsaw Talks. Planned U.S.–North Vietnamese peace talks for late 1966 that did not take place when the North Vietnamese protested U.S. air strikes.

See also: Lewandoski, Januscz; Marigold, Operation.

War Zones. In the early 1960s, before the United States entered the Vietnam War, the South Vietnamese referred to two areas north of Saigon that were under the control of the Viet Cong as War Zones C and D.

Washington Green, Operation. Code name for April 1969 U.S. Army 173rd Airborne Brigade pacification effort that also involved training South Vietnamese Regional/Popular forces (RF/PF) in Binh Dinh Province.

Washington Special Actions Group (WSAG). Nixon administration Vietnam War advisory committee formed in April 1969 and chaired by National Security Adviser Henry Kissinger, made up of second-ranking officers from the other national security agencies.

See also: Kissinger, Henry.

Watergate. The term for the scandal that engulfed President Richard Nixon after the 17 June 1972 break-in at Democratic National Committee headquarters in the Watergate office building in Washington, D.C.

The causes of the Watergate break-in were rooted in the Vietnam War. Antiwar and congressional critics had profoundly disturbed the president, national security adviser Henry Kissinger, and others in the administration, and they reacted with stern and illegal methods to repress that criticism. These included sponsorship of the Huston Plan to centralize surveillance and domestic intelligence activities; the use of the Federal Bureau of Investigation (FBI), Central Intelligence Agency (CIA), and U.S. Army personnel and resources to spy on antiwar protest groups. Daniel Ellsberg's leaking of the Pentagon Papers in June 1971 was the immediate occasion for creating the plumbers. The break-in was carried out by the "plumbers," a clandestine group that used illegal methods to gain compromising information on antiwar foes. The Watergate break-in and its cover-up led to an impeachment charge brought by the House Committee on the Judiciary in July 1974, and eventually forced Nixon's resignation.

See also: Central Intelligence Agency; Colson, Charles; Ehrlichman, John; Ellsberg, Daniel; Federal Bureau of Investigation; Ford, Gerald R. Jr.; Liddy, G. Gordon; Mitchell, John N.; Nixon, Richard M.; Paris Peace Accords; Pentagon Papers; Plumbers; Richardson, Elliot; Saturday Night Massacre; Appendex F, "Paris Peace Accords."

Wayne, John (1907–1979), Hollywood actor and director. Wayne, much admired for his portrayal of U.S. fighting men in WWII movies, directed *The Green Berets* (1968), the only Hollywood Vietnam War combat film made during the war. Many American men of the Vietnam War generation were influenced by Wayne's film persona; untold numbers joined the military to emulate his screen exploits. In Vietnam, "doing a John Wayne" meant the act of spontaneously charging the enemy or otherwise exposing oneself dangerously in combat.

See also: Green Berets, The.

Weathermen. A small, violent radical group led by Bernardine Dohrn and Mark Rudd. The Weathermen split off from Students for a Democratic Society in 1969. Taking their name from a lyric in the Bob Dylan song, "Subterranean Homesick Blues," the Weathermen sought to bring the Vietnam War home to the United States through violent protest and guerrilla attacks. After a spree of vandalism and attacks on police, the Weathermen formed small cells and went underground, surfacing occasionally to plant bombs at corporate, military, and government targets. They caused several fatalities and many injuries. Most of the Weathermen were arrested or had surrendered by the early 1980s.

See also: Dohrn, Bernardine; New Left; Students for a Democratic Society; Rudd, Mark.

Webb, Catherine B. (Kate)
(1943–), journalist. Webb, the
United Press International
bureau chief in Phnom Penh,
was captured by Viet Cong
guerillas in 1971. She was held
for 23 days before being released.
Webb's book, *On the Other Side*
(1972), tells the story of her captivity.

Webb, James (1946–), attorney; writer, government official;
minority counsel, U.S. House
Committee on Veterans Affairs,
1984–1987; assistant defense
secretary for Reserve Affairs,
1984–1987; secretary of the
Navy, 1987–1988. Webb, who
served as a U.S. Marine lieutenant in Vietnam, is the author
of several novels, including the
acclaimed Vietnam War combat
novel, *Fields of Fire* (1978).

See also: *Fields of Fire.*

Weigl, Bruce (1949–), poet.
Weigl, who served with the
United States 1st Cavalry
Division in Vietnam in
1967–1968, is the author of sev-
eral collections of prize-winning
poetry influenced by his Vietnam
service, including *The Monkey
Wars* (1984), *Song of Napalm*
(1988), and *Sweet Lorain* (1996).
He teaches writing at
Pennsylvania State University.

Wei Guoqing, Chinese general
sent with a military advisory
mission to aide Ho Chi Minh's
Vietminh forces in 1950.

See also: China, People's
Republic of.

Weinberger Doctrine. A vari-
ant of the "Vietnam Syndrome,"
stated by Secretary of Defense
Caspar Weinberger, in a 28
November 1984 speech.
Weinberger's doctrine held that
U.S. forces would only be committed on behalf of a "vital
national interest," and only with
the "clear intention of winning."
Political and military objectives
must be clearly defined in
advance, Weinberger said, and
troop commitments made with
the support of Congress and the
people.

See also: Vietnam Syndrome.

Weiner, Lee. See Chicago Seven

Weinglass, Leonard. See
Chicago Seven

Weiss, Cora. See New Mobe

**Westmoreland-CBS Libel
Suit.** Gen. William
Westmoreland sued the
Columbia Broadcasting System
(CBS) for libel after a January
1982 documentary charged that
in 1967, prior to the Tet
Offensive, Gen. Westmoreland
had directed a conspiracy to
underreport the strength of
North Vietnamese and Viet Cong
forces. The case went to trial; a
settlement was reached before
the jury began deliberations.
CBS issued a statement that
said that the network "never
intended to assert, and does not
believe, that General
Westmoreland was unpatriotic or
disloyal in performing his duties

as he saw them." Westmoreland and CBS stood by their charges and claimed victory.

See also: Adams, Sam; Central Intelligence Agency; Komer, Robert W.; McNamara, Robert; Tet Offensive; Westmoreland, William C.

Westmoreland, William C.

(1914–), general, U.S. Army; commander, U.S. Military Assistance Command, Vietnam (COMUSMACV), 1964–1968; U.S. Army chief of staff, 1968–1972. William C. Westmoreland was first captain, commander of the Corps of Cadets) in the West Point class of 1936. Commissioned in the field artillery, Westmoreland served with distinction in WWII, commanding an artillery battalion during the North African campaign and serving as chief of staff of the 9th Division in the final assault against Germany.

After holding many of the most visible and important positions in the U.S. Army, Westmoreland became superintendent of the U.S. Military Academy at West Point in 1960. Gen. Westmoreland replaced Gen. Paul Harkins as COMUSMACV in June 1964 after six months as Harkins' deputy. In 1965, when North Vietnamese regulars threatened to cut through the country in the Central Highlands, President Johnson, acting upon the advice of Westmoreland and the Joint Chiefs of Staff (JCS), increased the level of U.S. combat forces in

South Vietnam to more than 100,000.

From 1965 to 1967 Westmoreland was instrumental in raising the level of U.S. forces in South Vietnam and developing the military strategy of attrition for the ground war. During the 1968 Tet Offensive, Westmoreland's command, though taken by surprise, reacted quickly and decisively defeated the attackers. Westmoreland then asked for 200,000 additional troops, a request President Lyndon Johnson rejected. Westmoreland was then recalled and made Army chief of staff. Westmoreland retired in 1972, but remained a central figure in the debate over the Vietnam War, vigorously defending the war's conduct in his 1976 memoir, *A Soldier Reports.*

See also: Abrams, Creighton W. Jr.; Attrition Strategy; Defense, Department of; Joint General Staff; Johnson, Lyndon B.; Khe Sanh; Krulak, Victor; Military Assistance Command, Vietnam; Pacification; Rolling Thunder, Operation; Search-and-Destroy; Summers, Harry G. Jr.; Taylor, Maxwell D.; Tet Offensive.

"We Won't Go" Petitions.

Petitions first circulated in 1964 among draft-age men primarily on college campuses by the radical antiwar group, Students for a Democratic Society (SDS). In 1967, some two dozen "We Won't Go" groups were on college campuses, consisting of men who vowed to refuse to serve in Vietnam.

See also: Selective Service; Students for a Democratic Society.

Weyand, Frederick C.
(1916–), general, U.S. Army; commander, U.S. Military Assistance Command, Vietnam (MACV), 1972–1973; U.S. Army chief of staff, 1974–1976. The last MACV commander, Gen. Frederick Weyand had previously commanded the 25th Infantry Division and the II Field Force in Vietnam, and was instrumental in defeating the Viet Cong attack on Saigon during the 1968 Tet Offensive. He replaced Gen. Creighton Abrams in June 1972, and supervised the final withdrawal of U.S. forces.

See also: Tet Offensive.

Wheeler, Earle G. (1908–1975), general, U.S. Army; chief of staff, 1962–1964; chairman, Joint Chiefs of Staff (JCS), 1964–1970. Gen. Earle "Bus" Wheeler was a lifelong staff officer with no combat experience when President Kennedy appointed him U.S. Army chief of staff in 1962. He shared Kennedy's enthusiasm for counterinsurgency warfare and Secretary of Defense Robert McNamara's penchant for statistics, having taught mathematics at West Point. For his support of the controversial Limited Test Ban Treaty, Wheeler was appointed chairman of the JCS in 1964. Soon after being appointed JCS chairman Wheeler began promising success in Vietnam through further escalation. He resented

President Johnson's reluctance to use the full might of U.S. power against North Vietnam. After the 1968 Tet Offensive Wheeler advised Johnson to call up the reserves and send 200,000 additional troops to Vietnam. After serving longer than any other JCS chairman, Wheeler retired in 1970.

See also: Attrition Strategy; Defense, Department of; Nuclear Weapons; Joint Chiefs of Staff; SIGMA.

Wheeler, John. *See* Vietnam Veterans Memorial

Wheeler/Wallowa, Operation.
Code name for November 1967 through November 1968 U.S. Army Americal Division operations against the Viet Cong and North Vietnamese Army in Quang Nam and Quang Tin provinces south of Da Nang.

White Horse Division.
Nickname of Republic of Korea (ROK) 9th Infantry Division, which fought in the Vietnam War from 1965–1973.

See also: Korea, Republic of.

Whiteside, Thomas
(1918–1998), writer. Whiteside's 1970 articles for *The New Yorker* on the health and environmental consequences of U.S. use of the herbicide Agent Orange in Vietnam led to U.S. Senate hearings and the subsequent ending of the spraying by the Pentagon.

See also: Agent Orange.

Wild Weasel. Code name for U.S. aircraft, most often the F-105 and F-100, equipped with electronic countermeasure equipment that detected, suppressed and destroyed enemy missile and anti-aircraft sites.

See also: Electronic Countermeasures.

White Star Mobile Training Teams. Code name for U.S. Special Forces training of local Lao militias and the Royal Lao Army to fight the communist Pathet Lao. The program began in 1959 and ended in 1962.

See also: Pathet Lao; Special Forces, U.S. Army.

Williams, Samuel T. (1897–1984), lieutenant general, U.S. Army; commander, U.S. Military Assistance Advisory Group, Vietnam, 1955–1960. A strict disciplinarian known as "Hanging Sam," Williams continued the U.S. policy of training South Vietnamese troops to repel a conventional invasion from the north. Williams dismissed the Viet Cong guerrilla threat as diversionary tactics. He cultivated close relations with South Vietnamese President Ngo Dinh Diem while feuding constantly with U.S. Ambassador Elbridge Durbrow. Williams retired in 1960.

See also: Durbrow, Elbridge; Trang Sup.

Willson, David A. (1942–), novelist, bibliographer. Willson, who served as a clerk at U.S. Army Vietnam headquarters in Vietnam in 1966–1967, is the author of three well-received comic autobiographical novels: *REMF Diary* (1988), *The REMF Returns* (1992), and *In the Army Now* (1995). He is co-editor of the bibliography, *Vietnam War Literature* (1996).

Wilson, Charles E. (1890–1961), U.S. Secretary of Defense, 1953–1957. Wilson, the former head of General Motors, argued against U.S. military intervention in Vietnam during his tenure as defense secretary, which included the last two years of the French Indochina War.

See also: Eisenhower, Dwight D.

Wilson, (James) Harold (1916–1995), British prime minister, 1964–1970, 1974–1976. Wilson received many requests from the United States for military aid in Vietnam, but refused them all. Although he never officially opposed the U.S. war effort, Wilson repeatedly criticized the bombing of North Vietnam and privately called for negotiations. He was central to the Operation Sunflower negotiations in 1967, but his efforts to encourage Soviet prime minister Alexei Kosygin to pressure North Vietnam to negotiate failed when President Johnson adopted a tougher negotiating stance.

See also: Great Britain; Kosygin, Alexei.

Winners and Losers (1976). Book that won the National Book Award by former *New York Times* Vietnam War correspondent Gloria Emerson. It takes an in-depth look at the war and at Vietnam veterans, Vietnamese refugees, and others in America touched by the war.

See also: Emerson, Gloria.

Winter Soldier Investigation. 31 January to 2 February 1971, meeting in Detroit sponsored by Vietnam Veterans Against the War meant to show that U.S. troops committed war crimes and atrocities in Vietnam. About one hundred veterans and sixteen civilians presented testimony. Discussions also were held on such topics as racism and the effect of the war experience on soldiers. Although the media paid little attention to the investigation, Sen. Mark O. Hatfield (R-Oreg.) entered the testimony in the *Congressional Record* and urged that official hearings be held about the conduct of U.S. forces in Vietnam.

See also: Vietnam Veterans Against the War.

Wiretaps. *See* Cointelpro, Operation.

Wisconsin Bombing. *See* University of Wisconsin Bombing

Wise Men. Nickname given to a group of elder statesmen who met periodically from 1965 to 1968 to advise President Lyndon Johnson. Drawing upon their vast collective experience in government and the military, Johnson relied upon the "wise men" for insightful analysis of the Vietnam situation and policy options.

The group included Dean Acheson, John McCloy, Clark Clifford, Robert Murphy, Arthur Goldberg, George Ball, McGeorge Bundy, Henry Cabot Lodge, Abe Fortas, Douglas Dillon, Maxwell Taylor, Cyrus Vance, Omar Bradley and Matthew Ridgway. The "wise men" first met in July 1965 and endorsed Secretary of Defense Robert McNamara's proposal for escalation. In a November 1967 meeting, the wise men, with the exception of Ball, continued to back Johnson's Vietnam policies. After the 1968 Tet Offensive, Clifford, then secretary of Defense, convened a meeting for 25 March. The next day, the group advised Johnson to begin disengaging from Vietnam. Fortas, Murphy, and Generals Taylor and Bradley dissented. The change of opinion from this generally pro-war group profoundly affected Johnson.

See also: Acheson, Dean; Ball, George W.; Bundy, McGeorge; Clifford, Clark; Fortas, Abe; Harriman, W. Averell; Goldberg, Arthur J.; Lodge, Henry Cabot Jr.; McCloy, John; Murphy, Robert D.; Ridgway, Matthew B.; Rostow, Walt Whitman; Taylor, Maxwell D.; Vance, Cyrus R.

Wolff, Tobias (1945–), former U.S. Special Forces soldier;

writer. Wolff's novels, memoirs and short stories, including *The Barracks Thief* (1984), *Back in the World* (1985), and *This Boys' Life* (1989), have won critical acclaim and literary prizes. Wolff's *In Pharaoh's Army* (1994) is a revealing, literary memoir in which the author writes about his 1967–1968 Vietnam tour.

See also: In Pharaoh's Army.

Women, U.S. Military.

American military women during the Vietnam War era were segregated into separate branches of the U.S. armed forces, and excluded from combat. The Pentagon estimates that 7,465 women served in the military in Vietnam, of whom 80 percent were in the U.S. Army, Air Force, and Navy nurse corps. The vast majority (6,250) were Army nurses.

Unlike doctors, many of whom were drafted into the military, the vast majority of nurses were volunteers. In 1963, the U.S. Army's nurse corps numbered only 2,928 nurses, but by 1965 the Army began extensive recruiting of civilian volunteers. The nurses, who had to be at least 21 years old, were all commissioned officers and generally served one-year tours in Vietnam. Many served in Vietnam after being recruited into student nurse programs, whereby the Army, Air Force, or Navy paid for their final years of education in return for service. Before being assigned to Vietnam, Army nurses had to

attend basic training for eight weeks, Navy nurses were required to serve two years in the nurse corps, and Air Force nurses received flight training for two months. Despite these preparations, military nurses were generally inexperienced. Anna Mae Hayes, assistant chief of the Army Nurse Corps, reported that 60 percent of the Army nurses in Vietnam had less than two years of nursing experience, and 60 percent of these had less than six months.

In Vietnam, army nurses were stationed in hospitals throughout South Vietnam. Navy nurses were assigned to hospital ships off the coast, such as the USS *Repose* and USS *Sanctuary,* and to the Naval Support Activity unit in Da Nang. Air Force nurses cared for patients on evacuation flights within and outside of the country and at casualty staging facilities.

Some 700 members of the Women's Army Corps (WACs) served in Vietnam, reaching a peak strength of 20 officers and 139 enlisted women in January 1970. WAC advisers were first brought to Vietnam to help the government of South Vietnam with the planning and development of its Women's Armed Forces Corps (WAFC). WACs advised the WAFC on organization, recruitment, training, and administration. For additional training, WAFC officer candidates traveled to the United States and attended courses at the WAC school. WACs were assigned to clerical and administrative positions.

More than five hundred Women in the Air Force (WAFs) served in Southeast Asia between 1967 and 1973, providing administrative and technical support for the Seventh Air Force (Vietnam) and the Thirteenth Air Force (Thailand). Enlisted WAFs generally performed secretarial and clerical work while officers performed technical duties in fields such as communications, logistics, and information service. Nine Navy WAVES (Women Accepted for Voluntary Emergency Service) served in Vietnam during the war, all officers; no noncommissioned WAVES served in Vietnam. Most were assigned to the Military Assistance Command, Vietnam (MACV), in Saigon with either the commander of naval forces or the Communications Information Center. A few WAVES also served at Cam Ranh Bay with the Naval Support Activity unit. Thirty-six Women Marines (WMs) served in Vietnam between 1967 and 1973.

Eight women, all military nurses, died in Vietnam; one nurse, U.S. Army Lt. Sharon Lane, was killed by hostile fire. Nurses and other medical personnel often treated a steady flow of severely wounded soldiers, working long and grueling shifts. After returning to the United States, some nurse veterans, like many other Vietnam veterans, suffered from symptoms often diagnosed as Post-traumatic Stress Disorder (PTSD).

See also: Lane, Sharon; Nurses.

Women, Vietnamese. South Vietnamese women played a minimal role in the war. Madame Ngo Dinh Nhu organized the Women's Solidarity Movement, which supported official policy, and whose younger members dressed as female militia, mainly for show. Women in North Vietnam and those fighting for the communist cause in South Vietnam took a very active role in the conflict, serving as nurses, guerrilla fighters, entertainers, cooks, construction workers, and weapons carriers. The Viet Minh's Women's Unions spread propaganda and organized support for the Indochina War. Women served with the Viet Minh during the Indochina war, and with the Viet Cong guerrillas in the South during the Vietnam War.

Women in what is now Vietnam have participated in wars for independence from the earliest years, building upon traditional legends of heroines such as the Trung sisters, who fought in a war against China nearly 2,000 years ago. Ho Chi Minh, leader of the Viet Minh's nationalist movement against the French in the 1950s, emphasized women's equality with men. The communist-supported Viet Minh organized Women's Unions to spread propaganda and organize support for the Indochina War. Women served with the Viet Minh during the French war, with the Viet Cong guerrillas in the South during the Vietnam War, and virtually all North Vietnamese women were extensively involved in resistance to the southern government and the Americans on some level. Since no one could escape the ravages of war, some younger women actually joined the fighting forces, marching with men to form artillery battalions on the Ho Chi Minh Trail. They acted as nurses and served in repair crews, keeping the intermeshing trails open and repairing bomb damage. The intensive bombing of the North brought women other duties. Many learned to fire the antiaircraft weapons that defended Hanoi from U.S. bombers. Other women took groups of children to live in the countryside to escape the bombings, continuing their education, instructing them in the principles of revolution, acting as surrogate mothers, and nursing and comforting those who had lost parents or siblings.

In the South, women actively served with the Viet Cong, in some places accounting for one-third of its membership. Women were most useful as couriers and liaisons because they could go from one area to another disguised as peasants bringing goods to market and were less suspect than men. They transported weapons, food, and clothing, and were especially active in the tunnel area of Cu Chi, where they served as nurses, entertainers, cooks, and construction workers, and

carried weapons and information to and from Saigon.

Postwar Vietnam has been slow to acknowledge the role of its women warriors, although the Women's Union, organized in the 1930s and active today in health, education, family planning, and propaganda is building museums to honor the heroines of the past.

See also: Ngo Dinh Nhu (Madame Nhu); Nguyen Thi Binh.

Women's Armed Forces Corps. South Vietnamese female armed services branch set up with the advice and training in 1964 of U.S. Women's Army Corps (WAC) advisers.

See also: Women, U.S. Military.

Women's Liberation Association of South Vietnam. *See* Nguyen Thi Dinh

Women's Movement for the Right to Life. Broad-based South Vietnamese women's group formed 25 July 1970 to work for the dignity of Vietnamese women, for peace and the right to life, and against U.S. participation in the Vietnam War and the military government of President Nguyen Van Thieu.

See also: Ngo Ba Thanh.

Women's Solidarity League, Vietnamese. Anti-communist para-military organization headed by Madame Ngo Dinh Nhu formed in 1955 consisting mostly of the wives of government officials who supported the regime of Madame Nhu's brother in law, Ngo Dinh Diem.

See also: Ngo Dinh Nhu (Madame Nhu).

Women's Strike for Peace (WSP).

U.S. antiwar group founded in 1961 to work for nuclear disarmament. During the Vietnam War the WSP actively protested the war, taking part in demonstrations and sending delegations to North Vietnam.

Women's Union.

Vietnamese women's group organized in the 1930s and active today in health, education, family planning, and propaganda. The Women's Union is building museums to honor the heroines of the past.

See also: Nguyen Thi Binh; Nguyen Thi Dinh; Women, Vietnamese.

World Bank. *See* Embargo

World War I.

France conscripted some 48,000 Vietnamese laborers and sent them to the western front in Europe during WWI; some 10,000 died and 15,000 were wounded. After the war, Ho Chi Minh tried unsuccessfully to plead his case for Vietnamese independence at the Paris peace conference.

See also: France.

World War II.

Japan occupied Vietnam during WWII, but permitted the French to govern the colony's affairs. The communist-led Viet Minh, supported during the war's later stages by the U.S. Office of Strategic Services (OSS), fought the Japanese in Vietnam. During the war the United States bombed Japanese installations in Haiphong. In August 1945, the Viet Minh seized power in Hanoi and proclaimed an independent nation. Soon after, Great Britain and China accepted the Japanese surrender in Indochina and helped reestablish French power.

See also: Great Britain; Roosevelt, Franklin Delano; Viet Minh; Vo Nguyen Giap.

WRL. *See* War Resisters League

X-Y-Z

Xa Loi Pagoda Raid. 21 August 1963 armed attack on the Xa Loi pagoda, the main Buddhist sanctuary in Saigon. The raid was led by the armed forces of Ngo Dinh Nu, the brother of South Vietnamese President Ngo Dinh Diem. Some four hundred monks and nuns were arrested.

See also: Buddhists; Thich Tri Quang.

Xuan Loc. South Vietnamese city, 60 kilometers (37 miles) northeast of Saigon. The site of a South Vietnamese command center protecting the air base at Bien Hoa, Xuan Loc was attacked on 9 April 1975 by North Vietnamese Army (NVA) troops and artillery. Army of the Republic of Vietnam (ARVN) forces fought back, aided by air support from the South Vietnamese air force. Although the defenders inflicted severe casualties on the NVA troops, the ARVN forces withdrew on 22 April. One week later, on 30 April 1975, the Republic of Vietnam officially surrendered.

See also: Army of the Republic of Vietnam; Ho Chi Minh Campaign.

Xuan Thuy (1912–1985), foreign minister, Democratic Republic of Vietnam (DRV), 1963–1965; chief delegate, Paris peace talks, 1968–1970. Xuan Thuy joined the Indochina Communist party in 1938 and spent WWII in prison. Upon his release in 1945, Thuy edited *Cuu Quoc,* the official Viet Minh newspaper, and traveled in Europe during the Indochina War to publicize the nationalist cause. As the DRV's chief delegate to the Paris peace talks in 1968 Thuy insisted that the United States withdraw immediately and that President Thieu resign.

See also: Le Duc Tho; Kissinger, Henry; Paris Peace Accords; Appendix F, "Paris Peace Accords."

XYX Project. Code name for failed effort headed by Undersecretary of State George Ball to arrange peace negotiations with North Vietnam in France in the summer and fall 1965.

See also: Ball, George W.

Yalta Conference. Meeting between WWII allied leaders held 4–11 February 1945 in Yalta during which U.S. President Franklin D. Roosevelt softened his previously stated resistance to post-war French recolonization of Indochina.

See also: Potsdam Conference; Roosevelt, Franklin D.

Yankee Station. U.S. code-name for the area of the South China Sea in international waters off the coast of North Vietnam. Yankee Station served as an operations area for Task Force 77, an aircraft carrier strike group of the U.S. Navy's Seventh Fleet. From this staging point, the Navy launched air operations against North Vietnam.

See also: Dixie Station; Task Force 77; Search and Rescue.

Yankee Team, Operation. Code name for U.S. Air Force and Navy photo reconnaissance flights over Laos that began in May 1964.

Yellowstone, Operation. Code name for U.S. Army 25th Infantry Division engagements against two Viet Cong regiments in Tay Ninh province from December 1966 to February 1968.

Yen Bay. Northwestern Vietnamese city, near the Chinese border. In 1965 North Vietnam began constructing a large military base at Yen Bay.

Yen Bay Mutiny. Unsuccessful revolt against the French staged by the Vietnamese Nationalist Party (VNDQQ) in February 1930 at Yen Bay and other military posts in northern Vietnam.

See also: Viet Nam Quoc Dan Dang.

Yippie. *See* Youth International Party

Young Americans for Freedom (YAF). A staunchly conservative national group of mainly college students that supported the U.S. war effort in Vietnam.

Young, David (1936–), Nixon White House aide. Young, a member of the White House Domestic Council, was assigned in 1971 to investigate the leak of the Pentagon Papers.

See also: Plumbers; Watergate.

Young Turks. Name given by the U.S. embassy in Saigon to a group of young South Vietnamese military officers, including Nguyen Cao Ky and Nguyen Van Thieu, who were loyal to Gen. Nguyen Khanh during his overthrow of the South Vietnamese government of Gen. Duong Van Minh.

See also: Duong Van Minh; Nguyen Cao Ky; Nguyen Khanh; Nguyen Van Thieu.

Youth International Party (Yippie). *See* Democratic Convention, 1968

Youth Liberation Association (YLA). Communist-sponsored group aimed at those aged 16 to 25 in South Vietnam. Formed 25 December 1961 near Saigon, the YLA's goals were to overthrow the South Vietnamese government, end South Vietnamese military operations in rural

Vietnam, and unify North and South Vietnam.

Zablocki, Clement J. (1912–1983), U.S. representative (D-Wisc.), 1949–1983. Zablocki chaired the House Foreign Affairs Committee during the Vietnam War. He was an early and strong supporter of South Vietnamese President Ngo Dinh Diem and the U.S. war effort in Vietnam.

See also: Congress, U.S.

Zais, Melvin (1916–), U.S. Army lieutenant general. General Zais commanded the U.S. Army's 1st Infantry Division in 1966, was commanding general, U.S. Army 101st Airborne Division, 1968–1969, and commanded the Army XXIV Corps in the northern zone of Vietnam in 1969–1970.

Zhou Enlai (1898–1976), premier, People's Republic of China, 1949–1976. At the 1954 Geneva Conference, Zhou broke a French-Viet Minh deadlock and successfully brokered a compromise that resulted in the partition of Vietnam. When hostilities resumed in Vietnam, Zhou supported the Vietnamese communists with substantial military aid and with political and economic support. When Zhou met Henry Kissinger in 1971 and President Nixon the next year, he insisted that U.S. troops had to be withdrawn from Vietnam.

See also: China, People's Republic of; Geneva Conference,

1954; Kissinger, Henry; Mendès-France, Pierre; Ngo Dinh Luyen.

Ziegler Ronald L. (1939–), White House press secretary, 1969–1975.

Zimmerman, Mitchell, Co-author, with Benjamin Spock, of the antiwar treatise, *Dr. Spock on Vietnam* (1968).

See also: Spock, Benjamin.

Zippo Squads. Slang term for U.S. troops on search-and-destroy missions who searched villages suspected of Viet Cong guerrilla activity. Sometimes, after searching for hidden weapons or other incriminating evidence, the squads set fire to the villagers' thatch huts with their Zippo lighters.

See also: Search-and-Destroy.

Zorthian, Barry (1920–), minister-counselor for information and director, Joint U.S. Public Affairs Office, 1964–1968. Zorthian conducted the daily U.S. Information Service press briefing, referred to by journalists as the "Five O'Clock Follies," in Saigon.

See also: Five O'Clock Follies; Joint U.S. Public Affairs Office.

Zuckert, Eugene M. (1911–), Secretary of the U.S. Air Force, January 1961-September 1965.

Zumwalt, Elmo R. Jr. (1920–), admiral, U.S. Navy; U.S. Navy commander, Vietnam, 1968–1970; chief of naval operations, 1970–1974. Zumwalt commanded the "brown water navy" of river boats that patrolled the Mekong Delta and coastal areas of South Vietnam. He planned and executed Operation SEALORDS, which cut riverine supply lines from Cambodia to the Viet Cong guerrillas, and ordered the spraying of Agent Orange defoliant over the Mekong Delta. As chief of naval operations in 1970, Zumwalt advocated U.S. withdrawal from Vietnam to meet the rising challenge of Soviet sea power.

See also: Agent Orange; Navy, U.S; Sealord, Operation.

Zumwalt, Elmo R. III
(1946–1988), U.S. Navy swift boat commander in Vietnam, 1969–1970. The son of U.S. Navy Admiral Elmo R. Zumwalt, Jr., who ordered the spraying of the herbicide Agent Orange in Vietnam, Elmo Zumwalt III was diagnosed with cancer in 1983. He died in 1988. Father and son believe the cancer was caused by the son's exposure to Agent Orange in Vietnam.

See also: Agent Orange.

Appendix A
Chronology

Early History

Date	Southeast Asia	United States	The War
Early 7th century B.C.	Dong Son era begins; the kingdom of Van Lang forms in the Red River Delta, eventually expanding into surrounding mountainous areas to form Au Lac.		
Late 3rd century B.C.	Chinese general Chao T'o (Trieu Da) conquers Au Lac and establishes the independent kingdom of Nam Viet ("Southern Viet") under his rule.		
111 B.C.	Chinese Han dynasty conquers Nam Viet.		
A.D. 39	Trung sisters lead unsuccessful revolt against Chinese rule.		
938 January	Battle of Bach Dang River; Vietnamese under Ngo Quyen defeat Chinese.		
939	Ngo Quyen becomes king of new independent Nam Viet.		
966	Bo Linh declares himself emperor, naming his empire Dai Co Viet.		
1009	Ly Thai To becomes emperor, establishing Ly dynasty.		
1225	Tran dynasty replaces Ly dynasty.		
1288 April	Second battle of Bach Dang River; Vietnamese under Tran Hung Dao defeat invading Mongols.		
1407	Chinese Ming dynasty re-occupies Vietnamese state, known as Dai Viet.		
1426	Le Loi defeats Chinese, re-establishing independent Dai Viet and establishing Le dynasty.		
1492 October		Columbus lands at San Salvador.	
Late 16th century	Vietnam fragments politically and is divided by the Trinh and the Nguyen.		

continues

Early History, continued

Date	Southeast Asia	United States	The War
1627	French missionary Alexandre de Rhodes codifies *quoc ngu,* an adoption of the Roman alphabet to the Vietnamese language.		
1771	Tay Son Rebellion begins under Nguyen Hue, deposing the Nguyen and later the Trinh.		
1776 July		Declaration of Independence signed.	
1778 December	Nguyen Hue declares himself emperor.		
1779 January	Nguyen Hue attacks and defeats Chinese forces at Thang Long (Hanoi) during Tet.		
1787 September		Constitution of the United States signed.	
1802 June	Nguyen Anh, after defeating Tay Son forces with the aid of French missionary Pgneau de Béhaine, becomes emperor Gia Long, establishing his capital at Hue.		

The Colonial Era

Date	Southeast Asia	United States	The War
1858	French fleet under Adm. Rigault de Genouilly bombards Tourane (Da Nang) and captures Saigon.		
1862 June	Vietnam cedes the three eastern provinces of Cochinchina to France under the Treaty of Saigon.		
1863 August	France imposes protectorate on Cambodia.		
1867	France occupies the three western provinces of Cochinchina.		
1883 August	France extends protectorate to Annam and Tonkin under the Treaty of Hue, effectively establishing control of Vietnam.		
1887	France creates the Union Indo-Chinoise, which administratively unifies Tonkin, Annam, Cochinchina, and Cambodia.		

Date	Southeast Asia	United States	The War
1893	France imposes protectorate on Laos.		
1930 February	Ho Chi Minh creates the Indochinese Communist Party.		
1940 March	Japan occupies French Indochina but retains French colonial administration.		
1941 May	Viet Minh established.		
1945 March	Japanese eliminate French rule; Bao Dai proclaims independent Vietnam under Japanese protectorate.		
1945 April		Franklin D. Roosevelt dies; Harry S. Truman becomes president.	
1945 August	Japan surrenders; August Revolution; Bao Dai abdicates.		
1945 September	Ho Chi Minh proclaims the creation of the Democratic Republic of Vietnam (DRV).		
1945 November	Ho Chi Minh dissolves the Indochinese Communist Party.		
1946 March	French declare Vietnam an independent state within the French Union.		
1946 May	Fontainebleau conference begins, lasting until September.		
1946 June	Argenlieu proclaims State of Cochinchina.		

The Indochina War

Date	Southeast Asia	United States	The War
1946 November			French naval forces bombard Haiphong, initiating the Indochina War.
1949 March	Élysée Agreement is signed, creating the nominally in dependent State of Vietnam under former emperor Bao Dai.		
1950 January	The DRV is recognized by the People's Republic of China, the Soviet Union, and Yugoslavia.		
1950 February	The French-organized State of Vietnam is recognized by the United States and Britain.		
1950 July		United States begins providing military and economic aid to French effort in Indochina.	
1950 September		U.S. Military Advisory Group–Indochina established.	Battle of Cao Bang.

continues

The Indochina War, continued

Date	Southeast Asia	United States	The War
1950 October			Battle of Lang Son.
1951 February	The Lao Dong Party is created.		
1951 November			Battle of Hoa Binh begins, lasting until February 1952.
1952 November		Dwight D. Eisenhower elected president.	Battle of Na San.
1954 March			Battle of Dien Bien Phu begins, lasting until May 1954.
1954 April		Eisenhower rejects French request for U.S. military intervention at Dien Bien Phu.	
1954 June	Ngo Dinh Diem is chosen as the State of Vietnam's prime minister by Bao Dai.		
1954 July	Geneva agreements signed, partitioning Vietnam at the 17th Parallel pending a national referendum; International Supervision and Control Commission established.		
1954 September	Southeast Asia Treaty Organization (SEATO) established.		
1954 October		J. Lawton Collins sent as special envoy to Diem government, bringing assurances of direct U.S. aid.	Final withdrawal of French troops from Hanoi.
1955 April	Binh Xuyen and Cao Dai defeated by Diem's forces.		
1955 July	Diem refuses to proceed with national elections, rejecting the Geneva accords.		
1955 September	Cambodia becomes independent; Norodom Sihanouk abdicates as king to become prime minister.		
1955 October	Diem deposes Bao Dai by referendum; declares the establishment of the Republish of Vietnam.		

Prelude to U.S. Combat Intervention

Date	Southeast Asia	United States	The War
1955 November		U.S. Military Advisory Group–Vietnam formed from U.S. Military Advisory Group–Indochina.	
1957 June			Last French military advisers leave Republic of Vietnam.

Date	Southeast Asia	United States	The War
1957 October			Communist insurgency commences in Republic of Vietnam.
1959 May			Group 559 established.
1959 July		First U.S. casualties of the Vietnam War, Maj. Dale Buis and Sgt. Chester Ovnand, killed at Bien Hoa.	
1959 August	National Assembly Law 10/59 enacted.		
1959 September			Group 959 established.
1959 October			Group 759 established.
1960 April	Caravelle Group petitions Diem.		
1960 August	Laotian government overthrown by Kong Le.		
1960 November	Unsuccessful coup attempt against Diem.	John F. Kennedy elected president.	
1960 December			National Liberation Front established.
1961 April		Frederick Nolting replaces Elbridge Durbrow as ambassador to South Vietnam.	
1961 May	Geneva Conference convened in response to Laotian crisis, lasting until July 1962.		
1962 February		U.S. Military Assistance Command, Vietnam formed from U.S. Military Advisory Group–Vietnam, with Paul D. Harkins as commander.	Strategic Hamlet program initiated.
1963 January			Battle of Ap Bac.
1963 April	Buddhist demonstrations begin and continue into August.		
1963 June	First of seven Buddhist monks commits self-immolation to protest Diem's policies.		
1963 November	Diem and Nhu assassinated; Duong Van Minh, as head of Military Revolutionary Council, assumes control of South Vietnam.	Kennedy assassinated; Lyndon B. Johnson becomes president.	
1964 January	Nguyen Khanh seizes power from Minh.		
1964 June		William C. Westmoreland replaces Harkins; Maxwell Taylor replaces Lodge.	
1964 August		Congress adopts Gulf of Tonkin Resolution.	Gulf of Tonkin incidents.
1964 December			Viet Cong bomb U.S. officers quarters at Brinks Hotel, Saigon; battle of Binh Gia.
1965 February	Khanh flees South Vietnam; Phan Huy Quat becomes prime minister.		Viet Cong attack U.S. base at Pleiku; United States retaliates with FLAMING DART air attacks; Viet Cong attack U.S. billet at Qui Nhon.

The Vietnam War

Date	Southeast Asia	United States	The War
1965 March		University of Michigan faculty organize first teach-in.	Rolling Thunder begins; U.S. Marines, the first U.S. combat troops committed to Vietnam, land at Da Nang; Viet Cong bomb U.S. embassy at Saigon.
1965 April		Johnson delivers Johns Hopkins speech.	
1965 May		Johnson announces six-day pause in the U.S. bombing of North Vietnam.	
1965 June	Nguyen Cao Ky becomes South Vietnamese prime minister.		First Arc Light strike launched, the first use of B-52s in combat.
1965 July		Lodge reappointed as ambassador to South Vietnam, replacing Taylor; Johnson approves Westmoreland's request for an additional 44 maneuver battalions.	
1965 August		Henry Cabot Lodge replaces Nolting.	Operation Starlite. Operation Silver Bayonet begins, lasting until November.
1965 November		Antiwar demonstrations become widespread.	
1965 December		Johnson announces a 37-day bombing pause.	
1966 January			Operation Masher/White Wing begins, lasting until March.
1966 February		Honolulu conference.	
1966 March	Buddhist antigovernment protests begin in Hue and Da Nang, lasting until June.		
1966 April			First use of B-52s against targets in North Vietnam, in strikes on the Mu Gia pass.
1966 October		Manila conference.	
1967 January			Operation Cedar Falls.
1967 February	Bernard Fall killed.		Operation Junction City begins, lasting until May.
1967 March		Guam conference.	Battle of Con Thien begins, lasting until October.
1967 May		Ellsworth Bunker replaces Lodge; Robert W. Komer becomes Westmoreland's deputy as head of CORDS. Johnson meets with Soviet Prime Minister Alexei N. Kosygin at Glassboro, New Jersey.	
1967 August		Trial of the Chicago Seven begins, lasting until February.	

Date	Southeast Asia	United States	The War
1967 September	Nguyen Van Thieu elected president of South Vietnam, Ky vice president.		
1967 Autumn			"Border battles" of Song Be, Loc Ninh, and Dak To.
1968 January	Sihanouk meets with U.E. emissary Chester Bowles.		Siege of Khe Sanh begins, lasting until early April; Tet Offensive begins, lasting until late February; North Korea seizes USS *Pueblo*.
1968 February		Westmoreland requests 206,000 additional U.S. troops; Clark Clifford replaces Robert McNamara.	
1968 March		Creighton Abrams replaces Westmoreland; "wise men" meet; Johnson announces a partial bombing halt and that he will not seek reelection as president.	My Lai massacre.
1968 April		Martin Luther King Jr., assassinated.	
1968 May	U.S. and DRV begin negotiations in Paris.		
1968 June		Robert F. Kennedy assassinated.	Khe Sanh abandoned.
1968 August		Democratic National Convention at Chicago.	
1968 October		Johnson announces a total cessation of bombing of North Vietnam.	
1968 November		Richard W. Nixon elected president.	
1969 January	Republic of Vietnam and Provisional Revolutionary Government join Paris peace talks.		
1969 February			Communist forces implement "high point" strategy, rocketing and mortaring South Vietnamese cities. Secret bombing of Cambodia begins, lasting until August 1973.
1969 June		Midway Island conference; Nixon announces Vietnamization.	
1969 September	Ho Chi Minh dies.		
1970 October		First Moratorium antiwar protest.	
1970 November		"Silent majority" speech; My Lai massacre revealed.	
1970 March			ARVN forces begin cross-border operations into Cambodia. Incursion into Cambodia begins, lasting until June.
1970 April	Lon Nol seizes power in Cambodia, deposing Sihanouk.		

continues

The Vietnam War, continued

Date	Southeast Asia	United States	The War
1970 May		Widespread antiwar protests; Kent State; Jackson State.	
1970 November		Trial of Lt. William L. Calley Jr. begins, lasting until March 1971.	
1970 December		Congress repeals Gulf of Tonkin Resolution.	
1971 January			ARVN Operation Lam Son 719 begins, lasting until April, supported by U.S. Operation Dewey Canyon II.
1971 April		Massive antiwar protests occur in Washington, D.C., and San Francisco, including Dewey Canyon III protest by Vietnam veterans.	
1971 June		*New York Times* begins publication of the Pentagon Papers.	
1971 October	Thieu reelected president of South Vietnam.		
1971 December			U.S. aircraft begin attacks on PAVN forces in North Vietnam massing in preparation for the Easter Offensive.
1972 February		Nixon visits the People's Republic of China.	
1972 March			Easter Offensive begins.
1972 April			Siege of An Loc begins, lasting until June.
1972 May			Quang Tri City is captured by PAVN forces; Operation Line-Backer begins, lasting until October.
1972 June		Watergate break-in; Frederick C. Weyand replaces Abrams.	
1972 August			The last U.S. ground combat troops withdraw from Vietnam.
1972 September			ARVN forces recapture Quang Tri City.
1972 November		Nixon reelected president.	
1972 December			Operation Linebacker II.
1973 January		Draft ends.	Paris peace accords signed.
1973 February			Communists release 588 U.S. POWs in Operation Homecoming.
1973 March			The last U.S. troops leave Vietnam.
1973 April			The last U.S. POWs are released.
1973 June		Graham Martin replaces Bunker; Congress bans bombing of Cambodia as of August.	
1973 October		Vice President Spiro T. Agnew resigns and is replaced by Gerald R. Ford, Jr.	

Date	Southeast Asia	United States	The War
1973 November		Congress overrides Nixon's veto of the War Powers Act.	
1974 January	Fall of South Vietnam's Phuoc Long province.		
1974 August		Nixon resigns; Ford becomes president.	
1974 September		Ford pardons Nixon.	
1975 March			Fall of Ban Me Thuot; Thieu orders abandonment of northern South Vietnam; fall of Hue and Da Nang; Ho Chi Minh Campaign begins.
1975 April	Khmer Rouge assume power in Cambodia; reunification of Vietnam under communist rule.		Fall of Phnom Penh; fall of Saigon.
1975 May			*Mayaguez* incident.
1975 August	Pathet Lao assume control of Laos.		

Aftermath

Date	Southeast Asia	United States	The War
1976 November		Jimmy Carter elected president.	
1977 January		Carter pardons most Vietnam War draft evaders.	
1978 November	Vietnam and the Soviet Union sign mutual defense pact.		
1978 December	Exodus of "boat people" from Vietnam begins.	U.S. establishes full diplomatic relations with People's Republic of China.	Vietnam invades Cambodia.
1979 February			Chinese invasion of Vietnam begins, lasting until March.
1980 November		Ronald Reagan elected president.	
1982 November		Vietnam Veterans Memorial dedicated.	
1984 May		A $180 million out-of-court settlement between seven manufactures of Agent Orange and Vietnam veterans is announced; an unknown U.S. casualty of the Vietnam War is interred at Arlington National Cemetery.	
1984 November		A statue of three servicemen, added to the Vietnam Veterans Memorial after protests by veterans, is dedicated.	

continues

Aftermath, continued

Date	Southeast Asia	United States	The War
1986 December	Vietnam initiates economic reforms.		
1988 November		George Bush elected president.	
1989 September			Vietnam withdraws the bulk of its troops from Cambodia.
1990 August	Under United Nations auspices, Cambodian factions agree to form a coalition government and to hold national elections.		
1992 November		Bill Clinton elected president.	
1994 February		Clinton lifts embargo on trade with Vietnam.	
1995 July		Clinton announces recognition of Vietnam.	

Appendix B
Order of Battle, U.S. Military

This appendix is not intended to be a complete order of battle of U.S. military forces in the Vietnam War. It is only a brief overview of the major commands.

For more detailed information, see the sources cited in the bibliography.

Service/Field Headquarters

Military Assistance Command, Vietnam. Formed on 8 February 1962 the Military Assistance Command, Vietnam (MACV), was the joint service headquarters for U.S. military forces in Vietnam. The commanding general of the U.S. Military Assistance Command, Vietnam (COMUSMACV), reported to the Commander-in-Chief, Pacific (CINCPAC) located in Hawaii. COMUSMACV's authority was limited to U.S. operations within South Vietnam and along its immediate borders. Therefore, CINCPAC attempted to coordinate military operations throughout Southeast Asia through MACV, the Seventh Fleet, and a confusing chain of command for air operations.

The complex command structure within South Vietnam also seriously complicated military matters. In May 1964 MACV absorbed the responsibilities of the Military Assistance and Advisory Group–Vietnam (MAAG-V), which had been advising the South Vietnamese military since September 1950. With the deactivation of MAAG-V, the advisory effort lost its central direction. MACV also played a dual role as both a joint service headquarters and the U.S. Army's field headquarters in Vietnam. Finally, the South Vietnamese armed forces remained independent of U.S. control. Such a decentralized and disorganized command arrangement undermined MACV's effectiveness.

The following elements fell under MACV's direct authority: Field Advisory Element, MACV; U. S. Army, Vietnam (USARV); Naval Forces Vietnam; Seventh Air Force; III Marine Amphibious Force; I Field Force; II Field Force; XXIV Corps; and 5th Special Forces Group. A wide range of political and civil projects existed as well. MACV departed South Vietnam on 29 March 1973.

Commanding Generals, U. S. Military Assistance Command, Vietnam

Officer	Term
General Paul D. Harkins	February 1962 to June 1964
General William C. Westmoreland	June 1964 to July 1968
General Creighton W. Abrams	July 1968 to June 1972
General Frederick C. Weyand	June 1972 to March 1973

U.S. Air Force

2d Air Division. Reporting to MACV, the 2d Air Division controlled U.S. air operations in South Vietnam between October 1962 and the establishment of the Seventh Air Force on 1 April 1966. Until the rapid U.S. military buildup began in 1965, the 2d Division relied on propeller-driven aircraft to provide air support for the Army of the Republic of Vietnam (ARVN). Jet fighters arrived in the spring of 1965, and by the end of the year the United States had deployed nearly 500 U.S. combat aircraft in South Vietnam. When eventually transformed into the Seventh Air Force, the 2d Division consisted of nearly 1,000 aircraft and roughly 30,000 personnel.

Commanding Generals, 2d Air Division

Officer	Term
Brig. Gen. Rollen H. Anthis	October to December 1962
Brig. Gen. Robert R. Rowland	December 1962 to December 1963
Brig. Gen. Milton B. Adams	December 1963 to January 1964
Lt. Gen. Joseph H. Moore	January 1964 to March 1966

Seventh Air Force. Organized on 1 April 1966 to replace the 2d Air Division, the Seventh Air Force was responsible for U.S. air operations in Southeast Asia until its departure in March 1973. Headquartered at Tan Son Nhut Air Base near Saigon, the Seventh Air Force took its orders from the COMUSMACV for missions conducted within South Vietnam, along its immediate borders, and in southern Laos. The commander of the Seventh Air Force also served as the deputy COMUSMACV for air.

For air operations against targets in northern Laos and North Vietnam, however, the commanding general of the Seventh Air Force reported to the Commander-in-Chief of the Pacific Air Force (CINCPACAF), who reported to CINCPAC. Under CINCPACAF's direction, the Seventh Air Force and the Thirteenth Air Force in the Philippines also shared a joint command in Udorn, Thailand—the Seventh/Thirteenth Air Force. The Strategic Air Command (SAC) retained direct control of its B-52 bombers deployed against targets in Southeast Asia. The lack of a single headquarters for all air operations handicapped efforts for effective coordination.

Subordinate commands of the Seventh Air Force included: the 3d Tactical Fighter Wing in the III Corps Tactical Zone (CTZ); the 12th, 31st, and 35th Tactical Fighter Wings in the II CTZ; the 366th Tactical Fighter Wing in the I CTZ; the 834th Air Division; and the Air Force Advisory Group.

Commanding Generals, Seventh Air Force

Officer	Term
Lt. Gen. Joseph H. Moore	April to June 1966
General William W. Momyer	June 1966 to July 1968
General George S. Brown	August 1968 to August 1970
General Lucius D. Clay, Jr.	September 1970 to July 1971
General John D. Lavelle	August 1971 to April 1972
General John W. Vogt, Jr.	April 1972 to September 1973

Seventh/Thirteenth Air Force. Stationed in Udorn, Thailand, the Seventh/Thirteenth Air Force was organized on 6 January 1966. It was an independent air division taking orders from two different commands. The commander of the Seventh/Thirteenth Air Force reported to the Seventh Air Force on operational matters and to the Thirteenth Air Force on logistical and administrative matters.

At its peak in 1968, the Seventh/Thirteenth Air Force numbered 35,000 personnel and 600 aircraft. Its major combat units included the 8th Tactical Fighter Wing, the 355th Tactical Fighter Wing, the 388th Tactical Fighter Wing, the 432d Tactical Reconnaissance Wing, the 553d Tactical Reconnaissance Wing, and the 56th Special Operations Wing.

Commanding Generals, Seventh/Thirteenth Air Force

Officer	Term
Maj. Gen. Charles R. Bond	January 1966 to May 1967
Maj. Gen. William C. Lindley, Jr.	June 1967 to May 1968
Maj. Gen. Louis T. Seith	June 1968 to May 1969
Maj. Gen. Robert L. Petit	June 1969 to March 1970

continues

continued

Officer	Term
Maj. Gen. James E. Kirkendall	March to October 1970
Maj. Gen. Andrew Evans, Jr.	October 1970 to June 1971
Maj. Gen. De Witt R. Searles	July 1971 to September 1972
Maj. Gen. James D. Hughes	September 1972 to April 1973

Strategic Air Command. The Strategic Air Command (SAC) retained direct control of its strategic bombers employed against targets in Southeast Asia. The B-52 strategic bomber was the mainstay of U.S. strategic forces in the 1960s and 1970s and was used extensively during the Vietnam War for tactical and strategic missions. B-52 strikes began on 18 June 1965 and ended on 23 January 1973. Between 1965 and 1973, B-52s flew more than 126,000 sorties in Southeast Asia.

SAC initially controlled the employment of B-52 bombers via the 3d Air Division in Guam, but after July 1970 the Eighth Air Force assumed responsibility. Widely scattered subordinate units included the 4133d Bombardment Wing out of Guam, 4258th Strategic Air Wing (later designated the 307th Strategic Air Wing), which began flying out of Thailand in 1967, and the 4252d Strategic Air Wing out of Okinawa.

Military Airlift Command. The Military Airlift Command (MAC) transported a large percentage of the supplies, equipment, and personnel deployed to South Vietnam. MAC's resupply missions to Southeast Asia totaled 340 million kilometers (210 million miles) in 1967 and accounted for nearly 348,000 passengers. This airlift included the transportation of the entire 25th Infantry Division in 1965 and the 101st Airborne Division in 1967. Equally significant was the transport of more than 400,000 medical evacuees flown to the United States between 1963 and 1973.

Prior to 1973 the MAC and the Tactical Air Command divided airlift responsibilities. MAC retained direct control of its aircraft rather than turning them over to the operational control of area air commanders. The result was a divided airlift effort with duplicate responsibilities and functions and intense competition for limited ramp space, fuel, and ground crews.

Tactical Air Command. The Tactical Air Command (TAC) was responsible for meeting the U.S. Air Force's tactical airlift needs in the Vietnam War. Tactical airlift delivered more than 7 million tons of passengers and cargo within South Vietnam between 1962 and 1972. Unlike the MAC, TAC placed its aircraft under the operational control of units in the combat theater. The 834th Air Division handled tactical airlift within South

Vietnam and reported directly to the Seventh Air Force. It received support from the 315th Air Division stationed in Japan.

834th Air Division. Organized on 25 October 1966 and placed under the Seventh Air Force, the 834th Air Division provided centralized control for tactical airlift within South Vietnam until its departure in November 1970. Its duties included logistical airlift, airborne operations, and medical evacuations. Subordinate units included the 315th Special Operations Wing, the 483d Tactical Airlift Wing, and the Airlift Control Center (ALCC). The ALCC was a flexible headquarters that controlled transport aircraft rotated into South Vietnam by the 315th Air Division.

315th Air Division. The 315th Air Division was activated at Tachikawa Air Base in Japan on 25 January 1951 and reported to the Thirteenth Air Force stationed at Clark Air Base in the Philippines. Subordinate units of the 315th Air Division included the 374th Troop Carrier Wing in Taiwan and the 463d Troop Carrier Wing at Clark. The division was deactivated on 15 April 1969.

U.S. Army

I. Support and Advisory Elements

Field Advisory Element, Military Assistance Command, Vietnam. Following the deactivation of MAAG-V in May 1964, the advising and training of the ARVN became the primary function of the Field Advisory Element, MACV. No single individual coordinated the training and advising effort; central direction came from diverse elements within the MACV staff and from senior advisers in the CTZs. This arrangement left the advisory effort virtually ignored for several years, and the development of the South Vietnamese military suffered accordingly. It was not until after the Tet Offensive of 1968 that the ARVN's combat capabilities became a fundamental concern. The selection and training of advisory teams subsequently received a higher priority and reached a broader array of defense forces. Despite these changes, the inability to make wholesale changes in the ARVN command structure doomed the advisory program to failure.

U.S. Army, Vietnam. Established on 20 July 1965, the U.S. Army, Vietnam (USARV), was intended to be the field headquarters for the U.S. Army's combat units in Vietnam, but MACV retained direct operational control of those forces. Without a combat role, USARV developed into an administrative and logistical support command and played a pivotal role in the U.S. buildup. Although the commanding general of MACV was technically the commander of USARV as well, in reality his deputy exercised that responsibility. Units under USARV control included the 1st Logistical Command, 1st Aviation Brigade, 18th Military Police Brigade, 34th General Support Group, 525th Military Intelligence Group, and a wide variety of other commands. USARV was dissolved on 15 May 1972.

Deputy Command Generals, MACV

Officer	Term
Maj. Gen. John Norton	July 1965 to January 1966
Lt. Gen. Jean E. Engler	January 1966 to July 1967
Lt. Gen. Bruce Palmer, Jr.	July 1967 to June 1968
Lt. Gen. Frank T. Mildren	June 1968 to July 1970
Lt. Gen. William J. McCaffrey	July 1970 to September 1972
Maj. Gen. Morgan C. Roseborough	September 1972 to March 1973

II. Tactical Corps Headquarters

I Field Force, Vietnam. Headquartered at Nha Trang, the I Field Force, Vietnam (I FFV), exercised operational control over U.S. Army and allied units in the II CTZ from 15 November 1965 to 30 April 1971. Originally it was called Field Force, Vietnam, but the name change became necessary in March 1966 with the formation of II Field Force, Vietnam. The U.S. Army employed the designation of Field Force to denote the command's flexibility as a tactical organization and to avoid confusion with the geographically defined corps tactical zones established by South Vietnam. Each field force was an army corps headquarters.

Major combat units that served under the control of the I FFV included the 1st Cavalry Division, 4th Infantry Division, 25th Infantry Division, 101st Airborne Division, and 173d Airborne Brigade.

Command Generals, I Field Force

Officer	Term
Lt. Gen. Stanley R. Larson	November 1965 to March 1968
Lt. Gen. William R. Peers	March 1968 to March 1969
Lt. Gen. Charles A. Corcoran	March 1969 to March 1970
Lt. Gen. Arthur S. Collins, Jr.	March 1970 to January 1971
Maj. Gen. Charles P. Brown	January to April 1971

II Field Force, Vietnam. Organized on 15 March 1966, the II Field
Force, Vietnam (II FFV), exercised operational control over U.S. and allied
units in the III CTZ. A significant U.S. presence was required in the region
to protect Saigon and the vast number of key military installations.
Headquartered at Bien Hoa and later Long Binh, the II FFV became the
largest U.S. Army field element in South Vietnam. It frequently conducted
multidivisional operations against North Vietnamese and Viet Cong
strongholds in War Zones C and D and in the Iron Triangle. In May 1970
the commanding general of the II FFV organized and executed the invasion of Cambodia.

Major combat units that served with the II FFV included the 1st, 4th,
9th, and 25th Infantry Divisions, the 1st Cavalry Division, the 101st
Airborne Division, the 3d Brigade of the 82d Airborne Division, the 196th
and 199th Infantry Brigades, and the 173d Airborne Brigade. The II FFV
was deactivated on 2 May 1971.

Command Generals, II Field Force

Officer	Term
Lt. Gen. Jonathan O. Seaman	March 1966 to March 1967
Lt. Gen. Bruce Palmer, Jr.	March to July 1967
Maj. Gen. Frederick C. Weyand	July 1967 to August 1968
Maj. Gen. Walter T. Kerwin, Jr.	August 1968 to April 1969
Lt. Gen. Julian J. Ewell	April 1969 to April 1970
Lt. Gen. Michael S. Davison	April 1970 to May 1971

XXIV Corps. In February 1968, General William C. Westmoreland temporarily sent MACV's forward headquarters to the I CTZ to exercise
control over the substantial number of Army units recently deployed there.
He eventually transformed the headquarters into the U.S. Army
Provisional Corps, Vietnam. Finally, on 15 August 1968, MACV activated
the XXIV Corps to replace the Provisional Corps. Since the III Marine
Amphibious Force directed U.S. operations in the I CTZ, the XXIV Corps
came under its command.

The XXIV Corps conducted operations along the demilitarized zone
(DMZ) and the Laotian border in conjunction with U.S. Marine units. By
March 1970 the U.S. Army's maneuver elements in the I CTZ outnum-
bered the marines three to one, and the XXIV Corps became the senior
U.S. headquarters in the region. Major combat units that served with the
XXIV Corps included the 23d (Americal) Infantry Division, 1st Cavalry
Division, 101st Airborne Division, several separate infantry brigades, and
Marine Corps units. The XXIV Corps departed Vietnam on 20 June 1972.

Command Generals, XXIV Corps

Officer	Term
Lt. Gen. William B. Rosson	February to July 1968
Lt. Gen. Richard G. Stilwell	July 1968 to June 1969
Lt. Gen. Melvin Zais	June 1969 to June 1970
Lt. Gen. James W. Sutherland Jr.	June 1970 to June 1971
Lt. Gen. Welborn G. Dolvin	June 1971 to June 1972

III. Combat Divisions

1st Cavalry Division (Airmobile). The 1st Cavalry Division (Airmobile) was the first U.S. Army division to enter combat in South Vietnam. It arrived on 11 September 1965 and was immediately sent to the II CTZ to stem a growing North Vietnamese Army (NVA) threat in the critical Central Highlands. The 1st Cavalry Division relied totally on helicopters for mobility. It established headquarters at An Khe and proceeded to challenge the NVA for control of the Ia Drang Valley. Although the division's mobility and firepower resulted in a tactical victory, that success masked fundamental weaknesses in U.S. strategy and doctrine. The division served throughout South Vietnam and participated in the 1970 invasion of Cambodia. It earned a reputation for aggressive and successful combat operations. The bulk of the 1st Cavalry Division withdrew on 29 April 1971, but a brigade task force remained until June 1972.

Command Generals, 1st Cavalry Division

Officer	Term
Maj. Gen. Harry W. B. Kinnard	July 1965 to May 1966
Maj. Gen. John Norton	May 1966 to April 1967
Maj. Gen. John J. Tolson III	April 1967 to July 1968
Maj. Gen. George Forsythe	July 1968 to May 1969
Maj. Gen. Elvy B. Roberts	May 1969 to May 1970
Maj. Gen. George W. Casey	May to July 1970
Maj. Gen. George W. Putnam, Jr.	July 1970 to April 1971

1st Infantry Division. The oldest of the U.S. Army's combat divisions, the 1st Infantry Division arrived in South Vietnam on 2 October 1965 and established headquarters at Bien Hoa in the III CTZ. Under the control of the II FFV, the division participated in some of the largest combat operations of the Vietnam War including operations Attleboro, Cedar Falls, and Junction City. The 1st Infantry Division developed a reputation for relying on a preponderance of firepower to overwhelm the opposition. Although this kept casualties low, the doctrine was not well suited for maintaining contact with elusive NVA and Viet Cong forces in the jungle. The division withdrew from South Vietnam on 15 April 1970.

Command Generals, 1st Infantry Division

Officer	Term
Maj. Gen. Jonathan O. Seaman	October 1965 to March 1966
Maj. Gen. William E. DePuy	March 1966 to February 1967
Maj. Gen. John H. Hay, Jr.	February 1967 to March 1968
Maj. Gen. Keith L. Ware	March to September 1968
Maj. Gen. Orwin C. Talbott	September 1968 to August 1969
Maj. Gen. Albert E. Milloy	August 1969 to March 1970
Brig. Gen. John Q. Herrion	March to April 1970

4th Infantry Division. Arriving in South Vietnam on 25 September 1966, the 4th Infantry Division established headquarters at Pleiku in the II CTZ. A significant portion of the division, however, never reached Pleiku. The division's 3d Brigade and supporting armor were ordered to the II CTZ and were later exchanged for elements of the 25th Infantry Division. The 4th Division spent the next four years in the Central Highlands and earned a reputation for steadfast dependability. In June 1970, when the 4th Division was on the coast awaiting shipment home, it received orders to participate in the invasion of Cambodia. The division took less than three days to move to the border and launch the operation. It departed Vietnam on 7 December 1970.

Command Generals, 4th Infantry Division

Officer	Term
Maj. Gen. Arthur S. Collins, Jr.	September 1966 to January 1967
Maj. Gen. William R. Peers	January 1967 to January 1968
Maj. Gen. Charles R. Stone	January to December 1968
Maj. Gen. Donn R. Pepke	December 1968 to November 1969
Maj. Gen. Glenn D. Walker	November 1969 to July 1970.
Maj. Gen. William A. Burke	July to December 1970

9th Infantry Division. The 9th Infantry Division landed in South Vietnam on 16 December 1966, only eleven months after being activated. Sent to the III CTZ, the division established headquarters at Bear Cat, south of Saigon. In June 1967 the 9th Division lost its 2d Brigade to the Mobile Riverine Force (MRF) in the IV CTZ. The MRF was a joint U.S. Army-Navy operation designed to deny the Viet Cong control of the waterways of the Mekong River. The force employed river gunboats and amphibious assault forces to patrol the region and attack Viet Cong strongholds. The 9th Infantry Division returned to the United States on 27 August 1969, but its 3d Brigade remained in the III CTZ until October 1970.

Command Generals, 9th Infantry Division

Officer	Term
Maj. Gen. George C. Eckhart	December 1966 to June 1967
Maj. Gen. George C. O'Connor	June 1967 to February 1968
Maj. Gen. Julian J. Ewell	February 1968 to April 1969
Maj. Gen. Harris W. Hollis	April to August 1969

23d (American) Infantry Division. Reactivated in Vietnam on 25 September 1 967, the 23d (American) Infantry Division was the brainchild of General William C. Westmoreland. Early in 1967 the Marine Corps was stretched to its limit in the I CTZ and needed urgent reinforcement. Westmoreland decided to send a collection of U.S. Army infantry brigades to the region and placed them under a division-size headquarters named Task Force Oregon. The task force was transformed into the 23d (American) Division, first raised on New Caledonia during World War II. Consisting of the 11th, 196th, and 198th Infantry Brigades plus other supporting units, the division handled security for Quang Nam and Quang Tri provinces. Intense NVA and guerrilla activity provided a serious challenge, and the American Division suffered from weak leadership and low morale. Deactivated on 29 November 1971, the division is probably best known for the My Lai massacre.

Command Generals, 23d (American) Infantry Division

Officer	Term
Maj. Gen. Samuel W. Koster	September 1967 to June 1968
Maj. Gen. Charles M. Gettys	June 1968 to June 1969
Maj. Gen. Lloyd B. Ramsey	June 1969 to March 1970

Maj. Gen. Albert E. Milloy   March to November 1970

Maj. Gen. James L. Baldwin   November 1970 to July 1971

Maj. Gen. Frederick J.   July to November 1971
Kroesen, Jr.

25th Infantry Division. Initially stationed in Hawaii as the ready-reserve for the Pacific, the 25th Infantry Division moved to Vietnam in several stages. Its 3d Brigade arrived late in 1965 and went to the II CTZ. The 2d Brigade landed in January 1966 and went to Cu Chi in the III CTZ; the rest of the division followed in March. The 25th Division remained in the III CTZ and eventually exchanged its 3d Brigade for elements of the 4th Division. It took part in Operation Junction City and participated in the 1970 invasion of Cambodia. The bulk of the 25th Division withdrew from Vietnam on 8 December 1970, but the 2d Brigade remained until April 1971.

Command Generals, 25th Infantry Division

Officer	Term
Maj. Gen. Frederick C. Weyand	March 1966 to March 1967
Maj. Gen. John C. F. Tillson III	March to August 1967
Maj. Gen. Fillmore K. Mearns	August 1967 to August 1968
Maj. Gen. Ellis W. Williamson	August 1968 to September 1969
Maj. Gen. Edward Baultz, Jr.	September 1969 to December 1970

101st Airborne Division (Airmobile). The 1st Brigade of the famed 101st Airborne Division (Airmobile) arrived in Vietnam on 29 July 1965 and began operating in the II CTZ. It later temporarily joined Task Force Oregon. The bulk of the division arrived on 19 November 1967 and established its headquarters at Bien Hoa in the III CTZ. Initially earmarked for conversion to an elite airmobile division, the 101st Airborne Division arrived short of trained personnel and aviation assets, which forced MACV to postpone the conversion until mid-1969. During the 1968 Tet Offensive, the division shifted north to the city of Hue and remained in the I CTZ. In 1970 and 1971, it took part in Operation Jefferson Glenn—the last major U.S. ground operation of the war. The division began to withdraw from Vietnam in December 1971 and completed the process by 10 March 1972.

Command Generals, 101st Airborne Division

Officer	Term
Maj. Gen. Olinto M. Barsanti	November 1967 to July 1968
Maj. Gen. Melvin Zais	July 1968 to May 1969
Maj. Gen. John M. Wright Jr.	May 1969 to May 1970
Maj. Gen. John J. Hennessey	May 1970 to January 1971
Maj. Gen. Thomas M. Tarpley	January 1971 to March 1972

Task Force Oregon. Activated in the I CTZ on 12 April 1967, Task Force Oregon was a provisional division deployed to support the U.S. Marines in the northern provinces. Its combat elements consisted of the 3d Brigade, 25th Infantry Division, the 1st Brigade, 101st Airborne Division, and the 196th Infantry Brigade. The task force was replaced by the Americal Division on 22 September 1967.

Command Generals, Task Force Oregon

Officer	Term
Maj. Gen. William B. Rosson	April to June 1967
Maj. Gen. Richard T. Knowles	June to September 1967

IV. Independent Combat Brigades

1st Aviation Brigade. Activated in Vietnam on 25 May 1966, the 1st Aviation Brigade flew helicopter air support for U.S. and allied forces throughout the four corps tactical zones. At peak strength it consisted of more than 24,000 personnel and 4,000 combat and support helicopters. Headquartered at Tan Son Nhut and Long Binh, the 1st Brigade departed Vietnam on 28 March 1973.

11th Infantry Brigade (Light). The 11th Infantry Brigade (Light) arrived in Vietnam on 19 December 1967 and joined the Americal Division. Stationed in Hawaii since 1966 as the strategic reserve for the Pacific, the division was completely unprepared for combat deployment. Poor leadership and lack of training earned the 11th Brigade a reputation during the war for its morale problems and brutality, including its involvement in the massacre at My Lai. The brigade departed Vietnam on 13 November 1971.

173d Airborne Brigade. Specially trained for warfare in Southeast Asia, the 173d Airborne Brigade was the first major combat unit sent to

Vietnam. It arrived on 7 May 1965 and began providing security for the extensive military facility at Bien Hoa. Although intended for short-term deployment, the brigade remained in Vietnam until 25 August 1971. Generally considered one of the most elite units to serve in the Vietnam War, the 173d Brigade won acclaim for its parachute jump into Tay Ninh province during Operation Junction City in February 1967. In November of that same year the brigade won a Presidential Unit Citation for its conduct during the Battle of Dak To.

196th Infantry Brigade (Light). Originally slated for duty in the Dominican Republic, the 196th Infantry Brigade (Light) was the first light infantry brigade formed by the U.S. Army. Activated in September 1965, the brigade suffered from shortages of training cadre and of experienced noncommissioned officers. It arrived in Vietnam on 26 August 1966 not completely prepared for combat.

The 196th Brigade was initially assigned to the III CTZ but moved north to the I CTZ in the spring of 1967 to form Tusk Force Oregon. On 25 September 1967 it became part of the Americal Division and remained part of the division until 29 November 1971. The brigade remained in Vietnam until June 1972 providing security for the region surrounding Da Nang.

198th Infantry Brigade (Light). Activated to man the proposed "McNamara Line" infiltration barrier along the DMZ, the 198th Infantry Brigade (Light) was sent to Vietnam several months ahead of schedule and arrived on 21 October 1967. It immediately joined the Americal Division in the I CTZ. Because the barrier never materialized, the brigade remained with the division until it departed Vietnam on 13 November 1971. Hampered by a hurried training schedule and poor leadership, the 198th Brigade suffered from lack of discipline and low morale throughout the war.

199th Infantry Brigade (Light). To provide badly needed ground support in the III CTZ, the 199th Infantry Brigade (Light) was rushed to Vietnam in December 1966 after an abbreviated training period. The brigade, however, overcame its initial shortcomings and participated in one of the most intense battles of the Tet Offensive in 1968, successfully defending the vast U.S. military installation at Long Binh, outside Saigon, from an attack by the 275th Viet Cong Regiment. One battalion was sent by helicopter into Saigon to help regain control of key areas of the city. The 199th Brigade returned to the United States on 11 October 1970.

1st Brigade, 5th Infantry Division (Mechanized). The 1st Brigade, 5th Infantry Division (Mechanized), arrived in Vietnam on 25 July 1968 as an emergency deployment to meet MACV's dire need for combat units.

Sent to the I CTZ to serve with the Marine Corps, the brigade's heavy fire-power and mechanized mobility provided the capabilities necessary to combat the regular units of the NVA encountered along the DMZ. It also supported South Vietnamese forces during the January 1971 invasion of Laos. The 1st Brigade, 5th Division, withdrew from Vietnam on 27 August 1971.

3d Brigade, 82d Airborne Division. Arriving in Vietnam on 18 February 1968, the 3d Brigade, 82d Airborne Division, provided emergency reinforcement during the Tet Offensive. A massive airlift of more than 140 aircraft flew the brigade to Vietnam from Fort Bragg, North Carolina, in only four days. The brigade, initially sent to Hue to provide security, was shifted to Saigon in September and remained there before returning to the United States on 11 December 1969.

The 82d Airborne Division was the only combat-ready division in the U.S. Army's reserve, and the option of deploying the entire division to Vietnam was rejected as too risky. Still, deploying a single brigade severely reduced the effectiveness of the entire division.

V. Special Forces

U.S. Army Special Forces, Vietnam (Provisional). Formed in Saigon in September 1962, the U.S. Army Special Forces, Vietnam (Provisional), supervised Special Forces activities in South Vietnam. Its mission was to assist in the development of the Civilian Irregular Defense Group (CIDG) forces. The South Vietnamese government and counterinsurgency experts hoped CIDG forces would provide adequate local security to allow the regular army to embark on large-scale operations. Popularly known as the Green Berets, the Special Forces were the U.S. Army's elite counterinsurgency branch. Detachments from various Special Forces groups went to Vietnam on a rotating basis. The provisional group was replaced by the 5th Special Forces Group (Airborne) on 1 October 1964.

5th Special Forces Group (Airborne), 1st Special Forces. The 5th Special Forces Group (Airborne), 1st Special Forces, arrived from Fort Bragg, North Carolina, on 1 October 1965 and established headquarters at Nha Trang in the II CTZ. The group consisted of five companies, each consisting of several detachments. The command operations of each company were handled by a C-detachment, which directed several B-detachments; each B-detachment commanded several A-teams.

Company A was stationed at Bien Hoa in the III CTZ and consisted of 5 B-detachments and 23 A-teams. Company B established its headquarters in the II CTZ at Pleiku and deployed 4 B-detachments and 34 A-teams. The I CTZ was served by Company C headquartered at Da Nang with 2

B-detachments and 9 A-teams. Serving in the IV CTZ with headquarters at Can Tho, Company D consisted of 5 B-detachments and 20 A-teams. Company E was employed for special operations by MACV and included 7 B-detachments and a fluctuating number of A-teams.

Before departing Vietnam on 13 November 1971, the 5th Special Forces Group won a Presidential Unit Citation and the Meritorious Unit Citation for its exceptional service in the Vietnam War. Thirteen members of the group were awarded Medals of Honor and 75 were awarded Distinguished Service Crosses.

U.S. Coast Guard

Commander Coast Guard Activities, Vietnam. The U.S. Coast Guard arrived in South Vietnam in the summer of 1965. The position of Commander Coast Guard Activities, Vietnam, was established on 3 February 1967 to provide central direction to the growing Coast Guard presence. This officer commanded Coast Guard Squadron One, Coast Guard Squadron Three, and various detachments that provided port security, handled the unloading of ammunition and other explosive cargo, and flew search-and-rescue missions. Nearly fifty Coast Guard vessels served in Vietnam, participating in more than 5,000 combat support missions and boarding some 250,000 Vietnamese vessels. Beginning in May 1969 and continuing until August 1972, the Coast Guard transferred its assets to the South Vietnamese navy.

Coast Guard Squadron One. Formed in May 1965 for deployment to Vietnam, Coast Guard Squadron One arrived in July 1965 with seventeen 25-meter (82-foot) patrol boats; an additional nine arrived in February 1966. The squadron served with the U.S. Navy's Task Force 115 and provided coastal surveillance patrols as part of Operation Market Time.

Squadron One consisted of three separate commands. Coast Guard Division 11 was stationed at An Thoi in the IV CTZ with nine patrol boats. Division 12 with eight patrol boats established its headquarters at Da Nang in the I CTZ. Based at Cat Lo in the II CTZ, Division 13 consisted of nine patrol boats.

Before deporting Vietnam on 15 August 1970, the squadron had cruised more than 6.5 million kilometers (4 million miles) and transferred its 26 patrol boats to the South Vietnamese navy.

Coast Guard Squadron Three. The continued demand for coastal surveillance vessels resulted in a request for high-endurance cutters, and Coast Guard Squadron Three arrived in South Vietnam in May 1967. The squadron consisted of five heavily armed cutters whose shallow draft allowed them to cruise the Gulf of Thailand. Besides patrolling coastal waters, Squadron Three conducted fire support missions for ground forces and often provided logistical services to smaller vessels involved in Operation Market Time.

Coast Guard cutters typically spent six to nine months on duty with the squadron before being sent back to the United States. By the spring of 1970, the number of cutters on patrol had been reduced to three. Squadron Three officially departed South Vietnam on 21 December 1971.

U.S. Marine Corps

III Marine Amphibious Force. Formed on 7 May 1965 in Vietnam, the III Marine Amphibious Force (MAF) was a corps-level headquarters based at Da Nang with responsibility for U.S. combat operations in the I CTZ. Marines were initially deployed in South Vietnam in March 1965 to provide security for the Da Nang airfield. It quickly became apparent that the military situation in the northern provinces required a much larger commitment of ground forces. The lack of port facilities in the region meant the burden fell to the Marine Corps, and the 3d Marine Division arrived in May 1965.

The III MAF became involved in some of the largest battles of the Vietnam War. The most notable occasion was the extensive fighting at Khe Sanh that began in 1967 and lasted well into 1968. At its peak in late 1968, the III MAF had command of the U.S. Army's XXIV Corps, the 1st and 3d Marine Divisions, the 1st Marine Air Wing, and two Marine Corps regimental combat teams. The Marine Corps began to withdraw from Vietnam in 1969, and in April 1970, the overwhelming preponderance of U.S. Army personnel in the I CTZ required the III MAF to relinquish control of operations in the region to the XXIV Corps. The III MAF left South Vietnam on 14 April 1971.

Command Generals, III Marine Amphibious Force

Officer	Term
Maj. Gen. William R. Collins	May to June 1965
Maj. Gen. Lewis W. Walt	June 1965 to February 1966
Maj. Gen. Keith B. McCutcheon	February to March 1966
Lt. Gen. Lewis W. Walt	March 1966 June 1967
Lt. Gen. Robert E. Cushman	June 1967 to March 1969
Lt. Gen. Herman Nickerson, Jr.	March 1969 to March 1970
Lt. Gen. Keith B. McCutcheon	March to December 1970
Lt. Gen. Donn J. Robertson	December 1970 to April 1971

1st Marine Air Wing. Although a Marine Corps helicopter squadron arrived in South Vietnam in April 1962, it was not until May 1965 that the 1st Marine Air Wing (MAW) established headquarters at Da Nang and began operations. The 1st MAW provided tactical air support for ground forces in the I CTZ and took its orders from the III MAF. The independent command of Marine Corps aviation was an irritant for the Seventh Air Force.

The 1st MAW, at its peak strength, consisted of six Marine Air Groups—three helicopter groups and three fighter-bomber or attack aircraft groups. This amounted to approximately 225 helicopters and 250 fixed-wing aircraft. Although one Marine Corps air wing typically supported each Marine Corps division, the 1st MAW was reinforced to provide support for the entire III MAF. The air wing departed Vietnam on 14 April 1971.

Command Generals, 1st Marine Air Wing

Officer	Term
Maj. Gen. Paul J. Fontana	May to June 1965
Maj. Gen. Keith B. McCutcheon	June 1965 to May 1966
Maj. Gen. Louis B. Robertshaw	May 1966 to June 1967
Maj. Gen. Norman J. Anderson	June 1967 to June 1968
Maj. Gen. Charles J. Quilter	June 1968 to July 1969
Maj. Gen. William G. Thrash	July 1969 to July 1970
Maj. Gen. Alan J. Armstrong	July 1970 to April 1971

1st Marine Division. The 1st Marine Division arrived in Vietnam in February 1966 and established headquarters at Chu Lai in the I CTZ before shifting north to Da Nang in November. The division initially conducted operations against NVA and Viet Cong forces in the southern provinces of Quang Tin and Quang Ngai. During the Tet Offensive in 1968, it assisted South Vietnamese forces in recapturing Hue. The departure of the 3rd Marine Division in 1969 left the 1st Marine Division with sole responsibility for defending Da Nang and the surrounding provinces. The division withdrew from Vietnam in April 1971.

A powerful combat force, the 1st Marine Division at its peak consisted of four infantry regiments—the 1st, 5th, and 7th Marine Regiments, and beginning in February 1968, the 27th Marine Regiment detached from the 5th Marine Division. Its other combat elements included an artillery regiment consisting of six battalions, a battalion of tanks, an antitank battalion, and a reconnaissance battalion. On two separate occasions the division received a Presidential Unit Citation for gallantry in action.

Command Generals, 1st Marine Division

Officer	Term
Maj. Gen. Lewis J. Fields	February to October 1966
Maj. Gen. Herman Nickerson, Jr.	October 1966 to October 1967
Maj. Gen. Donn J. Robertson	October 1967 to June 1968
Maj. Gen. Ormond R. Simpson	December 1968 to December 1969
Maj. Gen. Edwin B. Wheeler	December 1969 to April 1970
Maj. Gen. Charles E. Widdecke	April 1970 to April 1971

3d Marine Division. Forward elements of the 3d Marine Division first landed in the I CTZ in March 1965, initially assigned to the defense of Da Nang and Quang Nam province. In October 1966 it moved north and deployed in the northern provinces and along the DMZ. Beginning in late 1967, elements of the 3d Marine Division successfully defended Khe Sanh against repeated assaults.

The 3d Marine Division was a heavily armed combat force of four infantry regiments—the 3d, 4th, and 9th Marine Regiments, and by April 1967, the 26th Marine Regiment detached from the 5th Marine Division. The division's artillery regiment controlled eight battalions, and at one point in 1967, had three Army battalions attached as well. Other combat elements included a tank battalion, an antitank battalion, a reconnaissance battalion, and an amphibious tractor battalion. The 3d Marine Division departed Vietnam on 30 November 1969, having been awarded a Presidential Unit Citation for gallantry in action.

Command Generals, 3d Marine Division

Officer	Term
Maj. Gen. William R. Collins	March to June 1965
Maj. Gen. Lewis Walt	June 1965 to March 1966
Maj. Gen. Wood B. Kyle	March 1966 to March 1967
Maj. Gen. Bruno A. Hochmuth	March to November 1967
Maj. Gen. Rathvon McC. Tompkins	November 1967 to May 1968
Maj. Gen. Raymond G. Davis	May 1968 to April 1969
Maj. Gen. William K. Jones	April to November 1969

U.S. Navy

Seventh Fleet. Subordinate to the Commander-in-Chief, Pacific Fleet (CINCPACFLT), the Seventh Fleet was stationed in Japan and deployed elements in the waters off Southeast Asia. It had responsibility for most naval operations in the western Pacific, but after 1 April 1966, Naval Forces, Vietnam, reporting directly to MACV, controlled naval activities deemed internal to the conflict in South Vietnam. Although both MACV and CINCPACFLT reported to CINCPAC in Honolulu, naval activities in the combat area lacked unity of command and direction.

Seventh Fleet task forces conducted a variety of missions to support the war effort. Carrier-based aircraft from Task Force 77 launched air strikes against targets throughout Southeast Asia. Cruisers and destroyers of Task Group 70.8 attacked enemy shipping and bombarded inland targets. Task Force 73 provided logistical support at sea for naval warships operating off Vietnam, while amphibious assault forces under Task Force 76 cruised the coast.

As early as 1961 the Seventh Fleet began to maintain a presence off the coast of Vietnam. This presence increased tremendously in 1965 and became fairly permanent until mid-1973.

Command Officers, Seventh Fleet

Officer	Term
Vice Admiral Roy L. Johnson	June 1960 March 1965
Vice Admiral Paul P. Blackburn Jr.	March to October 1965
Rear Admiral Joseph W. Williams	October to December 1965
Vice Admiral John J. Hyland	December 1965 to November 1967
Vice Admiral William F. Bringle	November 1967 March 1970
Vice Admiral Maurice F. Weisner	March 1970 to June 1971
Vice Admiral William P. Mack	June 1971 to May 1972
Vice Admiral James L. Holloway III	May 1972 to July 1973

Task Force 77. The Seventh Fleet's Attack Carrier Striking Force was Task Force 77. Before May 1966, the task force generally consisted of two to three attack carriers supported by escorts and deployed southeast of Cam Ranh Bay at a staging area called Dixie Station. From that vantage point, naval aircraft consistently supported ground operations throughout

South Vietnam. By the summer of 1966, Task Force 77 had shifted northward to Yankee Station, a staging point just north of the 17th parallel. This placed the carriers in a better position to conduct operations against North Vietnam, Laos, and the Ho Chi Minh Trail. Three to four attack carriers typically operated from Yankee Station, each holding 70 to 100 combat aircraft.

Task Force 77 did not rely on air power alone; as part of Operation Sea Dragon, cruisers, destroyers, and other warships from the task force conducted operations against shipping in the coastal waters off North Vietnam. These vessels also participated in search-and-rescue missions and provided naval gunfire support as part of Task Group 70.8.

After 1968 the strength of Task Force 77 decreased to two carriers, and the number of monthly sorties decreased from a peak of 6,000 to less than 2,500 by 1971. The task force briefly swelled to five carriers during the North Vietnamese Easter Offensive of 1972, but combat operations gradually halted in 1973.

Task Force 73. Task Force 73—technically Service Squadron 3, Service Force, U.S. Pacific Fleet—was the Seventh Fleet's logistical support element. Specifically designed for flexibility and versatility, the task force resupplied and repaired the fleet while at sea. More than 70 percent of the Seventh Fleet's supply requirements were satisfied in this fashion. The hospital ships *Sanctuary* and *Repose* were also part of Task Force 73. Located 50 kilometers (30 miles) off the coast of the I CTZ, the ships had modern medical facilities and nearly 300 doctors, nurses, and corpsmen aboard and saved thousands of American lives.

Task Force 76. Task Force 76, the Seventh Fleet's Amphibious Task Force, initially consisted of a Marine Corps Special Landing Force (SLF) and several vessels of an Amphibious Ready Group (ARG). The task force conducted amphibious landings along the coast of South Vietnam beginning with the initial landing at Da Nang on 8 March 1965. A second ARG/SLF joined Task Force 76 in April 1967, and the two were designated Alpha and Bravo.

Beginning in the fall of 1966, Task Force 76 was stationed off the DMZ in a position to flank the North Vietnamese Army. When NVA units launched strikes across the border, the task force countered with rear area raids or augmented existing ground forces in I CTZ. In early 1969 Task Force 76 conducted the largest amphibious operation of the Vietnam War—Operation Bold Mariner. Working in conjunction with the Americal Division, the task force sealed off Batangan Peninsula and conducted a massive search-and-destroy mission. Despite the size of the operation, the results were less than desired. Task Force 76 withdrew from the waters off Vietnam later in 1969.

Task Group 70.8. Task Group 70.8 was the Seventh Fleet's Cruiser-Destroyer Group. Elements of the task group participated in Operation Sea Dragon—attacking enemy shipping and bombarding military targets along the coast of North Vietnam. The Naval Gunfire Support Unit (Task Unit 70.8.9) was subordinate to Task Group 70.8 and operated in conjunction with MACV to provide gunfire support to allied ground forces in South Vietnam. In addition to the cruisers and destroyers from Task Group 70.8, the Naval Gunfire Support Unit relied on warships from the Royal Australian Navy, escorts from the carrier groups, and the battleship *New Jersey,* which had 16-inch guns.

Naval gunfire support began in May 1965 and ranged along the entire coast of Vietnam, but the highest concentration of activity was in the I CTZ where nearly one-third of the available targets were within range. Although typically consisting of 1 cruiser, 4 destroyers, and 3 smaller vessels, the Naval Gunfire Support Unit peaked at 22 warships during the Tet Offensive.

After early 1969, Task Group 70.8 played an increasingly smaller role in the war effort. Missions into North Vietnamese waters were restricted and gunfire support in the I CTZ was reduced. Targets near Haiphong, however, were hit sharply by naval vessels as part of Operation Linebacker in the spring of 1972.

Naval Forces, Vietnam. Advisers from the U.S. Navy had been in South Vietnam since 1950. The increasing role of naval operations in 1966 required the creation of a separate headquarters under MACV's control. On 1 April 1966, Naval Forces, Vietnam (NAVFORV), was established and assumed control of all naval activities in the II, III, and IV CTZs and along the coast of South Vietnam. The III Marine Amphibious Force had basic responsibility for naval operations in the I CTZ; the Seventh Fleet handled operations beyond the immediate coastal waters.

NAVFORV's major combat elements consisted of the Costal Surveillance Force (Task Force 115), the River Patrol Force (Task Force 116), and the Riverine Assault Force (Task Force 117). Other organizations under its command included the Naval Advisory Group, the 3d Naval Construction Brigade (Seabees), the Military Sea Transportation Service Office, Vietnam, and the Coast Guard Command, Vietnam. NAVFORV was deactivated on 29 March 1973.

Total U.S. Military Personnel in South Vietnam

DATE	ARMY	NAVY	MARINE CORPS	AIR FORCE	COAST GUARD	TOTAL
31 Dec. 1960 *	800	15	2	68	—	About 900
31 Dec. 1961	2,100	100	5	1,000	—	3,205
30 June 1962	5,900	300	700	2,100	—	9,000
31 Dec. 1962	7,900	500	500	2,400	—	11,300
30 June 1963	10,200	600	600	4,000	—	15,400
31 Dec. 1963	10,100	800	800	4,600	—	16,300
30 June 1964	9,900	1,000	600	5,000	—	16,500
31 Dec. 1964	14,700	1,100	900	6,600	—	23,300
30 June 1965	27,300	3,800	18,100	10,700	—	59,900
31 Dec. 1965	116,800	8,400	38,200	20,600	300	184,300
30 June 1966	160,000	17,000	53,700	36,400	400	267,500
31 Dec. 1966	239,400	23,300	69,200	52,900	500	385,300
30 June 1967	285,700	28,500	78,400	55,700	500	448,800
31 Dec. 1967	319,500	31,700	78,000	55,900	500	485,600
30 June 1968	354,300	35,600	83,600	60,700	500	534,700
31 Dec. 1968	359,800	36,100	81,400	58,400	400	536,100
30 April 1969	363,300	36,500	81,800	61,400	400	543,400 **
30 June 1969	360,500	35,800	81,500	60,500	400	538,700
31 Dec. 1969	331,100	30,200	55,100	58,400	400	475,200
30 June 1970	298,600	25,700	39,900	50,500	200	414,900
31 Dec. 1970	249,600	16,700	25,100	43,100	100	334,600
30 June 1971	190,500	10,700	500	37,400	100	239,200
31 Dec. 1971	119,700	7,600	600	28,800	100	156,800
30 June 1972	31,800	2,200	1,400	11,500	100	47,000
31 Dec. 1972	13,800	1,500	1,200	7,600	100	24,200
30 June 1973	***	***	***	***	***	***

SOURCE: U.S. Department of Defense, OASD (Comptroller), Directorate for Information Operations, Mar. 19, 1974.

*Between 1954 and 1960, U.S. military strength averaged about 650 advisers.

**Peak strength.

***Totals for all five services less than 250.

Command Officers, Naval Forces, Vietnam

Officer	Term
Rear Admiral Norvell G. Ward	April 1966 to April 1967
Rear Admiral Kenneth L. Veth	April 1967 to September 1968
Vice Admiral Elmo R. Zumwalt	September 1968 to May 1970
Vice Admiral Jerome H. King	May 1970 to April 1971
Rear Admiral Robert S. Salzer	April 1971 June 1972
Rear Admiral Arthur W. Price Jr.	June to August 1972
Rear Admiral James B. Wilson	August 1972 to March 1973

Military Sea Transportation Service. Responsible for the line of communication and supply to Southeast Asia, the Military Sea Transportation Service (MSTS) was an independent service command. By mid 1967, it controlled more than 500 supply vessels that served the 11,000-kilometer (7,000-mile) transoceanic lifeline between the United States and U.S. forces in Vietnam. With its Far East headquarters in Japan, the MSTS established an office in South Vietnam, operationally under the control of Naval Forces, Vietnam.

More than 99 percent of the ammunition and fuel and 95 percent of other supplies used by U.S. forces in the theater arrived by means of MSTS, which also shuttled cargo along the coast. During the evacuation of the northern provinces in 1975, MSTS elements from the Seventh Fleet transported 130,000 refugees to Saigon.

Task Force 115. Task Force 115, the U.S. Navy's Coastal Surveillance Force, attempted to cut the flow of seaborne supplies from North Vietnam to NVA and Viet Cong forces in the South. Organized on 11 March 1965 under the code name Operation Market Time, Task Force 115 initially reported to the Seventh Fleet but later came under the authority of the Naval Advisory Group in July 1965 and then Naval Forces, Vietnam. Its original headquarters was in Saigon, but it was transferred to Cam Ranh Bay in July 1967.

Nine patrol sections divided the 2,000-kilometer (1,200-mile) coast of South Vietnam. Each sector relied on a diverse collection of airplanes, warships, and small patrol boats to cover three different zones. The zone farthest out—160–240 kilometers (100–150 miles) offshore—was covered by air surveillance; the middle zone was patrolled by destroyer escorts, minesweepers, and Coast Guard cutters; and the zone closest to the coast relied on small, fast U.S. patrol boats and South Vietnamese navy coastal junks.

By the summer of 1967, Task Force 115 nearly succeeded in halting seaborne infiltration altogether. At its peak, the Coastal Surveillance Force employed 81 fast patrol boats, 24 Coast Guard cutters, and 39 other vessels. The South Vietnamese navy assumed a larger role in 1969 and assumed responsibility for the inner zone in September 1970. One year later it had complete control of the operation.

Task Force 116. Formed on 18 December 1965, Task Force 116, the U.S. Navy's River Patrol Force, reported to Naval Forces, Vietnam, and directed naval units involved in Operation Game Warden. The operation focused on denying the Viet Cong use of the critical waterways in the country, especially in the Mekong Delta region. It also tried to make navigation safe for friendly vessels.

River Patrol Squadron 5 served under Task Force 116 and commanded the patrol boats used on the rivers. The squadron was divided into five divisions—four in the IV CTZ and one at Da Nang. Each consisted of two ten-boat sections and a base ship, often a converted Landing Ship, Tank (LST). A crew off our manned the 8.5-meter (28-foot) patrol boats, which carried a variety of machine guns and a grenade launcher. Crews required several months of training, and full-scale operations did not begin until March 1966.

Task Force 116 also used direct air support. Initially the task force relied on U.S. Army helicopters, but by August 1966 the U.S. Navy's Helicopter Squadron 1 was assigned to it. Helicopter Squadron 1 was replaced by Helicopter Attack (Light) Squadron 3 on 1 April 1967.

Additional firepower came from other sources. A dozen or so small minesweepers from Mine Division 112 were attached to the task force to scour the inland waterways for mines. Task Force 116 also received assistance from Navy SEALs. By mid 1968, the Pacific Fleet's SEAL Team 1 had deployed four or five 14-man platoons to South Vietnam. Three platoons generally served under the task force commander and conducted reconnaissance patrols, ambushes, and special intelligence operations.

Task Force 116 kept the largest waterways open and forced the Viet Cong to divert significant resources to maintain their water communications in the IV CTZ. The patrol boats also played a critical role during the Tet Offensive in assisting villages under siege. In 1969 Task Force 116 began to turn over its resources and responsibilities to the South Vietnamese navy and was deactivated in December 1970.

Task Force 117. Task Force 117 was the Riverine Assault Force, and the U.S. Navy's component of the joint U.S. Army-Navy Mobile Riverine Force. Activated on 28 February 1967 and stationed in the Mekong Delta, it consisted of four river assault squadrons. Each 400-man squadron manned a variety of vessels to support operations of the Army's 9th Infantry Division. Armored troop carriers shuttled infantry along the waterways and heavily armed monitors provided critical fire support. The armor-plated monitors carried 40mm and 20mm cannons, grenade launchers, machine guns, and 81mm mortars.

The task force also included a floating base, which consisted of barracks ships, LSTs, repair ships, and other support vessels. One or two infantry battalions were held in reserve as well.

The Mobile Riverine Force played a key role in breaking up NVA and Viet Cong troop concentrations in the Mekong Delta and in recapturing cities taken by the Viet Cong forces in the first days of the Tet Offensive. Task Force 117 was the first large U.S. Navy command to turn over its responsibilities to the South Vietnamese navy. It was deactivated on 25 August 1969.

continued

Officer	Term
Maj. Gen. Le Van Nghiem	5 May 1960
Maj. Gen. Ton That Dinh	7 December 1962
Lt. Gen. Tran Thien Khiem	5 January 1964
Maj. Gen. Lam Van Phat	2 February 1964
Lt. Col. Tran Ngoc Tam	4 April 1964
Maj. Gen. Cao Van Vien	12 October 1964
Maj. Gen. Nguyen Bac Tri	11 October 1965
Lt. Gen. Le Nguyen Khang	9 June 1966
Lt. Gen. Do Cao Tri*	5 August 1968
Lt. Gen. Nguyen Van Minh	23 February 1971
Lt. Gen. Pham Quoc Thuan	29 October 1973
Lt. Gen. Du Quoc Dong	30 October 1974
Lt. Gen. Nguyen Van Toan	January 1975 to 25 April 1975

*Killed in a helicopter crash 23 February 1971.

IV Corps. Organized 1 January 1963, IV Corps, which encompassed the Mekong Delta, contained more than half of both the nation's population and cultivated land. It consisted of the following provinces: Go Cong, Kien Tuong, Dinh Tuong, Kien Hoa, Kien Phong, Sa Dec, Vinh Long, Vinh Binh, Chau Doc, An Giang, Phong Dinh, Ba Xuyen, Kien Giang, Chuong Thien, Bac Lieu, and An Xuyen. The semiautonomous 44th Special Tactical Zone coordinated ARVN military operations and security in the northwestern delta along the Cambodian border until late 1973. After a string of tactical successes that eliminated communist main-force units in the area, the STZ was abolished, its Ranger battalions deactivated, and their personnel sent to battalions further north. However, since the units had been recruited from the delta area, many personnel deserted rather than leave their home regions.

Commanding Officers, IV Corps

Officer	Term
Maj. Gen. Huynh Van Cao*	1 January 1963
Maj. Gen. Nguyen Huu Co	4 November 1963
Maj. Gen. Duong Van Duc**	4 March 1964

Appendix C

Order of Battle, Army of the Republic of Vietnam (ARVN)

As with the order of battle for communist forces, data for ARVN commanders' names, ranks, and dates of service are often incomplete or inconclusive. The following lists give the date an officer was officially appointed to command a unit, or, whenever possible, the date he actually assumed command; c. indicates that the officer in question held the position at the date noted. Ranks given are the highest known rank attained by the officer while in command of a specific entity. Province names are those in official RVN use during the war; see map of Vietnam, Republic of.

The origins of the Army of the Republic of Vietnam (ARVN) can be traced to the Vietnamese colonial units organized by the French to fight the Viet Minh. After the French defeat, some of these units were turned over to the noncommunist State of Vietnam. When incorporated into the armed forces of the new state, these units usually retained the designations of their French antecedents to retain a link with their past. With the creation of the Republic of Vietnam on 26 October 1955, the ARVN went through several of reorganizations. The result is a complex organizational history, in which unit designations change repeatedly. Light divisions, created on 1 August 1955, were redesignated on 1 November and abolished during the first half of 1959. Numerous units were created, converted, or merged. The following appendix provides an overview of the complex 30-year history of the ARVN's corps and divisions.

The ARVN was the largest combat component of the Republic of Vietnam Armed Forces (RVNAF). At its height, it consisted of eleven regular infantry divisions, each assigned to one of the four corps commands, or Corps Tactical Zones (CTZ), that divided the country. The airborne and marine divisions, under semi-independent command, served as South Vietnam's general reserve at the discretion of the president. Armor, artillery, and ranger units, nominally part of separate commands, were allocated to the various corps and operated under the control of corps commanders. Also under the control of corps commanders were local militia units, most importantly the Regional/Popular Forces (RF/PF). Several semi-autonomous Special Tactical Zones (STZ) existed within the CTZs, created to concentrate military resources in key areas.

ARVN Divisions, December 1972

The map shows ARVN divisional headquarters as located after the Easter Offensive. Note that the Airborne and Marine divisions, though headquartered in Saigon, were operating in and around Quang Tri City, which was retaken in the closing stages of the offensive. (Map adapted from William E. Le Gro, *Vietnam from Cease-Fire to Capitulation*. Center of Military History, 1981.)

Corps Commands

I Corps. Organized 1 June 1957, I Corps, directly south of the DMZ, consisted of the five northern provinces of the Republic of Vietnam: Quang Tri, Thua Thien, Quang Nam, Quang Tin, and Quang Ngai (transferred from II Corps in November 1963). The semiautonomous Quang Da Special Zone coordinated the security of the area around Da Nang.

Commanding Officers, I Corps

Officer	Term
Lt. Gen. Tran Van Don	15 October 1957
Maj. Gen. Le Van Nghiem	7 December 1962
Maj. Gen. Do Cao Tri	21 August 1963
Lt. Gen. Nguyen Khanh	11 December 1963
Maj. Gen. Ton That Xung	30 January 1964
Lt. Gen. Nguyen Chanh Thi	14 November 1964
Maj. Gen. Nguyen Van Chuan	14 March 1966
Lt. Gen. Ton That Dinh	9 April 1966
Maj. Gen. Huynh Van Cao	15 May 1966
Gen. Tran Thanh Phong*	20 May 1966
Lt. Gen. Hoang Xuan Lam	30 May 1966
Lt. Gen. Ngo Quang Truong	3 May 1972 to 30 April 1975

*Acting commander

II Corps. Organized 1 October 1957, II Corps, the largest in geographical area of all the corps, encompassed much of the Central Highlands as well as South Vietnam's narrow coastal plain. It consisted of the following provinces: Kontum, Binh Dinh, Pleiku, Phu Bon, Phu Yen, Darlac, Khanh Hoa, Quang Duc, Tuyen Duc, Ninh Thuan, Lam Dong, and Binh Thuan. The semiautonomous 24th Special Tactical Zone, to which the independent

42d Regiment was assigned, covered areas of heavy communist infiltration along the Laotian border. Established July 1966 and located in Kontum province in the Central Highlands, the 24th STZ was abolished 30 April 1970. During the 1975 Ho Chi Minh Campaign, the fall of Ban Me Thuot on 12 March impelled President Nguyen Van Thieu to abandon I and II Corps. The disastrous withdrawal of II Corps forces down Route 7B from Pleiku to Tuy Hoa, mishandled by corps commander Maj. Gen. Pham Van Phu, marked the beginning of the end for the Republic of Vietnam.

Commanding Officers, II Corps

Officer	Term
Maj. Gen. Tran Ngoc Tam	1 October 1957
Maj. Gen. Ton That Dinh	13 August 1958
Lt. Gen. Nguyen Khanh	20 December 1962
Lt. Gen. Do Cao Tri	12 December 1963
Maj. Gen. Nguyen Huu Co	15 September 1964
Lt. Gen. Vinh Loc	25 June 1965
Lt. Gen. Lu Lan	28 February 1968
Lt. Gen. Ngo Dzu	28 August 1970
Maj. Gen. Nguyen Van Toan	10 May 1972
Maj. Gen. Pham Van Phu	30 October 1974 to 1 April 1975

III Corps. Provisionally organized 1 March 1959 and permanently organized 20 May 1960, III Corps consisted of the following provinces: Phuoc Long, Long Khanh, Binh Tuy, Binh Long, Binh Duong, Bien Hoa, Phuoc Tuy, Tay Ninh, Hau Nghia, and Long An. Saigon, with neighboring Gia Dinh province, formed the semiautonomous Capital Military District (CMD), which also had a political dimension: it was intended as much to protect Saigon from coup attempts by ambitious corps commanders as from attack by communist forces. The Rung Sat Special Zone, an area of intense Viet Cong activity at the mouth of the Dong Nai River, protected the river approaches to Saigon.

Commanding Officers, III Corps

Officer	Term
Lt. Gen. Thai Quang Hoang	1 March 1959
Lt. Gen. Nguyen Ngoc Le	11 October 1959

continu

Officer	Term
Maj. Gen. Nguyen Van Thieu	15 September 1964
Lt. Col. Dang Van Quang	20 January 1965
Maj. Gen. Nguyen Van Manh	23 November 1966
Lt. Gen. Nguyen Duc Thang	29 February 1968
Lt. Gen. Nguyen Viet Thanh***	1 July 1968
Maj. Gen. Ngo Dzu	1 May 1970
Lt. Gen. Ngo Quang Truong	21 August 1970
Maj. Gen. Nguyen Vinh Nghi	4 May 1972
Maj. Gen. Nguyen Khoa Nam	30 October 1974

*Relieved in aftermath of 1 November 1963 coup.
**Attempted unsuccessful coup 13 September 1964.
***Killed in a helicopter crash 23 February 1971.

Divisions

The ARVN's divisions tended to develop local attachments, as they were usually based in the same locales for years, even decades, and often were formed with units and personnel drawn from the area around their bases. Military dependents of division personnel naturally lived in the vicinity as well. Such ties contributed to the general immobility and inertia of the ARVN, and had a significant impact on unit performance. For example, during the 1975 Ho Chi Minh Campaign, the 1st, 2d, and 3d divisions all collapsed as I Corps was overrun, partly because soldiers deserted in droves to protect their families. On the other hand, the 18th Division fought tenaciously in defense of its home base, Xuan Loc.

1st Division. Organized 1 January 1955, the 1st Division had its origins in the 21st Mobile Group, established by the French 1 September 1953 and raised in Thua Thien and Quang Tri provinces. The 21st Mobile Group provided the nucleus for the 21st Infantry Division, redesignated on 1 August 1955 as the 21st Field Division. Renumbered on 1 November 1955 as the 1st Field Division, the unit became the 1st Infantry Division in January 1959.

Considered to be one of the best units in the ARVN, the 1st Division conducted operations in Quang Tri, Thua Thien, Quang Nam, and Quang Ngai provinces throughout the war. The 1st also took part in Operation Lam Son 719, the South Vietnamese invasion of Laos in late January-March 1971. The division, headquartered at or near Hue throughout its history, supported the Buddhist-led Struggle Movement in Hue during the

1966 uprisings in I Corps. During the 1975 Ho Chi Minh Campaign, the 1st Division disintegrated during the fighting to cover the evacuation of Hue. The remnants of the division, two officers and forty men, were evacuated to Ba Ria, Phuoc Tuy province, captured 27 March.

Commanding Officers, 1st Division

Officer	Term
Lt. Col. Le Van Nghiem*	1 January 1955
Gen. Do Cao Tri	c.1963
Gen. Nguyen Chanh Thi	c.1964
Maj. Gen. Nguyen Van Chnan	c.1965 to 1966
Gen. Pham Xuan Nhuan	12 March 1966
Lt. Gen. Ngo Quang Truong	June 1966
Maj. Gen. Pham Van Phu	21 August 1970
Brig. Gen. Le Van Than	c.1973
Maj. Gen. Nguyen Van Diem	31 October 1974 to 30 April 1975

*Information on units commanders between 1955 and 1963 is unavailable.

2d Division. Organized 1 February 1955, the 2d Division was created from the 32d Mobile Group, established by the French 3 November 1953 in the Red River Delta of North Vietnam. After the 1954 Geneva agreements, the group was transported to Da Nang from Haiphong and reorganized as the 32d Infantry Division; the commander of the 32d Mobile Group became the new division's first commander. The unit was redesignated on 1 August 1955 as the 32d Field Division. Renumbered on 1 November 1955 as the 2d Field Division, the unit became the 2d Infantry Division in January 1959.

The 2d Division conducted operations in Quang Nam, Quang Tin, and Quang Ngai provinces throughout the war. First headquartered at Da Nang, the 2d Division alternated its headquarters between Da Nang and Quang Ngai before settling at Quang Ngai in May 1965. In early 1972, the 2d shifted its headquarters to the former U.S. base camp at Chu Lai, Quang Tin province. During the 1975 Ho Chi Minh Campaign, the 2d held Tam Ky until 24 March. The division was almost destroyed in the fighting, and its remnants were withdrawn to Da Nang and evacuated by sea. Reconstituted at Ham Tan, the 2d Division held Phan Rang until 16 April 1975, when the city and its defenders were overrun.

Commanding Officers, 2d Division

Officer	Term
Col. Ton That Dinh	1 January 1955
Lt. Col. Dang Van Son	22 November 1956
Lt. Col. Le Quang Trong	14 June 1957
Col. Duong Ngoc Lam	23 August 1958
Col. Lam Van Phat	8 June 1961
Col. Truong Van Chuong	18 June 1963
Brig. Gen. Ton That Xung	6 December 1963
Brig. Gen. Ngo Dzu	30 January 1964
Col. Nguyen Thanh Sang	29 July 1964
Maj. Gen. Hoang Xuan Lam*	15 October 1964
Maj. Gen. Nguyen Van Toan	10 January 1967
Brig. Gen. Pham Hoa Hiep	22 January 1972
Brig. Gen. Tran Van Nhut	27 August 1972 to 30 April 1975

*Concurrently commander of I Corps from 30 May 1966.

3d Division. Organized 1 October 1971, the 3d Division was established to make up for the withdrawal of U.S. forces from the heavily contested northern area of I Corps along the DMZ. The new division was formed from the newly raised 56th and 57th regiments and from the 2d Regiment, transferred from the 1st Division. First headquartered at Ai Tu, near Quang Tri City, the division had barely become fully operational when it was struck by the initial thrusts of the 1972 Easter Offensive. The division disintegrated, allowing Quang Tri to be overrun by communist forces. Reconstituted at Da Nang, the 3d operated in Quang Nam and Quang Tin provinces for the remainder of the war, with the defense of Da Nang as its primary responsibility. During the 1975 Ho Chi Minh Campaign, the bulk of the division was overrun and Da Nang captured on 30 March 1975.

Commanding Officers, 3d Division

Officer	Term
Brig. Gen. Vu Van Giai*	1 October 1971
Maj. Gen. Nguyen Duy Hinh	9 June 1972 to 30 April 1975

*Relieved of command 3 May 1972.

5th Division. Organized 1 February 1955, the division was formed from Nung veterans of French service against the Viet Minh transported south after the 1954 Geneva accords. Many Nung, members of an ethnically Chinese minority group, had fled China to escape the 1948 communist takeover. The unit, at first exclusively made up of Nung, was purposefully diluted with ethnic Vietnamese by President Ngo Dinh Diem. However, the division retained a number of Nung personnel throughout the war.

Originally designated the 6th Infantry Division, the unit was redesignated on 1 August 1955 as the 6th Field Division and on 1 September 1955 was renumbered as the 41st Field Division. Renumbered on 1 November 1955 as the 3d Field Division, the unit became the 5th Infantry Division in January 1959.

First headquartered at Song Mao in Binh Thuan province, the 5th was moved to Bien Hoa in May 1961. Troops of the division, directed by Col. Nguyen Van Thieu, participated in the 1 November 1963 coup that overthrew President Ngo Dinh Diem. Moved to Binh Duong province in July 1964, the 5th was first headquartered at Phu Loi and moved to Lai Khe in February 1970. The 5th, which operated in the northern provinces of III Corps, participated in cross-border operations into Cambodia in 1970 and 1971. During the 1972 Easter Offensive, the 5th successfully held the city of An Loc, besieged for more than two months. During the 1975 Ho Chi Minh Campaign, the 5th Division formed part of Saigon's defenses north of the city near Ben Cat on Route 13 until the city fell on 30 April.

Commanding Officers, 5th Division

Officer	Term
Col. Vong A Sang	I March 1955
Col. Pham Van Dong	25 October 1956
Lt. Col. Nguyen Quang Thong*	18 March 1958
Col. Ton That Xung	16 September 1958
Lt. Col. Dang Van Son	19 November 1958
Col. Nguyen Van Chuan	3 August 1959
Brig. Gen. Tran Ngoc Tam	20 May 1961
Col. Nguyen Duc Thang	16 October 1961
Col. Nguyen Van Thieu	20 December 1962
Brig. Gen. Dang Thanh Liem	2 February 1964
Brig. Gen. Cao Hao Hoa	5 June 1964
Brig. Gen. Tran Thanh Phong	21 October 1964

Officer	Term
Maj. Gen. Pham Quoc Thuan	19 July 1965
Maj. Gen. Nguyen Van Hieu	15 August 1969
Brig. Gen. Le Van Hung	14 June 1971
Brig. Gen. Tran Quoc Lich	4 September 1972
Col. Le Nguyen Vy	7 November 1973 to 30 April 1975

*Acting commander

7th Division. Organized 1 January 1955, the 7th Division traced its origins back to the 7th Mobile Group, raised by the French in the Red River Delta of North Vietnam. The unit was later redesignated as the 2d and then, on 1 September 1953, as the 31st Mobile Group. After the 1954 Geneva agreements, the group was transported to Da Nang from Haiphong and reorganized 1 January 1955 as the 31st Infantry Division; the commander of the 31st Mobile Group became the new division's first commander. Based initially at Tam Ky, the 31st was moved south during the summer of 1955. On 1 August 1955, it was redesignated as the 31st Field Division. It was redesignated only a few weeks later as the 11th Field Division and redesignated again on 1 November as the 4th Field Division. The 4th established its headquarters at Bien Hoa 11 November 1955. The 4th Field Division fought in early 1956 against the Hoa Hao military forces commanded by Ba Cut (Le Quang Vinh), operating in the Mekong Delta in an area that later became part of Chau Doc province. The 4th was redesignated as the 7th Infantry Division on 1 January 1959. The 7th moved its headquarters from Bien Hoa to My Tho, Dinh Tuong province, 20 May 1961; the 5th Division moved to Bien Hoa at the same time. On 1 September 1969, the division moved to Dong Tam, near My Tho. The former base camp of the 9th U.S. Infantry Division, Dong Tam was an island built by U.S. engineers from earth dredged from the My Tho branch of the Mekong.

The 7th Division conducted operations in the heavily populated provinces of Long An, Go Cong, Kien Tuong, Dinh Tuang, Kien Hoa, Kien Phong, Sa Dec, Vinh Long, Vinh Binh, An Giang, and Phong Dinh throughout the war. The 7th participated in cross-border operations into Cambodia in 1970 and 1971. In June during the 1972 Easter Offensive, the 7th fought in the Cambodian border area known as the Elephant's Foot, north of Moc Hoa, Kien Tuong province. In November, it fought in Kien Phong province. During the 1975 Ho Chi Minh Campaign, the 7th Division, fighting in the northern Mekong Delta, reinforced the defenders of Tan An with a regiment, the 12th Infantry. Tan An, southwest of Saigon in Long An province, formed part of the capital's defenses and held out until the capitulation of the Republic of Vietnam.

Commanding Officers, 7th Division

Officer	Term
Lt. Col. Nguyen Huu Co	1 January 1955
Col. Ton That Xung	15 June 1955
Lt. Col. Ngo Dzu	27 April 1957
Col. Tran Thien Khiem	17 March 1958
Col. Huynh Van Cao	30 March 1959
Col. Bui Dinh Dam	22 December 1962
Brig. Gen. Nguyen Huu Co	I November 1963
Col. Pham Van Dong	5 November 1963
Brig. Gen. Lam Van Phat	2 December 1963
Col. Bui Huu Nhon	2 February 1964
Col. Huynh Van Ton	7 March 1964
Brig. Gen. Nguyen Bao Tri	16 September 1964
Brig. Gen. Nguyen Viet Thanh	9 October 1965
Brig. Gen. Nguyen Thanh Hoang	3 July 1968
Maj. Gen. Nguyen Khoa Nam	16 January 1970
Gen. Tran Van Hal	30 October 1974 to 30 April 1975

9th Division. Organized 1 January 1962, the 9th Division was created, along with the 25th Division, as part of a program to increase the strength of the ARVN by 30,000 personnel. Its first headquarters were at Phu Thanh, Binh Dinh province, near Qui Nhon. The 25th operated in Binh Dinh, Phu Bon, and Phu Yen provinces until 20 September 1963, when it transferred its headquarters to Sa Dec. in IV Corps. On 5 April 1972, the division moved its headquarters to the former U.S. base at the town of Vinh Long.

The 9th operated in nearly every province of IV Corps, acting as the mobile force for the corps from 1969 on. During the 1963 coup that overthrew President Ngo Dinh Diem, the 9th, controlled by Diem loyalists, was blocked from moving to Diem's aid: one of the conspirators, Col. Nguyen Huu Co, took control of the 7th Division at My Tho and used it to seize the ferries that crossed the Mekong River. The 9th participated in cross-border operations into Cambodia in 1970 and 1971. During the Easter Offensive, the 9th Division detached a regiment, the 15th Infantry, to assist in an abortive attempt in May 1972 to relieve the besieged 5th Division at An

Loc. During the 1975 Ho Chi Minh Campaign, the 9th Division fought in the northern Mekong Delta until the capitulation of the Republic of Vietnam.

Commanding Officers, 9th Division

Officer	Term
Col. Bui Dzinh*	1 January 1962
Col. Doan Van Quang	7 November 1963
Brig. Gen. Vinh Loc	9 February 1964
Brig. Gen. Lam Quang Thi	29 May 1965
Maj. Gen. Tran Ba Di	3 July 1968
Brig. Gen. Huynh Van Lac	26 October 1973 to 30 April 1975

*Relieved in aftermath of 1 November 1963 coup.

18th Division. Provisionally organized 16 May 1965 and permanently organized August 1965, the 18th Division was formed at Xuan Loc, Long Khanh province, which served as its main headquarters throughout its existence. First designated as the 10th Division, it was redesignated on 1 January 1967 as the 18th because of the inauspicious connotations of the original name: "number 10" in both Vietnamese and American military slang meant "the worst."

The 18th, considered to be perhaps the worst division in the ARVN, generally operated in eastern III Corps throughout the war. During the 1972 Easter Offensive, elements of the 18th Division were moved to Binh Long province and fought at An Loc. During the 1975 Ho Chi Minh Campaign, the 18th Division held Xuan Loc from 17 March to 16 April, enduring repeated assaults as well as some of the heaviest artillery bombardment of the war. The battle proved to be the last stand of the Army of the Republic of Vietnam.

Commanding Officers, 18th Division

Officer	Term
Col. Nguyen Van Manh	5 June 1965
Brig. Gen. Lu Lan	20 August 1965
Brig. Gen. Do Ke Giai	16 September 1966
Maj. Gen. Lam Quang Tho	20 August 1969
Brig. Gen. Le Minh Dao	4 April 1972 to 30 April 1975

21st Division. Organized 1 June 1959, the 21st Division traced its origins back to the 1st and the 3d Light Divisions. The 1st, formed at Long Xuyen but soon moved to Sa Dec was redesignated the 11th Light Division on 1 November 1955. The 3d, formed at Thu Dau Mot (later Phu Cuong), was moved shortly afterward to Ben Keo, Tay Ninh, establishing itself in the former headquarters of the Cao Dai armed forces. The unit was also redesignated on 1 November, becoming the 13th Light Division. Both divisions fought against Hoa Hao military forces in the Mekong Delta in 1955 and 1956. The two units were officially combined as the 21st Infantry Division on 1 June 1959. The commander of the 11th was the new division's first commander and the Sa Dec headquarters of the 11th became the 21st Division's main headquarters. The 21st was dispersed throughout southern South Vietnam by late 1960, operating around Tay Ninh, Long An, Kien Tuong and Kien Phong, and Ca Mau in An Xuyen province. The division was later concentrated in IV Corps in the southern Mekong Delta, transferring its headquarters from Sa Dec to Bac Lieu.

The 21st, under Col. Tranh Thien Khiem, helped put down the 11 November 1960 coup attempt against President Ngo Dinh Diem, led by Col. Nguyen Chanh Thi, commander of the Airborne Division. The division fought in the U Minh forest in Kien Giang province in 1970 and 1971. During the 1972 Easter Offensive, much of the division was temporarily moved to Binh Dinh province. The 21st, along with the 25th Division, participated in an abortive attempt in May 1972 to relieve the besieged 5th Division at An Loc. During the 1975 Ho Chi Minh Campaign, the 21st Division fought in the southern Mekong Delta until the capitulation of the Republic of Vietnam.

Commanding Officers, 21st Division

Officer	Term
Lt. Col. Nguyen Bao Tri*	1 June 1959
Lt. Col. Tran Thanh Chieu	8 September 1959
Col. Tranh Thien Khiem	2 February 1960
Col. Bui Huu Nhon	December 1962
Col. Cao Hao Hon	November 1963
Brig. Gen. Dang Van Quang	1 June 1964
Col. Nguyen Van Phuoc**	20 January 1965
Brig. Gen. Nguyen Van Minh	21 March 1965
Maj. Gen. Nguyen Vinh Nghi	13 June 1968
Brig. Gen. Ho Trung Hau	3 May 1972

Officer	Term
Brig. Gen. Chuong Dzanh Quay	21 August 1972
Brig. Gen. Le Van Hung	9 June 1973

*Lt. Col. Tri became commander of the 11th Light Division, the predecessor of the 21st Division, on 16 October 1957.

**Acting commander.

22d Division. Organized 1 April 1959, the 22d Division traced its origins back to the 4th and the 2d Light Divisions. The 2d, formed at Kontum but manned almost entirely by troops from the Mekong Delta, was redesignated the 12th Light Division 1 November 1955. The troops of the 4th, formed at Ban Me Thuot, originally were overwhelmingly Montagnards. The 4th was redesignated the 14th Light Division 1 November. Transferred to Qui Nhon, the 14th fought in early 1956 against the Hoa Hao military forces commanded by Ba Cut (Le Quang Vinh) in the Mekong Delta. Later moved to Kontum, the 14th Light Division was redesignated as the 22d Infantry Division on 1 April 1959; the personnel of the 2d, which was disbanded the day before, were transferred into the new unit.

The 22d was responsible throughout most of the war for the five northern provinces of II Corps (Binh Dinh, Phu Bon, Phu Yen, and Kontum and Pleiku in the Central Highlands). Originally at Kontum, the 22d's headquarters were moved to Ba Gi, Binh Dinh province, in March 1965. During the Easter Offensive, the division, responsible for defending both Kontum and the coast, disintegrated 24 April 1972 at Tan Canh; the 23d Division had to be rushed in to hold the city. Later in 1972, the division, reconstituted in Binh Dinh, reopened coastal highway Route 1. During the 1975 Ho Chi Minh Campaign, the 22d Division held Binh Dinh province until cut off by the collapse of ARVN forces in the Central Highlands at Binh Khe. It broke through to Qui Nhon and was evacuated by sea to Vung Tau. Reconstituted, the 22d held out at Tan An and Ben Luc, southwest of Saigon in Long An province, until the capitulation of South Vietnam.

Commanding Officers, 22d Division

Officer	Term
Lt. Col. Tran Thanh Chieu*	1 April 1959
Lt. Col. Nguyen Bao Tri	8 September 1959
Col. Nguyen Thanh Sang	5 November 1963
Brig Gen. Linh Quang Vien	5 February 1964
Col. Nguyen Van Hieu	7 September 1964

continues

continued

Officer	Term
Brig. Gen. Nguyen Xuan Thinh	24 October 1964
Brig. Gen. Nguyen Thanh Sang	1 March 1965
Brig. Gen. Nguyen Van Hieu	28 June 1966
Brig. Gen. Le Ngoc Trien	I1 August 1969
Col. Le Dac Dal**	1 March 1972
Brig. Gen. Phan Dinh Niem	28 April 1972 to 30 April 1975

*Lt. Col. Chieu became commander of the 14th Light Division, the predecessor of the 22d Division, on 28 March 1958.

**Missing in action, April 1972.

23d Division. Organized 1 April 1959, the 23d Division had its origins in the 5th Light Division, established at Nha Trang and redesignated the 15th Light Division 1 November 1955. From January to May 1956, the 15th fought in the Nguyen Hue campaign launched by President Ngo Dinh Diem to suppress the Hoa Hao and Cao Dai religious armies. The division operated throughout the upper Mekong Delta in the Dong Thap Muoi area (later divided into Kien Tuong and Kien Phong provinces), as well as Tay Ninh and the areas that later became Long An, Hau Nghia, and An Giang provinces. After the campaign, the 15th returned to Nha Trang, but was moved to Duc My, Khanh Hoa province, 14 August 1956. On 1 April 1959, the 15th Light Division became the 23rd Infantry Division. The 23d was moved into the Central Highlands beginning in late 1960, transferring its headquarters to Ban Me Thuot, Darlac province, by June 1961.

The 23d operated throughout central South Vietnam from 1958 to 1969, both in the Central Highlands and along the coast from Quang Ngai to Binh Tuy, although the division's area of responsibility consisted of the seven southern provinces of II Corps (Darlac, Khanh Hoa, Quang Duc, Tuyen Duc, Ninh Thuan, Lam Dong, and Binh Thuan). Part of the 23d participated in cross-border operations into Cambodia in 1970 and 1971. In May 1972 during the Easter Offensive, the 23d, rushed to defend Kontum City after the defending 22d Division crumbled, held the city despite heavy communist artillery bombardment and repeated assaults. In 1975, the 23d attempted to retake the captured town of Ban Me Thuot but failed and was shattered in the attempt. The remnants of the division were evacuated by air to Camh Ranh, 21 March 1975, and then to Long Hai, Phuoc Tuy province, captured 27 March.

Commanding Officers, 23d Division

Officer	Term
Lt. Col. Tran Thanh Phong	19 May 1959
Col. Le Quang Trong	17 May 1963
Brig. Gen. Hoang Xuan Lam	14 December 1963
Brig. Gen. Lu Lan	14 October 1964
Brig. Gen. Nguyen Van Manh	20 August 1965
Brig. Gen. Truong Quang An*	24 November 1966
Brig. Gen. Vo Van Canh	9 September 1968
Brig. Gen. Ly Tong Ba	25 January 1972
Brig. Gen. Tran Van Cam	20 October 1972
Brig. Gen. Le Trung Tuong**	24 November 1973 to 10 March 1975

*Killed in action in a helicopter crash.
**Slightly wounded on 10 March 1975, Brig. Gen. Tuong had himself evacuated.

25th Division. Organized 1 July 1962, the 25th Division was created, along with the 9th Division, as part of a program to increase the strength of the ARVN by 30,000 personnel. It was formed in Quang Ngai province, with its first headquarters at Thuan Hoa, near Quang Ngai City. The 25th operated in Quang Ngai and Binh Dinh provinces until 28 October 1964, when it was transferred to Cay Diep, Gia Dinh province, near Saigon, and moved again 23 December 1964 to Duc Hoa, Hau Nghia province. On 13 December 1970, the division moved to Cu Chi, the former base camp of the 25th U.S. Infantry Division, also in Hau Nghia.

The 25th operated in the western provinces of III Corps throughout the war. Units of the 25th took part in the cross-border operations into Cambodia that began in April 1970, attacking down Route 1 into the "Parrot's Beak" area and advancing through Svay Rieng as far as Kampong Trabek. Other units of the 25th pushed into Krek and Chap along Route 7. During the Easter Offensive, the 25th, along with the 21st Division, participated in an abortive attempt in May 1972 to relieve the besieged 5th Division at An Loc. During the Ho Chi Minh Campaign, in April 1975, the 25th Division defended Tay Ninh City and Go Dau Ha, both along Route 22 west of Saigon, as part of the capital's defenses until the capitulation of the Republic of Vietnam.

Commanding Officers, 25th Division

Officer	Term
Col. Nguyen Van Chuen	July 1962
Col. Lu Lan	28 December 1962
Col. Nguyen Viet Dam	19 March 1964
Brig. Gen. Nguyen Thanh Sang	December 1964
Brig. Gen. Phan Trong Chinh	16 March 1965
Lt. Gen. Nguyen Xuan Thinh	10 January 1968
Brig. Gen. Le Van Tu	25 January 1972
Col. Nguyen Huu Toan	7 November 1973
Brig. Gen. Ly Tong Ba	to 30 April 1975

Airborne Division. Organized 1 May 1955, the Airborne Division traced its origins back to the 1st Airborne Battalion, formed by the French with Vietnamese members of the airborne *Troupes Aeroportées en Indochine,* 1 August 1951. This unit was combined with several other Vietnamese-manned units to form *Groupement Airport 3* (G. A.P. 3; equivalent to an airborne regimental combat team) on 1 May 1954, under the command of a Vietnamese officer, then-major Do Cao Tri. After the Geneva agreements, Lt. Col. Tri was named commander of airborne troops of the armed forces of the State of Vietnam, 1 March 1955; G. A.P. 3 was transformed into the Airborne Group, 1 May 1955, at Tan Son Nhut. It was expanded to a brigade on 1 December 1959 and to a division on 1 December 1965.

An independent command under the direct control of the JGS, the Airborne Division was headquartered at Tan Son Nhut throughout the war, where it also had its training base. Considered one of the best units in the RVNAF, its ranks were filled exclusively by volunteers. Many airborne officers went on to command infantry divisions and corps, among them Nguyen Chanh Thi, Ngo Quang Truong, and Do Cao Tri. As part of South Vietnam's general reserve, the Airborne Division operated throughout the country as reinforcement for ARVN units. It also took part in the cross-border operations into Cambodia in 1970 and 1971 as well as in Operation Lam Son 719. The division operated in I Corps from the 1972 Easter Offensive on, maintaining a forward headquarters in the area.

During the 1975 Ho Chi Minh Campaign, the Airborne Division was withdrawn from I Corps, a move that helped precipitate the collapse of ARVN forces in the region. The division's 3d Brigade, rushed to the defense of Nha Trang, was virtually destroyed 30-31 March. The 2d

Brigade, sent to reinforce the defenders of Phan Rang 9 April, was badly battered and later relieved by the 2d Division. The 1st Brigade attempted to break through to the 18th Division at Xuan Loc. Failing in the attempt, the brigade retreated to Ba Ria, Phuoc Tuy province, where it held out until the capitulation of the Republic of Vietnam.

Commanding Officers, Airborne Division

Officer	Term
Lt. Col. Do Cao Tri	1 March 1955
Col. Nguyen Chanh Thi	1 September 1956
Col. Cao Van Vien	12 November 1960
Lt. Gen. Du Quoc Dong	19 December 1964
Brig. Gen. Le Quang Luong	11 November 1972

Marine Division. Organized 1 October 1954, the Vietnamese Marine Corps (VNMC) was descended from the French-organized 1st and 2d *Bataillons de Marche*. The 1st Bataillon, raised in North Vietnam, was moved south following the July 1954 Geneva agreements, and both units were transferred by the French to the armed forces of the State of Vietnam l January 1954. The combat element of the VNMC, first designated as the Marine Infantry, was expanded to a group on 16 April 1956, to a brigade on 1 January 1962, and to a division on 1 October 1968. The VNMC, which essentially consisted of the Marine Division, was officially part of the Vietnamese Navy. In actual practice, however, the VNMC was an independent command under the direct control of the JGS and headquartered in Saigon.

All South Vietnamese marines were volunteers, and the Marine Division was considered one of the best units in the RVNAF. As part of South Vietnam's general reserve, the Marine Division operated throughout the country in support of ARVN units. It also took part in the cross-border operations into Cambodia in 1970 and 1971 as well as in Operation Lam Son 719. The Marine Division operated in I Corps from the 1972 Easter Offensive on, recapturing Quang Tri City 16 September 1972 after the 3d Division was driven out of the city in May. During the 1975 Ho Chi Minh Campaign, the remnant of the Marine Division was the last body of organized troops to leave Da Nang before the city fell 30 March 1975. Reconstituted in Vung Tau under their commander, Brig. Gen. Bui The Lan, the Marine Division held the city until the capitulation of the Republic of Vietnam. Many of the marines and their dependents were evacuated by U.S. forces with the country's collapse.

Commanding Officers, Marine Division

Officer	Term
Lt. Col. Le Quang Trong	1 October 1954
Maj. Pham Van Lieu	16 January 1956
Capt. Bui Pho Chi*	31 July 1956
Maj. Le Nhu Hung	30 September 1956
Maj. Le Nguyen Khang	7 May 1960
Lt. Col. Nguyen Ba Lien	16 December 1963
Lt. Gen. Le Nguyen Khang	26 February 1964
Brig. Gen. Bui The Lan	5 May 1972 to 30 April 1975

*Acting commander.

Appendix D

Order of Battle, People's Army of Vietnam (PAVN) and People's Liberation Armed Force (PLAF)

The available sources for this order of battle provide too little information on some units to make useful description possible. They also are sometimes imprecise, incomplete, or mute about commanders' names, ranks, and service dates. In the lists below, the word *before* signifies that service began or ended at an indeterminate time before the date; the word *after* signifies that service began or ended at an indeterminate time after the date; and *c.* (circa) indicates a date based on inference rather than specific mention in a source. Ranks are those that officers held at some time during the period of service. Province names are those in official use during the war; see the map on page 313.

People's Army of Vietnam (PAVN)

The PAVN High Command (*Bo Tong tu lenh*) consisted after January 1950 of a General Staff (*Bo Tong tham muu*), Political General Directorate (*Tong cuc chinh tri*), and Supply (Rear Services) General Directorate (*Tong cuc hau can*). Each directorate had a chain of command running from the center to regions and on down to basic units. A second major reorganization during 1958–1960, facilitated by assistance from the Soviet Union (USSR) and the People's Republic of China (PRC), created new technical services and branches, established universal military service, professionalized the officer corps, and introduced formal insignia of rank. Air and naval forces developed as integral parts of the army rather than as separate services.

The Military Affairs Party Committee (MAPC), composed of civilian and military members of the party central committee, wielded the party's authority over the high command. The party further exercised control through the membership of military personnel in party committees at all echelons. Nearly all officers were members of the party and subject to supervision by their unit committees.

Following standard communist practice, units had both a military commander and a political officer. Formally they had equal authority but separate responsibilities. Military commanders were responsible for unit administration and combat, political officers for motivation, morale, and liaison with civilian organizations. Although military commanders tended to enjoy precedence in the field, political officers had sufficient military training to take over a command when necessary. In a few instances a single individual held both positions simultaneously.

In March 1965 the central committee directed certain divisions to leave skeleton staffs in the North as "frame" units when the divisions left for the South. Frame units trained replacements while providing reserves for defense of the North. Replacement units received the designation of the frame unit that had created them plus a letter (e.g. Division 325B, Regiment 95D). The purpose was to reproduce the PAVN's oldest units, giving new units an instant lineage and troops a sense of continuity with the armed resistance against French colonialism during the 1946–1954 Indochina War. Further confusing the system of designations, units often took cover numbers upon entering the South and frequently changed numbers when moving to a different theater.

At the end of the Vietnam War in 1975, the entire military establishment of the Democratic Republic of Vietnam (DRV) consisted of 685,000 regular army troops organized into twenty-four divisions (plus three training divisions), one artillery command of ten regiments, ten independent infantry regiments, fifteen surface-to-air (SAM) missile regiments, and forty antiaircraft artillery (AAA) regiments; 3,000 troops in the navy; 12,000 troops in the air force organized into one light bomber squadron, four MiG-21 interceptor squadrons, two MiG–19 interceptor squadrons, six MiG–15/17 fighter-bomber squadrons, and support units; 50,000 troops of the Frontier, Coast Security, and People's Armed Security Forces; and militia numbering about 1,500,000. These figures excluded forces recruited in the South under the party's auspices.

From 1945 to February 1980 the combined office of commander in chief and minister of national defense was held by Gen. Vo Nguyen Giap. Two chiefs of staff served under General Giap: Maj. Gen. Hoang Van Thai from December 1945 to 1953 and Col. Gen. Van Tien Dung from 1953 to 1980.

People's Liberation Armed Force of South Vietnam (PLAF)

The People's Liberation Armed Force, formally established on 15 February 1961, was nominally the armed wing of the National Liberation Front (NLF) in the South, but it operated as a theater force of the PAVN under the direct command of the Central Office for South Vietnam (COSVN) regional headquarters. Although the distinction between the PAVN and PLAF was more formal than real at the top command level, PLAF personnel were distinctly different from their PAVN comrades. In order to lend plausibility to Hanoi's claim of noninvolvement with the PLAF, the PLAF had to rely initially on troops recruited locally and on southern "regroupees" returning from the North after 1959. PAVN fillers who began arriving in the B2 theater (see Southern Regional Headquarters, below) in 1965 joined existing PLAF units or fleshed out new ones. PLAF-designated units composed largely of southern troops carried the burden of combat until losses in the 1968 Tet Offensive led to greatly expanded use of entire former PAVN units that had been recruited and trained in the North. The PAVN formally absorbed the PLAF in June 1976.

Political General Directorate. A PAVN political department was first established in 1946. In 1950 it became a formal part of the high command with the assignment to assist the communist party to implement and administer political work and the party committee system in the army. Political officers installed in all units down to company level reported to this directorate.

Commanding Officers, Political General Directorate

Officer	Term
Gen. Nguyen Chi Thanh, director	June 1950 to 1961
Lt. Gen. Song Hao, director	1961 to after December 1975
Sen. Gen. Chu Huy Man, director	Before April 1977 to after October 1984

Rear Services General Directorate. Established in January 1950, the General Supply Directorate later evolved into the Rear Services General Directorate, with the primary functions of supporting units in the field, managing base and medical facilities, and providing construction services. The Rear Services General Directorate advised Group 559 and the rear services department of Southern Regional Headquarters, which organized logistics within the B2 theater.

Commanding Officers, Rear Services General Directorate

Officer	Term
Maj. Gen. Dinh Duc Thien, director	April 1971 to April 1975
Lt. Gen. Bui Phong, director	April 1975 to before June 1984

Technical General Directorate. This directorate was created in September 1974 to take over machine maintenance, defense industries, technical research and training, personnel management, and cartography from the General Rear Services Directorate.

Commanding Officers, General Technical Directorate

Officer	Term
Maj. Gen. Le Van Tri, director	Before September 1977 to after March 1988

Transportation Groups

Military Transportation Group 559. A directive dated 19 May 1959 established Group 559 to move troops, weapons, and materiel from the North to the South and to maintain support facilities at way stations (*binh tram*) en route. In 1962 the group's force level was 6,000 troops organized into two regiments and several smaller units equipped with 1,000 bicycles and a few trucks. Within a year the force level grew to 24,400 troops and six motorized transport battalions plus engineering, antiaircraft, and security elements. In 1965 Group 559 moved a volume of supplies nearly equal to the total volume of the preceding five years. Increased PAVN involvement in the war and U.S. interdiction of Group 759's transportation activities at sea sharply increased dependence on the group's overland route. In 1965, Group 559 acquired the status of a military region reporting directly to the MAPC and the General Staff, with three subordinate commands for the supply corridors through Laos.

Preparations for large-scale main force offensives after the U.S. withdrawal sharply increased logistical requirements. In July 1973 the group, redesignated the Truong Son Command, converted sectoral (*khu vuc*) and way station (*binh tram*) forces into divisions or regiments and established five additional regiments. By late 1974 forces under its command included AAA Division 377, Transportation Division 571, Engineering Division 473, Infantry Division 968, the sectoral divisions 470, 471 and 472, plus fourteen regiments and various repair facilities and hospitals with total personnel of 100,495.

Commanding Officers, Military Transportation Group 559/Truong Son Command

Officer	Term
Sen. Col. Vo Bam, commander	May 1959 to 1965
Maj. Gen. Phan Trong Tue, commander	1965 to 1967

Officer	Term
Sen. Col. Dong Sy Nguyen, commander	1967 to c. March 1975
Maj. Gen. Hoang The Thien, political officer	to before March 1975

Military Transportation Group 759. Group 759 originated in the assignment of several general staff officers in July 1959 to consider supporting forces in the South by sea. The group was formally activated on 23 October 1961 and for some time provided the only practical means of moving weapons, supplies, and high-ranking cadres to distant southern points such as the Mekong Delta. From 1962 to 1965, up to 70 percent of supplies from the North moved by sea.

The navy took over responsibility for the group in August 1963 and redesignated it Group 125. In the year prior to February 1965, when the U.S. Navy captured one of its ships in Phu Yen province, the group's twenty junks and trawlers delivered 4,000 tons of weapons to the South. Interdiction by the U.S. Navy's Operation Market Time forced the North to depend more on the land route, and the group suspended activities in 1973.

Commanding Officers, Military Transportation Group 759/125

Officer	Term
Doan Hoang Phuoc, commander	October 1961 on
Vo Huy Phuc, political officer	October 1961 on

Military Transportation Group 100/959. The Vietnamese communists advised and supported the Pathet Lao insurgency in Sam Neua and Phong Saly provinces after 1954 through Transportation Group 100. This group became Group 959 on 9 September 1959, when it acquired the additional duty of Commanding PAVN "volunteer" units in Sam Neua, Xieng Khoang, and Vientiane. The group, though not its activities, came to an end with the signing of a cease-fire with Laos in 1973.

Regional Commands

Military Region 1. Military Region 1 corresponded to the colonial resistance-era Viet Bac region of mountainous provinces on the border with the PRC. At the height of the air war, up to 100,000 Chinese troops and laborers helped the DRV keep road and rail links open through this region.

Military Region 2. Military Region 2 included the resistance-era Tay Bac region, from the Laotian border to the Red River northwest of Hanoi.

Commanding Officers, Military Region 2

Officer	Term
Lt. Gen. Vu Lap, commander	Before April 1979 to after December 1982

Military Region 3. This region initially encompassed the "right bank" area south and east of Hanoi, including the southern half of the Red River Delta, and by 1970 included parts of the "left bank" and coastal Dong Bac military regions.

Commanding Officers, Military Region 3

Officer	Term
Maj. Gen. Hoang Sam, commander	Before 1965 on
Sen. Col. Nguyen Quyet, political officer	Before 1965 to after May 1979

Military Region 4. North Vietnam's panhandle region came under exceptionally heavy U.S. bombardment because it was the staging area for the movement of reinforcements and supplies by Group 559 into Laos and the South. The bombing grow so severe that in October 1968 the political general directorate set up a special Command Headquarters 500 under major generals Nguyen Don and Le Quang Dao and reinforced the region with the antiaircraft artillery divisions 367, 377, and 368 to provide security for transportation and communications. PAVN units deployed from this region into the Route 9-Tri Thien Front remained under the region's command.

Commanding Officers, Military Region 4

Officer	Term
Maj. Gen. Tran Van Quang, commander	1965 to 1974
Lt. Gen. Dam Quang Trung, commander	c. December 1975
Lt. Gen. Le Quang Hoa, commander/political officer	Before December 1977 to after June 1979

Military Region 5. Military Region 5 covered the northern half of South Vietnam from 1954 until April 1966, when Quang Tri and Thua Thien provinces were split off to form the Tri-Thien-Hue Military Region. Throughout the war Military Region 5 coordinated two fronts, one for the Tay Nguyen highlands (B3 theater), the other for the lowlands stretching from Da Nang to Nha Trang (B1 theater). The region's strategic mission was to coordinate the varied forms of armed action in the densely populated lowlands with the main force offensives launched from the highlands, linking the two during general offensives to isolate ARVN forces farther north.

The region acquired a command headquarters in July 1961 and, with the first resources supplied to the South by Transportation Group 559, it organized regiments 1, 2, and 3 during 1962. Regiment I (minus a battalion) battled U.S. Marines in U.S. Operation Starlite, the first large offensive operation by U.S. forces in the war, on the Batangan Peninsula in Quang Ngai province in August 1965. In the fall of that year the region consolidated forces to form divisions 2 and 3 and Regiment 10 in the coastal provinces.

In January 1966 Region 5 organized a front command for Binh Dinh province under Sen. Col. Giap Van Cuong to coordinate resistance against U.S., South Korean, and ARVN forces. In 1968 the region strengthened this command with the appointment of Doan Khue as commander and set up another command for Quang Ngai province under Lu Giang. To direct attacks on Da Nang in 1968, it also set up Front 4 (Quang Da Front), which became the Quang Nam-Da Nang Front under the command of Le Trong Tan and Chu Huy Man on 25 March 1975.

Commanding Officers, Military Region 5

Officer	Term
Maj. Gen. Nguyen Don, commander	1961 on
Lt. Gen. Hoang Van Thai, commander/political officer	August 1966 to June 1967
Lt. Gen. Chu Huy Man, commander	Before late 1970 to after September 1975
Lt. Gen. Doan Khue, commander/political officer	Before May 1977

Tay Nguyen Front. This subordinate zone of Military Region 5, set up on 1 May 1964, became a front command in September. It covered the Central Highlands parallel to the Ho Chi Minh Trail in southern Laos and northeastern Cambodia. Control of the area would have allowed communist forces to link the trail with roads inside the South and increase the scale of offensives in the lowlands. This front comprised the B3 theater.

U.S. and communist forces struggled for control of the highlands in fierce battles at Pleime, Pleiku, and Ia Drang Valley, the first major clashes between U.S. forces and PAVN regulars, during 1965. In spring 1966 the Tay Nguyen Front received reinforcements of three regiments from divisions 304, 308, and 325B, plus one regiment and two battalions of artillery. But insufficient logistical support prevented the front from consolidating forces until spring 1972, when U.S. withdrawals and successful PAVN assaults on the outposts at Dak To and Tan Canh presented an opportunity to organize Division 10. In February 1975 the front command set up a campaign headquarters under Maj. Gen. Hoang Minh Thao with the objective of seizing Ban Me Thuot.

Commanding Officers, Tay Nguyen Front

Officer	Term
Sen. Col. Nguyen Chanh, commander	May 1964 to July 1965
Sen. Col. Doan Khue, political officer	May 1964 to July 1956
Maj. Gen Chu Huy Man, commander/political officer	July 1965 on
Maj. Gen. Hoang Minh Thao, commander	June 1967 to
Sen. Col. Tran The Mon, political officer	June 1967 to
Nguyen Hiep, political officer	c. 1975

Tri-Thien-Hue Military Region. This region was carved out of Military Region 5 in April 1966. The PAVN command attached special importance to the area, perceiving control of it as crucial to the defense of both the North and the PAVN's lines of communication through Laos. Two front commands set up in June 1966—the Route 9 front known as theater B5 and the rest known as theater B4—corresponded to the distinction between the conventional war of main forces near the Demilitarized Zone (DMZ) and the emphasis on the "people's war" in the rest of Quang Tri and Thua Thien provinces. The strategy was to divide U.S. and ARVN forces between the main force war on Route 9 and the peoples war in the lowlands, intensifying one or the other as circumstances required.

For a few months after June 1968 the region unified command over all the forces of B4 and B5, thus becoming the Tri-Thien Front, but the attempt proved premature and was abandoned. The regional leadership made the attempt again in March 1972 in order to sustain the momentum of the Easter Offensive, which also proved unsuccessful. The main forces were organized under the region's command as 2d Corps in May 1974.

Commanding Officers, Tri-Thien-Hue Military Region

Officer	Term
Maj. Gen. Le Chuong, commander	April 1966 to June 1967
Maj. Gen. Le Chuong, political officer	April 1966 to after April 1968
Maj. Gen. Tran Van Quang, commander	June 1967 on

Commanding Officers, Tri Thien Front Command

Officer	Term
Le Trong Tan, commander	March 1972 on
Le Quang Dao, political officer	March 1972 on

Southern Regional Headquarters. The communist party central committee set up the Central Office for South Vietnam (COSVN) in 1961 as a forward element of its operations in South Vietnam. The early COSVN contained a Military Committee (Ban quan su) which doubled as the Military Affairs Committee of the National Liberation Front and the command of the People's Liberation Armed Force (PLAF). The first head of COSVN's Military Committee, Maj. Gen. Tran Luong (aka Tran Nam Trung), a deputy director of the PAVN General Political Directorate, was also chairman of the Military Affairs Committee of the NLF and, after June 1969, minister of defense of the Provisional Revolutionary Government (PRG). Luong had come south in May 1961 with five hundred PAVN cadres to help set up the command headquarters at COSVN and its subordinate regions, military regions 6,7,8,9 and the Saigon-Gia Dinh Special Zone, known collectively as the B2 theater.

In October 1963 COSVN organized the Military Affairs Party Committee (Quan uy) and Regional Military Headquarters (Bo tu lenh Mien). COSVN first secretary Nguyen Van Linh served concurrently as secretary of the MAPC, while Col. Gen. Tran Van Tra became commander of the Regional Military Headquarters. Other PAVN officers who took key posts in Southern Regional Headquarters at this time were Maj. Gen. Le Trong Tan, Maj. Gen. Tran Do, and Sen. Col. Hoang Cam. Gen. Nguyen Chi Thanh, a member of the party political bureau, arrived at COSVN later in 1963 or early 1964 to serve as Southern regional political officer and was the dominant figure until his death in 1967. This regional command structure reported through Thanh to the PAVN general staff in Hanoi. When Pham Hung replaced Thanh as the political bureau's representative, he also became first secretary of COSVN and of the MAPC.

The headquarters' jurisdiction covered communist military regions 6 through 9 and the special zones within them. On the eve of the 1968 Tet Offensive, it directly controlled three infantry divisions and one artillery division. Two forward command centers, one for main forces operating northeast of Saigon, and one for forces entering the city from the south and west, coordinated the attacks. In spring 1972, the region directed attacks by divisions 5, 7, and 9 northeast of Saigon, drawing the 21st ARVN Division out of the Mekong Delta so that guerrillas and four main force regiments could disrupt the pacification program. For the final offensive of the war, it organized these forces under two corps-level commands, the 4th Corps and Group 232.

First Secretaries, COSVN Military Committee

Officer	Term
Maj. Gen. Tran Luong, first secretary	May 1961 to October 1963

First Secretaries, COSVN Military Affairs Party Committee

Officer	Term
Nguyen Van Linh	October 1963 to 1964
Sen. Gen. Nguyen Chi Thanh	1964 to June 1967
Pham Hung	June 1967 to May 1975

Commanding Officers, Southern Regional Military Headquarters

Officer	Term
Col. Gen. Tran Van Tra, commander	October 1963 to January 1967
Lt. Gen. Hoang Van Thai, commander	January 1967 to 1973
Col. Gen. Tran Van Tra, commander	1973 to May 1975

Military Region 6. This region covered the southern part of central Vietnam, including Quang Duc, Tuyen Duc, Ninh Thuan, Binh Thuan, Lam Dong, and Binh Tuy provinces.

Commanding Officers, Military Region 6

Officer	Term
Sen. Col. Nguyen Trong Xuyen, commander	c. January 1975

Military Region 7. This region, more commonly known as the Eastern Nam Bo Region, comprised Phuoc Long, Long Khanh, Phuoc Tuy, Binh Long, Binh Duong, Bien Hoa, Tay Ninh, and Hau Nghia provinces. The Ho Chi Minh Trail brought forces and supplies close to Saigon in this region, which absorbed the Saigon-Gia Dinh Special Zone in October 1967 for the Tet Offensive.

Commanding Officers, Eastern Nam Bo Military Region

Officer	Term
Nguyen Van Xuyen, commander	c. 1946 to 1960
Col. Le Van Ngoc, commander	Before Jan 1975 to after April 1975
Col. Gen. Tran Van Tra, commander/political officer	Before 1976 to March 1978
Maj. Gen. Duong Cu Tam, political officer	Before December 1978

Military Region 8. This region lay southwest of Saigon, stretching from Cambodia to the South China Sea and including Long An, Kien Tuong, Sa Dec. Dinh Tuong, Go Cong, and Kien Hoa provinces. The boundary between regions 8 and 9 bisected the Mekong Delta.

Commanding Officers, Military Region 8

Officer	Term
Tran Van Tra, commander	c. 1946 on

Military Region 9. Military Region 9 covered the southern tip of Vietnam, including Chau Doc, An Giang, Vinh Long, Vinh Binh, Phong Dinh, Ba Xuyen, Kien Giang, Bac Lieu, and An Xuyen provinces.

Commanding Officers, Military Region 9

Officer	Term
Le Duc Anh, commander	c. December 1965 on
Pham Ngoc Hung, commander	Before 1975 to after January 1983

Route 9–Northern Quang Tri Front. The Route 9 or B5 Front was established in June 1966 to command forces just south of the Demilitarized Zone (DMZ). Short supply lines from the North made it possible for the PAVN to wage set-piece battles with U.S. forces on this front. Until late 1967, the front reported to the command of Military Region 4, which lay north of the DMZ; after that it reported to Tri-Thien-Hue Military Region command. In the 1966–1967 dry season, the front organized attacks on strong points south of the DMZ with PAVN divisions 325C and 324, and infantry regiments 27 and 31. In December 1967 elements of the PAVN divisions 304 and 320 joined the front for assaults on outposts along Route 9 to distract U.S. and ARVN attention from preparations for attacks against the cities. A western sector commanded 304 and 325C, and an eastern sector commanded 320 and 324. The region combined the commands of B4 and B5 theaters in November 1972.

Commanding Officers, Route 9–Northern Quang Tri Front

Officer	Term
Sen. Col. Vu Nam Long, commander	June 1966 to December 1967
Maj. Gen. Nguyen Xuan Hoang, political officer	June 1966 to December 1967
Maj. Gen. Tran Quy Hal, commander	December 1967 on
Maj. Gen. Le Quang Dao, political officer	December 1967 on

Saigon-Gia Dinh Special Zone. This region organized intelligence and "special activity" operations inside the South's largest urban area. In 1965 this special zone had two "security" units under its command, and later its special action units coordinated with sappers (infiltration and demolition commandos) in the Rung Sat Special Zone to attack shipping in the Long Tau river and harass Tao Son Nhut airfield and the U.S. and ARVN base at Long Binh. In October 1967 it merged with Military Region 7 to form part of the Main Target Region (Khu trong diem) for the Tet Offensive.

Military Branches

Air Defense–Air Force Branch. The establishment on 3 March 1955 of an Airfield Studies Committee to advise the General Staff marked the beginning of a North Vietnamese air force. The committee had responsibility for civil as well as military aviation and received its first aircraft (five Soviet and Czech transports donated by China) in early 1956. It also organized the dispatch of personnel for training in the PRC and the USSR. The committee was upgraded to a department and given command of Military Air Transport Regiment 919 in January 1959.

Meanwhile, the PAVN's antiaircraft artillery forces had grown to about 7,500 men organized into six antiaircraft and two radar regiments. On 22 October 1963 these forces were combined with the air force to form the Air Defense-Air Force Branch (Quan chung Phong khong-Khong quan). Soviet training, advice, and equipment were crucial to development of both forces. In August 1964, the branch organized troops who had returned from training abroad into Air Force Regiment 921. A year later it established Regiment 923. The first 11-28 bombers (Ilyushin-28) and MiG-21 fighters arrived about the same time. In mid 1965 the branch also deployed the first two antiaircraft missile regiments, raising in one year the total of personnel under its command from 22,500 to 52,700.

In June 1966, the branch organized the air defense units into "strategic" divisions 361, 363, 365, and 369 and "mobile" Division 367 to improve coordination of antiaircraft and air force operations. Air, missile, and radar forces became separate services with their own commanders reporting to the branch in March 1967. Air force regiments 921 and 923 combined to form Air Force Division 371. Regiment 925 emerged in February 1969, Regiment 927 in February 1972. The force organized a bomber unit equipped with eight IL-28s in October 1968, but it had no mission until October 1972, when two of its planes carried out a single strike near the Laotian border. In general, antiaircraft artillery and ground-to-air missiles posed a much greater threat than did MiGs to U.S. aircraft. The PAVN air force's main role in spring 1975 was to take over the airfields and equipment abandoned by the ARVN. The Air and Air Defense forces became separate branches on 6 May 1977.

Commanding Officers, Airfield Studies Committee/Air Force Department

Officer	Term
Sen. Col. Dang Tinh, commander	September 1955 to October 1963
Col. Hoang The Thien, political officer	September 1956 to October 1963

Commanding Officers, Air Defense–Air Force Branch

Officer	Term
Sen. Col. Phung The Tai, commander	October 1963 on
Sen. Col. Dang Tinh, political officer	October 1963 to April 1970
Sen. Col. Le Van Tri, commander	April 1973 to May 1977
Hoang Phuong, political officer	Before April 1975 to May 1977

Commanding Officers, Air Force

Officer	Term
Col. Nguyen Van Tien, commander	March 1967 on
Col. Phan Khac Hy, political officer	March 1967 on
Col. Dao Dinh Luyen, commander	March 1977 to after 1984
Lt. Col. Do Long, political officer	March 1977 to after 1984
Sen. Col. Dao Dinh Luyen, commander/political officer	March 1977 to after 1984

Commanding Officers, Air Defense Force

Officer	Term
Maj. Gen. Hoang Van Khanh, commander	Before December 1979 to before October 1983
Maj. Gen. Nguyen Xuan Man, political officer	Before December 1979 to before July 1981

Armored Branch. The PAVN's first tank regiment, 202, was commissioned on 5 October 1959, though the armored service did not achieve branch status until 22 June 1965. Regiment 202 and its sibling unit, 203, developed into brigades, and 203 in particular fought extensively in the South from January 1968 onward. Two tanks of Regiment 203, numbers 390 and 843, broke into the grounds of Saigon's presidential palace on 30 April 1975.

Commanding Officers, Armored Branch

Officer	Term
Dao Huy Vu, deputy commander/commander	June 1965 to after September 1984

Artillery Branch. The PAVN established an artillery force on 29 June 1946 to defend Hanoi from the returning French. In 1955 artillery regiments of the "heavy" Division 351 were redesignated as divisions 675, 45, and 349 and placed under a new Artillery Command. By 1960 this command had organized 17,500 men into artillery brigades 364, 368, 374, and 378; four long-range artillery regiments; and four antiaircraft regiments.

Commanding Officers, Artillery Branch

Officer	Term
Maj. Gen. Le Thief Hung, commander	1955 on
Maj. Gen. Doan Tue, commander	Before June 1972 to after April 1975
Sen. Col. Nam Thang, commander	February 1978 to before September 1979

Engineer Branch. The Communications Bureau in the General Staff commanded engineering regiments 333, 444, 555, and 506 in 1955. Forces of about 4,500 were assembled into construction regiments 229, 239, 219, and 249 during the reorganization of the PAVN in 1958–1960.

Commanding Officers, Engineer Branch

Officer	Term
Maj. Gen. Tran Va Dang, commander	Before December 1979 to after July 1984
Maj. Gen. Nguyen Huan, political officer	Before March 1981 on

Navy Branch. The PAVN established a Coastal Defense Department on 7 May 1955 to train officers and technical personnel for the North's tiny fleet of patrol boats and motorized junks. Renamed the Navy Department in January 1959, with Soviet help it began developing patrol boat bases, mobile coastal artillery, and radar stations. The Ministry of Defense renamed it the Navy Branch on 3 January 1964.

At 9:15 P.M. on 1 August 1964 the navy received orders from the General Staff to attack ships that radar had detected repeatedly entering the North's territorial waters. The orders apparently made no distinction between ARVN commando and naval activities and maneuvers by U.S. warships in the same general area. The execution of these orders by three PAVN torpedo boats against the U.S. destroyer *Maddox* constituted what Americans came to know as the Gulf of Tonkin Incident.

U.S. air and naval dominance subsequently left the PAVN navy little role at sea. In spring 1967 the Ministry of Defense attached the naval command to the Northeast Military Region (MR 3) and reassigned one-third of the navy's personnel. In 1972 the PAVN captured Cua Viet, a village port just south of the DMZ, allowing the navy to ferry men and supplies directly into Quang Tri province from then until the war's end.

Commanding Officers, Navy Department/Branch

Officer	Term
Maj. Gen. Ta Xuan Thu, commander/political officer	January 1959 to January 1964
Maj. Gen. Ta Xuan Thu, commander/political officer	January 1964 to March 1967
Sen. Col. Nguyen Ba Phat, commander	March 1967 to late 1974
Sen. Col. Doan Phung, political officer	March 1967 to April 1970
Hoang Tra, political officer	April 1970 to late 1974
Sen. Col. Doan Ba Khanh, commander	late 1974 to March 1977
Sen. Col. Tran Van Giang, political officer	late 1974 to March 1977

Sapper Branch. Sappers (*dac cong*) consisting of small teams and units, attached to political or military commands, developed early during the war with France. A subcategory of sappers known as special activities (*biet dung*) forces operated in towns and cities. Several hundred sappers (infiltration and demolition commandos) from the South who regrouped in the North formed two battalions attached to Division 338 and Military Region 4. Some of these men began returning to the South in small numbers to gather intelligence as early as August 1955. Military regions in the South began developing their own sapper companies and battalions in 1961, and the General Staff organized a uniform sapper training program in July 1962.

The special training requirements and role that sappers were to play in the Tet Offensive were recognized with the establishment of the Sapper Branch (Binh chung Dac cong) on 19 March 1967, with direct control over the Brigade 305, Regiment 426, (naval) Group 126, and nine battalions. The branch primarily trained sappers for attachment to other PAVN commands and units. In its first year it trained and dispatched over 2,500 sapper officers and troops to the South, and it doubled this output within two years.

Southern Regional Headquarters maintained its own sapper department, known as J16, and for a time it trained as many sappers as the branch. In 1973 B2 controlled eight sapper "groups" equivalent to regiments, including one in Cambodia. On the eve of the 1975 Spring Offensive, 12 sapper regiments or their equivalents, 36 battalions, 121 companies, 15 groups of bier dung, and hundreds of squads, teams, and cells were scattered across the South. The entire dac cong-biet dong "brigade" 316 was operating inside Saigon or its outskirts by war's end.

Commanding Officers, Sapper Branch

Officer	Term
Sen. Col. Nguyen Chi Diem, commander	March 1967 to after May 1973
Sen. Col. Vu Chi Dao, political officer	March 1967 to after May 1973

Signals Branch. This branch traced its origins to an army signals office set up on 9 September 1945 and later absorbed into a signals department of the high command. Many of the department's personnel received training abroad to prepare for the PAVN's modernization. In 1958 the department organized the PAVN's first signals regiment, the 205 (initially designated the 303). One of this regiment's missions was to maintain a station for radio communications with the South, known as B18. Regiment 205 also maintained the link with the groups 559, 759,959 and other transportation groups supplying PAVN forces in distant theaters.

The department's radios often provided the North's only working communications during the air war. The department commander was himself killed while traveling to Military Region 4. The increased demand for communications led to the establishment of Regiment 26 in February 1965 specifically to serve air and antiaircraft defense forces and to the creation by August 1966 of two more signals regiments (132 and 134) and four battalions under the department's direct command. The Ministry of Defense elevated the department to a branch on 31 January 1968.

Commanding Officers, Signals Branch

Officer	Term
Hoang Dao Thuy, commander	June 1949 to 1962
Hoang Buu Dong, political officer	Before October 1954 on
Nguyen Anh Bao, commander	1962 to August 1965
Hoang Niem, commander (acting)	August 1965 to January 1969
Le Cu, political officer	Before 1965 on
Col. Ta Dinh Hieu, commander	January 1969 to mid-1973
Pham Nien, commander	Mid-1973 on
Sen. Col. Nguyen Duy Lac, political officer	Before December 1976 on

Main Force Combat Units

1st Military Corps (Quyet Thang Corps). The 1st Corps was established in the North on 24 October 1973 to command infantry divisions 308, 312, and 320B, Antiaircraft Division 367, Artillery Brigade 45, Tank Brigade 202, Engineer Brigade 299, and Signal Regiment 140. In March 1975 the corps was building dikes in the North when the PAVN overran the Central Highlands. Ordered into the fighting on 25 March, it traveled 1,700 kilometers to reach South Vietnam just in time for the final push on Saigon.

Commanding Officers, 1st Corps

Officer	Term
Maj. Gen. Le Trong Tan, commander	October 1973 on
Maj. Gen. Le Quang Hoa, political officer	October 1973 on
Maj. Gen. Nguyen Hoa, commander	Before March 1975 on
Maj. Gen. Hoang Minh Thi, political officer	Before March 1975 on

2d Military Corps. The 2d Corps was established on 17 May 1974 in the Tri Thien Front area in preparation for the final offensive of the war. Forces under its command included infantry divisions 304, 324, and 325, Antiaircraft Division 367, Tank Brigade 203, Artillery Brigade 164,

Engineering Brigade 219, and Signals Regiment 463. Following success in Quang Tri and Hue, the 2d Corps seized Da Nang, and a branch of the corps under Lt. Gen. Le Trong Tan, commander, and Lt. Gen. Le Quang Hoa, political officer, proceeded down the coast, taking Phan Rang and Phan Thief on the way.

Commanding Officers, 2d Corps

Officer	Term
Lt. Gen. Hoang Van Thai, commander	October 1973 on
Maj. Gen. Le Linh, political officer	October 1973 to after March 1975
Maj. Gen. Nguyen Huu An	c.1974 to after March 1975

3d Military Corps (Lay Nguyen Corps). The command staff of the Tay Nguyen Front became the staff of the 3d Corps on 26 March 1975. The corps supervised infantry divisions 10, 320, and 316, artillery regiments 40 and 675, antiaircraft regiments 234 and 593, Tank Regiment 273, Engineer Regiment 7, and Signal Regiment 29 during their approach to Saigon through eastern South Vietnam in the final offensive of the war. In June 1976 the corps returned to Military Region 5 and established headquarters in Nha Trang.

Commanding Officers, 3d Corps

Officer	Term
Vu Lang, commander	March 1975 on
Dang Vu Hiep, political officer	March 1975 on

4th Military Corps (Cuu Long Corps). Southern Regional Headquarters began forming its first regiments (1 and 2) in 1962. Further growth in forces allowed the region to organize divisions 5, 9, and 7 in 1965–1966. In March 1971 the region placed these and other forces under the command of Group 301, which became the nucleus of the 4th Corps at its founding on 20 July 1974. The corps grouped divisions 5,9, and 7, Mobile Artillery Regiment 24, Antiaircraft Artillery Regiment 71, Engineer Regiment 25, Sapper Regiment 429, Signals Regiment 69, and support elements, consisting altogether of 35,000 officers and men.

In late December 1974, 1st Corps moved to seize Route 14 in Phuoc Long province. The accomplishment of this aim in early January allowed forces and supplies to move swiftly toward Saigon. Division 341 reinforced the corps for the drive on Saigon from the northwest, while Division 5 was reassigned to Group 232. Divisions 341, 7, and 9 remained the main units of the corps after war's end.

Commanding Officers, 4th Corps

Officer	Term
Maj. Gen. Hoang Cam, commander	July 1974 to c. May 1975
Maj. Gen. Hoang The Thien, political officer	March 1975 on

70th Military Corps. The 70th Military Corps appeared in October 1970 to coordinate the operations of divisions 304, 308, 320, and several regiments along Route 9 and in Laos.

Group 232. Group 232 was set up in February 1975 to serve as a forward element of Southern Regional Headquarters during the final phase of the war. Equivalent to a corps command, it organized the attacks by divisions 3 and 5 west and southwest of Saigon in coordination with 4th Corps.

Commanding Officers, Group 232

Officer	Term
Le Duc Anh, commander	February 1975 to March 1975
Le Van Tuong, political officer	February 1975 to March 1975
Maj. Gen. Nguyen Minh Chau, commander	March 1975 on
Maj. Gen. Tran Van Phac, political officer	March 1975 on

Group 301. Established on 18 March 1971, this group incorporated divisions 5, 7, and 9 plus Artillery Regiment 28. Essentially a campaign headquarters, it coordinated the regroupment and counterattack of COSVN's main forces against ARVN operations in Cambodia. The group served as the nucleus for the formation of 4th Corps in 1974.

Commanding Officers, Group 301

Officer	Term
Tran Van Tra, commander	March 1971 on
Tran Do, political officer	March 1971 on

Division 1. The Tay Nguyen Front command formed Division I on 20 December 1965 with regiments 33, 320, and 66, which had taken heavy casualties in fighting for control of the Central Highlands. Most of these forces had entered the South as elements of other units, principally Division 325A, in early 1965. Regiment 33 later operated independently and was replaced in the division by Regiment 88, which left Tay Nguyen to reinforce B2 theater in late 1967.

Division 2. This division, activated on 20 October 1965 in Quang Nam province, was based on PLAF Regiment 1, PAVN Regiment 21, and Battalion 70. Regiment 1 had originated in Military Region 5 in the early 1960s, Regiment 21 had recently arrived from the North, and Battalion 70 consisted mainly of regroupees. PAVN Regiment 31 joined the division in 1966.

Division 2 was supposed to complement guerrilla and political action in the lowlands, thwarting "pacification" and tying down ARVN forces. Under increasing pressure after the introduction of U.S. and South Korean troops, it did not mount division-level operations until August 1967. Devastating strikes by helicopter gunships killed many of the division's top officers in December, and it went into the Tet Offensive under the command of officers dispatched from region headquarters.

The division retreated to Laos in mid 1970, received PAVN Regiment 141 to replace the 21st, and fought in Laos until early March 1971. In spring 1972 it fought in the Tay Nguyen highlands, after which it returned to Quang Ngai and incorporated Regiment 52 from Division 320. The divisional command suffered a second decimation when a B-52 strike scored a direct hit on its headquarters in September 1972.

A major reorganization of Military Region 5 forces in mid-1973 transformed Regiment 52 into a brigade and left Division 2 with regiments 141, 31, and 38, and some remnants from the disbanding of Division 711. Strengthened by the addition of the PAVN's Infantry Regiment 36 and Artillery Regiment 368 in late 1974, the division participated in the capture of Da Nang on 29 March 1975. It subsequently participated in the defense of the western border and intervention in Cambodia.

Commanding Officers, Division 2

Officer	Term
Nguyen Nang, commander	October 1965 to before August 1967
Nguyen Minh Duc, political officer	October 1965 to December 1967

continues

continued

Officer	Term
Le Huu Tru, commander	Before August 1967 to December 1967
Giap Van Cuong, commander	December 1967 to before February 1969
Nguyen Ngoc Son, political officer	December 1967 to before February 1969
Le Kich, commander (acting)	Before February 1969 to August 1969
Ho Xuan Anh, commander	August 1969 to before March 1971
Nguyen Huy Chuong, political officer	October 1969 to before April 1972
Nguyen Chon, commander	Before March 1971 to June 1972
Le Dinh Yen, political officer	Before April 1972 on
Quong Ba Loi, commander (acting)	June 1972 to September 1972
Nguyen Viet Son, commander	September 1972 to June 1973
Nguyen Chon, commander	June 1973 on
Mai Thnan, political officer (acting)	Before March 1975 on

Division 3. Infantry regiments 2, 12, and 22 plus mortar, antiaircraft, engineers, and signals battalions formed the Sao Vang (Gold Star) Division on September 2, 1965, the National Day of the DRV. Regiment 2 had been organized in Quang Nai province in 1962, Regiment 12 (formerly 18 of PAVN Division 312) had come from the North in February 1965, while Regiment 22 had come into existence in summer 1965 by combining troops from the North with local forces from Military Region 5. The division's primary mission was to tie down ARVN forces in Quang Ngai, Binh Dinh, and Phu Yen provinces while the PAVN built offensive capability in the highlands.

U.S. occupation of the highlands blocked that strategy until late in the war. In the 1968 Tet Offensive the 3d played mostly a support role for provincial and local forces that attacked the towns but had to disperse its forces until mid 1971. Regrouped in June (with Regiment 21 replacing the 22d), it participated in the capture of several district capitals in Binh Dinh during spring 1972. PAVN Regiment 141 replaced the 21st in the 3d during a reorganization of Military Region 5 forces in June 1973. In spring

1975 the division participated in the capture of Phan Rang and Vung Tau, joining 2d Corps on April 18.

In mid 1976 the division moved to Military Region 3, and in July 1978 to Lang Son in Military Region 1, where it met the Chinese attack in February 1979.

Commanding Officers, Division 3

Officer	Term
Sen. Col. Giap Van Cuong, commander	September 1965 on
Dang Hoa, political officer	September 1965 on
Lu Giang, commander	Before May 1968 to July 1970
Nguyen Nam Khanh, political officer	Before May 1968 to July 1970
Huynh Huu Anh, commander	July 1970 to before June 1974
Mai Tan, political officer	June 1971 on
Tran Trong Son, commander (acting)	Before June 1974 on
Do Quang Hung, commander	Before March 1975 on
Tran Van Khue, commander	Before April 1975 on

Division 4. This unit appeared in Military Region 9 during the 1975 Spring Offensive. It returned to region 9 from "internationalist duty" in Cambodia in 1969.

Division 5. PLAF Infantry Division 5 was formed in Ba Ria base area on 23 November 1965 by combining the Dong Nai (4th) Regiment of Military Region 7 with Regiment 5, which had been assembled from regional units in Nam Bo. The division operated only at regimental level for some years. Two regiments of this division coordinated with regional forces to attack Route 15 and the U.S. base at Vung Tau in 1966. In March 1971 it became part of Group 301 for operations in Cambodia. It was a major component of the forces that attacked Route 13 and Loc Ninh in spring 1972.

Commanding Officers, Division 5

Officer	Term
Bui Thanh Van, commander	Before April 1972 on
Nguyen Van Cuc, political officer	Before April 1972 on

continues

continued

Officer	Term
Tran Thanh Van, commander	c. 1975
Vu Van Thuoc, commander	c. 1975
Nguyen Xuan On, political officer	c. 1975

Division 6. This unit appeared in Military Region 6 during the Spring Offensive.

Commanding Officers, Division 6

Officer	Term
Dang Ngoc Si, commander	August 1974 on

Division 7. Southern Regional Headquarters established PLAF Division 7 on 13 June 1966 in the area of Phuoc Lon, Eastern Nam Bo (South Vietnam). The 7th's first regiments were the 16th, formerly the IOIA of PAVN Division 325; the 141st, formerly of PAVN Division 312; and the 165th, also of PAVN Division 312. Regiment 52 of PAVN Division 320 soon replaced the 16th.

In spring 1967 the division moved to Tay Ninh province to resist the joint U.S./ARVN Operation Junction City. For the Tet Offensive, the 7th's mission was to distract attention from Saigon with attacks in Tay Ninh and Binh Long provinces, helping assault forces achieve surprise in the city. While that mission was successful, the division suffered heavy casualties in the counteroffensive that followed. After reorganization in late 1968, the 7th was composed of three regiments descended from PAVN Division 312. Units of the 7th took the brunt of the U.S./ARVN "incursion" into Cambodia in spring 1970, Regiment 141 seeing particularly heavy action around Snoul and Mimot. In March 1971 the 7th joined Group 301 for the spring 1972 attacks in Binh Long province that seized Loc Ninh and nearly overran An Loc. Regiment 209 of the 7th took the brunt of the B-52 and tactical airstrikes while serving as the main blocking force south of An Loc.

Division 7 joined 4th Corps in Eastern Nam Bo in July 1974 and participated in the 1975 Spring Offensive in Phuoc Long province. Regiments 141 and 165 of the 7th entered the provincial capital on January 6, and a large part of the division assisted in overcoming the last major ARVN resistance at Xuan Loc on April 20.

The division redeployed from Saigon to the border with Cambodia in mid 1977 and entered Cambodia with the rest of 4th Corps on 1 January 1979. The division returned to Vietnam in May 1983.

Commanding Officers, Division 7

Officer	Term
Nguyen Hoa, commander	June 1966 on
Duong Thanh, political officer	June 1966 on
Nguyen The Bon, commander	1967 to c.1970
Vuong The Hiep, political officer	1967 to c.1970
Dam Van Nguy, commander	c. 1970 to September 1972
Le Thanh, political officer	c. 1970 to after 1972
Le Nam Phong, commander	September 1972 to 1977
Tu Vinh, political officer	Before July 1974 on
Phan Liem, political officer	Before March 1975 to 1977

Division 8. This unit appeared in Military Region 8 during the 1975 Spring Offensive.

Commanding Officers, Division 8

Officer	Term
Sen. Col. Huynh Van Nhiem, commander	August 1974 on

Division 9. PLAF Division 9 had its origins in two battalions organized by regroupee officers in 1961. These battalions became PLAF regiments 1 and 2 in 1963. With RPG-2 rocket launchers, 82 mm mortars, and recoilless rifles supplied by Group 759, elements of these regiments defeated a larger ARVN force at the pivotal battle of Binh Gia village in December 1964. These regiments plus a third received formal commissioning as Division 9 on 2 September 1965. The 9th was the first communist main force division formed entirely in the South under COSVN's supervision.

Attempting to maintain a case close to Saigon, the division had its first engagement with U.S. forces at the strategic hamlet of Bau Bang in December 1965. Elements of the division took heavy casualties but emerged intact from the U.S.-led search-and-destroy operations Attleboro and Cedar Falls in 1966 and 1967. Plagued by shortages of supply, weapons, and manpower, it regrouped in Tay Ninh province, closer to the Cambodian border.

The division's assignment at the beginning of the 1968 Tet Offensive was to distract U.S. and ARVN posts on the outskirts of Saigon while sappers and special forces attacked inside the city. This limited success led to the use of elements from two Division 9 regiments in direct attacks on the city in May, with disastrous results. One 500-man battalion retreated with only 43 troops not dead or wounded.

Replenishment the following year brought in Regiment 95C of Division 325C (redesignated Regiment 3) to replace Regiment 3B (formerly Regiment 88 of Division 308). The U.S./ARVN "incursion" in 1970 pushed the division deep into Cambodia, where in March 1971 as part of Group 301 it helped defeat the Phnom Penh government's Operation Chen-La 2. Elements of the division returned to battle inside Vietnam in spring 1972 along Route 13 near Loc Ninh and An Loc. Reinforced with infantry and both ground and antiaircraft artillery, Division 9 became a component of the 4th Corps in July 1974 and participated in the seizure of Phuoc Long province in January 1975. The division's intervention in Cambodia after 1978 corroded the morale of the new southern recruits who composed it.

Commanding Officers, Division 9

Officer	Term
Sen. Lt. Col. Hoang Cam, commander	September 1965 to 1967
Sen. Col. Le Van Tuong, political officer	September 1965 to 1967
Ta Minh Kham, commander	1967 to 1969
Nguyen Van Tong, political officer	1967 to 1969
Le Van Nho, commander	1969 to c. 1969
Nguyen Thoi Bung, commander	c. 1969 to c. 1972
Nguyen Van Quang, political officer	c. 1969 to c. 1972
Vo Van Dan, commander	c. 1972 on
Pham Xuan Tang, political officer	c. 1972 on
Tam Tang, political officer	Before July 1974 on

Division 10. This division emerged from the concentration of forces in the Tay Nguyen Front for the 1972 Easter Offensive. An "Eastern Command Staff" set up to supervise regiments 28, 66, and 95 in attacks in northern Tay Nguyen in February became the command of Division 10 upon activation on 20 September 1972. The division incorporated Regiment 24 in spring 1973. Along with elements of Division 320 the 10th pushed ARVN forces out of areas near Pleiku and Ban Me Thuot in 1974.

In spring 1975, the 10th participated in the final assault on Ban Me
Thuot, and Regiment 95B transferred from the 10th to Division 320 for
the pursuit of ARVN forces down Route 7 to Nha Trang. The division
became a part of the 3d Military Corps upon the carps' formation on 26
March 1975 and fought as part of that corps in Eastern Nam Bo during
the final stage of the war, reaching Tan Son Nhut airbase on the outskirts
of Saigon on April 30.

Following the war the division moved to Lam Dong province, where it
concentrated on economic reconstruction, the suppression of remnant montagnard dissidence, and defense of the border against Khmer Rouge
attacks in 1977. It participated in the intervention in Cambodia in
December 1978, and its units were among the first to enter Phnom Penh.

Commanding Officers, Division 10

Officer	Term
Nguyen Manh Quan, commander	September 1972 to May 1973
Sen. Col. Dang Vu Hiep, political officer	September 1972 to May 1973
Do Duc Gia, commander	May 1973 to mid-1974
La Ngoc Chau, political officer	May 1973 to 1975
Ho De, commander	mid-1974 to April 1975
Hong son, commander	April 1975 to September 1976
Luu Quy Ngu, political officer	1975 to March 1979
Sen. Col. Phung sa Thuong, commander	September 1976 on

Division 303. Southern Regional Headquarters organized Division 303
to prepare for the final offensive of the war. Briefly designated Division 3
after establishment on 19 August 1974, the division comprised PLAF
infantry regiments 201,205, and 271, and PAVN Artillery Regiment 262.

The division's first assignment was to cut Route 14 and isolate Phuoc
Long province, which it accomplished by March 1975. With the ARVN
falling back more rapidly than communist strategists had expected, the
303d advanced almost immediately into Tay Nih province and the Plain of
Reeds, and in April it was attached to Group 232 for the attack on Saigon.

Following the war the bulk of the division returned to Phuoc Long
province, where it worked in economic reconstruction as the Phuoc Long
Unified Economic Group. It was reconstituted in August 1978 for the intervention in Cambodia and redeployed a year later to defend the Red River
Delta in the brief border war with China.

Commanding Officers, Division 303

Officer	Term
Do Quang Hueng, commander	August 1974 on
Sen. Col. Tran Hal Phung, commander	1977 to September 1977
Col. Cao Hoai sai, commander	September 1977 to August 1978

Division 304. The 304th, the second of six infantry divisions organized during the resistance against France, was commissioned on 4 January 1950 in Thanh Hoa province. During the resistance against the French it fought in the Red River Delta and also saw action in Laos and Dien Bien Phu. The division received orders in August 1965 to march south, and regiments 24 and 66 entered the Tay Nguyen Front around the end of the year while Regiment 9 served briefly in Laos. The 304th was picked in September 1967 as one of four PAVN divisions to support the Tet Offensive. Regiment 24 helped to overrun the U.S. Special Forces camp at Lang Vei in February 1968, while Regiment 9 joined the attack on Hue and Regiment 66 participated in the siege of Khe Sanh.

Gravely depleted, the division returned in June 1968 to the North. In October 1970 it was attached to the newly formed 70th Military Corps of the Route 9 Front and Laos and participated in the counterattack on ARVN Operation Lam Son 719 in spring 1971. In 1972 it participated in the capture of Quang Tri province and the following year became part of the 1st Military Corps. In the final offensive of the war it traveled down the coast from Hue as part of the 2d Army Corps, and elements of Infantry Regiment 66 and Tank Brigade 203 under its command seized the presidential palace in Saigon.

At the same time that the 304th departed for the South, Military Region 3 received orders to organize the "second" 304th, designated the 304B. This division entered the fighting in early 1968 around the western end of Route 9 including Khe Sanh.

Commanding Officers, Division 304

Officer	Term
Hoang Minh Thao, commander	February 1950 to November 1953
Tran Van Quang, political officer	February 1950 to 1951
Hoang Sam, commander	November 1953 to late 1955
Le Chuong, political officer	1951 to late 1955
Nam Long, commander	late 1955 on

Officer	Term
Truong Cong Can, political officer	late 1955 on
Ngo Ngoc Duong, commander	to March 1965
Tran Hay, political officer	to March 1965
Mai Hien, commander (acting)	March 1965 to August 1965
Hoang Kien, commander	August 1965 to c. 1967
Truong Cong Can, political officer	August 1965 to January 1968
Thai Dung, commander	1967 to June 1968
Tran Nguyen Do, political officer	January 1968 to June 1968
Hoang Dan, commander	June 1968 on
Hoang The Thien, political officer	June 1968 on
Le Cong Phe, commander	c. 1973 on
Nguyen An, commander (acting)	c. 1974 on

Commanding Officers, Division 304B

Officer	Term
Nguyen Thai Dung, commander	September 1967 on

Division 308. The 308th, the first of six infantry divisions organized during the resistance, was established in August 1949. Significantly upgraded with artillery, tanks, engineers, and communications in 1961–1962, the 308th contributed one of three battalions in late 1964 that formed Regiment 320, which then infiltrated the Tay Nguyen Front, followed in 1966 by Regiment 88. In September 1967, the 308th was picked as one of four PAVN divisions that would participate in the Tet Offensive. Regiment 36 joined the Quang Da Front in Military Region 5 while regiments 102 and 88 entered the Route 9 Front in 1968 and saw action at Khe Sanh.

Commanding Officers, Division 308

Officer	Term
Vuong Thua Vu, commander	August 1949 on
Song Hao, political officer	August 1949 on

continues

continued

Officer	Term
Thai Dung, commander	June 1968 on
Nguyen Huu An, commander	c. 1972

Division 312. The Chien Thang (Victorious) Division, established 27 October 1950, fought at Dien Bien Phu. A battalion of the 312th crossed the Ben Hal river into Quang Tri province in spring 1963, and a year later a second battalion entered Military Region 5, where it participated in the early fighting with U.S. forces on the Batangan peninsula in August 1965. Regiments 141 and 165 were dispatched to the B2 Front in 1966 to serve as the nucleus of PLAF Division 7. In September 1967, the 312th was picked as one of four PAVN divisions that would participate in the Tet Offensive. From 1963 through 1968 the 312th supplied a total of four regiments, nine battalions, and numerous teams of officers to the fighting in the South.

Regrouped near Hanoi after the Tet Offensive, regiments 141, 165, and 209 finally fought as a single unit when sent to enlarge the PAVN's logistical corridor through Laos in 1969–1970. In late 1971 it fought in Laos, supported, for the first time, by T-34 tanks and 130 mm long-range artillery. The 312th's regiments entered the Tri Thien Front in July 1972 as attachments of divisions 325, 308, and 304 and later replaced the 308th and 304th as the defense force south of the Thach Han river. Stationed in the North when the 1975 Spring Offensive began, the 312th was among the forces that the high command ordered into the South in late March to sustain the offensive's momentum.

Commanding Officers, Division 312

Officer	Term
Le Trong Tan, commander	October 1950 to 1954
Sen. Col. Hoang Cam, commander	1954 to 1964
Tran Do, political officer	Before 1954 to after July 1958
Nguyen Nang, commander	Before September 1969 to October 1971
Le Chieu, political officer	Before September 1969 to October 1971
La Thai Hoa, commander	October 1971 to July 1972
Pham Sinh, political officer	October 1971 to July 1972

Officer	Term
Nguyen Chuong, commander	Before April 1975 to after December 1977
Nguyen Xuyen, political officer	Before April 1975 on

Division 316. Nearly half of the troops in Division 316 at the time of its founding were from ethnic minorities of the Viet Bac region near Vietnam's border with China. The division was formally established on 1 May 1951 with regiments 98, 174, and 176. One regiment operated in the Tay Nguyen highlands in 1967, and two of them helped expand the Pathet Lao zone of control in December 1968. But for most of the war the 316th was a light infantry division that fought in Laos. It joined the 3d Corps for the attack on Ban Me Thuot in spring 1975, returned to the North after the war, and was among the forces stationed on the border when China attacked in February 1979.

Commanding Officers, Division 316

Officer	Term
Chu Huy Man, deputy political officer	May 1951 to after 1953
Le Quang Ba, commander	1953 to 1958
Lt. Gen. Vu Lap, commander	
Sen. Col. Dam Van Nguy, commander	Before March 1975 on
Col. Ha Quoc Toan, political officer	Before March 1975 on

Division 320. Division 320, the Dong Bang (Delta, or Plains) Division, was organized in the delta region south of the Red River on 16 January 1951. The division sent its Antiaircraft Battalion 14 to Laos in late 1964, and in August 1965 one of its mortar battalions entered the South to form the core of a PLAF artillery unit in the Eastern Nam Bo Region. In February 1966 Regiment 64 went into combat in Quang Ngai and Quang Nam provinces, and later in the year Regiment 52 reinforced the B2 Front. In September 1967, the 320th was one of four PAVN divisions picked to participate in the Tet Offensive. Under the Route 9-Northern Quang Tri Front Command (B5), it attacked along Route 9 in coordination with assaults by divisions 304 and 325 on Lang Vei and Khe Sanh. It withdrew to the North in October 1968, returned to action in October 1970, and part of it joined the 70th Corps to fight around Route 9 and in southern Laos in 1971. After another period of regroupment in the North, the division

moved to the Tay Nguyen Front, arriving there in January 1972. In spring 1975, it pursued ARVN remnants down Route 7 toward the coast, became part of the 3d Corps in March, and moved entirely by truck to Tay Ninh for the final push on Saigon.

The 320th's frame unit trained 153,000 men from 1965 through 1970, sending many to the South in battalion strength. However, because of the force requirements of the 1972 Easter Offensive, regiments of Division 320B were sent into combat as integral units. The 320B withdrew to the North's Thanh Hoa province in September 1973 and became part of the newly formed 1st Military Corps in October. Regiment 48 of the 320B, then a training unit, participated in the defense of the northern border against the attack by China in February 1979. The 320B was officially redesignated Division 390 on 4 May 1979.

Commanding Officers, Division 320

Officer	Term
Van Tien Dung, commander/political officer	January 1951 on
Sung Lam, commander	c. 1967 to c. 1971
Sen. Col. Luong Tuan Khang, political officer	c. 1965 to c. 1971
Kim Tuan, commander	c. 1971 to March 1975
Phi Trieu Ham, political officer	c. 1971 to March 1975
Bui Dinh Hoe, commander	March 1975 on
Col. Bui Huy Bong, political officer	March 1975 on

Commanding Officers, Division 320B

Officer	Term
Pham Thanh Son, commander	September 1965 to early 1966
Nguyen Duy Tuong, political officer	September 1965 to early 1966
Bui Sinh, commander	Early 1966 to 1969
Nguyen Huan, political officer	Early 1966 to 1969
Ha Vi Tung, commander	Mid-1969 to c. 1973
Tran Ngoc Kien, political officer	Mid-1969 to c. 1973
Sen. Col. Luu Ba Xao, commander	c. 1973 to c. 1976

Division 324. Formed with regroupees from the South in June 1955, Division 324 trained specially to attack fortified strong points. In late 1966 it moved to the Route 9 Front, where its artillery supported assaults on U.S. Marine outposts. Regiment 3 of the 324th participated in fighting in Hue during the Tet Offensive. In spring 1975 the division fought as part of the 2d Corps in the Tri Thien Front but remained in Hue and Da Nang to provide security while the rest of the corps proceeded to Saigon.

Commanding Officers, Division 324

Officer	Term
Nguyen Don, commander	c. 1955
Duy Son, commander	c. 1975
Nguyen Trong Dan, political officer	c. 1975

Division 325. Activated on 11 March 1951, the 325th was the only resistance-era division organized in what was to become South Vietnam after 1954. In 1961, elements of this division expanded Pathet Lao control around Tchopone, permitting easier passage by Group 559 through southern Laos. In November 1964 regiments 95 and 101 of the 325th left the North to enter Military Region 5 while Regiment 18 went to the Tay Nguyen Front. The division took the designation 325A as the skeleton staff it had left behind began to build Division 325B, and later divisions 325C and 325D, regiments 95B, 95C, 95D, and so forth.

Division 325B entered the South in spring 1966. Two regiments of this division, the 95B and 101B, reinforced the Tay Nguyen Front, where the 95B pushed U.S. Special Forces out of the A Shau valley during March. Heavy losses, however, forced regiments 101B and 101C to combine as Regiment 33. The 33d, 24th, and 95B operated for a time as independent regiments in Kontum, Gia Lai, and Quang Duc provinces. Regiment 33 moved to Eastern Nam Bo in late 1968, while the 95B remained in Tay Nguyen until the end of the war.

Division 325C comprising regiments 101D, 95C, and 18C began entering the Route 9-Tri Thien Front in late 1966, and the 95C and a battalion of the 18C fought around Khe Sanh a year later. Regiment 18C spearheaded the attack on Hue while elements of regiments 95C and 101D participated in attacks on Lang Vei and around Khe Sanh in February 1968. The 95C and 10 ID were redeployed farther south following the Tet Offensive, while divisional headquarters returned to the North to build Division 325D.

Division 325D was built around three regiments raised in Military Region 3. Although the 325D sent Regiment 18D to help Group 559 expand supply routes through Laos and sent Regiment 95D to Route 9 in early 1969, it was essentially a training and reserve unit until the 1972

Easter Offensive. The 325D played a large role in the seizure of Quang Tri province, and from that time on—other offspring of the 325th having disappeared or merged into new units—it dropped the "D" from its designation. In May 1974 the 325th became part of the 2d Corps, and in spring 1975 it helped take Hue and Da Nang before joining the assault on Saigon. Most of the division moved down the coast, taking Phan Rang, Phan Thief, Long Thanh, and Long Trach along the way. Elements of the division were stationed in Laos until 1977 and saw action on the border with Cambodia in 1978–1979.

Commanding Officers, Division 325

Officer	Term
Tran Quy Hal, commander	c. 1953 on
Chu Van Bien, political officer	c. 1951 to 1955
Hoang Van Thai, political officer	1955 on
Quach Si Kha, political officer	1961 to 1964
Maj. Gen. Nguyen Huu An, commander	1964 to May 1964
Nguyen Minh Duc, political officer	1964 to May 1964

Commanding Officers, Division 325B

Officer	Term
Vuong Tuan Kiet, commander	c. 1964 on
Quoc Tuan, political officer	c. 1964 on

Commanding Officers, Division 325C

Officer	Term
Chu Phuong Doi, commander	c. 1965 on
Nguyen Cong Trang, political officer	c. 1965 on

Commanding Officers, Division 325D

Officer	Term
Thang Binh, commander	1968 to c. 1971
Vu Duc Thai, political officer	1968 to c. 1971

Officer	Term
Le Kich, commander	c. 1971 to May 1974
Sen. Col. Nguyen Cong Trang, political officer	c. 1971 to May 1974
Col. Pham Minh Tam, commander	May 1974 on
Col. Le Van Duong, political officer	May 1974 on

Division 330. Infantry Division 330 was formed in January 1955, partly with regroupees from the South's eastern, central, and Mekong Delta regions, and served for a time after 1959 as a training unit for troops preparing for operations in the South's populated lowland areas.

Commanding Officers, Division 330

Officer	Term
Maj. Gen. Tran Van Tra, commander	Before 1958 on

Division 338. This division at its founding on 12 December 1956 consisted largely of troops who regrouped from Nam Bo to the North in 1954. From 1959 to 1963 it was the main training unit for troops, cadres, and officers preparing to enter the South, especially for assignment in their native provinces of Western Nam Bo.

Division 341. Brigade 341 of Military Region 4 became Light Infantry Division 341 in February 1962. It was disbanded when several of its units left for the South, reconstituted in March 1965, disbanded again in late 1966, and finally established with some permanence in November 1972. In January 1975 five hundred trucks of Transportation Division 571 moved the entire division from its base in Nghe Tinh province to Eastern Nam Bo to reinforce the 4th Corps for the attack on Saigon.

Commanding Officers, Division 341

Officer	Term
Tran Van Tran, commander	c. January 1977
Tran Nguyen Do, political officer	c. January 1975

Antiaircraft Artillery Division 361. The 361st "Hanoi Air Defense Division" was founded on 19 May 1965 and designated a "strategic" or fixed site division in June 1966 to defend the capital.

Antiaircraft Artillery Division 363. Division 363 was a "strategic" anti-aircraft artillery division established in June 1966 and provided the main Antiaircraft defense of Haiphong.

Antiaircraft Artillery Division 365. Division 365 was a fixed site anti-aircraft artillery division established in June 1966.

Antiaircraft Artillery Division 367. The 367th, established in 1955, was the nucleus of what would become the PAVN's Air Defense-Air Force Branch. A "mobile" air defense division consisting of four regiments of antiaircraft artillery and one of missiles (added in June 1966), the 367th was assigned to Military Region 4 in 1968 to bolster defenses against intensified U.S. bombardment.

Antiaircraft Artillery Division 368. Division 368, its date of establishment not known, was assigned to Military Region 4 in 1968 to bolster defenses against intensified U.S. bombardment.

Antiaircraft Artillery Division 369. Division 369 was a fixed site anti-aircraft artillery division established in June 1966.

Antiaircraft Artillery Division 371. Air force regiments 921 and 923 were combined on 24 March 1967 to form Air Force Division 371 when the air force became a separate command within the Air Defense-Air Force Branch.

Antiaircraft Artillery Division 377. Division 377 was formed with three regiments taken from fixed site divisions in 1968 for the purpose of bolstering antiaircraft defenses in Military Region 4.

Divisions 470, 471, 472, 473 (of Group 559). Group 559 organized these divisions to administer key segments of the Ho Chi Minh Trail complex. The 470th, for example, came into existence in spring 1970 to organize an alternative source of supply for units in Cambodia and Nam Bo when the PAVN lost use of the Cambodian port of Sihanoukville. The 470th, 471st, and 472d were "sectoral" or "areal" (khu vuc) divisions until late 1974, when the 470th and 472d were designated engineering divisions and the 471st became a transportation division modeled on the 571st. The 473d was an engineering division from the time of its establishment. The 471st was abolished after the war.

Transportation Division 571. The expansion and reorganization of Group 559 to meet the increased logistical requirements of corps level operations included the establishment of the PAVN's first motorized transportation division on 12 July 1973. The division had been a sectoral command of the Ho Chi Minh Trail known as the Rear Service Command 571 after October 1972.

The main duty of the 571st was long distance hauling to trail termini where other units took over distribution to the field. In mid 1974 it had 2,600 vehicles and 8,500 officers, men, and women. The division's trucks operated on roads running through southern Laos to Stung Treng in Cambodia and over parts of Route 14 in South Vietnam. After PAVN victories in Phuoc Long province and the Central Highlands in early 1975, the division's mission shifted to the deployment and direct support of troops in battle.

The 571st avoided being decommissioned after the war by becoming, under the command of the Rear Services General Directorate, a conduit of assistance and trade with Laos as well as of logistical support for PAVN "volunteers" there.

Commanding Officers, Division 571

Officer	Term
Col. Nguyen Dam, commander	August 1973 to November 1973
Hoang Tra, commander (acting)	November 1973 to 1975
Col. Phan Hun Dal, political officer	August 1973 on
Sen. Col. Phan Huu Dal, commander/political officer	1975 on

Division 711. Military Region 5 organized Division 711 on 29 June 1971 in Binh Dinh province. The region decommissioned the division in late June 1973 during a general reorganization of Military Region 5 main forces, forming Brigade 52 out of its remnants.

Commanding Officers, Division 711

Officer	Term
Nguyen Chon, commander	June 1972 to June 1973

Tank Brigade 202. Upon being commissioned 5 October 1959 under officers who had trained abroad, Tank Regiment 202 consisted of two battalions equipped with World War II-vintage T-34s and one battalion of self-propelled artillery. The 202d's main combat role in 1965–1968 was to support air defenses around Vinh Linh. In 1969 a thirty-man team patched up half a dozen PT-76 amphibious tanks to form Group 195, which helped push the Hmong warlord Vang Pao and Thai mercenaries out of the Plain of Jars. A year later, Battalion 397 saw action in the counterattack on ARVN Operation Lam Son 719.

Regrouped near Vinh Linh in March 1972, the regiment crossed the Ben Hal River to support attacks by Division 308 on Dong Ha and Division 320B on Cua Viet. The 202d was officially designated an "armored and tank brigade" on 25 October 1973. In December it became a part of 1st Corps. After a period of recovery in the North and the acquisition of T-59 tanks, the 202d joined the 1975 Spring Offensive in late March. With the ARVN's collapse, tanks were able to move freely over the South's roads for the first time and arrived with Division 320B at the ARVN General Staff compound on 27 April.

Commanding Officers, Tank Brigade 202

Officer	Term
Dao Huy Vu, commander	October 1959 to June 1965
Dang Quang Long, political officer	October 1959 to June 1965
Le Xuan Kien, commander	June 1965 to November 1971
Vo Ngoc Hal, political officer	June 1965 to November 1971
Nguyen Van Lang, commander	November 1971 to 1972
Vo Ngoc Hal, political officer	November 1971 to 1972
Do Phuong Ngu, commander	1972 to 1980
Hoang Khoai, political officer	1972 to 1980

Tank Brigade 203. The PAVN's first tank brigade gave birth to its second, the 203d, sometimes before June 1965. Battalions 297 and 198 of the 203d saw action against Operation Lam Son 719 in early 1971. The brigade participated in the 1975 Spring Offensive under Tri Thien Front command as part of 2d Corps.

See also entries on individual communist military services.

Appendix E
The Gulf of Tonkin Resolution

[Introduced on 5 August by Rep. Thomas E. Morgan (D-Pa.), chairman, Committee on Foreign Relations, after President Lyndon B. Johnson requested "appropriate congressional action" that same day. Passed the House of Representatives 6 August after testimony by Secretary of State Dean Rusk, Secretary of Defense Robert S. McNamara, and General Earle G. Wheeler, chairman, Joint Chiefs of Staff; passed the Senate on 7 August. Source: U.S. *Code Congressional and Administrative News*, 88th Congress-Second Session, 1964.]

PUBLIC LAW 88-408; 78 STAT. 384

[H.J. Res. 1145]
JOINT RESOLUTION

To promote the maintenance of international peace and security in southeast Asia.

Whereas naval units of the Communist regime in [North] Vietnam, in violation of the principles of the Charter of the United Nations and of international law, have deliberately and repeatedly attacked United States naval vessels lawfully present in international waters, and have thereby created a serious threat to international peace; and

Whereas these attacks are part of a deliberate and systematic campaign of aggression that the Communist regime in North Vietnam has been waging against its neighbors and the nations joined with them in the collective defense of their freedom; and

Whereas the United States is assisting the peoples of southeast Asia to protect their freedom and has no territorial, military or political ambitions in that area, but desires only that these peoples should be left in peace to work out their own destinies in their own way: Now, therefore, be it

Resolved by the Senate and House of Representatives of the United States of America in Congress assembled,

That the Congress approves and supports the determination of the President, as Commander in Chief, to take all necessary measures to repel any armed attack against the forces of the United States and to prevent further aggression.

Sec. 2. The United States regards as vital to its national interest and to world peace the maintenance of international peace and security in southeast Asia. Consonant with the Constitution of the United States and the Charter of the United Nations and in accordance with its obligations under the Southeast Asia Collective Defense Treaty, the United States is, therefore, prepared, as the President determines, to take all necessary steps, including the use of armed force, to assist any member or protocol state of the Southeast Asia Collective Defense Treaty requesting assistance in defense of its freedom.

Sec. 3. This resolution shall expire when the President shall determine that the peace and security of the area is reasonably assured by international conditions created by action of the United Nations or otherwise, except that it may be terminated earlier by concurrent resolution of the Congress.

Approved August 10, 1964.

Repeal of the Gulf of Tonkin Resolution

[Passed the Senate 30 June 1970 as the twelfth of thirteen amendments to Public Law 91-672; the House bill contained no comparable provision. The amendment repealing the resolution was added in conference committee on 31 December 1970 and passed the same day Source: *U.S. Code Congressional and Administrative News,* 91st Congress—Second Session, 1970.]

PUBLIC LAW 91-672; 84 STAT. 2053

[H. R.15628]

An Act to amend the Foreign Military Sales Act, and for other purposes. Be it enacted by the Senate and House of Representatives of the United States of America in Congress assembled, That:

Sec. 12. The joint resolution entitled "Joint resolution to promote the maintenance of international peace and security in Southeast Asia," approved August 10,1964 (78 Stat. 384; Public Law 88–408), is terminated effective upon the day that the second session of the Ninety-first Congress is last adjourned.

Approved January 12, 1971.

Appendix F

Paris Peace Accords—
27 January 1973

[Source: U.S. Treaties and Other International Agreements. Vol. 24. (1973).]

AGREEMENT ON ENDING THE WAR AND RESTORING PEACE IN VIET-NAM

The Parties participating in the Paris Conference on Viet-Nam,
With a view to ending the war and restoring peace in Viet-Nam on the basis of respect for the Vietnamese people's fundamental national rights and the South Vietnamese people's right to self-determination, and to contributing to the consolidation of peace in Asia and the world,
Have agreed on the following provisions and undertake to respect and to implement them:

Chapter I

THE VIETNAMESE PEOPLE'S FUNDAMENTAL NATIONAL RIGHTS
Article 1

The United States and all other countries respect the independence, sovereignty, unity, and territorial integrity of Viet-Nam as recognized by the 1954 Geneva Agreements on Viet-Nam.

Chapter II

CESSATION OF HOSTILITIES—WITHDRAWAL OF TROOPS
Article 2

A cease-fire shall be observed throughout South Viet-Nam as of 2400 hours G.M.T., on January 27, 1973.

At the same hour, the United States will stop all its military activities against the territory of the Democratic Republic of Viet-Nam by ground, air and naval forces, wherever they may be based, and end the mining of the territorial waters, ports, harbors, and waterways of the Democratic Republic of Viet-Nam. The United States will remove, permanently deactivate or destroy all the mines in the territorial waters, ports, harbors, and waterways of North Viet-Nam as soon as this Agreement goes into effect.

The complete cessation of hostilities mentioned in this Article shall be durable and without limit of time.

Article 3

The parties undertake to maintain the cease-fire and to ensure a lasting and stable peace. As soon as the cease-fire goes into effect: (a) The United States forces and those of other foreign countries allied with the United States and the Republic of Viet-Nam shall remain in-place pending the implementation of the plan of troop withdrawal. The Four-Party Joint Military Commission described in Article 16 shall determine the modalities.

(b) The armed forces of the two South Vietnamese parties shall remain in-place. The Two Party Joint Military Commission described in Article 17 shall determine the areas controlled by each party and the modalities of stationing.

(c) The regular forces of all services and arms and the irregular forces of the parties in South Viet-Nam shall stop all offensive activities against each other and shall strictly abide by the following stipulations:

– All acts of force on the ground, in the air, and on the sea shall be prohibited;

– All hostile acts, terrorism and reprisals by both sides will be banned.

Article 4

The United States will not continue its military involvement or intervene in the internal affairs of South Viet-Nam.

Article 5

Within sixty days of the signing of this Agreement, there will be a total withdrawal from South Viet-Nam of troops, military advisers, and military personnel, including technical military personnel and military personnel associated with the pacification program, armaments, munitions, and war material of the United States and those of other foreign countries mentioned in Article 3 (a) Advisers from the above-mentioned countries to all paramilitary organizations and the police force will also be withdrawn within the same period of time.

Article 6

The dismantlement of all military bases in South Viet-Nam of the United States and of the other foreign countries mentioned in Article 3 (a) shall be completed within sixty days of the signing of this Agreement.

Article 7

From the enforcement of the cease-fire to the formation of the government provided for in Article [sic] 9 (b) and 14 of this Agreement, the two South Vietnamese parties shall not accept the introduction of troops, military advisers, and military personnel including technical military personnel, armaments, munitions, and war material into South Viet-Nam.

The two South Vietnamese parties shall be permitted to make periodic replacement of armaments, munitions and war material which have been destroyed, damaged, worn out or used up after the cease-fire, on the basis of piece-for-piece, of the same characteristics and properties, under the supervision of the Joint Military Commission of the two South Vietnamese parties and of the International Commission of Control and Supervision.

Chapter III

THE RETURN OF CAPTURED MILITARY PERSONNEL AND FOREIGN CIVILIANS, AND CAPTURED AND DETAINED VIET-NAMESE CIVILIAN PERSONNEL

Article 8

(a) The return of captured military personnel and foreign civilians of the parties shall be carried out simultaneously with and completed not later than the same day as the troop withdrawal mentioned in Article 5. The parties shall exchange complete lists of the above-mentioned captured military personnel and foreign civilians on the day of the signing of this Agreement.

(b) The parties shall help each other to get information about those military personnel and foreign civilians of the parties missing in action, to determine the location and take care of the graves of the dead so as to facilitate the exhumation and repatriation of the remains, and to take any such other measures as may be required to get information about those still considered missing in action.

(c) The question of the return of Vietnamese civilian personnel captured and detained in South Viet-Nam will be resolved by the two South Vietnamese parties on the basis of the principles of Article 21 (b) of the Agreement on the Cessation of Hostilities in Viet-Nam of July 20, 1954. The two South Vietnamese parties will do so in a spirit of national reconciliation and concord, with a view to ending hatred and enmity, in order to ease suffering and to reunite families. The two South Vietnamese parties will do their utmost to resolve this question within ninety days after the cease-fire comes into effect.

Chapter IV

THE EXERCISE OF THE SOUTH VIETNAMESE PEOPLE'S RIGHT TO SELF-DETERMINATION
Article 9

The Government of the United States of America and the Government of the Democratic Republic of Viet-Nam undertake to respect the following principles for the exercise of the South Vietnamese people's right to self-determination:

(a) The South Vietnamese people's right to self-determination is sacred, inalienable, and shall be respected by all countries.

(b) The South Vietnamese people shall decide themselves the political future of South Viet-Nam through genuinely free and democratic general elections under international supervision.

(c) Foreign countries shall not impose any political tendency or personality on the South Vietnamese people.

Article 10

The two South Vietnamese parties undertake to respect the cease-fire and maintain peace in South Viet-Nam, settle all matters of contention through negotiations, and avoid all armed conflict.

Article 11

Immediately alter the cease-fire, the two South Vietnamese parties will:

– achieve national reconciliation and concord, end hatred and enmity, prohibit all acts of reprisal and discrimination against individuals or organizations that have collaborated with one side or the other;

– ensure the democratic liberties of the people: personal freedom, freedom of speech, freedom of the press, freedom of meeting, freedom of organization, freedom of political activities, freedom of belief, freedom of movement, freedom of residence, freedom of work, right to property ownership, and right to free enterprise.

Article 12

(a) Immediately after the cease-fire, the two South Vietnamese parties shall hold consultations in a spirit of national reconciliation and concord, mutual respect, and mutual non-elimination to set up a National Council of National Reconciliation and Concord of three equal segments. The Council shall operate on the principle of unanimity. After the National Council of National Reconciliation and Concord has assumed its functions, the two South Vietnamese parties will consult about the formation of councils at lower levels. The two South Vietnamese parties shall sign an agreement on the internal matters of South Viet-Nam as soon as possible and do their utmost to accomplish this within ninety days after the cease-fire comes into effect, in keeping with the South Vietnamese people's aspirations for peace, independence and democracy.

(b) The National Council of National Reconciliation and Concord shall have the task of promoting the two South Vietnamese parties' implementation of this Agreement, achievement of national reconciliation and concord and ensurance of democratic liberties. The National Council of National Reconciliation and Concord will organize the free and democratic general elections provided for in Article 9 (b) and decide the procedures and modalities of these general elections. The institutions for which the general elections are to be held will be agreed upon through consultations between the two South Vietnamese parties. The National Council of National Reconciliation and Concord will also decide the procedures and modalities of such local elections as the two South Vietnamese parties agree upon.

Article 13

The question of Vietnamese armed forces in South Viet-Nam shall be settled by the two South Vietnamese parties in a spirit of national reconciliation and concord, equality and mutual respect, without foreign interference, in accordance with the postwar situation. Among the questions to be discussed by the two South Vietnamese parties are steps to reduce their military effectives and to demobilize the troops being reduced. The two South Vietnamese parties will accomplish this as soon as possible.

Article 14

South Viet-Nam win pursue a foreign policy of peace and independence. It will be prepared to establish relations with all countries irrespective of their political and social systems on the basis of mutual respect for independence and sovereignty and accept economic and technical aid from any country with no political conditions attached. The acceptance of military aid by South Viet-Nam in the future shall come under the authority of the government set up after the general elections in South Viet-Nam provided for in Article 9 (b).

Chapter V

THE REUNIFICATION OF VIET-NAM AND THE RELATION-SHIP BETWEEN NORTH AND SOUTH VIET-NAM

Article 15

The reunification of Viet-Nam shall be carried out step by step through peaceful means on the basis of discussions and agreements between North and South Viet-Nam, without coercion or annexation by either party, and without foreign interference. The time for reunification will be agreed upon by North and South Viet-Nam.

Pending reunification:

(a) The military demarcation line between the two zones at the 17th parallel is only provisional and not a political or territorial boundary, as provided for in paragraph 6 of the Final Declaration of the 1954 Geneva Conference.

(b) North and South Viet-Nam shall respect the Demilitarized Zone on either side of the Provisional Military Demarcation Line.

(c) North and South Viet-Nam shall promptly start negotiations with a view to reestablishing normal relations in various fields. Among the questions to be negotiated are the modalities of civilian movement across the Provisional Military Demarcation Line.

(d) North and South Viet-Nam shall not join any military alliance or military bloc and shall not allow foreign powers to maintain military bases, troops, military advisers, and military personnel on their respective territories, as stipulated in the 1954 Geneva Agreements on Viet-Nam.

Chapter VI

THE JOINT MILITARY COMMISSIONS, THE INTERNATIONAL COMMISSION OF CONTROL AND SUPERVISION, THE INTERNATIONAL CONFERENCE

Article 16

(a) The Parties participating in the Paris Conference on Viet-Nam shall immediately designate representatives to form a Four-Party Joint Military Commission with the task of ensuring joint action by the parties in implementing the following provisions of this Agreement:

– The first paragraph of Article 2, regarding the enforcement of the cease-fire throughout South Viet-Nam;

– Article 3 (a), regarding the cease-fire by U.S. forces and those of the other foreign countries referred to in that Article;

– Article 3 (c), regarding the cease-fire between all parties in South Viet-Nam;

– Article 5, regarding the withdrawal from South Viet-Nam of U.S. troops and those of the other foreign countries mentioned in Article 3 (a);

– Article 6, regarding the dismantlement of military bases in South Viet-Nam of the United States and those of the other foreign countries mentioned in Article 3 (a);

– Article 8 (a), regarding the return of captured military personnel and foreign civilians of the parties;

– Article 8 (b), regarding the mutual assistance of the parties in getting information about those military personnel and foreign civilians of the parties missing in action.

(b) The Four-Party Joint Military Commission shall operate in accordance with the principle of consultations and unanimity. Disagreements shall be referred to the International Commission of Control and Supervision.

(c) The Four-Party Joint Military Commission shall begin operating immediately after the signing of this Agreement and end its activities in sixty days, after the completion of the withdrawal of U.S. troops and those of the other foreign countries mentioned in Article 3 (a) and the completion of the return of captured military personnel and foreign civilians of the parties.

(d) The four parties shall agree immediately on the organization, the working procedure, means of activity, and expenditures of the Four-Party Joint Military Commission.

Article 17

(a) The two South Vietnamese parties shall immediately designate representatives to form a Two-Party Joint Military Commission with the task of ensuring joint action by the two South Vietnamese parties in implementing the following provisions of this Agreement:

– The first paragraph of Article 2, regarding the enforcement of the cease-fire throughout South Viet-Nam, when the Four-Party Joint Military Commission has ended its activities;

– Article 3 (b), regarding the cease-fire between the two South Vietnamese parties;

– Article 3 (c), regarding the cease-fire between all parties in South Viet-Nam, when the Four-Party Joint Military Commission has ended its activities;

– Article 7, regarding the prohibition of the introduction of troops into South Viet-Nam and all other provisions of this Article;

– Article 8 (c), regarding the question of the return of Vietnamese civilian personnel captured and detained in South Viet-Nam;

– Article 13, regarding the reduction of the military effectives of the two South Vietnamese parties and the demobilization of the troops being reduced.

(b) Disagreements shall be referred to the International Commission of Control and Supervision.

(c) After the signing of this Agreement, the Two-Party Joint Military Commission shall agree immediately on the measures and organization aimed at enforcing the cease-fire and preserving peace in South Viet-Nam.

Article 18

(a) After the signing of this Agreement, an International Commission of Control and Supervision shall be established immediately.

(b) Until the International Conference provided for in Article 19 makes definitive arrangements, the International Commission of Control and Supervision will report to the four parties of matters concerning the control and supervision of the implementation of the following provisions of this Agreement:

– The first paragraph of Article 2, regarding the enforcement of the cease-fire throughout South Viet-Nam;

– Article 3 (a), regarding the cease-fire by U.S. forces and those of other foreign countries referred to in that Article;

– Article 3 (c), regarding the cease-fire between all the parties in South Viet-Nam;

– Article 5, regarding the withdrawal from South Viet-Nam of U.S. troops and those of the other foreign countries mentioned in Article 3 (a);

– Article 6, regarding the dismantlement of military bases in South Viet-Nam of the United States and those of the other foreign countries mentioned in Article 3 (a);

– Article 8 (a), regarding the return of captured military personnel and foreign civilians the parties.

The International Commission of Control and Supervision shall form control teams for carrying out its task. The four parties shall agree immediately on the location and operation of these teams. The parties will facilitate their operation.

(c) Until the International Conference makes definitive arrangements, the International Commission of Control and Supervision will report to the two South Vietnamese parties on matters concerning the control and supervision of the implementation of the following provisions of this Agreement:

– The first paragraph of Article 2, regarding the enforcement of the cease-fire throughout South Viet-Nam, when the Four-Party Joint Military Commission has ended its activities;

– Article 3 (b), regarding the cease-fire between the two South Vietnamese parties;

– Article 3 (c), regarding the cease-fire between all parties in South Viet-Nam, when the Four-Party Joint Military Commission has ended its activities;

– Article 7, regarding the prohibition of the introduction of troops into South Viet-Nam and all other provisions of this Article;

– Article 8 (c), regarding the question of the return of Vietnamese civilian personnel captured and detained in South Viet-Nam;

– Article 9 (b), regarding the free and democratic general elections in South Viet-Nam;

– Article 13, regarding the reduction of the military effectives of the two South Vietnamese parties and the demobilization of the troops being reduced.

The International Commission of Control and Supervision shall form control teams for carrying out its tasks. The two South Vietnamese parties shall agree immediately on the location and operation of these teams. The two South Vietnamese parties will facilitate their operation.

(d) The International Commission of Control and Supervision shall be composed of representatives of four countries: Canada, Hungary, Indonesia and Poland. The chairmanship of this Commission will rotate among the members for specific periods to be determined by the Commission.

(e) The International Commission of Control and Supervision shall carry out its tasks in accordance with the principle of respect for the sovereignty of South Viet-Nam.

(f) The International Commission of Control and Supervision shall operate in accordance with the principle of consultations and unanimity.

(g) The International Commission of Control and Supervision shall begin operating when a cease-fire comes into force in Viet-Nam. As regards the provisions in Article 18 (b) concerning the four parties, the International Commission of Control and Supervision shall end its activities when the Commission's tasks of control and supervision regarding these provisions have been fulfilled. As regards the provisions in Article 18 (c) concerning the two South Vietnamese parties, the International Commission of Control and Supervision shall end its activities on the request of the government formed after the general elections in South Viet-Nam provided for in Article 9 (b).

(h) The four parties shall agree immediately on the organization, means of activity, and expenditures of the International Commission of Control and Supervision. The relationship between the International Commission and the International Conference will be agreed upon by the International Commission and the International Conference.

Article 19

The parties agree on the convening of an International Conference within thirty days of the signing of this Agreement to acknowledge the signed agreements; to guarantee the ending of the war, the maintenance of peace in Viet-Nam, the respect of the Vietnamese people's fundamental national rights, and the South Vietnamese people's rights to self-determination; and to contribute to and guarantee peace in Indochina.

The United States and the Democratic Republic of Viet-Nam, on behalf of the parties participating in the Paris Conference on Viet-Nam, will propose to the following parties that they participate in this International Conference; the People's Republic of China, the Republic of France, the

Union of Soviet Socialist Republics, the United Kingdom, the four countries of the International Commission of Control and Supervision, and the Secretary General of the United Nations, together with the parties participating in the Paris Conference on Viet-Nam.

Chapter VII

REGARDING CAMBODIA AND LAOS
Article 20

(a) The parties participating in the Paris Conference on Viet-Nam shall strictly respect the 1954 Geneva Agreement on Cambodia and the 1962 Geneva Agreements on Laos, which recognized the Cambodian and the Lao peoples' fundamental national rights, i.e., the independence, sovereignty, unity, and territorial integrity of these countries. The parties shall respect the neutrality of Cambodia and Laos.

The parties participating in the Paris Conference on Viet-Nam undertake to refrain from using the territory of Cambodia and the territory of Laos to encroach on the sovereignty and security of one another and of other countries.

(b) Foreign countries shall put an end to all military activities in Cambodia and Laos, totally withdraw from and refrain from reintroducing into these two countries troops, military advisers and military personnel, armaments, munitions and war material.

(c) The internal affairs of Cambodia and Laos shall be settled by the people of each of these countries without foreign interference.

(d) The problems existing between the Indochinese countries shall be settled by the Indochinese parties on the basis of respect for each other's independence, sovereignty, and territorial integrity, and non-interference in each other's internal affairs.

Chapter VIII

THE RELATIONSHIP BETWEEN THE UNITED STATES AND THE DEMOCRATIC REPUBLIC OF VIET-NAM
Article 21

The United States anticipates that this Agreement will usher in an era of reconciliation with the Democratic Republic of Viet-Nam as with all the peoples of Indochina. In pursuance of its traditional policy, the United States will contribute to healing the wounds of war and to postwar reconstruction of the Democratic Republic of Viet-Nam and throughout Indochina.

Article 22

The ending of the war, the restoration of peace in Viet-Nam, and the strict implementation of this Agreement will create conditions for establishing a new, equal and mutually beneficial relationship between the United States and the Democratic Republic of Viet-Nam on the basis of respect for each other's independence and sovereignty, and non-interference in each other's internal affairs. At the same time this will ensure stable peace in Viet-Nam and contribute to the preservation of lasting peace in Indochina and Southeast Asia.

Chapter IX

OTHER PROVISIONS

Article 23

This Agreement shall enter into force upon signature by plenipotentiary representatives of the parties participating in the Paris Conference on Viet-Nam. All the parties concerned shall strictly implement this Agreement and its Protocols.

Done in Paris this twenty-seventh day of January, one thousand-nine hundred and seventy-three, in English and Vietnamese. The English and Vietnamese texts are official and equally authentic.

[separate numbered page]

FOR THE GOVERNMENT OF THE UNITED STATES OF AMERICA:

William P. Rogers
Secretary of State

FOR THE GOVERNMENT OF THE DEMOCRATIC REPUBLIC OF VIET-NAM:

Nguyen Duy Trinh
Minister for Foreign Affairs

[separate numbered page]

FOR THE GOVERNMENT OF THE REPUBLIC OF VIET-NAM:

Tran Van Lam
Minister for Foreign Affairs

FOR THE PROVISIONAL REVOLUTIONARY GOVERNMENT OF THE
REPUBLIC OF SOUTH VIET-NAM:

Nguyen Thi Binh
Minister for Foreign Affairs

PROTOCOL TO THE AGREEMENT ON ENDING THE WAR AND RESTORING PEACE IN VIET-NAM CONCERNING THE RETURN OF CAPTURED MILITARY PERSONNEL AND FOREIGN CIVILIANS AND CAPTURED AND DETAINED VIET-NAMESE CIVILIAN PERSONNEL

The Parties participating in the Paris Conference on Viet-Nam,
In implementation of Article 8 of the Agreement on Ending the War and
Restoring Peace in Viet-Nam signed on this date providing for the return
of captured military personnel and foreign civilians, and captured and
detained Vietnamese civilian personnel,
Have agreed as follows:

THE RETURN OF CAPTURED MILITARY PERSONNEL AND FOREIGN CIVILIANS

Article 1

The parties signatory to the Agreement shall return the captured military personnel of the parties mentioned in Article 8 (a) of the agreement as follows:

– all captured military personnel of the United States and those of the other foreign countries mentioned in Article 3 (a) of the Agreement shall be returned to United States authorities;

– all captured Vietnamese military personnel, whether belonging to regular or irregular armed forces, shall be returned to the two South Vietnamese parties; they shall be returned to that South Vietnamese party under whose command they served.

Article 2

All captured civilians who are nationals of the United States or of any other foreign countries mentioned in Article 3 (a) of the Agreement shall be returned to United States authorities. All other captured foreign civilians shall be returned to the authorities of their country of nationality by any one of the parties willing and able to do so.

Article 3

The parties shall today exchange complete lists of captured persons mentioned in Articles 1 and 2 of this Protocol.

Article 4

(a) The return of all captured persons mentioned in Articles 1 and 2 of this Protocol shall be completed within sixty days of the signing of the Agreement at a rate no slower than the rate of withdrawal from South Viet-Nam of United States forces and those of the other foreign countries mentioned in Article 5 of the Agreement.

(b) Persons who are seriously ill, wounded or maimed, old persons and women shall be returned first. The remainder shall be returned either by returning all from one detention place after another or in order of their dates of capture, beginning with those who have been held the longest.

Article 5

The return and reception of the persons mentioned in Articles 1 and 2 of this Protocol shall be carried out at places convenient to the concerned parties. Places of return shall be agreed upon by the Four-Party Joint Military Commission. The parties shall ensure the safety of personnel engaged in the return and reception of those persons.

Article 6

Each party shall return all captured persons mentioned in Articles 1 and 2 of this Protocol without delay and shall facilitate their return and reception. The detaining parties shall not deny or delay their return for any reason, including the fact that captured persons may, on any grounds, have been prosecuted or sentenced.

THE RETURN OF CAPTURED AND DETAINED VIETNAMESE CIVILIAN PERSONNEL

Article 7

(a) The question of the return of Vietnamese civilian personnel captured and detained in South Viet-Nam will be resolved by the two South Vietnamese parties on the basis of the principles of Article 21 (b) of the Agreement on the Cessation of Hostilities in Viet-Nam of July 20, 1954, which reads as follows:

> "The term 'civilian Internees' is understood to mean all persons who, having in any way contributed to the political and armed struggle between the two parties, have been arrested for that reason and have been kept in detention by either party during the period of hostilities."

(b) The two South Vietnamese parties will do so in a spirit of national reconciliation and concord with a view to ending hatred and enmity in order to ease suffering and to reunite families. The two South Vietnamese parties will do their utmost to resolve this question within ninety days after the cease-fire comes into effect.

(c) Within fifteen days after the cease-fire comes into effect, the two South Vietnamese parties shall exchange lists of the Vietnamese civilian personnel captured and detained by each party and lists of the places at which they are held.

TREATMENT OF CAPTURED PERSONS DURING DETENTION

Article 8

(a) All captured military personnel of the parties and captured foreign civilians of the parties shall be treated humanely at all times, and in accordance with international practice.

They shall be protected against all violence to life and person, in particular against murder in any form, mutilation, torture and cruel treatment, and outrages upon personal dignity. These persons shall not be forced to join the armed forces of the detaining party.

They shall be given adequate food, clothing, shelter, and the medical attention required for their state of health. They shall be allowed to exchange post cards and letters with their families and receive parcels.

(b) All Vietnamese civilian personnel captured and detained in South Viet-Nam shall be treated humanely at all times, and in accordance with international practice.

They shall be protected against all violence to life and person, in particular against murder in any form, mutilation, torture and cruel treatment, and outrages against personal dignity. The detaining parties shall not deny or delay their return for any reason, including the fact that captured persons may, on any grounds, have been prosecuted or sentenced. These persons shall not be forced to join the armed forces of the detaining party.

They shall be given adequate food, clothing, shelter, and the medical attention required for their state of health. They shall be allowed to exchange post cards and letters with their families and receive.

Article 9

(a) To contribute to improving the living conditions of the captured military personnel of the parties and foreign civilians of the parties, the parties shall, within fifteen days after the cease-fire comes into effect, agree upon the designation of two or more national Red Cross societies to visit all places where captured military personnel and foreign civilians are held.

(b) To contribute to improving the living conditions of the captured and detained Vietnamese civilian personnel, the two South Vietnamese parties shall, within fifteen days after the cease-fire comes into effect, agree upon the designation of two or more national Red Cross societies to visit all places where the captured and detained Vietnamese civilian personnel are held.

WITH REGARD TO DEAD AND MISSING PERSONS
Article 10

(a) The Four-Party Joint Military Commission shall ensure joint action by the parties in implementing Article 8 (b) of the Agreement. When the Four-Party Joint Military Commission has ended its activities, a Four-Party Joint Military team shall be maintained to carry on this task.

(b) With regard to Vietnamese civilian personnel dead or missing in South Viet-Nam, the two South Vietnamese parties shall help each other to obtain information about missing persons, determine the location and take care of the graves of the dead, in a spirit of national reconciliation and concord, in keeping with the people's aspirations.

OTHER PROVISIONS
Article 11

(a) The Four-Party and Two-Party Joint Military Commissions will have the responsibility of determining immediately the modalities of implementing the provisions of this Protocol consistent with their respective responsibilities under Articles 16 (a) and 17 (a) of the Agreement. In case the Joint Military Commissions, when carrying out their tasks, cannot reach agreement on a matter pertaining to the return of captured personnel they shall refer to the International Commission for its assistance.

(b) The Four-Party Joint Military Commission shall form, in addition to the teams established by the Protocol concerning the cease-fire in South Viet-Nam and the Joint Military Commissions, a subcommission on captured persons and, as required, joint military teams on captured persons to assist the Commission in its tasks.

(c) From the time the cease-fire comes into force to the time when the Two-Party Joint Military Commission becomes operational, the two South Vietnamese parties' delegations to the Four-Party Joint Military Commission shall form a provisional sub-commission and provisional joint military teams to carry out its tasks concerning captured and detained Vietnamese civilian personnel.

(d) The Four-Party Joint Military Commission shall send joint military teams to observe the return of the persons mentioned in Articles 1 and 2 of this Protocol at each place in Viet-Nam where such persons are being returned, and at the last detention places from which these persons will be taken to the places of return. The Two-Party Joint Military Commission shall send joint military teams to observe the return of Vietnamese civilian personnel captured and detained at each place in South Viet-Nam where such persons are being returned, and at the last detention places from which these persons will be taken to the places of return, the examination of lists, and the investigation of violations of the provisions of the above-mentioned Articles.

Article 12

In implementation of Articles 18 (b) and 18 (c) of the Agreement, the International Commission of Control and Supervision shall have the responsibility to control and supervise the observance of Articles 1 through 7 of this Protocol through observation of the return of captured military personnel, foreign civilians and captured and detained Vietnamese civilian personnel at each place in Viet-Nam where these persons are being returned, and at the last detention places from which these persons will be taken to the places of return, the examination of lists, and the investigation of violations of the provisions of the above-mentioned Articles.

Article 13

Within five days after signature of this Protocol, each party shall publish the text of the Protocol and communicate it to all the captured persons covered by the Protocol and being detained by that party.

Article 14

This Protocol shall come into force upon signature by plenipotentiary representatives of all the parties participating in the Paris Conference on Viet-Nam. It shall be strictly implemented by all the parties concerned.

Done in Paris this twenty-seventh day of January, one thousand nine hundred and seventy three, in English and Vietnamese. The English and Vietnamese texts are official and equally authentic.

[separate numbered page]

FOR THE GOVERNMENT OF THE UNITED STATES OF AMERICA:

William P. Rogers
Secretary of State

FOR THE GOVERNMENT OF THE DEMOCRATIC REPUBLIC OF VIET-NAM:

Nguyen Duy Trinh
Minister for Foreign Affairs

[separate numbered page]

FOR THE GOVERNMENT OF THE REPUBLIC OF VIET-NAM:

Tran Van Lam
Minister for Foreign Affairs

FOR THE PROVISIONAL REVOLUTIONARY GOVERNMENT OF THE
REPUBLIC OF SOUTH VIET-NAM:

Nguyen Thi Binh
Minister for Foreign Affairs

PROTOCOL TO THE AGREEMENT ON ENDING THE WAR AND RESTORING PEACE IN VIET-NAM CONCERNING THE CEASE-FIRE IN SOUTH VIET-NAM AND THE JOINT MILITARY COMMISSIONS

The parties participating in the Paris Conference on Viet-Nam, In
implementation of the first paragraph of Article 2, Article 3, Article 5,
Article 6, Article 16 and Article 17 of the Agreement on Ending the War
and Restoring Peace in Viet-Nam signed on this date which provide for the
cease-fire in South Viet-Nam and the establishment of a Four-Party Joint
Military Commission and a Two-Party Joint Military Commission, Have
agreed as follows:

CEASE-FIRE IN SOUTH VIET-NAM
Article 1

The High Commands of the parties in South Viet-Nam shall issue
prompt and timely orders to all regular and irregular armed forces and
the armed police under their command to completely end hostilities
throughout South Viet-Nam, at the exact time stipulated in Article 2 of the
Agreement and ensure that these armed forces and armed police comply
with these orders and respect the cease-fire.

Article 2

(a) As soon as the cease-fire comes into force and until regulations are
issued by the Joint Military Commissions, all ground, river, sea and air
combat forces of the parties in South Viet-Nam shall remain in place; that
is, in order to ensure a stable cease-fire, there shall be no major redeploy-
ments or movements that would extend each party's area of control or
would result in contact between opposing armed forces and clashes which
might take place.

(b) All regular and irregular armed forces and the armed police of the
parties in South Viet-Nam shall observe the prohibition of the following
acts:

(1) Armed patrols into areas controlled by opposing armed forces
and flights by bomber and fighter aircraft of all types, except for
unarmed flights for proficiency training and maintenance;

(2) Armed attacks against any person, either military or civilian,
by any means whatsoever, including the use of small arms, mortars,
artillery, bombing and strafing by airplanes and any other type of
weapon or explosive device;

(3) All combat operations on the ground, on rivers, on the sea and in the air;

(4) All hostile acts, terrorism or reprisals; and

(5) All acts endangering lives or public or private property.

Article 3

(a) The above-mentioned prohibitions shall not hamper or restrict:

(1) Civilian supply, freedom of movement, freedom to work, and freedom of the people to engage in trade, and civilian communication and transportation between and among all areas in South Viet-Nam;

(2) The use by each party in areas under its control of military support elements, such as engineer and transportation units, in repair and construction of public facilities and the transportation and supplying of the population;

(3) Normal military proficiency training conducted by the parties in the areas under their respective control with due regard for public safety.

(b) The Joint Military Commissions shall immediately agree on corridors, routes, and other regulations governing the movement of military transport aircraft, military transport vehicles, and military transport vessels of all types of one party going through areas under the control of other parties.

Article 4

In order to avert conflict and ensure normal conditions for those armed forces which are in direct contact, and pending regulation by the Joint Military Commissions, the commanders of the opposing armed forces at those places of direct contact shall meet as soon as the cease-fire comes into force with a view to reaching an agreement on temporary measures to avert conflict and to ensure supply and medical care for these armed forces.

Article 5

(a) Within fifteen days after the cease-fire comes into effect, each party shall do its utmost to complete the removal or deactivation of all demolition objects, mine-fields, traps, obstacles or other dangerous objects placed previously, so as not to hamper the population's movement and work, in the first place on waterways, roads and railroads in South Viet-Nam. Those mines which cannot be removed or deactivated within that time shall be clearly marked and must be removed or deactivated as soon as possible.

(b) Emplacement of mines is prohibited, except as a defensive measure around the edges of military installations in places where they do not hamper the population's movement and work, and movement on waterways, roads and railroads. Mines and other obstacles already in place at the edges of military installations may remain in place if they are in places where they do not hamper the population's movement and work, and movement on waterways, roads and railroads.

Article 6

Civilian police and civilian security personnel of the parties in South Viet-Nam, who are responsible for the maintenance of law and order, shall strictly respect the prohibitions set torch in Article 2 of this Protocol. As required by their responsibilities, normally they shall be authorized to carry pistols, but when required by unusual circumstances, they shall be allowed to carry other small individual arms.

Article 7

(a) The entry into South Viet-Nam of replacement armaments, munitions, and war material permitted under Article 7 of the Agreement shall take place under the supervision and control of the Two-Party Joint Military Commission and of the International Commission of Control and Supervision and through such points of entry only as are designated by the two South Vietnamese parties. The two South Vietnamese parties may select as many as six points of entry which are not included in the list of places where teams of the International Commission of Control and Supervision are to be based contained in Article 4 (d) of the Protocol concerning the International Commission. At the same time, the two South Vietnamese parties may also select points of entry from the list of places set forth in Article 4 (d) of that Protocol.

(b) Each of the designated points of entry shall be available only for that South Vietnamese party which is in control of that point. The two South Vietnamese parties shall have an equal number of points of entry.

Article 8

(a) In implementation of Article 5 of the Agreement, the United States and the other foreign countries referred to in Article 5 of the Agreement shall take with them all their armaments, munitions, and war material. Transfers of such items which would leave them in South Viet-Nam shall not be made subsequent to the entry into force of the Agreement except for transfers of communications, transport, and other non-combat material to the Four-Party Joint Military Commission or the International Commission of Control and Supervision.

(b) Within five days after the entry into force of the cease-fire, the United States shall inform the Four-Party Joint Military Commission and the International Commission for Control and Supervision of the general plans for timing of complete troop withdrawals which shall take place in four phases of fifteen days each. It is anticipated that the numbers of troops withdrawn in each phase are not likely to be widely different, although it is not feasible to ensure equal numbers. The approximate numbers to be withdrawn in each phase shall be given to the Four-Party Joint Military Commission and the International Commission of Control and Supervision sufficiently in advance of actual withdrawals so that they can properly carry out their tasks in relation thereto.

Article 9

(a) In implementation of Article 6 of the Agreement, the United States and the other foreign countries referred to in that Article shall dismantle and remove from South Viet-Nam or destroy all military bases in South Viet-Nam of the United States and of the other foreign countries referred to in that Article, including weapons, mines, and other military equipment at these bases, for the purpose of making them unusable for military purposes.

(b) The United States shall supply the Four-Party Joint Military Commission and the International Commission of Control and Supervision with necessary information on plans for base dismantlement so that those Commissions can properly carry out their tasks in relation thereto.

THE JOINT MILITARY COMMISSIONS
Article 10

(a) The implementation of the Agreement is the responsibility of the parties signatory to the Agreement.

The Four-Party Joint Military Commission has the task of ensuring joint action by the parties in implementing the Agreement by serving as a channel of communication among the parties, by drawing up plans and fixing the modalities to carry out, coordinate, follow and inspect the implementation of the provisions mentioned in Article 16 of the Agreement, and by negotiation and settling all matters concerning the implementation of those provisions. (b) The concrete tasks of the Four-Party Joint Military Commission are:

(1) To coordinate, follow and inspect the implementation of the above mentioned provisions of the Agreement by the four parties;

(2) To deter and detect violations, to deal with cases of violation, and to settle conflicts and matters of contention between the parties relating to the above-mentioned provisions;

(3) To dispatch without delay one or more joint teams, as required by specific cases, to any part of South Viet-Nam, to investigate alleged violations of the Agreement and to assist the parties in finding measures to prevent recurrence of similar cases;

(4) To engage in observation at the places where this is necessary in the exercise of its functions;

(5) To perform such additional tasks as it may, by unanimous decision, determine.

Article 11

(a) There shall be a Central Joint Military Commission located in Saigon. Each party shall designate immediately a military delegation of fifty-nine persons to represent it on the Central Commission. The senior officer designated by each party shall be a general officer, or equivalent.

(b) There shall be seven Regional Joint Military Commissions located in the regions shown on the annexed map [not reproduced] and based at the following places:

Regions	Places
I	Hue
II	Danang
III	Pleiku
IV	Phan Thiet
V	Bien Hoa
VI	My Tho
VII	Can Tho

Each party shall designate a military delegation of sixteen persons to represent it on each Regional Commission. The senior officer designated by each party shall be an officer from the rank of Lieutenant Colonel to Colonel, or equivalent.

(c) There shall be a joint military team operating in each of the areas shown on the annexed map [not reproduced] and based at each of the following places in South Viet-Nam:

Region I
Quang Tri
Phu Bai
Region II
Hoi An
Tam Ky
Chu Lai
Region III
Kontum
Hau Bon
Phu Cat

continues

Region III, continued

Region III

Tuy An

Ninh Hoa

Ban Me Thuot

Region IV

Da Lat

Bao Loc

Phan Rang

Region V

An Loc

Xuan Loc

Ben Cat

Cu Chi

Tan An

Region VI

Moc Hoa

Giong Trom

Region VII

Tri Ton

Vinh Long

Vi Thanh

Khanh Hung

Quan Long

Each party shall provide four qualified persons for each joint military team. The senior person designated by each party shall be an officer from the rank of Major to Lieutenant Colonel, or equivalent.

(d) The Regional Joint Military Commissions shall assist the Central Joint Military Commission in performing its tasks and shall supervise the operations of the joint military teams. The region of Saigon-Gia Dinh is placed under the responsibility of the Central Commission which shall designate joint military teams to operate in this region.

(e) Each party shall be authorized to provide support and guard personnel for its delegations to the Central Joint Military Commission and

Regional Joint Military Commissions, and for its members of the joint military teams. The total number of support and guard personnel for each party shall not exceed five hundred and fifty.

(f) The Central Joint Military Commission may establish such joint sub-commissions, joint staffs and joint military teams as circumstances may require. The Central Commission shall determine the numbers of personnel required for any additional sub-commissions, staffs or teams it establishes, provided that each party shall designate one-fourth of the number of personnel required and that the total number of personnel for the Four-Party Joint Military Commission, to include its staffs, teams, and support personnel, shall not exceed three thousand three hundred.

(g) The delegations of the two South Vietnamese parties may, by agreement, establish provisional sub-commissions and joint military teams to carry out the tasks specifically assigned to them by Article 17 of the Agreement. With respect to Article 7 of the Agreement, the two South Vietnamese parties' delegations to the Four-Party Joint Military Commission shall establish joint military teams at the points of entry into South Viet-Nam used for replacement of armaments, munitions and war material which are designated in accordance with Article 7 of this Protocol. From the time the cease-fire comes into force to the time when the Two-Party Joint Military Commission becomes operational, the two South Vietnamese parties' delegations to the Four-Party Joint Military Commission shall form a provisional sub-commission and provisional joint military teams to carry out its tasks concerning captured and detained Vietnamese civilian personnel. Where necessary for the above purposes, the two South Vietnamese parties may agree to assign personnel additional to those assigned to the two South Vietnamese delegations to the Four-Party Joint Military Commission.

Article 12

(a) In accordance with Article 17 of the Agreement which stipulates that the two South Vietnamese parties shall immediately designate their respective representatives to form the Two-Party Joint Military Commission, twenty-four hours after the cease-fire comes into force, the two designated South Vietnamese parties' delegations to the Two-Party Joint Military Commission shall meet in Saigon so as to reach an agreement as soon as possible on organization and operation of the Two-Party Joint Military Commission, as well as the measures and organization aimed at enforcing the cease-fire and preserving peace in South Viet-Nam.

(b) From the time the cease-fire comes into force to the time when the Two-Party Joint Military Commission becomes operational, the two South Vietnamese parties' delegations to the Four-Party Joint Military Commission at all levels shall simultaneously assume the tasks of the Two-Party Joint Military Commission at all levels, in addition to their functions as delegations to the Four-Party Joint Military Commission.

(c) If, at the time the Four-Party Joint Military Commission ceases its operation in accordance with Article 16 of the Agreement, agreement has not be[en] [sic] reached on organization of the Two-Party Joint Military Commission, the delegations of the two South Vietnamese parties serving with the Four-Party Joint Military Commission at all levels shall continue temporarily to work together as a provisional two-party joint military commission and to assume the tasks of the Two-Party Joint Military Commission at all levels until the Two-Party Joint Military Commission becomes operational.

Article 13

In application of the principle of unanimity, the Joint Military Commissions shall have no chairmen, and meetings shall be convened at the request of any representative. The Joint Military Commissions shall adopt working procedures appropriate for the effective discharge of their functions and responsibilities.

Article 14

The Joint Military Commissions and the International Commission of Control and Supervision shall closely cooperate with and assist each other in carrying out their respective functions. Each Joint Military Commission shall inform the International Commission about the implementation of those provisions of the Agreement for which that Joint Military Commission has responsibility and which are within the competence of the International Commission. Each Joint Military Commission may request the International Commission to carry out specific observation activities.

Article 15

The Central Four-Party Joint Military Commission shall begin operating twenty-four hours after the cease-fire comes into force. The Regional Four-Party Joint Military Commissions shall begin operating forty-eighty hours after the cease-fire comes into force. The joint military teams based at the places listed in Article 11 (c) of this Protocol shall begin operating no later than fifteen days after the cease-fire comes into force. The delegations of the two South Vietnamese parties shall simultaneously begin to assume the tasks of the Two-Party Joint Military Commission as provided in Article 12 of this Protocol.

Article 16

(a) The parties shall provide full protection and all necessary assistance and cooperation to the Joint Military Commissions at all levels, in the discharge of their tasks.

(b) The Joint Military Commissions and their personnel, while carrying out their tasks, shall enjoy privileges and immunities equivalent to those accorded diplomatic missions and diplomatic agents.

(c) The personnel of the Joint Military Commissions may carry pistols and wear special insignia decided upon by each Central Joint Military Commission. The personnel of each party while guarding Commission installations or equipment may be authorized to carry other individual small arms, as determined by each Central Joint Military Commission.

Article 17

(a) The delegation of each party to the Four-Party Joint Military Commission and the Two-Party Joint Military Commission shall have its own offices, communication, logistics and transportation means, including aircraft when necessary.

(b) Each party, in its areas of control shall provide appropriate office and accommodation facilities to the Four-Party Joint Military Commission and the Two-Party Joint Military Commission at all levels.

(c) The parties shall endeavor to provide the Four-Party Joint Military Commission and the Two-Party Joint Military Commission, by means of loan, lease, or gift, the common means of operation, including equipment for communication, supply, and transport, including aircraft when necessary. The joint Military Commissions may purchase from any source necessary facilities, equipment, and services which are not supplied by the parties. The Joint Military Commissions shall possess and use these facilities and this equipment.

(d) The facilities and the equipment for common use mentioned above shall be returned to the parties when the Joint Military Commissions have ended their activities.

Article 18

The common expenses of the Four-Party Joint Military Commission shall be borne equally by the four parties, and the common expenses of the Two-Party Joint Military Commission in South Viet-Nam shall be borne equally by these two parties.

Article 19

This Protocol shall come into force upon signature by plenipotentiary representatives of all the parties participating in the Paris Conference on Viet-Nam. It shall be strictly implemented by all the parties concerned.

Done in Paris this twenty-seventh day of January, one thousand nine hundred and seventy-three, in English and Vietnamese. The English and Vietnamese texts are official and equally authentic.

[separate numbered page]

FOR THE GOVERNMENT OF THE UNITED STATES OF AMERICA:

William P. Rogers
Secretary of State

FOR THE GOVERNMENT OF THE DEMOCRATIC REPUBLIC OF
VIET-NAM:

Nguyen Duy Trinh
Minister for Foreign Affairs

[separate numbered page]

FOR THE GOVERNMENT OF THE REPUBLIC OF VIET-NAM:

Tran Van Lam
Minister for Foreign Affairs

FOR THE PROVISIONAL REVOLUTIONARY GOVERNMENT OF THE
REPUBLIC OF SOUTH VIET-NAM:

Nguyen Thi Binh
Minister for Foreign Affairs

PROTOCOL TO THE AGREEMENT ON ENDING THE WAR AND RESTORING PEACE IN VIET-NAM CONCERNING THE INTERNATIONAL COMMISSION OF CONTROL AND SUPERVISION

The parties participating in the Paris Conference on Viet-Nam,
In implementation of Article 18 of the Agreement on Ending the War and
Restoring Peace in Viet-Nam signed on this date providing for the forma-
tion of the International Commission of Control and Supervision,
Have agreed as follows:

Article 1

The implementation of the Agreement is the responsibility of the parties signatory to the Agreement.

The functions of the International Commission are to control and supervise the implementation of the provisions mentioned in Article 18 of the
Agreement. In carrying out these functions, the International Commission
shall:

(a) Follow the implementation of the above-mentioned provisions of the
Agreement through communication with the parties and on-the-spot observation at the places where this is required;

(b) Investigate violations of the provisions which fall under the control
and supervision of the Commission;

(c) When necessary, cooperate with the Joint Military Commissions in
deterring and detecting violations of the above-mentioned provisions.

Article 2

The International Commission shall investigate violations of the provisions described on Article 18 of the Agreement on the request of the Four-Party Joint Military Commission, or of the Two-Party Joint Military Commission, or of any party, or, with respect to Article 9 (b) of the Agreement on general elections, of the National Council on National Reconciliation and Concord, or in any case where the International Commission has other adequate grounds for considering that there has been a violation of those provisions. It is understood that, in carrying out this task, the International Commission shall function with the concerned parties' assistance and cooperation as required.

Article 3

(a) When the International Commission finds that there is a serious violation in the implementation of the Agreement or a threat to peace against which the Commission can find no appropriate measure, the Commission shall report this to the four parties to the Agreement so that they can hold consultations to find a solution.

(b) In accordance with Article 18 (f) of the Agreement, the International Commission's reports shall be made with the unanimous agreement of the representatives of all the four members. In case no unanimity is reached, the Commission shall forward the different views to the four parties in accordance with Article 18 (b) of the Agreement, or to the two South Vietnamese parties in accordance with Article 18 (c) of the Agreement, but these shall not be considered as reports of the Commission.

Article 4

(a) The headquarters of the International Commission shall be at Saigon.

(b) There shall be seven regional teams located in the regions shown on the annexed map [not reproduced] and based at the following places:

Regions	Places
I	Hue
II	Danang
III	Pleiku
IV	Phan Thiet
V	Bien Hoa
VI	My Tho
VII	Can Tho

The International Commission shall designate three teams for the region of Saigon-Gia Dinh.

(c) There shall be twenty-six teams operating in the areas shown on the annexed map [not reproduced] and based at each of the following places in South Viet-Nam:

Region I

Quang Tri

Phu Bai

Region II

Hoi An

Tam Ky

Chu Lai

Region III

Kontum

Hau Bon

Phu Cat

Tuy An

Ninh Hoa

Ban Me Thuot

Region IV

Da Lat

Bao Loc

Phan Rang

Region V

An Loc

Xuan Loc

Ben Cat

Cu Chi

Tan An

Region VI

Moc Hoa

Giong Trom

Region VII

Tri Ton

Vinh Long

Vi Thanh

Khanh Hung

Quan Long

(d) There shall be twelve teams located as shown on the annexed map [not reproduced] and based at the following places:

Gio Linh (to cover the area south of the Provisional Military Demarcation Line)

Lao Bao

Ben Het

Duc Co

Chu Lai

Qui Nhon

Nha Trang

Vung Tau

Xa Mat

Bien Hoa Airfield

Hong Ngu

Can Tho

(e) There shall be seven teams, six of which shall be available for assignment to the points of entry which are not listed in paragraph (d) above and which the two South Vietnamese parties choose as points for legitimate entry to South Viet-Nam for replacement of armaments, munitions, and war material permitted by Article 7 of the Agreement. Any team or teams not needed for the above-mentioned assignment shall be available for other tasks, in keeping with the Commission's responsibility for control and supervision.

(f) There shall be seven teams to control and supervise the return of captured and detained personnel of the parties.

Article 5

(a) To carry out its tasks concerning the return of the captured military personnel and foreign civilians of the parties as stipulated by Article 8 (a) of the Agreement, the International Commission shall, during the time of such return, send one control and supervision team to each place in Viet-

Nam where the captured persons are being returned, and to the last detention places from which these persons will be taken to the places of return.

(b) To carry out its tasks concerning the return of the Vietnamese civilian personnel captured and detained in South Viet-Nam mentioned in Article 8 (c) of the Agreement, the International Commission shall, during the time of such return, send one control and supervision team to each place in South Viet-Nam where the above-mentioned captured and detained persons are being returned, and to the last detention places from which these persons shall be taken to the places of return.

Article 6

To carry out its tasks regarding Article 9 (b) of the Agreement on the free and democratic general elections in South Viet-Nam, the International Commission shall organize additional teams, when necessary. The International Commission shall discuss this question in advance with the National Council of National Reconciliation and Concord. If additional teams are necessary for this purpose, they shall be formed thirty days before the general elections.

Article 7

The International Commission shall continually keep under review its size, and shall reduce the number of its teams, its representatives or other personnel, or both, when those teams, representatives or personnel have accomplished the tasks assigned to them and are not required for other tasks. At the same time, the expenditures of the International Commission shall be reduced correspondingly.

Article 8

Each member of the International Commission shall make available at all times the following numbers of qualified personnel:

(a) One senior representative and twenty-six others for the headquarters staff.

(b) Five for each of the seven regional teams.

(c) Two for each of the other international control teams, except for the teams at Gio Linh and Vung Tau, each of which shall have three.

(d) One hundred sixteen for the purpose of providing support to the Commission Headquarters and its teams.

Article 9

(a) The International Commission, and each of its teams, shall act as a single body comprising representatives of all four members.

(b) Each member has the responsibility to ensure the presence of its representatives at all levels of the International Commission. In case a

representative is absent, the member concerned shall immediately designate a replacement.

Article 10

(a) The parties shall afford full cooperation, assistance, and protection to
the International Commission.

(b) The parties shall at all times maintain regular and continuous liaison with the International Commission. During the existence of the
Four-Party Joint Military Commission, the delegations of the parties to
that Commission shall also perform functions with the International
Commission. After Four-Party Joint Military Commission has ended its
activities, such liaison shall be maintained throughout the Two-Party Joint
Military Commission, liaison missions, or other adequate means.

(c) The International Commission and the Joint Military Commissions
shall closely cooperate with and assist each other in carrying out their
respective functions.

(d) Wherever a team is stationed or operating, the concerned party shall
designate a liaison officer to the team to cooperate with and assist it in
carrying out without hindrance its task of control and supervision. When a
team is carrying out an investigation, a liaison officer from each concerned
party shall have the opportunity to accompany it, provided the investigation is not thereby delayed.

(e) Each party shall give the International Commission reasonable
advance notice of all proposed actions concerning those provisions of the
Agreement that are to be controlled and supervised by the International
Commission.

(f) The International Commission, including its teams, is allowed such
movement for observation as is reasonably required for the proper exercise
of its functions as stipulated in the Agreement. In carrying out these functions, the International Commission, including its teams, shall enjoy all
necessary assistance and cooperation from the parties concerned.

Article 11

In supervising the holding of the free and democratic general elections
described in Articles 9 (b) and 12 (b) of the Agreement in accordance with
modalities to be agreed upon between the National Council of National
Reconciliation and Concord and the International Commission, the latter
shall receive full cooperation from the National Council.

Article 12

The International Commission and its personnel who have the nationality of a member state shall, while carrying out their tasks, enjoy privileges
and immunities equivalent to those accorded diplomatic missions and
diplomatic agents.

Article 13

The International Commission may use the means of communication and transport necessary to perform its functions. Each South Vietnamese party shall make available for rent to the International Commission appropriate office and accommodation facilities and shall assist it in obtaining such facilities. The International Commission may receive from the parties, on mutually agreeable terms, the necessary means of communication and transport and may purchase from any source necessary equipment and services not obtained from the parties. The International Commission shall possess these means.

Article 14

The expenses for the activities of the International Commission shall be borne by the parties and the members of the International Commission in accordance with the provisions of this Article:

(a) Each member country of the International Commission shall pay the salaries and allowances of its personnel.

(b) All other expenses incurred by the International Commission shall be met from a fund to which each of the four parties shall contribute twenty-three percent (23%) and to which each member of the International Commission shall contribute two percent (2%).

(c) Within thirty days of the date of entry into force of this Protocol, each of the four parties shall provide the International Commission with an initial sum equivalent to four million, five hundred thousand (4,500,000) French francs in convertible currency, which sum shall be credited against the amounts due from that party under the first budget.

(d) The International Commission shall prepare its own budgets. After the International Commission approves a budget, it shall transmit it to all parties signatory to the Agreement for their approval. Only after the budgets have been approved by the four parties to the Agreement shall they be obliged to make contributions. However, in case the parties to the Agreement do not agree on a new budget, the International Commission shall temporarily base its expenditures on the previous budget, except for the extraordinary, one-time expenditures for installation or for the acquisition of equipment, and the parties shall continue to make their contributions on that basis until a new budget is approved.

Article 15

(a) The headquarters shall be operational and in place within twenty-four hours after the cease-fire.

(b) The regional teams shall be operational and in place, and three teams for supervision and control of the return of the captured and detained personnel shall be operational and ready for dispatch within forty-eight hours after the cease-fire.

(c) Other teams shall be operational and in place within fifteen to thirty days after the cease-fire.

Article 16

Meetings shall be convened at the call of the Chairman. The International Commission shall adopt other working procedures appropriate for the effective discharge of its functions and consistent with respect for the sovereignty of South Viet-Nam.

Article 17

The Members of the International Commission may accept the obligations of this Protocol by sending notes of acceptance to the four parties signatory to the Agreement. Should a member of the International Commission decide to withdraw from the International Commission, it may do so by giving three months notice by means of notes to the four parties to the Agreement, in which case those four parties shall consult among themselves for the purpose of agreeing upon a replacement member.

Article 18

This Protocol shall come into force upon signature by plenipotentiary representatives of all the parties participating in the Paris Conference on Viet-Nam. It shall be strictly implemented by all the parties concerned.

Done in Paris this twenty-seventh day of January, one thousand nine hundred and seventy-three, in English and Vietnamese. The English and Vietnamese texts are official and equally authentic.

[separate numbered page]

FOR THE GOVERNMENT OF THE UNITED STATES OF AMERICA:

William P. Rogers
Secretary of State

[separate numbered page]

FOR THE GOVERNMENT OF THE REPUBLIC OF VIET-NAM:

Tran Van Lam
Minister for Foreign Affairs

FOR THE GOVERNMENT OF THE DEMOCRATIC REPUBLIC OF VIET-NAM:

Nguyen Duy Trinh
Minister for Foreign Affairs

FOR THE PROVISIONAL REVOLUTIONARY GOVERNMENT OF THE
REPUBLIC OF SOUTH VIET-NAM:

Nguyen Thi Binh
Minister for Foreign Affairs

Appendix G

Vietnam War Medal of Honor Recipients

Recipient	Date of Action
Maj. William E. Adams, USA	25 May 1971
†Pfc. Lewis Albanese, USA	1 December 1966
†Pfc. James Anderson, Jr., USMC	28 February 1967
†L. Cpl. Richard A. Anderson, USMC	24 August 1969
Sfc. Webster Anderson, USA	15 October 1967
†Sfc. Eugene Ashley, Jr., USA	6–7 February 1968
†Pfc. Oscar P. Austin, USMC	23 February 1969
Sp4c. John P. Baca, USA	10 February 1970
S.Sgt. Nicky Daniel Bacon, USA	26 August 1968
Sgt. John E Baker, Jr., USA	5 November 1966
HC2c. Donald E. Ballard, USN	16 May 1968
AL. Cpl. Jedh Colby Barker, USMC	21 September 1967
†Pfc. John Andrew Barnes III, USA	12 November 1967
Capt. Harvey C. Barnum, Jr., USMC	18 December 1965
Sgt. Gary B. Beikirch, USA	1 April 1970
†Sgt. Ted Belcher, USA	19 November 1966
†Pfc. Leslie Allen Bellrichard, USA	20 May 1967
S. Sgt. Roy P. Benavidez, USA	2 May 1968
†Capt. Steven L. Bennett, USAF	29 June 1972
†Cpl. Thomas W. Bennett USA	9 February 1969
†Sp4c. Michael R. Blanchfield, USA	3 July 1969
†2d Lt. John P. Bobo, USMC	30 March 1967
S. Sgt. James Leroy Bondsteel, USA	24 May 1969
†S. Sgt. Hammett L. Bowen, Jr., USA	27 June 1969
Maj. Patrick Henry Brady, USA	6 January 1968
Sfc. Daniel D. Bruce, USMC	1 March 1969
†Sfc. William Maud Bryant, USA	24 March 1969
Capt. Paul William Bucha, USA	16–19 March 1968

† Posthumous award.

continues

continued

Recipient	Date of Action
†Sgt. Brian L. Buker, USA	5 April 1970
†Pfc. Robert C. Burke, USMC	17 May 1968
†Lt. Vincent R. Capodanno, USN	4 September 1967
†HC3c. Wayne Maurice Caron, USN	28 July 1968
†Pfc. Bruce W. Carter, USMC	7 August 1969
S. Sgt. Jon R. Cavaiani, USA	4–5 June 1971
Pfc. Raymond M. Clausen, USMC	31 January 1970
†Pfc. Ronald L. Coker, USMC	24 March 1969
†S. Sgt. Peter S. Connor, USMC	25 February 1966
Capt. Donald G. Cook, USMC	30 December 1964
†L. Cpl. Thomas E. Creek, USMC	13 February 1969
†Cpl. Michael J. Crescenz, USA	20 November 1968
†Sp4c. Nicholas J. Cutinha, USA	2 March 1968
†Sp4c. Larry G. Dahl, USA	23 February 1971
†Sgt. Rodney Maxwell Davis, USMC	6 September 1967
Sgt. Sammy L. Davis, USA	18 November 1967
Col. George E. Day, USAF	26 August 1967
†L. Cpl. Emilo A. De La Garza, Jr., USMC	11 April 1970
Maj. Merlyn Hans Dethlefsen, USAF	10 March 1967
†Sp4c. Edward A. Devore, Jr., USA	17 March 1968
†Pfc. Ralph E. Dias, USMC	12 November 1969
†Pfc. Douglas E. Dickey, USMC	26 March 1967
†S. Sgt. Drew Dennis Dix, USA	31 January to 1 February 1968
†1st Lt. Stephen Holden Doane, USA	25 March 1969
Sgt. David Charles Dolby, USA	21 May 1966
Capt. Roger Hugh C. Donlon, USA	6 July 1964
Maj. Kern W. Dunagan, USA	13 May 1969
†2d Lt. Harold Bascom Durham, Jr., USA	17 October 1967
†S. Sgt. Glenn H. English, Jr., USA	7 September 1970
†Capt. Michael J. Estocin, USN	20 and 26 April 1967
†SP4c. Donald W. Evans, Jr., USA	27 January 1967
†Sgt. Rodney J. Evans, USA	18 July 1969
CWO Frederick Edgar Ferguson, USA	31 January 1968
†Sp4c. Daniel Fernandez, USA	18 February 1966

Recipient	Date of Action
Maj. Bernard Francis Fisher, USAF	10 March 1966
Sp4c. Michael John Fitzmaurice, USA	23 March 1971
†Sgt. Charles Clinton Fleek, USA	27 May 1967
Capt. James P. Fleming, USAF	26 November 1968
Capt. Robert F. Foley, USA	5 November 1966
†Cpl. Michael Fleming Folland, USA	3 July 1969
†Sgt. Paul Hellstrom Foster, USMC	14 October 1967
†1st Lt. Douglas B. Fournet, USA	4 May 1968
†Pfc. James W. Fous, USA	14 May 1968
Capt. Wesley L. Fox, USMC	22 February 1969
†Cpl. Frank R. Fratellenico, USA	19 August 1970
Capt. Harold A. Fritz, USA	11 January 1969
†1st Lt. James A. Gardner, USA	7 February 1966
†S. Sgt. John G. Gertsch, USA	15–19 July 1969
†Sgt. Alfredo Gonzalez, USMC	4 February 1968
†Capt. James A. Graham, USMC	2 June 1967
†P. Sgt. Bruce Alan Grandstaff, USA	18 May 1967
†Capt. Joseph Xavier Grant, USA	13 November 1966
†2d Lt. Terrence Collinson Graves, USMC	16 February 1968
†Sp4c. Peter M. Guenette, USA	18 May 1968
Sp5c. Charles Cris Hagemeister, USA	20 March 1967
†1st Lt. Loren D. Hagen, USA	7 August 1971
†S. Sgt. Robert W. Hartsock, USA	23 February 1969
†Sp4c. Carmel Bernon Harvey, Jr., USA	21 June 1967
Sp4c. Frank A. Herda, USA	29 June 1968
†2d Lt. Robert John Hibbs, USA	5 March 1966
†Sgt. John Noble Holcomb, USA	3 December 1968
S. Sgt. Joe R. Hooper, USA	21 February 1968
†M. Sgt. Charles Ernest Hosking, Jr., USA	21 March 1967
G. Sgt. Jimmie E. Howard, USMC	16 June 1966
1st Lt. Robert L. Howard, USA	30 December 1968
†L. Cpl. James D. Howe, USMC	6 May 1970
†SP4c. George Alan Ingalls, USA	16 April 1967
P.O. Robert R. Ingram, USN	28 March 1966
Lt. Col. Joe M. Jackson, USAF	12 May 1968

† *Posthumous award.*

continues

continued

Recipient	Date of Action
Capt. Jack H. Jacabs, USA	9 March 1968
S. Sgt. Don J. Jenkins, USA	6 January 1969
†Pfc. Robert H. Jenkins, Jr., USMC	5 March 1969
S. Sgt. Delbert O. Jennings, USA	27 December 1966
†L. Cpl. Jose Francisco Jimenez, USMC	28 August 1969
Sp6c. Lawrence Joel, USA	8 November 1965
Sp5c. Dwight H. Johnson, USA	15 January 1968
†Pfc. Ralph H. Johnson, USMC	5 March 1968
†SP4c. Donald R. Johnston, USA	21 March 1969
†Col. William A. Jones III, USAF	1 September 1968
†1st Lt. Stephen Edward Karopczyc, USA	12 March 1967
†Cpl. Terry Teruo Kawamura, USA	20 March 1969
Pfc. Kenneth Michael Kays, USA	7 May 1970
†SP5c. John J. Kedenburg, USA	13 June 1968
†L. Cpl. Miguel Keith, USMC	8 May 1970
Sgt. Leonard B. Keller, USA	2 May 1967
Lt. Comdr. Thomas G. Kelley, USN	15 June 1969
G. Sgt. Allan Jay Kellog, Jr., USMC	11 March 1970
Lt.(jg) Joseph R. Kerrey, USNR	14 March 1969
Sp4c. Thomas James Kinsman, USA	6 February 1968
S. Sgt. Paul Ronald Lumbers, USA	20 August 1968
Sp4c. George C. Lang, USA	22 February 1969
†Pfc. Garfield M. Langhorn, USA	15 January 1969
†SP4c. Joseph G. LaPointe, Jr., USA	2 June 1969
Lt. Clyde Everett Lassen, USN	19 June 1968
†Pfc. Billy Lane Lauffer, USA	21 September 1966
†Sp4c. Robert D. Law, USA	22 February 1969
Maj. Howard V. Lee, USMC	8–9 August 1966
†Pfc. Milton A. Lee, USA	26 April 1968
†2d Lt. Robert Ronald Leisy, USA	2 December 1969
Sgt. Peter C. Lemon, USA	1 April 1970
†P. Sgt. Matthew Leonard, USA	28 February 1967
Sgt. John L. Levitow, USAF	24 February 1969
Capt. Angelo J. Liteky, USA	6 December 1967
Sfc. Gary Lee Littrell, USA	4–8 April 1970

Recipient	Date of Action
Capt. James E. Livingston, USMC	2 May 1968
†Sgt. Donald Russell Long, USA	30 June 1966
†Pfc. Carlos James Lozada, USA	20 November 1967
†Lt. Col. Andre C. Lucas, USA	1–23 July 1970
Sgt. Allen James Lynch, USA	15 December 1967
P. Sgt. Finnis D. McCleery, USA	14 May 1968
†Pfc. Phill G. McDonald, USA	7 June 1968
2d Lt. John J. McGinty III, USMC	18 July 1966
†Sgt. Ray McKibben, USA	8 December 1968
†SP4c. Thomas J. McMahon, USA	19 March 1969
1st Sgt. David H. McNerney, USA	22 March 1967
†Sp5c. Edgar Lee McWethy, Jr., USA	21 June 1967
1st Lt. Walter Joseph Marm, Jr., USA	14 November 1965
†Pfc. Gary W. Martini, USMC	21 April 1967
†Cpl. Larry Leonard Maxam, USMC	2 February 1968
†Sp4c. Don Leslie Michael, USA	8 April 1967
S. Sgt. Franklin D. Miller, USA	5 January 1970
†1st Lt. Gary L. Miller, USA	16 February 1969
Maj. Robert J. Modrzejewski, USMC	15–18 July 1966
†S. Sgt. Frankie Zoly Molnar, USA	20 May 1967
†Pfc. James H. Monroe, USA	16 February 1967
†Cpl. William D. Morgan, USMC	25 February 1969
S. Sgt. Charles B. Morris, USA	29 June 1966
†S. Sgt. Robert C. Murray, USA	7 June 1970
†Pfc. David R. Nash, USA	29 December 1968
†Pfc. Melvin Earl Newlin, USMC	4 July 1967
†L. Cpl. Thomas R. Noonan, Jr., USMC	5 February 1969
Lt. Thomas R. Norris, USN	10–13 April 1972
CWO Michael J. Novosel, USA	2 October 1969
Sgt. Robert E. O'Malley, USMC	19 August 1965
†Pfc. Milton L. Olive III, USA	22 October 1965
†Sp4c. Kenneth L. Olson, USA	13 May 1968
†Seaman David G. Ouellet, USN	6 March 1967
Sgt. Robert Martin Patterson, USA	6 May 1968
†L. Cpl. Joe C. Paul, USMC	18 August 1965

† *Posthumous award.*

continues

continued

Recipient	Date of Action
Sgt. Richard A. Penry, USA	31 January 1970
†Cpl. William Thomas Perkins, Jr., USMC	12 October 1967
†Sgt. Lawrence David Peters, USMC	4 September 1967
†Sp4c. Danny J. Petersen, USA	9 January 1970
†Pfc. Jimmy W. Phipps, USMC	27 May 1969
†Sgt. Larry S. Pierce, USA	20 September 1965
Sgt. Richard A. Pittman, USMC	24 July 1966
†Capt. Riley L. Pitts, USA	31 October 1967
Maj. Stephen W. Pless, USMC	19 August 1967
†Sgt. William D. Port, USA	12 January 1968
†1st Lt. Robert Leslie Poxon, USA	2 June 1969
†L. Cpl. William R. Prom, USMC	9 February 1969
†S. Sgt. Robert J. Pruden, USA	29 November 1969
†S. Sgt. Laszlo Rabel, USA	13 November 1968
†HC2c. David Robert Ray, USN	19 March 1969
Capt. Ronald Eric Ray, USA	19 June 1966
†1st Lt. Frank S. Reasoner, USMC	12 July 1965
†Sgt. Anund C. Roark, USA	16 May 1968
Sgt. Gordon R. Roberts, USA	11 July 1969
†Sgt. James W. Robinson, Jr., USA	11 April 1966
WO Louis R. Rocco, USA	24 May 1970
Lt. Col. Charles Gavin Rogers, USA	1 November 1968
†Capt. Euripides Rubio, USA	8 November 1966
†Sp4c. Hector Santiago-Colon,USA	28 June 1968
†1st Lt. Ruppert L. Sargent, USA	15 March 1967
Sp5c. Clarence Eugene Sasser, USA	10 January 1968
†Sgt. William W. Seay, USA	25 August 1968
†Pfc. Daniel John Shea, USA	14 May 1969
†CB3c. Marvin G. Shields, USN	10 June 1965
†Capt. Lance P. Sijan, USAF	9 November 1967
†S. Sgt Clifford Chester Sims, USA	21 February 1968
†Sgt. Walter K. Singleton, USMC	24 March 1967
†1st Lt. George K. Sisler, USA	7 February 1967
†Sgt. Donald Sidney Skidgel, USA	14 September 1969
†Cpl. Larry E. Smedley, USMC	21 December 1967
†P.Sgt. Elmelindo R. Smith, USA	16 February 1967

Recipient	Date of Action
Capt. James M. Sprayberry, USA	25 April 1968
†1st Lt. Russell A. Steindam, USA	1 February 1970
†S. Sgt. Jimmy G. Stewart, USA	18 May 1966
Rear Adm. James B. Stockdale, USN	4 September 1969
†Sgt. Lester R. Stone, Jr., USA	3 March 1969
†Sgt. Michael W. Stout, USA	12 March 1970
†Sp4c. Robert F. Stryker, USA	7 November 1967
S. Sgt. Kenneth E. Stumpf, USA	25 April 1967
Capt. James Allen Taylor, USA	9 November 1967
†S. Sgt. Karl G. Taylor Sr., USMC	8 December 1968
1st Lt. Brian Miles Thacker, USA	31 March 1971
PO Michael Edwin Thornton, USN	31 October 1972
Lt. Col. Leo K. Thorsness, USAF	19 April 1967
Maj. M. Sando Vargas, Jr., USMC	30 April to 2 May 1968
†1st Lt. John E. Warren, Jr., USA	14 January 1969
†Maj. Charles Joseph Watters, USA	19 November 1967
†Sp4c. Dale Eugene Wayrynen, USA	18 May 1967
†L. Cpl. Lester W. Weber, USMC	23 February 1969
Sp4c. Gary George Wetzel, USA	8 January 1968
†L. Cpt. Roy M. Wheat, USMC	11 August 1967
†Cpl. Jerry Wayne Wickam, USA	6 January 1968
†Capt. Hilliard A. Wilbanks, USAF	24 February 1967
†Pfc. Louis E. Willett, USA	15 February 1967
1st Lt. Charles Q. Williams, USA	9–10 June 1965
†Pfc. Dewayne T. Williams, USMC	18 September 1968
POlc. James E. Williams, USN	31 October 1966
†Pfc. Alfred M. Wilson, USMC	3 March 1969
†Pfc. David F. Winder, USA	13 May 1970
†L. Cpl. Kenneth L. Worley, USMC	12 August 1968
Sp4c. Raymond R. Wright, USA	2 May 1967
†1st. Sgt. Maximo Yabes, USA	26 February 1967
†Sfc. Rodney J. T. Yano, USA	1 January 1969
†Sgt. Gordon Douglas Yntema, USA	16–18 January 1968
Capt. Gerald O. Young, USAF	9 November 1967
†S. Sgt. Marvin R.Young, USA	21 August 1968
Sfc. Fred William Zabitosky, USA	19 February 1968

† *Posthumous award.*

Number of Medal of Honor Recipients by Rank and Year

Rank	1964	1965	1966	1967	1968	1969	1970	1971	1972	Total
Rear Adm.						1				1
Col./Capt.				2	1					3
Lt. Col./Comdr.				1	2		1			4
Maj./Lt. Comdr.			3	3	2	2		1		11
Capt./Lt.	2	1	4	8	6	2			2	25
Lt./Lt.(jg)		3	3	5	3	6	1	2		23
WO					1	1	1			3
Sgt./PO		2	13	16	19	12	9	1	1	73
Specialist—Cpl.		3	1	14	18	18	7	2		63
Pfc./Seaman		1	2	10	7	10	3			33
Total	1	10	26	59	59	52	22	6	3	239

Number of Posthumous Medal of Honor Recipients by Rank and Year

Rank	1964	1965	1966	1967	1968	1969	1970	1971	1972	Total
Col./Capt.				1	1					2
Lt. Col./Comdr.							1			1
Maj./Lt. Comdr.				1				1		2
Capt./Lt.	1		2	5					1	9
Lt./Lt.(jg)		1	2	5	2	5	1	1		17
Sgt./PO		1	5	11	12	8	4			41
Specialist—Cpl.		2	1	11	12	17	5	1		49
Pfc./Seaman		1	2	10	7	10	1			31
Total	1	5	12	44	34	40	12	3	1	152

Army, Air Force, and Marine Corps ranks are listed first, followed by equivalent Navy rank separated by a slash. Not every possible equivalent rank is listed, only ranks held by medal recipients. Note that the Marine Corps did not employ specialist rank.

Abbreviations to List of Medal of Honor Recipients

Abbreviation	Meaning
Adm.	Admiral
Capt.	Captain
CB3c.	Construction Mechanic Third Class
Col.	Colonel
Cpl.	Corporal

Abbreviation	Meaning
CWO	Chief Warrant Officer
G. Sgt.	Gunnery Sergeant
HC2c.	Hospital Corpsman Second Class
HC3c.	Hospital Corpsman Third Class
L. Cpl.	Lance Corporal
Lt.	Lieutenant
Lt. Col.	Lieutenant Colonel
Lt. Comdr.	Lieutenant Commander
Lt.(jg)	Lieutenant (junior grade)
Maj.	Major
M. Sgt.	Master Sergeant
Pfc.	Pfc.
PO	Petty Officer
PO1c.	Boatswain's Mate First Class
P. Sgt.	Platoon Sergeant
Sfc.	Sergeant First Class
Sgt.	Sergeant
Sp4c.	Specialist Fourth Class
Sp5c.	Specialist Fifth Class
Sp6c.	Specialist Sixth Class
S. Sgt.	Staff Sergeant
USA	U.S. Army
USAF	U.S. Air Force
USMC	U.S. Marine Corps
USN	U.S. Navy
USNR	U.S. Naval Reserve

Appendix H
Bibliographic Guide

The vast body of literature on the Vietnam War continues to grow, and the improvement of relations between the United States and Vietnam can only aid in its expansion. This bibliographic guide is intended to point out selected further readings in English on significant topics addressed in the *Webster's New World Dictionary of the Vietnam War* and is by no means an exhaustive listing. The information is grouped into the following categories:

- Vietnam

  The Indochina War

  Dien Bien Phu and Geneva

- The Vietnam War

- Strategy and Tactics

  The Ground War

  Pacification

  The Air War

- The United States

  The Antiwar Movement

  The Media

- Biographies

Vietnam

Among English-language general histories of Vietnam, Joseph Buttinger's works are perhaps the best available. Most notable is his classic three-volume *The Smaller Dragon: A Political History of Vietnam* (1958), written well before Vietnam became a household word in the United States. Buttinger's also-useful other works include his two-volume *Vietnam: A Dragon Embattled* (1967), *Vietnam: A Political History* (1968), and *Vietnam: The Dragon Defiant: A Short History of Vietnam* (1972).

Vietnam's early history is both ethnographically and politically complex, traditionally dominated by Chinese intervention and colonial rule but also influenced by seafaring South Asian groups. Keith Weller Taylor, *The Birth of Vietnam* (1983), details the origins and early history of the Vietnamese from the third century BC to the tenth century. Georges Coedès' *The Making of Southeast Asia* (1967) and *The Indianized States of Southeast Asia* (1968) are also useful, the later clarifying the history of Vietnam's Cham ethnic minority. Useful reference works include Danny J. Whitfield, *Historical and Cultural Dictionary of Vietnam* (1976), and William J. Duiker, *Historical Dictionary of Vietnam,* 2nd Edition (1998).

Significant texts covering early French colonialism in Southeast Asia include John Cady, *The Roots of French Imperialism in Asia* (1954); Thomas E. Ennis, *French Policy and Developments in Indochina* (1956); and Milton E. Osborne, *The French Presence in Cochinchina and Cambodia: Rule and Response (1859-1905)* (1969). Ngo Vinh Long's *Before the Revolution: The Vietnamese Peasants Under the French* (1991) is also illuminating, as is his *Vietnamese Women in Society and Revolution* (1974).

The era of French imperialism in Indochina also saw the growth of Vietnamese nationalism and the rise of communism as the predominant anticolonialist movement in Vietnam; important texts include John T. McAlister, *Vietnam: The Origins of Revolution* (1969), and, with Paul Mus, *The Vietnamese and Their Revolution* (1970); David G. Marr, *Vietnamese Anticolonialism, 1885-1925* (1971), *Vietnam 1945: The Quest for Power* (1995), and *Vietnamese Tradition on Trial, 1920-1945* (1981); William J. Duiker, *The Rise of Nationalism in Vietnam, 1900-1941* (1976); Douglas Pike, *History of Vietnamese Communism* (1978); and Huynh Kim Khanh, *Vietnamese Communism, 1925-1945* (1982).

The Indochina War

Sparked by the 1946 French bombardment of Haiphong, the war of Vietnamese independence against French colonial rule has been extensively covered. Key works include Bernard Fall, *Street Without Joy* (1989), first published in 1961; Edgar O'Ballance, *The Indo-China War, 1945-1954: A Study in Guerrilla Warfare* (1964); Ellen Hammer, *The Struggle for Indochina, 1940-1955* (1966); and Lucien Bodard, *The Quicksand War: Prelude to Vietnam* (1967). McAlister, *Vietnam,* noted above, focuses on the August Revolution and the outbreak of the war, while Peter M. Dunn, *The First Vietnam War* (1985) provides a rare look at the 1945 occupation of southern Vietnam, and attempts to suppress the local Viet Minh, by British forces sent in to disarm the Japanese.

Among the works covering the United States' early involvement in Vietnam is Archimedes L. A. Patti's *Why Vietnam? Prelude to America's Albatross* (1980), written by one of the OSS agents who met with Ho Chi Minh during World War II. Other texts useful to understanding the United States' polities during the Indochina War, including its commitments to

France, include Ronald E. Irving, *The First Indochina War: French and American Policy, 1945-1954* (1975); Robert M. Blum, *Drawing the Line: The Origins of the American Containment Policy in East Asia* (1982); Ronald H. Spector, *Advice and Support: The Early Years, 1941-1960* (1983); Gary R. Hess, *The United States' Emergence as a Southeast Asia Power, 1940-1950* (1987); Andrew J. Rotter, *The Path to Vietnam: Origins of the American Commitment to Southeast Asia* (1987); and Lloyd C. Gardner, *Approaching Vietnam: From World War II through Dienbieuphu* (1988).

Dien Bien Phu and Geneva

The climactic battle of the Indochina War and the negotiations that put an end to it are intertwined in history. The battle itself has been covered by its victor, Vo Nguyen Giap, in his *Dien Bien Phu* (1962), while an alternate account is presented in *The Battle of Dienbieuphu* (1965), by Jules Roy, a senior French air force officer who served in Indochina. The most scholarly work on the battle is Bernard Fall's *Hell in a Very Small Place: The Siege of Dien Bien Phu* (1966), while Melanie Billings-Yun, *Decision Against War: Eisenhower and Dien Bien Phu, 1954* (1988), gives insight into the U.S. refusal to intervene militarily. The battle has also been placed in its wider context, including its impact on the Geneva negotiations, in such works as Melvin Gurtov, *The First Vietnam Crisis: Chinese Communist Strategy and United States Involvement, 1953-1954* (1967); Philippe Devillers and Jean Lacouture, *End of a War: Indochina 1954* (1969); and Denise Artaud and Lawrence Kaplan, ads., *Dienbieuphu: The Atlantic Alliance and the Defense of Southeast Asia* (1989). Other works that focus on the negotiations themselves include Robert E. Randle, *Geneva, 1954: The Settlement of the Indochinese War* (1969) and James Cable, *The Geneva Conference of 1954 on Indochina* (1986).

The Vietnam War

The most important published documentary source for the Vietnam War is perhaps *The Pentagon Papers* (1971), not least for its historical significance. Among the most important general histories of the Vietnam War are George C. Herring, *America's Longest War: The United States and Vietnam, 1950-1975* (1986), which concentrates on U.S. strategy and policy during the war. *Vietnam: A History* (1991), written by journalist Stanley Karnow and first published in 1983 to accompany the PBS special *Vietnam: A Television History,* is also important. Another significant work is Frances FitzGerald, *Fire in the Lake: The Vietnamese and the Americans in Vietnam* (1972); timely, lauded, and influential during the war, the book has been criticized in later years for its sometimes oversimplified portrayals of both the U.S. and the communists. The war as seen by the North Vietnamese and the National Liberation Front is depicted by William J. Duiker, *The*

Communist Road to Power in Vietnam (1981). Other useful works include James Pinckney Harrison, *The Endless War: Fifty Years of War In Vietnam* (1982);William S. Turley, *The Second Indochina War: A Political and Military History* (1986); Gary R. Hess, *Vietnam and the United States: Origins and Legacy of War* (1990). Both Gabriel Kolko's *Anatomy of a War: Vietnam, the United States, and the Modern Historical Experience* (1985) and Marilyn B. Young's *The Vietnam Wars 1945-1990* (1991) are strong indictments of U.S. intervention. Works that place the Vietnam War into a broader international context include Ralph B. Smith, *An International History of the Vietnam War* (1983), and Daniel S. Papp, *Vietnam: The View from Moscow, Peking, Washington* (1981).

The event that propelled the United States into the war in Vietnam, the Gulf of Tonkin incident, also prompted several books, among them: Joseph Goulden, *Truth is the First Casualty: The Gulf of Tonkin Affair—Illusion and Reality* (1969); John Galloway, *The Gulf of Tonkin Incident* (1970); Anthony Austin, *The President's War* (1971); and Edwin E. Moise, *Tonkin Gulf and the Escalation of the Vietnam War* (1996). U.S. escalation in the war is covered in George McT. Kahin, *Intervention: How America Became Involved in Vietnam* (1986). Other significant works on this period include Robert Scigliano, *South Vietnam: Nation under Stress* (1963); Bernard Fall, *Viet-nam Witness* (1966) and *The Two Viet-nams: A Political and Military Analysis* (1967); Robert Shaplen, *The Lost Revolution: The United States in Vietnam, 1946-1966* (1966); Chester A. Bain, *Vietnam: The Roots of Conflict* (1967);Jean Lacouture, *Vietnam: Between Two Truces* (1966); Leslie Gelb and Richard Belts, *The Irony of Vietnam: The System Worked* (1978); and Larry Berman, *Planning a Tragedy: The Americanization of the War in Vietnam* (1982).

Strategy and Tactics

Critics of U.S. strategy in the Vietnam War often divide over the nature of the war, debating whether it was primarily a conventional war or an insurgency. The most influential strategical examination of the war, Harry G. Summers Jr.'s *On Strategy: A Critical Analysis of the Vietnam War* (1982), holds the former, contending that the United States could have triumphed through a more effective application of conventional military force. Andrew F. Krepinevich Jr., in *The Army and Vietnam* (1986), holds the latter, maintaining that by neglecting pacification in favor of conventional operations, the U.S. effort doomed itself to failure.

Other significant works include Dave Richard Palmer, *Summons of the Trumpet: A History of the Vietnam War from a Military Man's Viewpoint* (1978); Allan R. Millett, ed., *A Short History of the Vietnam War* (1978); Timothy J. Lomperis, *The War Everybody Lost—and Won* (1984); Bruce Palmer Jr., *The 25-Year War: America's Military Role in Vietnam* (1984); Thomas D. Boettcher, *Vietnam: The Valor and the Sorrow* (1985); Shelby Stanton, *The Rise and Fall of an American Army: U.S. Ground Forces in*

Vietnam, 1946–1975 (1985); Thomas C. Thayer, *War without ⌐⌐ American Experience in Vietnam* (1985); Norman B. Hannah, *The ⌐⌐ Failure: Laos and the Vietnam War* (1987); and Phillip B. Davidson, *Vietna⌐. at War: The History, 1946–1975* (1988). Particularly notable is Douglas Kinnard's *The War Managers* (1977), a survey of more than one hundred generals who served in Vietnam. Jeffrey J. Clarke, *Advice and Support: The Final Years, 1965–1973* (1988), covers the U.S. advisory effort during the war. An invaluable resource is Shelby Stanton, *Vietnam Order of Battle* (1981), which details the units of the U.S. Army in Vietnam.

Works covering communist strategies and tactics include Vo Nguyen Giap, *People's War, People's Army* (1962) and *Big Victory, Big Task* (1967); George K. Tanham, *Communist Revolutionary Warfare* (1967); Patrick J. McGarvey, ed., *Visions of Victory: Selected Vietnamese Communist Military Writings 1965–1968* (1969); Jon M. Van Dyke, *North Vietnam's Strategy for Survival* (1972); the official history issued by the Socialist Republic of Vietnam, *Vietnam: The Anti-U.S. Resistance for National Salvation 1954–1975: Military History* (1980); Tran Van Tra, *Vietnam: History of the Bulwark B2 Theater* (1982); Duiker, *The Communist Road to Power,* previously cited; Douglas Pike, *Viet Cong: National Liberation Front of South Vietnam* (1986) and *PAVN: People's Army of Vietnam* (1986).

Among the works on specific battles and campaigns of the war are Robert W. Rogers, *Cedar Fall—Junction City: A Turning Point* (1974); Don Oberdorfer, *Tet!* (1971); Robert Pisor, *The End of the Line: The Siege of the Sanh* (1982); Ronald H. Spector, *After Tet: The Bloodiest Year in Vietnam* (1993); Nguyen Duy Hinh, *Lam Son 719* (1979); Ngo Quang Truong, *The Easter Offensive of 1972* (1980); and Dale Andradé, *Trial by Fire: The 1972 Easter Offensive, America's Last Vietnam Battle* (1995). Works on the most notorious atrocity committed by U.S. forces during the Vietnam War include Seymour M. Hersh, *My Lai 4* (1970) and Michael Bilton and Kevin Sim, *Four Hours in My Lai* (1992). The testimony of numerous U.S. veterans of atrocities is contained in Vietnam Veterans against the War, *The Winter Soldier Investigation* (1972), while Guenter Lewy, *America in Vietnam* (1978), is defends U.S. military actions against charges of atrocities.

The war's extension into Vietnam's ostensibly neutral neighbors is covered in William Shawcross, *Sideshow: Kissinger, Nixon, and the Destruction of Cambodia* (1979) and Timothy N. Castle, *War in the Shadow of Vietnam: United States Military Aid to the Royal Lao Government, 1955–1975* (1993). The final years of the Republic of Vietnam are detailed in Stuart A. Herrington, *Peace with Honor? An American Reports on Vietnam, 1973–1975* (1983). Among the best works on the collapse of South Vietnam are William E. LeGro, *Vietnam from Cease-Fire To Capitulation* (1981) and Arnold R. Isaacs, *Without Honor: Defeat in Vietnam and Cambodia* (1983), white Van Tien Dung, *Our Great Spring Victory: An Account of the Liberation of South Vietnam* (1977), gives the communist account of the end of the Vietnam War.

The Ground War

Vast numbers of books detail the experiences of U.S. soldiers in Vietnam combat. Perhaps the best is the widely acclaimed work by Harold G. Moore and Joseph L. Galloway, *We Were Soldiers Once . . . And Young* (1992). John A. Cash, *Seven Firefights in Vietnam* (1993), is highly useful for understanding the vast diversity of combat that took place in Vietnam. Other significant books include Al Santoli, *Everything We Had: An Oral History of the Vietnam War by Thirty-Three American Soldiers Who Fought It* (1981); Shelby Stanton, *Green Berets at War: U.S. Army Special Forces in Southeast Asia, 1956-1975* (1985) and *Rangers at War: Combat Recon in Vietnam* (1992); J. D. Coleman, *Pleiku: The Damn of Helicopter Warfare in Vietnam* (1988); Thomas J. Cutler, *Brown Water, Black Berets* (1988); Eric Hammel, *Khe Sanh: Siege in the Clouds An Oral History* (1989); R. D. Camp and Eric Hammel, *Lima-6: A Marine Company Commander in Vietnam* (1989); R. L. Schreadley, *From the Rivers to the Seas: The U.S. Navy in Vietnam* (1992); and Wallace Terry, *Bloods: An Oral History of the Vietnam War by Black Veterans* (1992).

Works covering the Vietnam War experiences of women in the U.S. military include Lynda Van Devanter with Christopher Morgan, *Home Before Morning: The Story of an Army Nurse in Vietnam* (1983); Kathryn Marshall, *In the Combat Zone: An Oral History of American Women in Vietnam, 1966-1975* (1987); and Elizabeth Norman, *Women at War: The Story of Fifty Military Nurses Who Served in Vietnam* (1990). Ian McNeill, *The Team: Australian Army Advisers in Vietnam 1962-1972* (1984), covers the little-known role of a key U.S. ally, while Michael Lee Lanning and Dan Cragg, *Inside the VC and the NVA: The Real Story of North Vietnam's Armed Forces* (1992), give considerable insight into the experiences of communist soldiers.

Pacification

As noted above, debate continues over the importance of the "other war." Important works include George K. Tanham, *War without Guns: American Civilians in Rural Vietnam* (1966); British counterinsurgency expert Robert Thompson, *No Exit from Vietnam* (1969) and *Peace Is Not at Hand* (1974); Jeffrey Race, *War Comes to Long An: Revolutionary Conflict in a Vietnamese Province* (1971); Douglas S. Blaufarb, *The Counterinsurgency Era* (1977); Charles R. Anderson, *Vietnam: The Other War* (1982); Stuart A. Herrington (who from 1972–1973 served as an adviser to South Vietnamese territorials) *Silence Was a Weapon: The Vietnam War in the Villages* (1982); Francis West, *The Village* (1985); Michael E. Peterson, *The Combined Action Platoons: The US. Marines' Other War in Vietnam* (1989); and Dale Andradé,

Ashes to Ashes: The Phoenix Program and the Vietnam War (1990). Important works detailing the communist view of pacification are Truong Nhu Tang, with David Chanoff and Doan Van Toai, A *Viet Cong Memoir* (1985), and David Chanoff and Doan Van Toai, *Portrait of the Enemy* (1986). For works on the experiences of U.S. POWs, see *The Air War,* below.

The Air War

One of the most controversial aspects of U.S. military involvement in the Vietnam War has been the bombing campaign. Important critiques include Drew Middleton, *Air War: Vietnam* (1978); William W. Momyer (who commanded the U.S. Seventh Air Force during the Vietnam War), *Airpower in Three Wars (WW II, Korea, Vietnam)* (1978); James Clay Thompson, *Rolling Thunder: Understanding Policy and Program Failure* (1980); Mark Clodfelter, *The Limits of Air Power: The American Bombing of North Vietnam* (1989), which gives particular insight into the Linebacker II Christmas bombings of Hanoi and Haiphong; and Earl Tilford, *Setup: What the Air Force Did in Vietnam and Why* (1991).

Official histories include Carl Berger, *The United States Air Force in Southeast Asia* (1977); John Schlight, *The United States Air Force in Southeast Asia: The War in South Vietnam—The Years of the Offensive, 1965-1968* (1988); and Jacob Van Staaveren, *The United States Air Force in Southeast Asia: Interdiction in Southern Laos, 1960-1968* (1993). Two complementary works that cover the air war from the viewpoint of the pilots are John B. Nichols and Barrett Tillman, *On Yankee Station: The Naval Air War Over Vietnam* (1987), and Ken Bell, *100 Missions North: A Fighter Pilot's Story of the Vietnam War* (1993), which focus respectively on the U.S. Navy's carrier war and the U.S. Air Force's war from bases in Thailand. Earl Tilford's *U.S. Air Force Search and Rescue in Southeast Asia* (1980) covers a little-known but crucial aspect of the air war. The majority of U.S. prisoners of war were pilots; an important text is John G. Hubbell et al., *P.O.W.: A Definitive History of the American Prisoner of War Experience in Vietnam, 1964-1973* (1976); while a moving personal memoir is James and Sybil Stockdale's *In Love and War* (1984).

The United States

[For the United States' early involvement in Vietnam, see above, *The Indochina War.* For U.S. intervention in Vietnam, see above, *The Vietnam War.* For the U.S. military role in Vietnam, see above, *Strategy and Tactics.*]

The Vietnam War caused social, political, and generational upheaval unprecedented in American history, and continues to affect the United States.

The Antiwar Movement

The communist precept that war is inherently political in nature was
borne out by the Vietnam War's hugely divisive effect on U.S. society and
politics. Contemporary accounts of the American antiwar movement
include Samuel Lubell, *The Hidden Crisis in American Politics* (1971);
William O'Neill, *Coming Apart: An Informal History of America in the 1960's*
(1971); Thomas Powers, *The War at Home: Vietnam and the American People,
1964-1968* (1973); Alexander Kendrick, *The Wound Within: America in the
Vietnam Years 1945-1974* (1974); Irwin Unger, *The Movement: A History of
the American New Left, 1959-1972* (1974); and Sandy Vogelsanger, *The Long
Dark Night of the Soul: The American Intellectual Left and the Vietnam War*
(1974).

   Among the most influential post-Vietnam works is *Chance and
Circumstance: The Draft, the War and the Vietnam Generation* (1978) by
Lawrence M. Baskir and William M. Strauss; however, the work's reliance
on anecdotal sources has perpetuated within the literature several myths
about the Vietnam War, particularly about the Vietnam-era draft program
Project 100,000. Other notable post-war works include Charles Meconis,
With Clumsy Grace: The American Catholic Left, 1961-1977 (1979); Lawrence
S. Wittner, *Rebels against War: The American Peace Movement, 1933-1983*
(1984); Nancy Zaroulis and Gerald Sullivan, *Who Spoke Up? American
Protest against the War in Vietnam, 1963-1975* (1984); Randall M. Fisher,
Rhetoric and American Democracy: Black through Vietnam Dissent (1985);
Kathleen Turner, *Lyndon Johnson's Dual War: Vietnam and the Press* (1985);
John Dumbrell, ed., *Vietnam and the Antiwar Movement* (1987); James
Miller, *"Democracy is in the Streets": From Port Huron to the Siege of Chicago*
(1987); Melvin Small, *Johnson, Nixon and the Doves* (1988); Charles
DeBenedetti and Charles Chatfield, *An American Ordeal: The Antiwar
Movement of the Vietnam Era* (1990); Mitchell K. Hall, *Because of Their
Faith: CALCAV and Religious Opposition to the Vietnam War* (1990); David W.
Levy, *The Debate over Vietnam* (1991); Melvin Small and William D. Hoover,
eds., *Give Peace a Chance: Exploring the Vietnam Antiwar Movement* (1992);
Tom Wells, *The War Within: America's Battle over Vietnam* (1994); and Adam
Garfinkle, *Telltale Hearts: The Origins and Impact of the Vietnam Antiwar
Movement* (1995). For the impact of the media on the antiwar movement,
see Gitlin, *The Whole World is Watching* (1980) and Small, *Covering Dissent*
(1994), cited below.

The Media

The influence of the media upon the conduct and the outcome of the
Vietnam War has been hotly debated. Important works on the subject
include Peter Braestrup, *Big Story: How the American Press and TV Reported
and Interpreted the Crisis of Tet in Vietnam and Washington* (1977); Todd
Gitlin, *The Whole World is Watching: Mass Media in the Making and*